T0329876

JOBS WITH INEQUALITY

Financialization, Post-Democracy, and Labour
Market Deregulation in Canada

Jobs with Inequality

Financialization, Post-Democracy, and Labour Market Deregulation in Canada

JOHN PETERS

UNIVERSITY OF TORONTO PRESS

Toronto Buffalo London

ISBN 978-1-4426-4619-3 (cloth)   ISBN 978-1-4426-6512-5 (EPUB)
ISBN 978-1-4426-6511-8 (PDF)

Library and Archives Canada Cataloguing in Publication

Title: Jobs with inequality : financialization, post-democracy, and labour market
    deregulation in Canada / John Peters.
Names: Peters, John, 1963– author.
Description: Includes bibliographical references and index.
Identifiers: Canadiana (print) 20220175985 | Canadiana (ebook) 20220176051 |
    ISBN 9781442646193 (cloth) | ISBN 9781442665125 (EPUB) |
    ISBN 9781442665118 (PDF)
Subjects: LCSH: Income distribution – Canada. | LCSH: Wages – Canada. | LCSH:
    Financialization – Canada. | LCSH: Deregulation – Canada. | LCSH: Labor
    market – Canada. | LCSH: Labor policy – Canada.
Classification: LCC HC120.I5 P48 2022 | DDC 339.20971–dc23

This book has been published with the help of a grant from the Federation for the
Humanities and Social Sciences, through the Awards to Scholarly Publications
Program, using funds provided by the Social Sciences and Humanities Research
Council of Canada.

We wish to acknowledge the land on which the University of Toronto Press
operates. This land is the traditional territory of the Wendat, the Anishnaabeg, the
Haudenosaunee, the Métis, and the Mississaugas of the Credit First Nation.

University of Toronto Press acknowledges the financial support of the Government of
Canada, the Canada Council for the Arts, and the Ontario Arts Council, an agency of
the Government of Ontario, for its publishing activities.

Canada Council   Conseil des Arts
for the Arts   du Canada

ONTARIO ARTS COUNCIL
CONSEIL DES ARTS DE L'ONTARIO

an Ontario government agency
un organisme du gouvernement de l'Ontario

Funded by the   Financé par le
Government   gouvernement
of Canada   du Canada

Contents

Figures and Tables

Figures

Tables

Acknowledgments

This book is the result of research on the political economics of inequality and labour decline that I have carried out since the 2008 financial crisis. In its aftermath, I was struck by how the rich fared so well while working people faced rising unemployment or poorer jobs. Writing this book was my attempt to understand this process and, along the way, I relied on the generosity of many scholars, writers, students, government researchers, and activists.

The foundation for this book was laid in *Boom, Bust, and Crisis: Labour, Corporate Power, and Politics in Canada*, which I edited in 2012 as part of the Labour in Canada series. I am grateful to Fernwood Publishing for supporting that collection. In preparing this volume, I owe great thanks to many colleagues. Bryan Evans at Toronto Metropolitan University encouraged me throughout the project. I also want to thank again those who read – and often reread – the manuscript's various chapters and provided valuable advice: Greg Albo, York University; Angela Carter, University of Waterloo; Colin Crouch, University of Warwick; Eric Helleiner, University of Waterloo; Chris Howell, Oberlin College; Christopher Kollmeyer, University of Aberdeen; Louis Phillipe Rochon, Laurentian University; Don Wells, McMaster University; and James Wickham, University College Dublin. Their comments, often made under their own time constraints and pressures, greatly improved the book's framework.

Likewise, colleagues and friends across Canada kindly talked with me at length about their provinces and often commented on the case study chapters. I would not have been able to understand developments in provincial politics without the guidance of Sean Cadigan, Memorial University; David Fairey, Labour Consulting Services; Sam Gindin, formerly of the Canadian Auto Workers; Tom Klassen, York University; Andrew Macleod and Tom Sandborn of the *Tyee* in British Columbia; Lana Payne, UNIFOR; and Mark Thomas, York University.

At the University of Toronto Press, Daniel Quinlan has always been helpful and encouraging. I thank him for his support for the project. I am also very appreciative of the support of the University of Toronto's production team, who took such care in preparing the book for press, most especially Ian Mac-Kenzie of ParaGraphics, as well as Christine Robertson. In the work that lies behind the manuscript, sincere thanks are owed to David Mitchell and Jenn Harris, who edited and proofread multiple iterations of the book and took great care to make it clearer and more compelling. In the final stages, I was very appreciative of the assistance of Andrew Cheng and Amy Adams in the preparation of the figures. Justin Panos and Sune Sandbeck – both now union researchers – provided precious research assistance. And so too are thanks owed to Phil Scrimger, formerly at Harvard Law School's Labor and Worklife program and now at Statistics Canada. Without the generosity and tenacity of these friends and colleagues in pursuing material, data, and literature, this book would have been impossible to write. I also thank the anonymous reviewers whose detailed comments challenged me to revise and strengthen the clarity of the book.

I have used many published data sources throughout this book, but I would like to express my sincere thanks to the many people who so graciously helped me access new data or shared it with me. I thank Brian Murphy, Marc Levesque, Francois Page, and Nathalie Caron for guiding me on Statistics Canada data questions, as well as Michael Forster and Paul Swaim at the OECD in Paris for their support on international data. I thank Trish Hennessy and Armine Yalnizyan at the Canadian Centre for Policy Alternatives, and Jordan Brennan of UNIFOR for sharing custom data sets on household incomes and financialization. I also wish to thank Anthony Shorrocks of Global Economic Perspectives and the Global Wealth team for sharing data on high net worth individuals in Canada. Finally, John Holmes of Queen's University and Brendan Sweeney of McMaster University were always open to discussing auto sector developments and sharing insights and data from their current research.

Laurentian University and the Laurentian University Faculty Association first provided research funds that were critical in supporting data purchases and research assistance. Toward the end of the project, I also relied on the support of Gregor Murray and his SSHRC partnership grant, "Institutional Experimentation for Better Work."

I presented early drafts of portions of the manuscript at a number of conferences: the "Austerity and Its Alternatives" conference at McMaster University in 2016; the Society for the Advancement of Socio-Economics' (SASE) Twenty-Eighth Annual Conference at Berkeley University in 2016; the Canadian Association for Work and Labour Studies, Third Annual Congress, University of Calgary, in 2016; the Centre de recherche interuniversitaire sur la mondialisation et le travail (CRIMT) conference in Montreal in 2015; the "Manufacturing and Framing Austerity" conference at McMaster University in 2014; the Canadian Association for Work and Labour Studies Annual Meeting in 2014, St. Catharines; the CRIMT conference, "New Frontiers for

Citizenship at Work," in Montreal in 2014; SASE's Twenty-Sixth Annual Conference in 2014 in Chicago; the FORBA Research Institute in Vienna in 2012; and SASE's Twenty-Third Annual Conference in 2011 in Madrid. I would like to thank the conference participants who offered insightful questions and comparative points of reference that improved this work.

I initially developed my arguments about financialization and its impacts on work and employment in "The Rise of Finance and the Decline of Organised Labour in the Advanced Capitalist Countries" in *New Political Economy* in 2011. All of the empirical analysis on financialization in this volume is new. My first attempt at explaining the impacts of debt and financial markets on public sector restructuring were first published in "Neoliberal Convergence in North America and Western Europe: Fiscal Austerity, Privatization, and Public Sector Reform" in *Review of International Political Economy* in 2012. Portions of the analysis in chapters 2 and 3 have been drawn from "Post-Democracy and the Politics of Inequality: Explaining Policy Responses to the Financial Crisis and the Great Recession" in *The Austerity State*, edited by Stephen McBride and Bryan Evans (University of Toronto Press, 2017), as well as from "Neoliberalism, Inequality, and Austerity in Rich World Democracies" in *Orchestrating Austerity*, edited by Stephen McBride and Donna Baines (Fernwood Publishing, 2014), and "Canada, Free Markets, and the Decline of Unions and Good Jobs," in my edited collection, *Boom, Bust, and Crisis: Labour, Corporate Power, and Politics in Canada*.

Recently, I have further developed the theories of financialization presented in chapter 2 in an article with Chris Kollmeyer, "Financialization and the Decline of Organized Labor: A Study of 18 Advanced Capitalist Countries, 1970–2012" in *Social Forces* 2019, as well as with Mathieu Dupuis and Phillipe Scrimger in "Financialization and Union Decline: The Influence on Core Sectors and Industries" via *Competition and Change* 2020.

On the provincial case studies, arguments about labour market developments were initially developed in collaboration with Angela Carter and Sean Cadigan in "The Political Economy of the Labour Market in Newfoundland and Labrador," a chapter in *Politics and Public Policy in Newfoundland & Labrador* edited by Alex Marland and Matthew Kerby (McGill-Queen's University Press, 2014). Likewise, my thinking about British Columbia came with working with David Fairey and Tom Sandborn in "The 'Biggest Roll Back of Worker Rights in Canadian History': The Campbell Government and Labour Market Deregulation in British Columbia," in *Boom, Bust, and Crisis* (2012). Finally, I have addressed recent Ontario developments in "The Ontario Growth Model: The 'End of the Road' or a 'New Economy'?" in *Divided Province: Ontario Politics in the Age of Neoliberalism* edited by Greg Albo and Bryan Evans (McGill-Queen's University Press, 2018). I thank my co-authors, the editors, and reviewers of these pieces for their support and insightful comments.

My last word of thanks is to Angela Carter, who gave me intellectual and personal support at every step over the past decade as she worked on her own writing projects. Angela's superb analytical and editorial skills greatly improved many of the book's arguments. But more importantly, she has added so much light to my life and strengthened my commitment to understanding the distressing and complex problem of inequality before us. We welcomed John Weston into this world as this book was initially taking shape and I hope he may someday see it as contributing to the task of improving the lives of working Canadians.

JOBS WITH INEQUALITY

Financialization, Post-Democracy, and Labour
Market Deregulation in Canada

1 Introduction

The conventional understanding of income inequality in Canada suggests that the gap between the rich and the poor is neither especially extreme nor growing. Indeed, research and commentary often claim that Canada is somewhere in the middle of the pack: inequality is not as high as in the United States, but nor is Canada as egalitarian as Scandinavian countries such as Sweden and Denmark. The typical view of Canada is that of a rich country, one that is relatively generous and fair.

For example, Fritzell (1993), reflecting on income inequality trends in the 1980s, argued that inequality rates in Canada and Germany remained stable while the United States and the United Kingdom saw greater income inequality. In more recent academic literature, scholars such as Card, Lemieux, and Riddell (2003, 27) argued that "unlike the U.S. and U.K. … overall inequality has remained very stable in Canada over time." Even in public commentary and research, we commonly read that, despite increases in inequality, Canada has not witnessed increases as dramatic as in the United States (Heisz 2015; Yakabuski 2013).

The evidence contrasts with this perception. Over the past few decades, income inequality has skyrocketed in Canada while the incomes of average households have deteriorated and the job quality for the majority of workers has plummeted. Indeed, in contrast to the view of Canada's economy as relatively equitable, Canada has instead closely followed trends in the United States, with inequality increasing in lockstep with the boom of the rich and super rich.

A few observations are particularly telling. Over the 2001 to 2015 period, the number of Canadians whose net worth was at least US$50 million nearly quadrupled, from 803 to 2,840. The number of billionaires also grew. At the start of the millennium, there were thirteen billionaires in Canada; as of 2015, there were thirty (Credit Suisse 2015). Similarly, considering just annual incomes, those in the top income brackets saw their pay and capital gains increase exponentially. Between 1990 and 2015, the top 1 per cent of income earners across Canada tripled their annual incomes, with average family incomes for this group reaching $729,000 by 2008, then declining slightly after the crisis, before rising again to $842,910 in 2015.

However, if these gains enjoyed by the rich (and the approximately 158,000 individuals in the top 1 per cent) are striking enough, the contrasts with the experience of average Canadian households are even more disconcerting. The majority of workers and their families saw their incomes stagnate and had to cope with a rising tide of unemployment, the loss of good jobs, and the expansion of low-paying precarious work arrangements. Indeed, as of 2015, Canada's labour market had become so polarized that out of a total workforce of more than 17 million people, 8.6 million Canadians (or 49 per cent of the workforce) were in jobs that paid them on average less than $17,833 per year.

Strikingly, this widening of the gap between the rich and the poor occurred across the country. In Ontario, for example, deindustrialization led to a significant decline in well-paid and unionized manufacturing jobs. The decline was so steep that by 2015, manufacturing's share of total employment was 11 per cent – a level not seen since the 1930s. Yet this disappearance of good, well-paying jobs occurred at the same time that the province saw billions of dollars in new foreign direct investment and soaring stock and housing markets.

In British Columbia, another province that did extraordinarily well over the course of the first two decades of 2000 through expanding resource exports and the massive influx of new dollars into housing and infrastructure construction, by 2015 some 40 per cent of jobs in the province offered low pay and little job security, and 30 per cent of workers were in jobs that could be categorized as "working poverty." In Newfoundland and Labrador, offshore oil brought billions of dollars to the province, and the provincial government implemented measures to lower poverty rates. But more than 42 per cent of the workforce was working in low-wage employment, and another 15 per cent was unemployed in 2015.

Thus, in stark contrast to the standard view of Canada as a relatively equitable society that has shared its prosperity, in reality the wealthiest in Canada have enjoyed almost exclusive benefit from recent economic growth, while the majority of workers have seen their economic fortunes worsen as they struggle with low-paying and increasingly insecure jobs.

What accounts for this staggering concentration of wealth and income? Why have incomes stagnated and job quality worsened for most Canadians? Is there a connection between the rise of this "super rich" and a growing low-wage labour force? If so, who or what is the cause? These questions are at the heart of this book.

Financialization, Labour Market Deregulation, and Post-Democracy

Over the past decade and more, researchers and policy advocates have asked many questions about the rise of inequality and its causes. Some emphasize technology and how it harms the less educated but allows the well trained to take advantage (Boudarbat, Lemieux, and Riddell 2010; OECD 2015a). Others stress the impacts of a global world economy and its effects on trade and manufacturing employment (Breau 2007; Breau and Rigby 2010). Still others point out how labour markets are segmented by gender and race, and women and racialized minorities are systematically underpaid and routinely hired into poorly paid jobs (Galabuzi 2006; Lightman and Gingrich 2013). But my argument suggests we turn in another direction.

I argue that while all these provide partial – and often very plausible – explanations for the growing gap between the rich and the majority of citizens, they all fall short. And the main reason for their weakness is their neglect of politics – and especially the changes to political power and policy that have lain behind recent economic and labour market outcomes.

In contrast, I argue that inequality is not an inevitable result of unstoppable "external" market forces, nor is it simply the result of discrimination against women or vulnerable minorities. Rather, I contend that inequality is the consequence of public policy decisions and how powerful corporations and financial interests have influenced the visible hand of government to tailor the rules of finance, corporate operation, and the labour market – in their favour. Indeed, over the past few decades, what is so notable is how an array of laws, regulations, and institutions have been rewritten to prioritize corporate power and short-term financial gains at the expense of long-term growth and good jobs for Canadians. And looked at over the long run, it is how governments have reshaped the rules governing financial and labour markets that best explains the rise of inequality in Canada – as much for the top 1 per cent of earners as for the millions now mired in low-wage work.

Unfortunately conventional understandings of Canada's government and politics often say little about any of these developments, instead painting a picture of public officials duly responding to what citizens want. But these are of little help in answering the many questions about the rise of inequality. In these perspectives, it is assumed that elections allow the people to choose, and, failing that, citizens can raise their voice to make officials listen and react in the public interest. It is this routine electoral competition and citizen engagement that is supposed to make politicians responsive to popular majorities and theoretically should pose a significant political hurdle to inequality and ever-worsening jobs.

The argument I advance here sees little such harmony. Quite the opposite, in fact. My core argument is that over the past few decades business and financial power has fundamentally recast policy to the advantage of a wealthy few – dynamics that are often hidden from public view and too little discussed. The political system that I detail sees a political system under the influence of money and economic power. Policy is made with the interests of the elite few in mind, and most citizens are either cut out of the policy process or are simply ignored.

This book addresses why this has occurred and explains how the relationships between politics, policy, and the economy had profound consequences for inequality. My argument is that governments – and those in positions of power – have an enormous influence on how economies and labour markets function and who gets what. Indeed, over the past century, democracy and capitalism have always been in profound conflict with one another, most typically over power, income, and social justice public policy. But in recent decades, capital's dynamics have once again begun to corrode citizen's rights and democratic state powers – so much so that a convincing political account of inequality today must again turn its focus to core questions of how business and the affluent are winning persistent patterns of advantage as much in labour and capital markets as in political voice, representation, and influence over the executive branch of government – a process I call "post-democracy."

Just as important are the consequences of post-democracy for understanding the dynamics and patterns of contemporary inequality. Many explanations of inequality simply assume that market changes and technology are responsible for the growing gap between the rich and the rest of Canadians. But such assumptions overlook how government has a wide array of policies that set the rules for business and the labour market alike, and many of these explanations pay little attention – if any – to how government rules shape income distribution as well as the capacity for organized action among economic interests.

As I show in this book, to explain inequality today it is necessary to turn our attention in a different direction and take the impacts of post-democracy on public policy seriously. Above all, it is essential to identify how and why changes to Canada's democracy have led to policies that have swelled private credit, corporate size, and profitability. But at the same time, if we are to come to grips with the deteriorating quality of jobs and wages, we must also delve into the reasons behind the failure of labour laws and employment policies to counter inequality. I characterize such changes as "financialization" and "labour market deregulation," and each, I argue, offers a far more persuasive explanation of rising inequality in Canada today than do more conventional accounts. Indeed, I argue it is these political and policy factors that do the most to help us account for why more and more income has been redirected to those at the top while millions of Canadians are routinely relegated to low-wage, precarious employment.

Post-Democracy

The first step to understanding the causes of inequality is a process I call *post-democracy*: how Canada's organizational landscape has shifted to forward the interests of business, finance, and employers at the expense of wider public concerns about good jobs and equality. It is post-democracy – and the recent changes to the power dynamics that have reshaped public policy to favour corporations and the super rich – I claim that is a prime mover of inequality.

Certainly, there is some evidence that – at least in formal terms – democracy continues to function, and citizens have resisted recent increases in inequality. Some citizen groups still question the consequences of an economic system run by and for finance. Occasionally, too, issues of labour law, regulations, and employment policy become matters of public debate, as, for example, in the recent efforts to "Fight for $15" where low-wage workers have launched protests in support of a living wage across the United States and Canada.

But my account suggests we need a more critical eye for how our democracy actually works today. Indeed, I argue if we are to begin explaining why inequality continues to rise, despite citizens' concerns, we have to look far more carefully at how and why narrow economic interests are routinely intervening and remoulding the outcomes of financial markets, corporate growth, and labour markets (Crouch 2006; Hacker and Pierson 2010a). Also required is close attention to why political parties and public officials are increasingly focused and dependent on business and wealth, and increasingly aware that their political success depends on catering to the better off. Delving further into these two processes takes us part of the way to understanding why public officials have continued to tie themselves more closely to business and finance, and why professional elites have crafted policies to appeal to these elite interests.

At the same time, it is also clear that the majority of working Canadians have become less – not more – organized. Workers and citizens who were once better represented by unions and civic associations have often seen them atrophy. More are cynical of the system. Few have the time to engage in politics. Even fewer have access to the organizations and associations that once brought citizens together and helped them engage in politics. These political variables are the first keys to helping us understand how and why our political system increasingly caters only to those with money and resources.

Nowhere can the outcomes of these political dynamics be more clearly seen than in how governments have changed public policies in favour of business in recent decades. Because over time and across political administrations, organized business and financial interests have overhauled the rules and institutional frameworks governing financial markets, corporate operation, and the labour market more generally.

As this book shows, the results of post-democracy have been pivotal – to the economy and to the major interests that make up today's economy. As business and the rich have begun to wield ever greater political power, so Canada's economic model has become based largely on finance-led growth, with an expanding financial sector and its profits leading the way, and more and more businesses using finance to extract wealth and value from the wider economy as well as workers.

Financialization

Such economic consequences are best characterized as *"financialization"* – which I argue is a second critical factor explaining Canada's rising inequality. In the post-war period, and the aftermath of war and depression, the story of finance was largely one of commercial banks turning people's savings into investments, and governments making significant efforts to ensure that finance was carefully regulated so that financial investments and trading smoothed out the economy's up and down cycles. In this era, banks lent, people and business borrowed, and credit helped realize long-term investments. Consequently, finance flowed largely in the service of the economy and society.

Today, none of this holds true. To the contrary, in recent decades finance has exploded into an almost limitless system of private credit, and, with wider efforts to loosen regulation by the United States and other countries, investment is more typically channelled into such things as short-term money markets and inflated bubbles in property, equity, and financial products, as opposed to long-term growth (Durand 2017). Moreover, companies are far less tied to long-term investments and capital assets than to the interests of investors and shareholders and their demands for rising profit margins and financial returns, often through the heavy use of debt and debt financing. Consequently, more and more of Canada's economy is beholden to finance, and much like in the United States, wealth creation is driven by financial markets and incentives, with the "takers" using the market system to enrich themselves at the expense of the "makers" – that is the companies and workers that do create real economic growth (Forhoohar 2016).

But such a reversal in the roles of finance and business has not been due to chance or inexplicable "market forces." Rather the expansion of private credit and debt and their growth by leaps and bounds has been due to how governments have "deregulated" and "liberalized" their financial sectors, and turned authority over credit to the banks and the many multiplying financial actors themselves. In contrast to the post-war period, where public officials sought to reign in the activities of private banks and make private credit institutions provide loans to households and businesses, in recent decades governments have reversed course and handed back the privilege of creating money to commercial banks and other financial actors, allowing them to issue increasingly astronomical sums of loans and credit. At the same time, national governments have overhauled international institutions and regulations to allow new financial intermediaries to explode in size and complexity. Sovereign wealth funds, money managers, investment banks, pension funds, and many other financial interests now dominate national and international economies alike – each using its ownership of assets and role in financial markets to secure increasing income and wealth. Indeed, the growth has been so rapid that finance itself has become more risky, opaque, and complex – as much to government as to everyday citizens (Lapavitsas 2014; Lin and Neely 2020).

Yet this rapid growth has sparked another major economic sea change – in the "non-financial sector" – that is among the businesses that make things in the real economy and work with their vast supply chains. Businesses no longer simply make products or deliver services. Rather the largest corporations and their monopolies now rely heavily on debt and financial assets and focus their attention on increasing their profits in money and financial markets, as well as distributing returns to shareholders, rather than paying and retaining their workforce. Indeed, because they have taken advantage of a host of policy reforms and international changes, multinational corporations rely less and less on their traditional enterprises. Instead corporations lean ever more heavily on financial activities and rely on financial markets to make money. Now, for example, companies from GM to Apple routinely earn nearly as much profit from financial markets and financial markets as they do from making their actual products (Forhoohar 2016).

For workers and the larger labour market, the consequences of such a shift have been profound. No longer do bigger and more profitable firms ensure good jobs or the wider redistribution of income – but the opposite. Rather, in Canada – as elsewhere – finance-led growth functions more on the basis of "trickle-up" economics, with the corporate pursuit of maximum profit and the redistribution of earnings away from workers and toward executives and investors. Increasingly, corporations focus their growth strategies on maximizing "shareholder value," and managers seek to implement a whole range of strategies to reduce labour costs, such as downsizing, layoffs, and concessions from their unionized workforces. Or private equity partnerships use debt to take over companies and subsequently strip the firm of assets while terminating higher-paid workers (Batt and Appelbaum 2013; Lin and Neely 2020; Milberg and Winkler 2013).

Making matters worse is how many financialized corporations routinely resort to squeezing their widening global network of suppliers and contractors to produce more with less, making them less able to pay workers and more likely to use non-standard employment contracts to keep labour costs at a minimum (Appelbaum 2017; Weil 2014). Continually sidelined in their efforts, workers and unions alike have been left with eroding bargaining powers, far fewer protections, and widening economic insecurity.

"Financialization" is the term widely used today to describe this host of changes, and how and why private financial actors, markets, and credit have come to play such leading roles in everything from housing markets and real estate, manufacturing and agriculture, to the growth of new information technology and global cities (Epstein 2015). But "financialization" is also a term used to characterize how companies in the "real" economy – that is, businesses that actually create goods from cars and social media apps, to gasoline and groceries – have begun turning their attention away from their earlier concerns with making productive changes and investing in machinery and workers, and instead prioritizing finance and "financial engineering" to maximize shareholder profits and to extract wealth from the economy and their workforces with increasing creativity (Durand 2017; Shaxson 2018).

It is these multi-sided developments to finance, firms, and the economy – as well as to how government has directly aided and abetted such financialization – I argue that can help us explain why average Canadians have seen no benefit from the growing power, size, and efficiencies of firms. Indeed, it is because of financialization that the astronomical salaries of the financial sector and corporate CEOs have gone hand-in-hand with low-wage work, precarious employment, and deindustrialization.

Labour Market Deregulation

But a third and final overarching factor to explain why more and more Canadians are struggling to make ends meet is how politics and power dynamics have led to the overhaul of labour laws, regulations, and policies that once supported good jobs and a more equal society – a process called *labour market deregulation*.

As we will see, financialization and globalization are certainly key parts of any economic explanation for why jobs have worsened and incomes have stagnated. But the other side of the equation is what further policy adjustments public officials have made to accommodate the new financially driven demands of corporations, suppliers, and service industries to lower labour costs and create more "flexible" labour markets. For as financialization has increasingly made big firms less willing and small firms often less able to pay, so governments have sought to increase employer power and enhance managerial discretion at work by changing labour laws and employment policies – or by failing to enforce them – in order to expose workers to the relentless forces of competitive global markets.

This too has been a profound change and helps us account for rising inequality. After the Second World War, Canada followed the United States and Western Europe in developing a broader labour regime that recognized worker's rights inside their workplaces (Eidlin 2018; Western 1997). Under the pressure of unions and progressive political parties, public officials established new labour laws alongside unemployment insurance, public pensions, and family allowance programs to support workers, but also to ensure the income security of the unemployed, the elderly, and families. Such laws and policies radically changed the power equation between capital and labour in Canada and other societies, in large measure by extending democracy from a rather limited sphere of civil society and into the heart of capitalism – the economy and the workplace (McAlevey 2020).

But in recent decades, this power equation has been slowly and consistently reversed: business has used its demands for "competitiveness" and greater profitability to push public officials to overhaul labour laws and employment policies or simply ignore the growing violations of basic labour standards and norms. Following neoclassical economic theories claiming that any interference in markets leads to less than optimal outcomes, governments have often listened carefully to such appeals and recast public policies to make labour and social policies conform more closely to market and business priorities (Baccaro and Howell 2017). Just as frequently, in an effort to promote better business conditions, as demanded by increasingly aggressive business lobbyists, officials have simply let non-standard employment and labour insecurity grow, fearing that any countermeasures will not be good for business and the economy (Weil 2014).

For labour markets in Canada and around the world, these trends have led to "deregulation" – the unwinding, erosion, and limited enforcement of laws, policies, and regulations governing labour markets that were once oriented to upholding workers' rights and bargaining power. Routinely, over the past four decades, public officials have sought to deregulate labour markets in order to maximize economic "efficiency" and boost employer profitability, making deregulation the dominant policy paradigm for government labour market policies around the world (Baccaro and Avdagic 2014; Crouch 2014). As we shall see, such deregulation varies greatly in form and scope, as much for economic reasons as for political ones. But changes to labour market laws and policies such as these also help us explain the growing number of poorer-quality jobs and the proliferation of low-wage work in a number of Canada's provinces.

Together, I argue it is this interlaced rise of post-democracy, financialization, and labour market deregulation that is the real story behind the rise of inequality in Canada today. Over the last thirty years, public officials have rewritten the rules of the market so that business and financial elites could accrue unprecedented amounts of capital and income. But of equal importance is how, with the growing pressures of financially pressured corporations and employers, governments made consistent efforts to deregulate and loosen the constraints of labour rules and policies for the benefit of employers. In each of these ways, this book shows that inequality is the inevitable result of governments recasting their priorities to support business and finance, and doing so in ways that assist the privileged few at the cost of poorer income distribution and worsening jobs and wages for the many.

Top Income Inequality and Low-Wage Work in Canada

Economic growth and globalization were intended to increase incomes and standards of living for all workers, but it is clear that in Canada and many other countries the gains have been heavily concentrated at the top. Indeed, income growth among the rich in Canada has been so profound that compared to the past forty years (as long as data on inequality have been collected), Canada has never seen higher levels of top income inequality than right now (Osberg 2008; Veall 2012; Yalnizyan 2010). This development follows international trends in rising income inequality among the richest across developed countries (OECD 2011a, 2014a). But as the data show in a wide variety of ways – from top income shares, to market incomes, after-tax household incomes, and hourly and annual earnings – Canada is at an extreme among advanced industrial countries, with only the United States regularly witnessing higher levels of top income inequality (OECD 2011a, 2014a, 2015a).

For example, the share of the top 10 per cent in earned pre-tax income soared from approximately 32 per cent in 1980 to more than 42 per cent in 2015 across Western Europe and North America (Alvaredo et al. 2018). At the same time, income became even more concentrated at the top, where once capital gains are included, the share of income that the top 1 per cent of earners has received has gone from 9 per cent to 18 per cent (Atkinson, Piketty, and Saez 2011). This trend was most marked in the United States, where the share of the richest 1 per cent in all pre-tax income more than doubled, reaching 23 per cent in 2011 (OECD 2014a), but rich households also did well in Canada, where the top 1 per cent income share rose from 8.8 per cent in 1980 to 15.6 per cent in 2015.

This rapid rise in income inequality at the very top can be seen in several countries, but most notably in North America. As figure 1.1 demonstrates, the United States and Canada had the greatest disparities in income distribution. In terms of income captured by the top 1 per cent of earners, the richest in the United States accrued more than 47 per cent of all economic growth over this thirty-year period; in Canada, the richest received more than 37 per cent. Canada's top 10 per cent of earners, meanwhile, gained more than 66 per cent of all income earned during this period, only behind the United States, where the richest 10 per cent took home more than 72 per cent of all pre-tax income. By stark contrast, in Scandinavian countries, the distribution of income growth was far more egalitarian, with the top 1 per cent of earners in Denmark

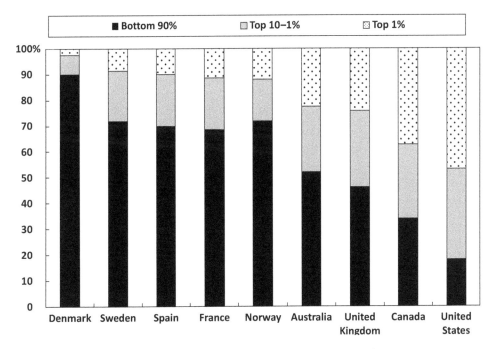

| ■ Bottom 90% | □ Top 10–1% | ▨ Top 1% |

Figure 1.1. Share of total income growth 1976–2007 captured by top income earners
Source: OECD (2014b), Trends in Top Incomes and Their Taxation.

capturing only 2.5 per cent of income, and the bottom 90 per cent earners earning 90 per cent of all income growth.

Unsurprisingly, given this uneven distribution of income, average economic gains were also heavily skewed toward those at the top. This was true in many countries, but particularly in Canada, where households at the bottom of the distribution did not keep pace with higher-income households and were left far behind by the richest individual earners (Lemieux and Riddell 2016).

Figure 1.2 portrays the scale of the disparity. It combines data calculated for working households, which is the most comprehensive measure for comparing household incomes, with family incomes of top income earners after tax. For the poorest 10 per cent of working families, average income was basically flat for more than twenty years, improving only in the wake of the financial crisis to $7,770. Those in the middle fifth did only slightly better, as their average income rose from $45,700 to $53,100 – an increase of 16 per cent. But this largely reflected the fact that the majority of households were working an additional 336 hours a year (Marshall 2009). Without these additional hours, household income would have fallen.

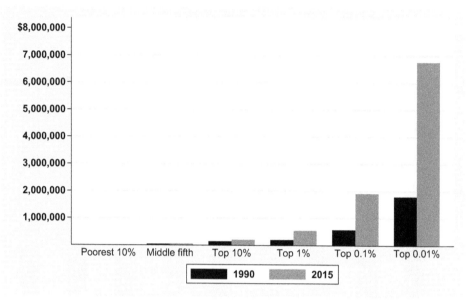

Figure 1.2. Average household and top income earner after-tax income in Canada, 1990–2015 (including capital gains)
Source: Author's figures based on a custom data request for "Market and After-Tax Incomes of Economic Families under Age 65," Survey of Labour and Income Dynamics, and custom data request "Market and After-Tax Incomes of Economic Families T1 Family File Tax Data," Statistics Canada.

In stark contrast, those at the top – and especially at the very top – witnessed exponential gains. Those whose family incomes put them among the richest 1 per cent of income earners increased their earnings 172 per cent over the twenty-five year period. The incomes of the richest 0.01 per cent (the richest 1500 families in Canada) grew even more, by 275 per cent to $6.75 million annually. And to put this in perspective, relative to what was happening in the rest of the labour market, in 1990, the richest 0.1 per cent had incomes twelve times larger than those of the average household; in 2015, the incomes of the rich were thirty-six times greater.

But the story of rising inequality in Canada does not just stop with the rich and how they have pulled away from everyone else. That is only part of it. Rising inequality in Canada has also been a story of the ongoing expansion of bad jobs and the systematic proliferation of low-wage non-standard employment. This disappearance of good jobs and their replacement by low-wage and non-standard jobs has also been key to rising inequality. And as we shall see, soaring incomes for the very rich and stagnating wages for the rest of the

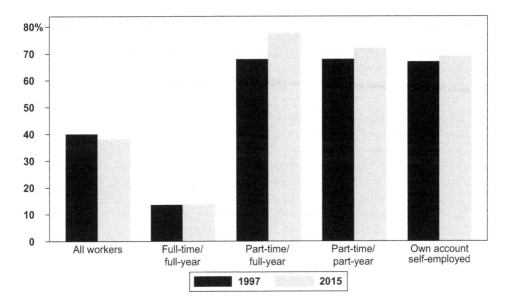

Figure 1.3. Low-wage work in Canada, 1997–2015 (% of workers below two-thirds of median full-time hourly wage)
Source: Author's figures from custom data request "Percentage of Workers with Low Annual Earnings and Low Hourly Wages, by Industry," Survey of Labour and Income Dynamics, Statistics Canada, custom table C749006; and Canadian Income Survey, "Percentage of Workers with Low Annual Earnings and Low Hourly Wages, by Industry, Canada, 2012–2015," custom table C858032.

labour force are not independent occurrences. Rather, rising inequality is due to an increasingly skewed economy that rewards owners for extracting wealth from the economy, rather than investing in their enterprises and good jobs.

One way of considering how little income many in the labour market receive is by calculating the number of people in low-paying jobs. The definition of low pay still differs considerably across countries, but the OECD has developed a widely used definition that defines low pay as workers earning less than two-thirds of the median hourly or annual earnings for all full-time workers. Using this definition, Canada currently has the third-highest level of low-wage work in the OECD, with 21.7 per cent of full-time workers in low-wage employment in 2015, behind only that of the United States and Ireland among advanced industrial economies (OECD 2015b, table O).

But as figure 1.3 demonstrates, looking more broadly at all employees (including those working in part-time and non-standard employment and "bogus" self-employment contracts), data demonstrate that in 2015 more than 37 per cent of workers in Canada were in jobs with hourly wages below what a full-time, full-year worker needed to maintain a decent standard of living. Again while full comparative data are limited (and notably the United States does not calculate low-wage work for those in non-standard employment), the International Labor Organization reports that only Panama and Honduras had comparable overall levels of low-wage employment in their workforce of more than 35 per cent (ILO 2011a, figure 21). Thus, explaining inequality in Canada also entails coming to grips with what has happened to the labour market more broadly, and what accounts for the exceptionally high share of low-wage work in the labour market.

What is so striking about figure 1.3 is how many Canadian workers were mired in low-paying, insecure jobs. Over the past few decades, the policy argument has been routinely made that governments should deregulate labour markets and promote "flexibility" – part-time, temporary, and self-employment – in order to have private business enthusiastically recruit new workers. In deregulating, it is argued, public officials can promote employment while also reducing income inequality, as the number of people earning no salary or relying on unemployment benefits would fall. Unfortunately, the reality in recent years has been different.

Most telling are the data for those in part-time, temporary, and own-account self-employment – who now make up over 40 per cent of the total Canadian labour market. While the Canadian Income Survey does not fully count all those who are precariously employed, the data still show that for these workers in 2015, a non-standard job has meant low wages, little security, and few long-term prospects. Indeed, so wide was the discrepancy in wages between those in secure, full-time/full-year jobs and those in part-time, temporary, and own-account self-employment, that even the OECD noted how Canada had the highest wage penalties among the advanced industrial economies (OECD 2015a, 152–3).

The data are most striking in comparisons with other rich world economies, where workers in non-standard work arrangements take home only 55–9 per cent of what a full-time worker regularly earns hourly. By contrast, in Canada over the course of a year, the earning levels of those Canadians in precarious jobs were far worse. Based on the Statistics Canada data noted in figure 1.3, in 2015 the more than six million Canadians in non-standard employment averaged only $15,725 – or only 29 per cent of what a full-time/full-year worker earned.

The Standard Debates on Income Distribution and Inequality

Such recent trends seem to belie the hypothesis that economic globalization and the opening of economies to rising levels of trade and investment by multinational corporations, alongside making the labour market increasingly flexible with less regulation and lower levels of social protection, would provide widespread benefit to those in the labour force. Indeed, these figures appear to show the opposite.

These data demonstrate that, like the United States, Canada has seen a steep upward concentration of income going to the very top. But at the same time, as in the United States, many ordinary Canadian workers have seen wages stagnate. Like in the United States, many Canadians are stuck in low-wage, non-standard employment. And as this book argues, such similarities in growing income inequality and the pervasive spread of low-wage work track very closely to those in the United States – trends that describe what has been called a "Winner-Take-All" economy (Hacker and Pierson 2010b; Reich 2015; Stiglitz 2013).

Yet while rising income inequality and the growth of low-wage work and non-standard employment have been recognized by the research community, the debate continues on the primary *causes* of these changes. The standard explanation in the scholarly literature attributes the widening gap between the rich and the majority of workers to "market forces," and above all to globalization and new technologies that have made many Canadians less "competitive" in the labour market. Some economists and many comparative political economists, for example, claim rising inequality is due to "skill-biased technological change" – a shift toward greater emphasis on specialized skills, knowledge, and education – that has fuelled a growing divide between the highly educated and the rest of the workforce (Autor, Katz, and Kearny 2005; Spitz-Oener 2006; Green and Sand 2015).

However, the standard explanation for externally generated technological change favouring the most educated does not appear to account for much of what has happened. Sweden and Denmark, for example – both among the most open and globalized economies in the world – have not seen similar increases in income concentration (OECD 2015a). Indeed as figure 1.1 shows, in Denmark, 90 per cent of income is still shared among 90 per cent of the working population. Thus, if their economies have faced the same pressures, an explanation based on globalization and adaptation to technology does not tell us why workers in these countries have not succumbed to these forces as quickly, and why these countries have the lowest levels of income inequality and almost no incidence of "working poverty."

Nor do arguments about the level of education take us very far. Certainly, Canada has a slightly lower rate of post-secondary education or vocational school completion, and the gap between the wages of the high-skilled and low-skilled workers has increased in Canada compared to the OECD average (OECD 2013; Boudarbat, Lemieux, and Riddell 2010). But overall, Canada has one of the highest rates of workers with some post-secondary or vocational schooling, and during the first decade of 2000, levels of post-secondary and vocational education rose (Green and Sand 2015). This suggests that despite rising upper post-secondary attainment rates, and higher rates of educational completion among women in particular, the majority of Canadians have seen little return on their educational investments. Such trends challenge arguments about technology rewarding the better educated.

What, then, of sociological differences and social patterns of inequality in the labour market? Over the past decade or more, sociologists have often argued that inequality is affected by the changing composition of the workforce, most notably by the increased participation in the labour force by women and migrants, who are typically underpaid in comparison to non-migrant men (Crompton 2006; Esping-Anderson 1999). Sociologists have also examined how these trends in social inequality have been exacerbated by the rapid growth of service sector employment, which has often occurred on the basis of labour-intensive, low-skilled jobs, which are typically poorly compensated. Consequently, as atypical and low-paid employment among women, visible minorities, and migrants has become more widespread, the economic precarity of many socially disadvantaged groups has deepened (Jackson 2010; Oesch 2006; Vosko 2006a).

These arguments are clearly very important in accounting for why income inequality is so pervasive among individuals and households with specific social characteristics. In Canada, women, visible minorities, and recent immigrants are more likely to work in non-standard jobs and are far more likely to work for low wages and in jobs with little stability than others in the labour force (Galabuzi 2006; Jackson 2010; Noack and Vosko 2011; Vosko, MacDonald, and Campbell 2009).

However, as we shall see in chapter 4, non-standard work and low-wage employment cut across gender, ethnic, and immigrant divides. Male unionized manufacturing and resource sectors have also lost hundreds of thousands of good jobs. In construction – a traditional male area of good jobs – the dominant trend has been growing part-time and low-paid self-employment. Then there is the issue of the stratospheric rise of the top 1 per cent, which seems little associated with a sociological explanation of changing patterns of employment among women, minorities, or youth.

This suggests that the drivers of rocketing top income inequality and low-paid work are not just those of advantaged or disadvantaged social groups, but rather systematic – that is, the political and economic dynamics that have allowed business and finance to rise while putting many millions of Canadians at risk of falling into – and then remaining in – low-paid work. Indeed, most notable is how financialization and deregulation have promoted and deepened these other sociological variables that have helped institutionalize inequality across Canadian society.

Critical Political Economy and Inequality

What of the role of government and politics? Could public officials and the policies they enact – or fail to enact – have created this jobs-with-inequality economy? Certainly, over the past decade, more political scientists have begun to suggest as much, pointing out that politicians are doing much less to redress the imbalances of income and resources than they have in previous decades (Anderson and Beramendi 2008; Emmenegger et al. 2012; Kelly 2009; Banting and Myles 2014). Indeed, this research suggests that politics and public policy are contributing significantly to rising inequality and the dualization of labour markets.

Some of the changes to income and wealth distribution have been due to the changing politics of the welfare state, including how governments have introduced economic-oriented reforms or retrenched programs like health care or pensions to save public expenditure (Huber and Stephens 2001; Iversen 2006; Pontusson 2005), or how government-sponsored or mandated maternity leave and childcare have been legislated to boost women's labour market participation (Crompton 2006; Del Boca and Wetzels 2007), or how public officials have sought to reduce income security programs by tightening unemployment insurance and in their place institute activation programs (Huo 2009; Lindvall 2010). Scholarship has also explored the outcomes of different political-economic regimes, as well as how polities respond to the shocks of economic downturns, technological and corporate innovation, demographic change, and globalization (Amable 2003; Armingeon and Bonoli 2006).

But as a growing literature in critical political economy has illustrated, what has been most common to the global economy in recent years is the exponential growth of transnational firms and finance, and the ongoing transfer of income and wealth to the wealthiest few (Atkinson 2015; Panitch and Gindin 2013; Stiglitz 2013). Over the past few decades, governments have made deliberate policy choices that have given the banking and financial industries enormous new opportunities to profit from financial innovations and the generation of private credit with few limits. But public officials have also rebuilt regulatory and legal frameworks that have allowed finance to take over firms and allowed companies to construct global production networks across countries. These changes in how governments have supported business and financial systems – a process often referred to as "neoliberalism" – have led to multinational corporations outsourcing, developing global supply chains, and relying on the flexible labour of contractors and suppliers, all in order to maximize "shareholder value" and profits (Barker 2010; Batt and Appelbaum 2014; Cobb 2016; Lin 2016; Lapavitsas 2014).

In making these arguments, critical scholars acknowledge that different institutions – whether electoral, industrial relations, or social programs – shape conflicts among political and economic interests and continue to lead to different combinations of firm and market supporting public polices associated with "competitiveness" across countries (Jessop 2016; Neilson and Stubbs 2016; Cerny 2010; Streeck 2014). However, critical scholarship has distinctly highlighted how successful business and finance have been in generating increasingly unequal outcomes, regardless of institutional setting. And the key reason has been the ability of organized economic interests to reshape the political and policy priorities of governments around the world – away from the concerns of ordinary citizens and the less fortunate and toward the demands of business and finance (Coates 2014; Crouch 2010; Hacker and Pierson 2016).

In examining rising inequality and the increasing polarization of the labour market between well-paid good jobs and low-paid, insecure jobs in Canada, I draw on these critical political economy perspectives to advance a set of theoretical propositions about the role of powerful economic interests and the financial sector in compelling governments to rewrite the rules by which markets work. Like others in current political economy literatures, I am most interested in understanding the political dynamics that explain how finance and credit have strengthened capitalism, and how capitalism in turn has enhanced its capacity to extract wealth and value from workers and the wider economy in recent decades (Durand 2017; Lapavitsas 2014; Lin and Neely 2020; Panitch and Gindin 2013).

However, in pursuing these issues, this book looks to delve more deeply into how economic inequality results from and influences politics today. Looking beyond how governments shape income distribution through after-tax and transfer policies, I first focus my attention on how business and financial markets operate, and how government and policies have reshaped these rules to the benefit of the wealthy few. Front and centre in my account are the political forces and policies that have restructured the operation of financial markets, corporate governance, and firm operation at the expense of good wages and jobs – "financialization."

But of equal importance in my explanation are the complex relationships between class and politics that have reshaped labour markets and labour policies to create a more "flexible" low-cost labour force – "labour market deregulation." Together, I argue it is the new interconnections between post-democracy, financialization, and deregulation that help us explain "Jobs with Inequality." It is their mutual ties that best illuminate how and why capitalism's transformations have gone hand-in-hand with the decline of labour laws and employment policies. And as I demonstrate, such dynamics go a long way to clarify why and how economic inequalities have spilled over into the realm of democratic participation, producing persistent patterns of bias in political voice and political resources – a new politics of inequality that has consistently reversed the distribution of income upwards to a wealthy few over recent decades.

Explaining the Rise in Inequality in the Long Run

A final comment about causality. Typically, in conventional social science as well as much of critical political science and economics, researchers look for direct and immediate connections where x directly leads to y (Pierson 2003). But as other contemporary scholarship has begun to emphasize, it is important to consider how key developments occur over long periods of time (Mahoney 2003).

Crucially, explanations must be more comprehensive, because this is how real-world developments occur – over time, through numerous causal chains, occasionally with sudden ruptures, but more frequently with cumulative, snowballing effects, as change at one point sets the stage for future developments. In part, this explanatory strategy also captures how, over the long run, not only do policy reforms regulate markets, but rule changes also reshape and recast the capacity for organized action among business and labour (Hacker and Pierson 2010b).

This book tells a similar story. It focuses on the relationships between capitalism and democracy, and how changes in politics, the economy, and the labour market became self-reinforcing. Public policies explain such long-term outcomes, and their reform or non-enforcement pattern income distribution and jobs in the wider labour market – directly as well as indirectly. In the first instance, laws and policies directly influence who gets what and when – for example, minimum wage laws or unemployment insurance have direct everyday consequences on the income security of citizens. But in the long run as well, policies, laws, and regulations shape the resources available to organized economic interests and the resources that elites and citizens alike can use to colour the wider political culture (Hacker 2006).

Whether free trade and investment agreements or union certification regulations or other economic and labour markets rules and regulations, each has substantive and direct impacts on income distribution and economic inequalities and subsequently on the political resources and capacities of organized interests (Jessop 2016; Kelly 1998; Jacobs and Soss 2010). So too public policies can force business to compromise and strengthen the ability of workers to organize, or unleash market forces that provide business with the wealth and political resources to oppose regulation, taxation, or any broader cooperation with organized labour (Hacker and Pierson 2010ab; Martin and Swank 2012).

Here, in pursuing these ideas, I look to offer a more comprehensive and synthetic account of Canada's political economy. And in so doing, I seek to address an empirical puzzle that still limits contemporary thinking on inequality in Canada and elsewhere today – why capital over the past few decades has so routinely captured increasing portions of national income, and why citizens in their everyday jobs and organizations have so regularly lost the countervailing powers necessary to resist and initiate an economy that works for a wider common interest.

Canada and Its Provinces as Case Studies for Inequality and Labour Market Reform

It is also useful to provide a brief overview of why Canada – as well as three of its provinces – provides an especially valuable context for comparative political-economic and labour market analysis.

One of the most important reasons for examining Canada is that in the first decades of the twenty-first century, Canada experienced particularly strong economic and employment growth (OECD 2010). Among industrialized economies, it had among the best economic growth rates and employment performance, fuelled in large part by record resource exports and large inflows of foreign direct investment, combined with record-breaking housing and property markets.

Moreover, unlike many other countries, Canada avoided the worst impacts of the financial crisis and did not see a major economic slowdown or long-term rise in unemployment. Yet at the same time, the country witnessed one of the most dramatic increases in pre-tax and benefit income inequality among G20 countries (OECD 2008). Low-wage work and non-standard employment also continued to grow, and Canada retained one of the most inequitable labour markets in the OECD, despite above-average rates of economic growth (OECD 2011a, 2015a). Canada also has one of the highest rates of top income inequality and has witnessed a rapid increase in the wealth of top income earners (Credit Suisse 2015).

In recent years, economists have claimed that rather than redistribute income, policymakers should focus on policies that improve returns to business – make such economic reforms – and the "job creators" (i.e., business owners) will invest and generate prosperity for all (Reich 2015). But in Canada this has been far from the case. Despite economic growth and the creation of more jobs, inequality has continued its slow and steady rise. So insight is needed into how and why striking levels of growth in a wealthy, advanced industrial country were accompanied by an equally striking growth in inequality. Focusing on the major structural shifts to policy and the economy that have abetted big finance and big business, it is argued here, provides one important part of the explanation.

Second, Canada is an important case for studying how policy and power are key contributors to inequality because of what has happened to economic and labour policies in recent years. Theoretically, if only technology and market competition are to blame for rising inequality, there should be little evidence of policy reform, and equally little evidence of how such reforms may have contributed to the widening gap between the rich and the rest of the labour market.

But as we shall see, during the past few decades there is much evidence of sweeping federal and provincial economic reforms in Canada (Evans and Smith 2015b; McBride and Whiteside 2011). Beginning in the 1980s, Canadian officials signed onto and helped initiate regional and international trade deals (Clarkson 2002). Canada was also one of the first to follow the US lead in initiating mortgage-backed securities (Dionne and Harchaoui 2007) and worked with the United States to develop new international legislation for derivatives and debt-backed securities in the 1980s (Porter 2014). So too government officials under financial pressure overhauled monetary policy, changed banking regulations, and overhauled pension regulations. And in the wake of these policy reforms, credit markets soared and multinationals grew exponentially in size and market power (Brennan 2012). Digging into the reasons for how and why a smaller, advanced economy like Canada's adopted competitive reforms that in the end benefitted the few, allows us an ideal opportunity to explore the roles of major economic policy change to inequality and how it has contributed to rising precarity in the workforce.

Third, what also makes Canada such an especially interesting case for the study of public policy and power is how uncommonly decentralized it is, and how this allows for close comparative analysis of political power and policy and their influence on inequality and income distribution. Unlike many other advanced countries where labour law and institutions are overseen by national governments, for example, in Canada the provinces are largely responsible for collective bargaining and labour regulation in the private and public sector as well as for setting basic employment standards, health and safety, and equity for non-unionized private sector employees. Federal labour law covers only some 10 per cent of workers, while the remaining 90 per cent are under provincial or territorial bargaining and employment regulations (Warner 2013). As much conventional literature has suggested, this decentralization of political authority to Canada's provinces provides ample opportunity for analysts to examine how partisan, economic, and institutional variables are thought to influence policy development across the provinces (Banting and Myles 2014; Klassen and Haddow 2006).

But I argue that if Canada's provinces provide especially good cases for comparative study, the focus of most researchers on short-term variables comes at a heavy cost. Above all, as we shall see, economic cycles, "external" market forces, partisanship, and institutions do little to explain soaring inequality. At the same time, too much of Canada's conventional social science simply misses the major social forces driving political-economic change, largely because it ignores how political-economic change occurs over longer periods of time.

However, shifting our attention to the changing composition and activities of business and labour, as well as to the interaction between parties and citizens across the provinces does provide us with an entirely new perspective. Economic, electoral, partisan, and institutional variables, which are all fairly constant across these provinces, are perhaps necessary in understanding general patterns and developments, but cannot explain political and policy outcomes, whether for economic or labour policies and laws. Rather, I argue, variations in labour law and employment policy far better reflect complex political configurations within post-democracy and financialization than other alternative explanations can.

Indeed, in looking at Canada's provincial economies closely, we can see not only how businesses organize politically, and how and in what ways parties seek to mobilize powerful political-economic interests to gain or hold power. We can also begin to understand how pro-labour actors and citizens can articulate and defend their preferences in the policy process or – just as frequently – how they fail to do so. Thus, it is by taking post-democracy seriously, and how it is tied to wider financialized industries and sectors in three of Canada's provinces, that we can get a far better grasp on how and why governments recast their labour law and policy models and approaches, whether through "reform," "drift," or "stasis."

Overview of the Book

To explain how inequality has become such a widespread and deep-seated problem in Canada, this book advances in two steps, each of which has its own section, and which interested researchers and readers may choose from first.

Part 1 addresses in detail how rising business power and new economic policies transformed Canada's market economy, creating almost limitless credit, and opened the way for financialization with its wide-ranging impacts on firms, income distribution, and labour markets. Chapter 2 discusses the theoretical underpinnings for understanding financialization and summarizes reasons for its recent rise and impacts on income distribution. The chapter sketches a conceptual model for how – as government support evolves and financialization advances – there are four key channels through which inequality progresses: the growth of private credit and assets that boosts the size of corporate assets alongside the salaries and compensation of top income earners; financial ownership that undermines unionized employment; corporate focus on "shareholder value," which increases rent extraction at the cost of investment and good jobs; and how financialization in many industries fissures jobs and employment contracts through outsourcing and supplier networks, with contractors and producers resorting to low-wage work and non-standard employment.

In chapter 3, I turn my attention to how financialization developed in Canada, and how under the pressure of business and financial interests, government officials rewrote economic policy to favour private financial and corporate interests. As I demonstrate, not only were the rules of Canada's monetary and financial systems overhauled in recent decades, allowing finance and credit markets to grow exponentially. But so too were tax, pension, investment, and trade rules reformed to allow corporations to manage their operations across borders, with little oversight by regulatory authorities. It was with these policy changes that private financial markets, techniques, and financial ways of thinking began to penetrate corporations and businesses in the "real" economy. At the same time, with the increasing resort of managers to financial assets for greater profits, and the growing focus of business owners on short-term stock prices and cash flows, managers and employers throughout widening supply chains began to push for more flexible labour forces to improve their returns and roll over their debts.

In chapter 4, I use the best statistical data available to test my claims about financialization and its impacts on the labour market and income inequality in Canada. Placing Canada in a comparative context, I employ a wealth of quantitative evidence to evaluate the argument that growing private credit and asset markets, alongside the new financial logics of corporations and their suppliers, are linked to the rise of low-wage work and the growing gap between the rich and the rest of Canada's workforce. Rather than independent phenomena, I claim there is much evidence to suggest that the rising incomes for the top 1 per cent and bad jobs for workers are interconnected dynamics of a political economy that today systematically rewards a few at the expense of the many – a growth model of "jobs with inequality."

Having analysed the wide-ranging effects of public policy on business and financial power and their role in initiating a finance-driven capitalism in recent decades, the second part of the book shifts its focus to domestic politics and how the emergence of organized, financially driven business interests have helped recast labour laws and employment regulations in increasingly inegalitarian ways. In the second half of the book, I seek to answer two questions: First, "How has finance-driven business in Canada been so successful in reshaping democracy and labour-related public policies to its advantage?" And second, "Why have democracies, citizens, and workers failed to counter rising inequality and the decline of good jobs?"

In answering these questions, I examine the distinct ways that post-democracy has contributed to "hard" neoliberal reforms of labour market deregulation; or led to the consolidation of policy "drift" and the blocking of progressive reforms to labour law and employment regulation; or opened the way to "stasis" and the failure to address wider problems of low-wage work and unemployment. Chapter 5 details the framework for understanding these patterns, and how the politics of post-democracy, coloured by financialization, has led to rollbacks, erosions, and circumventions to labour law and employment protection.

In the following provincial case study chapters, I explore in detail how the politics of post-democracy and the processes of financialization pattern labour market reform and generate rising inequality. In chapter 6, I examine how in British Columbia, post-democratic developments were strongest and resulted in the widespread "reform" of labour law, employment regulation, and social policy. In chapter 7, on Newfoundland and Labrador, I argue that the evidence suggests that the ruling Conservatives relied there on a booming oil sector as well as a more traditional brokerage strategy of appealing to many sectors to increase employment and reduce inequality. In this case, the Conservative government labour policy can be best characterized as one of "stasis," amid the renewal of bargaining frameworks and expansion of education and training opportunities for workers. But these policies did little to improve employment more widely in the province, where unemployment and temporary employment remain among the highest in Canada.

In chapter 8, I turn to Ontario to make the case that even though financialization drove aggressive demands for deregulation, employers were only strong enough to block reforms, but they were not united enough to drive a deregulatory agenda. This segmentation of organized business power was crucial to the development of a policy trajectory of "drift." That the Liberal Party sought to draw on urban constituencies as its base of support also limited the appeal of more extensive labour market reforms.

Finally, in chapter 9, I conclude by exploring what our understanding of financialization, post-democracy, and labour market deregulation in Canada can offer for the study of capitalism and inequality more broadly today, and I conclude by noting alternative policies and politics that could tackle recent inegalitarian trends. In particular, I highlight what a broader synthesis of critical political economy and literature on post-democracy and financialization can provide for new explanations of income inequality. I also briefly discuss more comprehensive economic, political, and labour market alternatives needed to go beyond recent "jobs with inequality" models.

Discussions of data, information on interviews conducted, and a discussion of my methodology – as well as the importance of new income data from tax and income surveys – are addressed in the appendices. Over the past decade or so, scholars have found several new sources of data to track inequality – especially tax and income data for the top 1 per cent of earners, as well as for those workers in low-wage employment. To shed light on income distribution and jobs in Canada I employ similar statistical data, and in the appendices I discuss the gaps in Canadian data and address my use of other national and international statistics, including government documents. I also note how these sources are used to evaluate the validity of my explanations on financialization and labour market deregulation. Scholars interested in these statistics – as well as my approach – what they offer, and how they go beyond more conventional accounts – may wish to begin with these issues first.

PART ONE

Financialization and Income Inequality

2 Bringing Finance into the Labour Market Inequality Debate

Democracy is premised on the idea that government decisions should meet the needs of the population, and that citizens are offered opportunities to participate in shaping public life. However, over the past three decades, not only has globalization deepened inequality, but government has also retreated from income redistribution and high-road labour standards. In the wake of the 2008–9 financial crisis over the past decade, these worrying trends have only worsened.

In this chapter I provide the theoretical foundations for why this occurred, and why government responses to rising inequality have been not just inadequate but have in fact exacerbated widening income inequality. In outlining my conceptual model, I argue that business power and neoliberal policy shifts have driven rising income inequality by uprooting older models of finance and firm operation, replacing them with new private credit models and finance-driven management strategies that emphasize the reduction of labour costs and the distribution of rents and profits to asset holders. The results I claim have been the "financialization" of the real economy, which has fundamentally changed the basic workings of capital accumulation and explains why labour markets and jobs have been skewed along far more unequal lines, with the prosperity for an elite few tied to the deepening of low-wage work and precarious employment for the many.

I present this overview of financialization and its impacts on labour markets and workers in four parts. I first review recent critical political economy debates about the origins, dynamics, and impacts of neoliberalism on public policy, with a specific eye to how they have contributed to rising inequality. Second, I explore the causes and consequences of financialization on income distribution and labour markets, arguing that a focus on finance improves critical accounts' understanding of how business has been able to maximize returns from global markets and labour alike. Third, I develop an explanation about why we might expect that, with such financialization, income is consistently redistributed upward to an elite few at the expense of better wages and jobs for the majority of workers. In the final section, I outline four ways that we might expect financialization to deepen income inequality, and how soaring returns for the top 1 per cent and stagnating wages and "bad" jobs for rest of the workforce are integral to a financialized economy.

The Political and Economic Foundations of Market Inequality: A Critical Perspective

Political scientists, economists, and sociologists have long debated the causes of economic inequality. And for many years, the primary reason given for rising inequality was economic globalization and the ways in which tax cuts, international trade, and capital mobility increased *external* pressures on firms to pursue higher rates of return at the expense of a broader working public (Strange 1996). Typically, the argument was made that rising trade in low-cost imports, most notably from Asia and particularly China, exposed domestic firms in developed industrial economies to heightened price competition. Faced with such constraints, many of these firms focused on sectors with higher value added and sought to lower labour costs and taxes paid (Boyer and Drache 1996).

At the same time, rising foreign direct investment was seen to put increased competitive pressures on domestic political economies (Western 1997). Since liberalization opened new opportunities for investment and finance, foreign capital movements increased exponentially across OECD economies from 1980 to 2007, and firms used the threat of their "exit" option to push governments to lower tax burdens, roll back regulatory interventions, and deregulate labour markets. Added to this mix were tax cuts, which firms pushed for under the rationale that more private capital would unleash a wave of investment and job creation. But as leading economies such as the United States and Great Britain cut corporate and high income taxes, this put pressures on other countries to follow suit, undercutting government revenues and authority, and cementing a policy model of "trickle-down" economics (Reich 2016; Saez and Zucman 2019).

However, since the global financial crisis of 2008–9, a new body of research has emerged on inequality, re-evaluating its causes, trends, and consequences (Boeri and van Ours 2013; Salverda, Nolan, and Smeeding 2009; Salverda et al. 2014). The scale of that crisis led many researchers to examine how and why credit and debt markets expanded so quickly, and how financial actors influenced the policy process and were able to muster so much financial support from public authorities in the wake of the collapse of major banks and debt markets (Duménil and Lévy 2011; Lapavitsas 2014; Stiglitz 2010). The crisis also directed new analytical interest into how economic growth has come to increasingly rely on finance, credit, and debt as its new driving forces – often with serious macroeconomic consequences, ranging from increasingly frequent economic crises, to unsustainable levels of debt and credit, faltering wages and inadequate economic demand, and growing monopolies that primarily feed off returns from existing assets like share values and government debt (Crouch 2009; Durand 2017; Guttmann 2016).

Rising inequality and the increasing upward distribution of income before and after the financial crisis also spurred new research into the political forces behind these policy changes, particularly the growing political power of large corporations, banks, and financial actors to shape markets within and across countries to their benefit (Hacker and Pierson 2010a; Hacker and Pierson 2016; Horn 2012; Lin and Tomaskovic-Devey 2013). Consequently, the most prominent perspectives in contemporary critical political economy have focused on how powerful, organized business interests have influenced governments, used public policy to create a far more unequal distribution of economic and political resources, and subsequently reaped the benefits from the increased power of corporations and finance (Glyn 2006; Harvey 2006).

Overwhelmingly, recent critical scholarly literature has begun to redirect its attention away from wider "external" market pressures and instead focus on the range of direct – and indirect – mechanisms that public officials have used to increase corporate power and funnel wealth to those at the top (van der Zwan, 2014). Here much critical work has countered older arguments about the "retreat of the state" or how states have "freed markets." In contrast, much current scholarship has focused on how economic inequalities result from and influence politics today (Jacobs and Soss 2010; Cafruny, Talani, and Pozo Martin 2016). Over recent years, it is argued market forces and business interests have corroded the workings of democracy in ways that have distributed income and power directly into the hands of owners, financial interests, and corporate executives (Duménil and Lévy 2011; Glyn 2006; Harvey 2006).

Despite the "free-market" image of official rhetoric, it is argued that the reality is far different: in recent decades, governments have consistently rolled out a host of new business-friendly policies in support of a more market-driven and globalizing economy (Aalbers 2017; Peck 2001). States, these scholars argue, have played a critical role in the retrenchment of public services and the rollback of corporate taxes. They have also played a significant part in expanding the freedom of capital by the institutionalization of global financial and product markets (Coe and Wai-Chung Yeung 2015; Panitch and Gindin 2013). So too have states blocked updates to public policies like labour law and post-secondary education, or simply undermined public policies by starving them of resources or by failing to enforce basic laws and standards (Hacker, Mettler, and Pinderhughes 2007; Hacker and Pierson 2010b).

Why did this occur? Recent critical literatures have begun to consider questions that go beyond free trade agreements, tax cuts, and social policy retrenchment. Rather, researchers now focus on the political organization of class interests and how, in the complex relationships between class and politics, finance-led growth became embedded in global capitalism.

Addressing Competitive Pressures through Economic and Structural Reforms

The conventional view of inequality is that it is simply a national problem and a result of what governments are not doing in response to the challenges of technology and global market competition. If income inequality is on the rise, it is commonly claimed, it's because governments are not doing enough to redistribute income through tax and social policies in recent years (Salverda et al. 2014). Varieties-of-capitalism studies, for example, have long highlighted how inequality is the consequence of poorly designed institutions and policies that fail to support citizens in coping with unemployment and increased family responsibilities that come with technological change, while also not offering business the flexibility and lower-cost structures necessary to compete in global markets (Beramendi and Anderson 2008; Beramendi et al. 2015; Borjas 2015; IMF 2016).

In these frameworks, the main challenge confronting many national officials is how best to deal with the competing trade-offs of equality and efficiency, as well as the conflicting objectives of public sector versus private sector growth within constantly changing technologies and globally competitive markets (Iversen 2006; Pontusson 2005). In such fraught circumstances, it is argued that inequality is the consequence of conflicting interests within countries that are unable to find the right "balance" of tax and transfer policy models that protect workers and families, but that can also support business in their efforts to shift investment to its most profitable uses (Thelen 2014; Iversen 2006).

However, as much recent critical political economy has argued, if this conception of the causes of inequality were correct, there would be little reason to delve deeper into the dynamics of advanced capitalist nations. The many economic and social policy reforms that governments have introduced over the past thirty years to boost competitiveness should have simply led to widespread growth and improved standards of living for the majority of workers. Instead, the most common trends have been the ratcheting up of wealth and income inequality, with corporate executives and financial elites capturing the majority of income growth (Alvaredo et al. 2017; Denk 2015; OECD 2015a).

To explain these developments, political economy scholars have countered that the causes of inequality have never simply been the result of governments failing to do enough. Nor is inequality primarily a consequence of citizens being unable to reach a consensus on how to best address the problems created by "external" markets – indeed, most in-depth surveys show that people would much prefer better public services and labour laws, if given the choice (Hacker and Pierson 2016; Page and Jacobs 2009). Rather, the major causes of inequality have been changes to capitalism and how governments, under the pressure of powerful organized business interests, have introduced more favourable policies that support profitability and growth at the expense of working people – a process called "neoliberalism" (Glyn 2006; Harvey 2006).

States, it is argued, have altered the nature of their policies and institutions to prioritize capital accumulation, and corporations and financial sectors have taken advantage by expanding their operations globally and seeking to cut costs – especially labour costs, which they have sought to lower by reducing wages, undermining unions, and increasing the intensity of production. And key to this transformation was how business and public officials effectively remade the economy to be far more friendly to global corporations, international investors, and finance, while creating more flexible labour laws and regulations, to the disadvantage of the workforce (Luce 2014; Lapavitsas 2014; Pettifor 2017).

How different contemporary neoliberal policy models are today can be seen in their sharp contrast with the more democratic and more employment-centred politics of the post–Second World War "golden age" of capitalism (Hobsbawm 1995; Reich 2015). Under the influence of Keynes and the wider public concerns for social welfare that evolved with the efforts to rebuild in the wake of war and depression, economic policy models typically revolved around a "mixed" economy based on money and financial markets tightly regulated by governments, and the government provision of public goods. Added were wider official commitments to more carefully balance labour and business interests through a range of labour laws and employment regulations (Pierson and Skocpol 2007; Western 1997). Because financial markets and monetary systems were inherently unstable, public officials acted under the belief that extensive government regulation and intervention through capital controls and fixed exchange rates was required to stabilize national economies, and that new international agreements and new institutions like the International Monetary Fund were also necessary to ensure that financial trading smoothed out economic fluctuations rather than provided opportunities for speculation. In addition, as citizens faced risks like unemployment, aging, and accident, state officials developed a "social wage" through the creation of increasingly comprehensive welfare systems that undergirded productive national economies.

But starting in the 1970s and continuing well into the first decade of 2000, governments fundamentally recast policy priorities to emphasize the profitability of business – most typically at the expense of workers' bargaining power and citizens' political clout – and sought to open their economies to big finance and big business (Harvey 2006; Glyn 2006). Critically important to these shifts were the general competitive pressures that pushed states to increase profits and productivity and rescue capitalism from economic stagnation. Arrighi

(2010) and Harvey (2006) argue that since the 1970s, declining profits and American efforts to boost global growth have led firms and American officials alike to push for regulatory reforms that would allow them to pursue new economic opportunities abroad. These theories have stressed that, because of falling profitability across industrial countries in the 1970s and 1980s, governments introduced policy reforms – from trade to investment, from banking to taxation, from finance to social services – that would spur growth and allow major economic sectors to find profitable investment opportunities and growing markets for consumption at home and abroad.

These theories about the rise of neoliberalism provide compelling arguments for why and how governments shifted their considerable resources in support of big business and finance. And in contrast to arguments suggesting that technology and the shift to more knowledge-based economies are the cause of a growing chasm between the rich and poor, critical scholars have argued that the problem lies in the political economics of capitalism itself (Hacker and Pierson 2016; Piketty 2014; Stiglitz 2013). Where states once sought to balance the demands of capital, labour, and society, because of major problems within capitalism, states definitively and consistently moved in support of capital to increase profits and productivity (Peters 2017). Instead of governments seeking to act in the wider collective interest through full-employment policies, better labour laws, and expanding social care, recent state interventions instead have given priority to the growth of finance and global capital, in turn redistributing income to favour the wealthy few. For critical political economy, it is these shifts in politics and economics – and not technology – that is at the heart of the story of skyrocketing inequality.

Spurring Economic Growth through Debt, Credit, and Finance

But apart from how governments remade "real-world" economic policies such as taxation, international trade, and employment regulations, it is also now clear that states overhauled their financial systems and worked to coordinate the reform of the wider international financial architecture in order to boost economic growth and expand global trade and investment. This is the second set of reasons why economic growth and politics has favoured only the wealthy few. And here, too, recent critical political economy literatures have begun to challenge traditional understandings of money, credit, and the operation of banking and financial systems (Durand 2017; Lapavitsas 2014; Pettifor 2017).

Most notable about this recent scholarship is its reconsideration of the role of money and finance in capitalist economies. Rather than consider money as simply "neutral" – an asset that represents an exchange value between buyers and sellers in a market and facilitates economic transactions – contemporary critical scholarship has examined how the private creation of money fuels new investment, creates speculative bubbles, and allows bankers and financial professionals to charge interest and fees at the expense of others (Durand 2017; Lapavitsas 2014). At the same time, critical political economy has challenged the view that banks and financial markets are simply market "intermediaries" between savers and borrowers and act largely independent of government regulation and involvement (Pettifor 2017).

Rather, it is argued, the financial sector is an active and politically aggressive economic force, and instead of simply providing funds for investments and job creation, or helping run a broader payment system, financial actors have sought to twist regulations and institutions to prioritize private asset speculation and market manipulation. Indeed, because of recent government reforms, the private financial sector has taken on a leading economic role, with enormous privileges and support, which have created a financial sector that works best for select groups of the powerful but often put economies at great risk because of dangerous speculation (Shaxson 2018; Stiglitz 2013, 2017).

In making these arguments, this new line of critical political economy scholarship has highlighted the contrast with the post-war regulation of money and credit (Durand 2017; Shaxson 2018). In the wake of the Great Depression and the Second World War, governments regulated their monetary and banking systems to ensure the expansion of credit and the growth of productive economic activity within nation states (Helleiner 1994). Central banks, capital controls, and developing national tax and government bond systems placed limits on the creation of private credit and prohibited risky speculation by banks and financial actors.

But policy reforms to monetary and credit systems in the 1980s and 1990s – alongside the non-regulation of tax havens and new financial products like "special purpose vehicles" and "credit default swaps" – overhauled regulations and their enforcement and unleashed finance and credit in ways that transformed them from being well-regulated and supportive economic activities to principal drivers of economies around the world (Forhoohar 2016; Lin and Neely 2020; Pettifor 2017). Instead of seeking financial sectors that would simply facilitate economic transactions or provide credit to fund long-term projects, government officials instead sought to deregulate financial markets and allow private finance to grow.

Part of the reason for this new emphasis on unleashing private credit markets was that with the recessions of the 1970s and 1980s, government officials sought to stimulate their economies directly through the expansion of a range of new debt and financial markets (Durand 2017; Jessop 2016; Streeck 2014). Officials made a series of reforms to pension funds and banking systems (Blackburn 2002), while loosening their monetary policies in order to spur new forms of finance capital and boost new investment in everything from information technology to biotechnology industries and global manufacturing (Guttman 2016). In enacting measures such as these, governments acted with the expectation that in releasing private finance, many other sectors from insurance to real estate to manufacturing would benefit from cheaper credit and more debt-financed investment (Crouch 2009; Bellamy Foster and Holleman 2010; Hay 2009; Schwartz 2009).

Government debt too was a major driver for unleashing credit in global economic activity, and it grew dramatically in the wake of major tax cuts and economic changes (Glyn 2006; Schafer and Streeck 2013). From the mid-1970s to the mid-1990s, with economic slowdown and the introduction of tax cuts, public indebtedness across advanced industrialized nations increased on average from 30 to 65 per cent of GDP (Streeck 2014). From 1995 to 2008, this ratio stabilized, as governments began to implement austerity measures, before abruptly rising again in the wake of the financial crisis to 100 per cent in 2015. But most notable is how such public debt was quickly absorbed by new financial markets, as government bonds were converted into money market funds, Eurocurrency deposits and loans, and a wide variety of other commercial paper credits (Guttmann 2016). In turn, states became increasingly dependent on deep secondary financial markets to sell bonds and reduce the costs of their debt financing (Streeck 2014).

One example of this was how, with the growth of new financial and credit markets, governments began to allow private lenders to "securitize" debt in order to sell it to investors, firms, and financial actors alike (Buchanan 2016; Guttmann 2016). Crouch argues that the origins of these policies lie in public officials enacting financial reforms to expand capital, mortgage, and corporate debt markets to stimulate economic growth – a model he characterizes as "privatized Keynesianism" (Crouch 2009). But unlike the 1970s and 1980s, when governments used public debt to fund infrastructure and social programs, he claims that, beginning in the late 1990s, public officials made further efforts to deregulate financial markets with the expectation that more liquid capital markets would provide joint benefits such as lower interest rates and easier terms of credit financing – benefits that public officials and households alike could agree on.

In addition, under American efforts to expand global economic activity, governments more widely deregulated their domestic financial markets and adopted new international standards for the private sector regulation of financial assets, debts, and securities. Pushed by American financial interests to remove restrictions on international capital mobility and expand financial and economic activity, international agencies and government coordination focused on securing "market-based" banking around the world (Panitch and Gindin 2013). Smaller countries were often forced to follow suit for fear of investment loss. Such international efforts at banking reform were a final factor in the exponential increase in financial market size and the growing influence of the private financial sector (Guttmann 2016).

In making such decisions, governments reversed decades of financial regulation and economic thinking, and changed financial rules to allow banks themselves to invest in stock markets and financial assets, and operate their own "shadow" or unregulated private entities and holding companies (Shaxson 2018). In addition, with bankers and financiers arguing for the loosening of rules to foster competitiveness, policymakers were persuaded to allow banks and new financial actors to operate in tax havens around the world, such as the Cayman and British Virgin Islands, and trade in unregulated "Euro" dollars. Through these new policy levers that downloaded responsibility onto private financial institutions themselves and allowed financial markets to operate largely outside public control, public officials enacted a private debt-growth model to boost falling macroeconomic demand, but also in many cases to act as a substitute for declining real wages that were no longer forthcoming in more flexible labour markets (see also Hay 2009; and Schwartz 2009).

Finally, the structural dependence between states and finance became so profound that public officials allowed banks to begin developing their own privately run but wholly unregulated financial system outside of official control – often characterized as the "shadow banking sector." Outside of traditional regulations and government monitoring, banks have used the shadow banking system in their race to profit from short-term financial operations and launched themselves into the "securitizing" of loans and other debt assets, ballooning the trade volume in the new securities markets, and helping drive global growth to record heights in the first decade of 2000 (Guttmann 2016). Unregulated private debt and credit markets have also enabled an explosion of housing markets, which have been a major driver of economic growth over the past two decades (Aalbers 2016; Schwartz 2009). It is this "market financialization" and the exponential growth of private credit markets that has been so central to recent developments in capitalism – often with calamitous consequences (Durand 2017; Guttmann 2016).

The result – as critical scholarship has detailed – has been the unparalleled development of finance – and financial power – around the world. Whether in government and corporate bonds, debt markets, and asset-backed securities, or short-term borrowing arrangements and shadow banking, governments now are tightly entangled in financial markets and strongly dependent on private credit markets for everyday operations. Driven by financial logics and forwarding financial innovations, government policy priorities are focused increasingly on the growth and health of their financial sectors. More and more, as recent critical literatures have detailed, these developments illustrate dramatically how states themselves are not only tied to finance but in fact are advancing institutions and policies that allow private credit to flourish.

The Limits of Recent Critical Accounts

As the outline of current critical political economy scholarship above demonstrates, there are many strengths to this literature's interpretation of the origins of neoliberalism and the recent growth in finance, and how they have favoured corporate and financial power while fostering income inequality. Critical literatures, for example, have offered powerful frameworks for thinking about how the sources of inequality lie with the interconnections between economics and politics (Cafruny, Talani, and Pozo Martin 2016). Recent political economy has also highlighted how, rather than there being some well-functioning relationship between markets and democracy, shifts in policy are due to how governments have responded to economic and business problems by consistently seeking solutions to improve profitability and growth – in response to long-term problems or to major crises, as in 2008–10 (Jessop 2016; Schafer and Streeck 2013).

But if critical scholars have done much to recast the debates on the causes of inequality, a number of questions remain unanswered. One such issue is how to explain variations in financialization, for even if states have generally converged on adopting neoliberal trade, investment, and tax policies, levels of income inequality and labour market inequality still diverge before taxes and transfers – often significantly (Alvaredo et al. 2018; Hall 2015; Roberts and Kwon 2017). This suggests that even with major pro-business and pro-finance policies, and the improvement to profitability in many capitalist economies, there is still variation between countries in how successful – or how widespread – neoliberal reforms have been in shifting income distribution to favour capital more generally. Thus, coming to grips with the different ways and different rates that economic inequality has grown also requires far closer attention to the political and institutional processes that underpin economic change. Here I delve into these recurring political and policy struggles, and how and why they have allowed a small elite in the financial and industrial sectors to reap massive financial gains.

Another noteworthy gap in recent critical literature has been its lack of attention to the key political shifts and economic policy developments that explain when and why financial sectors have grown so rapidly within countries and why the financialization of productive multinationals has occurred rapidly in some countries but not others (Flaherty 2015; Roberts and Kwon 2017). Although a number of authors have recently begun to pay more attention to the sources of variations within neoliberalism, the actual financial and monetary policies – and the politics behind them – have been little analysed (Birch and Siemiatycki 2016; Springer, Birch, and MacLeavy 2016). But without a closer examination of how and why states have actually supported finance and promoted corporate restructuring, we are left with no clear sense of why governments may have differed in their financial and monetary policies, and what this may have meant for finance and corporations alike.

We also have no clear understanding of how international developments have influenced national governments or how and why states have responded to the economic interests that have pushed for financial liberalization. What needs to be explained are what political and economic factors – international and national – might account for the liberalization of finance within national economies and how this did – or did not – release the power of private financial markets.

Finally, there is the issue of how and why finance and productive enterprises have increasingly merged and intertwined. In recent studies on finance, much emphasis has been directed to accounting for the increasing size of the financial sector, and the growing importance of the sector's profits to the overall economy (Lapavitsas 2014; Duménil and Lévy 2011). But typically, critical accounts have argued that the growth of finance and credit are due to slowdowns in capitalism: with declining profit rates, finance becomes a far more attractive asset, but in turn, financial markets begin to search out new and potentially profitable long-term investments, thus sparking a new cycle of capitalist growth anew (Arrighi 2010). Such a perspective certainly provides a much-needed and plausible explanation for the recent explosion in finance. However, it too requires far more thorough investigation of how and why multinational corporations have changed in recent decades, in ownership and operation.

Shifts between finance and the real economy indeed have taken place with the rise and fall of profits, and they do seem to have shaped the long-term cycles of capitalist development over the past century or more. Moreover, finance in its many forms – from government and private debt, to multiplying financial products, to soaring company share prices – is at the heart of how capitalism is organized today. But to understand how and why this has occurred, we require a political economy framework that can link the many aspects of finance – from the increasing internationalization of financial markets and the growth of financial corporate actors, to the governance and operation of global multinational corporations, and finally to dynamics of labour relations and job markets.

Neoliberalism and Financialization: A Conceptual Model

How then to account for the growing size and reach of finance into every corner of the globe? What best explains increasing international capital mobility? What are the reasons for public officials adopting finance and debt as solutions for economic growth?

A good place to start is with an understanding of political action and policy structures, and in particular with how governments, banks, and corporations have developed and deployed new policies and institutions to create debt and credit in order to propel innovative technologies, foreign investment flows, and new global markets (Durand 2017; Lapavitsas 2014; Milberg and Winkler 2013). Most striking about the current state of capitalist development is how contemporary states have deregulated financial sectors and downloaded responsibility onto private financial actors, allowing finance to outgrow the traditional means of commercial and merchant banking (Shaxson 2018). In compensating for industrial slowdown, advanced capitalist governments opted to fill the gaps with policies of financial loosening and deregulated global Eurodollar markets and tax havens – policy decisions that were crucial in allowing financial credit and debt to grow many times faster than the underlying economy.

As contemporary political economy research has demonstrated, government rules make markets and support firms, and public policies shape how, and in whose interest, the market operates (Hacker and Pierson 2010b; Hacker and Pierson 2016; Davis and Kim 2015; Epstein 2015). This is especially true of monetary systems and financial markets, for in pursuing "competitiveness" and growth, public officials have increasingly followed a common trajectory of promoting the mobility of financial capital at national, international, and global arenas (see table 2.1).

At the national level, this has resulted in the reversal of Central Bank monetary policy, from regulating bank lending – and the money supply more generally – to simply focusing on inflation within a context of loose public regulation allowing private financial actors to pursue a virtually unlimited money supply and new credit creation (Bieling 2013; Omarova et al. 2013; Palley 2013). This has been a critical transformative change to economic policy. In contrast to the post-war period, when governments sought full employment, regulated the money and credit supply, used capital controls extensively, and controlled the financial system through separate regulatory regimes for different categories of finance, with the shift to neoliberalism, public officials have tacked in a very direction.

Now the typical economic policy model in advanced capitalist countries is to promote the "efficient" functioning of capital markets and expand credit to increase demand and consumer spending (Duménil and Lévy 2004; Lapavitsas 2014). Rather than seek to control the amount of money in the economy, national monetary policies have more typically swung to a private sector–oriented "principle-based" model oriented to fighting inflation first and foremost, but with a relatively light touch, and a market-friendly regulatory framework for other financial services and markets that allows private financial actors to regulate themselves (Stiglitz 2010). In making these shifts, national monetary policies have moved far from the post-war banking practice of making banks "originate and hold" their loans to the benefit of national growth and toward

Table 2.1. Neoliberalism and market financialization: Actors and policy reforms

Policy Area	National Monetary Policy and Financial Regulation	Policy Transfer	International Institutions and Frameworks
Monetary Policy	Inflation targeting "Originate and distribute" model of banking End to controls on money supply	Coordination with major central banks	G7, G20 "Principle-based" banking regulation
Banking Regulation	Lower capital requirements End to commercial/ investment bank separation Expanded bank self-regulation Financial efficiency	Securitization Deregulation of national banking markets Financial liberalization Capital market liberalization	Bank of international settlements – Basel I-III IMF and World Bank – expansion of "non-market" finance
Capital Markets	Deregulation of "foreign investment reviews" Dergulation of funds for pension and insurance investment Tax treaties with tax havens	Free trade and international investment Tax and finance department coordination	US Federal Reserve/ European Central Bank End to restrictions on international capital movements Removal of currency exchange rate controls

to an "originate and distribute" framework, where national banks, private financial markets, and corporations are given the leeway to initiate, sell, and distribute loans and financial assets into national and international financial markets as needed and as they see fit (Konzelmann, Fovargue-Davies, and Wilkinson 2013).

At the same time, to move debt and finance to the centre stage of their economies, and to allow private financial actors and major non-financial companies to expand their enterprises, central banks and finance departments have introduced reforms to their financial systems. In part, central banks in the United States and elsewhere wanted deeper and more fluid capital markets to help companies grow and innovate (Krippner 2011). But Central Bank officials also saw deregulated capital markets as a solution to the problem of high borrowing costs for major firms (Konzelmann, Fovargue-Davies, and Wilkinson 2013). Thus, for states seeking ways to reboot their national economies, deregulated finance and the private sector self-regulation of the banking system were to support a policy revolution and provide a major new boost to the economy, but without the cost of high inflation (Lavoie and Seccareccia 2013).

Between states, the commitment to expand private credit has been just as intensive – a policy position often pushed by major American and British investment banks (Panitch and Gindin 2013; Shaxson 2018). Governments have used cooperation and coordination across borders to develop new policies and institutions in order to promote private credit creation and shift government intervention to "after the fact" crisis prevention (Stiglitz 2010, 2017). Officials have created reciprocal regulatory frameworks for financial market integration and capital market liberalization (Horn 2012; Panitch and Gindin 2013). Monetary and banking authorities also cooperated in making reforms that allowed their commercial and investment banking systems to integrate (Bieling 2006, 2013). They also coordinated efforts to reform their national securities regulation and mortgage industries to allow private financial institutions to sell debt into security markets (Buchanan 2016; Mugge 2010; Schwartz 2009). In addition, governments opened their banking markets (some more grudgingly than others), allowing national and international banks alike to compete in domestic economies (Tooze 2018; Panitch and Gindin 2013).

In making many of these changes, national regulatory agencies were often most concerned with drawing new financial institutions and investment into their domestic economies, rather than actually regulating those institutions. Many countries quickly copied legislation developed in the United States and Great Britain before going a few steps further (Engelen et al. 2011). This led to the rapid spread of the practice of securitization to disperse risk and boost liquidity (Buchanan 2016; Guttmann 2016).

Similarly, while the IMF and World Bank provided oversight, states under the pressure of fund managers worked prodigiously to financialize their pension contributions, allowing funds to invest in the stock market and new debt-backed securities (Blackburn 2002, 2011). This deregulation of pension industries was also crucial to financialization and the spread of finance into the real economy (Blackburn 2002; Ebbinghaus 2015; Hassel, Naczyk, and Wiß 2019). Under the lobbying of financial service industries as well as national stock markets, governments across North America and Western Europe loosened restraints on public pension plans and opened the door to private and occupational pension plans.

All such "marketization" and "privatization" of pension funds provided enormous reservoirs of capital at the disposal of financial actors and fund managers alike. In Canada, Great Britain, and the United States, the asset value of pension funds quickly exploded across the 1990s and the first decade of 2000 into the trillions, totalling more than 100 per cent of GDP (OECD 2019). In the Netherlands and Scandinavian countries, the growth of private pensions has been instrumental to capital market growth. Paving the way for such reforms was the growth and institutionalization of policy sharing among countries, driven by international agencies, major money funds, and investment banks (Panitch and Gindin 2013). The result was an increasing "disintermediation" – the redirection of savings and borrower funds away from commercial banks and into capital markets and new financial products – and especially into the increasingly global US and UK financial services industry and global credit markets (Lapavitsas 2014).

At the global level, economic reforms that have increased private credit and debt have been equally ubiquitous. Governments have worked with international financial actors to develop international – and often wholly self-governing – frameworks that standardize basic accounting and capital adequacy for private financial institutions (Panitch and Gindin 2013; Porter 2004). Already by the 1990s, there were strong deregulatory views being pushed by public officials and financial agencies and financial ministries alike (Stiglitz 2017). At the urging of major investment banks and business consultancies, faith was now placed in markets' self-regulation and a belief that government support for markets was essential in promoting the greater good. And under an international "principle-based" regulatory approach, officials were not to interfere with financial innovation, but instead seek to standardize practices for liberalized capital markets around the world (IMF 2010, 2014b).

In this context, officials working in conjunction with the US Federal Reserve, the IMF, and the World Bank, as well as the European Central Bank, set out new rules for the Bank of International Settlements, which included loosening international lending standards and restrictions on new financial and debt assets to boost financial lending and credit expansion (Konings 2011; Porter 2004). So too under the insistence of insurance and trust industries, the World Bank and IMF also advocated loosening national regulation of non-bank financial institutions to add liquidity and encourage investment. In these ways, governments and international institutions constructed a set of common rules for a debt-based growth model across countries and helped spur the financial innovation required to boost new financial markets and provide enormous new opportunities for a range of financial actors (Guttmann 2016).

Many accounts of financialization fail to identify the policies and institutions that can be plausibly linked to large increases in private credit and global capital mobility. Much of the increase in new financial assets and credit is assumed to be due to growing global markets and financial actor innovation. The conclusion often taken from this is that market changes, not public policy, are driving economic change.

But such conclusions neglect two critical facts. First, there is substantial evidence that direct government monetary, banking, tax, and pension policies directly abetted banks and the financial sector, and rewarded speculation and short-term gains. Second, government policies have not simply regulated money and financial markets, they have systematically structured those markets in ways that have fuelled greater inequality. As a result, finance has gone from serving the whole economy to only serving itself.

In chapter 3, I reverse the perspective of conventional accounts to trace how these monetary and financial policy developments have fuelled a new finance-led growth model. I argue that key to understanding the new mountains of private debt and the rising power of finance in Canada's economy is how the visible hand of government introduced a new institutional framework for the flourishing of financial markets, credit, and debt. For with these politically driven reforms, finance not only flourished, it also twisted incentives within the non-financial economy and pulled more of the economy's rewards into finance as well as into the profits and salaries of the wealthy few. Such changes to the rules governing the financial sector – including those that let financial markets write their own rules – are the first key to explaining the sky-rocketing salaries for those in the financial sector as well as to wider changes in the economy.

Financialization, Firms, and the Development of a "Taker" Economy

The widespread revision of financial policies and monetary institutions across countries helps us explain one reason for the transformation of capitalism across countries (Durand 2017; Lapavitsas 2014; Flaherty 2015; Volscho and Kelly 2012). But another big question remains: what accounts for changes in the rest of the economy – in the "non-financial" sector? Here too, as contemporary critical literatures have demonstrated, the changes to everyday business practice have been profound.

More and more multinational corporations are focused on maximizing "shareholder value" (Lin and Neely 2020). More and more, firms are focused on short-term performance and quarterly earnings. And more and more, multinationals have taken to using finance in their everyday operations, with executives and shareholders applying financial strategies to improve profit and to boost executive pay and payouts to stockholders (Forhoohar 2016). Now rather than investing in new capital or employees, or prioritizing innovation, the "shareholder revolution" across companies has translated into mergers and reduced capital investment, frequent corporate restructurings, and ever-rising corporate payouts – a "taker" economy rather than a productive one.

One reason for such shifts in corporate operation were the problems that capitalism itself ran into in the 1970s and 1980s. With falling returns, owners of capital sought increasingly innovative ways to increase returns, and using finance was one of the quickest ways that executives could find to shift the focus from the long-term performance of their enterprises to maximizing short-term gains (Lin and Tomaskovic-Devey 2013; Lin 2016). Rather than invest in capital and labour, executives turned to finance for mergers and acquisitions, or used finance to invest in short-term debt and money markets, then turned around and used debt to buy back stocks and redistribute wealth to shareholders (Forhoohar 2016). Similarly, finance provided the quickest way to build global operations and boost returns, offering the funds necessary to build global supplier networkers that could offshore and outsource production (Milberg and Winkler 2013). Finance, in these accounts, was a problem solver for capital to maximize cash generation and increase corporate profitability (Panitch and Gindin 2013).

But *corporate financialization* – that is, the financial ownership of non-financial corporations (NFCs), and the increasing use of finance as a tool for business operations and investment – was also a solution to improving returns to shareholders while undercutting wages and employment more generally (Durand 2017; Lapavitsas 2014). As institutional investors as well as pension and hedge funds expanded with liberalization, demands for returns increased as well. And as their investments grew, so too did demands for more active boards or new boards that would improve shareholder value and increase the proportion of profits returned to shareholders (Batt and Appelbaum 2014; Lin and Neely 2020). This was the second major long-term development responsible for the financialization of corporations worldwide.

Such arguments about how contemporary firms have "financialized" run counter to conventional varieties-of-capitalism perspectives that still see firms as neutral institutions shaped by their stakeholders – owners, workers, or community members (Aguilera and Jackson 2010; Barker 2010; Hall and Soskice 2001). In the standard view of the firm as a "stakeholder," conventional literature posits a sharp contrast between the "shareholder" model of corporate governance found in the United States and other liberal market economies that has long given priority to short-term returns to shareholders, and a European "stakeholder" model that is constrained by government and unions in the interest of suppliers, customers, and workers (Hall and Soskice 2001; Pontusson 2005).

But in questioning the benefits of different models of capitalism and the corporate governance of firms, much of this comparative debate has missed the obvious transformations in capitalism, and the fact that firms have never been simply neutral institutions brokering among different economic and societal interests, but rather institutions directed to maximizing profits (Harvey 2010; Lapavitsas 2014). For example, rather than being bound by different national systems, in seeking greater profits and competitiveness over the course of the late twentieth and early twenty-first century, some firms have used finance to offshore production, subcontract work, and acquire or ally with competitors

(Milberg and Winkler 2013). Others invested in financial assets and their own shares to make shareholders even richer (Forhoohar 2016; Stiglitz 2010). Others still built complex global value chains and financial lines of business, spinning off enterprises and using derivatives markets to mitigate risk while speculating heavily in commodity and money markets (Coe and Wai-Chung Yeung 2015; Gertel and Sippel 2016; McMichael 2013).

At the same time, with financial deregulation weakening the regulatory division between finance and everyday manufacturing, corporate ownership was rapidly transferred into financial hands, and corporations shifted to public equity and market-based debt for their operation – often to the enormous benefit of shareholders and owners themselves (Lin and Neely 2020; Peters 2011). This too has marked a major change to capitalism in recent years.

In these ways, as financial sectors across advanced capitalist economies swelled, the wider "real" economy was also transformed. Capitalism became focused on market power and short-term speculation. Financial and corporate actors sought to take a cut or "rent" out of future profits and future productive value (Durand 2017). And new financial actors and new financial instruments increasingly redirected rewards to asset holders and the financial sector more generally – typically at the expense of workers, and society more generally (Lin and Neely 2020).

As I argue, such financialization has done much to establish an economic system that enriches only an elite part of the population and does little for sustainable investment or income distribution. This transformation has been so profound that from the standpoint of investors, firms today are little more than assets to be rearranged to maximize shareholder value. Executives are paid extravagant rewards, regardless of how they boost share price. While for managers, under pressure to efficiently allocate capital, workers are increasingly disposable or simply an asset to be purchased at the lowest possible cost. Logics – as well as the new financial pressures and incentives – such as these help us account for the growing gap between wealthy business elites and the wider workforce – that is, inequality.

The Causes and Consequences of Financialization and Labour Market Inequality

In this book, I argue, it these interconnections – between government efforts at financial liberalization alongside the dynamics of global capitalism and corporate financialization – that are crucial to understanding increasing inequality in income distribution, and the erosion of job quality and wages today (figure 2.1). As this book argues, a driving agent of income inequality has been the politics of financialization, and how it has led to the marriage of finance with business. These new interconnections have occurred in a number of ways. But

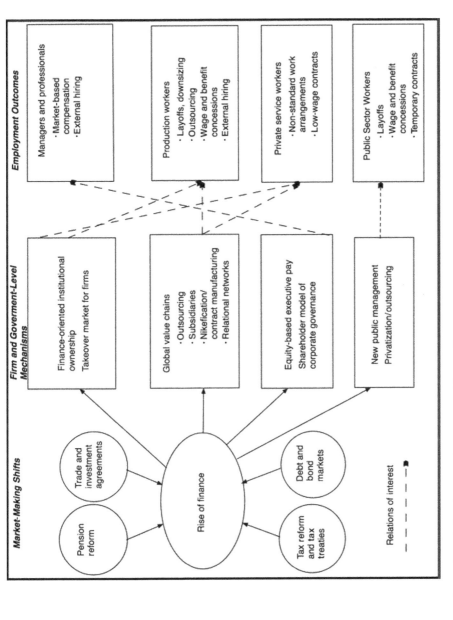

Figure 2.1. Financialization, employment, and inequality

to best explore how such political, policy, and corporate transformations do or do not emerge, I emphasize four channels through which finance and the wider economy can become entwined to the advantage of business and wealthy elites.

Growth of the Financial Sector and the Super Rich

For instance, a first key channel is how the financial sector has grown to become a key source of wealth creation for the very few. Over the course of the early 1990s to 2015, with major changes to policies and institutions shaping the financial sector, global finance grew many times over, with the stock of total lending, debt securities, foreign direct investment, and international equity swelling twelve-fold from just $15 trillion in 1995 to more than $180 trillion in 2015 (Lund et al. 2017). And as commercial and investment bankers specialized in these markets, facilitating deals, trades, and mergers, their businesses also developed exponentially. But such growth across advanced industrial economies in North America and Western Europe meant that the weight and size of financial sectors and their stock of assets ballooned from two or three times the size of gross domestic product to more than five or six times larger than GDP (Lapavitsas 2014). In Canada, too, as we will see in the next chapter, not only did traditional financial institutions expand their financial stock, but so too did "non-bank" financial institutions such as insurance companies more than double their holding of financial assets.

But as private credit and debt grew exponentially, so did the rewards for those working in the financial sector. As financial markets shot up and officials passed policies that distorted its power, the returns to capital through interest, fees, and commissions rose in tandem. These rewards help us account for the rising profitability of the financial sector and its growing economic importance to income inequality.

In North America and Western Europe, financial-sector profits as a percentage of profits regularly increased from 20 per cent to more than 30 per cent from the early 1990s to 2008 (Durand 2017; Lin and Neely 2020). Then, in turn, capturing returns along the lengthening financial chains, the rising profits for financial institutions meant constantly increasing wages, salaries, and bonuses for financial workers, who routinely earn more than 70 per cent than workers in other industries (Godechot 2016; Lin and Tomaskovic-Devy 2013). So, too, the rising fees and commissions that financial actors charged to firms for their mergers and acquisitions, the release of company bonds, and a growing number of market trades, added to the incomes of those in the financial sector (Durand 2017). Such growth in market finance fees has been essential to income inequality – especially to the incomes of the wealthiest few and those in the top 1 per cent of earners (Flaherty 2015; Godechot 2016; Lin and Tomaskovic-Devy 2013).

In stark contrast to the post-war period of industrial-led growth and restricted financial activity, over the past few decades the government push to deregulate finance and the wider economy led to the growth in finance and its new dominance. This represented a fundamental transformation to national economies and the global economy alike (Tooze 2018). It is in the financial sector that a new "super rich" have emerged (Flaherty 2015; Volscho and Kelly 2012). With the recasting of the laws and policies that structure economies, the financial, insurance, and real estate sectors all grew exponentially. In turn, white-collar workers experienced rising incomes, receiving growing incomes and compensation packages simply from their institutions capturing greater proportions of dividends, fees, interest, patents, and real estate rents and sales (Bellamy Foster and Holleman 2010; Roberts and Kwon 2017).

In the United States, for example, the wealthiest have earned exponential sums from rocketing stock markets and real estate prices and patents – in large measure because of how government introduced new rules governing the economy that favoured big business and bigger finance (Hacker and Pierson 2010a; Lin and Tomaskovic-Devey 2013). In Europe, the growth of finance has also seen outsize returns for those working in the financial sector, as financial executives and professionals have seen their compensation levels skyrocket (Godechot 2016; Hein 2015). The rapid rise in real estate around the world too has led to the returns on mortgages increasingly channelled to a wealthy few (Aalbers 2016; Stockhammer 2013a). Financialization – and its major government supports – has thus been a major contributor to income and wealth concentration across advanced industrial economies (Flaherty 2015; Hein 2015; Volscho and Kelly 2012). And in chapter 4, I document how the growth in financial assets and debt helps us similarly explain the rise of the top 1 per cent of earners in Canada.

Financial Ownership and the Decline of Good Jobs

A second reason for inequality in labour markets is the increasing integration of finance into production and its remaking of corporate governance and operation (Barker 2010; Kollmeyer and Peters 2019; Lin and Neely 2020; Peters 2011). Previously, corporations were held by wealthy families and operated on a national scale. However, over the past few decades, with governments liberalizing debt and capital markets, market finance has become far cheaper, and major corporations have expanded through waves of mergers and acquisitions, consequently institutionalizing independent boards of directors who are given the legal responsibility of maximizing shareholder value (Horn 2012; Wickham 2016).

Private equity investors across the United States and Western Europe have also taken advantage of tax reforms to aggressively take over companies, load companies with debt, and pursue the interests of shareholders over those of other established stakeholders (Batt and Appelbaum 2014; Watt 2008). At the same time, the liberalization of pension funds has allowed financial institutions to become the predominant owner of public and privately held corporations (Davis 2013). Now mutual funds and exchange-traded funds, but also global investment management corporations such as BlackRock (Davis 2013; Huizinga and Jonung 2005) are the dominant owners of multinational corporate equity and seek to use non-financial firms as liquid assets to make profits. The result is that firms are more unlikely to be tied to individual investors inside national economies (Shaxson 2018).

Institutional investors own approximately 75 per cent of the largest publicly traded corporations in the United States, more than 54 per cent of those in Western Europe (Celik and Isaksson 2014), and more than 80 per cent in Europe's largest economy, Germany (Deutsche Bundesbank 2014). At the same time, the rise of financially driven asset funds also led to the spread of private equity ownership and aggressive forms of corporate ownership based on debt and financial efficiencies. By 2014, there were 7,500 large multi-million-dollar companies owned by private equity firms in the United States; 1,300 in Canada; and more than 19,500 across Western Europe, with Germany having the most at 5,600 (Preqin 2015, 2016a).

Such a "financial" turn in corporate ownership led to major shifts in corporate strategies. Finance gains its profits from rents taken from production activities, investment in financial markets, and squeezing wages (Durand 2017; Krippner 2011). Business is no longer primarily about the production of real goods for the economy, but about serving finance. This has been most dramatically the case in the United States, where rather than use earnings for long-term capital investment and growth, firms now use profits to boost stock prices as well as simply reward shareholders, leaving few resources for company expansion or hiring (Forhoohar 2016; Lin and Neely 2020).

But in many other countries too, businesses changed their governance structures and priorities, and corporations began to look less like traditional enterprises tied to their home countries' markets, and more like vast global monopolies, with cross-border conglomerates of multiple enterprises around the world, headquartered in tax havens, and focused almost entirely on increasing their financial returns (Coe and Wai-Chung Yeung 2015). Leading examples of this new business model are – Facebook, Amazon, Apple, Netflix, and Google – the first corporations to all be nearly $1 trillion in value and to pay little tax worldwide (Saez and Zucman 2019). But companies across sectors – from manufacturing to oil to agriculture – have all witnessed massive growth in their size and have undertaken financial engineering to increase rewards for shareholders (Coe and Wai-Chung Yeung 2015; Durand 2017).

As a result, while corporate executives and shareholders have seen enormous benefits, workers have seen their share of income and wages decline

(Kristal 2010; Stockhammer 2013b). Looking to boost profits, firms have increasingly turned to financial investments to meet market demands for quarterly earnings (Krippner 2011). As firms have expanded globally and bought brands, patents, and subsidiaries, so their demand for higher-paid workers in advanced industrial countries to maintain production has decreased (Lin 2016; Milberg and Winkler 2013). This has typically led to widespread restructuring of labour forces across economies and regions, and forced unions to compete for investment by making wage and benefit concessions (Moody 2007). Consequently, the rise of financial ownership has long-run consequences for employment, and especially for the growth of good unionized jobs in advanced industrial economies, which are the most likely to be shed as shareholders seek to increase profits and restructure operations (Batt and Appelbaum 2013; Lin and Neely 2020).

Shareholder Capitalism and Labour Force Flexibility

A third key linkage between financialization and labour market inequality is the wider institutionalization of new shareholder models of business (Detzer and Hein 2014; Fligstein and Shin 2007; Davis 2009; Gunnoe 2016). Changes in firm ownership and equity holdings, it is argued, may not necessarily lead to changes in actual corporate governance (Gospel and Pendleton 2005; Gospel, Pendleton, and Vitols 2013). But if ownership change also results in an overhaul of corporate operations to a "shareholder model" of corporate governance, then a greater market orientation in employment relations is likely to follow. These changes to a shareholder model of corporate governance and labour management are key to widening income inequality (Cobb 2016).

Much evidence suggests that the internationalization of stock markets and the new finance-led ownership has had profound impacts on corporate governance, operation, and strategies (Dupuis, Peters, and Scrimger 2020; Forhoohar 2016; Peters 2011). Beginning in the 1980s, it became increasingly routine for firms to adopt equity-based compensation to spur corporate executives to focus on stock price and use finance to expand operation. Just as profound were the impacts of the financial turn on corporate operation and management. Because of takeovers or public listing, firms adopted a shareholder model and adopted "financial planning" models to meet "market expectations," as well as implement capitalization and restructuring strategies in order to grow and capture market share. In the United States and the United Kingdom, the money poured by financial institutions (banks, investment banks, and pension funds) into corporate equity led many NFCs to borrow heavily in order to buy their own stock so that dividends would rise and meet investors' expectations (Hein, Detzer, and Dodig 2016). Meanwhile, throughout Western Europe, the majority of managers willingly burned up "net present value" to meet short-term earnings benchmarks, and more and more firms sacrificed investment for share buy-backs and dividend payments (Durand 2017).

Equally important, the rapid growth of secondary money markets and new capital assets in real estate, as well as portfolio investments in currencies, bonds and stock futures, and financial derivatives provided a host of new opportunities for financially focused executives to increase returns and pursue new lines of business (Durand 2017; Batt and Appelbaum 2014). So, too, the entry of banks and institutional investors into international lending and equity markets placed new demands on firms to generate cash flows to justify companies floating record amounts of corporate bonds and commercial paper and higher debt loads – often by changing the composition of corporate boards or changing key corporate governance priorities. By the early to mid-1990s, for example, large projects from manufacturing and domestic enterprises had to meet the profitability benchmarks of institutional investors and professional analysts.

As a number of critical scholars have argued, non-financial firms have long been involved in financial markets throughout the twentieth century (Knafo and Dutta 2019; Krippner 2011; Panitch and Gindin 2013). Non-financial firms have extended credit to promote sales and help customers buy their products. To build conglomerates, firms required cheap credit to purchase competitors and extend new lines of business. Multinational firms have also used lines of credit to build production networks and manage their supply chains, and typically tie their suppliers to tighter and more rigorous timelines (Baud and Durand 2012). And by the 1980s, with financial deregulation providing official approval for NFCs to operate as banks and provide commercial loans, firms such as General Motors, General Electric, and Sears aggressively expanded their portfolios of financial services (Lin and Neely 2020).

But, unlike the "managerial" capitalism of the mid-twentieth century, where governments regulated national capital flows and protected their national industrial "champions" and firms realized profits through the operations of their own enterprises and sales, today's financialized firms have turned to shareholder models of corporate governance and invested in financial assets and financial markets to operate their enterprises. Here executives have sought to take advantage of growing debt markets by rapidly expanding their firms and resolutely focusing on maximizing returns to stockholders – often by using their firm's assets for financial investments rather than ongoing business operations (Batt and Appelbaum 2013; Lapavitsas 2014). Under pressure from financial interests to increase profits, and taking advantage of rule changes that allowed firms to grow globally and increase their market power with little regulation, firms have channelled their energies to paying growing dividends. All these developments have initiated a major "financial" turn for non-financial firms (Forhoohar 2016; Lin and Neely 2020).

In this context, financialization has also reshaped employment relations and employment contracts. In giving priority to shareholders and equity partners, and using finance and cheap debt to fuel global operations, firms have frequently altered their management and employment strategies – above all, by introducing cost-reduction human resource management strategies based on the idea that labour costs reduce the amount of income available to shareholders (Cobb 2016; Deakin and Rebérioux 2009). Essentially, workforces become costs to be reduced rather than assets to be utilized and developed (Darcillon 2015; Gospel and Pendleton 2005).

For labour, the emphasis on shareholder value has been a series of pressures on collective bargaining within and across firms (Dupuis, Peters, and Scrimger 2020). For example, with the vast expansion of corporate mergers and acquisitions where financially driven targets are key, workers are often laid off or forced to accede to outsourcing and offshoring (Peters 2011). Firms also routinely enact financial re-engineering and lean production systems to make workers "do more with less" (Moody 1997). Consequently, firms seek concessions from unions and from contractors and suppliers, who are also forced in turn to reduce wages and intensify working conditions for their workers. The result is that financialization undermines collective agreements and weakens union ability to uphold better wages (Grady and Simms 2018). This has been another major driver of wider inequality in labour markets (Kollmeyer and Peters 2019).

Financialization and the "Fissuring" of Employment

A fourth connection between financialization and worsening labour markets lies in how the growth of finance and globalization have increasingly "fissured" employment, allowing lead global firms to use a wide variety of organizational methods to shed their role as direct employers and onto smaller firms, which pay low wages, provide few if any benefits, and routinely avoid basic workplace standards (Weil 2014). Finance has been key to such fissuring, as across a range of industries – from private services to natural-resource extraction to agro-industries – major firms have relied on finance to access cheap sources of labour both locally and internationally (Milberg and Winkler 2013). Indeed, finance has facilitated business efforts to increase rents through traditional cost-cutting methods, as well as advanced more recent attempts by corporations and financial actors to offload employment onto contractors, suppliers, and third-party agencies, who cannot pay (Baud and Durand 2012; Coe and Yeung 2015).

For example, as finance and globalization have grown hand-in-hand, service jobs in transport, retail, wholesale, cleaning, and security have exploded, with firms hiring new workers to maintain capitalism's facilities and buildings as well as to ensure the circulation of goods and credit (Moody 2017; Standing 2011). Because neoliberalism encourages lead NFCs to adopt a range of financial engineering strategies to boost returns to shareholders, they have contracted millions of jobs to "second-tier" firms operating under competitive contracts. In turn, lower-level firms and third-party agencies have looked to control costs through many "traditional" managerial methods: low wages, temporary agency work, short-term contracts, on-call work, independent contracting (that is, bogus self-employment), and involuntary part-time work (Appelbaum 2010; Bernhardt et al. 2008). Global service industries – as in telecommunications and transport, which have expanded alongside global capital – are particularly notorious for their use of a low-wage workforce. But local cleaning and service providers that work to keep financial sectors – and many corporate actors – operating daily, routinely rely on low-cost labour power rather than technology to serve these growing markets, and routinely look to hire more workers at low wages with few or no benefits or severance costs.

Similar rent extraction from the labour force has occurred over the past few decades in the natural resource and agriculture sectors, where financial actors have played greater roles, and lower-tier contractors, firms, and employers can expand output only by hiring more workers at low wages and on non-standard employment contracts. In these industries, which have grown enormously with globalization, contractors and producers along the far-flung, finance-led supply chains have typically looked to increase their low-pay and low-skill labour force in order to meet increasingly competitive contracts (Forhoohar 2016). But because financial markets now influence resource and food prices so heavily (Ghosh, Heintz, and Pollin 2012; Fattouh, Kilian, and Mahadeva 2013), through everything from derivatives to commodity futures, multinational corporations in oil extraction and food retail work in increasingly volatile markets. Such volatility leads these corporate actors to dictate ever lower prices and cost-competitive terms to their suppliers, construction companies, and small-scale agriculture producers (Baud and Durand 2012; Forhoohar 2016). In response, contractors and producers in these industries find they can compete and produce more only by expanding their labour forces and by relying more heavily on low-wage, non-standard, and temporary foreign worker employment contracts (Castles 2006; Prebisch and Binford 2007).

These concurrent developments of neoliberalism and financial engineering across private service, natural resource, and agricultural industries have been key to the "fissuring" of employment relations. More and more, in the age of deregulated private finance, firm decisions on employment are made on the basis of financial revenue and debts, and even in the low-productivity service, agricultural, and resource sectors, such decisions have negative implications for employment relations and labour cost management (Baud and Durand 2012; Jung 2014).

At the top of the business chain, major multinationals shift their employment relations to outside firms and agencies in order to reduce costs and to push responsibility for upholding workplace standards onto outside agencies while putting more money into branding and financial investments (Appelbaum 2017; Weil 2014). In turn, small firms, suppliers, and producers are forced to move more of their workforces into cheaper non-standard employment relations and seek to maximize diminishing returns by exploiting vulnerable workforces (Coe and Wai-Chung Yeung 2015). This financially driven "fissuring" of employment in low-productivity, labour-intensive industries has been a final driving force in the rise of precarious and contingent employment around the world (Standing 2011, 2016).

Financialization and Labour Market Inequality

In sum, a number of theoretical reasons suggest that neoliberalism, financial deregulation, and the financialization of the "real" economy have changed the nature of capital and labour markets and how they operate. Over the past few decades, in the wake of major changes to the rules governing financial and capital markets, financialization has not only been critical for the growth of top incomes, especially for the super rich in the financial sector and corporate executives. Changes to economic policy have also led to the increasing integration of NFCs into financial markets – and their resort to financial techniques. This politically driven financialization of the "real" economy accounts for the growth of "bad" jobs and the skewing of income distribution to the advantage of business and a wealthy few. To see if developments such as these have occurred in Canada, my theoretical model generates four important predictions that I look to test in chapter 4.

First, the rise of finance can be expected to benefit those at the top in finance, insurance, and real estate, both in salaries and capital returns. Second, the emergence of institutional investors and private equity owners is likely to lead to profits being redirected to shareholders, with declining investments in human capital and good jobs. Third, shareholder and private equity models of corporate governance seek to increase returns by shedding labour costs and, where unions are in place, seeking concessions and the breakup of traditional collective bargaining arrangements. Finally, the use of finance within the accumulation process for service and labour-intensive industries imposes market discipline on labour relations across workplaces in supplier and contractor networks, typically leading to the fissuring of employment and a shift to low-wage work, most notably in the private service, natural resource, and agricultural industries where growing market pressures undermine the ability of employers to pay.

Through these four channels, I argue, we can expect that economies will have undergone dramatic transformations, and that as financial and financialized corporate actors have grown in size and importance, they have been able to increase their returns at the expense of workers through poorer jobs, lower wages, and weaker institutional protections. In chapter 4, I examine how these processes of market and corporate financialization are at the core of recent increases in income inequality in Canada.

Conclusion

In developing a theoretical framework of the political and economic causes of inequality, with soaring incomes for the wealthy rising alongside increasingly ubiquitous low-wage, precarious employment for the majority, my argument underscores how recent changes in politics and policy can affect income distribution. Those who claim that inequality is simply due to technology and growing trade pressures, or the constrained efforts of public officials to better redistribute income, overlook how recent changes in policy have reshaped financial markets and corporate operations to the advantage of top income earners, and have done so prior to any redistribution through taxes and transfers. They also underestimate how the growth of global financial and production systems have redrawn the capacity for organized action among citizens and economic interests, rewarding business and the wealthy with growing political superiority.

By contrast, my theory highlights how states have intervened in markets and workforces, seeking to boost the interests of finance and corporations, and how business has run with this opportunity to expand and increase their profits through a variety of financial strategies. My argument lays stress on how major corporations have adapted to policy changes by overhauling their operations, and how finance has led to changes in the ownership, operation, and strategic direction of these firms, redirecting corporate incentives and the reallocation of resources. Such processes, I contend, allow us to explain why the success of the few has come so regularly at the expense of the majority, as well as why unions and workers have been often sidelined in these processes.

I now turn to the empirical assessment of these theories. In the next two chapters, I examine the development of financialization in Canada and its impacts on jobs and income distribution.

3 Tracing the Rise of Financialization in Canada

The growing role of finance across advanced capitalist economies has been crucial to rising inequality. New forms of private market finance, debt, and credit have expanded exponentially – often to the benefit of a very few who have made returns from interest, fees, and commissions. But finance has also assumed major roles across economies, taking over companies and changing corporate strategies, while providing the debt-based financing and incentives necessary for multinational corporations to grow globally and take advantage of workers the world over. In Canada over recent decades, many of these same processes have occurred.

But how did they occur? Why did capitalism in Canada change in this way? What were the roles of politics, power, and policy in redirecting the economy toward finance and allowing the benefits to flow upward to a very few? These are the questions that a number of critical political economists are asking today and that are the central concerns of this chapter.

Here, I first highlight key dimensions in the expansion of financialization in Canada, and the rise of new policies that pumped credit into the economy. I initially present data on the rise of market finance in Canada and the massive rise of private financial assets and debt across the economy, as well as the growth in debt and credit within non-bank financial institutions and NFCs. This exponential growth in private credit has been critical for corporate expansion, but also for driving asset inflation in housing and real estate markets.

Second, I turn to assess how financial capital has overturned the ownership and operation of NFCs and led companies to increasingly focus on shareholder value and returns to investors – a process I characterize as "corporate financialization." With the vast expansion of market-based systems of private credit and debt, I examine how finance has shifted dramatically away from its former role as a provider of credit, and instead taken on new roles in the economy through ownership, with institutional investors and pension funds now having a controlling interest in corporations across Canada – at the same time that private equity investors have leveraged debt to play a growing role in major companies across the economy. I also evaluate the wider impacts of private finance on corporate operation, and how finance has affected how corporations earn and use their profits.

Such changes, I argue, strongly suggest that firms are increasingly using their profits not simply as resources to improve future investment or employment. But rather corporate managers are engaging in "financial engineering" and using debt finance to drive up short-term share prices in order to transfer growing proportions of corporate cash to shareholders and financial investors.

I conclude the final sections of the chapter by surveying some of the major domestic and international policy shifts that account for the exponential growth in private credit and finance, as well as the wider financialization of Canada's real economy. I assess the wide range of domestic and international deregulatory policy changes and moves to banking self-regulation that have been the key levers to this boom in financial markets and to the transformations in the financial context in which business operated. I also evaluate how governments in Canada, the United States, and internationally have fundamentally overhauled their monetary, financial, pension, and taxation policies over the past few decades – in large measure to promote growth but inevitably opening the door to the integration of finance and corporation operation in the real economy.

Market Financialization and the Debt Economy in Canada

Discussions of Canada's financial system often emphasize how "robust" and "well regulated" it is (Bordo, Redish, and Rockoff 2015; Puri 2012). Typically, these characterizations are made in comparison to the United States, where financial regulation is fragmented and private financial firms played a larger role in regulating their own activities. In contrast, it is often claimed that Canadian banks are better regulated by federal and provincial authorities, and that Canadian authorities have set higher regulatory capital ratios, leading Canada's banks to be far more "conservative" and hold more liquid assets (Liu, Papakirykos, and Yuan 2004; Allen and Liu 2007; Puri 2012).

But all such discussions have missed how finance has fundamentally transformed Canada's economy over the past few decades and led to a major shift away from activities that used to provide value like labour and production and toward an economy concerned with finance. Also missed is how financialization in Canada has grown in much the same regulatory context as in the United States and Great Britain – with major banks and a growing number of new financial market actors taking advantage of "light-touch" regulation and a wide dispersal of regulatory authority (Konzelmann and Fovargue-Davies 2013; Shaxson 2018). Jim Stanford has characterized this growth in finance as a "paper boom," and there is much evidence to suggest that the growth of finance has done more to boost profits in financial assets – and using money to make money – than real investment (Stanford 1999). But credit and debt across Canada's economy have also grown, and financial capital has begun to lead in economic growth through the development of asset bubbles and the financialization of productive firms.

Basic statistical evidence indicates how finance and its related insurance has become increasingly important in economic growth and replaced other industries as a driver of employment over the past few decades. As in other advanced industrial economies, value added by banks, real estate, and other business services as a percentage of total valued added in Canada increased from 17 per cent in 1980 to 26 per cent by 2010 (on the United States and the United Kingdom, see Konzelmann and Fovargue-Davies 2013). Financial profits as a percentage of total profits grew from approximately 18 per cent in the 1970s to more than a quarter of profits in the early 1990s and 30 per cent of profits by 2007 before declining slightly in the wake of the crisis. By contrast, manufacturing, which used to be a key driver of growth and employment, has seen its overall share of profits fall from over 30 per cent in the mid-1990s to less than 14 per cent in 2013–14 (Dupuis, Peters, and Scrimger 2020). These numbers provide some indication of the importance of finance to Canada's economy, though they are similar to those found across the advanced capitalist world (OECD 2016).

But digging more deeply reveals a host of different indicators of finance and debt's growing importance to the Canadian economy, including a disproportionate increase of the financial services sector, the explosion in the size and variety of financial markets, and the heavy accumulation of financial assets and liabilities within NFCs and a wide range of financial actors. Here Canada begins to appear less as a "conservative" financial system and one much more like the United States – the "taker" economy typically seen as the most financially driven by Wall Street (Forhoohar 2016).

Figure 3.1 provides one set of statistical evidence of this phenomenon, with total financial assets in the entire financial sector (from banks, insurance corporations, pension and insurance funds, and financial intermediaries such as investment funds) growing rapidly over the course of the 1990s and the first decade of 2000, from 247 per cent of GDP to more than 372 per cent of GDP and continuing to increase, despite the financial crisis in 2012 to more 533 per cent of GDP in 2012. As in the United States, finance in Canada grew at a rate faster than the rest of the economy, with its influence growing in tandem. Indeed, in comparative terms among the largest advanced industrial economies, the financial assets of Canada's financial corporations as percentage of GDP consistently ranked within the top four across the first decade of 2000.

Part of this credit growth was due to Canada's major chartered financial institutions allocating more and more of their credit for housing mortgages, as

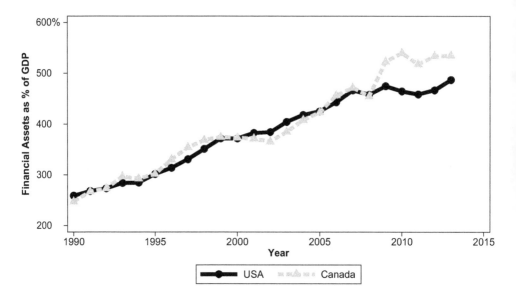

Figure 3.1. Canada/United States: Financial assets of financial corporations, 1990–2012 (% of GDP)

Source: OECD, Financial Dashboard, financial accounts, 720 financial balance sheets, author calculations.

well as investing in speculative activities such as money market funds, derivatives, corporate bonds and shares, as well as wealth funds. Canada's major "Big Five" chartered banks also began to move heavily into corporate underwriting and investment banking, with investment fees moving centre stage in their portfolios (Calmès and Théoret 2013). In addition, Canada's major financial institutions expanded into the United States and used their access to treasury bills and Canadian bond auctions for securities underwriting and trading in the tax havens of the Caribbean, where they sought to develop global operations with investment and financial services for all global companies and individuals seeking capital at lower rates and to conduct business in tax havens with little scrutiny and exceptionally low rates of taxation (Deneault and Sacher 2010; Deneault 2015). In these ways, Canada's major financial institutions followed trends in the United States and the United Kingdom, taking advantage of increasing international capital flows and light-touch regulation to spur credit growth and liquidity within the domestic economy as well as internationally (Coleman and Porter 2003; Konzelmann and Fovargue-Davies 2013).

But equally important to the mass expansion of finance was the development of capital liquidity outside of Canada's major chartered banks, often with little or no regulatory oversight – a process referred to as "shadow banking" or financial "disintermediation" (Calmès and Théoret 2013; Chapman, Lavoie, and Schembri 2011; IMF 2014b). Here the growth of finance companies, investment funds, hedge funds, and financial holding corporations – what are referred to as "non-bank" financial institutions – was critical to the increase in capital, share and bonds, and foreign exchange markets, as well as the new debt-based assets and securities. But also important was how NFCs began to engage and use capital markets. In this rapid mushrooming of shadow banking and unregulated capital markets, Canada followed American developments, with trusts, life insurance companies, and pension funds historically linked to turning personal savings into private sector investment, investing more heavily in financial markets, and using new debt-based assets to increase returns (Calmès and Théoret 2013; Guttmann 2016). But NFCs also increasingly engaged in financial arbitrage themselves, using the credit subsidiaries they had developed to attract consumers, as well as expanding their own bond and equity portfolios to boost corporate growth and profits.

As figure 3.2 demonstrates, over the course of the 1990s and the first decade of 2000, Canada's non-bank financial institutions and their corporate counterparts grew enormously, investing in public equity, venture funds, and private equity. In just over twenty years, financial assets in these institutions tripled to over 170 per cent of GDP, as savings and debt securities were funnelled into equity and capital markets through mutual funds and ETFs. At the same time, with new investments from Manulife and Sunlife (two insurance companies among the top ten largest in the world) as well as the Ontario Teachers' Pension fund (the eighteenth-largest pension fund globally), NFCs were able to tap into new sources of debt-based market capital to accumulate bonds, stocks, debt securities, and derivatives to boost their liquidity, but also to increase their alternative sources of income and provide their managers with greater market power. Discussions of Canada's financial system typically highlight only the size and market power of Canada's major chartered banks (Bordo, Redish, and Rockoff 2015; Puri 2012). But the increase in the financial assets and liabilities on the balance sheets of non-bank and non-financial actors in Canada to more than 330 per cent of GDP shows clearly how the non-banking sector of pension, mutual, and exchange trade funds were equally important suppliers of finance and credit, and equally crucial to engendering new liquidity and altering the growth pattern of the economy.

In taking on this new role, Canada's trusts, life insurance companies, and pension funds in many ways only expanded upon their long-standing practices of directing personal savings to private sector investment (Deaton 1989). In particular, private pension savings had long been central players in Canada's capital markets and a key source of investment capital for public and private companies alike. But with the growth of global capital and securities markets,

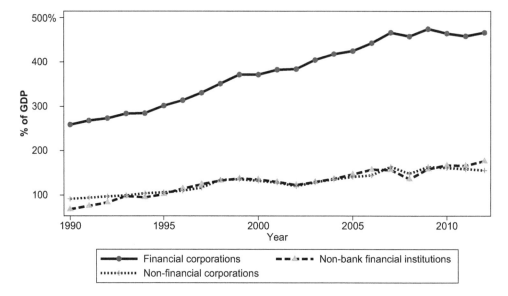

Figure 3.2. Canadian financial assets by sector, 1990–2012 (% of GDP)
Source: OECD, Financial Dashboard, financial accounts, author calculations.

and the expansion of their assets, non-bank financial institutions took on even greater importance in Canada's capital and equity markets. In the 1960s, institutional investor ownership of publicly trade stock was 10.5 per cent in 1965 and 22 per cent in 1979 (Deaton 1989). But by 2008, the importance of institutional investors and pension funds was far larger – as their ownership topped 50 per cent of the market capitalization of publicly listed firms on the Toronto Stock Exchange, a level of institutional ownership that was second only to the United States (Aggarwal et al. 2011). As I discuss in more detail below, the results of this channelling of savings and financial investments into securities and debt markets were profound, as institutional investors fundamentally changed firms and their corporate governance, changing executives, board structures, and firm priorities (Aggarwal et al. 2011).

But the growth in new financial products and services also expanded the availability of cheap credit for firms. Large corporations operating in Canada increasingly engaged in financial trading themselves to finance short-term funding requirements, but also used financial investments and corporate bonds to accelerate profits and increase dividends (Chapman, Lavoie, and Schembri 2011; Duprey, Grieder, and Hogg 2017). In many cases, non-financial firms invested primarily in debt securities and money markets for equity buy-backs and financial leverage rather than investment and capital expenditure

(Stanford 2011). In others, NFCs extended credit to consumers to promote increased spending and offer lower rates of interest. But with the vast increase of market finance, the investment functions of NFCs as well as pension and insurance funds and trust companies became critical for the emergence of finance-led growth in Canada – which mirrored financially driven processes in other advanced capitalist countries such as the United States and Great Britain (Durand 2017; Lapavitsas 2014).

The third element of Canada's recent financial boom was the growth in housing and construction – driven by government policies of financial deregulation and attempts to spur economic growth by creating higher levels of private consumer debt – and seized upon by the major banks to finance housing and commercial real estate. As in the United States and across Western Europe, beginning in the mid-1990s, the Canadian government sought to compensate for increasing income inequality and the weakening of broad-based economic demand by stimulating household borrowing and real estate markets (Baker 2009; Crouch 2009; Walks and Clifford 2015). With average earnings of Canadians stagnating in the late 1990s and early 1990s, the Mulroney government first deregulated mortgage markets to boost housing and consumer spending, then worked with the financial sector to find new ways to generate and sell consumer debt.

Here the remaking of property markets – and the role of homeownership in the overall economy – was enacted by major changes to the Canadian Housing and Mortgage Company as well as by the development of a mortgage securitization program. In Canada, as across advanced capitalist countries, this financialization of housing markets was driven by "securitization" and new regulations that have allowed financial institutions to sell – rather than hold – mortgage debt (Aalbers 2016). In Canada, the origins of securitization can be traced to the National Housing and Asset-Backed Securities Acts of 1986, which permitted banks and other financial institutions to use mortgage-backed debt securities provided by the government to lower risk and increase the proportion of funds available for the housing market (Walks 2014). At the same time, the Canada Housing and Mortgage agency was overhauled, and rather than an agency providing social housing, it was transformed to one that provided insurance and managed mortgage-backed securities to banks and private mortgage companies to expand private sector home construction and private homeownership.

As figure 3.3 shows, the initiation of the securitization market with the introduction of mortgage-backed securities and other asset-backed securities in the 1990s rapidly accelerated across the first decade of 2000. Using OECD data on private debt securities that captures their use across the chartered banks and other private mortgage banks, debt securities as a percentage of GDP increased from 10 per cent of GDP to 30 per cent by 2000 to more than 50 per cent in 2010. This acceleration reflected how quickly financial institutions and

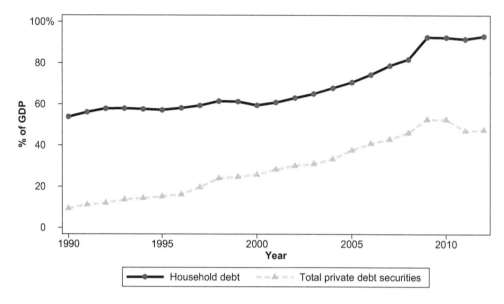

Figure 3.3. Canadian household debt and private debt securities, 1990–2012 (% of GDP)
Sources: Bank of International Settlements; OECD – Financial Dashboard, financial accounts; author calculations.

mortgage companies picked up the issuance of mortgage-backed securities to back mortgage lending. In turn, as securities provided financial institutions with credit and liquidity, and governments kept interest rates low, consumers were able to take on increasing amounts of debt for the purchases of houses and consumer goods. As in other advanced capitalist countries, household debt in Canada rose quickly over the course of the 1990s and the first decade of 2000, nearly doubling from 54 per cent in 1990 to more than 90 per cent by 2010.

In these ways, mortgage securitization was key to the "financialization of housing" (Aalbers 2016) as the new debt securities issued by the CMHC fuelled the growth of booming housing markets and rising house prices (Walks 2014). In addition, record low interest rates in the first decade of 2000 allowed more Canadian families to save less and borrow more to finance house purchases and other consumer purchases. At the same time, with repayment terms eased to thirty-five and forty years, investors bought housing, developers built more stock, and millions of homeowners got out of higher-priced mortgages through refinancing and bought second homes as investments. These changes fundamentally altered the economy to support housing-fuelled consumption. By 2008, housing-related spending – a broad category that includes not only home purchases but also repairs, renovations, furniture, appliances, and a host of other items – accounted for one-fifth of all economic activity (CMHC 2009).

Financialization and Corporate Ownership in Canada

If the rapid growth of new credit markets constitutes one side of the transformation of Canada's economy to increasing levels of market finance, the other is how finance grew in importance to the ownership, operation, and governance of non-financial firms – all key aspects of "corporate financialization" (Aalbers 2016). Corporations in Canada used to operate primarily within their own national borders, and ownership was passed generationally through a minority of wealthy families (Carroll 2008). But over the course of the 1990s and the first decade of 200s, this model was radically overhauled. The numbers are striking – even for Canada and the United States, which traditionally had far more concentrated ownership groups. In 1989–90, approximately half of publicly traded corporations were still held by individuals in Canada and the United States, far fewer than in the United Kingdom. But by 2008, more than 50 per cent of publicly traded firms had changed hands and come under the ownership of institutional investors (Aggarwal et al. 2011).

Today, institutional investors – wealth management companies, pension and mutual funds, and insurance companies, as well as private equity funds, exchange-traded and sovereign wealth funds – control the majority of corporate assets and debt (figure 3.4). ETFs like BlackRock, Carlyle, and Kohlberg Kravis Roberts, and mutual funds like State Street and Fidelity, rapidly expanded their holdings in thousands of companies and often became the largest public equity shareholders in the United States and the United Kingdom (OECD 2011b, 29–31). In Canada, major shareholders include Canada's chartered investment funds, but also major pension funds like the Canada Investment Pension Board, and the Ontario Teachers' Pension Plan (Bedard-Page et al. 2016; Skerrett et al. 2018).

Regarding the size of financial investment funds, the raw figures on the scale of institutional shareholders are staggering (figure 3.5). The OECD estimates that over the course of the first decade of 2000, the corporate assets under institutional investors more than doubled worldwide, and by 2011 the combined holdings of all institutions represented US\$84.8 trillion, approximately 38 per cent (US\$32 trillion) of which was held in the form of public equity (Celik and Isaksson 2014, 97). In Canada, the holdings of institutional investors were similarly immense and mushroomed over the 1990s and the first decade of 2000 (Jog and Mintz 2013). In 2005, for example, the total size of investment, insurance, and pension fund assets was \$1.6 trillion – or 142 per cent of GDP. By 2012, institutional assets grew to 152 per cent of GDP and by 2015 had ballooned to more than 208 per cent of GDP – or approximately \$3.7 trillion.

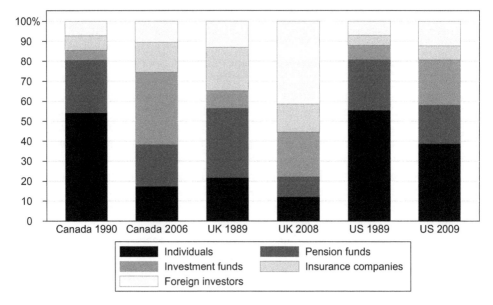

Figure 3.4. Ownership structure in Canada, the United Kingdom, and the United States, 1990–2009
Sources: OECD (2011b), figure 1.1; and Rydqvist, Spizman, and Strebulaev (2011).

The rise of financially driven asset funds has been fundamental in transforming the ownership structures beyond large, publicly traded companies. Over the course of the 1980s and 1990s, private equity and activist hedge funds emerged to take direct control of companies, or purchase large blocks of publicly traded companies, or make venture capital investments in young companies (Batt and Appelbaum 2014).

As figure 3.5 demonstrates, growth in institutional investor equity holdings was massive. In the early 1990s, pension, insurance, and investor funds had publicly traded equity holdings that totalled less than 17 per cent of GDP. By 2007, institutional investors were holding equity assets of more than 80 per cent, and by 2012 had expanded this to more than 87 per cent of GDP.

At the same time, growing amounts of market finance were critical for the emergence of new forms of private equity ownership. In the late 1980s, Michael Jensen predicted that private equity firms would become the major corporate organizational form (Jensen 1989). He argued that financial pressures, combined with high compensation incentives for managers, would lead to more efficient and profitable firms with lower costs. And by the late 1990s and early in the first decade of 2000, this prediction increasingly came true,

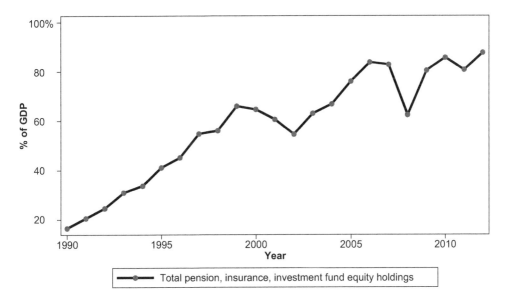

Figure 3.5. Total institutional investor equity holdings, 1990–2012 (% of GDP)
Source: OECD Financial Dashboard, "Institutional Investor Statistics," author calculations.

as record amounts of capital from institutional investors were committed to private equity (Kaplan and Stromberg 2009).

Drawing on new pools of capital from commercial and investment banks, as well as insurance companies and institutional investors, private equity firms took the opportunity to buy thousands of companies – both publicly traded and privately owned – with the goal of selling off underperforming divisions, reducing labour costs via downsizing or wage reductions, improving financial performance, and then exiting the investment in five years or less. Typically these deals involved high debt leverage (from 60–90 per cent debt) as equity managers used loans to purchase and run companies, while retaining high fees for themselves (Davis 2016). Moreover, in relying so heavily on debt, private equity firms often used financial engineering strategies to buy, run, and sell firms, many of which ended with managers adopting ruthless short-term measures such as the breaking up of firms, the raiding of pension funds, and layoffs (Batt and Appelbaum 2014). The only instances where private equity managers did not restructure firms was while providing venture capital, which was heavily invested in new information technology industries as well as other high-end manufacturing ventures (Torys LLP 2016).

In Canada, the shift to private equity ownership was pushed by institutional investors, especially pension fund organizations, which began backing private equity firms in the 1990s and continued to do so in the first decade of 2000 (Conference Board of Canada 2014). Banks and institutional managers such as the Caisse de dépôt et placement du Quebec (CDPQ) spun off their own private equity arms to buy, sell, and restructure firms. In addition, with the rapid rise of activist equity funds and leveraged buyouts in the United States, American activist fund managers bought and sold hundreds of companies in Canada over the course of the first decade of 2000 (Schertler and Tykvova 2009). Such private equity deals remained smaller than total financings on the Toronto Stock Exchange and Venture Exchange, rising from $5 to $26 billion (2000–8) in annual new financing of companies, or roughly 50 per cent of total financing on Canada's two major exchanges (Martineau 2012). But in terms of numbers of companies, private financing arrangements began to represent a sea change in how companies operated in Canada, as in many other countries (Siegel, Wright, and Filatotcheve 2011; Schertler and Tykvova 2009).

Dealing with primarily small and mid-market firms (less than $100 million and $100–$500 million, respectively), as well as providing venture capital to start-ups, private equity owners increasingly took over the direction of thousands of companies. On average, outside of major takeovers, it is estimated that each private equity deal involved five other portfolio companies (Schertler and Tykvova 2009) and were concentrated in oil and gas, mining, manufacturing, information technology/media, and private services (Torys LLP 2016). While data are still limited, the Conference Board of Canada reports 1593 deals between 2003 and 2010 (Conference Board of Canada 2014) and 1300 private equity firms by 2014 (Preqin 2016b). But this suggests that as of 2010, when discounting for annual exits of some 50 per cent of ownership, some 3500–4000 portfolio companies began to operate under new private equity owners – the majority Canadian and American in origin.

In contrast, in 2010 there were only 3985 large and medium-sized firms listed as public entities on the TSX and TSX Venture exchanges, approximately the same as the number of firms that came under the control private equity management over the course of the first decade of 2000. Still, given that all firms operating in Canada grew from 7,864 to 10,496 (2000–10), this suggests that with these new mergers and acquisitions some 15 per cent of all medium and large-sized firms in Canada were operating under private equity managers and investors by late in the first decade of 2000.

What accounts for this rapid transformation of corporate ownership for both publicly traded companies and new privately held firms? How and why did financial actors become the dominant owners of firms in Canada? Key to the rise of new institutional investors in Canada were public and private pension funds (Jog and Mintz 2013). As in the United States and Great Britain, pension deregulation and the redirection of pension funds to stocks, bonds, and financial assets were a major source of new capital for corporate and financial actors, allowing them to pool vast sums of savings into the industrial and financial sectors of the economy (Blackburn 2002, 177–85; Deaton 1989, 168). But over the course of the 1980s and 1990s, seeking new sources of finance, corporations turned away from retained earnings and increasingly turned to external sources of finance, provided through the sale of stock, issuing of debt, and via short-term debt instruments, many of which were funded by employer pension funds and private mutual funds.

In 1980, Canada – like the United States and Great Britain – already had extensive private employer tax-favoured pension plans, and Canadian institutional investors contributed more 27 per cent of total net business investment by the private sector and more than 46 per cent of all saving (Deaton 1989, 177). But driven by government efforts to have pension funds use equities, securities, and financial assets to fund pensions beyond payroll contributions, public and private pensions were reformed and restructured to provide an even greater source of capital for business growth and financialization. Officials argued that the growth of private employer plans, alongside individual retirement accounts based in mutual funds, and the direct investment of public pension monies into capital markets would all not only increase future pension returns, but also boost national saving and expand investment (Munnell and Sass 2006).

This resulted in the staggering growth of pension assets and new investments in capital markets. Total assets in the pension fund sector grew from approximately $250 billion in 1993 to $900 billion by 2007 and nearly $2 trillion by 2015 – or larger than annual GDP. Combined, the public Canada Pension Plan Investment Board and CDPQ, as well as public employer plans like the Ontario Teachers' Pension Plan, held more than two-thirds of all assets and became some of the largest institutional investors in the world, with three of them ranked among the twenty largest (Bedard-Page et al. 2016). Investing heavily in corporate equities, often with more than 50 per cent of their holdings, institutional investors drove the rapid growth in the stock market. But growing pension funds were also major drivers of new financial assets such as derivatives and private equity, doubling their holdings of "alternative assets" over the course of the first decade of 2000 (Bedard-Page et al. 2016).

Equally important for the rapid expansion of institutional investors was the rise of insurance companies and private mutual fund investors. Underpinned by billions of dollars in annual government tax expenditures for private individuals and their registered retirement savings funds, total net annual RRSP contributions rose from $3.7 billion in 1980 to $26.6 billion in 1998 and more than $34 billion in 2011 (CBC 2013). In turn, the total value of private mutual funds assets rapidly grew from $241.2 billion in 1998 to more than $775 billion in 2011. At the same time, the growth of insurance and private pension fund savings – along with the management of "high net worth" individuals – by Canadian insurance companies were poured into government bonds and corporate securities (Toronto Financial Services Alliance 2016). In this way, savings and investment were channelled into corporate and financial expansion, and pension savings became crucial to the operation of the economy and the financialization of corporate activity (Archer 2011).

As financial intermediaries, pension, insurance, and mutual funds were critical to the financialization of corporate ownership and operation. By 2006, domestic finance-based investors had contributed enormously to the growth of market capitalization and equity growth, with funds holding 50 per cent or more of the equity in the stock market. This has led rising pension contributions to track the growth of the stock market very closely (Clark, Monk, and Monk 2007). But pension funds were equally critical to the growth of the private equity market, investing heavily in hedge funds and private equity deals to boost returns (Archer 2011).

A final driver for the transformation of corporate ownership was the massive expansion of corporate mergers and acquisitions and the corporate use of finance to expand market share and extract supersized profits (Durand 2017; Shaxson 2018). One of the most common tactics companies used to achieve better returns in the face of new forms of finance and pressures from reformed corporate boards was to engage in a wave of mergers and acquisitions (M&As) and then subsequently restructure operations and workforces across regions and countries (Macaire et al. 2002). Using increasingly cheap sources of market credit, and typically with low interest payments, corporations massively expanded their size by acquiring others and developing wider global networks. In the OECD over the period 1987–2001, M&A sales represented more than 82 per cent of inward foreign direct investment (FDI), while purchases of foreign assets through M&A accounted for 71 per cent of outward FDI (Brakman, Garretsen, and van Marrewijk 2005). In these ways, companies bought out competitors, took ownership of patents and trademarks, and expanded into new areas of production and distribution, all in the effort to boost profits and returns to shareholders.

By 2007, M&A purchases made up 52 per cent of outward FDI, as financial institutions and multinationals increasingly used offshore financial hubs to lower taxation and redirect firm income to offshore holding companies (UNCTAD 2016). In buying mode, corporations and financial institutions expanded their outward FDI eleven-fold from US$513 billion in the early 1980s to US$6.1 trillion by 2000 to US$15 trillion by 2007. Over two-thirds of FDI in the 1990s and more than 50 per cent in the first decade of 2000 was directed to the purchasing of companies in other advanced capitalist countries, and despite a short decline of FDI inflows into the United States and Western Europe early in the first decade of 2000. In the wake of the financial crisis, M&A purchases did decline significantly. But by 2015, FDI flows returned to "normal" levels, while developed country OECD investments to the rest of world attained record peaks, pouring more than US$721 in mergers abroad (UNCTAD 2016).

American multinational companies were the largest overseas investors as well as largest host to European and Japanese investors, leading the way in their efforts to expand their enterprises and take increasing global profits (Panitch and Gindin 2013). And similarly, within North America, American cross-border investment in M&As in Canada was the driving force, with multinationals, hedge funds, and private equity firms snapping up hundreds of companies in the 1990s and the first decade of 2000. Over the course of the 1990s and early in the first decade of 2000, Canada ranked as one of the top ten global destinations in total value of inward foreign investment, and despite being the smallest economy in the G7, Canada ranked fifth in inward FDI flows over this period, ahead of larger economies such as Japan (Competition Policy Review Panel 2007, 11).

Led by private service multinationals and global manufacturing and mining firms, MNCs launched waves of corporate takeovers and buyouts across multiple sectors in the Canadian economy (Acharya et al. 2010). But debt-driven private equity deals also peaked just before the economic crisis in 2007 as favourable credit conditions helped fuel the increase in highly leveraged acquisitions. In Canada, mergers and acquisitions rose from 750 (1990–2004) to 2618 (2000–8) before declining to 899 (2010–14) in the wake of the financial crisis. Throughout this period, American investors were the largest purchasers of companies operating in Canada (Day et al. 2009) and built up the largest firms operating in Canada. For perspective, as a percentage of all business spending, mergers and acquisitions represented twice the amount firms spent on all of their expenditures on machinery, equipment, and buildings (Brennan 2012, 33).

Not content with simply buying up existing assets, leading MNCs and growing numbers of small and medium-sized enterprises in everything from chemicals to industrial machinery, instruments and food also expanded their operations abroad – a final key factor in the overhaul of global capitalism to extract greater wealth and income from workforces around the world (Milberg and Winkler 2013; Coe and Wai-Chung Yeung 2015). Global trends in production show the largest 100 transnational corporations vastly increasing their assets, sales, and employment over the course of the 1990s and the first decade of 2000 (UNCTAD 2013). The foreign assets of transnational corporations (TNCs) rose 400 per cent from 1990 to 2007 from US$5 trillion to US$20 trillion, before increasing again in the wake of the crisis to US$26 trillion in 2012. This was a rate more than triple their remarkable steady increase in domestic assets. Globally, TNC affiliates likewise skyrocketed more than five-fold, swelling from 190,000 in 1990 to more than 892,000 in 2010. These trends suggest how much TNCs globalized their operations and restructured firms and firm ownership worldwide in the effort to create global supersized firms that left their competitors behind or simply took over their competitors while growing their corporate operations.

In sum, over the course of the 1990s and the first decade of 2000, the evidence points to a dramatic change in firm ownership and operation in Canada. Where in the past individuals and wealthy owners often controlled ownership of their large public companies for long periods of time, with the rise of pension finance, mergers and acquisitions, and private equity partnerships, ownership was transferred to institutional investors and private equity owners (primarily domestic and American), where control was dispersed, subject to direct market pressures, and often rapidly turned over. Such ownership changes had a number of implications for corporate governance and operation, not the least of which were the new financial engineering strategies, shareholder models, and outsourcing strategies that companies adopted to deliver growing returns to shareholders and equity partners.

Corporate Financialization in Canada

While corporate ownership has moved in a far more financially driven direction, new types of corporate management based on shareholder returns were also introduced in Canada, as in many other advanced capitalist economies. Critical theorists have argued that the extent to which managers will take a long-term perspective or a market orientation toward employment practices, wages, and operation varies with corporate governance methods and domestic tax and regulations (Cobb 2016; Gospel and Pendleton 2005). Where individuals and block-holders are able to retain greater independence vis-à-vis external market participants, company owners will be theoretically more likely to work on improving productivity with other stakeholders, such as unions or skilled workers, in a more socially enlightened manner (Amable 2003). In contrast, where external market actors – like institutional investors – have taken over companies and forced changes in management, firms will be more likely to adopt strategies of shareholder value maximization, aggressively managing their cost base (Aggarwal et al. 2011; Goyer 2009; Jung and Dobbin 2014). Private equity is only a more aggressive shareholder model, which uses its capital to seek out high returns and lower costs in order to reward managers and fund partners (Batt and Appelbaum 2014).

But as growing evidence suggests, the financialization of ownership and use of financial engineering by firms has led to a significant convergence in corporate governance and management. And as major corporations have merged and acquired one another, while also seeking to leverage new finance to grow globally, more and more firms have rapidly taken to financial engineering and financial markets in order to grow and compete.

Barker has argued that there is no single quantitative indicator to assess the extent of changes to corporate governance and the financialization of MNCs on a comparative basis (Barker 2010). Nevertheless, he claims there are good basic proxies for financialization and changes to corporate operating procedures, and two of the better ones include stock market capitalization and values of shares traded. A more basic third indicator is the level of inward FDI and portfolio flows as a percentage of GDP – a figure that is readily available and comparable across countries (figure 3.6).

Rising market capitalization as a percentage of GDP is a good indicator of the extent to which publicly traded firms have grown massively while reorienting themselves to outside capital and a wide range of institutional investors and other minority stakeholders. Similarly, higher levels of share trading signal how active institutional investors and hedge funds, not to mention the firms themselves, were in the buying and selling of corporate shares on stock markets as part of a strategy of financial engineering intended to boost shareholder returns. Likewise, since FDI is the main mechanism for the international expansion of MNCs, domestic companies typically have to exhibit outsider-friendly governance if they are to draw investment. As figure 3.6 demonstrates, each of these indicators points to widening corporate financialization, and the growing importance of rents and benchmarked returns in production across advanced industrial economies (Durand 2017). But each also points to how corporations and investors alike have prioritized future returns in order to warrant investment.

As figure 3.6 shows, in North America and Western Europe, all three indicators grew exponentially between 1990 and 2015 – despite the financial crisis of 2007–8. Gross FDI increased more than five-fold as foreign institutional investors bought up the stock of the largest MNCs, and private firms sought to expand internationally through mergers and acquisitions. Indeed, the small export-oriented Nordic countries experienced the highest proportional increases in FDI debt and stock flows – a more than ten-fold rise in Finland, and a sixteen-fold increase in Sweden. In contrast, the United States saw only a doubling of financial and corporate investment, an increase similar to that seen in Canada (figure 3.7). But it is important to note that the United States still accounted for more than a quarter of world investment and only recently has fallen to a fifth of world investment as other global firms have expanded their international operations.

Overall, in thirteen advanced economies, FDI flows increased, on average, from roughly 11 per cent of GDP in 1990 to 56 per cent prior to the financial crisis in 2008, before growing again to more than 55 per cent of GDP in 2015. By comparison across the 1990s and the first decade of 2000, Canada's level of inward FDI was consistently greater than the OECD average, and the vast majority of that was tied to American institutional and private equity investors – the largest and most aggressive in the world. These investors undertook a record number of takeovers as well as new holdings in Canadian companies

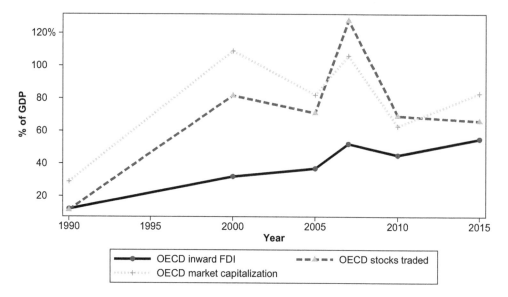

Figure 3.6. Corporate financialization OECD, 1990–2015 (inward FDI, value of
stocks traded, market capitalization of listed firms, as % of GDP, 13 country average)
Sources: IMF; World Bank world development indicators. Averages based on Austria, Belgium,
Canada, Denmark, Finland, France, Germany, Italy, the Netherlands, Norway, Sweden, Great
Britain, and the United States. Data incomplete 2015. Author calculations.

in order to integrate Canadian operations into North American and global operations. The result was that massive inflows of investment went into the largest
100 companies on the Toronto Stock Exchange, which now account for more
than 80 per cent of total market capitalization on the TSX (Nicholls 2006;
Peters 2011).

Matching these significant changes in the 1990s and the first decade of 2000
was the rising value of companies and stock markets throughout Canada, the
United States, and Western Europe, and over a twenty-year period, as firms
sought to grow rapidly, build global monopolies by acquiring others, and increase their market capitalization. Spurred by financial liberalization and the
loosening of restrictions on the international buying and selling of domestic
equity, investors and wealth funds spurred enterprises to restructure and expand (Carroll 2007). Consequently, whether in North America or Western
Europe, publicly listed companies began replacing bank loans and internal
financing with public equity and market-based debt. Such a turn can be clearly
seen in how companies began to rely on debt markets for finance. In 1990, for
example, there were just 610 hedge funds with $38.9 billion, but by 2006 there
9,462 managing $1.5 trillion (Ferguson 2008), and by 2015, there were 10,149
managing over $3 trillion (Preqin 2016a). Such new financial players allowed

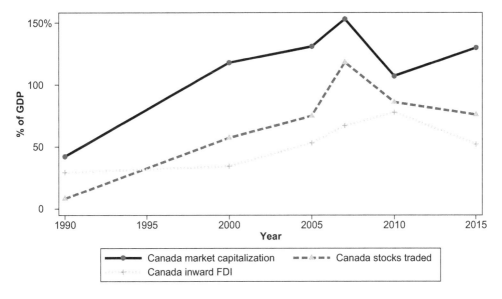

Figure 3.7. Corporate financialization in Canada, 1990–2015 (inward FDI, stocks traded, market capitalization of listed firms, as % of GDP in Canada)
Sources: OECD Stan indicators; World Bank world development indicators; UNCTAD International Finance; author calculations.

both private and public firms to use debt markets to finance mega-deals and corporate expansion.

With such easy credit available, beginning early in the first decade of 2000, more firms went private. And in the wake of the financial crisis, this trend continued. But already in the 1990s, many publicly traded firms had turned to new combinations of equity and debt in order to buy up their own stock and pay out dividends, pay off debts and merge with other global entities, or take advantage of tax credits for corporate debt. And in the wake of the crisis, helped along by banks that increasingly merged investment and commercial functions and that lent money on the basis of increasingly complex asset-back securities, firms used finance to expand and restructure operations.

Strikingly, the biggest transformations occurred in many of the social democratic countries of Finland, Denmark, Norway and Sweden, where businesses expanded their market capitalization nearly three-fold and turned to bond and equity markets for financing (Huizinga and Jonung 2005). But in Canada too the market capitalization of firms ballooned from 40 per cent of GDP to more than 150 per cent of GDP (1990–2008) then declined and rose again to 130 per cent of GDP in 2015. Such growth implies that major multinational firms were very successful in orienting their governance and growth strategies to the needs of outsider capital and using this capital to produce more and take increasing proportions of market share.

Unsurprisingly, with the growth in firm capitalization rates, equity trading also exploded. Seeking better rates of return and profit differentials, fund managers moved quickly to dump underperforming shares for those with higher returns. Exempt from capital gains taxes or often indifferent to tax rates, institutional investors rapidly turned over portfolios on the basis of short-term movements in stock price (Blackburn 2002, 130; Jacoby 2005, 35). With investment banks backing growing leverage ratios – and often themselves joining in the speculative surges – firms and traders alike bought and sold securities with the belief that the asset-price boom would go on endlessly.

The OECD estimates that over the course of the 1990s and first decade of 2000, institutional investors reduced their average holding period to less than a year (OECD 2011b, 31). High-frequency trading contributed to this decline, but so too did the active role of institutional investors who routinely adjusted portfolios to maximize returns. Overall in Canada, equity trading exploded from 15 per cent of GDP to more than 118 per cent of GDP (1990–2008), suggesting a greater orientation of corporate ownership toward outsider capital, as investors turned over their portfolios seeking quick returns, and hence corporations had to more closely align their priorities to the interests of external minority shareholders. Most notable for Canada was the growth of the oil and gas sectors, which led the TSX in equity and capitalization growth (Cross 2008; Cross 2010).

The consequences of this internationalization of stock markets and asset ownership for corporate operations in Canada were profound. From 1990 to 2008, stock trading on the TSX rose to over $1 trillion annually, exceeding the entire value of the Canadian economy by 20 per cent in 2008, before falling in 2009. Foreign direct investment in oil and natural resources climbed in Toronto and the other "junior" stock exchanges to record levels, making the Toronto stock and venture exchanges among the most natural-resource heavy in the world (Cross 2008; Nicholls 2006). Wages and fees in the banking and brokerage industry took off in the late 1990s, skyrocketing throughout the last decade. The size of Canadian listed companies grew by more than $3 trillion. All such developments signal a profound shift in the operation of NFCs, ranging from the introduction of new shareholder strategies, to the use of debt markets for finance, and the resort of financial engineering to maximize returns from firms operating in Canada.

Shareholder Value, Financial Engineering, and Corporate Operation

A third and final set of considerations for how finance transformed the nature of corporate operations is how NFCs began to engage in balance sheet engineering and global tax dodges to boost short-term corporate profits while funding global mergers and restructuring – all processes critical to "corporate financialization" and a "taker" economy (Forhoohar 2016). There is still a shortage of reliable statistics on corporate operations in Canada – not least because of the aggressive tax planning of firms that channels ownership and profits to multiple subsidiaries and tax havens that do not publish data (Tax Justice Network 2015). But there is still much evidence to strongly suggest that the many domestic, American, and international non-financial companies operating in Canada have taken to finance to improve returns for the wealthiest shareholders.

Such corporate financialization of firms operating in Canada can be seen in (1) the expansion of corporate debt; (2) the use of financial assets and portfolio income for firm and share price growth; (3) the use of finance within global value chains; and (4) the increasing reward for shareholders by diverting income to dividends. In each of these areas, there is evidence to demonstrate that corporations have changed dramatically in how they earn and use profits to increasingly prioritize finance, but also how this approach has been part of a longer-term trend to redistribute greater profits to shareholders and extract greater wealth from the wider economy as well as their workforces.

Over the past few decades, non-financial companies have increasingly used – and actively participated in – financial markets. Because of expanding financial opportunities available with ever-cheaper credit, and the pressures from financial owners and stock markets, firms have increasingly reshaped their managerial priorities away from national to international growth as well as away from long-term to short-term profits (Davis 2013; Lin 2016). In making this shift, managers have sought to maximize shareholder value and often used debt and securities markets as prime measures to increase stock price through stock buy-backs as well as to increase revenues through mergers and acquisitions (Krippner 2011; Tomaskovic-Devey, Lin, and Meyers 2015). In other cases, hedge funds and corporate takeover specialists have used cheap capital to take over firms and subsequently strip the companies of assets by selling off less-profitable divisions (Jung and Dobbin 2014). In these ways, even despite the massive expansion of market capitalization rates, firms have often substituted debt and debt-backed securities for equity as their chief source of financing.

As figure 3.8 demonstrates, already by the 1990s, non-financial firms were heavily leveraged, with the average across OECD countries exceeding more than 400 per cent, and Canadian non-financial firms nearly 600 per cent. This ratio is important, as it measures the capacity of NFCs to meet the cost of debt repayments and reflects how firms shifted their priorities to using debt for general operation and how gross operating surplus was used to service and turn over debt financing. With growing tax advantages provided to firms to use debt, firms increasingly turned to credit markets in order to operate, acquire other

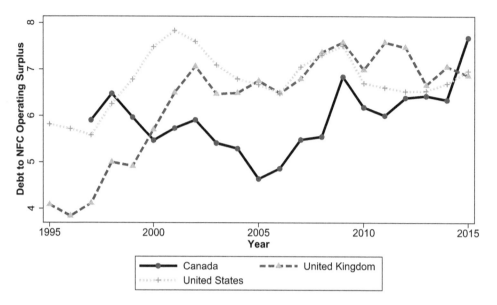

Figure 3.8. Consolidated debt to NFC operating surplus (ratio), 1995–2015
Source: OECD Financial Dashboard, "Financial Indicators-Stocks"; author calculations.

firms, and purchase assets. But it is noticeable that over the course of the 1990s and the first decade of 2000, with cheaper credit and growing profitability, the ratio continued to increase even after the boom of early in the first decade of 2000, so that by 2015 debt to operating ratios neared seven-fold.

Similarly, if we look more closely at the operating accounts of non-financial firms in Canada, we see a similar trend of debt and debt-based assets replacing equity as the chief means of corporate finance. The conventional depictions of corporate financing typically cite the falling debt-to-equity ratios of firms in Canada as evidence of the economic "soundness" of non-financial companies (Canada 2009). However, if the calculation is widened beyond standard liabilities like loans and bonds to also include debt securities, repos, and special drawing rights – which firms increasingly used to turn over and refinance debt – the picture changes dramatically. In 1990, the ratio of non-financial firm debt securities to listed equity was 2:1, by 2000, 4.4:1, and by 2012, it had climbed to 6:1 (Statistics Canada, CANSIM table 36100850). Such expansion shows how rapidly non-financial firms have aggressively turned to new forms of debt finance and leverage to boost short-term prospects, and turned to increasingly risky investment strategies to boost global returns while often avoiding repatriating cash for tax purposes. By 2016, non-financial corporations operating in Canada were estimated to have the largest gross debt to income ratio of any among advanced industrial countries – at nearly 500 per cent (IMF 2017).

Another way of thinking about the increasing resort to financial engineering among corporations is to consider how non-financial firms turned to the financial assets to seek out increasing profits. For example, it is possible to gain a sense of how important financial revenues and investments have become for firms by assessing the growth of portfolio income relative to profits and corporate cash flow (Krippner 2011, 34). Portfolio income measures firm earnings from interest, dividends, and capital gains on investment. Thus an increasing trend indicates the rising importance of financial revenues relative to returns from productive activities. In a comprehensive review of corporate activities in Canada, Jordan Brennan (2015), provides a calculation that approximates this ratio, but also adds returns from investments abroad.

The ratio of portfolio income to profits was consistently low throughout the post-war period of rapid corporate growth. In the 1950s, 1960s, and 1970s, portfolio income was generally less than 10 per cent of total profits. But beginning in the 1980s, the ratio began to rise sharply, passing 30 per cent in 2000, and 45 per cent in 2010 (Brennan 2015, 20). The ratio retreated during the financial crisis, as financial markets, stocks, and bonds fell sharply, but it soon rocketed again, as governments bailed out banks and bought up bad debt, re-inflating asset prices and boosting corporate bottom lines.

Figure 3.9 considers more broadly how non-financial companies extended their profit-making activities into new financial assets and markets. Over the course of the past few decades, many firms expanded their operations into trading, lending, and consumer finance (Krippner 2011), and corporations often turned to new commercial paper and mortgage markets for short-term finance. Likewise, companies have increasingly used derivatives to limit exchange-rate and interest-rate risks. And new sources of credit have allowed major multinationals to turn over debt without having to go to traditional bank loans or corporate bonds for finance. So understanding these dynamics of financialization – and specifically how firms have acquired and benefitted from growing portfolios of securities and credits lent to suppliers and consumers – and how they changed their corporate growth strategies is critical to understanding why income inequality has risen (Baud and Durand 2012; Milberg and Winkler 2013).

As figure 3.9 shows, NFCs have long relied on an extraordinary amount of financial assets, even more than those in the United States and the United Kingdom. But in all three countries, over the course of the 1990s and the first decade of 2000, NFCs turned to a widening assortment of market-based financial products for operation and profitability, increasing their holdings of short-term paper, advances, and money market assets, primarily by using their debt to fund purchases of financial assets (Detzer and Hein 2014; Hein 2015). The general trend across the OECD for non-financial companies was an increase

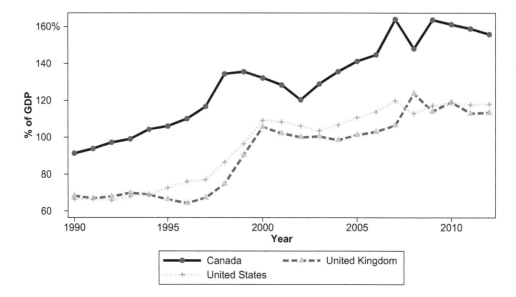

Figure 3.9. Non-financial firm financial assets, 1990–2012 (% of GDP)
Source: OECD, national accounts, financial accounts, financial balance sheets – non-consolidated; author calculations.

of some 70 per cent of GDP between 1990 and 2010 (Godechot 2016). In the Anglo-American countries, along with growing debt levels, the average increase in the financial assets of NFCs was 60 per cent over this period. But in Canada, NFCs quickly took to using an array of financial assets to boost returns, with corporations increasing the financial assets on their revenue balance sheets from 91 per cent of GDP in 1990 to more than 160 per cent of GDP in 2010.

A third facet in how finance transformed corporate operations is in the expansion of global production networks and the widespread use of offshore finance mechanisms. Led by the explosion of investment and capital mobility, global GDP doubled between 1980 and 2007; trade grew twice as fast as GDP; and FDI grew twice as fast as trade (Panitch and Gindin 2013). Corporations sought to take advantage of cheap credit by increasing productivity through lean production and the purchase of new machinery and improved technology. But firms also sought to take advantage of growing financial markets by expanding their outsourcing and offshoring in order to lower production costs. In these ways, finance became intimately entwined with corporate global growth and new corporate operating strategies.

Critical to this expansion were new offshore financial mechanisms, whereby firms used offshore financial institutions and special purpose entities to lower taxes, shelter profits, and redirect investments to the benefit of shareholders as firms globalized (Palan, Murphy, and Chavagneux 2013; Shaxson 2012). Over the course of the 1990s and first decade of 2000, profits of the largest 100 transnational corporations rocketed from US$100 billion to more than US$1.4 trillion (UNCTAD 2013) – and this occurred as more than one-third of FDI and intra-firm trade was funnelled through tax havens, while billions more were "parked" in offshore tax shelters (Shaxson 2018).

Conventionally, Canada's corporate sector is seen to have comparatively low participation in global value chains and offshore finance (Boileau and Sydor 2011; OECD 2009). In contrast to many European countries, Canadian-based firms are said to be characterized as having few connections with the United States and other countries. In part, this may be because many of the extensive service and financial industries are domestically located in cities such as Toronto, Vancouver, and Montreal. But such a characterization may have more to do with the data used and with the basic fact there are officially only some 10 per cent of firms actively involved in offshoring and outsourcing, and foreign-owned affiliates are also approximately 10 per cent of total firms operating in Canada.

However, a broader perspective on how global production networks are working to the advantage of global corporations, how they have concentrated in specific industries (like manufacturing, oil and gas, and mining), and how offshore finance has grown, gives a more developed sense of how widespread globalization and financial engineering have become in Canada as well. One issue most notably overlooked is the market power and size of major transnational corporations in manufacturing and natural resources, and their extensive financialization.

As of 2013, the top 10 per cent of exporting firms in the United States and the European Union accounted for more than 80 per cent of global trade, much of it intra-firm, and the rest part of intermediate processes, and in the United States less than 1 per cent of firms are responsible for 80 per cent of exports (UNCTAD 2013). Thus rather than the total number of foreign companies and their affiliates representing the influence of globalization and global value chains, the more important issue to understand is how key dominant international firms dominate global markets, both for inputs and exports, and also how these corporations are tied to a wide variety of financial actors from hedge and pension funds to insurance companies seeking to increase portfolios (Coe and Wai-Chung Yeung 2015).

Looking more specifically at Canada, it is clear that its economy is similarly led by a small number of transnational corporations with extensive global operations and connections in offshore financial centres. Canada's largest sectors are dominated by major global transnationals that are among the largest in the world. In Canada's oil and gas sector, the largest global transnationals of Royal Dutch Shell, BP, Chevron, and Exxon all have extensive investments in Canada and, along with ten other companies, generate 60 per cent of the revenues in the sector (Carroll 2017). In auto, Toyota and Honda, as well as the American "Big Three," all have extensive operations in Canada, tied to exporting autos and auto parts into the United States (Rutherford and Holmes 2014; Stanford 2010). Meanwhile in Canada's world-leading mining sectors, foreign mining giants Glencore, RioTinto, Vale, and BHP Billiton run the largest mining operations and account for the majority of exports (Peters 2010; PricewaterhouseCoopers 2010a). These companies are not only among the largest non-financial firms in the world, they are also among the most globally interconnected, with extensive operations around the world (Dicken 2015). And these few top firms, along with the other top sixty corporations listed on the Toronto Stock Exchange, regularly garner more than 60 per cent of total net corporate profits (Brennan 2012).

As table 3.1 suggests, by 2007, with massive conglomerate firms such as these, it is little surprise that in manufacturing (where there are the most reliable data), TNCs operating in Canada had developed a host of new global capacities and productive operations, and account for much of the activity in the sector. Prior to the crisis in 2007, global multinationals and their affiliates accounted for 30 per cent of gross operating revenues ("turnover") in host economies, more than 50 per cent in Canada, and approximately 20 per cent in the United States, as well as Finland and Italy. After the crisis, global firms still accounted for more than 52 per cent of turnover in Canadian manufacturing. The impacts of these global value chains was profound, and estimates of the impacts of outsourcing and offshoring suggest that the import content of exports now exceeds 75 per cent across industrial economies (Koopman et al. 2010). But outsourcing is also widespread: more than 80 per cent of manufacturing firms operating in Canada use outsourcing or offshoring in their activities (Innovation 2009). Likewise, foreign affiliate sales of goods and services outside of Canada equal 86 per cent of the total value of domestic Canadian exports, indicating the extensive global – and in particular American – integration of Canadian production and related services (Johansson 2009).

But in tying themselves to global value chains and production networks, multinationals have aggressively embraced financial engineering and tax avoidance strategies to boost their profit seeking (Palan, Murphy, and Chavagneux 2013; Shaxson 2018). At the centre of these corporate strategies has been their widespread use of tax havens alongside their restructuring of global operations to reduce tax payments. Typically, firms have shifted profits to lower tax jurisdictions, transferred prices, and set up elaborate ownership structures around the world in the effort to boost their bottom line and provide investors with greater gains (Cobham and Jansky 2015). In the United States alone, this has led to the growth of total profit shifting as a percentage of total

Table 3.1. Share of foreign-controlled affiliates in manufacturing, 2007 and 2011

	Turnover 2007	Turnover 2011
Ireland	79	76
Canada (2006)	51.5	52
United Kingdom	45.1	45
Netherlands (2005)	41.3	40
Sweden	39.6	39.9
Austria	39.3	41
Spain	30.4	26.9
France	29.7	28.5
Norway	27.8	25
Germany (2006)	27.2	28.5
Denmark	26.0	26.1
United States	21.2	23
Italy	18.7	17.8
Finland	18.4	16.5
Median	30.1	28.5

Source: OECD FATS Database.

profits from less than 10 per cent in 1994 to 40 per cent in 2007, and more than 50 per cent in 2012.

More broadly, financialized global firms have used a variety of tax avoidance strategies to benefit company shareholders (Batt and Appelbaum 2014). They include passing more than 30 per cent of all FDI through tax havens, as well as establishing affiliates in major tax havens, and shifting debt and debt securities to jurisdictions with the largest tax exemptions. Firms and their executives have also used tax havens to sell their shares and pay no tax, while corporations have increasingly "parked" their cash holdings in tax havens to avoid being taxed (Zucman, Fagan, and Piketty 2015). The primary reason that banks and firms alike establish subsidiaries in tax havens is their corporate tax rates: Barbados (0.25–2.5 per cent corporate income tax), Cayman Islands (0 per cent), Ireland (12.5 per cent), Bahamas (0 per cent), and Bermuda (0 per cent) all offer serious discounts on conventional industrial rates (Oxfam GB 2016).

Similar trends in tax avoidance can be seen in Canada over recent decades, indicating the extent of financial engineering. In Canada, the sixty biggest companies on the TSX have more than a thousand subsidiaries in tax havens (Chown Oved 2018). Canadian foreign direct investment in tax havens has risen from less than 5 per cent of total FDI in the early 1990s to more than 25 per cent by 2007 (Deneault 2015). Many Canadian corporations have also received billions of virtually tax-free dividend income from their affiliates in tax havens (Chown Oved 2016b), so much so that current estimates put the annual cost to taxpayers of such corporate tax avoidance at more than $10 billion annually

(Chown Oved 2016a). And among the most aggressive corporations to deploy tax havens to improve their profitability are those in the financial sector, manufacturing, and mining (Alepin 2012; Deneault and Sacher 2010).

Non-financial Corporations and Rent Extraction

A final issue to consider when assessing the extent of financial engineering of firms is whether profits have increasingly flowed out to shareholders – rather than to capital investment and employment. Here, because of takeovers or public listing, there is much evidence to suggest that firms have been pressed to adopt "financial planning" to meet "market expectations," as well as implement capitalization, restructuring, and acquisition strategies in order to grow and capture market share for better equity prices.

In the United States, these developments can be seen in the money poured by financial institutions (banks, investment banks, and pension funds) into corporate equity, and how this led many non-financial corporations to borrow heavily in order to buy their own stock so that dividends rise to meet investors' expectations (*Economist* 2014; Lazonick 2014; Wang and Bost 2014). Rather than reinvest in their firms or innovation, or for that matter, provide higher incomes for their workforces, NFCs in the United States increasingly shifted tack to emphasize shareholder primacy, and 85 per cent of corporate earnings were redirected to purchasing dividends and stock buy-backs (1998–2013).

In Canada a similar transformation took place over the course of the 1990s and first decade of 2000, with the largest firms paying out 87 per cent of all corporate earnings, and stock buy-backs escalating dramatically in the middle of the first decade of 2000 (Kent Baker et al. 2013, 178–80). Such buy-backs became increasingly popular with companies that took advantage of massive tax breaks by purchasing their own shares and boosting the earnings per share rather than reinvest in their productive activities. For executives and major shareholders, share buy-backs were a lower-risk and more lucrative option, as the lift in earning per share meant rising compensation and returns through their stock options and awards. The impact of such a shift on firms and investment was dramatic.

Even as business after-tax cash flows rose to record levels in the hundreds of billions, Canadian business investment declined steadily, falling to all-time lows in the first decade of 2000 or 5 per cent or less as a percentage of total cash flows reinvested (Stanford 2011). This was part of a global trend of rapidly expanding transnational corporations sitting on record levels of cash and failing to invest, while buying their own stock in record amounts to increase firm's market capitalization (UNCTAD 2012). By 2011, it was estimated that TNCs' cash levels reached more than $5 trillion, including earnings retained overseas, and had cut their expenditures significantly in the wake of the financial crisis.

Similarly aggressive were the new private equity models of corporate management that increased returns for executives and partners, often at the expense of firm growth. With the rapid rise in leveraged buyouts and private equity, managers – especially those from activist hedge funds – typically sought significant returns within a shorter time period (Batt and Appelbaum 2014; Celik and Isaksson 2014). Private equity managers used their concentrated ownership stakes and mandates from funders to seek returns, including exorbitant fees for their efforts. For example, in one study, it is estimated that private equity firms in the United States drew more than $20 billion in fees (1996–2014) from their purchased firms (Phalippou, Rauch, and Umber 2016). Performance of private equity companies exceeded that of publicly held ones in Canada (Conference Board of Canada 2013; McKinsey and Company 2010), but these figures often overlook the fees and stock rewards that private managers charge. Wider comparative studies of the performance of private equity takeovers routinely show that gains have come from layoffs, the sale of parts of firms and subsidiaries, and financial engineering (Batt and Appelbaum 2014; Gospel, Pendleton, and Vitols 2013).

But the widespread shift to corporate financialization can also be seen in how company profits were increasingly redistributed as dividends to shareholders, rather than invested in labour or capital. These changes have meant that as firms have taken on a growing number of financial priorities, a higher proportion of corporate cash has been redirected to shareholders and the purchasing of financial assets. This too has subsequently reduced the capital necessary for employment and productive capital.

Crucial to such shifts have been the spread of financial ownership and the consolidation of shareholder management strategies, which have led firms to emphasize the growth of financial assets and payouts to shareholders (Duménil and Lévy 2011; Lazonick and O'Sullivan 2000; Lazonick 2014). More and more frequently, with overhauls in ownership and governance, firms are being driven by shareholders to maximize profits and share value in order to fund higher dividends and returns from selling shares (Lazonick 2017).

Under the theory of maximizing shareholder value, it is assumed that only shareholders are making contributions to the company and are therefore the only ones who have a claim on corporate profits when they appear (Lazonick 2011). However, this has meant an increasing redistribution of capital to top income holders, as well as a decline in important sources of investment finance for corporations (Lin 2016). In Canada, as rising share price became the core concern of firm management, executives increasingly shifted to redistributing dividends to shareholders.

As figure 3.10 shows (although the data are incomplete for some years and their breaks in surveys but also periods of exceptional dividend payouts, as during the recession in 1982–4), over the period from the early 1970s through to the boom years of the first decade of 2000 and in the wake of the financial

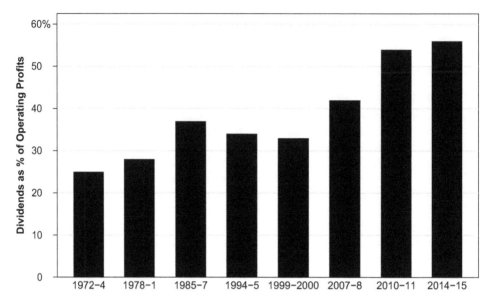

Figure 3.10. Average dividends paid to shareholders in corporations registered in Canada, 1972–2015
Source: Statistics Canada, CANSIM tables 1870002, 1870004; author calculations.

crisis, the long-term trend was a steady increase of cash being redistributed to shareholders, rising from an average of 25 per cent in the 1970s to more than 30 per cent in the mid-1980s and 1990s before peaking at more than 50 per cent in 2010–11. As we shall see in chapter 4, this shift in shareholder payouts and the increasing use of financial assets has had long-term impacts on investment, jobs, and employment.

Overall, it appears that the development of new, finance-driven modes of governance has been far from a transitory phenomenon in Canada or elsewhere. Rather, there is growing evidence that major TNCs operating in Canada increasingly took to debt and finance in their operations and enacted direct actions to increase returns to shareholders. Certainly, institutional investors and financial intermediaries displayed a wide range of ownership engagement and employed different business models with differing time frames for returns. However, Canada lacks the extensive business research on changing corporate practices required to further assess the impacts of these strategies in each and every sector.

Nevertheless, the data presented here demonstrate that the trends were of firms largely abandoning their traditional corporate governance structures and moving closer to highly financialized shareholder models that emphasized the use of market finance to maximize short-run returns and the distribution of a greater share of profits back to executives and shareholders. With rising market capitalization, publicly traded firms shifted ownership to institutional investors and other minority stakeholders. Booming stock markets led to the growing role of institutional investors and hedge funds in developing finance-driven models of corporate operation. In turn, firms made themselves more investor friendly, were subject to a wave of takeovers, and foreign investor ownership and private equity operations became widespread. At the same time, the increasing ease of access to cheaper forms of market finance provided private equity partnerships with the credit and funds necessary to buy, merge, and restructure thousands of firms.

The results were that major NFCs and many within their supply chains increasingly began to substitute financial for productive assets and to transfer income from longer-term productive investment to short-term strategies intended to increase returns to capital. And in these ways, firms increasingly shifted away from models focused on investment and toward models focused on wealth extraction and the capture of economic rents.

Policy Reform and Market Financialization

What accounts for this rapid growth in finance and the equally rapid transformations to business ownership and operation? How did governments create a financial environment conducive to exponential growth in credit and debt markets? What policies provided the opportunities for business –multinational and Canadian – to become obsessed with finance, share prices, debt, and new mergers and acquisitions?

The answers I claim come down to how states did – or did not – adopt and expand upon their regulatory functions and institutions to develop credit markets and support the wider growth of the financial industry. International developments in financial markets – and above all those in the United States and Great Britain – certainly played a role. But of equal importance was how states and business embraced "light-touch" neoliberal policies that boosted capital flows domestically and expanded the links to major financial centres like the United States and Great Britain. Once in place, these policies and international regulatory regimes provided financial actors with the means to generate and access new forms of debt and capital, as well as provide multinational corporations with financial assets necessary to increase their investment, leverage, and ability to extract greater wealth from their productive processes.

First, government adoption of financial deregulation and a new international financial policy architecture conducive to expanding capital and credit flows were two critical components for a major shift in monetary policy toward a more finance-driven economy (Stiglitz 2010). These moves toward financial liberalization were driven in the first instance by the breakdown of the Bretton

Wood system in the 1970s – which had profound effects on the basic economic policies of all advanced capitalist countries (Helleiner 1994; Ingham 2013; Wray 2011). Previously, under Keynesian economic management, to ensure full employment and the efficiency of government interventions, governments had established international capital controls that prioritized international trade over global finance and allowed officials to introduce and enforce national regulations on domestic finance. These regulations on international and domestic finance were not only extensive, they also tightly constrained the international financial system and prevented major crises for over three decades (Konzelmann and Fovargue-Davies 2013).

However, in the 1970s with rising inflation driven by oil prices, and stagnation in production, officials found it increasingly difficult to fend off the demands of major financial interests for wider deregulation (Panitch and Gindin 2013). At the heart of the problem was the fact the ongoing growth of Euromarkets funds as well as new investment form Asian and Middle East countries meant that officials could no longer use their older means of capital controls to maintain a stable international exchange system (Brenner 2002; Glyn 2006). In addition, British and American financial markets were seeking to take advantage of these changes to boost their own financial markets while financing their budget and current account deficits. Consequently, despite efforts to coordinate capital controls, the United States and Great Britain continued to push for a liberalized financial order and the end to national and international restrictions on the movement of finance capital around the world (Helleiner 1994). As a result, countries like Canada, as well as those across Western Europe, quickly followed the American and British lead, fearing that without similar policy reform their own banks and corporations would increasingly shift to New York or London (Strange 1996).

Added to these international pressures were political developments that were increasingly in favour of more "light-touch" finance-friendly policies (Hacker and Pierson 2010b; Fuchs 2007; McBride 2005). In Canada, by the 1980s, the Conservative Mulroney government pushed strong deregulatory views, often backed by key financial agencies and financial ministries, on the grounds that markets were essential for the public good, and financial efficiency was key to revitalize growth (Clarkson 2002). But across advanced industrial economies, the visible hand of governments introduced attempts – direct and indirect – to boost national and global growth by abandoning capital controls on foreign exchange and derivatives trading; loosening restrictions on the international buying and selling of domestic equity; lowering bank liquidity ratios; recognizing hedge funds; and reforming pension funds and stock market legislation to boost new equity investment (Guttman 2016; Panitch and Gindin 2013).

Faith was now placed in markets' "invisible" self-regulation and a belief that government support for markets was essential in promoting a wider good.

And despite periodic downturns, governments and financial agencies now prioritized cutting taxes, increasing credit, and clear inflation targets as the critical policy measures necessary to increase demand and stimulate renewed consumer and business spending (Durand 2017; Glyn 2006). Direct government oversight of banks and financial markets was secondary to the priorities of the free flow of capital (Shaxson 2018).

In looking at such changes, it is clear that there was no single economic actor, no single government administration, and no single policy reform to account for the growing role of private credit and private financial actors. Rather, there were cumulative processes. Over the course of the thirty-year period from the early 1980s to the first decade of 2000, economic interests – national and international – consistently pushed for policy and institutional changes to promote capital growth. But in successfully overhauling the rules governing money and credit markets, market forces then often opened the door to further and more comprehensive reforms. Over the long run, such policy changes did much more than simply structure how markets operated. They also overhauled the economy in ways that benefited private credit and wealthy elites.

Financial Liberalization in Canada

As Lavoie and Seccareccia (2006, 2014) have argued, in Canada officials introduced many policy reforms to deregulate the monetary and credit systems of the post-war period. Much as in the United States, in Canada this entailed major institutional reforms to the banking and financial services sectors that were previously extensively segregated and segmented since the Depression of the 1930s. The thinking behind these Depression- and Keynesian-era policies was that such segmentation would promote financial stability and prevent financial malpractice (Puri 2012).

In the post-war period, major chartered banks were prevented from dealing in non-governmental securities. Trust and loan companies could only specialize in residential mortgages and deposits. Insurance companies were limited to only offering insurance services for a fee. Pension funds were also limited to only holding government bonds and securities (Deaton 1989), while the banking sector – like almost all post-war banking sectors – was regulated to keep out foreign competitors and international banks. As a consequence, nationally based banks limited themselves to credit "intermediation": they took deposits from households and corporations and in turn they loaned out these funds to homebuyers and business. Similarly, trust and loan as well as insurance companies were restricted to their lines of business. And pension funds remained small and directed to providing savings for retirees.

But under the Mulroney government, all of these former regulations were first watered down, and then by the late 1980s were liberalized, allowing for the vast financial expansion and the restructuring of the financial sector (Brean 2003). The first set of reforms to transform the financial system was how money and credit systems were redesigned, moving from a model focused on regulating the supply of credit to instead fighting inflation and supporting the flows of international capital (Lavoie and Seccareccia 2013) – a first step in enacting financial deregulation along the lines of recent American and British developments.

Henceforth, Canada's Central Bank would follow US policies of lowering interest rates and liberalizing bank regulation to allow financial institutions to distribute credit as necessary and where profitable – as long as it remained financially sound (Seccareccia 2012). Under this new monetary framework of private market regulation, the Central Bank, and new financial institutions such as the Canadian Office of the Superintendent of Financial Institutions (OSFI), the primary goals were financial efficiency and limited regulation of private banking and credit markets to ensure market fundamentals. The Central Bank would focus on reducing inflation in major items that were consumed, such as food, material goods, and services. But assets and earnings based on financial assets – such as housing, shares, and financial and equity securities – were removed from this equation.

Indeed, for the securities and mortgage industries, financial system goals were quite the reverse – the expansion of finance at lower rates of interest and the deepening of private credit markets. Financial markets were now no longer to be based on an older model of government regulation and banks and lenders holding onto their loans and debt instruments to further national economic growth. But rather, financial institutions were supposed to be able to sell such debt as securities in open markets – an "originate and distribute" approach of fostering "deeper" financial markets (Lavoie and Seccareccia 2013). This, it was claimed, was the best way to boost critical sources for liquidity in financial markets. And in undertaking this major policy and institutional shift of deregulation and de-supervision of financial markets, public officials in Canada began to follow the American lead in turning their economies from being grounded in manufacturing and small business to ones based on banking, housing, and consumption (Omarova et al. 2013).

In developing this new model of growth through expanded private credit and financial markets, the second key set of reforms to expand capital markets was to remove restrictions on international capital mobility and allow financial institutions to offer a wider range of services and to deal in more diversified portfolios of debt and debt-based assets within and across countries (Helleiner 1995). In Canada, a series of new financial regulations was rolled out under Mulroney government to globalize Canada's economy and make it more competitive (Carroll 1989). Successive changes to the Bank and Insurance Acts in 1987, 1992, and 1997 officially ended any segmentation of the financial system between commercial and investment banking, trusts, and mortgage lending, and allowed Canada's chartered banks to engage in corporate underwriting while removing any foreign ownership restrictions between the United States, Japan, and other European countries with similar bilateral investment openness (Calmès 2004).

The result was that over the course of the late 1980s and 1990s, Canadian banks began to invest in corporate securities as well as redistribute government bonds and sell mutual funds in the billions (Calmès and Liu 2009). All major banks made substantial investments in the securities business and purchased control of most of the large investment dealers. This allowed the emergence of integrated financial conglomerates that combined commercial and investment banking operations, along with trust, insurance, and other commercial enterprises, and the expansion of their operations in Canada and abroad (Boreham 1989). The 1987 revision also allowed banks to invest directly in financial markets through their subsidiaries, and the 1992 reforms allowed banks to offer new services in portfolio management and investment advice. Finally, with the entry of the major American investment banks Goldman Sachs and Salomon Brothers in the late 1980s and 1990s, Canadian and American financial and investment firms alike were quick to respond to demands from business for new sources of finance and credit risk management such as bonds, options, collateralized debt obligations, and interest-rate and currency swaps. The market for these products ballooned during the 1990s and the first decade of 2000 (Calmès and Liu 2009).

The third pillar of a private credit–led growth model for a more global economy was the unleashing and redirection of workers' savings into capital markets – what has been characterized as "grey capital" (Blackburn 2002). In Canada, the move to boost pensions began in 1986, with new regulations to standardize pensions across Canada and increase contributions to public and private pensions alike (Little 2008) At the same time, new tax credits associated with RRSPs boosted the popularity of the program, more than doubling the number of contributors. In the early 1990s, governments further boosted private employer pension plans and mutual funds by raising annual contribution limits and expanding tax credits for individual and employer contributions (Archer 2011; Fougère 2002). Then in 2003 officials again raised contribution rates – a change that those of high incomes quickly took advantage of. Similarly, the introduction of TFSAs in 2009 in the wake of the financial crisis provided yet another avenue for savings to flow into capital markets (Messacar 2017). In these and other ways, government policy reforms sought to incentivize individuals to put their money into capital markets while offering greater contribution possibilities.

But if one side of the equation was redirecting workers' savings toward a globalizing economy, the other was consistent official efforts to ensure that pension funds were active contributors to private credit markets. Here, the major policy shift was away from restrictions that limited pension funds to only invest in domestic government bonds and non-marketable securities. And in its stead, governments sought to ensure that funds were placed at the disposal of Canada's and the world's leading banks and brokers (Skerrett 2017).

Under the pressure of Canada's recently deregulated banking sector that allowed Canada's major banks to engage in security trading, legislation eased – and then overhauled – many of the restraints on the types of assets that pension fund managers could invest in were lifted, while pension funds and insurance companies were allowed to actively trade in capital markets (Archer 2011, 2017). Part of this liberalization of finance was done at the provincial level, where the Ontario government was the first to restructure public pension plans into "trusts" that allowed the investment of funds into equities and financial assets. Equally important was the removal of restrictions on foreign security and asset holdings in private sector pension plans.

Pension liberalization was also driven by Federal and Quebec officials deregulating the public pension fund investments such as the Canada and Quebec Pension Plans in 1997 and the launch of the Canada Pension Plan Investment Board (Skerrett 2017). This allowed the investment board to shift from low-risk government bonds to active private sector stocks and financial assets (Mendelson 2005). Removing almost all restrictions on foreign holdings and assets in 2005 further boosted pension fund investments (Bedard-Page et al. 2016). As noted above, this allowed for the rapid expansion of institutional investor financial assets as well as for their growing role in public and private equity markets – so much so that by 2015, Canada had the fifth-largest private pension market in the world, with assets of more than $1.6 trillion dollars (Willis Towers Watson 2020).

Sealing the new role for worker savings as capital for the financial services industry and equity markets was how officials sought to promote "accommodative" monetary policies by fostering non-bank financial institutions (NBFIs). Backed by a series of World Bank and the International Monetary Fund reports recommending the loosening of restrictions on new financial assets to boost financial lending and credit expansion in the 1980s and 1990s, officials rewrote the Office of the Superintendent of Financial Institutions Act and the Insurance Acts, placing insurance companies under the OSFI and introducing new risk-based capital standards that allowed insurance companies to broaden their investments and expand their involvement in international markets (Coleman and Porter 2003). Life insurance companies had long been purchasers of government bonds and corporate securities. But over the course of the 1990s and the first decade of 2000, this activity increased significantly.

Led by Manulife, Sunlife, and Great West Life, insurance companies became major contributors to the financial sector and the corporate flow of funds.

Not only did insurers provide coverage for banks and corporations alike. They also became major purchasers of public and private securities, as well as derivatives, in order to generate the assets to cover their insurance and private pension liabilities. Following global trends in the insurance industry, Canada's major insurance companies also moved the majority of their new underwriting and investment abroad into international markets, especially into South-East Asia to make up for falling interest rates and lower returns on government bonds (OECD 2016). Insurance companies thus became diversified financial firms, expanding the size and resilience of the financial system, while also underwriting some of its risk.

International Liberalization

A final set of policy factors for the wider financialization of the economy and the development of private market finance were new international standards of banking self-regulation, the limited international regulation on debt-based financial assets, and the institutionalization of private self-monitoring by financial actors of their capital requirements and credit risks across advanced industrial economies – all key factors for the emergence of new financial assets like derivatives, credit default swaps, and mortgage-backed securities (Guttmann 2016). In contrast to the post-war period, where governments made serious efforts to regulate the money and credit supply and to constrain private finance across borders more generally, the objectives of financial liberalization were fundamentally different. Now officials turned to focus on creating an international framework conducive to the "efficient" functioning of private capital markets and using credit to increase demand and consumer spending within and across the global economy (Konzelmann, Fovargue-Davies, and Wilkinson 2013; Omarova et al. 2013).

By the end of the 1980s and early 1990s, policymakers' main priority was to expand markets, private credit, and flows of international capital (Durand 2017; Lapavitsas 2014). And by the early 1990s, public officials in Canada – as much as those in Western Europe – feared that American financial services were expanding so rapidly that they would overtake domestic capital markets. At the same time, governments worried that any significant attempts to regulate developing debt and debt-based security markets would limit the liquidity of markets and long-term economic growth. The solution was to remove legal and regulatory powers, prevent any new ones from emerging, and adapt an international framework agreement that simply monitored private financial actors – rather than regulated, supervised, and restricted – and their financial activities (Konzelmann and Fovargue-Davies 2013). In large measure, policy officials then shifted from telling banks what they could and could not do, to simply asking banks and the growing number of unregulated financial institutions what they were doing (Shaxson 2018).

The point was not so much to ensure that finance grew slowly in tandem with the economy as regulators had tried to ensure throughout much of the post-war period (Lavoie and Seccareccia 2013). Rather, as the World Bank argued, the new goal for domestic financial authorities was to give new private financial actors – and private non-bank financial actors – as much leeway as possible in order to foster liquidity and boost consumption and capital growth (Carmichael and Pomerleano 2002).

In shifting to a focus on international monitoring – rather than national regulation and international cooperation to uphold such regulations – little emphasis was placed on limiting the build-up of financial risks, or preventing system-wide financial excesses in credit and collateral risks before they occurred (Konzelmann and Fovargue-Davies 2013). Indeed, policymakers typically deferred to financial experts themselves in accepting that private market solutions – such as derivatives and private credit-rating agencies – were the only measures needed to provide the insurance and necessary information for markets to keep on working (Panitch and Gindin 2013). "Rational" actors in the financial system, it was argued, had a self-interest in preventing speculation or growing levels of risk taking (Carmichael and Pomerleano 2002).

The only key difference in this new regulatory set-up was that monitoring would be coordinated by a new international authority – the Bank of International Settlements (Porter 2004). The new bank was established to ensure that there would be more systemic information gathering. Financial reporting across borders on new debt and financial assets was to help enhance private investor confidence in bank balance sheets and improve the transparency in increasingly complex capital markets. In Canada, pushed by their financial sectors, Canadian and American governments established new international supervisory frameworks for banking and derivatives (Porter 2004, 2014). As a member of the G10, Canada signed the Basel Capital Accord in July 1988, committing to a minimum ratio of capital to risk-weighted assets of 8 per cent, and to supervising banks' international activities in derivatives. This was complemented by the creation of the International Organization of Securities Commissions (1984) headquartered in Montreal, which set out new international rules for derivative and securities markets, rating agencies, and offshore hedge funds (Porter 2014).

But while sounding impressive, these acts collectively paved the way for the proliferation of cheap private credit and new financial assets that traditional commercial banks, non-bank institutions (like insurance companies and pension funds), as well as corporations could use to back global expansion. In implementing these measures, public authorities did little more than privatize the regulatory burden by asking banks to report and retain the necessary regulatory capital, rather than actually oversee whether they did so (Duménil and Lévy 2011; Panitch and Gindin 2013). But governments also went a few steps further in loosening regulatory oversight in order to boost private bank lending and the expansion of largely unregulated private financial markets.

Most notably, under the Basel Accord, nationally regulated banks and financial actors were allowed to overlook any of the risks associated with corporate loans and mortgages and set their own equity reserves and capital requirements as well as calculate their own appetites for risk (Shaxson 2018). In this way, banks were able to significantly cut their capital requirements and lend out far larger volumes of debt into capital markets, allowing them to boost their returns. Similarly, even if the new securities commissions issued general principles, they did not establish any international regulatory agency nor set out rules for national governments do so. The result was countries like Canada – following the US and UK lead – doing nothing else to regulate the new private financial markets for debt, credit, or "securitization" other than ask that firms make public disclosure statements for each new securities issuances.

In these circumstances, private finance and credit expanded quickly and exponentially outside of any direct public supervisory authority (Young Chang et al. 2016). This was especially true of all the "off-balance sheet" and "short-term money instruments" that banks, non-financial institutions, and corporations began to use, as these were not covered under new regulations, and regulatory authorizes made no effort to either effectively monitor or limit their use by financial institutions – effectively creating a second "shadow banking" system (Gravelle, Grieder, and Lavoie 2013). In this, Canadian developments followed those in the United States and Great Britain (IMF 2014b). And with split jurisdictional authority between federal and provincial regulatory authorities, there were no attempts to better regulate the numerous new private financial assets that emerged over the course of 1990s and first decade of 2000 (Lavoie 2011).

Unsurprisingly, the impacts of such financial liberalization were profound. Using debt securitization, banks took loans and other debts and repackaged these as securities and sold them on to markets or to their non-regulated subsidiaries, effectively taking the debt off bank balance sheets. Non-financial corporations also used securitization to sell off their short-term debt to fund further leverage for mergers or share buy-backs. Securities dealers, hedge funds, and money market mutual funds also quickly sought to take advantage of the new "originate and distribute" model with no supervision or regulations, to quickly expand their issuances of "asset-backed commercial paper" (Young Chang et al. 2016).

By the mid-1990s in Canada this set off a boom in securitizations of government bonds, loans, credit-card receivables, and conventional residential mortgages. These increased the total value of debt instruments and market-based assets from $350 billion in 1996 to more than $1.3 trillion in 2010 (Chapman, Lavoie, and Schembri 2011). By 2007, such market-based or "shadow banking" activity represented about 60 per cent of traditional bank debts and liabilities (Gravelle, Grieder, and Lavoie 2013). And Canada was one of the most active national markets for derivative trading in the world, with a specialization in interest-rate and foreign exchange credit swaps (Mueller and Usche 2016). These developments in market finance were critical for the massive expansion of financial assets in Canada.

At the same time, the growth of financial markets, and the close ties of Canadian actors with those in the United States and Great Britain, allowed Canada's major banks and pension funds to expand exponentially. Through the issuance of debt-backed securities and securitized assets, Canada's major banks quickly expanded their mortgage lending and security businesses (Walks and Clifford 2015). Using new government-issued mortgage-backed securities, banks took their income-generating assets like mortgages and credit-card debt, bundled them together, and sold them on to financial markets. Once sold, the mortgages were no longer on the bank's books, allowing them to go out and issue mortgages and sell them on again. Repeating these transactions, Canada's major bank's grew into global financial players, among the largest in the world, with global business operations, predominantly tied to the United States, the United Kingdom, and the Caribbean (IMF 2014a).

"Pro-Growth" Policy Reform and Corporate Financialization

But of equal importance to financialization of the "real economy" were a series of "pro-growth" policies. Over the course of more than thirty years, government officials in Canada, the United States, and elsewhere adopted a wide range of legislative and institutional changes intended to foster "competition" and provide greater support for business (Panitch and Gindin 2013). In almost all cases, public officials did not introduce them with the explicit intent of expanding the role of finance inside of corporate activities. Nor were the reforms passed as a means to provide new and profitable financial assets for corporations. But in removing tight bank regulations and generating growing levels of cheap liquidity, the policy moves to promote private credit growth were crucial stepping stones for finance to become even more intimately entwined with corporate operation and for financial logics to become increasingly central to business management. The result was that the waves of policy, institutional, and legal changes effectively provided the opportunity for finance to reconfigure the way firms worked.

The Competition Act

One such "competitive" economic policy shift that had long-run consequences for the financialization of the real economy can be seen in the rolling backing of competition regulation and the blunting of foreign takeover and acquisition reviews. They opened the door to the massive expansion of global multinationals in Canada backed by the newly deregulated pension and institutional investment market. Prior polices to attract investment and greater economic benefit had focused on controlling economic monopolies while extracting commitments from foreign investors to satisfy performance rules for local content and exports, transferring technology or patents to domestic firms, and hiring Canadian management and labour (Anastakis 2005; Carroll 1989). But the signing into law of the Investment Canada Act (ICA) of 1985 and the Competition Act of 1986 signalled a much more aggressive approach to attracting international capital and ensuring the dominance of corporations over large swaths of the economy.

The new Competition Act 1986 shifted from an act that sought "to ban monopolistic, predatory practices" to one that looked "to maintain and encourage competition" (Day et al. 2009). For corporations this shift meant that all mergers and monopolies were decriminalized, and instead a competition tribunal would issue advance advice and certificates to all companies proposing mergers. Similarly, the new ICA reversed previous regulatory concerns for significant benefit to all Canadians, by removing all foreign ownership restrictions and any performance requirements. This was a flagship moment for the new Conservative government and its adoption of neoliberal ideas, as it signalled that there would be restrictions on neither foreign direct investment nor new financial assets and debt-backed financing arrangements (Clarkson 2008). The rollback of such regulatory instruments was the first step in the government's new approach to promoting market-oriented solutions to capital and economic development. By 2007, for example, only 0.2 per cent of the hundreds of mergers and acquisitions that were annually taking place in Canada were subject to any change or reform such as divestitures of assets or sale of businesses (Competition Policy Review Panel 2008, 55).

But such a change came at exactly the same time that top financial institutions, money managers, and pension fund executives were looking to jump into capital markets and diversify their holdings. Corporations had long used finance to grow operations and subsidiaries. But critical to the transformation of corporations into multinationals and subsequently transnationals was the ability of firms to take advantage of liberalized ownership rules and new sources of credit and investment.

The same was true in Canada. As international conglomerates in auto and auto parts, as well as oil and gas, sought to grow, they relied on the vast new amounts of equity financing made available by pension and insurance markets (Deaton 1989). In the aftermath of changes to the Competition Act in 1986 and federal and provincial pension liberalization, institutional investors rapidly started taking larger stakes in corporations.

Institutional investor equity holdings grew in lockstep with the publicly traded equity of major international multinationals, with both tripling in size over the period 1990–2008. And how important institutional investors' stakes were in the rise can be seen in their total holdings of publicly traded equity: 45 per cent in 1990 and 55 per cent in 2007. Major funds preferred the largest corporations and those with the fastest rising dividends. And as funds had to diversify their holdings, the growing number of institutional investors all bought stock in the largest firms. In this Canada followed trends in Great Britain and the United States, where top financial actors similarly directed their investments to the largest and safest of companies and quickly became the largest shareholders of corporate stock and equity (Blackburn 2002).

Free Trade and Investment Treaties

A second critical set of policy reforms to foster globalization and financialization was the government's new commitment to creating a bilateral – and then continental – free trade agreement that would loosen trade and investment barriers between Canada, the United States, and Mexico. Again the initial efforts of such reforms were simply to expand the productivity and profitability of capital across borders. But the results were not only the growth of multinational and supplier networks. They were also the increasing interconnection of finance to corporate operation and priorities.

The initial push to secure free trade was certainly based upon the corporate priorities of growth and increasing productive scale. Following the economic crisis of the late 1970s and recession of the early 1980s, leading manufacturing firms began to push for wider global integration and freer trade, hoping to capture larger shares of markets and boost returns (Chase 2004; Clarkson 2008). American auto, transport, and computer and machinery manufacturers – which operated as conglomerates and long used their own financial services to underwrite dealers and customer purchases – in particular wanted to expand and integrate their operations across the United States, Canada, and Mexico in order to compete with Japanese and European competitors (Chase 2003). But Canadian manufacturers as well wanted to secure greater American access and expand their multinational enterprises and regional production networks (Richardson 1992).

These efforts led to conglomerate enterprises in all three countries to mobilize their interest associations to create a common strategy toward bilateral trade and investment treaties that would boost assets and profits of MNCs in North America, while integrating their supplier and contractor networks (Brownlee 2005; Chase 2009). The Business Council on National Issues in Canada and the U.S. Chamber of Commerce were the main drivers behind this establishment of an international regime that eliminated tariffs and non-tariff barriers alike, guaranteed investor rights, and gave all corporations – whether foreign or domestic – access to similar state support while preventing the possibility of any future policy reversals. But these activities were only part of wider business cooperation across countries as major multinationals sought to remake market regulations and guide regulatory cooperation for global corporate growth through the initiation of the World Trade Organization, as well as through reforms to the European Union in the 1980s and 1990s (George 2015).

However, firms quickly realized that if they were to take advantage of such institutional reforms, they would also require common financial frameworks and investment rules that increased the growth of capital markets (Helleiner 1995; Panitch and Gindin 2013), for in building conglomerates, more and more multinational corporations were already adopting financially oriented governance strategies, where separate lines of their enterprises were evaluated on the basis of their profitability and returns to shareholders (Knafo and Dutta 2019). Company time horizons were also shortening, and the emphasis on financial returns was increasingly entrenched at all levels of corporate operation (Batt and Appelbaum 2014; Lin 2016). If major firms were to realize the benefits of free trade, then standard financial frameworks were also required, as well as easy access to private credit and especially to cheap credit across countries. International trade and investment agreements were the key policy solutions.

In addressing these issues in the 1980s and 1990s, successive Canadian provincial and federal governments worked with the financial industry and American officials to relax controls on the international mobility of capital. The objective of new regulations was to turn the financial system away from the protection of national markets and stakeholders, and to create a framework conducive for the efficient functioning of global capital markets (Carroll 1989; Porter 2014). And from the mid-1980s onwards, a range of reforms were initiated to further credit markets in Canada and advance corporate and financial growth across North America, including the signing of more than ten free trade agreements and more than fifty bilateral and international investment agreements (UNCTAD 2012).

Under the Canada-US Free Trade Agreement (1989) and then the North American Free Trade Agreement (1994), for example, governments aimed to expand the cross-border movement of goods and services, as well as improve the framework for corporate integration, expansion, and investment (Clarkson 2008; Panitch and Gindin 2013). A host of new rules and arbitration committees strongly emphasized a common market system, and for major multinationals looking to undertake new investments in technology, equipment, and logistics, the new international trade arrangements locked in state commitments of economic support and coordination – often to the benefit of American firms seeking global expansion (Panitch and Gindin 2013). But for Canadian firms as well, the new trade agreements were critical in laying out the institutional framework for expansion, lowering tariffs, ending domestic production regulations, and securing intellectual property, under which they could exploit scale economies by deepening cross-border production networks and specialize production for larger American markets (Chase 2003, 2004).

The result was the increasing integration of finance into multinational corporate operation (Milberg and Winkler 2013; Coe and Yeung 2015). For manufacturing, the new agreements underpinned their global growth strategies and their need for increasing amounts of finance and credit. In the auto sector, transportation equipment, electronic components, and chemicals, for example, globally expanding firms were increasingly reliant on finance to make acquisitions, boost profits, and increase shareholder value. But business executives also quickly saw the advantages of maximizing returns through an increased engagement with financial activities – such as derivative trading, leasing, and lending – and to increase their holdings in financial assets (Krippner 2011; Orhangazi 2008). And in Canada – as in the United States – globalizing corporations quickly increased their holdings of financial assets relative to productive assets, realizing growing returns from their financial holdings (Brennan 2014; Krippner 2011).

These trends can be seen most clearly in two of Canada's leading economic sectors: auto and natural resources (oil and gas and mining). Each is capital intensive, entry barriers are high, and costs of exit are high. Each operates in international markets and is highly integrated into the United States economy (Peters 2011; Stanford 2011). MNEs in these sectors also have the highest proportion of private sector jobs, larger workplaces, and high demands for capital and foreign direct investment. And in the wake of the free trade and global integration, financial assets as a percentage of total sector assets increased dramatically in the late 1990s and early in the first decade of 2000 from 18 per cent to more than 32 per cent (Dupuis, Peters, and Scrimger 2020). These financial assets declined during the Great Recession, but firms quickly increased their holdings with the growth of financial markets in 2014. Such evidence strongly suggests that non-financial corporations have increasingly engaged in financial activities to drive operational goals and profit-making as they have globalized their operations.

Tax Reforms and Tax Treaties

A final critical set of policy factors in fostering the development of financialization and a new rentier form of capitalism was the reform of Canada's contemporary tax system, and how it benefitted and indeed empowered corporate interests and the wealthy at the expense of the general population. One side of this process involved reforms to the domestic corporate tax regime in order to underwrite the increasing resort of non-financial companies to debt and financial assets. But equally important were overhauls to the wider international systems of tax havens and tax treaties, which not only often harmonized advanced countries' tax rates with those in tax havens, but also largely removed any supervision and regulation of multinational corporations that began registering in tax havens to operate their global enterprises and new lines of financial business (Palan, Murphy, and Chavagneux 2013).

In general, through these two tax policy reforms, Canadian government tax policy for the corporate sector has greatly facilitated wider corporate financialization. Not only do all corporations – Canadian and foreign – enjoy extremely low headline corporate tax rates, but MNCs operating in Canada also benefit from further tax credits and subsidies; light-touch regulation, especially in corporate debt and financial assets; and a new international tax architecture that assists global tax avoidance and the financialization of corporate operations. Ultimately, these schemes have done a great deal to foster even further tax competition among countries, enabling the upward redistribution of income to investors and shareholders rather than to labour in the form of wage increases.

Tax issues offer important examples of the way in which the non-market processes of government have been routinely used to redistribute income upward under neoliberalism and foster corporate financialization. Indeed, changes in tax rates such as cuts that favour corporations are straightforward political decisions, not market processes. Seeking to accommodate to industry demands to improve the investment climate for investors, Canada's governments have followed international trends in lowering statutory corporate rates from 48 per cent of profits in 1992 to 27 per cent by 2015 (Devereux et al. 2016). However, this does not take into account the generous depreciation rules, exemptions, deductions, and credits (sometimes termed "loopholes") that corporations may be eligible for (Brooks 2016). Those special provisions lower corporations' effective tax rate, or the share of their profits they actually pay in taxes. And here too Canada has seen a consistent decline, with effective rates of corporate taxation falling from 35 per cent in the early 1990s to an estimated 21 per cent by 2015 (Devereux et al. 2016).

Canada's tax codes have also been rewritten or left to languish as firms have engaged in financial engineering – whether through the sale of assets, tax arbitrage, dividend recapitalizations, or bankruptcy proceedings – to maximize their own returns and expand their global operations (De Mooij 2012). The favourable treatment of debt in the tax code has been a major incentive for firms to engage in financial engineering (Batt and Appelbaum 2014; Forhoohar 2016). Because a company's interest payments on its debt are tax deductible, its tax liabilities are reduced. There are no compelling legal, administrative, or economic rationales for this treatment of debt. Nevertheless, interest write-off has been a key component for MNCs investing abroad and acquiring companies, as well as well as for private equity partnerships, allowing dealmakers to supplement their capital firepower with tax-advantageous leverage on target companies (Congressional Budget Office 2017).

Also notable has been the role of Canada's federal government in creating a wider global financial tax architecture that has tacitly supported corporate tax avoidance (Deneault 2015). Seeking to attract or retain mobile capital within a context of supporting cross-border trade and investment, successive Canadian governments have employed new regulations and international tax treaties to boost corporate returns (Deneault and Sacher 2010).

New tax reforms and treaties have been passed to allow financial transactions to be booked in low-tax or lightly regulated jurisdictions such as the Cayman Islands, the Bahamas, and Barbados. Canadian officials have also adopted tax haven legislation, offering to foreign companies that register in Canada, no tax on their profits, removal of duties and taxes, and the deferring or waiving of GST/HST (Tax Justice Network 2015). Canada has also lured taxpayers and taxable transactions through a whole series of exemptions that allow firms and individuals to reduce or completely sever their connection to their country of origin, effectively allowing companies to avoid all taxation (Cribb and Chown Oved 2017; Seguin 2013). And by the 2010s, Canada had a world-leading number of ninety-three tax treaties and twenty-two tax information exchange agreements with tax havens that allowed corporations to claim profits elsewhere and move money into Canada tax free (Chown Oved 2016a, 2018).

Since the 1980s, tax havens that have signed tax agreements with Canada have received a rising share of Canadian "investments," as firms and financial institutions operating in Canada have made loans, shifted corporate headquarters, opened new corporations, and moved profits to lower tax jurisdictions. In 1987, outward flows from Canada to tax havens totalled 7 per cent of foreign investments. By 2014, total foreign investments in tax havens equalled 25 per cent of all Canadian investment abroad, and total foreign direct investment in tax havens throughout the Caribbean totalled more than $100 billion (Deneault 2015). Canada's major banks were among the most aggressive of firms in using offshore financial centres, with their subsidiaries in tax havens enabling them to massively expand the tax-exempt portion of their income into the billions, resulting in major tax reductions (Rogenmoser, Lauzon, and Lauzon 2012). But major non-financial companies also routinely used elite law firms and tax specialists to help them engage in aggressive tax planning, in order to reduce their costs and increase returns to investors.

By making these transactions, firms removed billions of dollars of income from taxation in order to fund dividend payments and buy-backs. There are no Canadian data on the extent to which firms use transfer pricing as part of their corporations, but in the United States, it is reported that 59 per cent of MNCs with foreign operations had tax haven subsidiaries to channel their investments, and 77 per cent use transfer pricing through tax havens as the first key to their tax strategy (Palan, Murphy, and Chavagneux 2013). Given the extensive corporate ties between Canada and the United States, it can be reasonably expected that similar results could be found here.

Looked at in terms of total annual tax avoidance – or the "tax gap," which is the amount that should be collected, compared to the actual amount that is collected – the Conference Board of Canada estimates that the total tax gap could be equivalent to that of the United States at roughly 2.5 per cent of GDP (Conference Board of Canada 2017). But the vast majority of MNCs now route profits and investments through a variety of investment vehicles and tax havens around the world (Clausing 2016; Haberly and Wójcik 2014). Companies direct 50 per cent of their FDI through offshore havens, using it to circumvent tax and regulatory regimes, and lower taxation on profits and investments. This profit shifting is best described as tax avoidance, rather than outright fraud. Nevertheless, estimates suggest that because of these corporate tax strategies, the gross annual tax gap is close to 6 per cent of GDP in the United Kingdom, 2 per cent in the United States, and 2–2.5 per cent in the European Union (Palan, Murphy, and Chavagneux 2013). These numbers may be even higher, though, as profits booked in tax havens have soared in recent years (Oxfam GB 2016).

In sum, the evidence demonstrates clear signs that multinational firms operating in Canada have used reductions in corporate taxation, interest-deduction loopholes, and loose regulation of tax havens to boost returns to investors from investments and acquisitions. In restructuring their companies and using tax planning to reduce tax payments, companies have generated substantial tax savings that have been subsequently passed to shareholders. Taking advantage of policy changes and new international tax treaties, many of Canada's largest domestic and foreign MNCs have used these tax structures to engage in financial engineering, used debt to multiply gains, and redirected profits to their investors.

Conclusion

With regard to the direct effects of financialization, the preceding analysis offers much evidence to support the critical view that shifts in Canada's economy and corporate operation were systematically related to the massive expansion of finance, as well as the rise of new financial ownership, and financially driven corporate governance models. Fostered by the neoliberal restructuring of economic policy, financial and non-financial sectors alike quickly overhauled their operations, dove into new financial markets, and began to use new debt and financial assets to boost the size of their institutions and increase profits. These findings support the notion that financialization has been strongly influenced by a wide range of policy reforms, and that subsequent reforms created new incentive structures for firms and financial actors alike.

As we have seen, crucial for these economic transformations were the major policy shifts that opened new sources of debt and credit for banks and NBFIs alike. So too, policy reforms to monetary policy, pensions, trade agreements, and tax as well as tax treaties allowed global multinationals to take up financial strategies, others to be bought by private equity partners, and others still to take on more debt in the effort to acquire firms or increase share buy-backs to increase returns and reward investors. Thus, it was with this range of public policies that Canada's economy increasingly financialized over the past few decades, often with profound impacts on corporate operation.

But were changes to companies' ownership, governance, and operation equally significant to firms' employment strategies? Did the growing role of finance within the economy affect income distribution to the advantage of business and the wealthy? Critical political economy theorizes that with corporate financialization, firms should adopt much more aggressive employment and labour cost-reduction strategies. At the same time, market financialization, our theoretical propositions suggest, should also lead to more destructive trends, such as increasing profits and rents that increase income of top earners. In the next chapter, I explore these issues for Canada.

4 Canada in International Context

This chapter explores the impacts of financialization on the labour market and income inequality in Canada. Here I argue that the rise of market financialization across the economy as well as the spread of financially owned and engineered MNCs and their supplier networks have significantly increased top income inequality while undermining jobs, wages, and traditional employment practices – all of which have cumulatively contributed to widening income inequality.

Key to this redistribution of income upward to the wealthy are four major channels: how finance boosts the earnings of corporate executives and financial professionals; how corporate focus on "shareholder value" increases rent extraction and pressures managers to reduce labour costs; how financial ownership and logics within business undermine unionized employment; and how financial engineering strategies fissure jobs and employment contracts with managers and employers resorting to low-wage work and non-standard employment.

Equally notable is how these channels of financialization actually affect jobs and labour market inequality across different national sectors. Many critical scholars have underscored how financialization has been a major contributor to rising inequality. However, little research has examined its varied impacts across the economy and the labour market. My argument addresses this limitation by examining the financialization–labour market link in Canadian manufacturing, private services, and extractive industries. Using Statistics Canada and OECD data as well as other secondary literature, this chapter assesses the evidence for how the dynamics of financialization did – or did not – affect jobs and employment across major national sectors. It finds that for the average working Canadian, there have been no benefits from the "financial" turn within the wider economy.

I begin by examining whether financialization and the new corporate priorities of shareholder value resulted in global MNCs and their production networks reshaping Canadian employment relations and weakening job security and good unionized jobs. I then evaluate private services to see whether as firms channelled resources from productive to financial activities, they increasingly set yet more onerous terms for their workers, suppliers, and third-party agencies, leading to the "fissuring" of employment contracts and the rise of non-standard, low-wage jobs. In the third section, I extend this analysis of financialization to analyse their impacts on the jobs and wages in natural resource and global agri-food industries and if there are links to the reliance of these sectors on an growing and low-paid temporary foreign workforce.

The chapter concludes by turning to an assessment of wider macroeconomic issues concerned with income inequality. Here, I review the broader evidence linking financialization to income inequality in Canada's national labour market. Whereas conventional arguments point to technological changes, educational levels, and social and familial constraints to explain rising income inequality, I examine evidence that indicates a primary cause of inequality in Canada has been the rise of finance and its benefit for an increasingly rich financial sector. Of equal importance I look at how finance has contributed to a fundamental reversal in the balance between capital and labour, with more and more income being systematically redistributed to the benefit of business but at the cost of mass layoffs for unionized workers, stagnant wages, and more precarious employment conditions.

Manufacturing

Conventional wisdom contends that globalization has not created uniform market pressures across countries, nor has it completely eroded the institutional differences that matter to labour market outcomes and income equality. Research has often argued that firms typically adapt to national systems of labour regulation, and that firms acquired by more active financial investors tend to continue with existing employee voice and representation practices (Gospel, Pendleton, and Vitols 2013; Lane and Wood 2012). Nonetheless, there is much evidence to suggest that as firms have financialized, they have significantly influenced employment relations, and that employers in many countries (including Canada) have been a driving force behind the wider polarization of jobs in the labour market (Dupuis, Peters, and Scrimger 2020; Peters 2011; Hyde, Vachon, and Wallace 2018; Kollmeyer 2018; Meyer 2019).

Two important trends influencing these outcomes are (1) the increasing extent to which finance-driven public and private equity manufacturing firms turned to finance for growing profits rather than reinvesting in productive activities and employment (Cobb 2016; Lin 2016; Lapavitsas 2014), and (2) how financializing manufacturers have used outsourcing, offshoring, and regional restructuring to slash input and labour costs, in order to redirect resources to financial assets, share buy-backs, and returns to shareholders (Milberg and Winkler 2013). These two factors are often connected, and both have driven the decline of unionized employment and increased convergence across national employment systems (Kollmeyer and Peters 2019).

Research on employment relations has found that manufacturing firms have regularly used downsizing as a strategy to increase share price (Jung 2015) or built subcontractor networks and franchises to offload costs on small employers under heavy competitive pressures (Milberg and Winkler 2013). Private equity funds, too, have contributed to manufacturing operations pushing for lower labour costs, purchasing and restructuring thousands of companies on the basis of heavy debt financing in an effort to boost returns for executive shareholders (Batt and Appelbaum 2014). Consequently, because of financialization, there have been several reasons that firms have pursued new managerial strategies to reduce labour costs and seek labour policy and institutional reforms that would make their workforces more "flexible" (Glyn 2006; Gall, Hurd, and Wilkinson, 2011).

Auto manufacturing was the sector most notable for how its firms rapidly adopted new financially driven models of business while expanding production networks around the world, and especially into low-wage jurisdictions such as Mexico and China – often at the expense of well-paying unionized auto jobs in Canada and the United States (Froud et al. 2006; Murphy and McDonough 2012; Stanford 2010). Working under models that sought to maximize shareholder value and employ financial engineering to boost returns, auto assembly and parts firms created global value chains that operate around the world and produce on constantly shortening time horizons and through growing subcontracting operations.

Many global auto companies sought to deal with these cost pressures by offshoring or outsourcing to the southern United States, Mexico, and China (Milberg and Winkler 2013; Moody 1997, 2007). Other assembly and parts manufacturers introduced new technology and intensified output through lean production practices and negotiating more "flexible" wage agreements, especially in sectors with stagnating markets and large factories (Moody 2007; Visser 2019). And many firms such as Ford and GM jumped into financial markets, initially to extend financing for the purchase of their products, but then extending their financial enterprises into leasing and mortgage markets (Froud et al. 2006; Orhangazi 2008). And over the course of the 1990s and the first decade of 2000, auto as the leading manufacturing industry in Canada increasingly turned to financial assets, outside share capital, and debt markets in its efforts to grow globally while also coping with major global and national crises (Dupuis, Peters, and Scrimger 2020).

In Canada, the globalized and (for many years) American-run auto sector has long played a leading economic role. Much like Japan, Germany, and Spain, in Canada the auto sector was a major contributor to exports as well as GDP, and in 1999 Canada ranked as the fourth-largest auto-maker, with an output of three million vehicles (Stanford 2010). However, by 2010, production was more than halved, as auto firms moved production to lower-cost countries such as China, Brazil, and Mexico, and the Big Three auto-makers lost market share to Japanese producers (Murphy and McDonough 2012). The global financial crisis of 2008–9 dramatically enhanced this restructuring, with the massive sales decline, government bailouts, and government-enforced concessions on unionized workers, which included significant permanent layoffs (Rosenfeld 2009; Siemiatycki 2012).

Part of the cause of this restructuring was the ongoing globalization and financialization of the auto industry, as major companies and suppliers sought to take advantage of global deregulation and expand production networks around the world, and then integrate their production and retail networks to achieve cost savings. For example, in the United States over the course of the 1980s and 1990s, the American Big Three downsized, outsourced, stripped out managerial layers, shed thousands of jobs, and then bought other companies (Moody 1997). Consequently, US unionized membership in auto manufacturing declined from 450,000 in the late 1970s to 73,000 in 2005 despite the fact that the number of auto production workers actually rose by some 200,000 over the 1980s and 1990s. In Canada the decline started later but was equally rapid in the first decade of 2000. In 2000, there were 112,000 unionized workers in the auto sector. But by 2010 there were thousands fewer as companies like GM closed facilities and sought concessions along with job cuts and outsourcing (Siemiatycki 2012).

The other cause for restructuring was the rapid development of new low-cost auto regions adjacent to high-income countries. In North America, for example, auto and aerospace firms as well as suppliers began investing heavily in Mexico, seeking cost savings by reallocating production. Consequently, by 2013, Mexico ranked as the eighth-largest automobile producer, with extensive supply networks and labour costs among the lowest in the world (Alavarez-Medina and Carrillo 2014). In contrast, American autoworkers were forced to contend with the closure of fifteen plants; Canadian autoworkers with one. In addition, car production dropped and jobs in unionized auto assembly and auto parts continued to decline, with the number of unionized jobs in Canadian assembly operations cut by 40 per cent. Over the course of the first decade of 2000, as Canada dropped to the tenth-largest auto producer in the world, and the Big Three auto-makers laid off approximately 38 per cent of their unionized workforces in assembly and parts – a decline that was only partially compensated by the small rebound of jobs among non-unionized Japanese auto-makers in the wake of the financial crisis (Holmes and Hracs 2010; Rutherford and Holmes 2014).

But the role of finance is also clear in all such developments (Froud et al. 2006; Krippner 2011; Dupuis, Peters, Scrimger 2020). Working under models that sought to maximize shareholder value and enhance financial operations, auto assembly and parts firms created global value chains that operate around the world and produce on constantly shortening time horizons and through growing subcontracting operations (Borghi, Sarti, and Cintra 2013). But auto manufacturers have also dived into financial markets to mitigate risk, expand sales, and improve profitability. Indeed, by early in the first decade of 2000, auto manufacturers like Ford drew the majority of their profits from financing cars rather than their direct production (Krippner 2011).

And over the course of the 1990s and the first decade of 2000 such trends were increasingly widespread as evidenced by the fact the largest sixty non-financial firms in Canada (of which the Big Three, Honda, and Toyota were among the top twenty) used debt to grow in value from 20 per cent of GDP (or some $136 billion) in 1990 to 80 per cent of GDP in 2010 (or approximately $1.3 trillion). At the same time, these largest non-financial firms increasingly relied on their financial investments for growth, with total financial returns as a percentage of total pre-tax profit rising to 47 per cent. This not only resulted in huge cash holdings for companies, often totalling hundreds of billions of dollars, but also in firms retaining this cash and failing to reinvest in their fixed capital (Stanford 2011).

As figure 4.1 demonstrates, the general results for employment were that as non-financial firms substituted financial activities for investment in production and grew their global value chains through debt and credit chains, manufacturers froze hiring and then, in the wake of the financial crisis, rapidly cut their unionized workforces through mass layoffs. In 1995, there were 644,000 well-paid, unionized manufacturing jobs paying more than two-thirds of the median full-time hourly wage. By 2010, there was only slightly more than half this number – 357,000. This decline more than exceeded the total decline in manufacturing jobs of 275,000 (1995–2011) as manufacturers replaced full-time, unionized positions with non-unionized and lower-paid employment. As figure 4.1 shows, there is a strong and consistent negative association of -0.78 between firms increasing their market capitalization and portfolio income and declining levels of well-paid, unionized manufacturing employment. This association also appears just as strong if we plot firms' financial assets and share capital against overall manufacturing employment (Dupuis, Peters, Scrimger 2020).

How do these Canadian developments compare with those elsewhere? There are no comparable comparative financial data on firms and their financial revenues and assets readily available for auto or manufacturing. However, as table 4.1 shows, there was widespread decline of industrial manufacturing as a proportion of overall civilian employment that correlates very strongly with

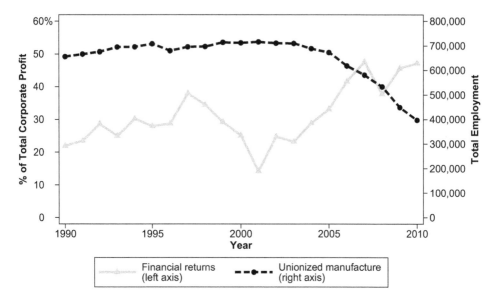

Figure 4.1. Financialization and manufacturing employment, 1990–2010

Correlation: -.78

Sources: Manufacturing employment: Statistics Canada, CANSIM tables 282-0012, 282-0078, 380-0027; financial returns: CANSIM tables 380-0016, 376-0012; financial data calculations by Jordan Brennan, UNIFOR.

the decline in union density. In addition, the loss of unionized manufacturing jobs was typically greatest in the auto sector.

Overall, throughout thirteen advanced capitalist countries, even if we still lack conclusive comparative evidence, we can surmise that as the financialization of non-financial firms expanded and firms expanded their global value chains, firms looked to shed their higher-cost unionized workforces (Kollmeyer and Peters 2019). Across the advanced industrial countries, manufacturing employment fell, as a percentage of civilian employment, from 23 per cent in 1980 to 11 per cent in 2015. At the same time, as manufacturing firms increased their market capitalization, investment banks and pension funds cross-promoted manufacturers' shares, and as CEO compensation was tied to share value and stock options, major auto producers focused on capital growth and dividend payments as their top priorities and rapidly developed flexibility and global restructuring strategies to reduce labour costs (Bartram et al. 2015; Murphy and McDonough 2012).

The impacts of such operational shifts were often highly damaging: the loss of industrial and manufacturing jobs, the disappearance of

Table 4.1. Decline of manufacturing jobs and union density, 1980–2015

Manufacturing Share of Total Employment				
	1980	1990	2005	2015	Change
Canada	19.1	15.6	13.0	9.5	-9.6
Germany	31.2	28.3	19.4	19.4	-11.8
Sweden	23.7	20.2	16.5	10.4	-13.3
United Kingdom	24.7	17.8	10.8	9.9	-14.8
United States	19.1	14.9	10.3	8.7	-10.4
OECD Average	23.2	19.3	14.5	12.4	-10.8

Union Density				
	1980	1990	2005	2015	Change
Canada	35.0	33.0	29.0	26.5	-8.5
Germany	35.0	31.0	21.0	17.6	-18.4
Sweden	78.0	81.0	76.0	67.0	-11.0
United Kingdom	51.0	39.0	28.0	23.6	-27.4
United States	22.0	15.0	12.0	10.1	-11.9
OECD Average	51.0	44.6	39.5	36.5	-14.5

Correlation: .99
Source: OECD Stat and author's figures from Custom Survey of Labour and Income Dynamics. Canadian numbers based on labour force, including self-employed with no employees or capital income.

unionized manufacturing jobs, and an overall decline of union density from 51 to 36 per cent from 1980 to 2015. The loss of unionized manufacturing jobs was greatest in Canada, the United States, and the United Kingdom, but across Europe as well, where more than three million manufacturing workers lost their jobs in the wake of the financial crisis. The United States, Germany, and the United Kingdom experienced the greatest declines in manufacturing employment and union membership, falling nearly 50 per cent from 1980 to 2015. But Canada was not far behind, with declines of more than 40 per cent in manufacturing as a share of employment and a 33 per cent fall in private sector union density 1980–2010. The strong correlation of .99 shows the intimate relationship of declining manufacturing employment to declining union density.

The impacts of such financialization on collective bargaining were profound. Unions increasingly lost their power to enforce wider sectoral patterns of collective bargaining and were increasingly forced to make major concessions in wages, benefits, and jobs for new hires (Dribbusch and Birke 2019; Moody 2007; Peters 2011; Rosenfeld 2009). As companies increasingly focused on the market valuations of companies and returns to investors, unionized auto manufacturers began to demand "all-in" concessions to reduce labour costs and that individual plants and their workers compete for investment and jobs in the auto sector (Murphy and McDonough 2012; Siemiatycki 2011). Multinationals demanded that unionized workers accept wage, benefit, and outsourcing conditions similar to those in non-union operations of Honda, Nissan, and Toyota. Then in the wake of the crisis, which led to massive wage concessions, two-tier bargaining, and outsourcing in the US plants, in Canadian operations, the Canadian Auto Workers were forced into concessions, accepting a massive wave of early retirements, lower pay for new hires, and reduced benefit and medical payouts (Albo, Gindin, and Panitch 2010).

Subsequently, union strategies have been forced to make a U-turn, away from the growth of good jobs and benefits, toward arguing for subsidies for auto plant investments, in return for flexibility in plant bargaining as a means to compete for new investment throughout North America and Mexico (Rosenfeld 2009). In this context, plants have successfully reoriented bargaining away from better wages for more productivity and have instead sought to boost returns to shareholders, instituted concessions in pay, outsourcing, benefits in return for higher productivity, and fewer long-term jobs. Meanwhile unions – facing growing insecurity in their employment prospects – have increasingly embraced plant cooperation and concessions for greater productivity as essential for their survival (Holmes 2015).

In terms of inequality, as figure 4.2 shows, with the exception of Nordic countries, this loss of unionized manufacturing jobs meant a rise in earnings inequality. Overall, a 1 per cent decline in manufacturing employment as a share of total employment correlates with a 0.66 per cent increase in earnings inequality before taxes and transfers. In Canada, a 1.9 per cent decline in manufacturing employment was accompanied by a rise of 4 per cent in market income inequality – a clear indicator of how transformations to manufacturing affected income distribution. This was due to the ability of firms to establish their priorities of greater flexibility, job relocation, and lower wages and benefits in employment contracts.

Have other variables such as technology and increasing capital intensity, or events such as the financial crisis contributed to the elimination of well-paying, unionized manufacturing jobs? Certainly, the data suggest all three have been important in the rapid growth and restructuring of manufacturing capital – in Canada and the United States. In the industrial sectors of both countries, real private stock of fixed, machinery, and equipment assets rose by over 66 per cent over the course of the 1990s and early in the first decade of 2000. Similarly, in both countries manufacturing output increased by more than 100 per cent from 1982 to 2007 (Clarke and Couture 2017; Moody 2017). With industrial exports increasing in both countries as well, it is clear that over the course of the late twentieth and early twenty-first centuries, capital became far more productive, and increasing technology and capital intensity were major contributors to job loss in manufacturing, especially unionized manufacturing.

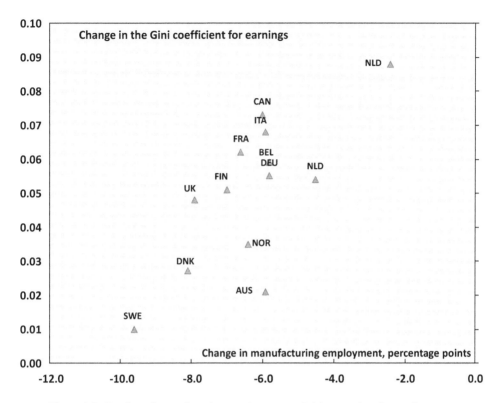

Figure 4.2. Decline of manufacturing employment and rising earnings inequality, mid-1990s to mid-2015
Correlation: -.73
Sources: OECD 2011, 2015, active labour force series; US data from Bureau of Labor Statistics.

Big job losses also occurred in Canada and the United States during slumps. In the United States, there were major jobs losses during the recession of 1980–2, and more than two million jobs were shed by manufacturing firms in the wake of the financial crisis 2008–9. In Canada, major job losses in manufacturing occurred during its early 1990s downturn and again in the wake of the crisis in 2008–9, where the core of the manufacturing workforce shrank by more than 20 per cent. Slumps were thus equally crucial to the ongoing accumulation in North American manufacturing, where recessions often destroyed jobs, but productivity increases due to the introduction of new technology, constrained the growth of well-paying manufacturing jobs when economic growth resumed (Moody 2017).

However, if capital growth drove the productivity and cycles that cut manufacturing jobs, it is important to place this in the context of the financialization of manufacturing. It was only with the vast expansion of financial assets and debts that major manufacturers expanded their production networks and supply chains, and in North American auto shifted new investment and output into Mexico and the US South. At the same time, even with downsizing of operations and reductions of labour costs, major non-financial firms in both countries vastly expanded the size and capitalization of their firms – all the while increasing their dividend payouts to wealthy shareholders. This suggests that the key to understanding the impacts of technology and economic downturns is not so much their unique and independent impacts on jobs, but rather to assess how they are connected to the wider processes of financialization, capital growth, and job loss.

In sum, the data presented in this section support the critical argument that with financialization and the development of global value chains, firms in Canada turned their focus from domestic growth to financial revenues and new production in low-wage jurisdictions. As a result, managers increasingly diverted resources away from reinvesting in productive activities and toward financial activities – typically at the cost of good manufacturing jobs. Such a shift helps account for the decline of jobs that once formed the backbone for wider economic prosperity during much of the post-war period, as well as partly explaining the rise of income inequality in Canada. The rise of low-wage, precarious service work is a second factor in explaining worsening employment and distribution outcomes.

Low-Wage Private Service Employment

This section considers the relationships between finance, corporate globalization, and expanding low-wage private service employment. While there is a lack of adequate long-run financial and ownership data for private service industries in Canada, there is much secondary quantitative data and sectoral reports that strongly suggest that financialization and increased low-wage service employment have been strongly connected (Appelbaum 2010; Weil 2014; Dupuis, Peters, and Scrimger 2020). These developments have had implications for labour market growth and for wider income inequality.

Figure 4.3 shows the positive relationship between finance and private service employment in Canada and twelve other countries, 1990–2015, and indicates our theory that financialization increases employment in financial, insurance, real estate, and private service industries as it fuels global capital growth and the need for service sectors to expand alongside. Overall, a 16 per cent increase in financial market activity per annum translated into a 1.4 per cent increase in private service employment. But around this average, there were wide differences in financialization and private service employment.

Austria and Sweden were clear outliers, with little financialization reported but high service employment increases. However, many of the largest firms in these

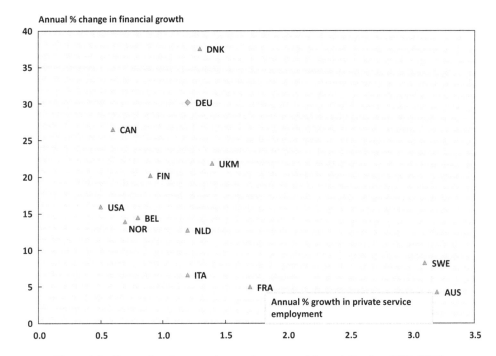

Figure 4.3. Change in private service employment and financialization, 1990–2015
Correlation: .68
Sources: Financial indicator based on World Bank and UNCTAD Stat; employment figures from
OECD Stat active labour force series; US data from BLS; French data from Eurostat.

outlier countries operate as privately held entities, while European multinationals
operate throughout Western European financial markets. Therefore, they may
account for the underreporting of financial market data. In addition, Canada and
the United States also saw below-average private service employment growth
during this period. But both economies have had above-average rates of private
service employment in their labour markets since the 1980s, reflecting their more
flexible labour market policies and active financial markets. Overall, as figure 4.3
illustrates, increases in finance correlate rather closely with changes in private
service employment on a cross-national basis – a correlation that is even more
significant when the outliers of Sweden and Austria are removed.

The aggregate evidence presented in the table has been supported by a growing number of case studies and comparative research that has closely examined
the links between firm finance, growth, and new employment in private services
(Thompson 2013). Food, housing, and business construction employment have
increased as firms expanded their global enterprises (Bernhardt et al. 2008).

The expansion of multinational corporations has required more managers, accountants, engineers, and IT specialists (Dicken 2015). Likewise, giant firms and their supplier networks have needed more accounting and legal services to track growth and sales (Coe, Lai, and Wójcik 2014). Moreover, to fulfil the final sale of goods through global value chains, businesses had to hire more people to transport, store, and retail goods (Appelbaum 2010). This brought on larger clerical workforces in addition to firms hiring more managers, sales persons, and professionals. Together, the growth of finance-fuelled corporate globalization and the massive increase in global production and distribution chains led to the vast expansion of private service sector and construction industries. As a result, employment growth in these industries outpaced industrial employment by a more than three-to-one ratio in many countries between 1990 and 2010 (Moody 2007, 38–43; Wren 2013, 7–14).

Moreover, just as in the financialized manufacturing sector, multinationals in the financialized service sectors operated under increasingly short time horizons to boost profits, and sought lower costs and more flexible labour markets – especially as they turned to contractors and third-party agencies to fulfil contracts (Baud and Durand 2012; Coe, Lai, and Wójcik 2014). Franchising, supply chains, and network alliances, as well as subcontracting in service industries, increased the polarization of jobs, with second- and third-tier firms using non-standard and contingent work arrangements to boost profitability throughout North America and Western Europe (Weil 2014). But growth in private services had an additional twist.

Unlike capital-intensive manufacturing industries that routinely increased mechanization in pursuit of greater productivity, in the private service industries greater profits could be generated only in one of three ways: longer hours, greater intensity of work, or lower wages. This has meant that second- and third-tier private service firms in highly financialized and competitive market contexts have had even less commitment than manufacturing establishments to industrial relations frameworks and employment regulations, and an even greater interest in expanding their non-standard labour force through subcontracting, licensing, and temporary employment agencies, than manufacturing establishments (Appelbaum 2010, 186; Weil 2014, 159–80). And these employment relations have been backed by the high levels of debt and credit offered by lead service multinationals to their supplier networks, putting additional pressure on suppliers to seek efficiencies through the increasingly ruthless use of low wages and temporary contract labour (Baud and Durand 2012).

The typical model followed by service-sector firms is that of competing on the basis of lower labour costs and expanded workforces, which has meant that employers have increasingly hired temporary and part-time workers while shifting their workforces away from standard employment relationships to atypical employment (Standing 2011). Retail giants like Walmart, for example, have expanded their operations nationally and internationally by integrating advanced contracting and inventory systems with low-cost suppliers through vast credit and financial arrangements in China and elsewhere, and then opening big-box stores staffed by low-wage workers on non-standard work contracts (Appelbaum, Bernhardt, and Murnane 2003; Jaehrling and Mehaut 2013). At the same time, temporary employment agencies servicing major firms, providing everything from clerical and cleaning to IT and administration, expanded their pools of employees on temporary and short-term contracts by the millions (Standing 2011, 26–38). Similarly, franchised restaurant and hotel employers increased their flexibility and productivity by hiring more workers on a part-time basis (Arrowsmith 2013), while private service firms in administration and clerical have routinely used fixed-term contracts as a source of cheap labour (Baud and Durand 2012). All such examples reveal the close association between financialization and the "fissuring" of standard employment contracts.

Canada saw similar trends: as firms globalized and expanded their production networks (most significantly between Canada and the United States), private services followed, expanding offices, partnerships, and low-wage service work. Business services such as banking, accountancy, insurance, law, advertising, and business consultancy constructed more complex and geographically diverse operations to serve business, especially to support the burgeoning commerce between Canada and the United States (Milway et al. 2007). But Canada's insurance companies were also among the largest in the world and moved to provide finance and investment in international markets. In these business sectors, there was a notable increase in good full-time jobs during the first decade of 2000.

Figure 4.4 displays the role of low-wage private services to overall low-wage employment and total employment in Canada (missing data in the Canadian Income Survey prohibits extension into the 2010s). It is based on the Survey of Labour and Income Dynamics data, and it shows that from 1998 to 2011, overall employment grew by three million new jobs. But of these jobs, one million earned less than two-thirds of what a full-time, full-year worker earned hourly – or put another way earned in the range of $12,000–$17,000. And of these, private services were the key driver of low-wage work. Over the course of the late 1990s and the first decade of 2000, private service firms hired some 768,000 workers into new jobs that paid little and offered little security.

And firms' increasing use of low-wage, non-standard employment contracts was common across private service industries. In Canada's retail and wholesale trade, for example, where more than half of retailing is in foreign firm hands (Office of Consumer Affairs 2013), low-wage employment made up approximately 42 per cent of the workforce, with more than 1.1 million workers paid $17,100 or less annually. In Canada's hotel and food industries (dominated by five American transnational chains that have the majority of market share), more

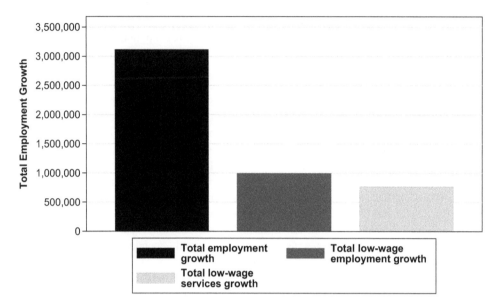

Figure 4.4. Low-wage work and private services employment in Canada, 1998–2011 (total employment growth).
Source: Author's figures based on a custom survey request from the Survey of Labour and Income Dynamics, Statistics Canada, "Low-Wage Work by Sector, Unionization, Gender, and Visible Minority Status," table C749006.

than 80 per cent of workers were in jobs with low incomes, no benefits, and little job security, paying on average less than $13,100 a year. Likewise, in low-end business services including clerical and administration, cleaning, and repair, the majority of workers were employed in jobs that left them working poor.

In terms of employment relations, there is also evidence of private service firms' increasing resort to non-standard employment and extensive use of third-party agencies to reduce labour costs – processes that have done much to undermine standard employment contracts and institutionalize low-wage work. While direct evidence of the varied contractual forms that employers have used to increase the flexibility of their labour force is limited, there are other indirect indicators of how employers in services fissured employment.

Employment service agencies, for example, increased substantially during the first decade of 2000, doubling their operating revenues and expanding by 50 per cent their number of establishments to nearly 5000 by 2011. At the same time, temporary employees – those in seasonal, casual, and contracts jobs – grew across Canada from 1.5 million to more than 1.9 million. And as evidence from interviews with workers employed by temp agencies in Ontario demonstrate, the most typical motivations for employers to use temporary employees was to avoid overhead and benefit costs, as well avoid paying vacation, overtime, sick pay, and vacation pay (Workers' Action Centre 2015). Such just-in-time staffing was especially prevalent in trucking, transport, courier, and business services. And in Ontario, where occasional employment standards "blitzes" of temporary agencies occurred, it was found that 72 per cent of all temp agencies had violations of employment law (Mojtehedzadeh 2015b).

But employers also began to lower labour costs simply by hiring workers not as employees but as self-employed contractors. Routinely, employers in transport, and professional, scientific, and technical services, as well as business, security, and cleaning services hired workers as self-employed contractors with no employees, and from 1995 to 2010 the numbers of workers who were so categorized expanded from 1.3 million to 1.8 million. Legally, employers were not supposed to shrug off their statutory obligations. But the benefits to business – and the fact that there were effectively no costs to using workers as self-employed contractors – were substantial.

By shifting employment costs to the workers themselves, employers avoided mandatory social payments such as employment insurance and Canada Pension Plan, and avoided liability for workplace injuries. In Ontario, just over a two-year period in the wake of the financial crisis, it was estimated that employers failed to pay $1.4 to $2.4 billion in social contributions because of the ease with which they misclassified workers (Workers' Action Centre 2015). As critical political economists have argued, such employment fissuring is typical of conditions when suppliers, agencies, and contractors are under competitive market conditions, when lead firms do not wish to pay, in their efforts to boost returns to investors, and they create profitability by offloading employment to firms that cannot pay (Weil 2014).

However, the role of finance and wider value chains across many of the private service industries is also notable. Figure 4.5 tests for some of the wider direct connections between financial expansion and the growth of low-wage service employment. It demonstrates that over the course of the late 1990s and the first decade of 2000, as the finance, insurance, and real estate industries grew in economic importance, overall low-wage private employment also increased (paying less than half of median annual earnings, or approximately less than $17,000). While the data break in 2011 shows a proportionate decline in low-wage work in the service industries (largely because the data are unable to account for workers with irregular or unnoted employment contracts), the correlation of .58 shows a consistent relationship between financialization and low-wage service jobs. And CIS data for 2011–15 (which exclude millions of part-time and temporary employees) reveal a similar relationship of increasing FIRE share driving the growth of low-wage service employment. Such developments strongly suggest that the finance-led model of growth and its impacts

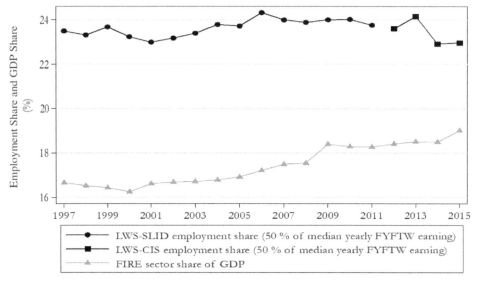

Figure 4.5. Growth in FIRE and low-wage private service employment in Canada, 1997–2015
Statistics: Correlation between LWS-SLID and FIRE share of GDP: $r(15) = .5812$, $p < .05$.
Correlation between LWS-CIS and FIRE share of GDP: $r(4) = .9673$, $p < .05$.
Source: LWS employment estimates from custom data request to Statistics Canada for Survey of Labour and Income Dynamics (SLID) and the Canadian Income Survey (CIS); FIRE sector share of GDP (Statistics Canada table 36-10-0434-01). Author compilation.

on private service firm labour markets were another key contributor to increasing labour market inequality in Canada.

What, then, of the overall impacts of growing private service employment on income inequality? As figure 4.6 makes clear, the shift from goods production to private service-employment in an era of financialization and global production networks typically led to a significant rise in income inequality. Overall, a 1 per cent annual increase in private services employment correlated with a 0.24 per cent rise in the Gini coefficient after taxes and transfers. Certainly, many other factors are associated with rising inequality. But as figure 4.6 illustrates, plotting increases in disposable income inequality against the rise of private service employment produces a very strong positive correlation across countries.

There were still clear cases of regulated labour markets and collective bargaining offsetting some of the impacts of rising non-standard employment. The Netherlands and Belgium, for example, retained the best protection for non-standard workers. With coordinated central collective agreements between

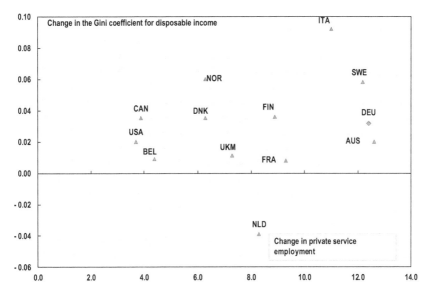

Figure 4.6. Growth of private service employment and disposable income inequality, 1990–2015

Correlation: .87

Sources: Author's figures from OECD Stat active labour force series; US data from BLS; French data from Eurostat strong tax and transfer programs. The largest increases came in many of the economies long associated with coordinated bargaining or institutionalized labour markets: Sweden, France, and Germany. But significant increases were also seen in the more deregulated economies of Canada and the United States.

governments, employers, and organized labour, workers in non-standard employment were less likely to experience wage penalties (Thelen 2014). But overall, despite many government efforts to support the growth of service employment through a variety of "flexicurity" programs intended to offset the impacts of low-wage work, the rise in inequality is consistent with expectations about increasing private services and its polarizing effects on employment growth.

These developments strongly illustrate how a finance-led model of growth and its impacts on the strategies of private service firms for reducing labour costs were a key contributor to increasing inequality and to the rising number of low-wage jobs in Canada and other advanced capitalist countries. Certainly, the expansion of service employment did produce some high-skill, high-quality jobs, particularly in high-end financial and business services. And in some small countries such as Belgium and the Netherlands, extensive collective bargaining coverage and government-led coordinated bargaining arrangements did offer some protection for service workers. But in Canada, the United States, and much of Western Europe, the more dominant trend was service firms increasing their "flexibility" and low-wage workforce and the fissuring of their employment relations (Heyes and Lewis 2013; Howell 2016).

Critics might argue that without such employment growth, inequality might well have been higher, as without deregulation or the enforcement of labour standards, more workers would have been unemployed. But even they would be forced to concede that the expansion of private service employers has not been without costs – above all the continued growth of large numbers of poor-quality, low-paying jobs, often poorly compensated – if at all – by tax and transfer policies.

Global Extractive and Primary Commodity Industries and Low-Cost Labour

A third major consequence of the ascendancy of financial capitalism was the massive growth of primary commodity and agri-food industries and the subsequent development of poorly paid, global temporary labour forces and the fissuring of labour markets. In this section, I examine the ongoing rise of highly financialized global primary-commodity and agri-food industries and their impact on low-wage work and inequality in Canada.

Both natural resources and food industries are critical for the functioning of modern economies, and both are central to the concerns of public officials across all countries. Indeed, because they need adequate and secure supplies of energy and food, most countries adopted extensive regulatory and fiscal policies to support, promote, and in many cases protect these key industries (Karl 1997; Weis 2007). As a consequence, resources, agriculture, and land have all become central to the acquisition concerns of major private investors and financial institutions, as new financial actors have sought novel areas of profit growth and creative ways to make resources and commodities conform more closely to safe and increasingly profitable portfolio assets (Clapp and Helleiner 2012; Gunnoe 2014; UNCTAD 2009a).

In Canada, the conventional policy view on natural resource and food industries has been that highly capital-intensive firms and producers facing fluctuating market prices require extensive public support in order to attract new foreign direct investment, ensure maximum economic benefit, and achieve long-term competitiveness (Arcand, Burt, and Crawford 2012; Mintz and Chen 2012). Most notably, Canada's federal and provincial governments have focused on major reductions in corporate taxation, heavy public infrastructure spending to support the transport of goods by private firms, massive direct subsidies to firms, and targeted research and development (Natural Resources Canada 2014; Angevine and Cervantes 2010). This suite of supply-side policies is believed to provide the best opportunity to maximize wealth from Canada's extensive natural resources and food and agricultural industries, as well as en-sure strong employment gains and productivity improvements.

However, such policies and their socio-economic impacts have become increasingly controversial. A large literature has argued that countries depending heavily on oil, gas, and other primary commodity exports have been marked by a "resource curse," tainted by uneven economic growth, inequality, immense environmental problems, and inflation, as well as rising currency exchange rates that squeeze out good manufacturing jobs (Humphreys, Sachs, and Stiglitz 2007; ILO 2011b). Countries that depend primarily on primary commodities often face adverse shocks in trade, and far greater economic uncertainty, undermining long-term growth (van der Ploeg and Poelhekke 2009).

Moreover, an over-reliance on natural resources and primary commodities has been strongly correlated with reducing the competitiveness of the manufacturing sector through higher exchange rates that subsequently diminish the positive impacts of high capital intensity and higher-quality jobs (Sachs and Warner 2001; Stiglitz 2006). Finally, countries and regions with abundant primary commodities are more likely to have firms and employers develop rent-seeking behaviour that relies on low-cost labour and undermines domestic demand and skill development (Humphreys, Sachs, and Stiglitz 2007).

In Canada, with the rapid growth of primary commodity industries in the 1990s and first decade of 2000, many of these political and economic problems associated with an over-reliance on these commodities became notable in the first decade of 2000 (Campbell 2013). Given the lack of comparative international data on resource and agri-food industries, and that Canada is one of a few advanced industrial countries to have both extensive fossil fuel wealth and highly developed agri-food industries (the others are the United States and Australia), I limit my discussion here to the rising importance of primary commodity and agricultural industries and their impacts on labour markets and job quality in Canada.

As much research has shown, Canada and other resource- and food-exporting countries benefited greatly from the globalization and financialization of these industries (Nikiforuk 2008; Roberts 2009; Roberts 2013). From 1970 to 2010, the extraction or production of primary commodities – oil and gas, ores/industrial minerals, forest products, and food production – nearly doubled worldwide (Moomaw et al. 2012; UN Department of Economic and Social Affairs 2010). Driven by increasing wealth and economic productivity in the rapidly growing economies of South-East Asia and China, global firms and their supply chains rapidly expanded their "ecological footprint" by extracting and consuming primary commodities faster than increases in global GDP.

The Canadian boom in natural resources and primary commodities, for example, was on such a scale that by 2008, the direct and indirect impact of resource output was equivalent to 19.9 per cent of Canada's GDP (Cross 2015). Agribusiness accounted for another 8 per cent of GDP (Agriculture and Agri-Food Canada 2013). Together, Canada's reliance on primary commodities was among the highest (along with Norway and Australia) across the advanced industrial economies (Radetizki 2010).

This dominance was driven by capital investments in the resource and agriculture sectors, as well as by new investments in associated construction and support services. And complementing this reliance on resource exports were imports of critical resource components necessary for processing. The result: between 1990 and 2008, oil exports more than tripled, mineral exports grew four-fold, and food exports increased by 70 per cent. These increases made Canada one of the world's leading exporters of primary commodities in everything from oil and gas (sixth in the world), to metals and non-metal ores (fourth), to primary agriculture products and processed food (fifth) (Agriculture and Agri-Food Canada 2013; Natural Resources Canada 2008).

Driving such developments were the rapid growth of global oil corporations and the financial sector that drove up spot prices in Canada and other oil exporters (Gkanoutas-Leventis and Nesvetailova 2015). Many oil majors themselves became global financial traders, further driving up oil prices (Forhoohar 2016). British Petroleum, for example, became one of the biggest oil derivatives and swaps players, gaining more than 20 per cent of its income from financial dealing, while at the same time becoming notorious for its cost-cutting in all its operations (Watts 2014). Also contributing to increasing prices was the rapid rise in demand from China and the developing world (Cross 2008). And with the creation of new financial markets and new sources of credit for oil companies, oil companies poured billions of dollars into new efforts to discover and transport recently discovered sources of fossil fuels (Carter, Fraser, and Zalik 2017). Combined, these processes lifted Canada's trade surplus to near-record levels – above C$45 billion per year for much of the decade (Carter 2020; Stanford 2008).

It was with this vast expansion of speculation on future commodity markets and oil's rise above $100 a barrel that resource majors increased their efforts to extract more resources from difficult geographical areas. Beginning in the 1990s and continuing through the first decade of 2000, corporate efforts focused on the exploration of marginal and offshore fields like the Hibernia development in Newfoundland and the oil sands of northern Alberta (Carter 2011, 2016). Similar financial developments and growing global demand also led to the rapid price rise for potash and metal ores, and Canada exporting record amounts of primary commodities (Stanford 2008).

The financialization and conglomeration of agri-food was also notably rapid and followed the trends of oil and other resources, with speculation playing an increasing role in inflating prices (Forhoohar 2016; Gertel and Sippel 2016).

Over the past few decades, the production, distribution, and consumption of food has been rapidly industrialized by the dominance of very large transnational firms (Roberts 2013; Weis 2007). The financialization of the industry has also created large speculative bubbles that favoured the consolidation of global corporate giants to weather the ups and downs in price markets and seasonal disruptions (McMichael 2012).

Historically, food and agriculture were local or regional, directed by fragmented companies and producers. However, the rise of giant transnational firms and global futures markets over the past few decades reshaped how food is produced, how it is marketed and distributed, and who produces it. The leading 100 global food retailers now have 35 per cent of world grocery sales (Dicken 2015), and while directly engaging in commodities future markets – along with hedge funds – firms have speculated heavily in commodity markets, driving up the real price of food and other basic consumables to record levels in the first decade of 2000, reaching their highest level in the twentieth century (Forhoohar 2016). Taking advantage of rapidly rising commodity prices, firms built massive global operations, acquiring operations around the world. For example, a quarter of the global packaged food market is directed by the ten largest firms (Dicken 2015). New food-processing and packaging assembly lines were also built across international boundaries, leaving workers in agri-food industries subject to lean and flexible production. In Canada, food distribution has been rapidly industrialized and consolidated among six multinational grocery/retail corporations, four of which are American (Roberts 2013; Weis 2007).

However, whereas manufacturing became a global activity through outsourcing and global value chains, the resource extraction and agriculture and agri-food businesses all developed by international financial markets, pressuring national corporations and distributors to increase their use of low-skill labour forces inside of domestic economies and limiting their use of higher-paid, skilled trades (Castles, De Haas, and Miller 2014; Clapp and Helleiner 2012; Dicken 2015). With increasing financial speculation and increasing swings in prices, the preference of many employers in resources, agriculture, and food processing turned to low-cost or easily controlled temporary workers – almost all of which was beyond standard employment regulation.

Consequently, in terms of labour markets, the growth and development of global primary industries has often been entwined with national suppliers and producers expanding their reliance on non-standard employment and the polarization of jobs – relatively few high-paying jobs offset by the expansion of low-wage and non-standard service-industry jobs (Emmenegger and Careja 2012; Foster and Barnetson 2015; Oxfam America 2004; Preibisch 2010). Under these pressures, many governments turned to the solution of regulated (and, in some countries, unregulated) labour migration to provide scarce low-skill workers and increase the competitiveness of their economies (Castles 2006).

Typically, officials did so by creating special labour contracts outside of their traditional systems of employment protection and collective bargaining – contracts that have left millions of temporary workers vulnerable to exploitation.

In Canada many of these dynamics can be seen in the profound changes to the construction and infrastructure industry that supported the resource and agri-food sectors. From 2001 to 2006, construction employment averaged 4.5 per cent growth, nearly triple the rate of overall employment. During the first decade of 2000, when Canada led the G7 nations in annual employment growth, employment in construction rose from 9.2 per cent of total employment in 2000 to more than 12 per cent by 2008 (Peters 2012c). But aggregated data on construction employment – which include those categorized as self-employed but without employees, as well as a range of non-standard workers – show that low-wage work and job polarization remained the norm in the industry. Despite the creation of more than 300,000 construction jobs in the first decade of 2000, 43 per cent of all construction jobs in 2011 still paid working-poverty wages of below $20,186 per year. Likewise, even though more full-time/full-year jobs were created, 85 per cent of new construction jobs were non-unionized, with earnings that were typically only half of what unionized construction workers earned.

The resource sector also saw lower wages and deteriorating job quality. With the rapid expansion of natural resources, employment in support industries and service industries (such as cleaning, waste removal, building management, janitorial, and retail) more than tripled, with annual growth rates of more than 7 per cent per annum, while in accommodation and food, employment expanded at a rate of 2.4 per cent a year – all jobs that are typically low-paying, part-time, or temporary (Mason and Salverda 2010; Vosko 2006b) – another example of how booming resource industries and related construction industries typically contribute to the fissuring of employment and expanding low-wage work (Foster and Barnetson 2015).

Likewise, under new financial pressures and fluctuating price markets, agri-food industries expanded their low-wage labour force and became the largest employer of casual, temporary, and foreign labour in Canada (Binford 2013; Oxfam America 2004; Preibisch 2010). While a small number of jobs in processing and packaging are full-time, two-thirds of all agriculture jobs in Canada are temporary, with low wages, long working hours, and no benefits. The vast majority of these jobs are worked by migrants, who, because of their precarious legal status, and work permits linked to specific employers and areas, tend to suffer from widespread workplace abuses (Fairey et al. 2008; Oxfam America 2004). In addition, the preference of many agricultural employers for undocumented workers has only served to worsen the problem of increasingly vulnerable migrant workers with few rights, as they are outside of the protection of normal labour laws and employment regulations (Castles 2006).

Canada – like other advanced industrial economies – dramatically expanded temporary migrant worker programs as a means of managing low-wage workforces (Castles 2006; Emmenegger and Careja 2012; Binford 2013; Hennebry 2012; Fudge and Strauss 2014). In the 1990s and throughout the first decade of 2000, numerous advanced industrial economies developed new guest-worker policies for the temporary entry of migrant workers in order to meet specific industry needs (Plewa 2007; Preibisch 2010). This expanded use of legalized precarity has been intended to ensure that migrant workers make little demand on social infrastructure, have little access to unionization and employment protection, and return home once their work permits have expired (Menz 2010). Information technology, finance, and hospitals have also pushed for special immigration work permit systems to recruit specialists, though in this case offering workers opportunities for permanent settlement and family reunion. In all cases, powerful employer interests have been key in developing special immigration rules to serve their growing demand for low-cost labour outside of regular employment laws and rules.

To investigate the relationship between financialization and low-wage work across extractive industry sectors here I track share capital as a proportion of total equity. Share capital consists of all funds raised by a company in exchange for shares of either common or preferred shares of stock. As such, an increasing ratio should suggest increased influence of shareholders and of the shareholder value model of corporate governance. This figure is compared against the rising number of temporary foreign workers in agriculture, private services, construction, and low-end manufacturing (figure 4.7). Rising share capital captures how corporations increasingly depend on shareholders for financing (as opposed to banks, for example) and the extent to which firms are oriented to external shareholders – that is "outsider capital" or short-term investor interests (Barker 2010). For Canada, share capital rose for all major non-financial corporations over the course of the 1990s and the first decade of the 2000s. But the trend was especially notable in the capital intensive industries of oil, gas, mining, and forestry (Dupuis, Scrimger, and Peters 2020).

At the same time, over the past decade, the numbers of temporary foreign workers who were covered under the international mobility program soared, recently exceeding the numbers of permanent migrants applying for permanent residency. There is no full data set of the program, but we do know that in the 2010s, 40 per cent of the workers in the TFW program were either agricultural workers or low-skilled workers, 40 per cent higher-skilled who typically worked in construction, and 20 per cent caregivers (Citizenship and Immigration Canada 2013). The TFW program does not include students, professionals, or intra-company transfers, who find temporary employment permits under a range of other programs.

As figure 4.7 demonstrates, total temporary foreign workers more than tripled, from 161,388 to 490,852 – mostly concentrated in Ontario, Alberta,

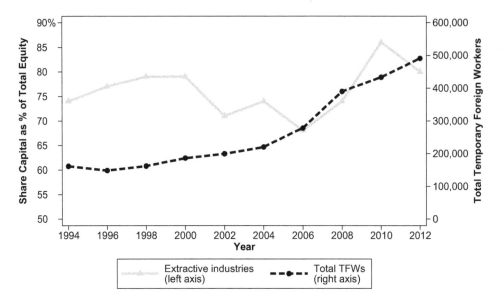

Figure 4.7. Financialization and growth of temporary foreign workers in Canada, 1994–2012
Correlation: .58
Sources: Citizenship and Immigration Canada, *Facts and Figures 2013*; Intercontinental Exchange, market data.

British Columbia, and Quebec. In the wake of the financial crisis, between 2010 and 2011, approximately 75 per cent of new jobs were filled by temporary foreign workers (Canadian Labour Congress 2013) – some 40,000 of these in agriculture (Preibisch 2012). By 2012, workers on temporary permits accounted for 3.2 per cent of the employed workforce.

Overall, the correlation between rising financialization and expanding temporary foreign work permits is strong and suggests a close association of financialization to the growing use of TFWs in extractive industries. As extractive industries financialized, they increased their cost pressures on contractors, suppliers, and small producers. In turn, this evidence suggests that Canadian suppliers and producers – like in other advanced industrial economies – dramatically expanded temporary migrant worker programs as a means of managing low-wage workforces in its financialized extractive and related service industries (Castles 2006; Emmenegger and Careja 2012; Binford 2013; Fudge and Strauss 2014).

For temporary migrant and recent immigrant workers employed in extractive industries, construction, and agriculture, such developments have commonly meant low wages, substandard working conditions, and new kinds of managerial discipline (Galabuzi 2006; Sharma 2005). Across Canada, the United States, and Western Europe, data show that immigrant workers earn significantly less than native-born workers, with estimates of the differential in earnings of immigrants at arrival and citizens with the same characteristics of up to 50 per cent or more (Adsera and Chiswick 2006; Galabuzi 2006). Moreover, with the expansion of the global labour pool, employers regularly engage in "country-surfing," threatening foreign countries that they will recruit migrant workers elsewhere unless labour costs and contracts are kept at a minimum (Prebisch and Binford 2007).

This has kept wage rates low, with temporary migrant workers typically earning only the legislated minimum, and all agricultural workers for which we have tax data in Canada (which often exclude TFWs) averaging less than $15,500 in annual incomes in 2011. Many employers also imposed productivity targets or piece rate systems that limited even standard minimum pay scales. Furthermore, workers often pay private recruiters to find them jobs, creating further, and often heavy, additional expenses (Preibisch 2010). Thus, migrant status is one major determinant of poverty and social exclusion, even after controlling for other socio-economic variables (OECD 2015a). And combined with the wider trends in resource industries, global financialization in these sectors was thus another key contributor to rising labour-market inequality in Canada, remaking Canada's labour market by expanding non-standard labour outside of regular employment law, and using foreign workers on temporary contracts with limited rights to do so.

Canada, Income Inequality, and Low-Wage Work in a Macroeconomic Perspective

As chapter 3 and the previous sections have detailed, Canada and many other rich world economies have often followed the liberal prescriptions for financial and trade liberalization with great vigour. These policy reforms have done much to change the way firms and finance operate. But have their expectations that policy reform would bring about economic dynamism been borne out? Supply-side economic theory suggests that greater financial liberalization and free trade should introduce greater investment, and in turn enhance labour productivity growth that generates rising living standards for workers. The common assumption is that workers and business interests should both benefit similarly from more free trade, wider financial liberalization, and greater market integration.

In this section, I question these commonly held assumptions. Drawing on Canadian and OECD data, I show that productivity growth has certainly expanded total income. But in Canada, as well as many other countries, much of this income has gone to the richest income earners – most notably to those in finance and to corporate executives. At the top, the growth of the financial economy, and the mass expansion of rents and profits in the sector, have contributed to enormous benefit for financial sector workers – and the richest executives and professionals. And the growth of firms and new structures of executive compensation have also benefitted the top 1 per cent of earners.

In contrast, median wages for the majority have been generally flat. Moreover, contrary to common economic assumptions that compensation tracks productivity, I demonstrate how labour's share of national income has fallen in tandem with the decline of labour's bargaining position and the growth of low-wage work. Finally, the evidence suggests that, rather than improving jobs, financially driven firms have generally replaced good jobs with non-standard ones – jobs that not only cost employers less but have contributed to greater income inequality.

Rise of the Financial Sector and Inequality

Evidence for the impact of financialization on income inequality continues to accumulate (Duménil and Lévy 2011; Flaherty 2015). One key reason that income inequality has risen over the past three decades is the widening gulf in wages between top income earners – those in the upper 1 per cent – and all other workers (Alvaredo et al. 2013; OECD 2011a). As noted in the introduction, the average annual earnings and capital gains of the top 1 per cent of income-earning families in Canada grew 172 per cent from 1990 to 2015, and by 283 per cent for the top 0.01 per cent between 1990 and 2008 before declining slightly in the wake of the financial crisis. In contrast, working families exactly in the middle of the income distribution grew only at a far more painful rate of 16 per cent, while those in the bottom 20 per cent stayed generally the same at $12,000. Even more notable was how for the bottom 10 per cent of working families, incomes actually fell by 10 per cent. Explanations of overall changes in income inequality can thus be markedly enriched by considering the role of top income earners.

This is particularly the case when considering the impacts of the growth in financial activity on the very rich. Over the past decade, a large literature has emerged indicating how the growth of finance, insurance, and real estate industries have increased income inequality and especially boosted the incomes of a few the "super rich" (Flaherty 2015; Godechot 2016; Volscho and Kelly 2012). As new forms of credit and market finance have expanded, those who work in financial sectors and draw income from investments have seen their profits, compensation, and returns rise (Atkinson and Piketty 2010; Piketty 2014). But the role of politics has also been critical, and how elites have been able to secure favourable regulatory structures that have delivered growing total income – what has been characterized as a "winner-take-all" economy (Hacker and Pierson 2010b). And where elites have been most successful in securing investor-friendly macroeconomic policies, investor and financial institutions reaped the rewards from new debt-based investment (Shaxson 2018).

The impact of economic policy reforms and financialization on skewing the distribution of incomes to an elite few is thus a key issue in considering the impacts of liberalization, which have been theorized to stimulate economic growth with widespread benefits, for if rising top income inequality is due less to globalization and skill-based wage premiums and instead to the politics of inequality, and how the top 1 per cent of earners have been able to change market and debt structures – in particular, the tax and financial policies and regulations that underwrite the use of debt – to boost their own incomes, then other policy reforms such as progressive economic policies and more effective international tax enforcement are required (Stiglitz 2013, 2017). Such considerations have led to examinations of how financial revenues have grown and in turn generated rising private sector compensation for financial sector workers (Lin and Tomaskovic-Devey 2013; Kaplan and Rauh 2013). But they have also led to studies of how the expansion of credit and debt markets has been a source of increasing rentier incomes for banks, large corporations, and their executives (Duménil and Lévy 2011; Lapavitsas 2014).

Figure 4.8 provides strong evidence of rising credit expansion and rising asset prices contributing to top income inequality. It compares the incomes of the top 1 per cent of earners with the total credit to the private non-financial sector. Increasing leverage and private sector credit can increase windfall profits for the financial sector and wealthy. Most generally, with the deregulation of housing loans, there was an explosion in household credit, as households took out larger and larger mortgages to purchase homes. But in doing so, banks and executives gained more profit through the collection of mortgage interest (Aalbers 2016; Walks and Clifford 2015). In addition, with lowering borrowing costs, firms and wealthy households began to use debt and leveraging to invest in the stock market, new financial assets, and money markets (Flaherty 2015; Kwon 2018).

With the run-up of asset prices and stock markets in the 1990s and again in the first decade of 2000 with the emergence of asset bubbles prior to the financial crisis, such leveraging provided the potential for large returns to financial institutions and wealthy global elites, as debt-aided investments in assets provided massive financial gains with rising prices (Volscho and Kelly 2012). And there is much evidence to suggest that the private sector debt growth through investments typically benefits the incomes of the wealthy, as increasing asset prices provide financial workers with the rents and allow executives to claim greater compensation with the rising stock price of firms (Atkinson, Piketty, and Saez 2011; Nau 2013). In Canada, the correlation of .79 between the growth of non-financial-sector debt and credit and the incomes of the top 1 per cent of earners strongly suggests similar outcomes, with increasing debt

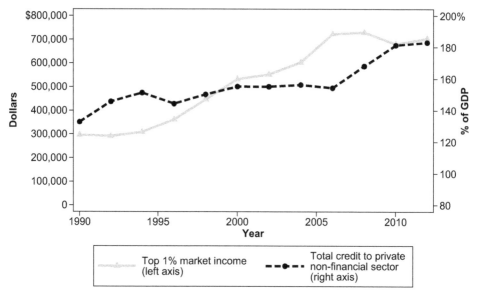

Figure 4.8. Private sector credit and the top 1%, 1990–2012
Correlation: .79
Sources: Author's figures from Bank of International Settlements, Statistics "Total Credit to the Non-Financial Private Sector, 1980–2015" and top income data based on author's figures from a custom data request from Statistics Canada, "T1 Family Filers, 1990–2015."

in the wider economy playing a fundamental role in redirecting income flows to wealthy individuals.

A second and more general set of evidence looks at the financial assets of the total financial sector for everything from banks, to international investment banks, hedge funds, capital market traders, and so on. Anglo-Saxon countries, like Canada, Ireland, the United Kingdom, and the United States, all witnessed the enormous expansion of income-producing assets and debt securities over the course of the 1990s and first decade of 2000 (a trend that has continued since 2010) (Konzelmann and Fovargue-Davies 2013). The growth of "super" banks, hedge funds, and institutional investors pursued highly speculative investments, using borrowed funds in the pursuit of large capital gains (Lapavitsas 2014). This contributed to the dramatic rise in financial profits around the world, and a boom in employment in the financial sector (Flaherty 2015; Godechot 2016). Financial and "non-bank" financial institutions also drew rents from loans to the non-financial sector, while the massive growth of hedge funds has also grown through their investments in public and private equity, money and commodity markets, and real estate (Shaxson 2018). But

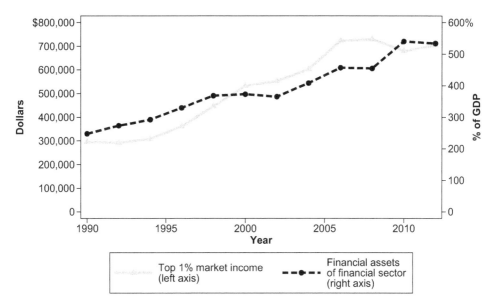

Figure 4.9. Financial assets and top incomes, 1990–2012
Correlation: .92
Sources: Author's figures from OECD, Financial Dashboard; top income data based on author's
figures from a custom data request from Statistics Canada, "T1 Family Filers, 1990–2015."

in investing in new debt-based securities and derivative markets around the
world, financial sectors were able to significantly increase their leverage to expand their income-producing wealth – a phenomenon most dramatically seen
in the world-leading financial centres of New York City, London, Tokyo, and
Amsterdam (Durand 2017; Shaxson 2018).

Figure 4.9 confirms similar trends in Canada. It compares the growth of financial assets in the financial sector with the market incomes of the top earners.
Again, the correlation of .92 is very strong, highlighting how growing financial
assets generated profits for financial institutions – and in particular its major
banks and insurance companies – that in turn increased the compensation for
those working in the sector. And other evidence confirms the association between rising financialization and top incomes in the financial sector.

At the top, executives across all financial institutions pocketed cash from bonuses and stock options, and of the best-compensated chief executive officers,
roughly 25 per cent of the top thirty were from the financial sector, with record
compensation for the CEOs of Canada's major banks (Mackenzie 2012, 2017).
And in privately held financial institutions, Eric Sprott, for example, the chair
and CEO of the mutual and hedge fund company Sprott Asset Management,

earned $27 million in 2010, roughly 11 per cent of the $200 million that the firm earned in performance fees alone (*Toronto Life* 2011). Lawyers and accounting firms also benefitted from the financial sector growth, with huge fees for managing money and taxes.

In these ways, with an increasingly favourable investment and tax climate, the financial sector in Canada underwent enormous growth in the 1990s and first decade of 2000, which contributed to skyrocketing compensation levels for those in the banking and investment industries. While financial investments do not make up the entire portfolio of top income earners, they do constitute a significant portion of top income wealth (Saez and Veall 2005). Thus rising assets provide a second good gauge for how investors and executives increased returns over time, further fuelling rising top incomes. Such evidence also helps us account for the dramatic rise of top earners working in the finance industries, which rose from 5.4 per cent of total top income earners in 1986 to 10.8 per cent in 2006 (Lemieux and Riddell 2016).

Executive Compensation, Financialization, and Inequality

The other major issue to consider for top income inequality is rising executive compensation. Over the past few decades, there have been many, such as professional athletes, actors, and investment bankers who saw their pay dramatically increase (Reich 2015; Stiglitz 2013). However, data show that in most countries it is non-financial corporate executives and upper-level managers who make up the vast majority of highest earners (OECD 2011a, 351). The data also reveal how, across countries, the relative pay of executives in comparison to that of the median worker rose dramatically over the course of the 1990s and first decade of 2000. For example, in the United States, the ratio of CEO-to-worker compensation rose from 59 to 1 in 1990 to more than 345 to 1 in 2007, before declining to 235 to 1 in 2011 (Economic Policy Institute 2015). In Germany, CEO pay had risen to 147 to 1.

In Canada, similarly, executive compensation skyrocketed between 1998 and 2007 from approximately 62 to 1 to 218 to 1, and while it fell after the financial crisis, by 2013 CEOs in Canada were again making more than 171 times more than an average worker earned in a year (Mackenzie 2008, 2016; IGOPP 2012). Consequently, the growth of CEO and executive compensation was a major factor in the near-doubling of the income shares of the top 1 per cent and top 10 per cent of earners – the second-highest rate in the OECD behind only the United States (OECD 2014a). If we factor in the ongoing reductions in top marginal tax and corporate tax rates, it is clear the top 1 per cent gained the most from economic growth over the past few years – in fact, as of 2007, the top 1 per cent captured more than 31 per cent of all recent income growth (Yalnizyan 2010, chart 2; OECD 2014a).

Conventional economic wisdom suggests that such differences in incomes are simply the result of unequal endowments in productive capacities between individuals, with higher-skilled individuals earning higher incomes, while those with identical skills obtain relatively equal earnings, regardless of job or occupation (Borjas 2015). But the exponential rise in top incomes challenges this theory, as human capital and expertise develop collectively across populations and often slowly (OECD 2013). Critical theories of financialization, however, suggest that firms generate income inequality through how they reward workers for their labour, and how they set compensation for executives and owners (Cobb 2016; Flaherty 2015; Kus 2013).

This has occurred for two reasons. First, as a result of shifts in ownership to institutional investors and minority shareholders, executives are incentivized by compensation packages that are linked to short-term stock performance. Consequently, executives have very strong incentives to distribute profits to shareholders rather than retain surpluses for investment or labour compensation (Davis 2009; Murphy 2013). Second, the shift in ownership to financial actors has created further pressures to reward shareholders and turned firms' strategic focus away from internal growth and development to debt financing, stock buy-backs, and financial investments (Epstein 2005; Lapavitsas 2014). In both cases, resources are drained away from firms to financial managers and equity holders, and the income gap between executives and workers widens (Economic Policy Institute 2015).

Figure 4.10 provides a test of these arguments for Canada. It is based on correlations between the development of firms' market capitalization, the rise in stock trading, and the growth in incomes of the top 1 per cent and the richest within the top 1 per cent. As noted above, under shareholder value systems, firm growth, stock trading, and the market capitalization of firms as a percentage of GDP are tightly correlated with rising financial incomes such as dividends, interest payouts, and portfolio income.

Here I average two indicators: first, the market capitalization of the top sixty publicly listed firms on the TSE, as they accounted for more than half of all firm capitalization on the TSE. Second, stock trading as a percentage of GDP is also a good indicator of firm financialization and a shareholder regime, as executive compensation is based on market-oriented compensation packages linked to stock options, and firms often manipulate their equity prices through debt financing and stock buy-backs. By averaging the two financial variables together here, I follow other recent literature that uses such a "financialization index" to test for the growing role of financial activity (Roberts and Kwon 2017; Kwon 2018). In averaging this way, jumps in stock trading or sudden bursts in firm growth are smoothed out and reflect the presumption that even if independent in their everyday operation, both are tightly bound to wider financial markets developments that better reflect the long-run influence of finance on socio-economic variables.

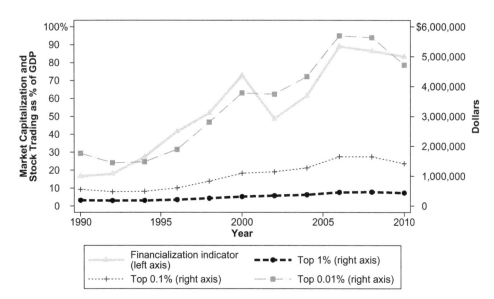

Figure 4.10. Stock trading, market capitalization, and top income growth, 1990–2010
Correlations: .93 top 1%; 0.94 top 0.1%; 0.94 top 0.01%
Sources: Market capitalization data drawn from the World Bank, courtesy of Brennan (2014);
stock trading from IMF; top income data based on author's figures from a custom data request
from Statistics Canada, "T1 Family Filers, 1990–2015."

As figure 4.10 illustrates, all the correlations are exceptionally strong, and
the trends in the data lend support to the growing number of critical arguments that suggest greater income inequality is strongly correlated to financialization. Over the course of the 1990s, as firms rapidly expanded and stock
trading exploded, top income rose in tandem. Those at the very top – the
top 0.01 per cent – did the best, with annual family incomes rising to nearly
$6 million as firms grew and stock trading increased. But those in the top
1 per cent also did well, with annual incomes increasing to more than $400,000
by 2010.

Such bivariate correlations, however, overlook other institutional and structural factors that might account for rising top income inequality, most notably
the growth of employment in the financial sector itself, as well as increasingly
favourable tax regimes for the rich (Flaherty 2015; Volscho and Kelly 2012).
Nevertheless, it is apparent that the growth of top incomes has been an integral part of new financially driven business models, and that the emergence of
shareholder models has facilitated top income capture and a surge in rentier
income. This suggests that the growth in top income has been less due to the

unique features of a few highly skilled individuals, and far more the result of structural changes that rewarded firms, their executives, and their shareholders at the expense of other income earners.

Financialization and the Decline in Labour's Share of Income

If there is much evidence about the effects of financialization on income distribution as seen in the bivariate dynamics between firms and top income earners, what then of the relationship between financialization and the fate of the majority of workers? Is there evidence to suggest that financial globalization and shareholder corporate models have also eroded workers' share of economic rewards overall? It is commonly held in economic theory that economic expansion will make most workers better off, and that over the long run labour productivity should grow at roughly the same rate as average compensation. But evidence for the impact of financialization on increasing income inequality and especially on declining wage shares continues to grow (Atkinson 2009; Kristal 2010; Stockhammer 2013b).

Recent scholarship has underscored the importance of studying labour's share of income in determining income inequality and overall macroeconomic stability (Stockhammer 2015; Dabla-Norris, Kochhar, et al. 2015; ILO 2014). Studies have shown the negative impact of labour's share of income on personal income inequality (Gini), stressing the long-term importance of strong collective bargaining in sustaining greater rewards for labour, and a more equitable distribution of income (Daudey and García-Peñalosa 2007; Kristal 2010; Stockhammer 2013b). At the same time, scholars have investigated how, with financialization and rising profits, income inequality has increased as top income earners have taken growing shares of national income, and earnings for the majority of workers have stagnated (Hein 2015; Volscho and Kelly 2012; Wolff 2015).

With financialization and the institutionalization of shareholder corporate governance models across advanced economies, it is argued, firms and top managers not only retain more income through greater profits, dividends, and interest payments, but the broader functional distribution of income overall is also transformed, as firms reduce domestic investment and employment to focus on cutting labour costs and wage compensation. These changes in the distribution of income have been most noticeable in the liberal market economies such as the United States and Canada. But European countries have also seen major declines in wage share with the growing importance of finance-driven business models.

The combined impacts of financial market liberalization alongside increasing rewards for top management and shareholders can be seen clearly in the failure of incomes to grow for the majority of low- and middle-class income earners – regardless of unionization or systems of employment protection. As figure 4.11 illustrates, across the advanced economies, the labour share of income declined in relation to the capital share (OECD 2012). The wage share in the business sector demonstrates this best, with recent OECD data showing steady deterioration over the past three decades.

In the 1970s and early 1980s, wage share of income reached highs of 89 per cent in Sweden and Austria, and the peak average for the thirteen countries reached 78 per cent. Since then, the wage share has steadily fallen as income from profits, stocks, shares, and rents have risen. In 1990, wage share had fallen to 71 per cent on average. In 2005, it fell further to 63 per cent. For the thirteen advanced industrial countries surveyed in figure 4.11 the average decline in labour share was 10.6 per cent, with the steepest declines seen in the Nordic countries. Throughout much of the 1980s and 1990s, the decline in wage share in Canada mirrored wider trends, with a decline of 8 per cent between 1980 and 2005, and if the wages of the top 1 per cent are discounted, the decline was even steeper (Brennan 2014; ILO 2012a). This declining labour share reflects the highly uneven growth in productivity returns to labour.

Several cross-national studies have confirmed that the decline in wage share contributed strongly to the rise in household income inequality across the OECD, as the majority of households had little wealth, and the majority of household income – typically more than 80 per cent – was derived from labour income (Salverda and Haas 2014; Hein 2015; Stockhammer 2013b;- Stockhammer 2015). In general, across the thirteen OECD countries surveyed here, a 1 per cent decline in wage share correlated with a 0.7 per cent rise in the Gini coefficient for market income between 1995 and 2005.

Another confirmation of how the distribution of income has become skewed is how wages have stagnated despite productivity growth – clearly illustrating how the rewards of increased worker productivity have gone to employers at the expense of the wider working population (Dencker and Fang 2016; Kochan and Riordan 2016; Reich 2015). Conventional wisdom suggests that productivity growth not only provides more employment opportunities but also improves workers' compensation. But as figure 4.12 illustrates, while productivity grew by approximately 25 per cent, real compensation for hourly workers in Canada increased only by about 10 per cent, with much of the increase occurring only just prior to the financial crisis. As Uguccioni, Sharpe, and Murray (2016) argue, a good part of this widening gap can be correlated with higher earnings inequality between those at the top and the rest of the labour market. And while some of this widening gap may be due to skill-based technological change and rising demand for highly skilled workers leading to a rise in earnings inequality (OECD 2015a), the other half is due to capital's growing share of income.

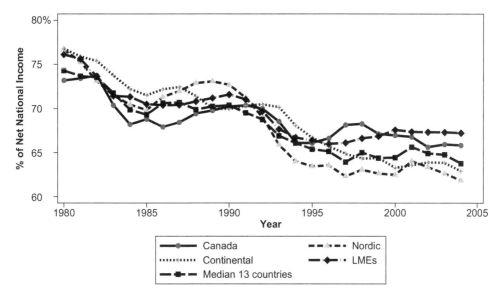

Figure 4.11. Decline in wage share (% of net national income)
Source: OECD Economic Outlook, courtesy of Paul Swaim, Economics Department OECD.
Averages and median based on Denmark, Finland, Norway, Sweden; Austria, Belgium, France,
Germany, Italy, the Netherlands; Canada, Great Britain, and the United States.

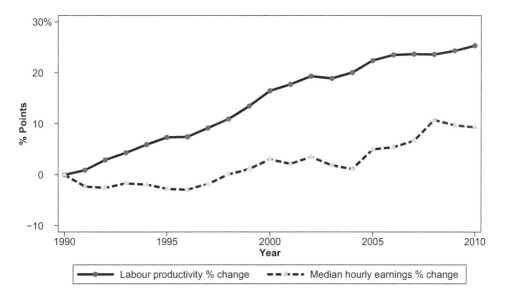

Figure 4.12. Unequal growth in productivity and median wages, 1990–2010
Sources: Author's figures from custom data request of Survey of Labour and Income Dynamics;
CANSIM table 383-0030; CANSIM table 384-0038.

This rise in capital's share, as we have seen, correlates well with the dynamics of financialization. Recall that critical political economy suggests that growing financialization is strongly associated with a substantial rise in CEO pay and an increase in the ratio of CEO-to-average-worker wages as firm surpluses are directed upward to corporate officers and shareholders. One manifestation of this is firms taking productivity gains at the expense of workers' compensation. This widening gap between productivity growth and wage growth has been significant not only in Canada, but in the United States, Germany, Japan, and the United Kingdom as well (ILO 2014; Dabla-Norris et al. 2015). This gap would likewise be far wider if the earnings of the top 1 per cent were dropped from the equation.

Financialization, Non-standard Employment, and Market Income Inequality

A final issue of relevance to the widening dispersion of income between capital and labour is the growth of non-standard employment, which has led to far lower hourly wages and annual earnings than standard jobs, especially for those at the bottom of the earnings distribution (OECD 2015a). As we have seen over the course of the 1990s and the first decade of 2000, nearly 60 per cent of all employment growth has been in the form of non-standard work. But throughout advanced industrial economies, median hourly wages of non-standard workers have averaged 70 to 80 per cent of those of standard workers – yet only 55–9 per cent in Canada. But the most noticeable difference is in annual earnings.

Employers have rapidly deployed non-standard employment as a means to lower wage and benefit costs. Among advanced economies, the annual pay level for workers in atypical work is 52 per cent, but far lower for women, young workers, and recent immigrants. However, Canada stands out as the country with the greatest wage penalties for non-standard work (there is no comparable data for the United States), with employers typically paying non-standard workers only 32 per cent of what standard workers make annually (figure 4.13).

This has meant that, as non-standard employment has grown, hourly wages and annual pay have lagged, especially for those workers in the bottom 40 per cent of the income distribution. This growth in low-wage, non-standard employment has contributed to wider overall wage inequality, since it increases inequality at the bottom of the labour market (OECD 2015a, 167–9). In Canada, lower earnings are especially notable among the bottom 10–40 per cent of the workforce. Single-parent families, families with two adults in non-standard employment, and families with only one adult in non-standard employment have some of the lowest earnings in the OECD. Consequently, once all

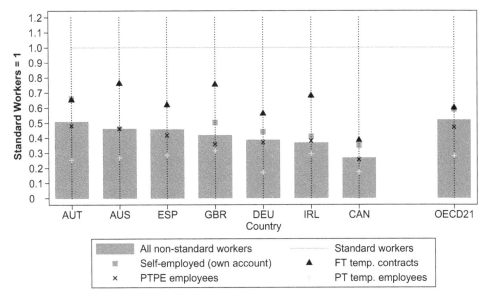

Figure 4.13. Earnings ratio between standard and non-standard workers annually, 2012 (standard workers = 1)

Source: OECD 2015, chapter 4, figure 4.10; author's figures for Canada from custom request, Statistics Canada, Survey of Income and Labour Dynamics, "Percentage of Workers with Low-Annual Earnings and Low-Hourly Wages," table C749006.

non-standard, low-wage workers are factored into analyses, Canada has one of the highest levels of income inequality within households in the OECD, with the impact of non-standard working households adding another 5 per cent to the Gini coefficient to earnings inequality (OECD 2015a, 175; 2011a, 170).

The Shortcomings of Alternative Explanations

Can other explanations that attribute inequality to faltering education levels and the lack of skill among low-wage workers and their inability to adapt to a "high-technology" economy help explain such trends (Boudarbat, Lemieux, and Riddell 2010; Beaudry and Green 2005)? Lack of education is often theorized as a key variable to inequality, as workers are theorized to lack the necessary "human capital" to adapt to new technology and machinery. And certainly those who are top income earners do generally see economic benefits from higher education. But if Canadian education levels are put in a wider comparative perspective, it is clear that education is not a factor in the explanation for low-wage work in Canada.

For example, Canada has one of the highest levels of post-secondary education in its workforce, of more than 54 per cent. By comparison, in Denmark and Sweden, which have among the lowest levels of low-wage work, only 45 per cent of their workforces have attained upper-level education levels (OECD 2018). Similarly, in terms of educational expenditures per student, Canada spends above the EU and OECD average, and while it does not spend as much as more equitable countries such as Norway and Sweden, it also spends more than others such as France and Finland (OECD 2018). Looking at these results suggests that while education is likely to matter for income differences in certain sectors and top income earners, there is little evidence to suggest that the lack of education has been a cause of employers paying workers little and employing them in non-standard jobs.

What of race or gender? Can theories that hypothesize that race and gender are major fault lines in the labour market help us account for the high levels of low-wage work and non-standard employment in the labour market? Certainly, there is much evidence to suggest that as the workforce in Canada – as in the United States – has become more diverse, women and racialized workers have continued to be underpaid and have lost ground (Galabuzi 2006; Kalleberg 2011; Lightman and Gingrich 2013). In both countries, women and racialized workers are not only typically paid less, but they are also more likely to be employed in non-standard jobs, with no benefits or pension plan (Healey, Stepnick, and O'Brien 2018; Vosko 2006b).

And wider comparative research has underscored how higher levels of immigration and racial composition of the workforce have typically hindered unionization but also been a part of more liberalized and unequal labour markets (Brady 2009; Pontusson 2005). Race and gender are thus important variables to explaining the high levels of income inequality in Canada and the United States. And in Canada in particular, data show that over the course of the 1990s and first decade of 2000, as low-wage work continued to growth, visible minority workers made up a growing share of those in low-wage work, increasing from 10 per cent in 1993 to 24 per cent by 2011.

However, it is important to view such socio-economic developments from a wider perspective. Even though women and racialized minorities were more likely to suffer the consequences of low-wage work, the more profound change was the general decline in living standards and job quality for the entire workforce. From this perspective, it is striking how many jobs and households across the labour market are in the low-income range, with a majority of families in working poverty or closely within range of it. Typical statistics for Canada commonly overlook this economic insecurity, citing, for example, that the median income for Canadian households was $70,336 (Statistics Canada 2017).

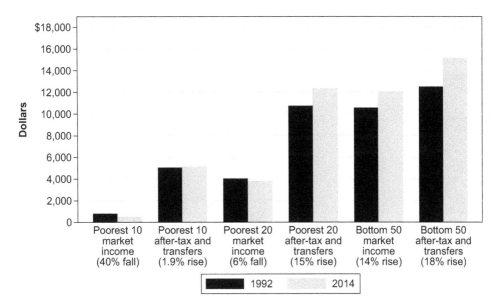

Figure 4.14. Average household real market income and after-tax and transfer income for bottom 50% of Canadian households, 1992–2014 ($)
Source: Author's figures based on a custom data request for "Market and After-Tax Incomes of Economic Families T1 Family File Tax Data," Statistics Canada.

However, using tax data and real constant dollars that assess the thresholds in terms of total number of households shows a very different picture.

Employing this method – which looks only at incomes for those below each cut-off rather than aggregating the very rich and the very poor into a final calculation – reveals the growing chasm within the economy. Here using the most generous method of considering total incomes available to workers – households – figure 4.14 portrays the scale of low wages and income security in real incomes. For the poorest 20 per cent of census families – covering roughly three million households – real market income actually fell by 6 per cent. And even though tax and a range of transfers helped shore up negligible wage incomes, for millions of households average real annual incomes still amounted to only $12,337 in 2014.

To put how inadequate such incomes were in a broader perspective, a living income for a family of four in real 1992 dollars would range from $30–$40,000, and $18,000–$22,000 for a single-parent household in 2015. For the bottom of 20 per cent of households this represents a gap of more than 75–150 per cent in annual incomes. Such little income for the vast majority of households represents

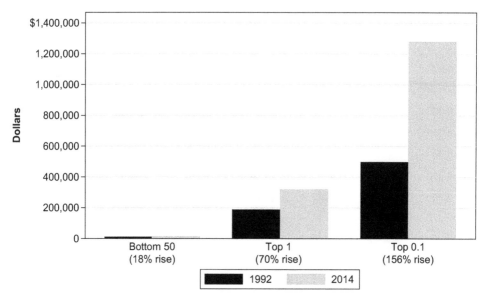

Figure 4.15. Average household real after-tax and transfer incomes for wealthiest and bottom 50% of Canadian households, 1992–2014 ($)
Source: Author's figures based on a custom data request for "Market and After-Tax Incomes of Economic Families T1 Family File Tax Data," Statistics Canada.

dramatically how widespread low-wage work and income insecurity are for millions of Canadians. But it also demonstrates how, even if tax and transfer programs marginally increased over the course of the 1990s and the first decade of 2000, these policies were inadequate in actually addressing the depth of working poverty and shortages of incomes that many families and individuals face.

In contrast, for top income earners, and especially for those at the very top (figure 4.15), the average real after-tax and transfer incomes increased from $189,120 in 1992 to more than $322,095 in 2014 – an increase of 70 per cent, almost doubling in twenty-two years. But the gains were really concentrated at the top 0.1 and top 0.01 per cent – i.e., corporate CEOs and financiers. Between 1992 and 2014, the average real household incomes of the very richest more than doubled, rising to $1.27 million – an increase of 156 per cent. However, for the bottom 50 per cent of households, the story was far different – an increase of only 18 per cent for an average income of only $15,157 in 2014. These statistics are arresting. But they demonstrate clearly the limitations of "business first" policies – unequal growth that not only contributed to jobs that paid little and provided little security, but that also redirected the vast majority of benefits upward to the rich and the very wealthy few.

Conclusion

This chapter has explored income and employment consequences of market and corporate financialization models. I have examined Canada in a largely international context, analysing the increasing role of the financial sector in the overall economy, as well as how corporate financialization and the increasing importance of financial assets, debts, and market capitalization affected employment relations, labour markets, and income inequality. In undertaking this analysis, I explored whether there were systematic impacts of financialization and the spread of global production networks on manufacturing, private services, and resource and agri-food industries. In addition, I considered the effects of a growing financial sector, as well as increasingly financialized corporations on the incomes of the very wealthiest.

The evidence presented in this chapter strongly underscores the fact that the rise of a powerful financial sector as well as highly financialized MNCs were major contributors to income inequality. Outside of the rising returns in the financial sector and exploding CEO compensation, the systematic impacts of financialization on employment relations and labour markets were incremental in each sector in contributing to rising inequality. However, the cumulative effects of financialization in displacing good jobs with bad, while redirecting income to the top, have been large.

In Canada, there are two parts to this story. First, with the massive growth in market-based finance and credit, alongside the financialization of corporate operations in the real economy, financial and corporate executives have captured a disproportionate share of national income through greater profits, more fees, interest, increased equity shares, and expanding capital gains. "Market financialization" thus helps us account for the rise of the "super rich" in Canada and is a key factor for the widening gap between the rich and everyone else. Indeed, where Canada stands out in particular is in how the rise of financialization has triggered the rapid growth of income for the top 1 per cent of earners – most notably among financial and corporate executives. In terms of growing top income inequality, Canada now ranks third only behind the United States and the United Kingdom.

Second, and by contrast, labour's share of national income has not only declined, but real earnings have increased much more slowly than productivity. This has been largely due to the displacement of good jobs – many in manufacturing, which experienced the heaviest losses. But declining labour income is also due to the growth of precarious low-wage jobs, which have continued to expand as financialized firms have sought to reduce labour costs by expanding their international operations and increasing the flexibility of their non-standard workforces – most typically by "fissuring" their employment relations or, in extractive industries, by increasing the size of their labour force outside of standard employment regulations.

It is this remaking of the labour market to better meet the demands of finance and wider "corporate financialization" that has done so much to undermine income security throughout the labour force and widen income inequality more generally. As a result, within the OECD, Canada not only has one of the most financialized economies, it also has one of most polarized labour markets, with one of the largest gaps between those with good jobs and those in low-wage non-standard employment.

Part One Summary

Explanations for income inequality have developed in variety and sophistication. Some have considered technology, others the roles of tax and transfers, and others still the role of race and gender. But for all their in-depth examination of potential causes, many of these explanations fall short.

Most missing in conventional explanations are the distinctive features of Canada's economic policies – and how the reform of monetary, financial, investment, pension, and taxation regulations and institutions has vastly expanded the opportunities for financial and corporate actors to grow their operations and profitability. Similarly lacking in social science literatures is any sustained attention to what is happening in markets, finance, and the economy before taxes, transfers, and labour market regulations take effect. Because of financialization, corporate ownership, operation, and functioning have all undergone significant change. But little of this change has been investigated by researchers in Canada. And perhaps most problematic in many perspectives is how inequality is often assumed to be due to "outside" global forces, rather than public policy and how governments are deeply involved with finance and corporate firms alike. The unspoken assumption is that markets autonomously produce inequality, and only afterwards do public officials seek to moderate its impacts (Hacker and Pierson 2010b).

My analysis of financialization has sought to challenge such assumptions about inequality in Canada. In particular, I have underscored how politics and policy should be at the centre of our accounts of income inequality. Rather than "external" market forces, key to rising inequality has been how international, federal, and provincial governments have used a wide range of tools to affect the intensity and growth of new financial assets and debt markets. Rather than simply inadequate tax and transfer policies failing to counter the effects of technology, government financial, investment, and tax policies have opened the door to new financial actors taking a growing role in corporate governance, and have provided a wealth of new incentives for corporate executives to turn to finance. These political and policy shifts are at the heart of the story of how and why business and finance have extracted greater profitability and productivity from the labour force to the benefit of a privileged few.

Certainly, conventional arguments for how technology harms under-skilled workers do have a role to play in our understanding of rising inequality. But they do not explain much. All advanced industrial countries faced similar pressures, but Canada and the United States stand out for the rate of growth of top income inequality and for the depth of low-wage work in their labour markets. If technology really were such a critical variable, it is far from clear why Canadian workers – who are among the best educated in the world – would see so little reward for their efforts to improve their qualifications. There is also much evidence that new capital investment increased capital-labour ratios in industries like manufacturing, and the growth of information technology industries did allow a few in these sectors to reap rewards. But this only raises the question of why the gains from new technology were not more broadly shared, or why the gains were not invested into lines of enterprise that had far better long-term impacts for workers, the economy, and the environment alike.

Turning next to sociological explanations, race and gender do figure as important variables that contribute to inequality in Canada – as in many other countries. Labour markets in Canada are clearly segmented by race and gender, and women and visible minorities are universally underpaid and routinely relegated to insecure non-standard jobs. Likewise the rise of immigration and temporary foreign workers has contributed to a pool of low-wage labour.

However, looking more broadly, the extent of low-pay and non-standard employment in Canada appears more as a function of the recently changed legal, institutional, and regulatory environment in which employers operate than of actual higher levels of sexist and racist employer attitudes. Low-wage and precarious employment with high levels of income insecurity for households is deeply entrenched across Canada's labour market – so much so that – as we have seen – Canada has among the highest levels of low-wage work and most inadequate standards of pay for non-standard employees among advanced economies. But the evidence presented here suggests this has more to do with how policies have been devised to favour business and finance, and how recent policy reforms – or the non-enforcement of laws and regulations – have come to exclude workers from economic opportunity – a model of "jobs with inequality" with serious consequences for income inequality.

What does the foregoing analysis allow us to conclude? My analysis points to a rather different set of factors for explaining inequality in Canada than conventional explanations, and highlights three interconnected political, policy, and economic processes that have driven a growing gap between the rich and the rest of the workforce:

1. Neoliberal economic policies have not only reformed the older "mixed economy" model; officials have also drafted new policies to serve financial and corporate interests, and have done so in ways that have redirected income to those at the top. Because of financial liberalization and new international frameworks for finance, financial markets and assets have gained power and prominence, and the gains in the financial sector have been highly concentrated to the benefit of a few financial professionals. Through these policy tools and rule changes, governments have powerfully shaped the extent and growth of upward income distribution and top income inequality. Political and policy factors have thus been key in altering the economic outcomes produced in the market and in implementing policies that direct more income to those at the top.

2. In addition, the efforts of officials to expand credit and debt and let enterprises operate globally with few restraints has led to significant changes to how corporate interests operate in the "real" economy, with many business enterprises becoming deeply integrated into speculative systems of finance and investment. Major policy shifts to tax, trade, and pensions have contributed to the "financial" turn among non-financial companies, propelling financial ownership, shareholder governance, and corporate reliance on credit and financial assets forward.

   As a result, corporate executives – domestic and foreign – now routinely operate their firms on debt and invest in financial assets and financial markets to boost dividends, and subsequently seek out new opportunities to increase "rents" throughout the production process – from outsourcing, to increasingly profitable financial assets, to mergers and acquisitions and monopolization of greater market share. This growth in global financialized operations in both the real economy and financial markets has provided firms with the revenues necessary to pay corporate executives and shareholders growing shares of income.

3. Finally, with these major shifts in power and the rules governing markets, financialization has become a major contributing factor to the erosion of good jobs and incomes for workers across the labour market. Because of the massive overhaul of economic policies and regulations, firms have become increasingly integrated with finance and have looked for greater cost efficiencies, by shedding unionized employment contracts, expanding their non-standard labour forces, or outsourcing production to supply chains, as well as developing temporary foreign-worker hiring systems.

   This financialization of corporate operation and labour management has been a final root cause of much labour market inequality. Such finance-led growth has not only been a major contributor to the decline of unions and good jobs, as firms have focused on increasing returns to shareholders rather than investing and paying their workforces. The financial turn among non-financial companies has also seriously diminished workers' leverage, allowing companies to fissure employment contracts and expand their "flexible" labour forces of low-wage, precarious employment.

Yet here we need to ask two further questions. If the balance of power among organized economic interests has shifted so decisively in favour of business and finance, what has this meant for other public policies such as labour law and employment policies? Political economy frameworks have inspired scholars to question not only changes to tax and transfer programs and their effects on income inequality, but also to examine how the stunning rise of corporate power has reshaped government policies structuring labour markets and labour bargaining, employment regulations, and their enforcement (Baccaro and Howell 2017; Weil 2014). If financialization has transformed employment relations, we might expect to see similarly dramatic and systematic shifts on labour law and employment regulation that provide employers with greater flexibility and lower labour costs. This is the first key question of part 2.

A second related issue is whether such economic inequalities have influenced politics and corroded the workings of democracy more generally. Labour laws, employment regulations, minimum wages, and other labour-related public policies affect millions of people. Labour market rules are of significant political importance and often subject to debate and partisanship, as democracies grapple with the tensions of capitalist growth and democracy. So if democratic politics and organized labour have been unable to challenge recent economic development or improve inadequate labour or social policies, a key question is why?

In part 2, I argue it is the development of post-democracy – and how organized interests, citizens, and political parties have been influenced by the pressures of financialization and the demands for a more cost-efficient and flexible labour force – that explains recent patterns of labour market deregulation. Answering questions about the impacts of financialization on policy and democracy means having to pay attention to the long-term interconnections between politics, business, unions, and citizens.

Examining how finance-driven business – now largely antagonistic to pro-labour government regulation – has begun to influence politics and the policy process, whether through lobbying and political finance, or by simply bypassing laws and regulations provides a first step. So too exploring how unions have lost members and discovered new difficulties in protecting members or organizing new workers in the age of financialized capitalism adds to our understanding of how post-democracy has eroded union power and weakened its voice with government officials. Last, to explain the politics of inequality today, it is necessary to tackle the obstacles that exclude workers and their families from good jobs and secure employment and what such exclusion actually means for workers' democratic involvement and their capacity to influence wider democratic debates. It is these dynamics and their causal impacts on the politics of inequality that I address in part 2.

PART TWO

Post-Democracy and Labour Market Deregulation

5 The Unequal Politics of Deregulation

Governments could have cushioned the blows of rising corporate power and expanding finance by improving wages, passing better labour laws, expanding public sector employment, or extending social distribution to cover gaps in current policies. But over the past three decades, public officials have either reformed labour law and employment policies to make them conform more closely to market and business priorities, or they have simply let corporations and financial actors grow, while allowing labour markets to drift into greater insecurity and expanding levels of non-standard employment. These tendencies have been reinforced by the post-2008 financial crisis and the ongoing austerity drive. Why?

Here in part 2, I argue that to understand these developments it is necessary to look at "post-democracy" and how business has been able to influence the state and policymaking, while organized labour and the broader public have lost the resources to succeed in interest group politics, or have simply been marginalized out of politics because of widening inequality and distrust. I claim that these changes to the power dynamics within democracy can help us make sense of why governments have failed to introduce policies that would counter rising inequality and instead have gone on to implement "labour market deregulation" – a set of policy priorities that seek to roll back, reform, or water down a host of labour laws and employment and social policies to better improve business profitability.

But as we will see, post-democracy has not meant a single common set of labour market reforms. Rather, over the past few decades, officials have introduced reforms to increase the flexibility of their labour markets in a variety of ways – everything from overhauling labour law and social policy, to blocking basic updates, to renewing legislation despite its flaws, or simply passing legislation that exempts employers and allows them to hire workers outside of standard employment law. Common explanations for this variety often highlight differences in collective bargaining, union strength, or political party orientations. But, as I argue, all such explanations are incomplete.

To come to terms with this variety, my second core argument is that we must examine the actual dynamics of "post-democracy" and how its political patterns shape labour law and employment policies. How business has mobilized, how parties have catered to business and upper-income earners, and how organized labour and citizens have tried – and often failed – to counter these trends, are all part of a new politics of inequality. Yet each have varied across national and (in the case of Canada) provincial polities, and in doing so, have generated an array of rollbacks, erosions, and circumventions to labour law and employment protection.

It is these differences within post-democracy I argue that can allow us to account for many of the distinct "varieties of deregulation" in use today. We can see that such varieties range along a spectrum from:

1. *reform* of labour markets in pursuit of greater flexibility; to
2. *drift*, where governments undertake a more limited number of neoliberal reforms, block progressive policy options, and do little to address growing inequalities, while frequently opening new exemptions to standard employment contracts; to
3. *stasis*, where public officials maintain regulations and institutional arrangements (most notably for organized labour) but largely fail to address the widening gap between good and bad jobs in the labour market, or between rich and poor more widely.

To develop this argument, I begin by discussing recent scholarship on deregulation and some of its shortcomings, most notably how it fails to take varieties of deregulation seriously, but also how it lacks a more developed account of the politics and organized business interests behind deregulation. I then frame a conceptual model that identifies ways to empirically study post-democracy and its consequences for deregulation. I conclude by outlining how and why governments are likely to differ in their implementation of a range of reforms to their labour laws and employment policies.

Explaining Labour Market Deregulation

Over the past three decades, public policies have been gradually reformed to make them conform more closely to market and business priorities (OECD 2006; Boeri and van Ours 2013). This tendency has been reinforced by the post-2008 fiscal crisis of the state and the ongoing austerity drive (Crouch 2014). Initially, policymakers and scholars were concerned primarily with the impact of tax and transfer programs and social policies on employment growth and business investment. But by the early 1990s, with the slowing of economic growth in most countries, policymakers focused increasingly on the labour market behaviour of workers and the impacts of collective bargaining and other regulatory measures and social programs on economic growth and business productivity (OECD 1994). And with the economic expansion and employment growth in the United States in the 1990s and early in the first decade of 2000, economists and international policy agencies regularly argued that other countries should emulate American practices and expose labour forces to wider market forces if they wished to prioritize economic growth (Crouch 2014).

The outcomes of such reasoning have seen governments introduce policy reforms to address employer concerns, from wage "rigidities" associated with collective bargaining to non-wage social costs such as unemployment insurance and pension benefits. Deregulation policies have likewise been directed at lifting restrictions on non-standard employment, and loosening rules for dismissal protection. In undertaking these changes, government policymakers have been concerned primarily with lowering wage pressures on price inflation in the overall economy, as well as expanding employers' right to maximize efficiency by hiring, working, and terminating workers as they see fit (Crouch 2014).

Why? Conventional explanations have highlighted the need for governments to implement reforms that improve "economic efficiency." Governments, it is claimed, should overhaul institutions of industrial relations such as collective bargaining to allow greater employer flexibility in hiring and more efficient labour markets (OECD 2006). Other collective employment relations like extension agreements, work councils, and tripartite training arrangements should also be reformed, as they were said to lead to inefficient wage setting and inflation. Employment protection laws, such as on severance payouts or company notice, were to be deregulated, as they inhibited firms from rapidly adjusting to changing market conditions (Bassanini, Nunziata, and Venn 2009; OECD 2004). Unemployment insurance and training programs were likewise to be reduced, with more responsibilities placed on individuals in order to ensure they retained their incentive to work (OECD 1994, 2004). Policy recommendations also included reducing other forms of social protection to a minimum, for fear that they would impede job creation and firm hiring, especially in the service sector (OECD 2006, 2010).

Key to many explanations in favour of deregulation is their emphasis on the "macroeconomic" problems created by unions and other protective labour market policies. For example, by increasing wages and subsequently labour costs, unions and labour policies are argued to hinder – if not directly undermine – economic growth (Borjas 2015; OECD 1994). On the basis of standard neoclassical economic theories, unions and labour-related policies and regulations are claimed to "artificially" raise the price of labour and create other "rigidities" that inhibit employers from quickly responding to consumer demand and competitive markets (Boeri and van Ours 2013).

Economists have also argued that because the majority of new jobs are being created in the private service sector, it is necessary to change a wide range of employment security laws and employment policies in order to lower the costs for employers to hire or lay off workers (Iversen 2006). Economists have also become preoccupied with the "unemployment trap" and cutting employer social costs, ostensibly because income support systems are argued to discourage the unemployed from finding work, and that social charges inhibit new hiring by employers, as benefits provided a "reserve" wage that blocks the natural adjustment of wages in the labour market (OECD 2013).

However, as critical scholarship has argued, there are a number of problems with these accounts about the causes and benefits of deregulation. Most notably they have pointed out that what business and economists often consider as "rigidities" are in fact key policies that ensure wider economic and social security for workers (Standing 2002). Throughout the post-war period and indeed until the late 1970s, governments under the pressure of labour movements passed new legislation recognizing the rights of employees against employers through collective bargaining frameworks and provided workers with a range of employment protection regulations. In large measure, these acts provided far better wages and lowered income inequality. But better labour laws and employment policies also ensured more efficient working relations between business and labour, as well as increased economic prosperity by stabilizing economic demand across economies (Sassoon 2010; Western 1997).

Deregulation undermined these institutional supports leaving labour markets more flexible than in decades past, with far less security for workers and far greater segmentation between "winners" and "losers" (Emmenegger et al. 2012; King and Rueda 2008; Standing 2011). Indeed, so dramatic has been the change that standard, full-time jobs have increasingly disappeared across countries, and non-standard jobs that pay lower wages and offer far fewer hours, are increasingly the norm (Kalleberg 2018; Weil 2014). Between 1995 and 2007, for example, more than 50 per cent of jobs created were non-standard across the OECD, and in countries such as Canada, Ireland, and Spain more than 60 per cent of jobs were non-standard.

In addition, critical scholarship has argued that theories that highlight the benefits of deregulation for lower labour costs confront the problem of explaining why deregulation has not led to a wider shared prosperity or to employment growth that provides some modicum of greater equality. Instead, as we have seen, while firms have grown enormously in size, scale, and productivity, earnings have generally been redistributed to only a very privileged few at the top (Flaherty 2015; Hyde, Vachon, and Wallace 2018). Through reforms that increase "flexibility" while restricting wage gains, wages have been generally flat, and the wage share of income in countries is in rapid decline across countries (Hein 2015; Stockhammer 2015). In addition, in privileging economic efficiency and corporate productivity, governments have generally done little to correct the market-generated inequalities in income and earnings that have often resulted from such reforms (Atkinson 2015), and the increase in inequality is undermining the conditions necessary for long-term growth (Reich 2015; Stiglitz 2017).

The argument that reforming social policy programs from "passive" to "active" will improve income security and income distribution has also been shown to have problematic and serious consequences for workers (Brady 2009; Moreira and Lodemel 2014). Rather, when governments create a growing number of "conditions of entitlement" that the unemployed must pass in order to acquire benefits, while cutting income-replacement rates and reducing the maximum duration of benefits, more of the unemployed are simply denied income support, and more workers are forced into jobs with poorer wages and working conditions (Standing 2002). In the United States and Canada in the 1970s, for example, approximately 80 per cent of the unemployed could receive benefits if they lost their job. By 2010, only 42 per cent of the unemployed in Canada and 30 per cent in the United States were able to access benefits, because of reforms that restricted eligibility (Whittaker and Isaacs 2013; Yalnizyan 2009). But if this has cut off workers from public programs of income security, it has not improved the functioning of labour markets. Rather, it has only increased stress, poor health, crime, and child poverty – all of which bring their own public costs and limit the ability of workers to improve their human capital.

Globalization, Financialization, and Deregulation: Causes and Consequences

So if conventional explanations have mischaracterized many of the dynamics driving deregulation, what are its major causes? Here critical scholarship has set out a very different account, highlighting two very basic points about the economic and political forces driving recent reforms: (1) global firms – which are not just one interest group among many –have more political power than all others in society, and now under financial pressures they have clear economic objectives to boost profits and satisfy investors and stock markets (Cobb 2016; Glyn 2006), and (2) governments have sought to accommodate firms' concerns by changing labour law, employment policy, and hiring-and-firing regulations (Baccaro and Howell 2017). To understand why, how, and when public officials have set out to reform their labour markets, critical scholars have argued that the focus should not be on workers, but rather on capital – and specifically on multinational corporations and their vast supplier networks, franchises, and contractors who drive economies, hire and pay workers, and set the trends that other smaller firms follow.

Shifting the attention to these global economic actors and their associated suppliers and service industries – which are now not the exception, but the rule worldwide – it is argued provides a far better starting point to understand what is driving labour policy reforms across countries and when. With global firms seeking increasing gains, and under growing market and financial pressures, executives now routinely emphasize cost-saving perspectives to reduce work-forces, scale back wages, and increase labour market flexibility to enhance shareholder value or private equity returns (Batt and Appelbaum 2014; Sjoberg 2009; Stockhammer 2013b; Coe and Wai-Chung Yeung 2015).

In turn, because of concerns with national competitiveness and under pres-sure from employers themselves, governments have been much more willing to adopt deregulation and much more open to expanding employer discretion, removing constraints on employers, and limiting labour law and collective regulation. This has resulted in policies that are far more liberal than egalitar-ian, and states have stepped back from balancing the interests of business and labour, instead more actively supporting business interests in order to boost growth while maintaining macroeconomic price stability.

Such political-economic dynamics can be seen in the labour market re-form efforts of advanced industrial governments over the past two decades (table 5.1). Looking first at labour law and collective bargaining over the past two decades, firms have vigorously organized, lobbied, and pushed aggressively for labour policy that better meets their needs of profitability and flexibility (Dundon and Gall 2013; Hacker and Pierson 2010b; Kinderman 2016). North American and German multinationals, with their huge finan-cial resources have argued very forcefully that unions cause "rigidities" in the labour market, for with a union contract, employers are not as flexible in responding to changing consumer and market demands and are constrained in their decisions (Kinderman 2005, 2016; Behrens and Dribbusch 2013; Stanford 2010; Dundon and Gall 2013).

In Canada and the United States, firms have routinely launched political coalitions pushing for labour reform and used business councils and their own lobbyists to advance reforms. In Germany, firms have worked at regional, national, and the European Union level to push for reforms, in their attempt to substitute individual rights over collective systems of labour law and em-ployment protection. This has led many West European governments to de-centralize collective bargaining frameworks down to firm levels, in order to give employers greater discretion in wage bargaining (Baccaro and Howell 2011). Meanwhile in North America, there have been several efforts by public officials to limit collective labour rights and implement a more limited regu-lation of the labour market, in the form of individual legal rights, enforceable through courts or government agencies (such as equity or human rights tribu-nals) (Howell 2015).

Table 5.1. Role of government in labour markets

Policy Area	Keynesian Post-War Model	Neoliberal Policy Model
Wagos and Economic Demand	Expand collective wage-setting; stabilize consumption	"End wage rigidity" – Limit collective wage setting; productivity agreements; two-tier arrangments; lower inflation
Employment Protection	Expand employment protection; regulate working hours; increase incentives for firms to hire full-time workers and increase investment and training	"Flexibility" – Limit employment protection; create "flexible" working hours; recognize and expand temporary labour contracts
Income Security and Risk Prevention	Expand income security programmes; smooth consumption through economic downturns; improve the quality of job matches	"Activation" – Limit and "activate" income security programmes; increase incentives for workers to reenter job market; reduce duration of unemployment

Likewise, for employment protection, since much of the expansion of highly financialized global operations happens through debt-financed mergers and acquisitions, scholars have noted how today firms routinely seek to persuade governments to weaken labour laws in order to reduce the costs of hiring and firing (ILO 2012b, 37–40). The rise of new global construction and agro-industrial conglomerates, for example, has been central to the push for governments to loosen labour laws and regulations for temporary work contracts and temporary foreign workers (Castles 2006; Castles, De Haas, and Miller 2014; Prebisch and Binford 2007). Service employers too – especially smaller firms in service and food industries – have regularly argued that restrictions on part-time and contractual workers limit their options for making use of flexible worktime arrangements, and their ability to shift new investments in low-skill labour-intensive service industries as well as emerging high-productivity ones (Bassanini, Nunziata, and Venn 2009; Carre et al. 2010). In turn, public officials have regularly and systematically overhauled policy to promote employer use of temporary contracts and promote worktime flexibility (OECD 1994, 2004).

Finally, critical theories attribute government efforts to create more "active" welfare states primarily to employer efforts to reduce their long-term social benefit costs, while also seeking to take advantage of workers' vulnerability because of the lack of a basic safety net (Handler 2004; Standing 2011). By limiting access to non-market sources of income, firms have been able to make the case for labour markets where workers are left with no other options but to accept poorer working conditions and fewer permanent jobs (Peck 2001; Moreira and Lodemel 2014). In winning reforms such as these, employers and their organizations have been very successful in overturning the post-war industrial relations and social policy regimes from full employment and income security, toward flexible labour markets responsive to employer demands and market pressures (Baccaro and Avdagic 2014; Crouch 2014).

In these ways, critical explanations have called attention to the way governments have routinely accommodated business concerns at the expense of the wider workforce. Whether through collective bargaining legislation, minimum wage laws, or union certification, governments have looked to reform and institutionalize change that limits the impact of collective bargaining and employment protection while lowering labour costs for business (Baccaro and Howell 2011; Glassner, Keune, and Marginson 2011; Marginson 2015). At the same time, government officials have reduced unemployment benefits and facilitated non-standard labour contracts, in order to define any job as suitable, irrespective of its terms and conditions (Handler 2004; Heyes and Lewis 2013).

Such policy reforms, it is claimed, have not only provided employers with much greater discretion in bargaining. They have also provided business with the opportunity to convert collective bargaining frameworks and individual employment contracts in ways that allowed them to lower costs, speed up production, ensure worker compliance, or avoid regulations and enforcement (Howell 2016; Kinderman 2017). It is these neoliberal political-economic dynamics that go a long way to explaining why governments have in fact implemented deregulation into their labour markets, and why in privileging economic efficiency and corporate productivity, governments have generally often done so little to correct the market-generated inequalities in income and earnings that have often resulted from such reforms.

Debt and Public Sector Restructuring

An equally important set of factors involved in rising labour market inequality has been how the policy priorities of states have changed in response to rising debt and the requirements to support the financial sector and the wealthy (Evans and McBride 2017; Streeck 2014; Schafer and Streeck 2013). Over the past two decades, many scholarly studies have stressed the resiliency of welfare states and the generally static nature of public programs and services in the face of global economic pressures (Castles 2004; Pontusson 2005; Thelen 2014). The widely accepted assumption of this literature has been that a climate of strong left political parties and unions makes governments wary of cutting popular redistribution programs (Huber and Stephens 2001; Swank 2002).

Levels of public services and redistribution, it is claimed, are likely to be determined less by the extent of need and available resources than by views of public officials and what they consider appropriate, and by how political parties look to support core business and middle-class constituencies with appropriate social policies (Beramendi and Cusack 2008; Cusack, Iversen, and Rehm 2008; Garrett 1998). Equally frequent is the claim that even where fiscal austerity measures have been introduced, unions have continued to restrain welfare state reform, either through wage-bargaining arrangements and politics, or, as in Western Europe, partnership agreements and national "social pacts" that have delivered wage restraint, flexible employment, and benefit concessions in return for job security and lower government spending and inflation (Molina and Rhodes 2008).

Critical scholarship has countered such claims by arguing that states have routinely restructured their public sectors either directly through outsourcing or more generally by modelling them along the lines of private business (Hermann and Flecker 2012; Leys 2003; Whiteside 2015). Financial globalization and debt management have often been two key drivers of these policy shifts, leading many governments to emphasize business and economic growth (Mercille and Murphy 2017; Peters 2012c). Among new right and third-way social democratic parties alike, there is now a consensus that expenditures on public services are a burden on the "productive" sectors of the economy and that tax cuts and "New Public Management" reforms are necessary for growth (Pollock and Leys 2005; Streeck 2014). Public sector reform has thus been the second major driver of labour market deregulation.

Rising deficits have driven this shift in emphasis (Genschel and Schwarz 2013), since lower taxes, unexpected increases in unemployment, and slower growth began to undermine government budgets by the mid-1990s (Streeck 2014, chap. 2). Consequently, with government debt levels rising on average from 50 per cent of GDP across major OECD countries in 1980 to 98 per cent of GDP by 2010, the response of governments has been to cut expenditures on general public services, social protection, and housing and community programs. At the same time, rating agencies that assess governments' "creditworthiness" have played an increasingly important and restrictive role in governments' fiscal policy decisions (Schwartz and Seabrooke 2008). Moreover, with greater capital mobility, financial actors, corporations, and high-income earners have moved profits and assets to lower tax jurisdictions, leading to a downward convergence of capital taxation as governments compete with each other to attract and retain industry (Genschel and Schwarz 2013). All of these developments, it is argued, have restricted the fiscal policies of North American and Western European governments, with the exception of the United States, which has a global currency whose value all governments and market actors have an interest in securing (Panitch and Gindin 2012).

Consequently, a number of critical authors have asserted that governments have now incorporated the preferences of financial actors and bond holders directly into policymaking, often at the expense of other domestic interests (Crouch 2011; Duménil and Lévy 2011; Krippner 2011; Schwartz 2009; Schafer and Streeck 2013). Over the past decade, a growing body of critical scholarship has underlined the transformation of government policymaking to meet capital's demand for greater profitability and productivity (Glyn 2006; Harvey 2006). For public services and public employment, this has meant that as debt levels have increased, government officials have chosen expenditure reductions over tax increases, as such austerity measures are seen to boost the confidence of business and increase employment in the private sector. Indeed, further tax cuts have been implemented in hopes of spurring new investment and providing economic growth to underpin government revenue (Schafer and Streeck 2013), while attempts to reduce public sector spending have sought to weaken labour's bargaining power and encourage people to work harder (Whitfield 2001; Panitch and Swartz 2003).

Indeed, what recent scholarship has most highlighted is how the new finance-oriented public sector model of management has led to the introduction of cost-reduction strategies of human resource management, based on the idea that higher labour costs increase taxes and consequently limit the funds available for business investment (Hermann 2014; Streeck 2014). And whether through balanced budget legislation, New Public Management, outsourcing, or public private partnerships, public service employment and public services have been undermined to focus less on public investment and public goods, and instead transformed to prioritize market "efficiency" and improvements to "human capital" (Hermann 2014; Whiteside 2015).

The impacts of these changes to government operation on public sector labour markets have been extensive (table 5.2). By adopting price and budget-oriented management throughout the public and public–private service sectors, governments sought to reduce labour costs through layoffs, wage freezes, and job-loading. By privatizing and marketizing services, governments gave administrators and new private owners enhanced workplace control in order to implement greater levels of employment and pay flexibility at local levels. Across the advanced industrial economies over the last twenty years, high levels of coordination – corporatist or otherwise – were no barrier to states introducing austerity and public sector restructuring in order to eliminate (or severely reduce) public sector mobilization and resistance to marketization, privatization, or "flexicurity."

States also learned from the private sector that "innovations" in systems of negotiation and bargaining were necessary to make pay and employment more flexible. Since many of the affected sectors, such as postal services, public transport, hospitals, and social services, are labour-intensive, with labour costs making up two-thirds of total production costs, states made the reduction of labour costs a core element in their strategies to improve competitiveness

Table 5.2. Public sector reform and deregulation

Public sector reform	Neoliberal labour policy model
Price and budget management	Layoffs of unionized workers
Privatization	Outsourcing
Marketization	Wage, job, and benefit concessions
New public management	Decentralization of bargaining and expanding non-standard employment

(Hermann and Flecker 2012; Whitfield 2001). Privatization, marketization, and outsourcing gave states and service employers enhanced means to enforce wage moderation. At the same time, through fragmentation, decentralization, and negotiated flexicurity arrangements, states differentiated collective agreements and shortened the coverage of public sector collective bargaining with the goal of creating flexible employment with lower wages and benefits.

"Flexible" bargaining and new corporatist arrangements have been the primary instruments for governments to restructure labour relations and weaken public sector labour power. Across North America and Western Europe, governments have routinely introduced "New Public Management" doctrines, emphasizing decentralization of public sector bargaining structures, expansion of individualized pay through bonuses and performance-related pay, and growth of temporary, part-time, and contracted employment (OECD 2008a). In addition, privatization has allowed companies to withdraw from central public sector collective agreements, and then either establish their own company agreements, or – in several cases – simply hire workers on an individual contract basis. This has created conditions where unions were unable to assist in new workplace agreements or oversee workplace developments, as many labour organizations lacked adequate staff or steward systems, while two-tiered agreements that protect remaining incumbents with good jobs have led to new hires being employed at lower wages and working conditions (Peters 2012c). The result is that in many public services across all countries a trend has been the growth in low-wage work, contracting out, and expanding flexible employment (Hellowell and Pollock 2007; Lethbridge 2005, 2008).

Such trends have put a number of post-war developments into reverse and undermined public sector bargaining powers. With the rise in part-time and temporary employment, workers have been subject to an average wage penalty of 15 per cent throughout the European Union, and over 45 per cent in other OECD countries (OECD 2006, 169). Where once governments used public services and industries alongside regulatory polices to reduce income inequality and promote job security, now public service employment is mirroring trends of private service industries, with rising levels of earnings inequality and volatility, increased part-time and temporary employment, and more low-wage work. Moreover, where in the past unions were able to improve the nature of jobs and the level of wages through collective bargaining, financial globalization and supply-side policies have pressured states to lower costs and to force through change that weakens labour power and lowers labour cost.

Varieties of Labour Market Deregulation

However, if labour market deregulation has become a more widely used public policy measure to improve competitiveness and advance business interests, a further question remains about why it has not been introduced everywhere at the same time and in the same way. Theoretically, financial ownership and the new short-term perspectives of firms to deliver greater returns to shareholders should lead firms to put greater political pressure on public officials for more flexible and lower-cost labour regulations. And the vast increase in public debt should provide public officials with the incentives to restructure public sector employment relations.

But what is clear is variety – and the facts that business has found numerous ways to force change in collective bargaining systems as well as successfully probed for new openings in unenforced rules to achieve greater flexibility (Baccaro and Howell 2017). Government collective bargaining systems and employment protection have also been transformed in ways from wholesale reform, to decentralization, to watering down (Thelen 2014). And firms and their transnational incarnations have given corporate managers like those at Ryanair in Europe the means to avoid national regulations and hire and employ workers in ways that allow them to take advantage of the employment contracts or third countries with the "lowest common denominator" in wages and employment protection (Weil 2014; Harvey and Turnbull 2015). Thus even as financialization and global firms have pressed governments for greater control in their workplaces and for lower costs, deregulation has occurred across regions, industries, and national governments with increasing variety.

To answer the question "Why varieties of deregulation?" thus requires a far richer appreciation of the politics of retrenchment and its varied paths than offered by critical political economy scholarship (Thelen 2014). Certainly in terms of wider literatures on policy retrenchment and public service reform, there is extensive academic debate about the political and institutional variables that help us account for the diversity of responses across the OECD and how policy reform has been implemented in specific areas and specific countries (Emmenegger 2014; Rehm, Hacker, and Schlesinger 2012; Baccaro and Howell 2011; Moreira and Lodemel 2014). As this research has shown, major reforms to public programs and to labour laws are still very much domestic choices, and politics and political institutions always play some role in accounting for the diversity in national responses (Hyman 2008; Thelen 2014; Wailes et al. 2016).

Consequently, to understand the complex reality of neoliberalism and policy change, this study argues that it is necessary to answer two key questions: (1) What are the strategies that governments have used to reform labour laws, and employment as well as related social policies? (2) And what changes to politics and the political power of organized interests might account for these differential repertoires?

To address these issues, I argue it is necessary to tackle the emergence of post-democracy and how financialized business – large and small – has been able to influence the state and policymaking, while organized labour and the broader public have either lost the resources to succeed in interest group politics, or have simply been marginalized out of politics because of widening inequality and distrust. It is these changes to democracy I claim that can help us make sense of why and how political advantage has shifted to favour those with wealth and power.

In making this argument, I distinguish between three different types of policy reform models as they affect labour markets and employer behaviour: active, drift, and stasis (table 5.3).

With "active" reforms, neoliberal, market-supporting governments have "rolled back" collective labour rights while also "rolling out" new market-supporting policies that have advantaged business despite widespread disapproval (Harvey 2006; Peck 2010). But with passive "drift" approaches, the most typical way public officials have sought to limit the burden of the minimum wage has been to simply fail to update it or to put off increases (Schulten 2014; Schmitt 2012). Routinely, governments look the other way or fail to enforce regulations in workplaces, providing employers with numerous "exit" options to employ workers in non-standard contracts with substandard wages outside of legal requirements (Bosch, Mayhew, and Gautié 2010; Vosko and Thomas 2014; Carre et al. 2010). Such drift may also be opened by states expanding new forms of temporary agency work or by doing little to improve the working rights of foreign workers, even as employers increasingly use them in their operations.

In contrast, a "stasis" approach is characterized by what appears to be institutional and regulatory stability, but in practice is typified by long-term erosion and gaps that fail to improve work and incomes for the majority of workers, as firms win concessions on wages, job quality, and benefits. As a result, even if there are few noticeable reforms to labour laws and regulations – and indeed there may be some surface improvements to workplace rules for a minority of skilled or public service employees – the reality is that balance of power continues to swing more favourably for employers because of their global size and increasingly financialized operations.

Table 5.3. Models of labour market deregulation and policy instruments

	Active	Drift	Stasis
Policy and Legislative Powers	Repeal of collective rights; introduction of new deregulation policy; direct legal intervention	Blocking of policy and legislative updates	Few or no changes to labour law, minimum wage, or employment regulations
Organization and Institutions	Privatization of government infrastructure and services;	Change in labour board/tribunal composition; reductions in scope	Few or no changes to labour boards
Administration and Enforcement Capacities	Removal of administrative oversight; increase of exemptions; two-tiering of policy and regulation	Reductions in funds and staff for administration and enforcement; introduction of self-enforcement	Few or no changes to enforcement

Which instruments are selected, how they will be implemented, and how widespread the reform efforts will be are a complex matter, and officials have had a wide range of policy choices and instruments with which to address labour and social costs and employment flexibility and improve the profit horizons of financialized enterprises. For example, in the United States, Republican-led state governments in Wisconsin, Michigan, and Ohio all repealed many of the collective bargaining rights of public servants, despite political protest and union mobilization (Rosenfeld 2014). In the United Kingdom, Margaret Thatcher not only dismantled the tripartite National Economic Development Council, her Conservative government also privatized public infrastructures, throwing thousands out of work, and overhauled labour legislation in the face of fierce resistance (Howell 2005). These instances of policy reform conform with the prediction that major and visible changes to labour rights and employment generated substantive opposition and popular mobilization. And this particular method of labour market deregulation has certainly generated studies of how neoliberal, market-supporting reforms have either entailed the "rollback" of collective labour rights or the roll-out of new market-supporting policies (Harvey 2006; Peck 2010).

But there is also much evidence to suggest that governments have also taken steps to freeze policies or to alter the institutional functioning of regulations and polices – a case of labour policy "drift" (Emmenegger 2014). In the case of minimum wages and countries with statutory systems, the most typical way public officials have sought to limit the cost of minimum wage has been to simply fail to update it or to put off increases (Schulten 2014; Schmitt 2012) – a situation that has been common across Canadian provinces (Battle 2011). And as employers have often mounted strong opposition to minimum wage increases, this has resulted in the minimum wage falling in real value over time.

Another passive approach to limiting wage costs has been for officials to provide numerous exemptions to collective agreements or collective agreement coverage (as in Western Europe) or to employment standards that govern hours of work, overtime, and benefits (Bosch, Mayhew, and Gautié 2010; Keune and Vandaele 2013; Law Commission of Ontario 2012). Exemptions and derogation clauses are often granted – and upheld – to small employers and sectors such as hotel and retail in order to limit wage costs in what are seen as occupations with particularly competitive conditions.

Complementing this approach is how governments have expanded their temporary labour forces through new foreign work permits or the "posting" of workers across jurisdictional boundaries, which limits the ability of unions and governments to regulate wages and working conditions. This creation of a growing non-standard labour force outside of regular employment law and institutions has produced another set of "exit" options for businesses and significantly enhanced the capacity of managers to shift work to non-standard employment contracts and unregulated subcontractors. Such indirect measures have also contributed significantly to labour market reform, and to wider inequalities in the labour market.

But this study argues that to make sense of these different patterns of deregulation – and why some public officials have introduced wholesale deregulation to labour rights institutions and enforcement, while others have made only passive changes to policy implementation, while others still have upheld labour rights and made only minor policy adjustments – requires tackling changes to democratic politics and the long-term decline of citizen influence. And to explain recent varieties of deregulation, I claim, entails a far more careful focus on organized interests, party politics, and citizen input, as well as on their key political transformations that have all contributed to the erosion of wider democratic influence and the growth in business power.

Post-Democracy and Labour Market Deregulation

Why have some governments changed course and overhauled laws and regulations, while others have adopted more passive "drift" approaches, or simply made no or few changes to labour and employment policies? As I argue in the provincial case studies of this book on British Columbia, Newfoundland and Labrador, and Ontario, many government labour-market policy responses reflect the changing interests and power of domestic actors within political systems, as well as the participation of voters and the shift in political partisanship to neoliberal policy models. Here in developing my theoretical framework below, I stress that the influence of financialization and business pressure on policymakers is strong – especially where organized labour has lost strategic capacity to influence parties and government.

But I also emphasize that the domestic policy impacts of business and finance differ substantially across countries (and across Canadian provinces) because of the varied political power of business interests and the fragmentation of organized labour and civic associations. At the same time, the capacity of other civil society organizations, as well as the political leanings of governing coalitions and citizen participation, can also influence patterns of labour law and employment policy reform. Globalization or socio-economic factors such as deindustrialization, skill-based change, or the rise of powerful service industries are not sole determinants of distributional outcomes. Instead I argue that the paths of labour market deregulation and reform in the three different Canadian provinces are based on the joint workings of these multiple and mutually reinforcing factors within post-democracy.

Coordination and Fragmentation of Business Interests

My first hypothesis is that the organizational capacity of business matters to when, why, and how labour market reforms are introduced. Despite the pressures and enhanced capacities of financialized industries, the degree to which governments have pushed or pulled labour policy in a more market-oriented direction has depended in the first instance on the political capacities of business and their corporate and political strategies. Business organizations with global connections and enormous financial resources have certainly developed new specializations in campaigns and lobbying, fundraising, and the development of policy and legal expertise. In these cases, financialization has allowed businesses as political actors to overturn previous political dynamics and push for greater flexibility and wage differentiation as well as a reduction in social costs. But assessing when, how, and why highly financialized firms as well as the smaller firms often in their supply chains coordinate their actions, I argue, is the first step required to explain differences in policy outcomes.

In making this argument, I take issue with the standard account of business interests – "varieties of capitalism" – that argues that institutional and political divergence are the norm because – in the right conditions – employers are quite willing and able to work with labour, government, and educational institutions, as long as the policies and institutions are in place that make them do so, and as long as they provide a "win-win" for business and the wider society alike (Hall and Soskice 2001). For example, in Western Europe it is common for many leading European firms to quite easily work with labour in more comprehensive forms of bargaining, and work with governments to direct innovation policies and training (Thelen 2014). In doing so, firms work with a higher unionized workforce to support better wage and working conditions, primarily as it allows them to compete in "high-quality/high-skill" product markets (Hancké, Rhodes, and Thatcher 2008).

But there are shortcomings to this explanation of how and when businesses engage in politics and why they vary. Most notably, as the work of Colin Crouch (2006, 2011, 2013) and Hacker and Pierson (2010a, 2010b, 2016) has pointed out, this framework fails to address what political actions firm do undertake and why and how financialization has boosted the capacity of business to act, as well as increased business interest in reducing labour costs. In North America, employers – across sectors – have pushed for reforms intended to erode the bargaining power of workers, while resisting changes that would improve workers' power or wages (Milkman 2013; Rosenfeld 2014). But in Europe as well, multinational corporations have also put their considerable organizational powers to work in pursuing market, tax, and social policy reforms that give them more opportunities to increase their use of outsourcing, subsidiaries, and temporary agency work. These efforts have had the common effect of undermining national bargaining structures by intensifying worker-to-worker and inter-firm competition across new market-mediated boundaries (Doellgast, Lillie, and Pulignano 2018; Greer and Doellgast 2017).

In addition, it is necessary to pay attention to the variations of business political activities across countries as well as to the differences in how firms work at the international level either on their own – such as Apple or Exxon – or as part of wider economic associations influencing public debate and government policy (Wilks 2013). Only recently have some literatures in critical political economy begun to look more systematically at how national economies and their businesses are intertwined politically (Bruff, Ebenau, and May 2015; Jessop 2013). As a first step, then, in tackling the political actions of business, a far deeper appreciation of what business and employer associations are doing and why is needed.

This appreciation requires detailing how far and how fast companies have attained reforms to collective bargaining and labour policies, and what kind of financial pressures alongside lobbying, party financing, coordination, and institutional strength has allowed them to successfully push for policy reforms and block improvements to labour regulation. Most notably in the LMEs, the institutional features that characterize the political economy – the growing size of the lobbying industry, the enormous campaign contributions, and the political power amassed by financially driven global corporations in contrast to that of national governments and nationally based unions – have had the effect of governments passing favourable corporate public policies that allow employers large and small to use cost-reduction and low-wage/low-skill strategies whenever they face any increase in international competitive pressure (Crouch 2014; Hacker and Pierson 2010a).

But in looking at these activities, it is also important to keep in mind the competitive conditions within industries and sectors, and how big firms with financial owners and small owners looking out for themselves seek to cope (Edwards 2013; Pulignano and Keune 2014). Evidence suggests that employers facing competition and serious declines in profitability have been more likely to push for policy change, while employers in industries that are growing and have healthy returns have been less inclined. Here I argue similarly that differing economic circumstances – and especially differences in financial circumstances – are crucial to determining the ways in which business coalitions have developed and operated.

A further feature for understanding post-democracy are the ways that business and government are actually intertwined, and how governments and political parties are increasingly recasting their focus onto one key priority above all: making their economies and labour forces fit for competition (Cerny 2010). Critical political economy literatures have long emphasized the "structural" power that capital has over governments (Poulantzas 1978). But if this can tell us much about the relationships that political economists should explore, such a focus often neglects the institutional setups that business and labour have created to deal with these issues. But also unnoticed is how over the past few decades these political-economic relationships and institutions have changed.

Now with the wider resort to neoliberalism, governments rely increasingly on corporations to achieve several policy goals, and policy focuses more tightly on maximizing the freedom and profitability of firms. But such developments still vary. Business has not "captured" governments all in the same way (Crouch 2015; Hopkin and Lynch 2016). Nor are firms across countries similarly in charge of major policies and infrastructures. The challenge then is not simply to note business influence on governments, but rather to detail how business and governments are integrated.

So another key component for understanding firm political involvement is how business develops its political alliances and uses new or current business organizations to seek labour market reform inside government. Only in specific contexts have businesses stepped up their political activism by funding and collaborating with centre-right parties and right-wing policy formation networks (Wilks 2013). Business organizations also varied in how they developed new specializations in campaigns and lobbying, fundraising, and the development of policy and legal expertise (Moran 2009). In these cases, where business has created the political resources to influence government officials, it can overturn previous political dynamics to push for greater flexibility and wage differentiation as well as reduction in social costs. But without such political mobilization, business will continue to work with labour institutions, or because of differences across sectors, firms will fail to develop a unified approach to labour market reform.

To account for these variations in business involvement in politics, my counterargument adds two key stipulations to critical accounts. My first hypothesis is that financialized multinationals have pushed for wider deregulation only when they were under conditions of intense product market competition, and generally the greater the number of business sectors facing economic difficulties, the more likely firms have been to work successfully together to push for reforms. In those situations where firms have pressed for changes to address market competition, governments have been far more likely to deregulate collective bargaining and employment protection with the expectation of increased investment and job creation.

Moreover, I argue, firms and business interests have succeeded only when they have developed a new range of organizational and political capacities to influence government policymakers – above all new political powers of coordination and active political coalitions of influence. Only in those countries (or those political regions like provinces in Canada that have primary legislative authority) where business interests were able to move public officials through lobbying, political ties, and business integration in the policy process did governments extend deregulation and weaken and erode employment-protection systems. In contrast, if employers could use international production chains to lower costs, remained in traditional institutions, or kept to traditional pluralist frameworks of interest group politics, then patterns of liberalization and deregulation were far slower to develop – situations that I characterize as "drift" or "stasis."

Organized Labour

The second factor influencing the development of post-democracy and labour market deregulation is the strength – or faltering role – of organized labour. In looking across countries, the power of organized labour is critical to the extent and scope of deregulation (Baccaro and Howell 2017).

However, as critical scholars have demonstrated, financialization and the globalization of production have led to a notable deterioration in the power resources and redistributive capacities of trade unions (Moody 2007; Standing 2011). In many countries, unions have not only lost thousands if not millions of members, but their decline has also meant the loss of progressive voters and the necessary political supporters of parties and candidates that could advocate on behalf of organized labour (Knutsen 2006; Moschonas 2002). Equally problematic has been the declining capacities of unions to reach out to civic organizations, which has left more communities without the community bodies that used to allow working- and middle-class workers to be deeply involved in their neighbourhoods and in local affairs (Rosenfeld 2014; Skocpol 2003).

Then there have been the organizational dilemmas that unions themselves have faced in retaining support from members and building solidarity among their members in the face of such declines. In the post-war era, unions used militancy and political mobilization to build support and solidarity with their members. But facing global corporations, unions have often backed away from militancy, fearing that strikes would further undercut public support or that wage gains would only undercut corporate profits and the long-term viability of the company. At the same time in the public sector, to ensure this defensive strategy, union leadership has reined in militancy and public campaigns over the past two decades, fearing further austerity measures and job loss (Piazza 2002; Scheur 2007; Upchurch, Taylor, and Mathers 2009). The results have been that many unions have lost legitimacy in the eyes of their own members, and this unravelling of internal solidarity has contributed to the foundering of labour movements and the inability of unions to work together and challenge governments to respond to their needs (Hacker and Pierson 2010a; Rosenfeld 2014; Upchurch, Taylor, and Mathers 2009).

To make matters more difficult, financialization has also led to many conflicting interests for workers – organized and not. For example, while workers have been able to access housing finance and consumers debt with increasing ease, many have turned to debt financing in order to make up for declining wages and incomes (Baker 2009; Crouch 2009). But increasing mortgage debt has made households more vulnerable, as job loss or industrial actions that threaten employers may lead to the loss of income and the inability to service debt. Higher indebtedness and mortgage debt may thus lower workers' propensity to take job actions, as many workers are only a pay check away from missing a mortgage payment (Kohler, Guschanski, and Stockhammer 2019; Wood 2017).

Workers' pensions and pension funds have also turned into double-edged swords. Workers initially won pensions to help cover inadequate public pension plans. But over the past few decades, as funds have been poured into a growing variety of plans, insurance and wealth management companies have used these monies to fuel financial markets and in turn corporate restructuring and layoffs (Blackburn 2011). This too has limited the ability of unions to take more militant stances in their negotiations with employers or in pushing governments to reign in their financial sectors for fear of pension losses on markets (Skerrett et al. 2018).

However, a more micro-perspective on union renewal and political revitalization suggests that despite these many challenges, organized labour is not without resources, nor are all union movements in a situation as dire as those in the United States (Frege and Kelly 2004; Hamann and Kelly 2010; Gumbrell-McCormick and Hyman 2013). Unions may indeed have lost members, political allies in government, and their special relationships with social democratic parties. But unions have continued to work to influence officials and policy in innovative ways, from lobbying to litigating (Tattersall 2010; Ross et al. 2015). Research has also shown that unions are still effective in making public officials enforce laws and regulations through new organizing, new union mergers that give labour officials more say in bargaining systems, and new transitional union partnerships that allow unions to counter pressures on their bargaining systems from employers by making solidaristic demands across borders (Ibsen and Thelen 2017).

Recent labour scholarship on union renewal has also foregrounded unions' innovative approaches to expand membership, develop community support, and educate and mobilize citizens about the impacts of corporate globalization (McAlevey 2015; Milkman 2013; Milkman and Voss 2004). This work has called attention to the ways many unions have shifted their range of activities toward more grassroots mobilization and solidarity actions with community groups in the effort to build wider solidarities (Ross and Savage 2012; Ross 2013; Luce 2014; Milkman and Voss 2004) to influence public officials on issues from the environment to community development (McAdam and Shaffer Boudet 2012). Unions have also adopted more aggressive organizing models, hiring staff to research and carry out new organizing while working with community members to build support for unions (Bronfenbrenner et al. 1998; Juravich 2007).

Finally, despite considerable difficulty, labour movements and citizens have sought out new ways to build solidarities that counter inequality and neoliberal reforms (Gumbrell-McCormick and Hyman 2013). Many have been of a traditional kind, with unions supporting citizens and immigrants in their efforts to raise the minimum wage or gain collective bargaining rights (Adler, Tapia, and Turner 2014). But there have also been recent efforts to support wider policy reforms for immigration, childcare, and income transfers that have joined unions, citizens, and immigrants in a movement to secure wider gains in public policy and to push politics in a more positive direction (Grimshaw et al. 2018). Living-wage campaigns, for example, as well as Fairbnb for affordable housing have sought to make the case that citizen interests are united behind progressive egalitarian policies and they to have pressed governments to reform (Wells 2016). Thus organized social mobilization has affected wider public debates and shifted some of the political terrain for unions, opening up new coalitions between unionized and non-union workers that challenge more general trends toward convergence on more post-democratic lines.

All such observations about union renewal and revitalization are at odds with power resource theories that emphasize declining memberships and fraying ties between organized labour and their political allies as evidence of declining union political resources and strength. Rather, evidence suggests unions have used unconventional repertoires of social mobilization to sway policymaking, and unions are increasingly adopting more aggressive social strategizing in their attempts to resist employer and government pressure (Murray and Cuillerier 2009; Levesque and Murray 2010).

But if critical literatures have suggested some of the reasons that we might expect some labour movements to better counter government and business efforts at deregulation, there is still no systematic analysis of when and how organized labour movements have succeeded. Scholars have looked at *how* some unions – and in particular how some union locals or branches – have "revitalized." But they have not considered why unions and labour movements have been able to take up new challenges in globalization and deregulation and instead build solidarity that draws all unions together around common objectives and modes of political action.

Here in engaging with these recent debates, my argument suggests that it is necessary to tackle the broader question of how unions and wider labour movements have mobilized the grassroots and initiated new kinds of political unionism and mobilization to boost membership and build solidarity between unions but also with other non-unionized workers. Most important is how unions actually suppress competition and their conflicting interests, and whether or not they can build alliances and institutions that represent the broader interests of unions and workers as a whole. Thus to understand when and where unions can retain economic and political influence, my second hypothesis is that unions have done somewhat better where they have continued to organize and advocate for a broad range of workers through political and social mobilization strategies, and where they could overcome their political differences to maintain the basic coordination of political resources and political strategies – a situation of institutional solidarity supporting political resources and challenges to political authority.

In the best of situations, where unions have kept their political and bargaining differences to a minimum and continued to integrate diverse and marginalized workers, I argue this has contributed to a trend of "stasis" and minimal change to bargaining and policymaking. Unions and labour movements in this situation are able to maintain solidarity, cross-union networks, and coordinated political efforts that challenge authority and seek to transform business practices and proposed deregulatory reforms. But where unions have faced a decline in organizing capacity and been riven by political differences that have limited their ability to undertake wider social and political mobilization and challenge employers and political authority, governments have been able to take advantage of such weaknesses to enact further policies and reforms to limit wages, make employment less secure, and facilitate the erosion of income support programs – an outcome that I characterize as "reform": the fundamental transformation of labour institutions and regulations.

Political Parties

Regarding the specific features of political parties, in contrast to classic median voter and national political dynamic models that have assumed little change in party operation, my post-democracy framework draws attention to how parties have sought to capitalize on the financialization of the economy and the labour market by devising policies that appeal to "insiders" and the wealthy few and by articulating new grounds for political allegiance based on race, religion, and morality for a select minority within the electorate (Hacker, Mettler, and Pinderhughes 2007; Soss and Jacobs 2009). Critical research has demonstrated how political parties today require substantial funds to conduct election campaigns, and party officials have responded by building up large budgets, permanent fundraising organizations, and central committees to oversee the recruiting and financing of candidates (Herrnson 2008). Consultants and party fundraising organizations are now at the core of party operations, where previously they were secondary.

As this literature has shown, the result is rather far from the common view of parties judiciously weighing the costs and benefits of education versus income security (Beramendi et al. 2015). Rather, political parties today increasingly seek to accommodate the interests of big business and the wealthy through tax cuts, trade liberalization, and financial deregulation in order to boost party fortunes (Hacker and Pierson 2005; Skocpol and Williamson 2012). Such dependency has reinforced political inequality, as the more parties target shareholder and financially driven donors for resources, expertise, and support, the more business and high-income groups enhance their influence over those parties.

In addition, critical literature has challenged general comparative assumptions that parties routinely seek to appeal to all voters (or, for that matter, a majority of citizens) by arguing that political leaders and powerful economic interests within parties have remade networks of supportive interests, established new patterns of institutional control, and built up large intellectual and policy advantages in public discourse, all in order to achieve electoral victory and lasting shifts in the political battleground (Hacker 2006; Teles 2009; Harvey 2006). Over the past generation, these internal sources of party influence have led to campaign politics taking on a high-tech nature, driven by advertising and polling (Crouch 2006) – again leading to an increasing reliance on private funding and private expertise.

Consequently, with the financialization of the economy, and the growing resources of business to influence politics nationally and internationally, contemporary political parties are more likely to advance neoliberal policy models in their efforts to build political coalitions that support the interests of upper-income earners in market-oriented public policy than ever before. And as reforms are structured to advance only a minority of interests, the negative impacts on "outsiders" mean that workers, women, immigrants, and young voters are systematically excluded. The result is a polarization of society, with policies crafted to treat different groups of citizens in highly unequal ways, insulating some portions of the workforce from growing inequality, while exposing others to new or greater risks – often on grounds of race and religion (Hacker 2006; Hacker, Mettler, and Pinderhughes 2007).

Thus my third hypothesis is that parties will adopt more pro-market labour and employment policies that maximize growth at the expense of equality when they are heavily reliant on business finance, when business people are directly involved in government, and when private firms are integrated into policymaking through privatization, subcontracting, or governance activities. In contrast, where parties are less reliant on direct business contributions, and firms and finance do not have an insider's role in government, parties will continue to develop policies that favour employment income security to appeal to a wider electorate – or at least parts of a wider electorate.

And this may be most true in the public sector, where officials can use public debt as a way to "buy time" or avoid fundamental problems in political economy. Wolfgang Streeck (2014) has argued that states have used rising deficits to put off unpopular policy reforms, even as they have enacted tax cuts for business and the wealthy, but still maintained public programs that have broad public support. This seemingly contradictory policy response, he claims, is due to governments using debt to cover the gap between revenues and expenditure, primarily to maintain social peace and retain public services.

Political Coalitions, Inequality, and Deregulation

Finally, this book explores the impacts of financialization and neoliberal public policy on the quality of democratic life, most notably on voter turnout and citizen participation, and how it has influenced the long-term decisions of political parties and government officials. My fourth hypothesis is that where high levels of civic affiliation and association continue to work and are often tied to organized labour, parties will be less likely to move in a post-democratic direction and more likely to take into account the interests of low- and medium-income citizens. Indeed, I argue that the resource and interpretive capacities offered by civic organizations as well as networks associated with labour organizations are likely to be instrumental in enhancing civic skills and fostering greater citizen interest in politics (Kelly 1998). Consequently, greater levels of civic association are likely to prompt political parties to lend access to such groups and to mobilize them politically (McAdam and Shaffer Boudet 2012).

In making this argument, I draw on research that argues that tax cuts, privatization, and means-tested programs, as well as the reform and undermining of collective bargaining, have all been critical to deepening income inequality (Bonica et al. 2013). Such policies, it is argued, are not simple "one-off" events, as is often assumed in conventional literatures. Rather, the passing of inegalitarian policies has reshaped political power and participation, inducing attitude and behavioural changes that have decreased citizen engagement and produced persistent and growing biases in political voice. The declining effectiveness or coverage of social programs has had negative implications for the values of citizens, including eroding civic involvement and general altruism, as well as wearing away at trust in democracy and democratic government (Hacker 2006).

At the same time, financialization and the market-making policies that have supported it have not only increased income inequality and deepened low-wage employment, but they have also widened the bias in political voice. With growing atypical employment, unemployment, and underemployment increasing economic precariousness, workers lack the time and security to participate in politics. Consequently, citizens in low-income and precarious employment have less connection to the political system, or even more negative attitudes toward government (Standing 2011). In addition, such financialization and its role in "fissuring" employment can exacerbate racial inequality, pitting one group of workers against another, and engendering greater mistrust and solidarity (Weil 2014). In these ways, I argue finanancialization can drive growing divides and distrust within the political system.

As a result, whereas citizens used to have great confidence that government was responsive to their demands, with the declining effectiveness of public policies to lower inequality or offset the growing instability of earnings, citizens have become far more cynical about politics and less attentive to policies (Pickett and Wilkinson 2010). Polices that have only benefitted finance and multinationals are leading to citizens losing trust in government and withdrawing from politics (Crouch 2013). As a wealthy few have reaped huge advantages from financialization, less advantaged citizens are now participating considerably less than they did in the post-war era, and, among lower-income voters, rates of voter turnout have fallen dramatically.

The results are that under these new conditions of declining turnout and declining support for redistribution, parties have changed their electoral and governing strategies – often dramatically – and citizens have seen many of their countervailing powers to influence public policy slowly erode (Mair 2013). Most importantly, as money from big corporations and finance has become more important to politics, and income a greater predictor of participation, parties have increasingly come to rely on mobilizing higher-income voters and well-organized business interests – a process that Crouch (2006) has characterized as highly indicative of post-democracy.

Elections and campaigns continue – but, he argues, where most citizens had been active and engaged, now parties and politicians use market research and opinion polls to shape their political image and subsequently turn to affluent donors and well-organized interests to finance spiralling campaign costs (Jacobs and Skocpol 2005; Page and Jacobs 2009), while developing single-issue policy ideas to draw in select groups of voters (Hacker and Pierson 2005). In contrast, the clout of ordinary voters, especially those who have been on the losing end of globalization and low employment, has fallen. Overall, these widespread changes to party operation are contributing to "post-democracy" and "winner-take-all" divides.

But we should also expect that post-democratic parties will resort to appeals and policies to mobilize support and retain legitimacy. Simply on their own, neoliberal policy models stressing the benefits of big business and even bigger finance are unlikely to draw much support (Blyth 2013; Crouch 2013, 2015). In the United States, scholars have emphasized the importance of race and re-ligion for neoliberal political mobilization, neither of which is incompatible with a post-democratic politics offering ways to restructure the state as well as broader private "choice" for individuals (Skocpol and Williamson 2012). And more secular neoliberal parties often appeal to nationalism and to consumerism more generally in their efforts to convince their share of the electorate (Leys 2003). More recently, scholars have also emphasized the importance of policies that support home ownership, providing individuals the opportunity to build wealth in rising property markets, while also securing housing and community participation (McCabe 2016; Fernandez 2016). These too have provided pow-erful ways for business-oriented political parties to broaden their support.

Given these possible political pathways to electoral success, we should expect that the political-coalitional underpinnings of post-democracy should vary across countries (or in Canada, across provinces) – even among the An-glo-American countries that are the most inequitable and have the highest levels of voter abstention (Bermeo and Pontusson 2012; Thelen 2014). For while voter participation has declined, the voting preferences of high-income individuals have continued to differ, as have the support of a variety of busi-ness interests. And citizen identities, race, and immigration have continued to influence winning party strategies, while unions and citizen groups have come together in new ways to force more progressive issues on to political agen-das. This suggests that the efforts of citizen and labour unions still matter to how parties seek coalitions among elites, high-income earners, and more mid-dle-class families, and such citizen efforts may counter government attempts to build support for their neoliberal policy strategies.

Political Variations in Post-Democracy and Deregulation

Much critical work on neoliberalism assumes that financialization, business pressure, and policy reforms create similarly flexible and individualized labour markets across capitalist countries. My analysis also emphasizes similar out-comes of deregulation, such as the undermining of collective bargaining and growing non-standard employment and low-wage work. However, thinking about financialization and deregulation as generally homogeneous overlooks significant differences in their development and implementation.

In this study, I analyse wider political-economic changes associated with financialization and the impacts of post-democracy on different models of labour market regulation. Because a wide number of shifts have advantaged business in the political process and marginalized citizens, governments have been far more open to the appeals of a "selfish" capitalism focused on increasing the rents of top firms and the financial sector. And this has resulted in the creation of more "flexible" or cheaper labour, with policy reforms opening the door to the growth of non-standard employment relationships, while limiting the power of unions to negotiate wages or improve workplace rights.

But as I argue, the development of financialization has occurred in many realms and in different ways across economic sectors. At the same time, depending on the politics of local organized business and labour interests, and the changing calculations of parties and voters, labour market deregulation and the choice of policy "model" has looked quite different across provinces, as well as across countries. The interplay of these local variables, I claim, has shaped the choice of deregulation pursued and the distributive consequences of labour market change (table 5.4).

If my argument is correct, the associations between financialization, corporate globalization, and labour market deregulation should be strongest in jurisdictions featuring coordinated business coalitions and post-democratic politics. Specifically, in countries or regions where the decline of traditional industries and increased competitive pressures have sparked fierce conflict, firms can be expected to join to press for lower labour costs and seek to roll back union bargaining rights altogether, as well as press for deregulation of employment regulations. Weak and fragmented unions in such contexts can be expected to lack the capacities and resources to respond effectively. Such policy shifts toward deregulation should lead to the widespread "reform" of bargaining, employment regulations, and related social policies. This should result in the individualization of employment relations, reduction of wages, and retrenchment of employment-related social policies. Long-term socio-economic outcomes include growth in low-wage jobs and income inequality.

However, given that political choice and state direction are critical in economic strategies to develop financialization and neoliberalism, we should also expect to see varied policy responses. From the perspective of organized business interests, where economies have experienced a decline in traditional sectors and growth in new financialized sectors like information technology, high-tech manufacturing, and private services, the fragmentation of policy demands from businesses and firms remaining in traditional-sector associations should lead to little direct reform of traditional bargaining frameworks. Moreover, if unions can negotiate layoffs and restructuring, and protect some good jobs while lowering long-term labour costs, firms will likely seek to retain bargaining systems. Thus, unlike the wholesale "active reform" policy

Table 5.4. Variations in post-democracy and deregulation

	Reform	Drift	Stasis
Business Coalitions and Economic Pressures	High pressures and Organized	Uneven pressures and Fragmented assoc'ns	Strong growth and sectoral associations
Organized Labour	Weak and Fragmented	Fragmented with some political resources	Coordinated with political and institutional strength
Party Electoral Strategies	Focus on upper income earners and single issue activists	Focus on upper income earners and broader interests	Focus on 'broad tent' appeal of policies
Voter Participation	Low and Falling	Falling in many ridings; stable in others	Stable

models of neoliberalism, in a policy model of "drift," officials do not look to overhaul collective bargaining or reform certification and strike laws in order to limit union influence and enhance flexibility, but rather do little, or will block implementation of policy alternatives – a situation of "drift."

We should also anticipate that a final policy variation is possible: "stasis" and the renewal or extension of bargaining frameworks alongside traditional efforts to mitigate inequality through social policy and education. With stasis, successful and growing financialized industries could be expected to maintain and renew cooperation with organized labour, while unions could be anticipated to seek gains in bargaining through new organizing or training. Likewise, lowering inequality and stable voter participation should enhance the representation and political capacities of low- and middle-income citizens alike – as in Western Europe. where lower income inequality, higher union density, and corporatist interest representation still underpin higher political engagement and support for redistribution (Hemerijck 2012). Theoretically, in this context, parties are expected to respond by maintaining broader brokerage strategies, and pursue growth policies that enhance employment and lower inequality, most typically through the expansion of social programs and services.

The policy results of stasis should be the upholding of labour law and stable union density, little or no deregulation of employment standards, and minimal enhancement of social policies to lower poverty and provide more educational opportunity. But despite this policy approach that continues to provide a modicum of redistribution, given the power of business, we should expect that governments would do little if anything to counteract wider income inequality, especially top income inequality, or to tackle wider underemployment and the more pervasive problem of low-wage work.

Conclusion

My argument about labour market deregulation stresses how democracy has changed, with many formal political institutions continuing to function, but with unions and citizens witnessing the decline of many of their countervailing sources of power, and corporations and financial institutions benefitting as the major active participants and shapers of policy. But we should also expect to see variation in the deregulation of labour and employment policy across democracies and polities. How and in what ways labour market inequality and low-wage work have grown, I argue, is due to the multidimensional political dynamics of post-democracy on labour law and employment policy.

Governments have created more "flexible" or cheaper labour, all in the effort to remake the standard employment relationship to the benefit of business. But depending on the politics of business and labour and the changing calculations of parties and voters, officials have implemented labour market deregulation through different models across countries (as well as across provinces, as in Canada). The interplay of these political variables, I argue, is critical in shaping the choice of public policies pursued and the distributive consequences of labour market change, especially for those in low-wage work and the growing numbers in non-standard employment.

In chapters 6 through 8, I explore statistical indicators, qualitative information, and secondary literatures to evaluate the role of post-democratic politics in labour law and labour policy change in British Columbia, Ontario, and Newfoundland and Labrador. In the following provincial case studies, I examine how labour market institutions across Canada – including collective bargaining, minimum wage laws, and employment standards – have been changed, left to stagnate, or simply avoided altogether. My post-democracy theory suggests reasons for government variation in their regulatory approach to unions and labour markets. The goal, then, is to determine whether the politics of "post-democracy" has been critical to labour market deregulation, and whether such processes can help us provide a second major part of the story for rising labour market inequality in Canada.

6 British Columbia: Neoliberal Reform and Deregulation

Between 1990 and 2010, British Columbia experienced one of the most rapid rises of income inequality among Canadian provinces. While nearly two-thirds of households saw their median earnings decline (1990–2008), the top 10 per cent of earners saw after-tax income grow by 40 per cent to $159,000 in 2008. For the top 1 per cent of earners, the upswing was even more pronounced: from 2000 to 2008, the top 1 per cent of individual income earners saw their average incomes rise from $289,000 to $392,000. In stark contrast, over the same time period, the number of workers in low-wage work rose to more than 1.2 million. Unsurprisingly, British Columbia also experienced a rapid rise in overall market income inequality – an increase that surpassed even that of the rapidly soaring Canadian average.

This chapter argues that a key reason for the rapid rise in income and earnings inequality in British Columbia was the wholesale shift in economic and policy models – from a more regulated capitalism to a deregulated capitalism based on flexible labour markets and widespread interaction between government and business – a model best characterized as neoliberal "reform." In the 1970s and 1980s, British Columbia's economic policy was still largely centred on fostering the resource sector and related manufacturing exports through generous tax concessions and extensive infrastructure development. This policy orientation depended on the government maintaining an arm's-length relationship with private firms, while modestly regulating business and labour relations through the expansion of collective bargaining and arbitration procedures to ensure productivity and wage growth, as well as ensuring support for property developers and small service enterprises (Allen 1986).

But in the first decade of 2000, after a decade of recession, deindustrialization, and NDP attempts to deal with growing deficits, government policies under the Gordon Campbell Liberals sought to gain from the liberation of financial forces and free markets, and looked to exploit the development of new global export markets, primarily in California, China, and South-East Asia. In the effort to move government closer to market-oriented forms of behaviour and increase business profitability, the Liberal government enacted a combination of supply-side and deregulation policies – including the widespread reform and deregulation of labour and employment policies. These measures were intended to boost the real estate and natural gas industries, while providing a low-cost labour force for Vancouver's tourism enterprises, then gearing up for the 2010 Winter Olympics. Government efforts were also focused on boosting residential housing and commercial building markets and new measures to draw foreign direct investment into natural resources and transport expansion. But to further these new economic goals, government fully supported business demands for a flexible labour market – including legislative and administrative reforms that lowered labour costs – most notably in the key domestic sectors of construction and private services, but in agriculture and the public sector as well, before and after the financial crisis.

As this chapter argues, political parties' new reliance on affluent voters and the growing organizational power of business interests were keys to this shift in economic models. Most important to collective bargaining and labour policy reforms was the emergence of strong business mobilization against unions and accompanying calls for labour market deregulation. Equally important to the transformed political landscape was organized labour's loss of membership and resources that undermined their capacity to respond effectively.

But also critical to the remaking of the political landscape in the province was partisan polarization and liberal efforts to recast their basis of political support towards the economically privileged, highly educated, and upper-middle-class earners. Finally, the chapter argues that the long-run effects of inequality on politics and especially on voter turnout among low-income and middle-class interests were critical to this trend towards post-democracy as the Liberal Party became highly responsive to the preferences of business and the affluent and little concerned with the preferences of middle-class voters and the poor. The argument is made that the combined impacts of these crucial political variables explain the policy shifts in government to wholesale "reform" and labour market deregulation.

Construction, Services, and the Rise of Non-standard Employment in BC

As in many rich world democracies, labour market segmentation and the rise of low-paid work in British Columbia were driven by two critical processes: deindustrialization and corporate restructuring (which accompanied financialization and economic globalization), and the expansion of non-union, non-standard employment (Gautie and Schmitt 2010). However, governments differed in the extent to which they sought to protect wage equality and enhance labour market participation. In Canada, as in other liberal market economies, increases in product market competition led many firms with low margins and limited investment solutions to seek productivity gains through increased work intensification, layoffs, and expanded non-standard employment contracts – and governments did little to offset these developments (Amable 2003; Marx and Eichhorst 2012). In the wake of implementation of the Canada-US Free Trade Agreement in the early 1990s, heightened international competition in BC led to resource, construction, and small manufacturing firms pushing for concessions from unionized workers. These firms were instrumental in driving policy change in the province.

The impacts of trade liberalization can be seen clearly in BC's manufacturing and resource industries, both of which underwent wrenching changes in the 1990s and early in the first decade of 2000 (Young and Matthews 2007; Sweeney 2010; Hayter 2000). In metal processing and metal manufacturing, expanding trade and investment competition were met with the merger of Teck and Cominco and the amalgamation of their operations in BC, as well as by other firms closing their smelters and processing plants along the West Coast (Wallace 1996; Barnes and Hayter 1992). With a more integrated North American market, small manufacturers of metal products were pressed by large retailers to lower costs as major multinational retailers and distributors began to source products from China and South-East Asia (BC retired union official 2, private sector; Hayter 2003; Hayter and Barnes 1992). Many small and medium-sized enterprises closed. Others merged with US operations, expecting gains from partnership arrangements, but instead were quickly centralized in the Western and Southern United States in non-union operations. US firms, in particular, were interested in efficiency and major productivity gains from downsizing and new technology (Sweeney 2010).

In forestry, BC's export-oriented logging, pulp and paper, and solid wood-processing industries all shed thousands of jobs in the wake of NAFTA and the Softwood Lumber Agreement (1996). Under global market pressures and financial pressures from US firms and new equity groups, firms were rapidly bought, sold, closed, and reintegrated in the attempts to maximize profits from US markets and lower labour and long-term pension costs (Hayter 2003; Sweeney 2010). With pension trusts and asset management groups seeking new opportunities stemming from government tax breaks and employment programs in the BC forest industry, new investors – many US based – took over firms, subsequently increasing new machinery investments and laying off or retiring older workers, while demanding concessions from unions to increase productivity, end seniority clauses, and contract out "non-essential" work (Hayter 2000). In the United States and globally, these processes were pushed even further by financial investors establishing new financial institutions for investment (timberland investment management organizations and real estate investment trusts) that by the middle of the first decade of 2000 bought up over half of all private industrial timberland (Gunnoe 2014). With this consolidation of financial control, timber firms moved quickly to focus on increasing the market value of their production in order to reward institutional investors.

Wood processing – the most capital intensive of the forestry industries – experienced the most dramatic losses of employment with the closure of mills and the centralization of production in the BC interior. Seeking to cut costs to accommodate American-led mergers and acquisitions, newly financialized ownership sought to reduce the costs of unionized forestry workers by downsizing and engaging in far more contentious collective bargaining. American-led firms led the break away from centralized sectoral bargaining in the late 1990s, in the attempt to lower labour and benefit costs to American levels. And by early in the first decade of 2000, forestry firms were also interested in labour reform, seeking longer work schedules, more outputs, and more flexibility through layoffs and unpaid short-term shutdowns (Sweeney 2010; Hayter 2000).

In fisheries, the impact of trade agreements was much less direct, though trade liberalization and the extension of national fisheries jurisdictions around the world, alongside the industrialization of fisheries vessels and services, with government programs to reduce capacity in the wake of global over-fishing, did lead to the rapid amalgamation of global fish operations and wholesaling markets (Deer 2000). In BC, the competition among national industrial fishing enterprises for global markets set off a dramatic decline of salmon and herring fisheries, and the mass sell-off of fleets as well as shutdowns of processing plants and canneries (Deer 2000; Egan 2001). The loss of fish stocks and the growing international trade in fish products also affected fisheries employment, as major fish-processing plants on the Lower Mainland and North Coast closed in the wake of massive conglomeration and consolidation across the industry. The growth of aquaculture and shellfish harvesting did partially compensate with jobs in new sectors. But as operators exported nearly 95 per cent of all seafood production in unprocessed, flash-frozen forms, former wage and job gains from processing were lost as the industry internationalized (Egan 2001). In the 1980s and 1990s, such processes had dramatic impacts on coastal communities, with mounting job losses and the decline of licences.

At the same time, driven by British Columbia's financialized housing bubble and construction boom, BC's labour market changed markedly in the first decade of 2000. Job growth in these non-unionized and low-wage sectors was extensive and had substantial impacts on the labour market. As in the rest of Canada, the United States, and Great Britain, the general context of housing-led consumer growth was set by the expansion of liquidity to highly securitized mortgage markets alongside low interest rates (Hay 2009; Schwartz and Seabrooke 2008). In Canada, the deregulation of domestic credit markets and the creation of the Canada Housing Trust in 2001 led to the rapid securitization of mortgages that stoked Vancouver's housing market – Canada's most expensive (Clarke et al. 2010). Backed by the federal securitization of mortgages and mortgage-backed securities, banks and mortgage lenders massively expanded their lending, fuelling a housing bubble and growing loan-to-value ratios (Walks and Clifford 2015).

With an increased supply of mortgage lending available to housing-market developers, resellers, and new entrants – including many of the wealthiest homebuyers from China – housing starts and housing prices rose rapidly in the first decade of 2000 as the expansion of domestic credit led to rapidly rising asset prices. In the course of seven years from 2000 to 2007, housing starts in BC nearly tripled from 14,418 to more than 39,000. Over the same time period, the average house price sold on the multiple listing service doubled from $300,000 to more than $625,000 (2000–7), and prime industrial land in Vancouver nearly doubled in price to $2.5 million per acre in Vancouver (RBC Economics 2012; Cushman and Wakefield Lepage 2007). The real estate boom was one of the first drivers of segmented employment growth in the first decade of 2000, as many construction firms established "double-breasted" operations, expanding their non-union establishments to hire lower-cost labour and bid for new contracts.

The third driver of new, segmented labour market growth was the Olympics, which in its preparation led to the construction of new facilities and infrastructure, much of it by contractors with low margins who readily used non-unionized and temporary foreign workers. An estimated $6 billion in provincial and federal spending on new highways, venues, and public transit spurred urban development and the construction industry (PWC 2010). Through its "Commerce Centre" program, the BC government sought to ensure that BC companies would benefit from procurement and that they would increase their hiring. The BC government also endeavoured to boost the province's export and tourism industries through the exposure provided by the games. In these ways, the province's debt-financed consumer-led growth dynamic was to be complemented with new infrastructure that facilitated future housing and commercial construction. Combined, this created a context of labour in-migration to meet the province's business needs, as firms attempted to deal with rising prices and skilled labour shortages through the expanded use of temporary foreign worker programs and by hiring more non-unionized labour.

The fourth dynamic underlying the province's growth model was the expansion of the natural gas and coal industries – the vast majority led by American firms that were highly financialized and the vast majority creating new, non-union workplaces. To spur growth and meet growing demand from California and China, the federal and provincial governments enacted policies to support resource extraction (Carter, Fraser, and Zalik 2017). BC officials cut corporate taxes and royalty rates for natural resource companies and enacted new investment incentives that allowed companies to write off 100 per cent of exploration and pre-production costs, as well as a further 33 per cent for new capital costs annually (Lee 2014). The Campbell government then introduced tax credits for the oil and gas and mining sectors to encourage further rapid resource exploitation (Marshall and Newnham 2004). These tax reforms were then supplemented by the federal government, allowing all mining companies to deduct 100 per cent of provincial mining taxes and royalties from federal taxes (PWC 2011, 2012).

At the same time, the introduction of a new Commodity Futures Modernization Act in the United States in 2000 created a financialized commodity market open to investments from investment banks, mutual funds, and insurance companies (Gkanoutas-Leventis and Nesvetailova 2015). As a result, many of the largest investment banks entered directly into the oil and gas markets, as did other large US hedge funds (Labban 2010). This encouraged major new investments in oil and gas markets, with financial investors anticipating major price increases (Lee and Ellis 2013). It was in this context that American-led firms operating in BC massively expanded their investments and increased their exports of coal to China and natural gas to California (Lee 2014). What followed was the growth of non-unionized firms in major resources sectors, which hired more skilled and unskilled construction workers into non-unionized and often underpaid employment.

As figure 6.1 shows, outlining total inputs into key sectors of construction, mining, oil, and gas, all grew rapidly in the first decade of 2000, with annual increases of more than 26 per cent, well above the Canadian averages for growth in these sectors. Combined with the regular growth of the FIRE sector, the three sectors accounted for more than $68 billion of new activity and 65 per cent of all economic growth in BC from 2000 to 2008. Their impact on employment was just as strong. Figure 6.2 demonstrates that more than 177,000 of the 336,000 new jobs in the province were construction and FIRE related. However, in the capital-intensive gas and mining industries, while profits for owners increased exponentially, only a limited number of new unionized jobs were created, and they did not offset the heavier losses of unionized jobs in manufacturing, forestry, and the pulp and paper industries.

Most notable in this rise of jobs in construction, housing, and FIRE industries was how closely associated it was with the development of non-unionized, non-standard employment, both directly and indirectly. Even though none of these sectors were immediately affected by global competition, employers sought to use non-standard employment vehicles such as part-time jobs, temporary agency work, and self-employment to lower labour costs. Employers in the construction and FIRE sectors increased part-time and temporary work as proportions of their labour force. In construction,

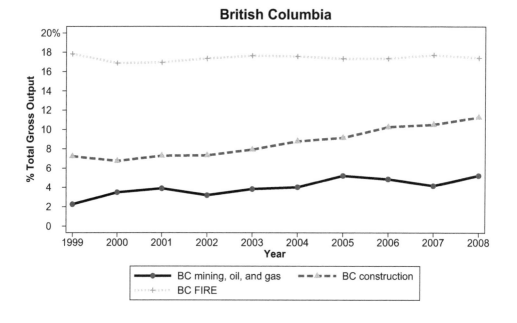

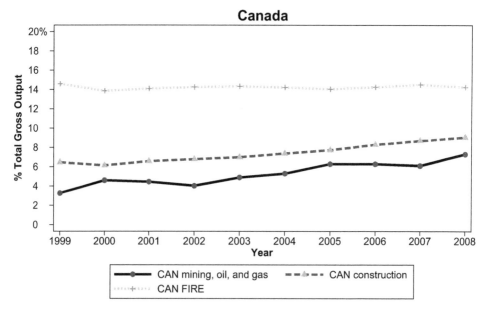

Figure 6.1. BC and Canada leading sectors of growth (% GDP)
Source: BC Stats, "BC GDP at Basic Prices, Current Dollars – NAICS Aggregations, 1997–2008"; Canada CANSIM table 3810016

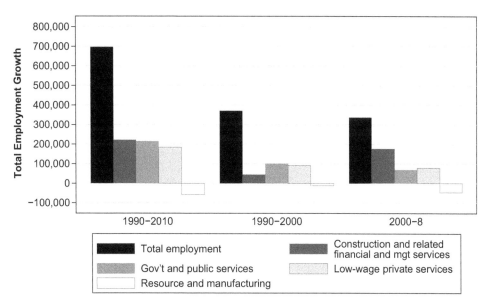

Figure 6.2. BC total employment and sectoral growth
Sources: Statistics Canada, CANSIM tables 2820055, 2820008

non-union and double-breasting construction firms dramatically increased the number of non-union and non-standard construction jobs, from 45,600 in 2001 to 115,500 in 2008.

Indirectly, employers in low-productivity service enterprises such as retail, food and beverage, hotel and accommodation, and private security looked to make a whole range of domestic inputs considerably cheaper for upper- and middle-income consumers by transforming standard employment into flexible jobs. As figure 6.3 illustrates, full-time, full-year jobs began to decline as a proportion of total employment during the recession in the early 1990s. But they declined even further in the first decade of 2000, to less than 50 per cent of total employment by 2010, as non-union, non-standard employment grew in tandem with labour force expansion.

With employers seeking to lower labour costs, low-wage work continued its steady rise (figure 6.4). The number of employees or self-employed workers earning less than two-thirds of median pay for a full-time/full-year worker rose by 147,000 between 2000 and 2008, accounting for 44 per cent of all new jobs. As a percentage of total employment, the number of jobs that earned less than the low-wage threshold of two-thirds of hourly pay of a full-time employee rose only slightly from 37 to 37.6 per cent 1997–2010, and did so as overall numbers of workers in low-wage hourly work remained largely static.

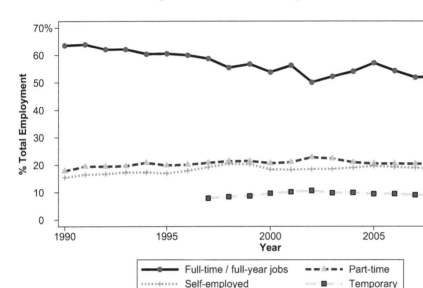

Figure 6.3. Rise of non-standard employment in BC, 1990–2010 (% total employment)
Sources: Statistics Canada, CANSIM tables 2020101, 2820080, 2820020.

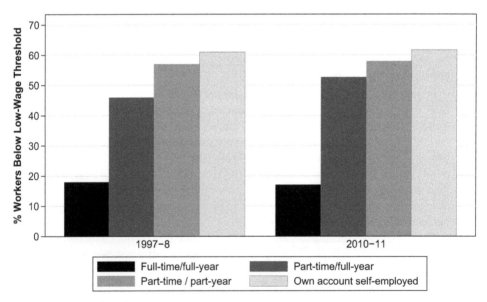

Figure 6.4. BC non-standard employment and low-wage work, 1999–2011 (% workers below hourly low-wage threshold of two-thirds of wages of full-time / full-year worker)
Source: Author's figures from custom request, Statistics Canada, Survey of Labour and Income Dynamics and Survey of Consumer Finances, "Percentage of Workers with Low Annual Earnings and Low Hourly Wages, Canada and Provinces," table C685593.

Those in full-time work actually saw a slight decline in the possibility of being in low-wage work to 17 per cent. But most affected were those in non-standard employment.

As figure 6.4 demonstrates, the number of workers in non-standard low-wage work grew over the course of the first decade of 2000. By 2011, more than 53 per cent of part-time workers were in low-wage work, and more than 61 per cent of the own-account self-employed earned low wages. People who worked part-time the entire year wound up with earnings 40 per cent below median earnings. Most affected were the age group twenty to twenty-four, who had median earnings of only $12,970. Statistics for August 2005 showed that only 34 per cent of the age group with employment income were full-time students (Kerstetter 2010).

Particularly noteworthy is who worked the majority of these jobs in the low-wage sectors. Early in first decade of 2000, low-wage employment was experienced largely by immigrants, youth (age twenty to twenty-four), and women (Kerstetter 2010). Between 2001 and 2008, the number of new landed immigrants in the workforce rose by 125,000 and that of temporary foreign workers by more than 45,000 (BC Ministry of Jobs 2012; Citizenship and Immigration Canada 2011). But median earnings of recent immigrants and those who had landed in the 1990s never rose above $21,000 per year, well below a low-wage rate and far below a living wage for those living in BC's Lower Mainland (Ivanova and Klein 2012).

Over the course of the first decade of 2000, the majority of women continued to work in low-wage jobs in both the public and private service sector. While more women with higher education credentials did begin to see wage returns more comparable to skill, over 60 per cent of all women worked in jobs that paid less than $29,900 (Statistics Canada CANSIM table 2020101). On average, BC women earned $1000 less than the Canadian average for women in 2000–9, and earned $2700 less in 2010 (Cohen 2012). Job creation in food, accommodation, clerical, and household-based personal services accounted for much of this segmentation of women in good and bad jobs. But the emergence of contracting out and non-standard employment in social services also contributed to the creation of inferior jobs in an employment field that overwhelmingly hires women (Cohen and Cohen 2004).

The high provincial rates of poverty stand as further evidence of the prevalence and persistence of low wages in BC over the first decade of the Liberal government. From 2001 to 2008, according to the National Council of Welfare, BC had the highest provincial poverty rate, reaching a peak in 2002 and 2003, when the provincial rates were 38 per cent and 33 per cent respectively above the national rate. The BC poverty rate declined slowly from 2004 to 2008, but remained 21 per cent above the national rate in 2008. High overall poverty rates have meant that child poverty rates in BC have also been the highest in the country in recent years (BC Campaign 2000, 2010). Low-wage work has been a major contributor to such trends (Kerstetter 2010).

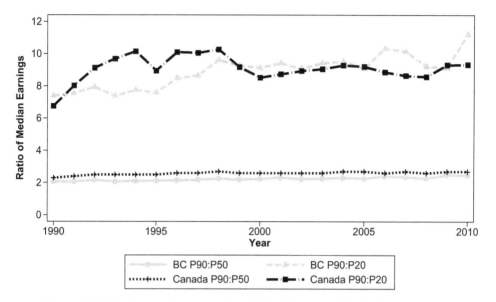

Figure 6.5. Widening earnings inequality in BC and Canada, 1990–2010 (economic families under 65)

Sources: Author's figures from custom tabulation from Survey of Labour and Income Dynamics and the Survey of Consumer Finances, "Median Incomes, Average Incomes, and Share of Incomes by Decile; P90:P10 Ratio, P90:P50 Ratio, P50:P10 Ratio," data shared by the Canadian Centre for Policy Alternatives.

As figure 6.5 illustrates, increasing earnings inequality was a basic consequence of rising non-unionized, non-standard employment, increasing immigration, and growing rates of female labour-market participation. Supply-side economic theory suggests that increasing rates of employment and more flexible labour markets should improve employment performance and earnings (OECD 2006, 2010). But as figure 6.5 shows, examining economic families under the age of sixty-five in BC, the ratio of median earnings between the wealthiest 10 per cent of earners and the bottom 20 per cent of regular income earners spiked during the 1990s recession and rose again in the first decade of 2000, especially after the financial crisis, with the wealthiest earning 7.8 times more than the bottom 20 per cent of earners in 1990, rising to 11.5 times more by 2010 – well above the Canadian ratio of 9. And most noticeable is where BC's top income ratio began to pull away from the Canadian average in 2006 – during the Campbell government's second electoral mandate.

The wealthiest 10 per cent of income earners also pulled away from middle-income earners. Following Canada-wide trends, the P90:P50 earnings ratio increased from 2.1 to 2.5 between 1990 and 2010. This increase in earnings inequality occurred despite declining unemployment in the first decade of 2000 and rising labour market participation among the core (twenty-five to sixty-four) labour force, both of which theoretically should have increased wages and led to greater wage compression. That such increases in earnings inequality between the top and bottom of the labour force were well above the Canadian average as well as other provincial economies that were also dependent on resources, real estate, and private services for growth, strongly suggests that political and institutional developments were important to these increases.

Business Mobilization and Labour Market Deregulation

Driving these changes in the labour market was a profound shift in provincial political forces in BC. The first decade of 2000 saw a rapid increase in the organizational resources of employers and business groups, as well as the rise of a more assertive, supply-side-oriented Liberal Party committed to deregulating labour market policy – both of which had significant impacts on the politics of inequality and the emergence of deregulation policies. In contrast to other provinces in the first decade of 2000, the Campbell government passed a host of legislative and regulatory changes to affect how labour markets functioned in the province. These ranged from reforms to employment standards that affected workers in private services, to legislative efforts to overhaul public sector collective bargaining, to policy and regulatory efforts to change how unions and labour boards operated.

Such policy change could occur only when powerful groups pushed effectively for policy reform over a long period time, often in the face of popular resistance and widespread criticism. In BC, the role of a mobilized business community in policy and politics was central to such changes.

The rapid mobilization of business resources began in the late 1980s and early 1990s, as the Business Council of National Issues, the Canadian Exporters Association, the Canadian Chamber of Commerce, as well as the Fraser Institute and other think tanks pressed for deregulation under the banner of "free trade" (Brownlee 2005; Newman 1998). Seeking to mobilize a broader front, businesses expanded their membership in coalitions in order to undertake national advocacy campaigns, foster coordination among the most powerful CEOs, and increase lobbying and political donations (Dobbin 1998). In BC, these initiatives opened the way for businesses to remake and expand their own networks, research, and lobby organizations. Led by the Vancouver-based Fraser Institute – a free market think tank that expanded membership and revenues over the course of the 1990s – business associations sought to similarly expand their research, marketing, and communications capabilities to influence government policy (Fraser Institute 1999, 2001).

The Business Council of BC (BCBC) rapidly expanded over the course of the 1980s, 1990s, and first decade of 2000 to become a leading advocacy and research organization. Similarly, the British Columbia Construction Association and the BC Chamber of Commerce expanded operations, providing business updates, editorials, newsletters, and backgrounders on public policies in order to influence public debate. Together, in the late 1990s and early in the first decade of 2000, they launched economic summits, funded policy research to shift public opinion in a business-oriented direction, and sought to set the political agenda with the creation of new advocacy coalitions (BC retired business consultant).

One of the most long-standing new business organizations to emerge was the Coalition of BC Businesses, established to push for labour market policy reforms and deregulation. Using the tools pioneered by public interest groups and emulating similar business organizations in the United States, the new groups poured vast new resources into a three-year public campaign, from 1998 to 2001, that pushed market-oriented and "practical" policy ideas based on the principles of free enterprise, limited government, reduced taxes, and a more "internationally competitive" economy (Clemens and Emes 2001; Coalition of BC Businesses 2011). Prior to the 2001 provincial election, the BCBC and Coalition of BC Businesses held regular advisory group meetings among Liberal Party officials, leading businessmen, and business associations. They culminated in the economic summits of 1998 and 2000/1, where businesses and business consultants presented major tax cut, labour, social policy, and regulatory proposals, gearing up for the 2001 provincial elections (British Columbia Business Summit 2000). According to one business official, "The entire business community was well represented" in all these meetings (BC retired business consultant). But most active was the Independent Contractors and Businesses Association, which represented the non-union construction sector and was a significant donor to the Liberal Party. The New Car Dealers Association was also active in the coalitions, as were mining and forestry companies, who were keen supporters of the Liberal Party and interested in labour and regulatory reforms.

On labour policy, the business coalitions worked with the Fraser Institute, the global business consultancy KPMG, and key Liberal supporters in the law firm of Heenan Blaikie to push for major changes to labour legislation and reforms to BC industrial relations and employment standards (Coalition of BC Businesses 2002; BC independent labour researcher 1). Provincial construction, restaurant, and agricultural associations were central to the coalition, pushing for major reforms that would give large and small employers alike far more opportunities to use non-union labour as well as immigrant labour where needed (BC retired business consultant; BC labour leader 1). Most active was the Independent Contractors and Businesses Association, which represented the non-union construction sector and was a significant donor to the Liberal

Party. The New Car Dealers Association was also active in the coalition, as were a number of mining and forestry companies who were keen supporters of the Liberal Party and interested in labour and regulatory reforms.

In the subsequent introduction of labour market deregulation, this anti-union stance of contractors and developers proved a striking difference to the situation in provinces such as Ontario and Newfoundland and Labrador, where contractors and unionized trades retained cordial relations. The animosity in BC was to have significant policy implications for the labour market. Also unique to BC were the demands of the restaurant association for a two-tier minimum wage for servers in bars and restaurants. Through fora, publicity, and regular meetings between employers and Liberal Party officials, business associations were able to build wide support among employers and develop advocacy and lobbying campaigns to achieve commitments to desired reforms in the lead up to the 2001 election (BC retired business lawyer). With the victory of the Campbell government, these new capacities in agenda setting, building business-wide support, and lobbying for policy changes were expanded, at the same time that employers sought to strengthen their connections with the government.

One area where business increased its influence with the new Liberal government was in political donations to the party, especially during election years. At the time when campaigns were becoming more reliant on expensive television advertising, business provided the Liberals with the resources to effectively run winning campaigns. As figure 6.6 shows, over the course of the decade, the Liberals not only regularly gained more than 97 per cent of all business support, they also used business donations to outspend the NDP on a 2-to-1 basis during election years, and a more than 3-to-1 ratio in non-election years. Just as importantly was how rapidly business donations expanded to give the Liberal Party the necessary revenue to advertise, campaign, and conduct polling every year, and to double this spending in election years. In 2001, the first election victory, business donations of $5.7 million to the Liberal Party represented 41 per cent of all political party revenues in the province. In 2005, business donations to the Liberals doubled to $10.1 million (the highest level in all provincial jurisdictions), making up 45 per cent of all political party revenues, and surpassing all funds donated to the NDP by individuals, unions, and business.

While business donations declined in 2009 in the wake of the financial crisis and the economic downturn, the $8.5 million raised from businesses alone for the BC Liberal Party still represented 42 per cent of all party revenues raised that year. During election years (2001, 2005, 2009), business donations never fell below $5.7 million, and exceeded $10 million in 2005, more than five times the amount that unions were able to raise for the NDP. In non-election years, business donations to the Liberal Party averaged more than $4.6 million,

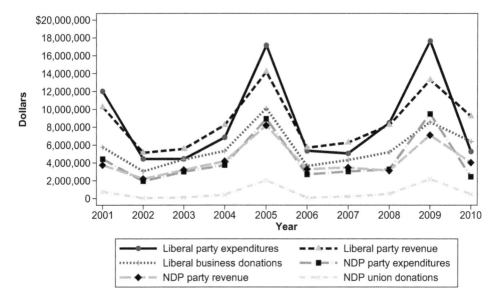

Figure 6.6. Political party revenues and expenditures in BC, 2001–2010 ($)
Source: Elections BC, annual political party statements.

compared to just $272,000 given by trade unions, a fifteen-fold financial advantage. Such advantages were invaluable in providing the Liberal Party with the resources to outspend the NDP throughout the first decade of 2000 in advertising, polling, and local and constituency-level party building – the activities that gave the party an organizational edge in elections.

Direct business donations were not the only way that economic leaders supported the BC Liberal Party. They also donated individually – often very generously and with the support of other corporate board members. Leading the way were real estate developers Francesco Aquilini (Aquilini Development Group and the Vancouver Canucks) and Terry Hui (Concord Pacific Group), whose companies not only regularly gave tens of thousands of dollars, but who during election years gave thousands more along with other family and corporate board members (Elections BC 2001–10; Modjeski and Gaboury 2009). Peter Brown and Paul Reynolds of Canaccord Capital would similarly "bundle" corporate and individual donations in order to provide more than $100,000 in financial support. Not to be outdone, contractors like Milan Ilich of Progressive Construction would donate thousands of dollars of their own money to the Liberal Party. Unlike the NDP, which relied on thousands more donors and smaller average donations, such monies from high-income earners were crucial to the Liberal Party's ability to allocate funds to critical, close-fought races.

Business and lobbyists also supported the Liberal Party through raising money for advertising campaigns as well as donating to party fundraisers that gave donors access to government officials and ministers (Tomlinson 2017). With no regulations on third-party spending prior to elections, millions of dollars were routinely raised by business organizations operating under titles such as "Future Prosperity for BC" for widespread television and social media campaigns attacking the NDP and promoting the message of the Liberal Party (Hager 2017). Lobbyists also gave thousands of dollars under their own names to party organizations and events – money that was subsequently reimbursed by their clients. And with no restrictions on the number of donations or caps on donations, business widely donated to the Liberal Party that repeatedly asked for further funding (Tomlinson 2017).

Business support for the Liberals extended into direct organizational support, within and outside government. The Liberal government institutionalized powerful new means to accommodate business interests and allow them to have direct input into policy decision-making (BC retired Liberal Party official). Government sought advice from individuals and organizations in the private sector on policy design, the introduction of privatization and market concepts in public service organizations, and basic fiscal and budgetary issues.

Immediately after the Liberals' 2001 election victory, Premier Campbell established a Fiscal Review Panel made up of private sector businessmen and business consultants to examine the province's finances. It forecast a "structural deficit" and recommended a review of program spending with the objective of expenditure reductions, privatization, and elimination of programs (British Columbia Fiscal Review Panel 2001). It also strongly emphasized that tax increases were not an option available to the government. Similarly, the international business consultant agencies PricewaterhouseCoopers and KPMG were repeatedly sought out for advice on public policy issues, setting out policy agendas and solutions. Whether on the Olympics and treaty settlements, or casino development, technology, and new management systems for health care, the government repeatedly contracted with these two agencies to conduct systemic reviews and make far-reaching recommendations.

At the same time, the government sought to "marketize" services. This too created a new dynamic that prioritized business needs at the expense of concerns for equality and the labour market. To put in place new infrastructure, the government created Partnerships BC, a government agency whose mandate included overseeing public private partnerships, including multi-million-dollar projects for the Olympics (McMartin 2011). BC Hydro contracted with the American accounting firm Accenture for a series of business service contracts that had little oversight and ultimately went over budget (McMartin 2010a). The government also sold BC Rail and BC Gas to private firms. Asset management companies that gave thousands of dollars in support to the Liberal Party were rewarded as they saw their investment vehicles for energy and forestry granted favourable contracts and land holdings (McMartin 2010b). In these ways, business solidified its control over major services formerly delivered by government, and firms gained increasing influence over the operation of key policy agencies.

Such transformations in government, alongside the emergence of powerful and coordinated business interests, were in many ways parallel to developments in the United States. Unlike provinces such as Ontario and Quebec, where business interests were often split between Liberal and Conservative Parties as well as between domestic and international ownership interests, in BC, business mobilization was far more cohesive and focused. As donors to campaigns and political activists in their own right, powerful business elites began to play major roles in reshaping the political terrain and shifting public opinion, most notably regarding tax cuts and labour market reform. Such mobilization also changed how political parties functioned and how elections were run – a second factor driving growing inequality in the province.

The New Economic Conservatism of the Liberal Party

Traditional scholarship on political parties and voters in Canada still assumes that there is a level playing field for all interests in policymaking and that voters have sufficient information to make reasoned choices (Anderson and Stephenson 2010; Bittner and Koop 2011). The median voter, it is argued, rationally chooses the best mix of policies; and Canada's brokerage parties still compete in an open, pluralist system by seeking the support of a large number of citizens. Such theories suggest that government policy should be tightly linked to the public preferences of the median voter, especially when those preferences are clear and strong.

But developments in BC from 2001 to 2010 suggest serious problems with such explanations, for rather than growing inequality leading to renewed pressure from the majority of citizens for a greater government role and improved public policies, the exact opposite occurred: the Campbell government continued to pass legislation that worsened inequality in the province and harmed job quality. At the same time, the Liberal Party targeted more affluent and high-turnout citizens, while low-income voters who were most harmed by changes to labour market policy were marginalized from the political process, and many began to abstain from voting. Moreover, even despite the clear preferences of many middle-class and low-income British Columbians for more redistribution and a greater role in ensuring employment, the government enacted policies counter to these preferences. Why?

Along with the emergence of powerful business interests, the ways that political parties brought organized groups into coalition and shaped citizen understanding of policy are key to an explanation. As in the United States, to be successful, business and elites depended upon the development of new voter blocs and electoral dynamics that would win over voters (especially higher-income voters) and ensure their long-term success (Hacker and Pierson 2010a; Pierson and Skocpol 2007). In BC, Liberal Party success in making major policy reforms came about only in the wake of the transformation of the party, its representatives, and its networks. But it also rested on the Liberal Party developing powerful new capacities to mobilize the economically privileged and create critical financial and organizational support. Understanding these political connections behind policy change requires a closer examination of the changing make-up of the party.

A sharp partisan divide between business-friendly political parties and more populist and labour-oriented ones has long characterized provincial politics in BC (Blake 1996; Phillips 2010). However, with the emergence of the Liberal Party in the 1990s in the wake of the defeat and dissolution of the Social Credit Party in 1991, this took an even more dramatic turn. Led by Gordon Campbell, the former mayor of Vancouver, who had extensive connections to the real estate and financial industries, the BC Liberal Party sought to construct a new centre-right coalition that would challenge the NDP government and better serve vested economic interests in the province. Consisting of an amalgam of former Social Credit and Reform Party members, as well as Conservative Party staff who had worked for the Ontario Conservative Party under Mike Harris, the newly renamed BC Liberal Party sought to fill the vacuum created by the political downfall of the Social Credit Party by calling for extensive tax cuts, labour policy reforms, and the retreat of government from regulation (McMartin 2005a; MacLeod 2008).

Unlike the federal Liberal Party and other provincial Liberal parties, BC MLAs came predominantly from small business, real estate, and former mayors and town councillors with small business background, and included few with legal training, university degrees, or educational occupations – backgrounds that have typically characterized other Liberal Party members in Canada. (On the educational profile of federal Liberal and Conservative governments, see Atkinson, Rogers, and Olfert 2016; Kerby 2009). And once in government, the Liberals also heavily recruited former Conservative politicians, agency directors, and administrative staff from Alberta and its strong Conservative Party to fill utility company directorships, agency positions, and deputy minister positions in order to provide advice, oversight, and direction to the new marketization and privatization reforms being introduced (McMartin 2004). In a fashion similar to the Republican Party and the development of conservatism in the United States, the BC Liberal Party changed internally with new senior officials taking control of the party, committed to advancing a deregulatory and tax-cutting agenda, and sought to take advantage of the resources and participation of the economically privileged and highly educated.

The impacts of these organizational changes were profound. Upon their election in 2001, the Liberal Party adopted a strong partisan orientation focused on making supply-side reforms that mirrored those of the Mike Harris Ontario Conservatives as well as that of centre-right parties in the United States (Beers 2005; Phillips 2010). The Liberals cut personal and corporate taxes, announcing on their first day in office they would reduce them by more than 25 per cent in their first term. Then they imposed tight constraints on public spending and reconfigured social programs to exclude many of BC's most vulnerable residents, including women, the disabled, and the homeless, while reducing the level of provincial public sector employment to the lowest in Canada (Ivanova 2010; McBride and Mcnutt 2007). Consequently, by 2010, BC not only had the highest rate of income inequality before tax, it also had the least effective tax and transfer programs in reducing income inequality (Sharpe and Capeluck 2012).

Such policies were intended to establish a new economic conservatism in the province, hobbling the ability of future governments to raise revenues and increase social spending. But the signature policy moves of tax cuts and balanced-budget legislation were also intended to ensure the long-term support of key sectors of the electorate (BC retired Liberal Party official). Crucial to Liberal mobilization was securing the support of corporate, small business, and highly wealthy interests from the North Shore and Westside of Vancouver. And with two of the most powerful figures in the new BC Liberal Party coming from West Vancouver – Gordon Campbell and Colin Hansen, both among the loudest voices for tax cuts and balanced budgets – the Liberal Party looked to realign traditional centre-right voters to the new party. Grounded in two of the wealthiest ridings in the province, and supported by voters who heavily favoured tax cuts and were far less likely to support a government role in redistribution, Campbell and Hansen were key to transforming the party into one that emphasized tax reductions as the first priority (McMartin 2005b).

With their election in 2001, the Liberal government made good on its promise and reduced taxes on those with economic clout. Cuts to corporate and personal income had a dramatic impact on effective tax rates for businesses and the wealthiest income-earners in North and West Vancouver ridings (Lee, Ivanova, and Klein 2011). For the wealthiest 1 per cent of households, tax cuts delivered an average of over $41,000 a year, while reducing their effective tax rates to the lowest among income earners. In contrast, lower-income households received an average tax cut of only $200 per year. For businesses, statutory rates for general corporations were slashed from 16.5 per cent to 10 per cent from 2001 to 2010, and small business taxes fell from 4.5 per cent to 2.5 per cent – among the lowest provincial rates in Canada (vander Ploeg and Vicq 2011).

As contemporary theorizing and research about "policy feedbacks" shows, fiscal and social policies can influence elite and mass understandings of political issues and possibilities, and can strongly influence voter preferences as

Table 6.1. BC voting and income polarization, 2001–2009

	2001	2005	2009	
Top 12 Wealthiest Electoral Districts				Totals
Liberal	12	11	11	34 or 94% of ridings
NDP	0	1	0	1
IND			1	1
Bottom 12 Low Income Electoral Districts				Totals
Liberal	9	4	3	16 or 44%
NDP	3	8	9	20 or 55% of ridings but 70% of ridings 2005–9

Sources: Author's figures from BC Stats Provincial Electoral District Profiles, based on the 2001 and 2006 census.

well as the goals of organized groups that get involved in subsequent rounds of policymaking (Gilens 2012; Hacker and Pierson 2010a). As the patterns displayed in table 6.1 confirms, the same appears to have held true in BC, with the dramatic impact of government policy on the wealthiest of British Columbians, who voted overwhelmingly for the Liberals and became increasingly opposed to redistributive policies.

Over the course of three provincial elections between 2001 and 2009, the Liberals won 94 per cent of the twelve highest-income ridings. In contrast, they won only 30 per cent of the lowest-income ridings in the province over the same period. While this evidence is limited to only the highest- and lowest-income ridings, the strong associations of policy influence on electoral mobilization and participation offer at least one highly plausible explanation for the new electoral and policy strategies the Liberal government pursued, particularly the ways it sought to respond to the demands of the top income strata at the cost of policies for a broader electorate.

Equally revealing of the new role of money in shaping provincial public policy was how government policies reflected the attitudes of the wealthiest voters. There is considerable debate about the role of money in shaping public policy (Gilens 2012). However, as table 6.2 demonstrates, upper-income earners in BC had very distinctive policy preferences on economic issues, diverging significantly from Canada-wide averages. Though few surveys regularly track the attitudes of rich Canadians over time, what evidence there is suggests that the rich in BC were more conservative economically – less supportive of economic redistribution and measures to provide economic security. As table 6.2, based on International Social Survey data, illustrates, upper-income voters were twice as likely to oppose income redistribution and a greater government

Table 6.2. Income and government's role in BC

Reduce Income Differences b/w Rich and Poor	Family Income under $65,000	Family Income over $65,000
BC		
Probably/Definitely Should	69%	34%
Probably/Definitely Should Not	31%	66%
Canada		
Probably/Definitely Should	78%	52%
Probably/Definitely Should Not	22%	48%

Source: Author's figures from International Social Survey Programme: Role of Government IV–ISSP, 2006.

role than were middle- and low-income British Columbians. And in comparison with the rest of the Canada, the economically privileged in BC were also far more likely to oppose more egalitarian policies.

Such findings suggest that public influence over policy was strongly concentrated within, if not entirely reserved for, the most affluent segment of the public. The fact that this same segment was the most likely to provide the majority of money that flows from businesses and individuals to politicians and lobbying organizations correlates well with other studies that show that high income and higher education were the most important determinants of voting and political participation in BC (Burgar and Monkman 2010).

These developments provide an explanation for the transformation of BC politics and how the disproportionate power of the wealthy limited the political influence of ordinary voters. For what the wealthy can more easily do – pool resources for sustained campaigns – allowed them to exercise enormous political influence within the Liberal government. Changing tax policy was one major focus of this influence, as we have seen, but of equal importance were changes to labour markets and labour policy. The Liberal government indeed proved especially effective at rewriting labour policy to favour business interests.

Deregulation of Employment Standards

With Liberals' success in mobilizing support of business and upper-income voters, the new government began to systematically chip away at collective bargaining, employment standards, and equality and protection in the labour market. Under growing influence of multinational and local employers, wealthy business owners, and upper-income earners, the BC Liberal government enacted a host of legislative and administrative changes affecting labour. Some of the most important reforms were to employment standards, and the changes were so dramatic that University of British Columbia Sauder School of Business professor emeritus Mark Thompson, a former independent employment standards review commissioner, characterized them as constituting "the biggest rollback of worker rights in Canadian history" (Sandborn 2010).

In its spring 2001 provincial election campaign, the Liberal Party of BC targeted employment standards and industrial relations legislation for change in its "New Era" platform. With a view to bypassing any of the informal veto powers held by unions through protests, strikes, or advocacy, the BC Liberals promised new employment policy: "To compete and prosper in the new economy, workers and employers alike need more flexibility and a modern work environment that encourages innovation and rewards creative thinking and increased productivity" (BC Liberal Party 2001, 11). The election platform went on to borrow heavily from the 1999 election campaign platform of the Progressive Conservative Party of Ontario, in which it promised to "modernize" the Ontario Employment Standards Act to make it "flexible" and adaptable to the contemporary labour market. Above all, the provincial labour strategy and workforce development plan were intended to address the "increasingly globalized marketplace where competition is tighter and competitive advantages more crucial" (British Columbia Ministry of Skills Development and Labour 2004). Policy changes were intended to send an "important message" to the labour relations community and to investors (BC Ministry of Skills Development and Labour 2002).

With Bills 37 and 48 in 2002 and 2003, the government made a comprehensive attempt to create new jobs in the low-wage sector, making forty-two substantive changes to the Employment Standards Act, thirty-five of which have had a negative impact on workers' conditions of employment (Fairey 2005). The first regulatory change, in 2001, was the introduction of the $6-per-hour minimum first-job entry-level wage for the first 500 hours of employment, $2 per hour below the general minimum wage of $8 per hour. Intended to reduce the youth unemployment rate, the first-job entry-level wage demonstrably did not have that effect. The unemployment rate for fifteen- to twenty-four-year-olds increased from 13.9 per cent in 2001 to 15.1 per cent in 2002 and remained above 10 per cent until 2005. During 2006 and 2007, when economic growth nudged higher, the youth unemployment rate fell to 7.6 per cent, but then in 2009 jumped dramatically to 13.2 per cent – double the overall unemployment rate for twenty-five- to fifty-four-year-olds. However, for employers, the lower minimum wage represented a new and lucrative pool of cheap labour. By 2005, 352,530 fifteen- to twenty-four-year-old workers earned less than $12,091 annually and made up 15 per cent of the workforce.

Another set of important changes came with the weakening of clauses regulating private, non-standard employment. A new "hours-averaging agreement" provision allowed employers to enter into agreements with individual employees to forego their rights to overtime pay after eight hours per day and/or forty hours per week, so that they might be compelled to work up to twelve hours per day without overtime pay, provided their hours of work did not exceed an average of forty hours per week over a four-week period (Fairey 2005). Similarly, the deregulation of statutory holiday provisions effectively eliminated statutory holiday pay for many part-time employees. In addition, the change in regulations allowed employers to opt out of providing employees with a paid day off in lieu of the holiday.

Subsequently, to modernize the Employment Standards complaint process, the government put the onus on workers to prove the violation of employment standards by their employer, and Employment Standards offices were closed and staff laid off. In their place, the government offered workers a "self-help/do-it-yourself" kit as the first step in filing complaints. This reversal of the complaint process effectively required employees to not only initially make their complaint to the employer, but to then oversee the protracted complaint processing procedures involving the Employment Standards Branch (Fairey 2005; BC union staff official 2, private sector). Unsurprisingly, with such onerous conditions, employment standards complaints by employees fell by 71 per cent between 2000 and 2005 (BC Ministry of Labour and Citizens' Services 2007).

Of equal significance were changes to minimum standards and protections for farm workers, especially those employed through farm labour contractors. The wide-ranging reforms affected everything from the complaint procedures to the elimination of requirements for growers to keep track of records of contractors and employees' wages, to the excluding of farm workers from overtime pay (Fairey et al. 2008). The provincial government also entered into an agreement with the federal government in 2004 to permit the employment of temporary agricultural workers by farm operators under the Seasonal Agricultural Workers Program. At the same time, the Campbell government removed protections for temporary foreign workers, denying them the ability to claim overtime pay, minimum wages, or vacation pay.

Within a few years, British Columbia growers in the Fraser and Okanagan Valleys had taken full advantage of the program, hiring some 3,400 temporary foreign workers and paying them at slightly above the minimum wage, and hiring contractors to employ immigrants to pick fruit at piece rates. By 2005, 80 per cent of immigrant harvesters were illegally forced to return some of their wages to contractors. In addition, many were paid less than the legal minimum piece rate, and many who resided at their worksites were being paid for only eight hours, five days a week, but were working ten hours per day, seven days a week. Because the ministry lacked the resources and staff to enforce regulations, to collect fines from negligent employers, or to pursue repeat offenders, employers continued to routinely contravene the act with little respect for working conditions or employment standards (BC Ministry of Labour official 1; BC member of the Legislative Assembly; Fairey 2005; Fairey et al. 2008).

Other private sector employers similarly sought to take advantage of the reforms to employment standards by defecting from open-ended contracts and full-time jobs. In accommodation and food industries, employers moved to fixed-term contracts and part-time work in the effort to lower hourly wages and increase their reliance on overtime (Cohen 2012; MacPhail and Bowles 2008; BC union staff official 1, private sector). From 1999 to 2010, temporary jobs increased at the same rate as permanent jobs, and of the permanent jobs created, more than 70 per cent had fewer than twenty-five hours during the week. In other private service industries, employers increased their temporary and part-time hiring to create greater flexibility and lower labour costs (Griffin Cohen and Klein 2011). Over the course of the first decade of 2000, employers sought to create larger buffers of flexible and cheaper labour by expanding the number of "core age" women (eighteen to fifteen-four years old) in part-time employment to over 31 per cent. Employers also sought new cost savings in their patterns of gendered hiring, as women were increasingly employed in casual and non-standard jobs.

Reforms and the Conversion of BC's Industrial Relations and Collective Bargaining Systems

In liberal market economies, governments have typically ensured business profitability and labour market growth by allowing wage levels to lag well behind productivity gains (Streeck 2012; Thelen 2012). In these policy regimes, it is believed that the most straightforward way to achieve employment growth is to suppress wages at the lower end of the earnings distribution.

The expansion of lower-paying jobs, however, can generally occur only if employment standards are deregulated or not enforced, or (when collective agreements are widespread) if industrial relations are adjusted to allow greater wage dispersion. In British Columbia, the Campbell government not only changed employment standards. It also chose to lower labour costs through direct reforms in the labour code that allowed companies to free themselves from the constraints of collective bargaining and the threat of job action.

The most significant Labour Relations Code amendments in 2001 (Bill 18) and 2002 (Bill 42) involved the reintroduction of mandatory union representation votes and the elimination of the card-check system of automatic certification of a union when the union could demonstrate majority workplace support for certification. These changes were intended to make it significantly more difficult for unions to organize and certify new workplaces, as representation votes give employers much greater opportunity to influence and intimidate workers. Along with these reforms, the government also introduced amendments to the unfair labour practices provisions, in order to give employers much greater leeway to conduct anti-union campaigns (BC union staff official 2, private sector;

BC labour leader 1; Slinn 2008). Changes to the labour code allowed these actions to escalate and gave the labour board fewer reasons to uphold the existing principles and regulations (Dickie 2005; Fairey 2005). Changes to the mandate of the labour board that led it to emphasize employment rather than contractual fairness also contributed to strengthening the code in favour of employers (Fairey 2009). Finally, new business appointments were made to the board that tilted the weight of representation in favour of employers (BC union staff official 2, private sector; BC independent labour researcher 1).

Such reforms contributed greatly to the decline in union density and to employers having more capacity to reduce labour costs (Slinn 2008). The ending of card certification and first-contract arbitration across the province proved enormously effective in weakening union attempts to organize new members. It meant that the era of the moderate employer campaigns against union organizing drives was now over. Henceforth, management could hire lawyers and consultants who ran campaigns that bordered on, and often crossed the line into, illegality with little opportunity for challenge or oversight (Dickie 2005) (BC union staff official 2, private sector).

With the labour code reforms, company law firms challenged the certification process with increasing frequency, often delaying certification procedures for months. Such delays provide a window of opportunity for employers and their managers to either change the hours and working conditions of internal workplace organizers, or to simply terminate those seen as troublemakers. Employees are then left without key internal mobilizers, and those who remain feel their jobs are at risk should they continue efforts to unionize.

The labour code reforms and overhauled labour boards thus made it harder for unions to win certification drives. These difficulties can be seen clearly in the declining number of employees granted union representation, from an average of 8,762 per year in the period 1994 to 2000 to an average of 4,000 per year in the period 2002 to 2009 (Dickie 2005; Fairey 2005). Despite attempts to adopt more forward-looking and aggressive organizing strategies, unions still saw the number of new certifications granted to individual workplaces decline from an annual average of 353 in the period 1993 to 2001 to 112 in the period 2002 to 2009. In addition, the certification success rate went from an average of above 65 per cent in the period 1993 to 2000 to an average of 50 per cent in the period 2002 to 2009.

This decline in new union organizing has led to a long-term and chronic pattern of falling union density in the private sector (figure 6.7). Faced with a hard choice – devote their dwindling resources to increasingly difficult organizing or to political lobbying to promote new rules and protect old ones – many unions retreated from organizing and instead sought to merge with other unions to make up for the shortfall of members. As figure 6.7 makes clear, union density in BC's private sector first fell with the loss of resource jobs in the 1990s after

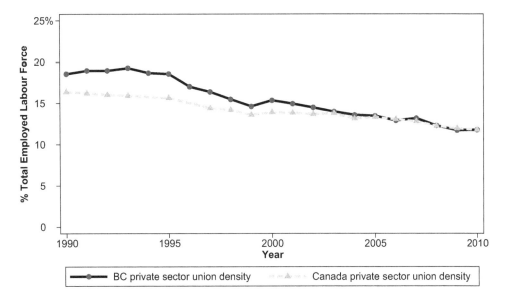

Figure 6.7. BC and Canada private sector union density (% total employed labour force)

Sources: Author's figures: 1990–7: (a) Statistics Canada, CANSIM Data Base II, Matrix 3529 CALURA "Number of Unionized Workers by Sex and Industry, Canada. Annual, 1976–1995"; and Matrix 3532 Labour Force Survey "Employees by Sex and Industry'"; (b) 1997–2010: Statistics Canada, CANSIM table 2820078.

the introduction of free trade, and then slowly declined from 1990 to 2010, as unions were unable to organize new members, given the reforms to the labour code. By 2010, private sector union density in the province had levelled off at approximately 12 per cent.

The 2002 repeal of the labour code's sectoral bargaining provisions for the construction industry also contributed to the waning of unionized work in the province. In many provinces, labour laws make special institutional arrangements to facilitate the orderly acquisition, operation, and retention of collective bargaining rights for construction workers. As construction companies and developers require skilled labour for short-term contracts, employers have worked to coordinate with unions to ensure apprenticeship and skill acquisition, in return for short-term contracts and the ability to name-hire unionized workers.

Employers have long sought to take advantage of a skilled labour surplus in construction, created in part by the fact that BC.s housing market has long been the most profitable, and that construction takes place year-round. Consequently, the Construction Contractors Association pushed hard for changes to the labour code that imposed card-check and vote certification in individual workplaces where they sought to keep unions out. Contractors also pushed for the repeal of the Skills Development and Fair Wage Act in August 2001 – legislation that had required fair wages and occupational training programs on all public construction projects (BC union president 1, private sector; Fairey 2009). Its repeal helped undermine employment conditions and labour relations in the construction industry. So too did the elimination of Highway Constructors Limited, a government company that provided centralized hiring of all construction labour on highway projects through a single agency, which led to fewer employees receiving adequate health and safety training and less priority given to equity hiring. With the introduction of these regulatory changes, unionization in the BC construction industry plunged from 34 per cent in 2001 to 20 per cent in 2009 (Fairey, Peters, and Sandborn 2012).

Public Sector Restructuring

Most scholarly studies on the welfare state have stressed that there is no "race to the bottom." Despite globalization and the rise of market-oriented politics, it is commonly argued that welfare state retrenchment and public policy reform have been slow and often patterned along partisan and institutional lines (Hay and Wincott 2012; Huo 2009; Pontusson 2005). Because unions and corporatist and collective bargaining systems influence economic and social policy reform, and political parties look to support core constituencies with appropriate social policies, welfare state change has been incremental, as domestic interests have defended existing institutions in the face of global economic pressures (Beramendi and Cusack 2008; Cusack, Iversen, and Rehm 2008).

But in BC, public policy reform and public sector restructuring were deep and widespread. Fiscal changes and a series of incremental reforms to public sector management and operation had significant negative impacts on public service employment, public sector collective bargaining, and public sector job quality. Claiming that expenditures on public services were a burden on the productive sectors of the economy and that tax cuts and New Public Management reforms were necessary for growth, the Campbell government introduced policies of fiscal austerity, attempted to rewrite collective bargaining contracts, centralized bargaining, and initiated purchaser-provider splits in public sector agencies (BC Liberal Party 2001). Such reforms were intended to alter the calculus and priorities of public officials, workers, and interest groups alike (BC retired Liberal Party official; BC labour leader 1). Above all, government efforts were directed at enforcing wage moderation and attenuating labour bargaining power through collective bargaining reforms, layoffs, early retirement, and the growth of "flexible employment." Under the pressure of business and seeking to meet the needs of high-income earners, the Liberal government's main policy goals were to lower public spending and boost economic growth.

Redistributive and employment concerns were of secondary importance, if noted at all.

This was far more a classical "liberal" perception of the public sector, which viewed expenditure on public services as a burden on the productive sectors of the economy, and believed that governments had a responsibility to deregulate markets, and that private responsibility for health and education would be more widely institutionalized. In 2001, the newly elected Liberal government instituted personal and corporate tax cuts that lowered revenue, increased deficits, and provided the rationale for reductions in public employment and the imposition of public sector bargaining reforms. Combined, the tax cuts reduced provincial revenue by more than $3.5 billion per year (BC Liberal Party 2001). In turn, the government enacted spending reductions that affected social programs and public services across the province.

As figure 6.8 demonstrates, over the course of the first decade of 2000, BC's government expenditures and public employment fell. With the introduction of the tax cuts, the province's consolidated revenues fell from 18.5 per cent of GDP in 2000 to only 15.3 per cent in 2008. Committed to balanced budgets, the government reduced expenditures from 18.5 per cent of GDP in 2001 to a low of 15.4 per cent in 2006, before expenditures rose proportionally in the wake of the economic crisis and slowdown of economic activity in 2009. This reduction in expenditure exceeded the general provincial government retrenchment of public spending by more than 1.5 per cent of GDP, and BC cuts were among the deepest in Canada, with significant negative impacts on the effectiveness of programs in reducing inequality (Sharpe and Capeluck 2012).

The impacts of spending reductions were less significant on overall levels of public employment, which fell by only 0.8 per cent of total employment (2001–5) before following Canada-wide trends of increasing proportions of public employment with the rise of unemployment and the decline of labour market participation after the 2008 economic crisis. However, in comparative terms, by 2008, BC had the lowest provincial level of public sector employment relative to population in Canada (Ivanova 2010). At approximately 90 public sector employees per 1,000 citizens, BC had only 64 per cent of the ratio of public sector workers that Manitoba employed, where 140 employees per 1,000 citizens worked in public services and public administration.

The Campbell government also introduced a significant number of measures intended to make public sector pay and employment more "flexible" and to lower labour costs. Like a number of other governments in the first decade of 2000, BC public officials focused on reducing labour costs as a core element in their strategy to improve competitiveness. As public services are labour intensive, and labour costs account for up to two-thirds of total production cost, governments like those of the Campbell Liberals looked to privatization, differentiated collective agreements, and "two-tier" bargaining as the primary

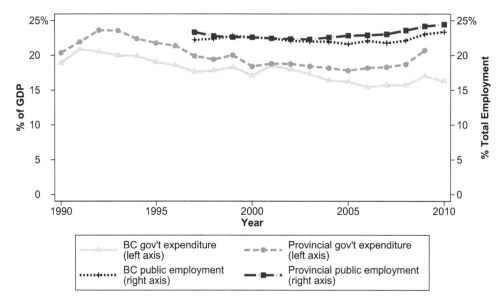

Figure 6.8. BC government expenditure and public employment, 1990–2010 (BC and provincial averages)
Sources: British Columbia Financial and Economic Review 2009, 2012; and Statistics Canada, CANSIM tables 2820078 and 3850002.

means to introduce flexible employment and lower labour costs. These had impacts ranging from the decline of public sector employment to the attenuating of collective bargaining institutions to the expansion of part-time and temporary employment and the widening of wage and income inequality (BC union president, public sector; Ivanova 2010).

The most dramatic changes occurred in health and long-term care, starting with Bill 29, the Health and Social Services Delivery Improvement Act, which was enacted in January 2002 (Camfield 2006). The goal of Bill 29 was to lay off thousands of workers, contract out work, and terminate the equity wage provisions of the community social services collective agreement, all in order to cut health-care labour costs. In addition, Bill 29 gave health employers the opportunity to opt out of job-security and contracting-out protections from master collective agreements and hire new employees at half the wage rate and with far fewer benefits, often with limited or no pension or long-term disability plans and very limited vacation, sick leave, and health benefits (Stinson, Pollak, and Cohen 2005). And to ensure that the newly privatized employees would not reorganize with existing unions, the government offered three multinational service organizations (Aramark, Sodexho, and Compass) the ability to negotiate with other private sector unions in order to sign "voluntary recognition agreements," in which the terms and conditions of employment were established by mutual agreement prior to hiring the workforce.

While almost all unions refused this offer, one local of the Industrial and Allied Workers of Canada (IWA) agreed to sign collective agreements with the companies for wages ranging from $10 to $11 an hour. The BC health unions did successfully challenge these agreements at the Labour Relations Board and managed to reorganize the vast majority of these new workers. However, the workers remained with the private firms at the wages and benefits levels agreed to by the IWA. As a result, in less than a year, BC went from having the highest-paid to the lowest-paid health-support workers in the country (Cohen and Cohen 2004).

From 2001 to 2010, private providers hired more than 40 per cent of all employees in the BC health-care sector, with significant impacts on pay and benefits, in some cases at wage rates 40 per cent below similar unionized positions (Stinson, Pollak, and Cohen 2005). Non-standard employment – which pays significantly less than full-time jobs, with far fewer benefits – also expanded notably in health care and social assistance. From 2001 to 2010, health care and social assistance gained more than 80,000 new jobs. But of these, more than 59 per cent were temporary, part-time, or self-employed. This was especially prevalent in hospitals, as regional health authorities began to act more like independent businesses and contract out many of their ancillary services, such as laundry, cleaning, and food preparation.

But in education as well, the Campbell government undertook major reforms. Through a series of bills in 2001 and 2002, the government removed rights and provisions from collective agreements that teachers had previously won governing class size, staffing ratios, and working hours – all key to establishing workloads and ensuring that education retain basic service components. The moves were so dramatic for the time that Canada's national newspaper described them as "legislative vandalism" (*Globe and Mail* 2002).

Such trends put a number of post-war developments into reverse and undermined public-sector bargaining powers. Where once provincial governments used public services and public utilities alongside regulatory polices to promote income equality and job security, now public service employment is mirroring trends of private service industries, with rising levels of earnings inequality and volatility, increased part-time and temporary employment, and more low-wage work. Moreover, where in the past unions were able to improve the nature of jobs and the level of wages through collective bargaining, the Campbell government's supply-side policies pushed through changes that weakened the power of organized labour. This attenuation of labour power had wider ramifications in the labour market as well as on the politics of the province.

The Waning Effectiveness of Union Response

Confronted by such political and economic trends, BC unions sought to establish new and more effective means of bargaining and to build provincial strategies that would allow them to pressure employers and governments. At the provincial level, the BC Federation of Labour and unions launched advocacy campaigns and developed new tactics to access community resources in the attempt to acquire more effective sources of political leverage. Many unions themselves tried out new organizing strategies, or commenced lawsuits hoping to influence government policy (BC labour leader 1; BC retired union president 1, private sector; BC union staff official 2). Moreover, in contrast to many other provincial jurisdictions, all the major private and public sector unions remained affiliated to the provincial federation, and the vast majority continued to support the NDP in working for measures to improve workers' rights and general conditions at work. However, the results were often much less than expected, and BC's labour movement found that many of these new measures were insufficient in opposing policy changes unfavourable to workers, and that they were simply inadequate in moderating the anti-unionism of employers.

Scholarship suggests that major national labour movements have faced increased challenges with economic globalization over the past few decades, and have had little success in improving collective bargaining or gaining greater political influence with the adoption of neoliberal public policies (Frege and Kelly 2004; Moody 2007). However, it is claimed that where unions have used well-conceived political and economic tactics, and strategically used their resources to influence governments, they have been able to translate their actions into the protection of collective bargaining arrangements and modest progressive policy reforms, especially when governments are facing defeat or the loss of other coalition partners (Hamann and Kelly 2010). In BC, evidence suggests that such conclusions may hold only under particular institutional and electoral contexts. Because despite significant union efforts, as well as wider labour solidarity between public and private sector unions, the BC labour movement was unable to make progress on key demands and continued to suffer from a steady decline in membership and bargaining power.

As in other North American provincial and state jurisdictions, the political and economic actions by BC unions took four main forms: advocacy campaigns backed by legal challenges; organizing and voter mobilization; lobbying of the provincial government; and links with the New Democratic Party. These were intended to influence the distribution of income in society and provide the institutional context for wage and benefit improvements. But the greatest success came with the legal challenges and advocacy campaigns.

The most notable labour victory was that of the Hospital Employees Union in court against Bill 29 (Camfield 2006). The legal challenge brought by health employees unions, including the BC Government and Service Employees

Union, the Hospitals Employee Unions, and other health-care union led to the Supreme Court of Canada striking down sections of the legislation because it denied the freedom of association guarantee of the Charter's section 2(d) (Centre for Constitutional Studies 2007). The court ruled that the new legislation violated citizens' rights "either by disregarding past processes of collective bargaining, by pre-emptively undermining future processes of collective bargaining, or both." Several public sector unions also successfully filed complaints with the International Labour Organization (ILO) of the United Nations, claiming that parts of Bills 15, 18, 28, and 29 violated international labour conventions protecting freedom of association, the right to collective bargaining, and the right to strike. However, despite the ruling by the ILO in March 2003 that the six pieces of labour legislation imposed by the Liberal government did violate international agreements, the provincial government took no action to repeal or rewrite the offending laws.

The BC Federation of Labour and unions also joined other community coalitions to campaign vigorously on behalf of agricultural workers who died in a tragic van accident in 2007 (BC union staff official 1, private sector; BC labour leader 1). Like other labour and community campaigns that have highlighted the dangers that new immigrant and temporary foreign agricultural workers face, unions coordinated with ethnic and faith-based partners to publicize the tragic facts of the event and the conditions that other agricultural workers face in the province. This resulted in an official inquest into the accident, and the finding of health and safety violations against several agricultural employers (BC Ministry of Labour official). It also led to new regulations requiring employers to provide health and safety training for agricultural workers. Similarly, the BC Federation of Labour along with other poverty groups, and non-governmental organizations conducted research, lobbied, and held rallies on the inadequacy of BC's minimum wage and the problems of a two-tier minimum wage. In 2011, under heavy pressure, the Liberal government of Premier Christie Clark ended the tiered minimum wage, and increased the minimum wage to $10.25, which remains 25 per cent below the basic poverty level for a single full-time employed worker.

Politically, unions also initiated efforts to get more union members involved in politics. The BC Federation of Labour has organized training and education for members to participate in municipal politics (BC labour leader 1). Unions have also targeted key ridings to have members participate as volunteers in municipal and provincial campaigns. The goal has been to create a new culture of involvement for union members, but also to show community members the active role of unions in providing education about key political issues (BC union staff official 2, private sector). As in other jurisdictions with first-past-the-post systems, where small swings in voter turnout in specific electoral ridings can influence electoral outcomes, BC unions have strong incentives to engage in targeted voter mobilization, as even small gains in turnout can make a significant difference to electoral results. Consequently, unions have sought new ways to engage members in their efforts to boost electoral activity and resources on behalf of the NDP.

To supplement these activities, while also trying to build bridges into immigrant communities, unions began to use community ESL and education programs on a limited basis to reach out to new Canadians, in order to provide recent immigrants with language skills while at the same time offering basic information on workers' rights in workplace issues. The BC Federation of Labour has also held health and safety courses and conducted community campaigns in a number of languages on the problems of employer violations of health and safety and employment standards. There have also been attempts to build up new community institutions such as low-income dental clinics and a local flea market, which have been intended to provide local services and give unions a face in local communities.

A minority of British Columbia's unions also sought to increase their financial and electoral involvement with the NDP, as a means to promote their long-term influence in policymaking. Traditionally, BC unions have had close ties with the NDP. Many senior union officials have been elected as NDP executive council members, and the vast majority of unions are affiliated to the NDP and seek to influence policy through regular channels of the party decision-making process. In the wake of the defeat of the NDP government in 2001, unions continued to provide the party with substantial electoral support. Though its overall annual political contributions were only a fraction of business contributions to the Liberals – $272,000 per year as opposed to $6.8 million given by business – the labour movement did increase its fundraising and participation in provincial elections, most notably in the years prior to the 2005 and 2009 provincial elections. Through their fundraising and campaign contributions, unions hoped that their assistance would give them access and influence with their elected representatives, but would also help elect a government that would enact more progressive and egalitarian legislation (BC union staff official 1, private sector; BC member of the legislative assembly).

Nonetheless, despite this extensive and coordinated response by sections of organized labour, unions continued to suffer a steady decline in union density and political power, and the Campbell government largely ignored labour concerns. This mirrored wider international trends of governments instituting reforms to industrial relations that have favoured business, implementing cuts in welfare provision, and restructuring public services to heighten the competitiveness of national economies at the expense of better jobs and working conditions (Gall, Hurd, and Wilkinson 2011; Lehndorff 2012). Consequently, BC unions – much like those in the rest of North America – have had little success in positioning themselves as major political actors with whom governments must interact and negotiate, nor have they been able to overcome key trends undermining bargaining strength and political power.

Part of the explanation for this diminution of influence has to do with the limits of strategies such as legal challenges and advocacy campaigns. Despite the successful legal challenge of Bill 29, and the ongoing anti-privatization campaigns in health care, many union efforts at advocacy campaigning were unable to shift opinions, increase member participation, or create new community bridge builders between social movements and labour unions. In the wake of the legal challenge to Bill 29, the Supreme Court ruled in 2007 that collective bargaining rights are protected by the Charter of Rights and Freedoms and that the BC Liberal government did not have the right to unilaterally strip provisions from the health-care unions' collective agreements (Centre for Constitutional Studies 2007).

However, while the court decision was a precedent-setting victory for the entire union movement and provided some monetary compensation for the laid-off workers, it did not reverse the very significant setback experienced by the 8,000 workers who were laid off. Nor did it help the privatized health-support workers, who were not allowed to bargain with other health-care workers and were subject to essential service legislation, which prohibited them from striking. In addition, as a result of the changes set off by Bill 29 and other health-care restructuring, the major public sector unions have continued to engage in increasingly destructive raiding drives, which have undermined solidarity in the BC labour movement and made it more difficult for unions to conduct effective, public advocacy campaigns in support of public health care and the end to privatization.

BC's labour movement also experienced difficulties in trying to boost union member involvement – difficulties that were in many ways similar to those experienced in the United States and Great Britain (Moody 2007; Daniels and McIlroy 2008). Membership losses in resource industries cut financial and staff resources in unions that were often the most militant (BC retired union official 2, private sector). Subsequently, declining union density has meant the cost of organizing new members has gone up (BC union staff official 2, private sector). Leadership difficulties and the lack of union mobilization have eroded union capacities to mobilize and undertake strikes and public protests, and often induced public anger. And politically, despite union efforts to raise campaign donations, organized labour lacks the financial clout and sophisticated lobbying techniques of big business.

Added to this were the typical political disputes among unions over strategy. Labour movements are often split on what concessions they are willing to make in negotiations, and when to walk away – typically, this is a divide between public and private sector unions (Garrett 1998; Boeri, Brugiavini, and Calmfors 2001). Union leaders also commonly disagree on political strategy:

some look to bargain with government on a set agenda; others only want to bargain after opposing the agenda from outside, and working with opposition parties to force through or block legislative reforms (Hamann and Kelly 2004). In BC, these tensions have affected the relationships between major public sector unions such as the Canadian Union of Public Employees, the Hospital Employees Union, the Health Sciences Association of BC, and the British Columbia Nurses Union, as well as the Canadian Auto Workers (now Unifor) and the United Steel Workers (BC union staff official 1, private sector; BC retired union official 2, private sector). Such divisions of opinion constrain efforts at wider mobilization and limit discussion of strategies in key urban labour councils as well as in the BC Federation of Labour (BC retired staff official 1, private sector; BC retired union president 1, private sector).

Moreover, because of the many setbacks and defeats of the last few years, organized labour has been unable to overcome the reforms to union certification and the ongoing employer animus to unionized workplaces. Overall, certification attempts dropped by more than two-thirds from mid-1990 averages of more than 600 annually to 175 between 2008 and 2010. Union success rates in certification also declined to below 50 per cent, while more than 20 per cent of all certification attempts were routinely dismissed because of procedural issues and employer interference in the wake of the financial crisis.

And in specific sectors that are hard to organize, the problems of mobilizing and certifying new workers were even more challenging. In agriculture, for example, recent union efforts have been remarkably free of the racism that has blemished labour responses to immigrant workers in times past, and BC's labour movement has organized new low-wage workers into existing unions, set up storefront service centres to meet their needs, and called on the government to allow guest workers a pathway to citizenship. These efforts have been led by the United Food and Commercial Workers through their Agricultural Workers Alliance, which operates ten storefront organizing centres across the country, including three in BC: in Surrey and Abbotsford in the Fraser Valley and in Kelowna in the Okanagan Valley, where several successful organizing drives have been conducted in recent years (Fairey et al. 2008; Sandborn 2008). For the first time in BC history, foreign workers imported to pick crops were allowed to join a union.

However, across the BC agricultural sector, hundreds of thousands of workers remain non-unionized. Even though the provincial government effectively reduced the minimum piece rates payable to farm workers by approximately 4 per cent in 2002, by deeming piece rates to include statutory holiday and annual vacation pay under the Employment Standards Act, many farm workers were not even paid the piece rates they contracted for. And even if they are paid the statutory minimum piece rates, their hourly pay often comes to less than the minimum wage. In addition, when the provincial minimum wage was finally

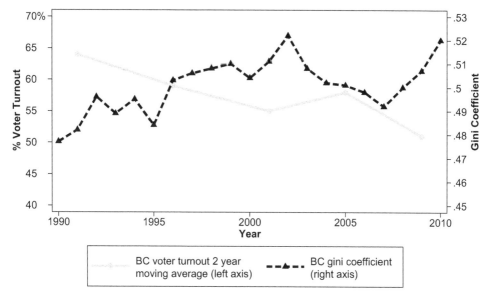

Figure 6.9. BC income inequality and declining voter turnout
Sources: Statistics Canada, CANSIM table 202-705; Elections BC, "General Elections Statistics in Comparison: 1928–2009."

increased in 2011, the agriculture association lobbies successfully pressured the government to exempt much of the agriculture from increasing the minimum wage for agricultural workers. This has not only limited the improvement of working conditions in this highly exploited sector. The failure to make organizing gains has also limited any political headway that unions are able to make in new immigrant communities in claiming to represent "all" workers (BC union staff official 1, private sector).

Finally, such reversals have been compounded by the ongoing decline of voter turnout and marginalization of low- and middle-income workers from the political process. As figure 6.9 shows, BC followed wider international trends of income inequality increasing electoral abstention, as poorer citizens either lacked the time and resources to participate, or increasingly perceived the political system as untrustworthy and unresponsive to their needs (Anderson and Beramendi 2008; McBride and Whiteside 2011). With the rise of inequality and the declining effectiveness of tax and transfer programs from 1990 to 2010, voter turnout declined from 64 per cent in 1991 to 51 per cent in 2009. Along with Ontario, which saw the highest rise in market income inequality over this period, this was the steepest decline in turnout among provincial voter participation. These data conform well with the econometric regression study by BC

Elections that also showed that income was the primary variable of importance in determining electoral participation (Burgar and Monkman 2010).

Consequently, not only did rising income inequality work to diminish political attention to the economic concerns of ordinary citizens. It also contributed to weakening the voice of organized labour in public policymaking and voter mobilization over the longer term. As recent scholarship has highlighted, increases in inequality have provided the opportunity for conservative parties to move further to the right and enact policy that weakens the interests of organized labour (Pontusson and Rueda 2008). These feedback mechanisms help explain the profound organizational shift seen in many countries that have favoured the expansion of business power and the exclusion of low- and middle-income voters (Crouch 2011; Hacker and Pierson 2010a).

In the BC context, unions represented by far the most significant organized interest with a stake in the material circumstances of those with modest means. However, the electoral victories of the Campbell government and the subsequent reforms to the labour code and to labour institutions greatly diminished the capacity of organized labour to pressure policymakers to sustain or refurbish commitments to good jobs or social provision that were made in the middle decades of the last century. Unions – as much in North America as in Western Europe – used to offer powerful organizational counterweights to the power of organized business interests and pushed governments to address wider economic and social concerns and implement policies that provided income and social security (Boeri, Brugiavini, and Calmfors 2001; Western 1997). But by the first decade of 2000, this was much less frequently the case.

Instead, the ongoing abstention of lower- and middle-class voters has left organized labour increasingly unable to counter wider policy and economic trends, or reverse legislation that contributed to declines in union density. The drop in the electoral representation of the poor and middle-income earners contributed to an electoral context where the influence and extra-electoral participation among the wealthy and business could be increased to ensure the political capacity of organized employer interests – so much so that in the 2005 and 2009 elections, the Liberal government required the support of only 28 and 25 per cent respectively of the eligible voting electorate to win majority governments.

Continuing Inequality and Flexibility after the Financial Crisis

In the wake of the financial crisis of 2008–10, many of these trends continued. As in all jurisdictions that depended on high mortgage debt and resource exports for prosperity, the financial crisis had significant negative impacts on British Columbia. Drops in foreign investment in real estate alongside the downturn in housing starts and house sales meant higher unemployment and rapid declines in provincial and municipal revenue. At the same time, the collapse of export markets for minerals, gas, and forest products, led to layoffs across resource sectors, and a rapid decline in resource royalties and taxes. Government deficits grew rapidly, and the province's Liberal government quickly committed to expenditure reductions as well as further public austerity measures. But rather than address the major problems revealed by the economic downturn, the Campbell government and then the new premier, Christy Clark, only further committed to business-friendly policy reforms.

Part of the reason for these renewed government commitments to high-risk economic sectors was the efforts of major businesses to win policy commitments. Led by oil and gas firms as well as global and local mining companies, firms massively expanded their lobbying of the provincial government, meeting with government ministers thousands of times over the course of 2010–16 (Graham, Daub, and Carroll 2017). And new levels of political donations to the liberal government that millions to party campaigns, and further cemented the ties of business to the Liberal Party. The result was new Liberal government efforts to increase liquefied natural gas exports to Alberta for oil sands processing as well as to China for conventional fossil fuel energy use (Lee and Klein 2020).

The other major reason for government commitment to economic sectors that benefitted only a few was how federal efforts to set record low interest rates, combined with vast new inflows of Chinese and Asian investment in real estate, fuelled hundreds of millions into provincial real estate markets. This was part of wider global trends where vast government backing of mortgage markets and secondary financial markets provided investors with enormous new opportunities to invest in high-return cities like Vancouver, London, New York, and Hong Kong (Dorfman 2015; Ley 2017). Such new capital inflows quickly led to a reboot of Vancouver's real estate market, and over the next decade, prices soared again, with loose borrowing rules and limited oversight fuelling ever-higher levels of mortgage debt and foreign investment – economic trends that benefit the very wealthy but only burdened the average household with hundreds of thousands dollars more in mortgage debt (Lee 2016).

For labour markets, the success of business and finance in finding new sources of accumulation in the aftermath of the crisis meant that the primacy of flexible labour markets was simply reinforced. In the public sector, the provincial government demanded greater austerity. In the private sector, the emphasis was on lower labour costs and continuing low-wage immigration into private services and agriculture. For workers, precarious work and low-wage jobs became the wider norm as more high-skilled and low-skilled workers were faced with greater insecurity, and temporary work increasingly began to characterize all types of occupations. And for the unemployed, the underemployed, and the homeless, the consequences of flexible labour markets and limited social protections only became more severe.

Across public services, as the Liberal government continued with its policies of low taxation, enacting austerity measures to keep wage costs low and public employment in check. With the Supreme Court overruling Bill 29, thereby countering the government's ability to overturn collective agreements, the government quickly introduced the "Public Sector Zero-Cost Compensation Mandate" (2009–11) to further restrict public services and public sector employment (Longhurst, Ponder, and McGregor 2020). With this new mandate in place, health care, long-term care, and education sectors were prevented from replacing retirees, and instead expanded the use of temporary and fixed-term contracts, and contracting out. Added to this was a "Compensation Review," which selected specific sectors such as cleaning and food services for further competitive bidding and contracting out. This was followed by the passing of a new "Economic Stability Mandate" that sought to bargain zero-cost five-year agreements. The results for the public sector were the continued decline of full-time jobs across the sector, and BC public sector workers in health, social work, and education facing among the highest levels of low-wage and precarious employment in the country.

In the formerly unionized private sectors, such as construction and forestry, workers in good jobs were terminated in the thousands, only to be replaced with non-unionized workers and growing numbers of workers in insecure jobs. In forestry, the deregulation of rules requiring the provincial milling of logs led to the closure of mills and a rapid increase in raw log exports (Parfitt 2017). Unionized workers lost jobs as sawmills and pulp and paper mills were closed, while temporary jobs increased as logs were directly loaded onto ships. In construction, a growing number of once unionized firms opened non-union operations to compete with the growing non-union construction companies and subcontractors that came to dominate the industry. By 2015, only 15 per cent of construction workers were still protected by collective agreements.

In private services, earlier deregulatory reforms continued to open the door for employers to find new ways to cheapen the cost of labour – whether through reducing their permanent workforce or by simply ignoring the laxly enforced employment standards of the province. With unions continuing to decline after the financial crisis, and no government commitment to uphold standards, employers largely acted with little to no consideration of the views of their workers. Part-time and temporary jobs grew in number, the vast majority of which lacked benefits, training opportunities, or any expectation of continuity. In restaurants, retail, and cleaning services, women and people of colour were forced to cope with the adverse effects of low wages and insecure employment. Indeed, even where workers were on the job for years, they still made only the minimum wage or little more than the minimum wage (BC Fair Wages Commission 2018). And as research study after research study demonstrated,

Vancouver (along with Toronto) had the highest rates of working poverty in Canada (Ivanova 2016).

By 2015, British Columbia's economy had resumed strong job growth as well as a rising labour force participation rate. But with the government's commitment to limited regulation of the labour market – combined with employer expectations of flexibility – a "jobs with inequality" model of employment growth had become firmly institutionalized in the province. Forty-two per cent of the province's labour force – the vast majority in non-standard employment – had median earnings of $15,200, a figure well below what any worker or family required to live in a city with globally high housing and rental prices. In such circumstances, for those stuck in such low-wage jobs, there were few opportunities to break out of the working poverty cycle. In contrast, in 2016 the top ten wealthiest families in British Columbia held $25 billion in net worth – more than the total wealth of 1.32 million provincial residents – and had seen that wealth grow by more than $3 billion in the previous four years (Hemingway and Macdonald 2018).

Conclusion

The net effect of BC's shifting political climate – the increasing organizational capacity of business, the shift of the Liberal Party to represent the interests of the highest-income earners, the decline of unions, and the ever-declining turnout of citizens – has been clear: it dramatically weakened the organized political voice of ordinary citizens on economic issues and increased the influence of organized business interests and the wealthy on public policy. Unions and other organizations representing the economic interests of voters from the middle to the bottom of the economic ladder, already weak, atrophied further, while the political clout of employers and the affluent in general greatly increased.

The result was that over the course of the 1990s and the first two decades of the 2000s, the structure of British Columbia's industrial relations, employment standards, and public sector changed profoundly. Union density – the share of the workforce covered by collective bargaining – fell dramatically, especially in the private sector. Employers offered fewer full-time jobs and increased their non-standard and often underpaid workforce. Public sector restructuring lowered wages and weakened the influence of public sector employment on the wider labour market. And with the erosion of the minimum wage and employment standards, more and more workers were relegated to low-wage precarious employment.

These changes were largely politically driven and had direct as well as indirect effects on the rise in income inequality and the severe decline in job quality in British Columbia. There were policy alternatives that could have reduced such negative impacts, and that had advocates within the province. However, opponents of such reforms, possessing formidable and growing organizational resources, could easily mobilize to stop them and used their organizational resources to launch a vigorous assault on British Columbia's unions and wider employment standards. In comparison with provincial developments elsewhere in Canada, this made BC unique in the extent to which shifts in organized interests and party representation contributed to the depth and continuation of neoliberal labour market policy reforms.

7 Newfoundland and Labrador: Institutional Stasis during the Oil Boom

Over the course of the late 1990s and early in the first decade of 2000, the province of Newfoundland and Labrador (NL) cast off its "have-not" status and became a "have" province. Fuelled by expanding offshore oil production and mining projects, public and private sector employment grew and poverty declined. Like other capital cities in the midst of resource booms, NL's St. John's experienced considerable growth, with a rise in new jobs in construction and highly skilled professions. But at the same time, unemployment in the province remained the highest in Canada, and long-term unemployment was especially high in rural communities hit by the collapse of fisheries, plant closures, and wind down of forestry companies. NL was also distinctive in that many of its labour force worked in temporary jobs and another 6 to 7 per cent of its labour force emigrated to work elsewhere in Canada, most notably to Alberta's oil patch.

The Progressive Conservative (PC) government of Danny Williams, first elected in 2003, responded to these developments in ways that were distinct from most other Canadian jurisdictions. Most strikingly, both government and business continued to work with organized labour. There was no major government effort to reform labour market institutions or lower employment standards. Union density remained among the highest in Canada, as did levels of public sector employment in the overall labour force. In addition, also in contrast to other Canadian provinces, the provincial government sustained policies that reduced income inequality across the province. Business "insiders" led by the oil multinationals were compensated with subsidies and extensive tax and royalty concessions, but low-income earners and the seasonally unemployed were also provided with income supports and educational opportunities. Nevertheless, NL's labour market remained strongly "dualized" labour market between those with good, unionized jobs in construction and the public sector, and those with low-wage work in industries and sectors that relied heavily on part-time and seasonal employment, such as the fisheries, hotel and accommodation, retail, and finance and business administration.

This chapter argues that politics, unions, and business interests were key in shaping these government responses to rising global demand for oil and maintaining labour-related policies and regulations – a case of "institutional stasis." Like other right and centre-right governments, Williams's PC party primarily represented the interests of business and adopted supply-side policies that sought to reduce business costs, enact fiscal austerity, and boost the economic competitiveness of resource and local service industries. However, organized labour in NL was better able than other provincial labour movements to influence the policies and redistributive efforts of government, especially through the training of unionized construction workers and other skilled workers. Moreover, in contrast to many international employers operating in Canada, large transnational resource companies in NL sought to gain access to skilled labour as well as constrain the costs of long-term capital investments by ensuring the agreement of unions to wage moderation through province-wide collective agreements. I argue that these unique features of business and labour were two keys to explaining why the government retained a labour market policy that favoured the status quo.

Another critical reason for the difference in NL politics was the nature of political organization within the province. Even though the Conservative government was strongly pro-business and had large legislative majorities, it retained traditional brokerage strategies that looked to use oil-generated revenues to reward domestic provincial businesses while providing job opportunities as well as at least minimal income security to the middle class and to vulnerable socio-economic groups, such as women, youth, and the long-term unemployed.

Two organizational features were crucial to such distinctive developments. One was the ongoing active role of traditional civic, commerce, and community associations in influencing party politics and policy. The second was the brokerage approach of the Conservative Party that allowed teachers and other middle-class professionals to take up important Cabinet portfolios. It is argued here that when such wider citizen interests overlap with party strategies of mobilization, policymaking was far more consensual and far less likely to adopt more radical reforms targeting labour regulations and institutions. In NL, these organizational developments of brokerage politics and civic mobilization help account for why the PC Party – unlike all other Conservative parties in Canada – remained committed to introducing a new poverty reduction strategy aimed at assisting students, women, and low-income families. While such policies did little to overcome the divide between good and bad jobs in the labour market, or reduce the number of temporary jobs in the province, they did offer some income support that lowered poverty and ameliorated income insecurity in rural areas of the province.

The Resource Boom and PC Economic Policy

Since the global recession of the early 1990s, Canada and other affluent countries witnessed the transformation of their economies. As in many countries, so too across Canada, deindustrialization and the decline of core manufacturing industries led to the loss of stable, well-paid, full-time jobs and the rise of long-term unemployment (Western 1997; Emmenegger et al. 2011; Jackson 1999). But in Canada and Norway, global competition and rising world demand for resources led to oil booms that boosted economic growth, but also led to the rapid mechanization of resource industries and the precipitous decline of industrial and manufacturing employment (Campbell 2013; Ross 2012; Stanford 2008). At the same time, economic globalization – especially the deregulation of finance – provided the context for rapid inflows of investment into resource-rich states, and the rapid growth of resource exports in countries like Canada (PricewaterhouseCoopers 2010b).

In response, many North American and Western European governments shifted from demand-side management to an emphasis on improving supply-side conditions for business, with the goals of boosting investment and employment through tax reductions and the deregulation of labour markets (Glyn 2006; Duménil and Lévy 2004). However, scholarship suggests that policies from different partisan governments demonstrated contrasting intellectual interpretations of the purpose of economic growth, and that different fiscal conditions patterned policymakers' actions (Beramendi and Cusack 2008; Pontusson 2005; Amable 2009). In general, governments of the Left adopted monetary and fiscal policies with the goals of counterbalancing economic cycles (Huo 2009); governments of the Right enacted policies that enhanced economic cycles, enacting greater spending and tax cuts during periods of growth or cutting spending and reducing deficits during downturns (Amable 2009).

From 2003 to 2010, similar partisan effects were evident in NL as Williams's PC government passed pro-cyclical policies in the name of "free commerce" and were attentive to business concerns (especially those of the global resource industry) for profitability. But new legislation did not create markets that were simply in the interests of a narrow corporate interest, as in British Columbia. Nor did the PC legislature block efforts to address inequities throughout NL. Rather, PC economic, resource, and human capital policy remained firmly traditional, emphasizing the government's role in managing resources and economic development for the interests of the "province" as well as for developing "self-reliance" (PC Party of NL 2003, 2007). The growth in oil and resource revenues backed this agenda, providing the context for some expansion of public sector and unionized private sector employment.

Certainly, PC actions were geared to removing tax, regulatory, and institutional constraints on the resource sector and those with economic clout. Both the federal and provincial PC government made significant efforts to push forward rapid, extensive resource development (Carter 2020). And influenced by a powerful, globally integrated industry, NL developed many of the typical characteristics of a booming resource economy – rapid oil development, for instance, as well as a government committed to "economic efficiency," with limited political capacity to capture resource rents and diversify, but with significant policy levers to spur foreign investment (Humphreys, Sachs, and Stiglitz 2007). Seeking to take advantage of the growing global demand for oil, the Williams Conservatives enacted standard fiscally conservative and pro-cyclical economic measures such as tax reductions and tax subsidies to oil MNCs and businesses.

In 2002, NL had among the highest rates of personal income tax in Canada, the highest rate of fuel taxes, and corporate income tax rates that ranked among the middle with other Canadian provinces (Norris 2003). However, by 2007, the province stated that it had delivered the biggest personal income tax reductions ever in the history of the province (Department of Finance 2011). For business, building on earlier corporate tax reforms in the 1990s, the Williams government sought to support business investment in the resource industries by introducing new tax credits and accelerated capital depreciation allowances. Accompanied by federal tax reforms, effective tax rates in oil and gas declined on average from approximately 40 per cent to 18 per cent between 2002 and 2010 (PricewaterhouseCoopers 2010a). Oil and gas companies were also given massive federal government write-offs for exploration and investment (Taylor, Bramley, and Winfield 2005; Taylor and Raynolds 2006). In mining, the effective tax rate fell from 10 per cent in 2008 to an approximate average of 7.6 per cent in 2008 (PricewaterhouseCoopers 2009).

At the same time, the other key driver of offshore oil and resource exploitation was the financialization of resource and commodity markets, and integration of global resource companies into financialized commodity markets (Gkanoutas-Leventis and Nesvetailova 2015; UNCTAD 2009b). Over the course of the 1990s and the first decade of 2000, the deregulation of commodity markets and pension funds led to major investment banks like Goldman Sachs and Morgan Stanley as well as many others pouring torrents of money into commodities and commodity-linked derivative and future markets (Forhoohar 2016). For example, in 2003 there was approximately $13 billion in commodity indexes; by 2008 more than $260 billion. Making billions off trading and speculation, the major financial institutions profited substantially. But they also drove the price of all commodities skyward, with prices nearly doubling in the middle of the first decade of 2000 alone (Forhoohar 2016).

This financialization of commodity markets provided new opportunities for oil and resource majors to not only profit, but also to expand production, especially into secondary areas and offshore oil fields around the world (Watts

2014). To diversify their portfolios and expand their sources of production, global resource companies launched major investment initiatives, buying up other firms and investing heavily in new areas (PricewaterhouseCoopers 2010a). And this was much assisted by investment banks, which as active players in resource markets also enormously increased their lending to resource companies to expand production further. It was in this context of booming prices and burgeoning financial markets that companies expanded their extractive activities into increasingly difficult geographies.

The result was that with the financialization of oil and resources alongside the government's fiscal changes led to rapid growth of offshore oil production and the expansion of iron and nickel mining in the first decade of 2000. From 1997, when pumping began, until November 2009, 1.08 billion barrels of oil were extracted from three fields in the North Grand Banks: Hibernia (the oldest field, producing since 1997), Terra Nova, and White Rose. From 2002 until 2008, annual production was fairly steady, ranging from 104 million to 134 million barrels per year (Canada–Newfoundland and Labrador Offshore Petroleum Board 2010). In mining, the growth of global demand for resources and the entry of global mining multinationals led to the upgrading of ore and processing facilities, a vast expansion of exploration, and – with the rise of nickel and iron prices – a more than four-fold increase in returns.

This expansion of global resources and global commodity futures markets strongly contributed to remaking the province, turning it from a traditional "have-not" Canadian province into a resource powerhouse. In 1999, the oil and gas (and related construction and manufacturing) industries accounted for 14.3 per cent of NL's GDP; by 2008, they accounted for more than 52 per cent (NL Department of Finance 2010; see figure 7.1). In 1999, mining contributed $972 million to the provincial economy. By 2010, mining had grown into a $3.7 billion industry, directly accounting for more than 7 per cent of GDP. Overall, oil and gas accounted for 58 per cent of total output growth between 1997 and 2010 (Atlantic Provinces Economic Council 2011). Resource exploitation revenues grew by more than 400 per cent between 1999 and 2008, before declining slightly in the wake of the financial crisis and the resulting fall in oil and resource prices (Locke 2010).

NL's transformation was part of Canada's emergence as a major resource exporter and the replacement of manufacturing with resources as the main engine of its economic growth (Cross 2008). In the 1980s, it appeared that Canada was diversifying its economy, but in recent years with the financialization of resource and commodity industries, the country has become increasingly dependent on its resource sector while seeing its manufacturing sector go into decline. China's growing demand for natural resources lifted Canada's trade surplus to near-record levels of exports: above C$45 billion per year for much of the decade. Foreign capital flowed into Canada's and NL's natural resources,

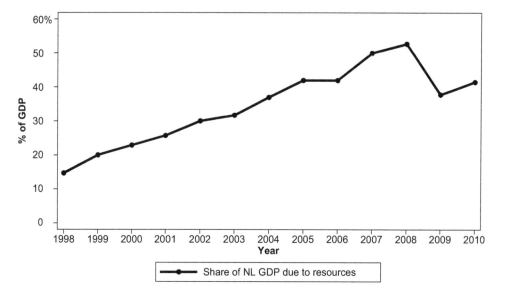

Figure 7.1. Growth of resources in NL (share of GDP due to oil, gas, and mining)
Source: Department of Finance NL.

and foreign multinationals bought companies outright or took controlling shares in smaller domestic companies (Peters 2012b).

In oil and gas in NL, hundreds of billions of dollars in new investment came from American giants Exxon, Chevron, and Norway's national company, Statoil (PricewaterhouseCoopers 2010a). Diversified mining giants like Vale and RioTinto entered into Canada and NL, yielding billion of dollars in profits and unprecedented share price returns in a little less than ten years (Peters 2010; PricewaterhouseCoopers 2010a).

The boom brought with it new areas of investment as well as new employment. In terms of the labour market, the resource boom immediately contributed an average of 5.1 per cent of total employment, with growth in oil and gas as well as construction jobs (figure 7.2). In 2010, oil, gas, and mining employment accounted directly for 4.7 per cent of the labour force in the province. But the indirect and induced impacts of the resource, construction, and financial and service-related industries were much larger, with an average of 10,600 new jobs per year between 2003 and 2008.

At the same time, more and more workers who were not employed in the oil, gas, mining, and construction industries began to hold jobs that supported those who were. Since the resource industries resulted in an estimated annual average of $663 million in new income for NL residents from 1997 to 2007

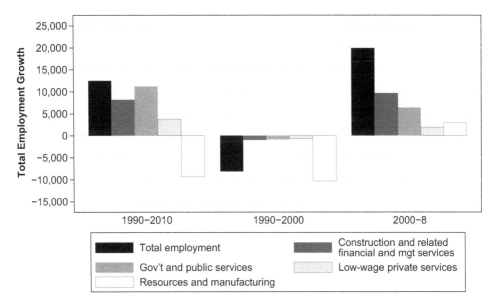

Figure 7.2. Employment and private sector employment growth in NL, 1999–2009
(thousands)
Sources: Statistics Canada, CANSIM table 2820008.

(Canadian Association of Petroleum Producers 2010), this money led to rising demand for food, clothing, and accommodation services. Over the course of ten years (2000–10), new jobs in low-wage private services, such as retail, accommodation and food, transport, and business services accounted for 10 per cent of all employment growth (figure 7.2).

In the first decade of 2000, NL's public sector also continued to grow, and even though NL has traditionally had a much larger public sector than the rest of Canada, averaging over 32 per cent of total employment during the past decade, public sector employment grew both before and after the economic crisis of 2008. While in other provinces, the public sector was also grew slowly and contributed good jobs, in NL the public sector made up the majority of job growth – and good job growth – between 1990 and 2010.

However, the emergence of oil and gas as well as mining in NL widened inequality between men and women in the labour market. The offshore sector's major impact on industries such as retail, food and accommodation, and hospitality was only to create a demand for far more low-paid service-sector workers rather than better-paid, highly skilled workers, while reinforcing the gendered dimension of work. Women occupied between 50 and 57 per cent of all service-sector employment since 1987 and never held more than 21 per cent of jobs in production.

Consequently, the demand for labour in the predominantly non-unionized service sector, with its characteristically high levels of part-time and temporary employment, reinforced a persistent disparity between the incomes of men and women. Since 1997, the average income derived by women from wages, salaries, and commissions ranged from 53 per cent to 60 per cent of men's income. In areas such as retail trade and the accommodations and food services industries, women often worked at much lower wages than men. In 2008, for example, over 70 per cent of employees in the accommodation and food services industry earned less than $10 per hour (NL Department of Finance 2008).

Moreover, despite rapid economic growth over the past decade, temporary and seasonal employment continued to account for a quarter of NL's employment (figure 7.3). With the fisheries, construction, and tourism industries playing key roles as employers in the province, much employment was seasonal and temporary. But temporary employment was also widespread in private service industries such as retail, food, and accommodation – all generally non-unionized industries. In NL, temporary employment as a percentage of total employment was twice the level of the Canadian average of 12 per cent (figure 7.3). But even outside of typical temporary contracts, part-year jobs were also more common across the province, as approximately 42 per cent of the workforce were in part-year jobs, working less than thirty-nine weeks per year (NL Department of Human Resources 2011). This compares with the Canadian average of 23 per cent in part-year jobs.

The socio-economic problems associated with temporary and part-year employment are well known (OECD 2008a). High levels of temporary employment mean that workers earn less, receive fewer benefits, and work irregular hours. Non-unionized temporary workers are also more likely to be laid off during downturns as employers hang on to skilled employees. Persistently high levels of temporary employment are known to reduce the relative bargaining power of other unskilled and low-wage workers (Gautie and Schmitt 2010). Higher levels of insecure employment are also associated with lower levels of training and education, as individual workers lack the time and resources to access post-secondary training and educational opportunities.

But NL remained different from BC and Ontario, as employers did not defect from full-time/full-year jobs. Rather, the labour market remained dualized between those with permanent jobs and those with fixed-term, part-time, and low-pay seasonal employment. As figure 7.3 demonstrates, full-time/full-year jobs remained at approximately 60 per cent throughout the 1990s and first decade of 2000. Part-time employment also remained at 14–15 per cent of the labour force. Self-employment, most notably of skilled trades, declined slightly, averaging 10 per cent at the end of the first decade of 2000, among the lowest levels in Canada. However, the decline in self-employment was related in large part to the out-migration of skilled workers to Alberta, where

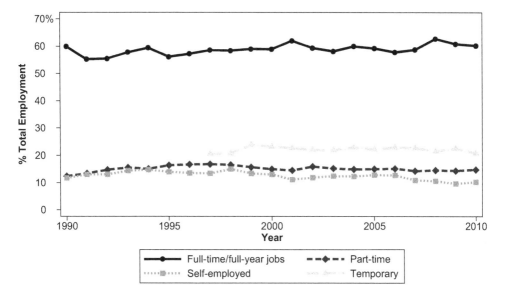

Figure 7.3. Stasis in non-standard employment in NL, 1990–2010 (% total employment)
Sources: Statistics Canada CANSIM tables 2820055, 2020101.

NL construction workers remained in demand throughout the first decade of 2000, with more than 13,000 workers categorized as "mobile" and working in Alberta or elsewhere in Canada each year, a figure that spiked above 20,000 in the wake of the financial crisis (NL Department of Human Resources 2011).

NL also saw a notable decline in low-wage work in the province, although levels of non-standard labour remained the highest in Canada. In the 1990s, with the collapse of the fisheries, skilled workers left the province to work elsewhere in Canada, and the number of low-wage/low-skill jobs rose accordingly, to account for more than 44 per cent of jobs in the province (figure 7.4). But with the development of the oil and construction sectors, wages and average working time increased, and led to a comparatively rapid decline of low-wage work across the province of more than 6 per centage points 1999–2007 (figure 7.4).

The rise of oil and new jobs also significantly reduced income inequality from its highs in the mid-1990s (figure 7.5). Low-earning households were particularly affected by fisheries closure and the recession of the mid-1990s, with earnings declining by more than 75 per cent for many households. But by 2000, median earnings began to recover for NL working families, and by 2010 had grown by more than 33 per cent since 2000. As figure 7.5 shows, this resulted in a rapid decline of earnings inequality between the top and bottom

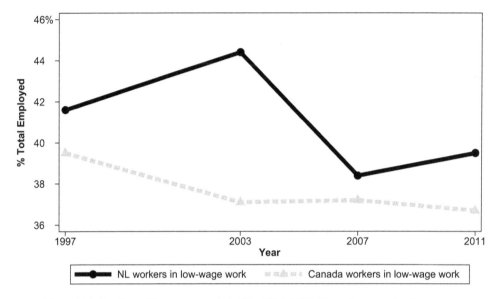

Figure 7.4. Decline of low-wage work in NL, 2000–2010 (% workers earning less
than two-thirds of median hourly wage of full-time/full-year worker)
Source: Author's figures from custom request, Statistics Canada, Survey of Labour and Income
Dynamics and Survey of Consumer Finances, "Percentage of Workers with Low Annual
Earnings and Low-Hourly wages, Canada and Provinces," CANSIM table C685593.

20 per cent of income earners. From average highs of more than 20 in the
D90:D20 ratio in the mid-1990s, this has had declined to 11 between 2009 and
2010. In comparison to BC and Ontario, NL was the only province to see a decline in earnings inequality between top- and low-income earners, and overall
the decline was the greatest among all provinces.

Big Oil and Government

Despite the rapid rise of oil wealth in the province, and the central role of
multinational resource companies and financialized commodity markets in
public policy, NL retained a more traditional model of dealing with corporate
influence, so the oil wealth of the companies was not converted into direct and
overt political power with influence over broader public policy. Given the ways
in which the economic power of oil and resource companies has been used
in other jurisdictions to buy political influence, theoretically the transnational
companies operating in NL could have been expected to seek ways to make
themselves richer still through pursuit of labour market deregulation, "open
shop" construction arrangements, and the lowering of labour costs. But this

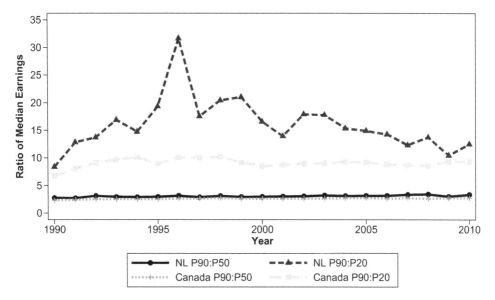

Figure 7.5. Declining earnings inequality in NL, 1990–2010 (among economic families, age 18–65, decile ratio)
Source: Author's figures from custom tabulation from Survey of Labour and Income Dynamics and the Survey of Consumer Finances, "Median Incomes, Average Incomes, and Share of Incomes by Decile; P90:P10 Ratio, P90:P50 Ratio, P50:P10 Ratio," data shared by the Canadian Centre for Policy Alternatives.

did not happen in NL. Instead, the province retained a highly dualized labour market characterized by well-paying union jobs accompanied by a larger number of low-wage, non-standard jobs in the non-unionized private sector. Why?

One reason for the growth of unionized jobs was government commitment to private oil development through supply management strategies, combined with a provincial concern with maintaining employment and for NL to see a "fair share" of return from oil and resource wealth. Keynesian supply management strategies were common in the post-war industrial powers. Seeking to plan infrastructure development, manage finance, and manage energy and telecommunications, governments routinely set up state-owned enterprises (Toninelli 2000). In the liberal market economies, in the post-war period, state intervention was always more limited as governments remained committed to the ideal that private enterprise was to generate jobs and investment.

Nevertheless, in Canada, provincial governments did undertake "province building" activities in electricity and telecommunications by establishing Crown corporations. And the federal government introduced the Auto Pact, a selective trade liberalization deal with the United States, which had import substitution qualifications that ensured production and sales ratios in Canada, while protecting auto parts producers from offshore competitors (Anastakis 2005; Brownsey and Howlett 1992). Such government activities made up for typical market failures of under-investment in less populated areas, and provided long-term infrastructure and social capital development for enhanced business productivity (Laux and Molot 1988).

However, in the 1980s and 1990s, as governments adopted models of economic liberalization, they privatized state-owned enterprises, and only a few continued to seek to manage investment and employment opportunities for major multinational enterprises, their branch plants, and related supplier industries (Bortolotti and Siniscalco 2004; Etchemendy 2011). In Canada, NL and Quebec were the only two provinces where governments retained modest inward-oriented goals of provincial development in their attempts to boost economic growth through global trade. In NL, this has meant that the development of natural resources has long been tied to aspirations of wider economic development. This government stance has shaped relations with business and created a context for greater provincial autonomy in labour and social policy (House 2002). But the trade-off has been a neoliberal development model that has prioritized low royalties and extensive tax breaks to global MNCs for resource development (Carter 2020).

With the rise of OPEC countries and oil prices in the 1970s, governments took increasingly active roles in managing the development, production, and distribution of oil wealth (Ross 2012). The vast majority nationalized the industry and established national petroleum companies to manage the resource. However, in Canada, since the discovery of oil in the 1970s, the approach has been – with only a few exceptions such as Saskatchewan in the 1970s – a purely private one, based on private corporations – predominantly American – developing and exploiting the resource, and governments seeking to uphold some minimal royalties from the industry as well as seeking companies to conform to minimal environmental regulation (Nikiforuk 2008).

In the 1980s, NL's Liberal representatives, provincial and federal, became interested in the Norwegian and British models of public development (Fossum 1997). But with the defeat of the federal Liberals in 1984 and the election of Conservative governments in both Ottawa and NL, a joint federal-provincial accord was struck for the development of offshore oil, and NL's development model shifted to government supporting large multinational oil companies, in return for capturing low royalties and equity stakes in offshore developments (House 2002).This left companies to extract large profits in return for the foreign corporations paying royalties and maintaining a largely neutral role in politics and other public policies in the province.

In NL, this private model of development, accompanied by provincial royalties, led to the provincial government receiving $12.9 billion in oil revenues from 1997 to 2011, and the federal government taking in approximately \$5.5 billion (Locke 2006, 2010, 2012). However, with few public documents, estimates vary on how favourable the province's royalty regime has been to the companies. Given how companies are protected under law from disclosing true returns, estimates are based on what little is known about specific royalty deals and oil company costs and expenditures. Yet by any of these estimated measures, private oil companies have done extremely well in the offshore oil business, paying minimal rents and taxes to government.

Statutory rates for combined royalties and tax to the federal and provincial governments are thought to be in the range of between 50 and 63 per cent of gross corporate revenues (Locke 2010; Mintz and Chen 2010). But in Canada, as in North America more generally, oil exploration is heavily subsidized by generous tax allowances for development. In addition, companies are not only allowed to write off all development, exploration, and capital costs, but borrowing costs over time can also be discounted under complex tax accounting procedures. In addition, companies can typically pay different royalties, depending on the price of oil, and they are given the further advantage to write off all royalties as well as corporate income taxes against their profits, depending on the production phase of the project (Mintz and Chen 2010). Once all of these are factored in, the actual "effective" rate of taxation and royalties (the real rate of taxation of company revenues) that oil companies operating in NL pay is far lower: approximately 13–14 per cent of company revenues (Mintz and Chen 2012). This compares with an effective non-resource company effective tax rate of 12 per cent in NL and 14 per cent nationally.

For ExxonMobil, Chevron, Suncor, and Husky Energy – the major oil MNCs operating offshore in NL – this meant high corporate profits throughout the first decade of 2000. While income figures provide only a snapshot of corporate profitability, oil companies regularly saw returns of \$4–5 billion annually, as figure 7.6 shows, generally taking in close to a quarter of all income in the province. In contrast, wages and other income for working people grew at well below productivity rates.

To maintain this arrangement of heavy subsidies to the oil industry and ensure the long-term private development of offshore oil, the federal and provincial governments sought to protect oil producers from further political or administrative interventions and established an arm's-length relationship between public officials and private firms, through a two-sided administrative structure that split operational issues from royalty questions. For exploration and production, the governments set up a joint petroleum board to manage competitive bids for leases and oversee the production licences for private corporate producers. For collecting royalties and overseeing the accounting of company costs, the provincial Ministry of Natural Resources was allocated the task, while the Federal Ministry of Finance collected corporate

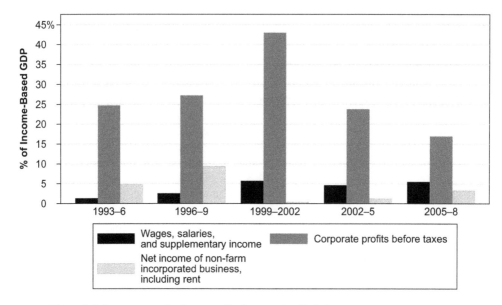

Figure 7.6. Percentage of select contributions to NL GDP (income based)
Sources: CANSIM tables 13-018-X and 3840037.

tax. Governments followed this structure to prevent corruption and to foster competitive exploration and production in the private offshore oil industry while maintaining a protective layer of civil servants between government and private business people.

Big Oil and Employment Policies

The province also sought to promote local development and employment growth. To stimulate employment, the province pushed for agreements with the oil companies to use a gravity-based system for offshore oil production and financed developments such as the Bull Arm construction site and the Marystown Shipyard – facilities built in the 1990s to construct and service the oil platforms as well as the later Terra Nova Floating Production Storage and Offloading vessel (Fusco 2007). The government also financed the construction of the NEWDOCK sub-sea systems fabrication centre and the Newfoundland Transshipment Terminal, both of which were to create local engineering and construction capacity (Carter 2011; House 2002). Similarly, the Government of NL looked to develop new research applications through its support of geological mapping and geoscience (Government of Newfoundland and Labrador 2008).

Then, with the establishment of Nalcor Energy, a provincially owned energy company created in 2007, the government utility became a minor partner in three offshore projects – Hebron, White Rose, and Hibernia – while initiating onshore oil exploration with the expectation of future oil and gas finds. Nalcor also became responsible for the Bullarm construction site, and is planning future hydro developments. This new public utility was the only one created by any provincial government in the first decade of 2000, after the wave of privatizations by provincial governments in the 1980s and 1990s (Boardman and Vining 2012).

The results were a clear separation of state and market, with the province collecting minimal royalties and overseeing any of the "backward-linkages" of construction and service development, at the same time that companies exported oil to the American oil market. When major issues arose such as delays in construction, oil spills, or other environmental damage, businesses engaged in "quiet politics," working behind the scenes to lobby, coordinate expertise with provincial ministries, and, when necessary, using their managerial authority to influence the tenor of press coverage. Unlike in BC, major oil MNCs did not establish political coalitions or campaign lobbies, or engage in political fundraising for pro-business political parties. Rather, with huge financial resources, the extensive global expertise of company managers, and the power of companies to set the terms of debate on oil and gas development, companies could work with the provincial government and the offshore petroleum board to realize construction and long-term production. This was especially true on issues of construction and maintenance employment.

Given the high costs and long time horizons of construction, it could have been expected that, as in other North American jurisdictions, powerful business actors would push the provincial government to enact policy reforms to create opportunities for non-unionized contractors through "open shop" labour policies that would lower wages (Belman and Smith 2008). However, oil companies (and other multinational resource companies) largely compromised with government and accepted provincial "special project" legislation that centralized oil producers, construction employers, and trade unions in project-specific bargaining councils that mirrored "project labour agreements" that were common in the 1960s and 1970s (Oakley 2012). Since 1990, the government has issued five special project orders that carved major oil and resource construction projects out typical liberal market labour relations frameworks and established centralized collective agreements for the length of the project, ensuring union coverage of workers and standardized wage and benefit rates.

Employers and resource companies cooperated with government and local and national unions, in part because of their concerns with cost, project completion, and the realization that unions were the key provincial intermediaries providing a skilled workforce (Oakley 2012). Employers were also willing to work with government as the special project orders included no-strike provisions that ensured stable construction relations and few if any work stoppages. In doing so, the government continued its efforts to see provincial benefits flow from the projects by introducing regulations that committed contractors to give consideration to NL workers for training and employment, and that ensured that all workers hired for projects became union members.

Consequently, employer and labour organizations, supported by "special project order" government legislation, consented to centralized sectoral bargaining frameworks to boost business competitiveness and job-creation capacity (Cadigan 2010; Cooper 2000). Led by the International Building Trades Petroleum Development Association, PCL Industrial Constructors, and oil companies, comprehensive construction agreements that centralized collective bargaining between major employers and building trades unions were signed for the five major offshore oil and gas platforms, as well as related fabrication and construction projects. Unions agreed to restrictions on strikes and to negotiate local wage rates in return for closed shop arrangements and coordination with government to ensure training and apprenticeships (NL union staff official 1, private sector). In return, oil companies and construction companies agreed to centralize bargaining to secure industrial stability, wage restraint, and orderly access to skilled labour. Both labour and business also agreed to binding arbitration arrangements (rather than strikes) during the lifetime of the projects.

Compared to province-wide bargaining arrangements in other jurisdictions, the new framework went further by ensuring that all jobs on the construction site would be unionized. It also centralized bargaining to a single table for all employers and building trades unions, in contrast to the majority of construction agreements that typically only involve single trades or a single employer with two or more trades (Peirce and Bentham 2009).

Employers readily accepted the new legislation early in the first decade of 2000, as the opportunity to retain predominantly sectoral bargaining in construction, and the coordination among sectoral organizations of employers and unions, offered skilled labour at an affordable and predictable cost. As figure 7.7 demonstrates, these expectations were largely met, as wage increases remained well below productivity gains, and below standard Canadian real wage costs. Between 2003 and 2005, increases in real unit labour costs lagged well below increases in GDP output and actually fell between 2006 and 2008. NL labour costs also remained – with the exception of 2006 – at well below average Canadian labour costs, which rose slightly over the course of the first decade of 2000.

Such institutional arrangements between big business and government in NL were fundamental in setting out a mode of political interaction that was

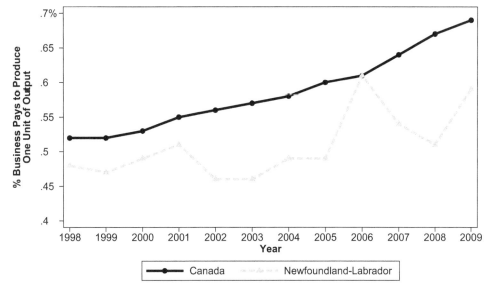

Figure 7.7. Real unit labour costs in NL, 1998–2009
Source: NL community accounts.

different from the one that became increasingly common in the rest of Canada and North America. Instead of large employers pushing for labour market deregulation, major industries operating in NL compromised, working with government within existing bargaining frameworks. Major resource industries also did not join provincial coalitions to push for structural reforms in government and its operation.

This created different dynamics of inequality that affected labour market growth and labour policy reforms. Oil and construction MNCs sought wage and production stability through government-supported labour and employer bargaining frameworks. Where they wanted to raise their profits by lowering government royalty and equity claims, MNCs engaged in the quiet diplomacy of lobbying and negotiating to establish favourable long-term deals. But big business influence was far more muted in its impact on labour policy. Such politics were one critical dynamic explaining the continuation of traditional, pluralist collective bargaining frameworks, and why the Williams government did not implement neoliberal policy reforms common elsewhere. Of equal importance was the influence of small business, community, unions, and cross-class associations on NL's Conservative Party in the first decade of 2000.

Business and Citizens in the Traditional Brokerage Politics of the Williams Conservatives

In examining the rightward shift of party politics across the rich countries, scholars have emphasized interrelated variables. For many, major recent policy shifts are seen to have required not just the electoral success of conservative centre-right parties, but also new long-term mobilization by organized interests and parties that changed voters' preferences and built support for neoliberal public policies. Examining how conservative and centre-right parties have increased their political influence, some scholars have highlighted how right-wing political leaders and economic interests have remade networks of supportive interests, established new patterns of institutional control, and built up large intellectual and policy advantages in public discourse, all in order to achieve electoral victory and lasting shifts in the political battleground (Hacker 2006; Teles 2009; Harvey 2006).

Others have explored the ways in which political parties have attempted to maximize the effects of money and advertising, and how this has influenced party agendas and strategies to win voter support (Gilens 2012; Lehman Schlozman, Verba, and Brady 2012). As this literature has shown, parties have expanded their organizational and fundraising capacities to accommodate the interests of business and the wealthy (Hacker and Pierson 2005; Skocpol and Williamson 2012). Because current political party mobilization depends more than ever on fundraising, mass mailing, and advertising, parties are increasingly reliant on financial interests and the wealthy. Such a mutually dependent relationship has strongly reinforced political inequality, because as parties target wealthy donors for resources, well-financed and high-income groups enhance their sway inside of political parties to articulate issues and set the policy agenda of party officials. The results, these studies conclude, are a new economic conservatism within party coalitions and a substantial shift to the right in government policymaking.

In NL, similar trends can be seen very clearly in the first decade of 2000. With the extensive support of the business community, the PC Party championed tax cuts and tax credits to the oil industry and to small business as keys to a new economic prosperity in the province. Like other centre-right parties in the first decade of 2000, the PCs framed themselves as the best "economic managers" for the province, emphasizing the importance of balanced budgets, public sector reform, and the removal of regulations on business to boost economic growth (PC Party of NL 2003, 2007). Moreover, the PCs built a formidable fundraising operation that allowed them to capitalize on their ties with business to better advertise policies, mobilize voters, and provide financial support to candidates (figure 7.8). However, unlike other conservative parties in North America, the PCs retained a more traditional brokerage organization

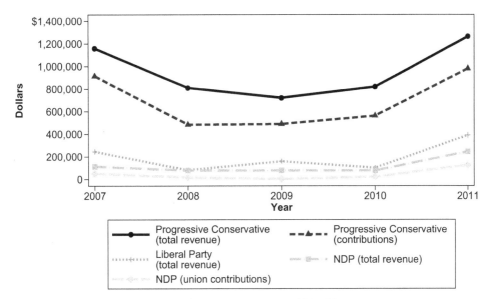

Figure 7.8. NL political party revenue and donations, 2007–2011
Source: Author's figures from Elections Newfoundland and Labrador, annual reports, political
party (contribution summary) and general election reports (contribution summary).

in order to mobilize interests and voters, and economic policies were framed on a more populist basis of what they would do to develop NL's ability to manage its "own wealth" and develop "self-reliance." Also unique was how the influence of provincial business interests was partly attenuated.

One reason for this more traditional "Red Tory" policy stance by NL's PCs was that, unlike in BC or the United States, provincial businesses in NL did not establish new think tanks, political action committees, or advocacy coalitions to influence politics and policy. Instead, Conservative power was rooted in small and medium-sized businesses that were tightly tied to local, community, and government-based organizations where businesspeople took the lead, but were constrained by other civic-political groups. This gave businesses significant organizational strength. But it also gave other organized and voluntary entities some influence in the institutions and policies of the PC government.

As figure 7.8 demonstrates, business support for the PC Party was exceptionally strong and consistent. While NL electoral financing regulation does not require comprehensive disclosure of business and union donations, tabulations based on data from 2007 to 2011 show that business donations to the PCs made up more than 68 per cent of all PC party revenue in 2008 and 2009, and more than 78 per cent of all PC Party revenues during election years. Business donations to the PCs totalled more than 50 per cent of all financial contributions to political parties and were consistently 2.5 times larger than the annual revenues of the Liberal and NDP Parties combined.

Small and medium-sized industries – many from the oil services and real estate sectors – were the most generous, donating thousands of dollars each year. But all businesses typically doubled or tripled their contributions during election years, donating to the central party association, as well as to local Conservative candidates' campaigns across the province. Overall, business donations to the Conservatives gave the PC Party an enormous financial advantage. In comparison, union donations to the NDP during election years were far smaller, with business donations eighteen times larger in 2007 and eight times greater in 2011 than those from organized labour. In non-election years, the business advantage was even larger, with business donations dwarfing those from organized labour by a more than thirty-fold advantage. Among the three provincial case studies here, this level of business support for the centre-right was the highest and most consistent.

Consequently, with their substantive advantage in fundraising and party revenues, the NL PCs invested heavily in voter mobilization. Unlike the Liberals and the NDP, who lacked the revenue, the PCs devoted extensive resources to direct-mail contact, aimed at all voters in the riding, with special mailings to those who had higher incomes and greater education. To then channel their money, the party built up a central election committee that hired staff, gave financial support to legislative candidates, and sponsored campaign seminars for prospective candidates. The PCs also far outspent the opposition parties in hiring campaign consultants to provide candidates with polling information and hired media firms to create advertising and campaign strategies.

But in contrast to other centre-right parties that lost many of their grassroots ties as they became more capital-intensive and more reliant on business donations, the NL PCs continued to rely on small business associations, community organizations, and voluntary government boards and councils. Such a reliance on local networks gave the PC Party markedly stronger populist roots than other provincial centre-right parties and led to a continuing emphasis on government intervention to improve small business opportunities in communities across the province.

In the 1980s and 1990s, the provincial and federal governments routinely developed regional economic development boards, programs, and health and labour regulations that promoted economic security and educational opportunity across broad segments of the population (House 2002). Such programs not only helped to generate wider civic engagement on policy issues. They also made government and local public officials more attuned to local issues, leading them to adopt more broadly generous policies than Conservative and Liberal Parties elsewhere.

Through the federal Atlantic Canada Opportunities Agency and under provincial direction, the province established regional economic development boards in twenty zones across the province. The provincial government also sought to develop community boards and a province-wide community-sector council that worked with the Premier's Office and the Cabinet to develop local strategic plans (Close, Rowe, Wheaton 2007). At the same time, regional health boards as well as regional community advisory boards allowed local actors access to government administrators and public officials in the development of policy (Department of Human Resources 2005).

Such programs offered avenues of access for local interests, spurring the involvement of local businesspeople and sectoral economic associations. But boards and councils also created new volunteer and civic involvement in economic and social issues. Meanwhile, federal and provincial programs encouraged provincial and local governments to contract with regional and community boards to develop long-term strategic plans for government and opportunities for local entrepreneurs (House 2002). This created new political opportunity structures for businesspeople, fishers, and voluntary groups, for with new modes of ongoing access to the provincial government, there was a proliferation of municipal committees and increased organization by the Fish, Food and Allied Workers that sought to influence local and provincial planning (NL union president 1, private sector).

Moreover, in contrast to other centre-right governments that centralized the policymaking process and sought to limit public input into policy processes (Lehman Scholzman, Verba, and Brady 2011), community issue networks developed in NL with substantial interaction among community leaders, businesspeople, fishers, and provincial policymakers (Vodden 2010). If leverage over the provincial government were desired, regional development boards, along with local chambers of commerce and the Fish, Food, and Allied Workers (FFAW) would gather information from across the districts and then press for new policies (NL municipal official). And despite business and policymakers' interest in supporting the major resource industries, much civic energy was still dedicated to shared endeavours, helping tilt agendas of public discussion and legislation away from cutbacks and instead towards policy measures that might broaden popular access to opportunity and security.

In addition, in 2004 the Williams government created a new "rural secretariat" to provide representation, policy input, and citizen involvement in policy formulation (Caledon Institute of Social Policy 2009). Seeking to implement a wider "strategic social plan," the secretariat established nine regional councils as well as a provincial council to involve community members in social and policy issues throughout the province. This was combined with a statistical division to develop detailed statistical profiles of each region. The goals of the secretariat included promoting the well-being of all regions in NL and ensuring that government took regional issues into consideration. Regional councillors who were interviewed did not always feel that regional issues were well addressed in such a format, but they did agree that the regional and local council provided for some accountability by government and improved the transparency of policy decision-making (NL regional councillor).

Development boards, regional councils, community boards, and health boards did not have the economic resources to drive their own initiatives forward (House 2003), but the existence of extensive community networks with direct ties to provincial government officials did allow a much wider array of local business and community interests to be a part of the PC policy coalition from the outset, and allow them influence plans to boost tourism, improve aquaculture and forestry programs, and introduce long-term care in smaller communities. Moreover, unlike other Conservative governments across Canada, in NL, community networks and institutions led local elected officials to listen intently to local concerns, and facilitated a greater openness from elected officials to local projects such as cooperatives, training, and the development of new technology (Vodden 2008).

These distinctive political features and the ability of local civic interests to have some voice in policy development help account for why the PC Party continued to view resource growth as a mechanism to engage in demand-side stimulation of the economy and to address long-term unemployment and poverty within their framework of fiscal conservatism. The impact on party policy was often significant. Whereas in BC, policies were increasingly directed to serve business and the wealthiest constituents, in NL traditional brokerage politics and policy feedback effects had an opposite impact. In a context of high unemployment and poverty, the Williams government sought to use the oil boom to increase public sector employment and lower poverty.

Fiscal Conservatism and "Strong Communities": Conservative Public Policy

As with other centre-right parties, the main emphasis of the PCs was on increasing growth and employment. However, the PCs also continued to pay attention to health, long-term care, and education as well as fisheries and rural development (Progressive Conservative Party of NL 2003, 2007). These programs were geared not so much to reducing income inequality, as to improving economic efficiency and reducing long-term costs to public expenditure. In seeking to improve the socio-economic conditions of the province, the Williams government attempted to appeal to upper-, middle-, and lower-income earners (NL Ministry of Finance official). This included Williams himself actively campaigning in a populist manner for improved transfer payments and better provincial control over federal programs on behalf of all NL residents (PC Party of NL 2007). The Ministry of Human Resources, Labour and Employment, in consultation with community groups, also developed policies to reduce poverty across the province, and the ministry also put forward a comprehensive social and education strategy with regular targets and progress reports (Department of Human Resources 2005, 2009).

Thus, instead of following a more standard neoliberal policy model focused on cost control and minimizing the state, the PCs emphasized fiscally prudent spending and the building of "strong communities" through new infrastructure, education, and better social programs. Helped by the surge in oil revenues, the PCs largely implemented their plans. In the late 1990s, direct oil revenues contributed less than 5 per cent of total provincial revenue. By 2007, oil revenues surged to 33 per cent of total revenues and continued to rise to 41 per cent of total provincial government revenues in 2008. Subsequent budget surpluses allowed the Williams government to enact corporate and personal tax cuts. But unlike other centre-right governments, public officials continued to engage in infrastructure spending, business investment incentives, and the building of new hospitals and long-term care facilities to spur economic growth in the public and private sectors alike. Such spending was to make up for the economic declines of the 1980s and 1990s, when NL's unemployment soared, and resource employers laid off thousands of workers (Cadigan 2009).

As tracked in the auditor general's reports on the provincial fiscal situation, over the decade from 1999 until 2009, there was a 51 per cent increase in spending, including a 77 per cent increase for health and a 71 per cent increase for education (Noseworthy 2009). Emphasis was also placed on infrastructure spending, primarily roads (with, for example, 38 per cent of the 2009 infrastructure stimulus package, $270 million, going to roads).

These more activist measures also helped prevent welfare and public service retrenchment, and unlike other right-wing governments facing debt problems, the Williams government neither reduced nor significantly restructured health, education, or social funding through privatization, contracting out, or New Public Management. In 2004, the government did impose a four-year contract settlement and wage freeze on its public sector workers (Cadigan 2012), but by 2005, the Williams administration sought to make investments in health care, long-term care, education, and training programs. Since that time, spending increases have grown steadily, with fiscal year 2009 representing the largest increase in spending: an 8.8 per cent increase over the previous year (Noseworthy 2009; Office of the Auditor General 2006). As figure 7.9 shows, even though government spending as a percentage of GDP fell to a fifty-year low of 18 per cent of GDP in 2008 with the rapid rise of oil and mineral industries, public expenditures rose by $2.8 billion from 1999 to 2009.

Reflecting the increases in spending, along with the new instrumental programs targeting access to education and a range of new policies for single mothers and students, the NL PCs remained the most effective of Canada's

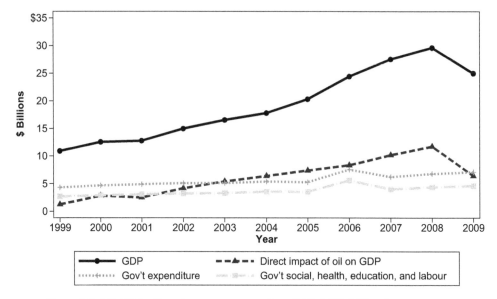

Figure 7.9. NL GDP, oil, and government spending, 1999–2009 (billions)
Source: Statistics Canada, CANSIM table 3850002.

provincial governments at reducing market income inequality in the first decade of 2000 (Sharpe and Capeluck 2012). All provinces – including NL –
saw declines in program effectiveness at reducing income inequality, and in
some provinces such as BC and Alberta, the declines were especially steep.
However, with the new fiscal and policy commitments, the NL PCs witnessed
the slowest retrenchment. By 2010, for Canada, the average effect of taxes
and transfers on reducing the Gini coefficient (a critical indicator of income
inequality) was 0.125. In NL, tax and transfer programs reduced income inequality by 0.176, a redistributive effort more than 34 per cent greater than the
Canadian average.

Conservative Mobilization, and the Impacts of Limited Inequality on Voter Preferences

As the patterns evident in table 7.1 show, in NL over the course of 2003–11,
such a policy platform had strong political effects. With the introduction of tax
cuts and highly favourable business policies for multinational resource companies that strongly favoured high-income and medium-income earners alike,
as well as some low-income earners, the PCs won over 93 per cent of NL's
thirteen highest-income ridings over the course of three provincial elections

Table 7.1. Voting and income polarization in NL

	2003	2007	2011	
Top 11 Wealthiest Electoral Districts				Totals
PC	11	13	11	30 or 94% of ridings
Lib	0	0	0	
NDP	1	0	2	3 or 6% of ridings
Bottom 15 Low-Income Electoral Districts				Totals
PC	9	14	12	35 or 81% of ridings
Lib	4	1	2	7 or 16% of ridings
NDP	0	0	1	1 or 3% of ridings

Sources: Statistics Canada, Community Accounts, Community Profiles, Census Tract Profiles 2005; NL Statistics Community and Municipality Profiles; Elections NL Election Reports 2003, 2007, 2011.
Low-income ridings: Baie-Verte Springdale, Burin Placentia West, The Isles of Notre Dame (2007), Bonavista South, Fortune Bay Cape La Hune, Lewisporte, Exploits, Bonavista North, Trinity Bay de Verde, Grand Falls Windsor Green Bay (2007), Port au Port, Cartwright L'anse au Clair, Grand Falls Buchans, Straits of White Bay North, Humber Valley
High-income ridings: Labrador West, Lake Melville, Topsail, St. John's East, Cape St. Francis, Conception Bay East, The Straits of White Bay North, South (2007), Mount Pearl North, St. John's North, Ferryland, Conception Bay South

between 2003 and 2011, typically sweeping all the wealthier, home-owning suburbs surrounding St. John's. As in many political jurisdictions, government was most responsive to the concerns of the affluent, introducing deep tax cuts and economic deregulation. Responding to lobbying, political donations, and the propensity of the affluent and educated to be more involved in party activities, officials adopted policies that were most consistent with and most beneficial to their upper-income supporters. Consistent with such preferences, the PCs adopted policy reforms that were upwardly redistributive and helped direct economic growth towards high-income earners. The top decile of family earners under sixty-five saw their average market income rise from $147,572 to $200,770, and their overall share of market income increase from 30.2 to 32.1 per cent – the only group of earners to see their share of provincial income grow.

At the same time, the PCs went against expected theoretical trends by seeking – and winning – the support of low- and middle-income voters as well. Two factors appear to explain the unexpected association between PC control and policy responsiveness to lower-income voters. First, the PCs sought to build an electoral coalition incorporating as many rural and coastal ridings as possible into their electoral base – a key for political power in the province

(Cadigan 2009). Under electoral pressures, the PCs continued to pursue policies popular with rural constituents.

Second, under pressure from civic associations and government committees, the Conservatives channelled increasing portions of tax revenues into rural development, health care, and income security policies. As noted above, this utilization of growing tax revenues for public services intensified from 2005 to 2008 as growth continued and the deficit fell. But in this way, the link between a role for government in promoting socio-economic redistribution and the public was emphasized on an ongoing basis. The result was that, over the course of three elections from 2003 to 2011, the PCs also won more than 80 per cent of the low-income ridings in the province. Only in the western part of the province were the Liberals able to make any electoral gains by consistently campaigning for greater resources to be directed to fishing and rural communities.

In contrast, the NDP was successful only in the capital, St. John's, where they would regularly win one of the highest-income ridings and two of the lowest-income ridings in the city. The traditional policy orientation of the NDP with middle- and low-income earners as well as with organized labour drew voter support in the urban ridings with high levels of poverty and low income, as well as higher levels of public services. More affluent voters and those in the public sector dependant on government redistribution and urban services were often far more supportive of the NDP than in other areas of the province. But outside of St. John's, the NDP had little political presence, in large measure because of the lack of electoral and organizing resources, but also because of the lower percentage of union members and lower level of public sector employment in many communities.

Of equal importance to the role of distribution in provincial public policy was how similar the attitudes of low- and higher-income earners in NL were. In contrast to BC and Ontario, where there were notable shifts in upper-income earner preference opposing redistribution, as table 7.2 demonstrates, upper-income earners in NL continued to only modestly oppose government efforts. Much like other upper-income earners in Canada, 47 per cent of the better off in NL still supported economic redistribution and measures to provide economic security. This evidence suggests the positive effect of government programs and wider civic participation on voter preferences, for rather than higher-income earners turning against government responsibilities, in NL the interaction between local institutions and committees with government officials, combined with fiscal expansion, not only maintained more traditional patterns of civic engagement. It also positively influenced the identity and goals of voters to support more modest, fiscally conservative policies intended to increase employment and reduce the deficit.

As expected, with more effective tax and transfer programs, middle- and lower-income Newfoundlanders – especially those facing regular spells of

Table 7.2. Income and government's role in NL

Reduce Income Differences b/w Rich and Poor	Family Income under $65,000	Family Income over $65,000
NL		
Probably/Definitely Should	79%	47%
Probably/Definitely Should Not	20%	53%
Canada		
Probably/Definitely Should	78%	52%
Probably/Definitely Should Not	22%	48%

Source: International Social Survey Program: Role of Government IV – ISSP 2006.

unemployment – were more supportive of policy changes that would redistribute resources more widely. On average, redistributive policies were strongly supported by 79 per cent of respondents with incomes less than $65,000. The strength of these preferences attests to the popularity of a number of redistributive policies passed during the PC tenure, including raising the minimum wage, increasing income benefits for low-income earners, boosting income supports for education and housing assistance, and the defence of pilot project legislation for EI for seasonal and temporary workers.

In contrast to BC, where rising inequality and declining program effectiveness were closely correlated to a steep decline in voter participation, in NL income inequality after taxes and transfers remained largely unchanged as the result of program redistribution, with the household income Gini value averaging .368 throughout the decade with the exception of 2008 and the financial crisis (figure 7.10). After 2008, while tax and transfer programs in NL remained the most redistributive among Canadian provincial governments, voter turnout declined by only 1 per cent: from 59 to 58 per cent. This finding suggests that – in line with our theory – low- and middle-income voter participation is driven largely by income and resources. And whereas in BC, with rising income inequality and declining voter turnout, the governing party redefined policies to better meet the needs of affluent voters, in NL the PCs continued to benefit politically from policies that addressed affluent voters as well as middle- and low-income voters.

These developments provide an explanation for the continuity in NL politics, and why the PC government retained its populist orientation and interest in provincial development and redistribution. Like other centre-right parties, the PCs in NL rapidly opened their economy to global forces under pressure from business interests. But as the NL case shows, business pressure was not sufficient to explain the variations in policy. In the context of global resource development and the rightward shift in policymaking, governments still had

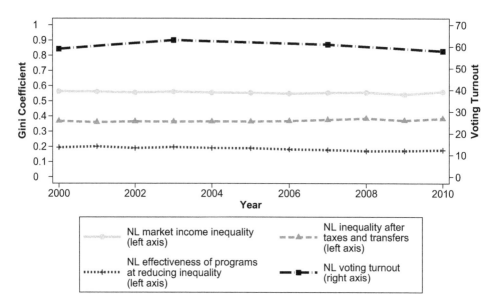

Figure 7.10. NL income inequality and voting
Sources: Statistics Canada, CANSIM table 202-705; NL Elections Election Reports 1999–2011.

to deal with a wide variety of social actors. In many jurisdictions, centre-right parties have been increasingly able to ignore them, relying on business support and professionally run advocacy organizations to win office and shape public agendas (Hacker and Pierson 2010a). In others, governing parties have had to engage in a number of strategic interactions and build coalitions with social actors (Hausermann 2010; Huo 2009). In NL, the political dynamics of civic institutions and activity followed along these more traditional lines and shaped how market reforms were buttressed and wider compensation was distributed. Such dynamics also help explain why the PCs remained more open than other centre-right parties to retaining and renewing existing labour regulations and social policies in the province.

Labour Market Policy and Bipartite Industrial Relations Frameworks in the Private Sector

During the 1980s and 1990s, led by parties that advocated a new economic conservatism, governments blamed high unemployment and the economic downturn on labour institutions (Freeman 2008; OECD 2006). Many countries deregulated labour markets to make lower labour costs; to weaken employment security and unemployment benefits; and to drive youth and the unemployed into service sector jobs (Standing 2011). Accompanying these measures, governments sought to boost "competitiveness" through a radical restructuring of institutional supports for collective bargaining, union organizing, and strikes (Bosch, Lehndorff, and Rubery 2009).

However, in NL, the Williams government remained committed to wage setting through centralized and sectoral collective bargaining practices in construction and the public sector; made only minor adjustments to employment standards; and introduced compensatory measures for low-wage workers and the underemployed. These measures did not reduce the split between good and bad jobs in the province, but they did result in the maintenance of unionized employment and modest declines in low-wage work and poverty. The strength of unions in enforcing these bargaining arrangements, combined with the development of a new business/labour "partnership council," were also critical to these developments.

Unlike other provincial and state jurisdictions in North America, with the exception of Quebec, NL had a history of collective bargaining conducted under bipartite frameworks beyond just the construction sector. Initially established in the construction industry to deal with major public works in the 1960s, coordinated bargaining frameworks among province-wide employers and labour associations became common in NL with the extension of collective bargaining rights to fish harvesters and public employees in the 1970s and the consolidation of bargaining institutions in the wake of a series of strikes in the 1980s (Oakley 2012). In addition, in the 1980s and 1990s, in the wake of a prolonged public sector strike and shutdowns in construction and the fisheries sector, province-wide employer organizations were established with bargaining power that sought to ensure common wage and benefit rates and industrial stability in the public and private sectors. Under government auspices, sectoral employer associations with coordinated bargaining power were institutionalized (Luchak 2003).

In the 1990s and early part of the first decade of 2000, these province-wide bipartite institutions were extended into the residential construction and fishery industries (Cooper 2000). In the fisheries, the combination of employers' councils and the strength of the FFAW/CAW in representing and mobilizing harvesters and processors across the province, accounts for the continuing development of centralized bargaining and price-setting frameworks in the industry. In the 1980s, FFAW/CAW was the first fishery local to have the government extend collective bargaining rights to all harvesters and processors under government jurisdiction (RMS Review Committee 2005). Then in 1998, with the government moratorium on cod fishing, rising unemployment, and strikes in the fishing industry, the government moved to create labour stability by introducing price arbitration between the FFAW/CAW workers and the provincial producer associations. Employing an interest-based binding arbitration system to settle impasses over the price of cod and other species such as crab and shrimp sold by harvesters to local processing plants across the province, the government sought cost stability at the price of the workers giving up the right to strike and companies having to pay a common floor price to harvesters.

In 2003, companies sought to break the arrangement and drive down costs by illegally locking out workers. This led to an end to the price arbitration system from 2003 to 2005 as well as the return of strikes and lockouts, with individual negotiations on prices. The Williams government then attempted to stabilize the industry by imposing a "catch" quota in the crab and shrimp fishery that was to be used across all species. But a massive five-week protest by the FFAW/CAW against the quotas, which they believed threatened to give all bargaining power to the companies and reduce fishing jobs, led the Williams government to appoint Richard Cashin, the former, long-serving president of the FFAW/CAW, to a special committee that would investigate and make recommendations on the fisheries.

In November 2005, Cashin recommended a central bargaining table with the FFAW/CAW and the processor association; the binding extension of agreement provisions on all processors if the largest processors signed on; a binding arbitration price panel; and accreditation of processor organizations before the labour relations board (RMS Review Committee 2005). In early 2006, the Williams government amended the Fishing Industry Collective Bargaining Act to centralize bargaining between the parties and introduce all the major recommendations of the Cashin committee (Overview of Proposed Amendments to the Fishing Industry Collective Bargaining Act Labour Relations Agency and Department of Fisheries and Aquaculture Feb 22 2006). That the FFAW was able to shut down the province's fisheries, and do so with support in hundreds of communities, played one part in the continuation of the centralized bargaining framework in the fisheries (NL labour leader). But that the Premier's Office and Cabinet caught flak from constituents as well as their own MHAs also played a part in the government maintaining the bargaining and price arbitration system (NL Ministry of Fisheries official).

In addition to unions' strength and employer acceptance backing centralized and sectoral bargaining councils and collective bargaining arrangements, a final reason that the Conservatives under Williams adopted a more consensual and accommodating attitude towards the labour movement was the growing networks and wider working consensus on current economic development and labour market strategies. Unions accepted the principle that greater business profit and budget surpluses would drive investment and jobs (NL union staff official 1, private sector; NL union president 3, private sector). In parallel, the acceptance on the employer side of the importance of maintaining sectoral bargaining and avoiding further state intervention left more employers open to the idea of other institutional forums where all "stakeholders" would discuss economic problems and possible coordinated solutions. At the same time, the government remained committed to expanding a number of tripartite committees and initiatives involving the government, business, and labour discussing economic, social, and labour issues.

The Strategic Partnership Council, initially established by the Roger Grimes Liberal government in 2002, was used throughout the first decade of 2000 to discuss long-term socio-economic plans for the province and initiate research on public policy. While it did not provide new avenues of communication between business and labour, it did provide organized labour with the opportunity to meet more regularly with government officials to address employment standards, poverty, and training issues (NL labour leader; NL union president 3, private sector). In conjunction with regional economic development boards and ongoing steering committees for worker adjustment and restructuring in the fisheries, the partnership council also provided a regularized context for discussions among government, employer organizations, and union officials to address province-wide policies and propose solutions. The consequence of such ad hoc and standing committees was that labour market issues were increasingly dealt with more openly and more cooperatively (NL union staff official public sector; NL labour leader; NL Agency of Labour Relations official). Thus in contrast to many conservative governments, Williams's PC government regularly held meetings with union officials and invited union officials to participate in planning and steering committees (NL union president 3, private sector).

The result was that rather than undertake typical measures to make union decertification easier and strengthen employer controls on workplaces, the PC government was more willing than any other provincial jurisdiction to work with unions and maintain industrial relations frameworks. Union density in NL remained at more than 37 per cent in total employment, more than 6 per cent above overall Canadian levels, and the highest in Canada. Likewise in the private sector, union density in NL remained the highest in Canada, above 21 per cent, whereas Canadian private sector union density fell to 17 per cent (figure 7.11). Moreover, in contrast to Canadian and North American trends in construction, the rate of union coverage in NL's construction industry continued to rise, from almost 22 per cent in 2003 to 29 per cent in 2008, while the rate in the mining and oil sectors remained higher than Canadian averages, with union density rates fluctuating between 55 per cent and 44 per cent in the first decade of 2000.

But beyond upholding sectoral bargaining in construction and the fisheries, the Williams government retained the traditional pluralist and decentralized system of industrial relations. Employers were to be free to hire and fire, and unions would organize workplaces where they had majority support. The PC government was anxious about productivity, but outside of construction and fisheries, the major concern of industrial relations policy was boosting labour market participation, not unionization (NL Agency of Labour Relations official). In private

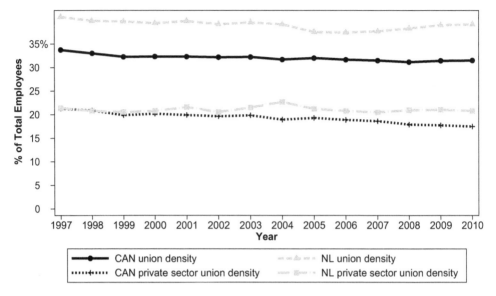

Figure 7.11. NL and Canada union density rates
Source: Statistics Canada, CANSIM table 2820078.

service sectors such as retail and wholesale trade, as well as food and accommodation, the small size of workplaces and the flexible nature of the workforce posed significant barriers to union organizing, and union density in the private service industries was less than 10 per cent. With firms able to respond to price changes by making "quantity" adjustments – most notably in the size of their workforces or in work schedules or layoffs – the PC government upheld managerial prerogatives to continue using non-standard employment. In this context, even without any reform efforts, employer voice remained dominant, and the Conservatives used their authority only to preside over labour relations in the key resource areas necessary to ensure growth and higher profits.

Public Sector Coordination and Bargaining

Over the past two decades, governments have widely introduced public management reforms (Bach and Bordogna 2011; Hermann and Flecker 2012). Through public sector layoffs, privatization and outsourcing of services, performance management and performance-related pay, and changes to collective bargaining legislation, governments have sought to lower labour costs and make their public sector labour forces more "flexible" through increasing non-standard employment. Scholars have debated the extent to which governments have adopted similar policy models of market-oriented reforms (Peters 2012c; Pollitt and Bouckaert 2004), but in the liberal market economies, New Public Management reforms have been consistently pursued (Bach, Givan, and Forth 2009; Ross and Savage 2013). Policymakers have also decentralized wage-setting systems and introduced two-tier pay and working arrangements for new hires.

Working from a common New Public Management template, governments have enacted restructuring and modernization measures according to the fiscal balances of government, its partisan orientation, and union response. In Canada, the provincial and federal governments used suspensions of the rights to bargain and strike, back-to-work legislation, and freezes or rollbacks of public sector wages in order to reduce government spending and retrench public services (Panitch and Swartz 2013). Citing the need for fiscal constraint, public officials either imposed or bargained wage increases below the rate of inflation, resulting in a decline of 4 per cent or more in the wages of public sector workers across Canada (Evans 2013).

In NL as well, the Williams government initially called for public sector reform. Promising a budget that would cut social expenditures and enact a two-year wage freeze, the Williams government also sought to eliminate 4,000 public sector jobs. But with oil monies raising government revenues, public sector workers pushed back in a bitter strike by more than 20,000 Canadian Union of Public Employees (CUPE) and the Newfoundland Association of Public Employees (NAPE) workers that ended with the government passing back-to-work legislation that imposed significant wage moderation: a two-year wage freeze, and 2 and 3 per cent increases in the following two years.

By 2005, however, the economic situation had continued to improve considerably, with ongoing economic growth, declines in unemployment, and new budget surpluses. This economic context helped change the government policy position and reshaped its microeconomic response to organized labour. Then, under Williams's direction, the government adopted a new strategy of working with organized labour at a central table that included the premier, the Treasury Board, and the minister of finance negotiating with public sector leaders over key wage and benefit issues (NL union executive, public sector).

In 2008, following the Williams administration's second election victory, fiscal austerity and pro-cyclical measures reduced budget deficits but also provided the context for patterned public sector bargaining across sectors that allowed for "wage catchup." In bargaining, the government's focus shifted from economic supply-side management and a concern with deficits to income and employment growth. First the government signed an agreement with CUPE, one of its most vocal opponents in the 2004 public sector strike, that provided an 8 per cent wage increase to its members in provincial hospitals and school boards in the first year of a four-year deal, with 4 per cent raises in each of the next three years. Overall, CUPE and NAPE workers would receive an approximately 20 per cent

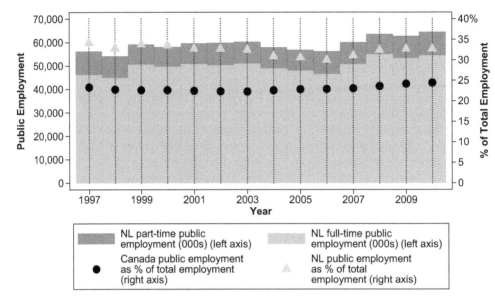

Figure 7.12. NL public employment and public employment growth, 1997–2012
Source: Statistics Canada, CANSIM tables 2820078, 282008.

wage increase over four years – the best collective agreement for public sector workers in Canada in more than twenty-five years (Cadigan 2012). While other public sector unions were unhappy with particular wage components of the deal, the contract became the template that NAPE, the teachers unions, and the nurses union all quickly came to accept as their basic wage rates and contract terms.

The result was, as figure 7.12 makes clear, the maintenance of high levels of public sector employment. In Canada, public employment as a percentage of the dependant-employed workforce remained at 24 per cent throughout the early twenty-first century. In contrast, in NL, after briefly declining in the wake of the 2004 collective agreement, public sector employment again rose to more than 33 per cent of the workforce in 2008. Public-sector wage increases also far outpaced inflation, with real wage increases of more than 4 per cent between 2006 and 2010. Unlike other provincial jurisdictions, part-time and temporary employees were also covered by new collective agreements and received benefits (NL union executive, public sector). Public boards also made commitments to expand the number of full-time, public-sector jobs while reducing part-time and temporary jobs.

Relief from wage freezes and the imposed contract of 2004 was due in large part to economic growth and the new oil royalties available to government. But also critical was a new bargaining climate between public sector labour leaders and the Williams government. By 2006, union officials realized that the problems created by the strike and back-to-work legislation would not be repeated in 2007 and 2008 (NL union staff official, public sector). Instead of the open conflict between government and public sector union leaders common to other provincial jurisdictions, union leaders in NL began to have open discussions with government and senior officials.

The government also feared that labour shortages in key services would hurt public service employment in the long run, and that budget surpluses should be used to raise the wages of NL workers to levels comparable to elsewhere in Canada, while providing an improved context for restructuring and amalgamation in health services (NL Ministry of Finance official). Most important to public sector unions was the government's commitment to use the Atlantic Accord to cover the massive $2 billion deficit in the public sector pension plan, a result of previous governments using workers' employee contributions as part of general revenue. The settlement of this issue generated increasing goodwill between public officials and union leaders.

The 2008 contract negotiations marked a substantive improvement in public sector jobs and wages across the province. My theory predicts that more centralized and coordinated union bargaining and political responses should have been a factor in this improvement in jobs. But this was only partly true. NL public sector unions had already developed informal coordination amongst themselves, engaging with governments from the late 1980s through to 2004 in central table bargaining with Treasury Board officials as well as with premiers (NL public sector union official). But in the 2007–8 negotiations, the major public sector unions negotiated at separate tables, as union leaders disagreed over major contract and political goals, most notably over whether union interests would be better served through negotiation and cooperation or protest and public advocacy. Nonetheless, government and unions accepted a pattern agreement across provincial public sector services, with the contract signed by NAPE providing the general wage and benefit template for other unions to work from. This more limited form of coordinated bargaining was compensated by unions engaging in much more active consultation with members prior to negotiations, and more active discussions involved in contract ratification in each of the unions (NL union executive, public sector).

Critical to success, then, in improving public sector jobs and wages in NL was a shared sense of economic well-being that forced actors to come together to explore the possibility of a joint positive solution to previous bargaining problems. The brokerage nature of the PCs was critical in the government developing this more accommodating stance. But for the advances in public sector jobs, unions only had to be strategically committed to negotiated solutions that would benefit the entire public sector. Given the splits between unions over bargaining and political options in 2008, this was neither inevitable nor automatic.

Past experience had taught union leaders that peak-level negotiations with provincial officials would not necessarily result in improvements or changes in government policy. But a strategic commitment to joint negotiations along with patterned agreements and member consultation did provide unions with the ability to make gains for public sector workers throughout the province.

Unemployment, Atypical Employment, and the Commitment to Passive Protection and Poverty Reduction

In NL, as was the case across Canada, policies to expand competitiveness and increase employment improved the labour market prospects for only a minority of occupations and sectors. For the majority of workers, unemployment and atypical employment continued to undermine job and income security. In the 1990s, unemployment was high across Western nations as they coped with deindustrialization, rising trade, and the entry of more women into the labour force, and corporate restructuring (Jackson 2010). In NL in the 1990s and first decade of 2000, unemployment averaged more than 15 per cent, by far the highest rate of any province, and more than double the Canadian average of the past decade (figure 7.13). This was due to the fishing moratoria and fishery closures, as well as the highly seasonal and sporadic nature of employment for many labour-intensive industries in the province, which meant more than a quarter of employment in the province was routinely temporary. In the first decade of 2000, unemployment, atypical employment, and poverty in NL still remained among the highest in Canada. The result was a labour market that was strongly "dualized" between those workers with good, full-time permanent jobs, and those in low-paying, non-standard ones.

Workers in resource industries and rural areas were most affected by global competition, industrial restructuring, and business downsizing as well as closures. In forestry and logging, for example, the emergence of international markets alongside global multinationals led to growing exports and capital intensification in the industry and the loss of jobs throughout North America and Western Europe (McLaren and Pollard 2009; Milley 2008). In NL in the early 1990s, approximately 1,600 people worked in forestry and logging; by 2009, in the wake of the financial crisis, only 500 remained. From the 1980s, with a decline in American demand for newsprint (the main paper product of the province), companies laid off workers, introduced mechanized harvesting, and implemented "lean" production methods in order to cut labour costs. By 2009, only one pulp and paper mill remained, at Corner Brook, and the mills at Stephenville, in 2005, and Grand Falls-Winsor, in 2009, closed completely (NL Department of Finance 2006; Morrissey 2007; *Telegram* 2008).

Further driving rapid restructuring and layoffs in the forest industry was the quick appreciation of the Canadian dollar, whose value was closely tied

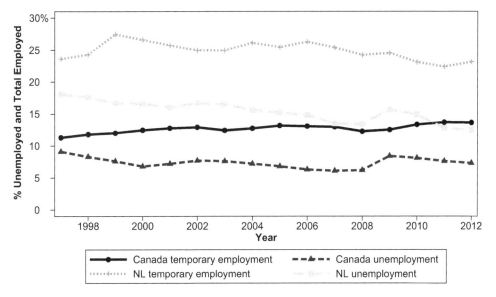

Figure 7.13. Unemployment and temporary employment rates in NL and Canada
Source: Statistics Canada, CANSIM tables 2820048 and 14100078.

to global movements in commodity prices. With increasing terms of trade and competition from low-cost producers from South America and South-East Asia, the pulp, paper, and wood product industry throughout the East Coast of Canada declined from $4.6 billion in 2000 to $2.6 billion in 2010 (Atlantic Provinces Economic Council 2011). This downturn in exports and revenues forced many of the American multinationals as well as the Corner Brook mill to downsize, restructure, and lay off unionized workers.

Similarly, in the fisheries, the 50 per cent appreciation in the real value of the Canadian dollar hurt processors and harvesters. With terms of trade turning against the industry, fishery employers laid off more than 4,000 workers in the 1990s and early in the first decade of 2000 (Cadigan 2012). The rise in the Canadian dollar came alongside long-standing problems in the fishing industry – particularly international over-fishing in the North Atlantic, which continued largely unchecked. While fishers diversified the species they caught, overall increases in the number and size of boats contributed to the collapse of many fish stocks and consequent moratoria on ground fisheries in 1992. The federal government's response to the moratoria was to use compensation programs and, eventually, quota systems to encourage people to withdraw from the fishing industry. But by diverting more effort down the food chain, the newer fisheries have proven more capital-intensive and led to the over-exploitation of some new species. The fewer fishers who survived the catastrophic events of the 1990s then became the new, if still small-scale, capitalists of the fishing industry, further limiting employment prospects.

With intense competition among domestic and international fisheries, rising input costs and debts, fewer and fewer fish harvesters were able to make sustainable annual incomes (Neis and Kean 2003; Murray, Neis, and Johnsen 2006; Ommer and the Coasts under Stress Research Project Team 2007). As in other resource industries, in fisheries the intense pressures of global competition as well as boom-and-bust cycles left only high levels of unemployment, underemployment, and depopulation in their wake, with better returns available for only a few.

The emergence of oil and gas as well as mining in NL did little to improve this situation for the majority of workers, often only serving to widen inequality between men and women in the labour market (Cadigan 2012). The offshore sector's major impact on industries such as retail, food and hotel accommodation, and hospitality was to create demand for more low-paid, non-unionized, service-sector workers rather than better-paid, highly skilled workers, while reinforcing the gendered dimension of work. With the growth of service employment, employer demand for part-time and temporary workers reinforced the persistent disparity between the incomes of men and women. As figure 7.14 demonstrates, while rates of low-wage work in non-standard employment fell over the course of the first decade of 2000, they still remained above 60 per cent, and by 2011, full-time low-wage employment had also witnessed a small increase to 31 per cent of all full-time/full-year workers.

Moreover, as it was for women across Canada, women in NL were disadvantaged in the labour market because Canada ranks last among advanced industrial countries in family support and quality of childcare programs (Friendly and Prentice 2009). Despite minimal PC tax credits as well as child benefits, the lack of universal childcare in the province only increased the poverty rate among families, especially among single-parent mothers. In addition, without basic childcare and elder-care facilities, women were often forced by necessity to stay out of the paid labour force, constrained to take poorly paid "flexible" employment, or in many cases, to live in poverty as they turned to social assistance for woefully inadequate income support (Friendly and Prentice 2009). According to the Child Care Coalition of NL, the province has roughly 49,000 mothers with children under the age of twelve, but only 4,400 regulated childcare spaces, a rate that compares with other provinces such as Alberta and Saskatchewan, which have the fewest childcare spaces per capita in Canada (Friendly and Prentice 2009).

Finally, despite rapid economic growth over the past decade, temporary and seasonal employment continued to account for a quarter of NL's employment. With the fisheries, construction, and tourism industries playing key employer roles in the province, much employment has remained seasonal and temporary.

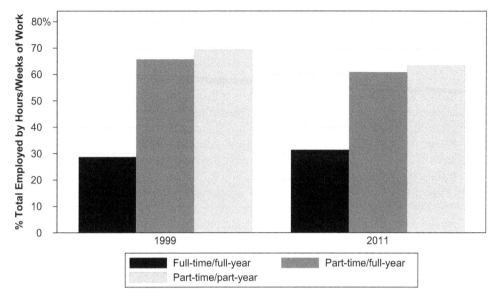

Figure 7.14. NL non-standard employment and low-wage work, 1999–2011
(% workers below low-wage threshold of two-thirds of median hourly wage of full-time/full-year worker)
Source: Author's figures from custom request, Statistics Canada, Survey of Labour and Income Dynamics and Survey of Consumer Finances, "Percentage of Workers with Low Annual Earnings and Low Hourly wages, Canada and Provinces," table C685593.

But temporary employment is also widespread in private service industries such as retail, food, and accommodation – all generally non-unionized industries. Consequently, in NL, temporary employment as a percentage of total employment has been twice the level of the Canadian average of 12 per cent.

Whereas most provincial governments in Canada sought to resolve these problems through deregulatory policies intended to increase pressures on workers to re-enter the labour market and lower costs for employers seeking to hire non-standard workers, in NL the government took a more distinct policy tack. With the return of budget surpluses in 2005, the Williams government launched a new "poverty reduction initiative" to improve the accessibility and levels of means-tested income replacement programs, and sought to develop new "active" labour market measures that would assist students and low-income individuals to enter the labour market (Department of Human Resources 2005). The minimum wage was raised by 66 per cent between 2005 and 2010, with a proviso for public officials to revisit increases every two years.

Also distinct was how NL retained a more traditional employment insurance system that ensured access to a modicum of income security for unemployed workers. With the introduction of reforms in 1996, employment insurance varied work requirements and the maximum duration of benefits according to regional unemployment rates. The regional variability of work requirements and duration of benefits created a labyrinth of qualifying conditions that led to widespread exclusion of the unemployed from receiving benefits. By October 2008, just prior to the financial crisis, only 43 per cent of the unemployed in NL received insurance benefits (Jackson and Schetagne 2010), while in provinces such as Ontario and British Columbia, only a third of the unemployed could qualify for employment insurance.

For provinces such as NL and New Brunswick, with resource industries based on seasonal production, increasing capital intensity, and lower employment needs, the regional variation of the employment insurance program, along with special pilot project legislation for workers in the fisheries, provided key means to support more than 90 per cent of the unemployed in much of the province's rural regions. Even if benefit levels have fallen and duration of benefits have been reduced, NL workers in the hardest hit industries of fisheries, forestry, and pulp and paper have been able to continue accessing employment insurance, allowing many in rural areas to remain in their communities, but with very low levels of annual income (Jackson and Schetagne 2010). As in other parts of Canada, unionized workers are best able to access EI benefits, because of union assistance to the unemployed and because of union advocacy and lobbying to maintain income security for their members. In NL, the FFAW/CAW provided all its members with extensive education and counselling on how to use the EI system to full effect (NL union president 2, private sector).

Alongside these policies, the PC administration tried to combat poverty by introducing new transition policies to promote employment, especially – but not exclusively – in the low-wage sector. In its attempts to develop "to-work" incentives, the Williams administration focused attention on single parents, disadvantaged families, and students leaving post-secondary education. New activation measures were designed to facilitate labour market entry for the unemployed and those who had been out of the labour force for some time. Supplementary measures were geared towards increasing the financial incentives to employers to hire young or unemployed workers, while others served to decrease family-related personal costs for those returning to work.

The young unemployed were a key target and were provided with the most resources for job skills and job search training. To improve employment prospects, the government remained committed to maintaining the lowest post-secondary tuition rates in Canada as well as steadily increasing the minimum wage from 2008 to 2010 (Department of Human Resources 2009).

Financial incentives were also directed to compensating employers for providing temporary training, educational opportunities, and direct job placements in the private sector. Graduate employment as well as placement programs offered wage subsidies to businesses that would cover up to 60 per cent of annual wages in the first year.

For the longer-term unemployed, the priority of government was to reduce benefit enrolment by improving training and educational opportunities in order to enhance the prospects for the unemployed in finding work (Department of Human Resources 2005). Traditional income security programs were left relatively untouched, and benefit levels marginally increased. But with the introduction of the poverty reduction initiative, the government expanded employment and job opportunities for the unemployed with little imposition of harsh penalties. NL Works provided employment counselling and wage subsidies for private and not-for-profit employers. Public assistance recipients also received support for work, transportation, training, and placement courses. Women were also offered rental subsidies and child tax benefits when returning to work.

Moreover, in order to activate single parents and low-income earners in households, the government introduced new pharmacare programs, functional increases to income support, and improvements to social housing (Government of Newfoundland and Labrador 2008, 2009). The Ministry of Finance and the restructured Department of Human Resources, Labour and Employment were particularly active after 2005 in targeting income towards those in low income, through lowering means-testing thresholds for passive benefits, as well as fiscal welfare measures similar to those used in other liberal welfare states like Great Britain and the United States, such as the targeted low-income tax reduction that in 2009 raised the low-income tax reduction threshold from $13,511 to $15,911 for individuals and from $21,825 to $26,625 for families (Government of Newfoundland and Labrador 2009).

Little direct information is available for the extent and take-up of these programs. But macro-evidence on poverty rates suggests that while Canada and NL's poverty rates remain among the highest in the industrialized world, nationally Canadian programs are still among the least effective in reducing poverty and in-work poverty. Poverty rates before taxes and transfers, as measured by the standard "low-income cut-off" ratio, have remained among the highest (more than 10 per cent of all persons) in the OECD, although Canada has one of the leading levels of economic growth (OECD 2008a).

However, as figure 7.15 shows, NL experienced a dramatic decline in poverty rates both before and after tax and transfers, suggesting that PC policies in NL were significantly more effective than those elsewhere in Canada. Since 2003, poverty among all low-income persons has decreased by more than 38 per cent in NL; in Canada, by 15 per cent. In 2003, social and fiscal measures reduced

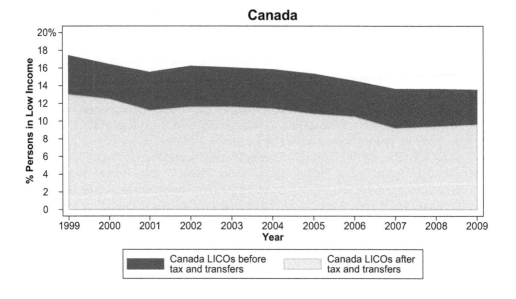

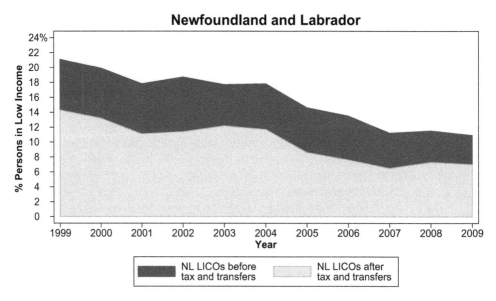

Figure 7.15. Poverty rates in Canada and NL, 1999–2009
Source: Statistics Canada, CANSIM table 202802.

income poverty by 31 per cent; in 2009, such measures decreased poverty by 36 per cent. Both reductions were better than those across Canada, and in comparative terms, they were well above the 13 per cent poverty reduction in the United States, but far below Sweden's rate of 82 per cent (Brandolini and Smeeding 2008).

In part, such changes to NL's unemployment and social protection systems were driven by the brokerage nature of the PC Party, and its efforts to reach out to lower-income groups and especially to low-income women and single parents. In 2003, seven women were elected for the Conservatives and four were named to Cabinet – the second-largest female representation in government in the province's history – with the majority in important Cabinet portfolios (Bittner and Goodyear-Grant 2013). Joan Burke served as the minister of human resources and employment and the minister responsible for the status of women, and in 2005, the minister of education; Kathy Dunderdale was minister of innovation, trade and rural development, minister of natural resources, and the minister responsible for the status of women.

Unlike in many centre-right parties, where predominantly male small business owners, lawyers, and developers sought to defend and expand corporate interests, these women came from education and social work backgrounds and were open to working with community organizations and anti-poverty organizations (NL Ministry of Finance official). To develop the new poverty reduction plan, government officials consulted extensively with anti-poverty organizations, and the ministry undertook new research on poverty for the development of an action plan in 2006 (NL labour leader). With the budget of 2005 and the publication of the Poverty Reduction Plan in 2006, the government began to push for reforms to reduce poverty in NL, which at the time was the second-highest in Canada.

The distinctive provincial government response was also due to the different political dynamics in the province. In contrast to the BC Liberal government, the Williams PCs were more dependent on retaining rural and low-income voters, and sought to develop incremental improvements to social and education programs. At the same time, the large number of church groups, anti-poverty organizations, women's associations, and unions sought to champion policies for the public good. And given that many PC politicians relied on local community networks, as well as the input from regional councils and community development boards, this gave many civic organizers more influence over legislators (NL labour leader). The results were an increase to income redistribution to poorer individuals and more tax credits for youth seeking educational opportunities. But because the PC's core constituencies were increasingly older and rural, the government's targeting prioritized the elderly and non-earners, and only in a more limited way did resources reach young low-income earners. Average after-tax incomes of families in the lowest decile, for example, only rose by $2,296 from 2003 to 2010. In contrast, average after-tax incomes of elderly families rose by more $12,600 over the same time period – an annual rate of more than 4.5 per cent per annum.

In sum, enhanced social security and continued commitment to retaining passive income security measures like employment insurance certainly did not eliminate insider/outsider divides in the labour market. But because these measures did lower poverty, NL's labour market adjustment path should be considered a case of "smoothed" dualization. Unique too was the fact that low-wage work did not increase over the course of the first decade of 2000, and instead there was a notable improvement in labour market performance. Much in contrast to Ontario and other provinces, even in the crisis year of 2009, NL's unemployment rate did not increase, nor did income inequalities worsen.

The Pragmatic Strategies of Organized Labour

Labour studies scholarship has underscored how reformist and oppositional strategies have been essential for union renewal and the continued relevance of organized labour in maintaining bargaining and political power (Fairbrother 2014; Upchurch, Taylor, and Mathers 2009). With the break – or fraying – of ties with left and centre-left parties, or aggressive attempts at deregulation undertaken by partisan governments, scholars have claimed that unions that have built up new political resources through renewed efforts in organizing and coalition building with other progressive organizations have been best able to maintain strength and influence. Unions that emphasize the education of activists, and the deepening of linkages with community groups alongside corporate and social issue campaigns are best able to organize and most likely to develop wider legitimacy that strengthens unions in their efforts to influence governments. But in NL, there have been no innovative campaigns, no unions tied to political parties, and few attempts at coalition building alongside a rapid decline in new organizing drives. Yet in density, policy reform, and recent job growth, NL unions have had far better results. The question is why.

One key has been the pragmatic political strategies that unions have accepted as their best hope for success. Unions have been intent on maintaining collective bargaining institutions and the protection of members' wages, benefits, and workplace rights. Union officials have also looked to maintain their influence on governments. But unlike many regions and countries, where political action has traditionally meant organizational ties to centre-left parties, voter mobilization, and lobbying, in NL, political action has focused primarily on lobbying and engaging in committee and parliamentary hearings, taking an "accommodationist" role where unions seek to benefit from resource and

construction booms while seeking strategic protection and state action to ensure jobs in the province.

Lobbying has taken on this important role because unions in NL are politically "non-partisan" and tend to distance themselves from political parties.
Though many members in private and public sector unions do vote for the
Conservative Party, unions have made a strategic choice to remain non-aligned,
fearing partisan shifts and their long-term impacts. Unions made this choice
over the course of the 1970s, as unions moved away from close affiliation with
the Liberal Party in the wake of government intervention in strikes as well as
bargaining and organizing issues. This allowed unions to avoid partisan debates internally and between unions, while also allowing the labour movement
more generally to pursue more pragmatic relationships with all parties (NL
labour leader).

But if unions opted to remain "non-partisan," they agreed that the provincial
government was the major focus of action, and they chose to work as lobby
groups or "partners," acting under the assumption that they could and would
take political strikes to protest government labour and economic policies. This
stance is argued to provide the best leverage to affect the general interest and
make public officials listen (NL union executive, public sector). Moreover, in
the context of continued government efforts to improve the labour market and
the welfare state, unions sought to expand and improve their status as privileged stakeholders. And in both the public and private sectors, unions have
occasionally resorted to the militant defence of members' interests. But since
the discovery of oil, the main goal for unions has been to find common ground
and advance resource development, while finding means to share the resulting
wealth (NL union president 1, private sector; NL union president 2, private sector; NL union president 3, private sector). This more accommodating position
is also reflected in the declining number of strikes, which fell from an average
of ten per year in the early 1990s to an average of five between 2006 and 2010.

At the government and legislative level, this pragmatic strategy meant that
unions do seek to initiate their own policies and work hard to block measures that are unfavourable to unions and workers. And unions work hardest
to influence policy when it has involved construction jobs, training, and unemployment benefits, and in fisheries price arbitration panels and collective
bargaining issues (NL union staff official 1, private sector). To achieve this, NL
unions have attempted to improve their lobbying by increasing the frequency
and formality of lobbying and regular meetings. Individual unions have also
taken formal steps to increase their input into government policy by acting as
partners in construction projects, and public sector growth and modernization.

In large measure, union officials have been able to maintain their voice
inside government. In contrast to British Columbia, where unions have few
working relationships with government officials, construction unions in NL

have had open and often excellent working relationships with government (NL union president 1, private sector). These relationships have been critical in developing the Special Order legislation that eventually provided collective agreement coverage for all industrial construction sites and companies. The Building Trades Council supported special order legislation and provided an initial forum for skilled trade unions to learn about and then plan ways to ensure jobs and training for members through collective agreements and government support.

Similarly, in the public sector, unions were able to have regular dialogue with the province on public sector investment and bargaining. Initially, with the attempt by the Williams government to cut public sector spending, the 2004 public sector strike worsened government–public sector relations, most notably with the imposition of fines for strikes and an imposed contract that included a pay penalty. But in the wake of the strike, public sector unions took a more consensual and non-confrontational approach to bargaining. This included improving relations with government officials and regular communication throughout the collective agreement. And by 2007, labour officials were able to "pick up a phone" and talk to ministers and ministry officials (NL union executive, public sector).

Complementing this was a centralized and often personal bargaining system with Premier Williams. While more coordinated public sector bargaining preceded the Williams administration, with the Conservative government coming to office, sectors bargained at separate tables, but during final negotiations over wages, jobs, and pensions, the premier often joined negotiations directly with union leaders (NL union executive, public sector). Indeed, by 2008, the union view of Premier Williams was that he believed the public sector was working hard and deserved a significant wage "catchup" and a major commitment to fund the public sector pension plan (NL labour leader). This has created a relationship where many issues could be discussed between the government and union before they reached the bargaining table and became points of contention during contract negotiations.

The Newfoundland and Labrador Federation of Labour (NLFL) also played a key role in giving organized labour a voice in policymaking as well as building inter-union alliances to support the labour movement. Working from an unwritten consensus that labour and government could work together for betterment of the province, the provincial labour council has played a regular role in unifying local unions around a common political and economic agenda. Backed by the major public and private sector unions, the provincial council has regularly advanced discussions on current issues of bargaining, and provided a forum for union leaders to discuss collective bargaining, training, and organizing issues in the province. In leading these discussions, it has not been riven by political or factional disputes, as happened in Ontario. Nor, given the support offered to the council across the province, has NLFL faced financial difficulties in conducting research or carrying out its lobbying and leadership roles.

Unlike in many provinces, where partisan governments have refused to meet with labour leaders, the NLFL regularly conducted meetings with government to develop and implement new minimum wage and anti-poverty plans with regular targets and updates. This included directly campaigning alongside community groups to raise the minimum wage in NL, which at that time was among the lowest in Canada. It also involved the NLFL participating in committee hearings and regular meetings to improve health and safety legislation in the province. Thus, in contrast to provincial council leaderships that have often been shut out by governments seeking to marginalize organized labour, the NLFL has been able to provide a clear voice to government on bargaining and training. Equally critical was the ability of the NLFL to bring in key leaders in unions and in major bargaining councils. Unlike many provincial labour councils, the NLFL has sought to have input from major leaders in order that key issues are addressed by decision makers, as opposed to representatives with little authority. This centralization of leadership authority in the province has been key in limiting interest-based and political factional conflicts, offering a forum for formal discussion as well as an informal social setting to meet and resolve issues.

Finally, the third key for continued union influence was how NL unions were able to insert themselves directly into vocational training, which has provided skilled trade locals with a way to retain unionized memberships. In combination with firms and governments, unions have played a key role in overseeing the growth of training opportunities for skilled and low-skilled workers alike. Governments have supported training as a mechanism to provide opportunities for youth and unemployed or underemployed workers to increase their qualifications and improve job prospects. But the emphasis of the Conservative government on lowering poverty and improving jobs for NL workers depended on consistent union pressure to expand employment and provide more training.

In 1999, under union pressure to meet company demands for workers on the Terra Nova project, the province agreed to set up a provincial apprenticeship and certification board that includes employers and union/employee representatives to oversee the designation of trades, the training and work periods, as well as final exams of apprentices (NL union staff official 1, private sector; NL union president 3, private sector). The board also had the authority to ensure training by employers and fixed rates of pay for apprentices. But most importantly, the creation of an apprenticeship board gave unionized skilled trades the right to oversee the training of their own members. Subsequently, a number of trades including the carpenters, plumbers and pipefitters, ironworkers, and operating engineers established separate trade-run colleges for vocational training, as well as developing a certification system for colleges offering trade certification. Trades locals also became directly involved in offering and overseeing the delivery of skilled vocational training inside the College of the North Atlantic.

Likewise, the new board was granted power to oversee firms and ensure that training complied with national standards set by the bipartite committees of business and unions. This authority was central to increasing the number of skilled workers for construction and value-added production. Under union direction, students rotate between classes and practical experience in a training firm. For small firms, the system was voluntary. But for construction associations, firms under obligations of collective agreements had to provide a fixed ratio of apprenticeships on work projects, giving young workers the opportunity to gain work experience and complete their vocational training in order to be certified as qualified journeymen.

Funding and support for training was also set up on a tripartite basis. The provincial government provided support for trade training, as well as more general training colleges in infrastructure, tuition waivers, and books. This funding was supplemented by the devolution of employment insurance funds to the province in 2008, which provided further provincial training dollars. In addition, unions received government support in pushing for training and stabilization fund clauses in collective agreements that have provided a direct private source of funds for training programs. Finally, trades themselves contributed to training through the provision and operation of training centres. This has led to the expansion of vocational education training, and the development of programs that led to jobs that are attractive to many youth.

The results were that business, labour, and government committed to working together to provide a growing percentage of workers with vocational training. Through the first decade of 2000, the number of apprenticeship registrations rapidly increased, from 5 per cent of the labour force to more than 21 per cent in 2005. The quality of apprenticeship training was also high, with four-year programs for skilled tradespeople and shorter one- and two-year programs for lower-skilled occupations. Apprenticeship spaces also rapidly increased, and by 2005 more than 25 per cent of the population had completed an apprenticeship program (Red Seal Secretariat 2014).

In union coverage and better wages for workers, the most notable outcome for workers was the rising coverage of skilled and temporary workers in the province (figure 7.16). For construction unions seeking new ways to bring in members and provide skilled workers to sites, these activities have been central in building up broader provincial alliances within the labour movement and certifying new skilled workers working the province. Unlike other provincial labour movements, such as in Ontario or Alberta (the other major oil construction province) – where organizing rates among young and temporary workers have held steady at low levels, declining only slightly in the wake of the financial crisis in 2008 – in NL they have continued to increase. As figure 7.16

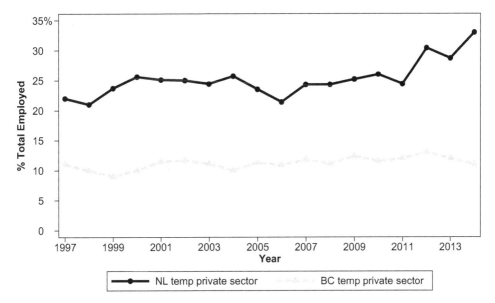

Figure 7.16. Union density in Newfoundland-Labrador and Ontario among temporary workers in the private sector, 1997–2013
Source: Author's figures from custom tabulation, Statistics Canada, Labour Force Division, "Union Coverage for Private Sector Employees in Canada and the Provinces, 1997 to 2014, Annual Averages."

shows, union density among temporary workers continued to climb and by 2013 was at 30 per cent for all temporary private sector workers. This reflects the strongly unionized nature of construction work in the province. In contrast, in Ontario, unionized private sector temporary work remained at approximately 11–12 per cent of all temporary workers, despite the near doubling of construction workers in Ontario during this time. The central role of NL unions in training provides a key reason for this comparative difference.

Thus, in contrast to other provincial union movements, NL's labour movement was able to retain moderate influence on government policy while also retaining collective bargaining coverage and ties to new members. This largely reflects three factors: the unions' role within training systems; the NLFL's ability to create consensus and mitigate marked ideological differences; and unions' established links to government officials. NL unions have resorted to militant and province-wide actions on occasion, but over the course of the first decade of 2000, they diminished significantly. Instead, NL unions sought to retain "accommodationist" strategies that provided them with a role in working as "partners" with government and business to realize local benefits. Such accommodationist strategies have limited wage increases and also meant that unions have not developed more oppositional strategies such as workplace organizing and more community-based mobilization. Instead, NL unions have received significant benefits with steady increases in public sector employment and regular wage increases. These trends have run counter to those in Ontario, British Columbia, and much of the rest of Canada.

"Stasis" after the Financial Crisis and the End of the Oil Boom

Unlike many jurisdictions in North America and Western Europe, NL experienced little of an economic slowdown in the wake of the financial crisis (2008–9). Prices for oil and metals did fall, but only temporarily, and government revenues and multinational investment into resource development continued to flow into the province (Carter 2020). With oil and mineral royalties – as well as corporate taxes – coming into the province, the provincial government continued to invest in public services and public infrastructure, and public employment held steady while construction employment grew, despite the one-sided nature of the tax, royalty, and development agreements with the companies.

Major foreign multinationals – among them Vale and ExxonMobil – launched new mining and offshore oil projects and signed special project orders with the provincial government to oversee the union contracts and ensure there were neither lockouts nor strikes during construction. Vale began construction of a new nickel processing facility at Long Harbour in 2009 that at its peak employed 6,000 unionized construction workers in its five years of construction. ExxonMobil – and other oil giants – signed onto the development of another offshore oil development (Hebron 2011), again under a Special Order agreement that provided good short-term unionized construction jobs and training funds. Thus where many countries struggled with downturns and debt crises, NL bucked the trend and realized steady growth that underpinned the continuation of employment relations in the province.

But by 2014, NL's economy began to turn with the further decline of oil and mineral prices, and the province entered a recession with falling investment and increasing unemployment that peaked at 15 per cent in 2017. Further worsening the fiscal situation of the province was the government decision to proceed with a multi-billion dollar hydroelectricity project in 2014 – at just the time that oil royalties plummeted with falling resource prices (Commission of Inquiry 2018). As in other oil-rich jurisdictions where governments depended on the twisting fortunes of natural resources, NL had little capacity to raise taxes or royalties on foreign multinationals during a price decline or economic downturn. And as the oil and mineral industries were highly capital intensive and there had been only minimal effort to ensure local value added, there were no alternatives for economic growth that the province could pursue (Carter 2020).

The results were rapidly escalating debts alongside government deficits – both of which led to the increasing "drift" in private and public sector employment relations in the province. In the public sector, with faltering revenues, the provincial government began to introduce austerity measures across the education and health care sectors. Rather than increase corporate taxes or windfall profits tax on resource multinationals, public officials shrank budgets in education and government agencies. Layoffs and concessionary collective agreements were met by walkouts and protest by public sector employees. So after a decade of better relations between government and public sector employees, the relationship again turned conflictual – though with no major legislative and labour law reform.

Similar "drift" also now characterized the situation of low-wage workers in the province. After officials had raised the minimum wage late in the first decade of 2000 and made new policy investments to lower poverty in the province, the minimum wage was frozen for five years (2010–15) and policy changes to reduce poverty were left to languish. Over the course of the 2010s, as resource revenues declined, former tax cuts and commitments to keep costs low for the major multinationals left budgets frozen and programs to introduce more means testing and eligibility requirements. After declining throughout the first decade of 2000, poverty rates rose again to the highest level in Canada at 14 per cent in 2015 (Hillel 2020). And after declining in the middle of the first decade of 2000, the numbers of workers in low-wage and insecure employment again topped 30 per cent by 2015.

Labour law and collective bargaining did not undergo a major overhaul, as seen in British Columbia during a time of economic downturn. But a key institutional feature of the earlier special project orders and company development agreements was dismantled – the Strategic Partnership Council. And when the Conservative government and employers both ended their support for wider tripartite negotiations and exchange, organized labour could no longer advance proposals for longer-term investments by companies through development agreements. Similarly, with the return to budget deficits, union officials could no longer directly contact ministry officials to discuss issues or problems related to collective bargaining. In these ways, the former "pragmatic" strategies of organized labour were eroded and its influence constrained.

Thus while the picture of NL's employment relations appeared to be one of "stability" in the wake of the financial crisis, by 2015 much of its trajectory was towards greater deregulation through institutional drift. No longer as distinct from Ontario during the boom period of the first decade of 2000 or the aftermath of the financial crisis, many of NL's long-term problems of high levels of low-wage work, unemployment, and poverty again returned – despite few overt reforms. Such developments show that trajectories of labour and employment relations do change – and can change in incremental ways that undo earlier gains. But to understand these developments it is necessary to enquire into changing economic circumstances, and how they influence the interests of governments, employers, and unions alike.

Conclusion

Overall, the NL pathway of "institutional stasis" and its later evolution into "drift" suggests that arguments about pronounced deregulation and rising non-standard employment as the natural policy outcomes of centre-right-led, liberal-market political economies are too one-sided. This qualification is supported by the way the PC Party initially responded to ongoing poverty problems, and how they did not extend neoliberal reforms into either social assistance or industrial relations. In line with our hypothesis, it was not merely partisanship or economic conditions that mattered for labour market outcomes, but rather how organized interests worked with and influenced government policy, and how middle-class and rural interests continued to influence public officials. These were the keys to why the PC government initially updated and upheld labour and social policies but then under downturns in international oil and mineral markets began to pull away from earlier commitments and policies – slowly and in piecemeal fashion.

Because of the way brokerage politics and resource management strategies operated within the province, government priorities were less labour policy reforms that would lower wages and reduce income transfer programs, and more the renewal of current industrial relations systems to take account of the demand of oil companies and contractors for skilled workers, and of the province's need for fresh investment in the public sector. Such politics made the government's strategy of dualization, which protected unionized workers and offered compensation to low-income workers, the most likely outcome of its labour and social policy. And so too such "dualization" helps explains the government's hesitant and limited efforts to boost employment in the province by taking on major resource multinationals.

In comparative political economy literatures, these political dynamics are often missed, as it is assumed that majoritarian centre-right parties can easily ignore or marginalize large proportions of the electorate. In BC case, this was certainly true. However, in NL it was not, as citizens and organized outsiders had modest influence on policymaking. Consequently, the ways in which the Williams government could pursue its goals was highly contingent only not on the economic preferences of major corporate actors, but also on government policy changes influenced by bargaining coordination among employers and unions, as well as by the actions of citizens and community groups across the province.

The result was that with the oil boom, the NL PC government sought to ensure wage moderation through a three-pronged approach that was unique in North America and throughout the liberal market economies. This included centralized, bipartite bargaining arrangements between multinational resource companies, construction companies (international and local), and major private sector construction unions. But it also involved centrally coordinated pattern agreements for public sector workers. And finally, oil revenues allowed new social investments and the continuation of income-securing labour market policies that would allow construction, resource, and low-wage service sector workers to easily circulate in and out of seasonal and private service employment. Only with the decline of oil and mineral revenues did this model begin to slowly unravel. But even as it did, former political commitments and relationships between employers, unions, and governments meant that no major labour or employment reforms were considered. Instead, the reform trajectory then shifted to one of "drift" as former institutions like the Strategic Partnership Council were not renewed and the minimum wage and social benefits were frozen.

A key implication of this analysis is that even in a liberal market policy regime, neither financialization nor centre-right incumbency is sufficient in understanding neoliberal policy shifts and patterns of labour market reform. Even though the changes brought about by financial markets and global resource development created strong preferences among economic actors, partisan policy preferences were also shaped by business political mobilization, party dynamics, and electoral preferences. Economic actors such as the powerful oil and construction industries – especially when capable of sustained collective action on behalf of shared material interests – did have a massive and ongoing impact on how political authority was exercised in the labour market and in the economy more broadly. But unionized and non-unionized workers as well as community and civic assertions could still make their interests felt – though only within the parameters of fiscal responsibility and extractive resource development as set by the party in power.

Public and private sector unions adopted strategies of cooperation based on the government renewing existing labour legislation, with occasional resorts to militancy as required. Unions have not had a strong centre-left party to represent their interests, and unions were in many ways willing to work with government as long as it sought to protect unionized jobs in the construction sector, as well as improve public sector contracts and employment within the context of growing oil revenues. Accepting that the benefits of bipartite sectoral collective bargaining arrangements would assist unionized workers, NL unions secured wage improvement and benefits for their members.

In doing so, however, unions had to accept the restraints that came with a populist centre-right government that, while willing to improve the minimum wage and social income programs, was not willing to improve certification procedures or employment standards. Such a strategic stance did expand wages and job quality for a minority of organized workers. However, it did not decisively counter the power of liberal market ideas within the Williams government, nor did it do anything to narrow the gap between good and bad jobs in the labour market. In these ways, NL's labour movement ran into real constraints into how active and effective it could be in the workplace and at the wider provincial policy tables – constraints that only grew with the economic downturn that began in 2014–15.

Consequently, the labour market situation remained largely one of "institutional stasis" with substantive improvement for only a minority of unionized workers until the decline of oil in 2015, and more modest improvements to jobs for those in private sector, non-unionized employment, but little change for the thousands of workers in low-wage temporary employment or stuck in long-term unemployment. Even though public policies, labour market institutions, and economic growth under the Williams government did provide a major boost to the labour market and to reducing poverty, "dualization" and insider/outsider divides remained throughout the province. High levels of unemployment, temporary employment, and non-standard employment in the labour market all affected workers across the province. And each of these problems was magnified with the decline in royalties and tax from the multinational resource corporations as well as the growing debt and deficit problems faced by the province by the mid-2010s.

8 Ontario: Policy "Drift" in Canada's Financial and Industrial Heartland

Neoliberalism is often conceived of as involving policies that roll back older redistributive models or that roll out new legislative measures that weaken unions and retrench social program spending. But as scholars such as Thelen (2014) and Hacker (2006) have argued, there is another path by which public officials can impose neoliberalism: drift. Government inaction and the absence of updates to policy in the face of major transformations to work, poverty, and the balance of power among economic interests, it is claimed, can often harm long-term job prospects, incomes, and wages of citizens.

In Germany and the United States, for example, the failure of the government to intervene in labour policy has played a key role in the dramatic decline of unions and the rise in low-wage work (Hacker and Pierson 2010b; Thelen 2014). In both cases, the argument is made that either because of the formidable organizational resources of organized economic interests, or because of the strategic considerations of political parties, public officials ignore – or avoid – problems rather than address them, with the intent to ward off alternative policies and avoid political controversy. Consequently, well-organized business interests often benefit from this pattern of little or no policy change, as they retain status quo policies and continue to exploit loopholes that profit them greatly.

In labour and employment regulation, Ontario saw similar developments throughout the first decade of 2000. Unlike the previous Conservative administration (1995–2003), or the Campbell BC Liberal government that focused on deregulation of the labour market, the Liberal government of Dalton McGuinty (2003–11) attempted to reverse the Conservative emphasis on flexibility and de-unionization, and adopted a more conciliatory and open approach to unions and employment regulations. However, despite this more conciliatory policy approach, private sector unions declined precipitously, low-wage work continued to rise, and growing numbers of workers found themselves in non-standard jobs or in non-standard jobs with little or no employment protection.

This chapter argues that a number of political variables contributed to this disconnect between policy response and outcomes. Above all, firms' efforts were critical to blocking updates or improvements to labour law and regulation. But also important was the influence of a "Third Way" policy model of the Liberal government that prioritized business growth at the expense of redistribution, which led government officials to downplay reforming labour policy in favour of a "balanced" approach that did little to address the growing number of low-wage workers and employers who sought ways to work around labour laws and regulations. Backing this approach was the support of a diverse coalition of interests in the exposed and sheltered domestic sectors as well as among urban homeowners in Toronto that benefitted from the new economic policies. Equally significant was the fact that the provincial labour movement – in many ways the strongest in the country – was often politically fragmented and organizationally constrained from expanding or pushing for new policies. This too furthered a trajectory of declining union density and eroding jobs and wages for the majority of workers.

The result was that while the Liberal government did not opt for across-the-board deregulation, the deterioration of job quality and the increasing individualization of employment relations was due to *drift* – a policy choice whereby the Liberal government routinely blocked updates to bargaining or employment standards, failed to adequately update policies, and more typically maintained bargaining legislation and regulations that included loopholes for employers to hire more workers on a non-standard basis. The fact that even when Liberal officials made new efforts to expand the enforcement of employment standards they generally failed to provide any real enforcement of policy, or simply engaged in multi-year "stakeholder" consultation without acting, also contributed to the erosion of good jobs and wages for many workers.

Such inaction meant was that during the first decades of the 2000s, collective bargaining arrangements increasingly lost their protective capacity as more and more firms in formerly unionized sectors shed their collective agreements. At the same time, with a minimum wage that failed to keep pace with economic growth, and the lack of effective policy updates along with flagging enforcement of employment standards, many employers increasingly sought to maximize their use of lightly regulated labour markets. Others began to undermine the formerly commonly accepted labour contract of full-time, full-year jobs with non-standard work arrangements. For workers, the outcomes were often negative: fewer well-paying full-time jobs, more low-wage and non-standard employment, and often little protection of workplace rights beyond the expensive and time-consuming court system.

Industrial Restructuring, Financial, Information, and Communications Technology, and the Construction Boom

After the global recession of the late 1970s, Ontario witnessed massive structural changes in its provincial economy (Peters 2018). Much as in other industrial regions, as detailed in chapter 4, industrial restructuring and the decline of core manufacturing industries were key drivers of the loss of stable, well-paid, full-time jobs and the rise of long-term unemployment in Canada's leading industrial province. But also key to the transformation of the labour market in the 1990s and the first decade of 2000 was how Canada's federal government pursued rising levels of foreign direct investment in auto, information and communications technology (ICT), and natural resources, and how Ontario's provincial government followed suit, providing tax credits and flexible labour markets to spur the expansion of economic growth of increasingly highly financialized companies. As in many other liberal market economies, these policies of liberalized trade and investment drove the expansion of the finance, service, and construction sectors. But they also opened Ontario's provincial economy to a rapid increase in income inequality and the expansion of low-wage, non-standard employment as labour-intensive employers sought greater flexibility and lower labour costs.

Industrial restructuring in the context of financialization and rising global competition was a major contributor to the worsening of the labour market. In the resource industries, rising global demand for resources led to the rapid mechanization of resource industries and the precipitous decline of employment, with greater productivity gains realized through a combination of capital investment and job shedding. In manufacturing, the globalization of auto firm operations, foreign investment, and inter-firm trade among Detroit's "Big Three" (GM, Ford, and Chrysler) led to the displacement of workers and unionized manufacturing in affluent countries and the equally rapid growth of manufacturing in the US South and Mexico (Brady and Denniston 2006; Kollmeyer 2009) (Rutherford and Holmes 2014; Stanford 2010). In North American manufacturing, in particular, non-financial firms' increasing use of financial activities to generate revenue, alongside their massive expansion of debt to fund mergers and acquisitions, and the increasing redistribution of revenues to shareholders and corporate executives, was critical to the mass layoff of workers and the declining quality of wages and jobs (Lin 2016; Lin and Tomaskovic-Devey 2013; Fligstein and Shin 2007).

Equally important, with the financialization of operations, many global enterprises closed unionized workplaces and transferred their activities to nearby non-union subsidiaries in the United States or to other offshore sites with low-wage labour (Milberg and Winkler 2013). For example, manufacturers in North American auto parts and consumer goods established production chains that contracted parts and component production to low-wage companies as well as to non-union contractors in nearby states and to other countries around the world (Moody 2007). But other executives, like those at General Electric, BMW, and Volkswagen, driven by shareholder-linked compensation schemes, also routinely redirected resources to financial activities such as leasing, lending, and mortgage markets, rather than capital and labour reinvestment (Froud et al. 2006). The increased use of corporate debt had similarly negative employment impacts, as high debt-to-equity ratios routinely forced businesses to use layoffs to cut costs (Gittell et al. 2006) – a problem magnified even further in firms run by private equity partners (Batt and Appelbaum 2014). As recent studies have confirmed, the turn by non-financial firms to finance and debt had negative consequences for total employment and new employment in non-financial industries in the United States as well as many other countries (Cecchetti and Kharroubi 2013; Lin 2016; Reich 2015).

In Ontario, as figure 8.1 shows, similar consequences of financialization for 1997–2010 can be seen with the rapid decline of the unionized private sector workforce. Total formal private sector employment grew by nearly 800,000 in the province, but manufacturing employment declined from its peak by more than 320,000. Unionized manufacturing underwent the most wrenching change, as firms laid off and retired more than 177,000 unionized workers – the majority formerly holding full-time jobs. In Ontario's Big Three auto plants, the Canadian Auto Workers (CAW) suffered the loss of roughly 38 per cent of their members in the assembly and parts sectors over the past ten years (Rutherford and Holmes 2014). In steel-making, centred in Hamilton and Sault Ste. Marie, and once the home to over 60 per cent of Canada's steel manufacturing, job losses of 63,000 totalled more than 40 per cent of employment in the steel sector during 1990–2006 (Livingstone, Smith, and Smith 2011). Northern Ontario's forestry, paper, and wood industries were similarly affected by corporate restructuring, higher automation, and shutdown, with the loss of thousands of jobs that accounted for the decline of more than 46 per cent of total employment in these industries.

Restructuring and job losses were most pronounced in the auto sector, as firms moved new production, assembly, and parts to Mexico and Eastern Europe, and turned to finance to offset production losses in a cyclical auto business (Stanford 2010; Froud et al. 2006). Seeking to boost sales, auto companies like Ford increasingly turned to credit, leasing, and derivative markets to boost demand for their products, which massively expanded their earnings. But many of the American firms found that, even despite these increases, actual returns from financial markets were low and forced the auto companies to engage in even more radical restructuring of their parts and assembly operations to low-wage jurisdictions.

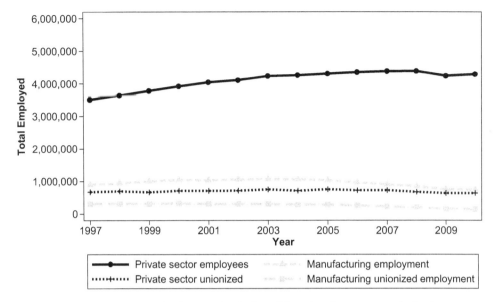

Figure 8.1. Deindustrialization and the decline of Ontario private sector unionized manufacturing employment, 1997–2010 (total labour force and % total employment)
Source: Statistics Canada, CANSIM table 2820078.

The financial crisis and subsequent recession (2008–11) had equally serious consequences for manufacturing – especially in unionized auto manufacturing (Albo, Gindin, and Panitch 2010; Rosenfeld 2009). With the collapse of financial markets in North America and Western Europe, there was not only a significant decline in American demand for Canadian exports. There were equally significant debts and credits that could be financed only with government bailouts. Across Canada, from late 2008 to November 2009, firms laid off more than 450,000 full-time workers, the majority in manufacturing and natural resources, as the seasonally adjusted number of unemployed workers jumped to over 1.5 million (Larochelle-Côté and Gilmore 2009).

Car sales plummeted to their lowest level in decades in 2008–9, and the Big Three auto-makers responded by shutting four plants and laying off thousands of workers from the major assembly plants. Auto parts manufacturers folded many more plants, and with the bankruptcies of General Motors and Chrysler in 2009, over 30,000 auto jobs were lost in the assembly and auto parts industry between 2008 and 2010 (Holmes and Hracs 2010). In mining, similarly highly leveraged global giants Vale and Xstrata laid off hundreds of workers as the downturn and credit crunch worsened. Vale then fought a twelve-month strike with the United Steelworkers Local 6500 that resulted in major wage

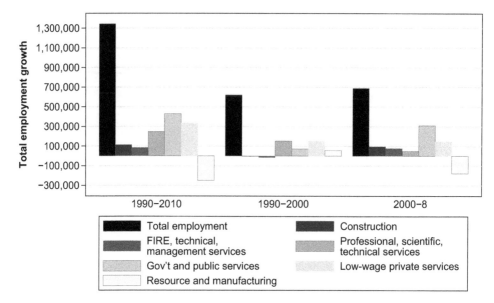

Figure 8.2. Ontario total employment and sectoral growth/decline, 1990–2008 (total employment in labour market)
Sources: Author's figures from Statistics Canada, CANSIM table 2820008.

concessions by the local, the retirement of another 10 per cent of their unionized labour force, and the continuing widespread use of part-time contractors (Peters 2010).

In Ontario's forest and paper industries, the collapse of US housing starts and the drying up demand for paper used in advertising led to the rapid decline of lumber, newsprint, and wood product exports (PWC 2010). In the wake of the financial crisis, the American firms in Ontario's forestry sector received little financial assistance from the federal and provincial governments to facilitate restructuring and to maintain employment and investment. Across Northern Ontario, forestry and lumbering firms closed to focus on core operations in other countries (many in Latin America and China), and workers were forced to leave in search of new employment. By 2010, manufacturing and resources had declined by nearly half from their peak of 26 per cent of GDP in 1985 to 13.8 per cent.

However, in stark contrast to the decline of manufacturing and resource industries, Ontario's finance, insurance, and real estate sector as well as its ICT, biotechnology, and pharmaceutical industries took on an entirely new level of economic importance, provincially and in the overall Canadian economy (figure 8.2). Echoing trends in the United States and the United Kingdom, one key reason for this rapid development in finance, real estate, and ICT was how governments in Canada – federal and provincial – deregulated financial markets and provided strategic supports and tax breaks. Over the course of the 1990s and the first decade of 2000, as in other advanced industrial countries in the late 1990s, Canadian governments sought to deal with declining profitability in manufacturing and primary industries by demand stimulus through financial deregulation, low interest rates, and support for housing markets (Brenner 2002; Duménil and Lévy 2011).

As noted in chapter 4, seeking to stimulate demand and new investment from multinationals, the federal and Ontario provincial governments enacted financial liberalization and loosened restrictions on the international buying and selling of domestic equity, with the hope that these reforms would boost foreign investment and spur domestic enterprises to restructure and expand, thereby increasing profits and employment growth (Carter 2015; Konzelmann and Fovargue-Davies 2013; Walks and Clifford 2015). The federal government also eased restrictions on the types of assets and equities in which public and private pension fund managers could invest in order to stimulate changes in corporate finance and corporate operation (CPP Investment Board 2005). The Ontario Securities Commission, following federal approval, passed new laws allowing the "securitization" of loans – that is, giving businesses the opportunity to package loans into bonds that were sold on capital markets to pension and mutual funds (Bank of Canada 2004, 2009), thus turning debts into assets. Other reforms included lowering of bank liquidity ratios, merger of commercial and investment banking, repeal of legislation regulating share buybacks, lower taxation on capital gains from equity sales, and formal approval of hedge funds.

With these legislative measures in place and the expanding freedom to use them, Canadian financial enterprises and non-financial firms rapidly developed new financial instruments and created astonishing opportunities to profit. Securitization – the buying and selling of corporate and mortgage market debt – was rapidly developed. Beginning in the late 1990s, companies both large and small issued thousands of new initial public share offerings on the Toronto Stock Exchange (TSX) to raise capital, fend off takeovers, and allow executives to "cash in their chips" with compensation totalling hundreds of millions of dollars. So too the expansion of foreign MNCs into Ontario and Canada led to massive inflows of investment into domestic stock markets, especially into the largest 100 companies on the Toronto Stock Exchange, which accounted for more than 80 per cent of total market capitalization on the exchange (Peters 2011; Nicholls 2006).

Adding to this financial transformation were companies using collateralized debt obligations and derivatives to drive up their leverage and profits. Canada's burgeoning investment banks, such as CIBC World Markets and RBC Capital Markets, allowed financial and manufacturing firms to increase their debt-to-equity leverage ratios to record levels (Milway et al. 2007). Institutional investors such as the public sector pension funds of Ontario Teachers and Ontario's municipal employees, along with insurance companies, also became major players on Canada's stock and financial markets and contributed to their growth (Boulay 2010). The results were the explosion of pension funds that increased in size from approximately 5 per cent of Canadian GDP to over 40 per cent from 1990 to 2000. Private equity and venture capital groups also grew rapidly, investing more than $2 billion in computer, software, and biotechnology industries, the vast majority in Canada's "research triangle" of Kitchener-Waterloo, Toronto, and Ottawa (Durufle 2009). The growth of these industries was so rapid that by 2009, Toronto was North America's third-largest financial services centre (after New York City and Chicago), with all of Canada's national banks, fifty foreign banks subsidiaries and branches, over 150 credit unions, and 115 securities firms (Milway et al. 2007).

New financial investment was also poured into ICT, life sciences, engineering, and biotechnology (Industry Canada 2009, 2010). With its open financial markets and firms run by CEOs on the basis of incentive compensation and stock options, international and domestic businesses quickly shifted to new areas of high profitability. In less than fifteen years, more than 16,000 ICT firms were established in Ontario, representing more than 50 per cent of Canada's total ICT industry. Ontario's life sciences industry also grew rapidly in the 1990s and by the middle of the first decade of 2000 was the ninth-largest pharmaceutical industry in the world (Industry Canada 2009).

As figure 8.3 demonstrates, one consequence of this rise in FIRE and tech industries was the steady increase in jobs in these sectors. After declining in the wake of the early 1990s, they saw employment rapidly increase, climbing by more than 150,000 from 1995 to 2010. The business, law, and scientific industries also rose rapidly, doubling in employment size from 1990 to 2010 to more than 544,000. Together, these two broad sectors accounted for 32 per cent of all new employment growth in Ontario between 1990 and 2010.

But residential and commercial construction was also crucial to employment and economic growth. Driven by the financialization of housing and mortgages, the housing sector exploded in Ontario's major urban markets (Walks and Clifford 2015). Federally, down payment requirements were lowered for homebuyers and eliminated for those who qualified. Tax breaks were given to property developers. Maximum mortgage amortization terms were extended to forty years. Variable rate mortgages were offered to buyers. Then in 2007, Canada's Housing and Mortgage Corporation (CMHC) not only insured more mortgages, it sold them back into markets in the form of "asset-backed commercial paper" to cover the growing amounts of precarious mortgage debt (Chapman, Lavoie, and Schembri 2011). Consequently, Canadian banks were

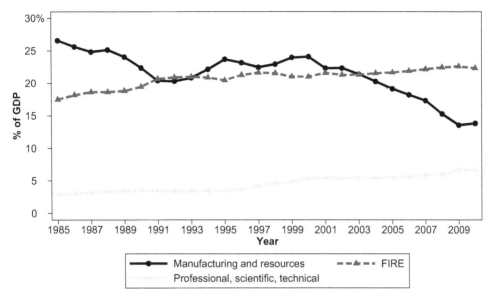

Figure 8.3. Ontario's new economy, sector changes (% GDP)
Sources: Statistics Canada, CANSIM tables 3790025 and 3700028.

very accommodating in providing record amounts of credit to Ontario and Canadian households.

Between 2000 and 2008, the value of outstanding mortgages grew from $427 billion to nearly $930 billion. From 1999 to 2005, consumer credit tripled, and variable rate mortgages climbed from 2 per cent of all residential mortgages to more than 25 per cent (CMHC 2009). Total household debt rose from 95 per cent of disposable income to 147 per cent in 2009, among the highest in the world (OECD 2010, 114). Thus, in a period of wage stagnation and growing economic inequality, deregulated credit markets became increasingly important to sustaining consumer demand, most notably for housing.

For Ontario in terms of employment, the securitization of mortgages and the growth of housing-driven financial assets expanded financial institutions' investments into housing markets and inflated the credit for construction firms and developers to take advantage of historic levels of borrowing to households to increase levels of new construction. With prices rising steeply – by more than 120 per cent in central Toronto – in 1996–2007, Ontario housing starts reached more than 80,000, over a third of all housing starts in Canada. Construction employment grew in tandem, expanding by more than 130,000 between 2001 and 2007, or nearly 19 per cent of total employment growth.

The Rise of Low-Wage and Precarious Employment in Ontario

With these transformations to Ontario's labour market underway, employers continued to hire more workers into both high-end and low-paid positions – with the majority of workers entering into low-wage and non-standard employment contracts. The result was an income "pyramid," with the ongoing growth of millionaires and ultra-high net-worth individuals who benefitted from expanding salaries and personal assets, and the continued expansion of workers with low-wage and low annual incomes (Credit Suisse 2013). While full data back to 1990 are unavailable, the share of workers earning below the two-thirds threshold of the full-time hourly wage in Ontario remained relatively consistent from 1997 to 2011, increasing from 37.5 to 38.5 per cent of the total workforce during that time (figure 8.4). But overall, this represented an increase of more than 579,000 workers in low-wage positions during the first decade of 2000. In addition, the intensity of low-wage work also increased. In 1997, only 2 per cent of workers of Ontario's workforce earned the minimum wage. But by 2010, more than 10 per cent of the workforce earned the minimum wage, and those earning within four dollars of the minimum wage (or roughly 80 per cent of the low-wage cutoff) more than doubled between 1997 and 2011 (Block 2015).

The majority of this growth in low-wage jobs came from the expansion of non-standard employment and the growth in non-union, private sector service jobs. Non-standard hours were the norm for low-wage workers, affecting more than 50 per cent of those in low-paying jobs. Wage penalties were common for workers in non-standard employment, with more than 63 per cent of workers in part-time and 68 per cent of those in self-employment earning less than two-thirds of the median wage in 2011. Employers in private services, agriculture, and construction – the growth industries reliant on low-cost labour – were the most likely to hire workers on a low-wage, non-standard basis. But wholesale and retail trade sectors, business services, cleaning, security, administration and clerical, and the agriculture sector – along with the many employers in agricultural and construction who employed foreign workers on temporary permits – also increased their workforces of low-wage and non-standard workers (Law Commission of Ontario 2012; Noack and Vosko 2011).

Temporary agency workers and workers in finance and ICT were also likely to be employed in low-wage work. Previously, employers hired only agency workers to temporarily fill positions for regular employees on leave or who were ill. However, with the vast expansion of temporary staffing and employment agencies in Toronto and Ontario to more than 2,500, employers increasingly resorted to flexible outsourcing. Major finance and ICT firms hired the vast majority of their administrative assistants, clerks, data entry workers,

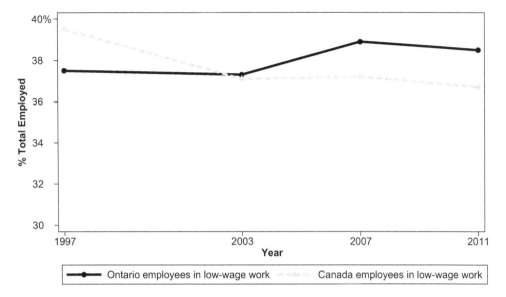

Figure 8.4. Percentage of employees in low-wage work in Ontario, 1997–2011 (workers earning less than two-thirds of median hourly wage of full-time/full-year employee)
Sources: Author's figures from custom request, Statistics Canada, Survey of Labour and Income Dynamics and Survey of Consumer Finances, "Percentage of Workers with Low Annual Earnings and Low Hourly Wages, Canada and Provinces," CANSIM table C685593.

researchers, paralegals, and other "service" providers on contract. Similarly, business, professional, and scientific industries doubled their part-time and temporary workforces. The rise of precarious employment was especially noticeable in finance and insurance, as over 600,000 of the million jobs in finance, insurance, business, and the new economy industries were clerical, where the average annual salary was only $36,000 in 2010.

As Noack and Vosko (2011) have demonstrated, women and racialized workers were more likely to be in low-wage, non-standard work, and these figures increased over the course of the 1990s and the first decade of 2000. But with employers increasingly hiring workers on a non-standard basis, and union coverage and organizing in decline, all workers in service sectors and lower-skill employment felt the impacts of lower earnings.

The result, as figure 8.5 shows, was a significant rise in income inequality. Between 1990 and 2010, the 90:20 ratio between top and bottom income earners increased by more than 50 per cent to 9.3. In contrast, Canada's 90:20 ratio fell slightly over the course of the first decade of 2000. Figure 8.5 also indicates that working households in the middle of the distribution did somewhat better

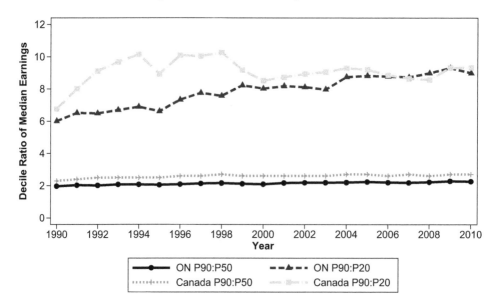

Figure 8.5. Rising earnings inequality in Ontario, 1990–2010 (among economic families, age 18–65)
Source: Author's figures from custom tabulation from Survey of Labour and Income Dynamics and the Survey of Consumer Finances, "Median Incomes, Average Incomes, and Share of Incomes by Decile," data shared by the Canadian Centre for Policy Alternatives.

than those in the bottom of the income distribution as the 50:20 ratio grew by more than 25 per cent between 1990 and 2010. This decline in the incomes of the lowest-income workers appears to be related to the rise in non-standard employment and the impacts of service, construction, and agriculture employers to use low-cost labour to underpin their competitive strategies.

Drift and the Pluralist Nature of Organized Business in Ontario

What accounts for this rise in low-wage work and non-standard employment? Why, despite the relative institutional stability of labour law and employment regulations throughout the first decade of 2000, did job and income security continue to worsen? Clearly, the role of employers was key: globalization and cost-competitiveness made labour costs a key concern for all companies and wider commerce. As noted in chapters 6 and 7 on British Columbia and Newfoundland and Labrador, so too in Ontario, increasingly financialized firms across the province enacted human resource strategies to ensure flexibility and cost constraint – most notably hiring more workers on a temporary or part-time basis. But employers and business associations did not achieve major reforms to legislation, as in British Columbia or elsewhere in the United States, such as Wisconsin or Pennsylvania. Nor did employers remain within formal bargaining and institutional frameworks, as in Newfoundland and Labrador.

Our theory suggests that unless firms develop overlapping associations and advocacy coalitions, while deepening their political networks with (and integration into) parties and government, it will be more difficult to achieve their goals of widespread labour policy change. However, as comparative frameworks propose, politically active firms and politically organized sector associations can still play critical roles in blocking policy updates or preventing improvements to basic employment standards and the minimum wage. This is because even though employers across manufacturing and service sectors may take different views of bargaining rules and employment regulations, major employer groups can more generally agree to prevent improvements to employment regulations that would make non-standard employment more expensive and can agree to prevent reforms that would improve the prospects of organized labour organizing or bargaining for better agreements (Thelen 2014). In Ontario, there is evidence that this holds true as well, for even though employers may not have agreed on a common set of reforms to press government officials to implement, they could often concur on opposing labour policy improvements that would improve jobs, close employer loopholes, and better balance collective bargaining in the province.

One key factor for employer success in Ontario in blocking improvements to labour legislation and regulations was the pluralist nature of interest representation and the growth and expansion of sectoral business associations that consistently advanced the importance of market growth, free trade, and low labour costs alongside circumscribed labour rights in order to maintain business competitiveness. In general, business in Ontario has long been strongly represented by a host of industrial and commercial associations. The Toronto Financial Services Alliance or the Canadian Automotive Partnership Council, for example, have regularly provided firms with information on policy updates, and conducted policy lobbying and advocacy. But these associations have also offered counselling and advice and provided networks for businesses to meet, share ideas, and interact with government officials. At a larger scale, national organizations such as the Canadian Council of Chief Executives and the Canadian Chamber of Commerce represent a mix of Ontario-based companies, global MNCS, and small business interests addressing trade and infrastructure and other social policy issues like workplace insurance with provincial officials (Brownlee 2005). In these organizations, global MNCs (the majority of which are American), international and domestic construction companies, and Canada's internationally competitive banks represent themselves in their regular meetings with provincial government officials (Brennan 2012).

Businesses have also strongly supported a cluster of business-directed research organizations such as the Conference Board of Canada, the C.D. Howe Institute, and the Global Risk Institute to undertake research and policy advocacy. Added to these have been the active role of global business consultancies such as PricewaterhouseCoopers (PwC), Deloitte, and KPMG, which have directly promoted business goals through research, consulting, and interactions with government officials on public policy (Hodge and Bowman 2006; Shaoul, Stafford, and Stapleton 2007). Beginning in 2004, under government policy direction to municipal governments, the provincial government recommended that municipal governments hire private sector consultants to provide advice on municipal service provision and possibilities for privatization and contracting out. Often regions and municipalities hired large consultant firms such as KPMG that regularly lobby for tax cuts for private sector firms and subsequently recommend that governments cut public spending through privatization, outsourcing, and elimination of services.

Finally, the most consistent political thrust of business has come through the growing number of consultant lobby organizations and business law firms such as Strategycorp, Hill and Knowlton Strategies, Hicks Morley LLP, Fasken Martineau LLP, McMillan LLP, Cassels Brock and Blackwell LLP, and Heenan Blaikie that have provided a wide range of "government relations" services to business, including lobbying, polling, and representing key firms and sectors during government negotiations with businesses (Gray 2011). For example, during the economic crisis, Cassels Brock and Blackwell LLP represented the major auto companies and auto dealers in negotiating compensation packages and government support (Cassels Brock and Blackwell LLP 2009; Gray 2014). Business strategy consultants and law firms have also led in hiring former federal and provincial Cabinet ministers and employing former party executives and staffs to better manage business government lobbying efforts. Leading employer law firms also represented numerous business associations and often went so far as to draft proposed legislation for officials and legislators to consider (Ontario NDP party official).

In line with trends elsewhere in Canada and in the United States, the expansion of these business associations, their networks, and resources had direct political effects. Business representation to government and lobbying increased significantly in the first decade of 2000, influencing both Conservative and Liberal governments. In 2000, there were 684 lobbyists registered with the Office of the Integrity Commissioner, who met with government officials some 1,400 times. By 2010, these numbers had more than tripled, with more than 1,900 lobbyists registered, holding more than 5,900 meetings with government officials, including more than 1,300 meetings with the premier of Ontario and other senior provincial officials (Ontario Office of the Integrity Commissioner). Research organizations like the Conference Board of Canada also significantly increased their resources and expenditures, more than tripling their annual expenditures on research publications, conferences, and other media over the course of the 1990s and first decade of the 2000s.

Moreover, with such resources at hand, firms developed and promoted their market views of the necessity of tax cuts, greater government subsidies to support enterprises, and increased investment in infrastructure through public-private partnerships to promote economic growth and boost business investment. For example, KPMG, an international business consultant agency, established a tax unit devoted to regularly publishing and publicizing the nature of tax competitiveness across countries and regions, ranking countries on the lowest tax structures, and making recommendations on how public officials can improve their international competitiveness (KPMG 2012). Similarly, the auto sector association – the Canadian Automotive Partnership Council – set up special working committees and research groups among major firms and executives, which produced wide-ranging "calls to action" arguing for governments to reduce taxation, remove environmental regulations, lower energy costs, and provide greater investment supports for the auto industry (Canadian Automotive Partnership Council 2013). The Ontario Agricultural Federation also regularly called for a host of tax reductions on property and inputs, while lobbying and meeting officials for agriculture to be exempt from labour relations and employment standards legislation.

Many business organizations also met with government officials, most notably on workplace safety and insurance issues, as well as the minimum wage, with the Canadian Restaurant and Food Services Association regularly opposing increases to the minimum wage, new union certification procedures, and any increases to pension plans (Canadian Restaurant and Foodservices Association 2005). Similarly, the Ontario Chamber of Commerce routinely polled its member firms on minimum wage and working hour issues, and subsequently made recommendations to make only minor changes to minimum wages, or to keep minimum wage increases pegged to inflation, and not to increase the minimum wage to a living wage. By 2013, the Ontario Chamber of Commerce was promoting the privatization of government services, covering everything from prisons to employment training (Ontario Chamber of Commerce 2013).

However, business organizations were most successful in advocating against reforms to labour policy and employment regulations, rather than advancing new reforms. In contrast to British Columbia, where business associations established a coalition to discuss and promote labour policy reforms to Liberal Party officials prior to and soon after the Campbell government came to power, the most typical pattern in Ontario has been that firms and employer associations establish new business coalitions to oppose legislative reforms. In 1992, a wide range of employer organizations including the Canadian Manufacturers associations as well as agricultural and small business associations joined under the banners of the "All Business Coalition" and "More Jobs Coalition" to lobby and publicly campaign against Bill 40, a labour legislation reform bill proposed by the short-lived NDP government (Galt 1992; Tobin 1992). In developing research, hosting public meetings, and lobbying government officials directly and in committee hearings, the coalition mobilized wider opposition to the bill. It also subsequently provided support and policies for the Conservative government elected in 1995, which removed all aspects of the reform labour legislation, including card certification, shorter first-contract arbitration, and bans on replacement workers during strikes (Klassen and Haddow 2006).

When the Liberal government of Dalton McGuinty came to power in 2003, business associations and new business coalitions campaigned against proposed reforms. In the view of one ministry official, business not only increased its lobbying in the first decade of 2000, it became increasingly well organized, meeting with individual representatives, bringing in experts, and launching public campaigns that were impossible for public officials to ignore (Ontario Ministry of Labour official). For example, in addressing proposed changes to employment standards legislation that would see a permit system reinstated for overtime above forty-eight hours a week and regular increases to minimum wages, the Canadian Federation of Independent Business (CFIB) lobbied ministry officials, released research reports, and held regular press conferences and committee meetings to press its view that any changes would reduce jobs and new investment.

Arguing that any restrictions on flexibility and any wage increases in industries such as restaurants and accommodation would cut into low profit margins for business, the CFIB argued that measures like labour regulations and minimum wages were "too blunt" to reduce poverty (CFIB 2004). And throughout the first decade of 2000, the CFIB and other service associations regularly opposed updates to the minimum wage. The evidence suggests that such business organizations were very successful in highlighting their position, as minimum wage and poverty policy reviews in 2007 regularly underscored business opposition to minimum wage increases. But more importantly, the success of business activities can be seen in the restricted increases to the Ontario minimum wage, which in real dollars remained below 1997 levels, and by 2012 had increased by only $1.42 – a rise of 10 per cent between 2004 and 2012 (Minimum Wage Advisory Panel 2014).

Organized business interests across the agricultural sector also mobilized against any labour law or labour policy reforms that would affect agricultural workers (Preibisch 2010). Traditionally, in Ontario – as in most Canadian provinces – agricultural workers have been denied the right to unionization and have had limited employment regulation under special legislation (Tucker 2008). However, over the past few decades, as unions faced increasingly restrictive legislation and found that traditional political processes were more closed, unions launched an increasing number of legal challenges and complaints to national and international courts and international organizations (Fudge 2007). In some provinces, as in Quebec, this led to new legislation that provided for some extension of collective bargaining rights and employment standards protection for agricultural workers.

But in Ontario, employers challenged the provision of collective bargaining rights to workers as well as the extension of minimum employment standards requirements for workers (Tucker 2012). This led to the introduction of limited new collective bargaining legislation for agricultural workers that does not include a formal requirement for employers to negotiate with unions, nor does it allow agricultural workers the right to strike (Walchuk 2009). Employer pressure was also instrumental to the legislative exemption of the agriculture sector from rules for overtime, rest periods, and maximum hours of work, as well as the Occupational Health and Safety Act until 2006 (Law Commission of Ontario 2012).

In Ontario, such employer success in blocking the update of agricultural collective bargaining regulation was due to activities of the Labour Issues Coordinating Committee (LICC). The LICC was the driving force for large and small farmers in blocking collective bargaining reform and maintaining employment standards exemptions. Established in 1991 in response to the NDP proposed legislation that included agricultural workers under collective bargaining legislation, it brought together leading employers from the Ontario Fruit and Growers Association, the Dairy Farmers of Ontario, and key members from the Ontario Federation of Agriculture to organize and advocate against labour reforms. Mobilizing members with regular meetings and fundraising campaigns, as well as with updates at Ontario Federation of Agriculture meetings, it made routine presentations to the Harris Conservative government that in 1995 led to the repeal of NDP legislation recognizing the bargaining rights of agricultural workers. Similarly, when the exclusionary Conservative legislation was challenged in court and overturned by the Supreme Court in 2001 (Dunmore v Ontario), the LICC hired a leading business law firm in Canada – Heenan Blaikie – to represent it in drafting new provincial legislation that would meet the bare minimum by providing precarious agricultural workers with restricted association rights, but no rights to certification of workplaces, to collective bargaining, to strike, or to health and safety protection.

In 2001, under LICC direction, Heenan Blaikie met several times with the Ministries of Labour and Agriculture, Food and Rural Affairs, and draft legislation was sent to the LICC for comment and approval (Ontario Integrity Commission). This consultation between government and the agricultural employer associations finally resulted in the Agricultural Employees Protection Act (AEPA 2002), which failed to provide agricultural workers with the right to collective bargaining. When this act too was challenged by the United Food and Commercial Workers (UFCW) several times in court over the next decade, the LICC continued to meet regularly with government officials and backed a costly Supreme Court fight over several years that eventually upheld the act in 2011, denying workers their basic collective bargaining rights and potentially limiting future court actions by denying fundamental practicalities necessary for unions to exercise their freedom of association (Tucker 2012).

Finally, critically influential in preventing any progressive evolution of labour law and policy in construction and trade-related industries were non-union construction firms that allied under their OpenShop Contractors Association and led in the most comprehensive employers' advocacy coalition called the Coalition for Democratic Labour Relations. In 2005, when the Liberal government was considering reforms to the Ontario Labour Relations Act and improving certification procedures and union representation, the Coalition for Democratic Labour Relations, backed by the Ontario Chamber of Commerce, launched an extensive advocacy and lobbying campaign against any return to card-based certification, as well as any return of remedial powers to the provincial labour board to provide for the reinstatement of workers who were dismissed during an organizing drive (Canada NewsWire 2004; Cameron 2004). In 1995, the Conservative government, taking direction from leading business coalitions, had removed card-based certification and the remedial powers of labour boards in order to foster a "more competitive business environment" (Slinn 2004). But when the Liberal government proposed reforming the Ontario Labour Relations Act, they faced extensive business opposition.

Seeking "balance" in its reopening of the legislation, the government introduced changes that took employer concerns seriously (Ontario Ministry of Labour official). Most notably, the new powers granted to the labour board were circumscribed, allowing employers to dismiss workers, and only in cases of "irreparable harm" were workers who had been dismissed during organized drives allowed to be reinstated (Ontario union organizer, private sector 1; Ontario union organizer, private sector 2; Ontario labour lawyer). In addition, the burden of proof in establishing that the dismissal was related to organizing activity was placed on the individual rather than the employer. The result was that even though labour boards gained new interim powers to reinstate workers under the Liberal government, the reality was that unions and individual workers continued to risk loss of employment, and that workers could be intimidated by aggressive employers attempting to stop union organizing drives.

Cathie Jo Martin and Duane Swank (2012) have argued that firms develop their policy interests in packs, and that employer or business associations can facilitate regular meetings with government and expose members to ideas about the benefits of bargaining and social policies for productivity growth and labour market stability. Because preferences are politically constructed, they claim, associations and their success can channel employers' long-term corporate and political strategies. This appears to also hold true of business associations in Ontario, where business associations were critical in upholding views that collective bargaining and employment regulations were inimical to competitive enterprises and limited employer options to respond to changing market conditions.

In BC, such views led to new business associations forming that pressured public officials to convert collective bargaining and employment regulations. However, in Ontario, business associations remained generally segmented by sector, while overarching employer associations such as the Canadian Chamber of Commerce and the Canadian Federation of Business mobilized not to rewrite minimum wages and collective bargaining legislation, but to leave it unchanged. Consequently, with few cross-sector coalitions pushing for labour policy reform, business associations were most successful in blocking or limiting reforms to collective bargaining and employment standards legislation.

Many businesses – especially those in non-union construction and small private service enterprises – may have been interested in seeing far wider reforms similar to those in the United States that would deregulate labour markets even further. However, without the development of long-lasting business coalitions committed to legislative and policy reform, there was no political impetus for government officials to enact major reform of this kind. Of equal importance, as argued in the next section, was Ontario's three-party system, which made it far easier to settle for preventing updates or improvements to labour policy than to undertake extensive business-friendly alterations.

Business and the Electoral Politics of Support for a "Third Way" Policy Model

Political economists have argued that because of the rise of globalization and finance capitalism, political parties are becoming increasingly alike in their support for business and the affluent, and their models of political economy more similar (Crouch 2014; Hacker and Pierson 2010b). However, party politics in Ontario in the 1990s and the first decade of 2000 shows that even though there is substantial merit to such critical explanations, there is also still a strong role for political parties and their strategic calculations in understanding trajectories of policy reform and the extent to which governments have sought to reform and restructure their labour markets. Indeed, as developments in Ontario demonstrate, how parties do or do not pursue deregulation is patterned by the partisan make-up of competing parties and their strategic considerations for wider electoral support.

This distinction is clearest in the policy priorities and policy approach of the Conservative and Liberal governments, for even though both the Conservative and Liberal parties of Ontario were committed to advancing market growth, free trade, and greater economic efficiency over the course of the 1990s and first decade of 2000, their means for achieving these ends often differed (Evans 2011; Evans and Smith 2015a). Most notably, whereas the Conservative Party sought to reverse union rights and rewrite employment regulation in the private and public sectors alike, the Ontario Liberal Party was committed to "Moving Forward Together" and securing wider class cooperation and compromise in order to advance economic prosperity – what has been termed as a Canadian version of "Third Way" politics evident in Great Britain, Germany, and a number of other countries (Coulter 2009). It was the political and electoral considerations behind these decisions that created a context for labour policy "drift" throughout much of the first decade of 2000, suggesting that political parties – despite pressures from the business lobby – can take a number of different policy positions in addressing labour and employment issues.

Nevertheless, before looking more closely at how the parties differed, it is revealing to look at the similarities in policymaking between the Conservative and Liberal Parties, and how the role of organized business interests and the priorities of the business community were critical to Ontario politics and to macroeconomic policymaking in the province. As in other liberal market economies with first-past-the-post systems (Amable 2003), similarly in Ontario well-organized political interests and their electoral coalitions have been able to exercise lasting influence on provincial governments. Taking advantage of Ontario's three-party system and how it narrowed the expression of political demands, the Ontario PC Party held office for sixty years between 1943 and 2003. Both the Liberals and the NDP provided electoral competition to the Conservatives, but organized business interests with greater financial resources, more political organization, and substantive input on agenda setting and legislation provided the Conservative Party with more than 60 per cent of all its political campaign funding throughout the 1970s and helped link interest groups with local candidates and riding associations (MacDermid 2009).

Likewise there is evidence to suggest that with the continuing success of Conservative business-oriented policies, other competing parties in Ontario were forced to adopt similar policies and political tactics, emulating the models of successful governments in the effort to win over an diminishing number of affluent and median voters within a shrunken and politically marginalized electorate. For example, forced to deal with an assertive and organized business community, beginning in the 1990s, the Liberal Party began to reach out to corporate and financial donors as never before and shifted their party into a tighter alignment with money-driven politics (Sorbara 2014).

Whereas, in the 1990s, more than two-thirds of Liberal Party revenue came from individuals and local riding associations, by early in the first decade of 2000, as figure 8.6 shows, the Liberals were matching Conservative corporate donations, and in the 2003 election drew more than 60 per cent of political financing from business donations. The impact of business funding for both

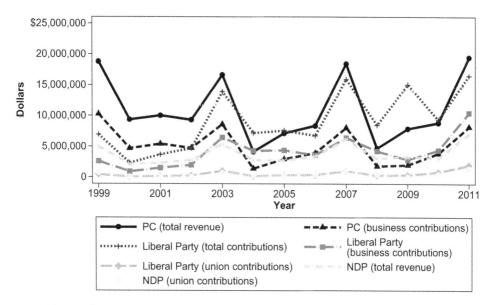

Figure 8.6. Political finance in Ontario, 1999–2011
Source: Elections Ontario, data compilation by Robert MacDermid, York University.

parties was significant, and business donations routinely made up more than 40 per cent of all party revenue in Ontario. When combined with individual donations from leading businessmen, real estate developers, and financial industry executives and professionals, this funding amounted to more than 50 per cent of all party revenue in Ontario provincial politics (MacDermid 2011).

In addition, over the course of the first decade of 2000, the Liberal government followed its Conservative predecessor in strengthening its connections with influential business consultancies. New political consultancies and public relations firms developed lists of prominent former premiers and politicians to make contact with key legislative figures. The public relations firms Strategy Corp, Hill and Knowlton Strategies, and Counsel Public Affairs, for example, all hired former Liberal politicians and party advisors to undertake lobbying services for business associations and to provide political advice for Liberal campaign and transition teams (DeMara 2004; Erwin 2005; Van Harten 2004). This growth in lobbying increased the influence of well-placed public relations firms and helped equip business groups with new political prominence.

The macro results on policymaking in Ontario thus appear comparable to developments in the United States (Hacker and Pierson 2010b), Great Britain (Leys 2003), and British Columbia. In 1994, when the Conservative Party returned to power, retooling their platform along more business-friendly lines, they placed heavy stress on tax cuts, deficit reduction, welfare reform, and labour market deregulation (Klassen and Haddow 2006). Public spending as a percentage of GDP, already among the lowest in Canada throughout the 1980s and early 1990s, fell even lower to 12.8 per cent by 2000 (Evans and Smith 2015a). Corporate and individual tax cuts in Ontario reduced annual revenue-raising capacity by more than $13 billion annually by 2002–3, and by more than $48 billion cumulatively in 1996–2003, substantively lowering the redistributive impact of transfers on income inequality in the province (CCPA 2007; Sharpe and Capeluck 2012).

However, when the Liberal government was elected in 2003, there was little change to tax or transfer policies. Despite regular electoral commitments to improving education and training and expanding innovation and infrastructure, and policy commitments to poverty reduction beginning in 2008, the Liberal Party did little to reverse shortfalls in tax revenue and remained one of the lowest public spending governments in Canada (Commission of the Reform of Ontario's Public Services 2012). Much as in British Columbia, throughout early in the first decade of 2000, the Liberal Party remained a key advocate of deficit reduction and retained all the previous administration's corporate and individual tax cuts, only expanding a range of indirect taxes and levies combined with tax credits and exemptions. This was followed in 2010 by a new set of proposals to match the federal government reductions in corporate taxes and reduce general and small business corporate tax rates (Mackenzie 2010). These policy moves meant that by 2009, Ontario retained the second-lowest overall tax load as percentage of GDP across Canada (Commission of the Reform of Ontario's Public Services 2012).

The low rates of taxation also meant that as Ontario's income inequality rose in the first decade of 2000, Liberal policies did little to offset it through increased spending or taxation, and the overall redistributive impact of taxes and transfers actually fell (Sharpe and Capeluck 2012). In policy areas such as social assistance, childcare, and housing, by 2010, Liberal spending was actually lower in real terms than it had been in 1994–5 (Mackenzie 2010). As in other liberal market jurisdictions, such developments in Ontario support critical political economy arguments that partisanship differences among parties were substantially narrowed over the course of the 1990s and the first decade of 2000 because of the growing influence of business and finance within parties and policy circles, and older ideas of a mixed economy were increasingly replaced by supply-side polices of low taxes and limited regulation (Evans and Smith 2015a; Glyn 2006).

Nevertheless, in labour policy and collective bargaining, policy differences remained between the Conservative (1994–2003) and Liberal (2003–15) governments. In the 1990s and early in the first decade of 2000, the Conservative government not only pushed for reduced taxation and regulation, welfare reform, and reliance on competition and market forces to "restore efficiency and encourage new investment." It also sought to overturn the power of trade unions and reverse the previous administration's attempt to balance employer and union powers in the province (Klassen and Haddow 2006). It pushed for wider deregulation and changes in collective bargaining. In the effort to politically dismantle previous legislative gains by unions, the Conservative government reinstated new voting procedures for certification, eliminated successor rights for public sector workers whose jobs were transferred to the private sector, and introduced requirements for workplaces to post information on how and when individual employees could decertify their union.

In contrast, the Liberal government, which ruled from 2003 to 2011, made few major election commitments to reform, modernize, or update labour legislation in the province (Ontario Liberal Party 2003, 2007, 2011). Instead, policy platforms noted that the Liberal Party would bring "fairness and balance" to Ontario labour laws and policies. It would achieve this by increasing employment in the health and education sectors, and under its economic growth plan, raise the minimum wage and introduce new employment standards to limit a standard sixty-hour workweek. In 2010 and 2011, in the wake of the financial crisis, the Liberal government did begin to take more substantive measures to restrain wage increases among elementary and secondary school teachers (Evans 2011; Thomas and Tufts 2016). But these policy measures were never central to their election campaigns, however. Only reforms and new investment in education were highlighted in all three election platforms (2003, 2007, 2011), but even in these policy areas, reforms to collective bargaining were never mentioned, and only limited reference was made to changing the new Ontario College of Teachers into a professional body run by teachers themselves rather than political appointees. These policies – and their limited impacts – are outlined in more detail in the following sections.

Political Coalitions and the Third Way Model

Why the significant difference in Liberal partisan policy response? The short answer is that the Liberal government pursued policies that diverged from the Ontario Conservatives or BC Liberals because the coalition of interests underpinning their economic strategy was far more particularistic and sought to appeal to a wider range of voters and taxpayers – especially those in urban areas such as Toronto. Made up of interests from the financial, development, and IT sectors, as well as those from more sheltered domestic economic sectors, the key supporters of the Liberals were less interested in wage flexibility and labour market reforms than the agricultural, private service employers and the non-unionized construction firms that were closely tied to the Conservative Party. In political terms, the preference of key interests that supported the Liberal Party was more in line with maintaining "status quo" policies of modest bargaining regulation and limited employment regulation – rather than their further reform or a fundamental overturn.

How did the Liberal Party build electoral support and maintain business backing in an institutional context that strongly promoted greater labour market deregulation and lower labour costs? Three reasons suggest themselves. This first is that the Liberal Party mobilized – and sought to attract – a set of business groups different from those that supported the Conservatives – most notably economic interests less affected by labour cost considerations. While both parties relied heavily on the financial contributions of developers and the major banks (MacDermid 2011), their core business supporters differed greatly.

Unlike in British Columbia, where all business support was unified behind the Liberal Party, in Ontario, business support and political ties were segmented between the Liberal and Conservative Parties. For the Conservatives, core supporters included the non-unionized construction industry, numerous agricultural associations, and retail chains such as Giant Tiger, all of whom were strongly committed to wage flexibility and cost competitiveness. In contrast, the Liberal base of financial and political support was led by the largest unionized construction firm in the province, Ellis Don, as well as by the largest information technology firm of the early 2000s, Research in Motion (MacDermid 2011). Similarly, while many non-unionized auto parts manufacturers were closely tied to Conservative fundraising efforts in the first decade of 2000 (Lilley 2006), large unionized manufacturing corporations were more than willing to work with the Liberals in developing industrial policies that would underwrite their new investments (Rutherford and Holmes 2014).

In this context, while many construction, manufacturing, and private service firms may have preferred the wider deregulation of labour markets as well as more direct political support to limit union powers and union growth, many others did not or were simply less concerned with labour costs as competitive priorities. For IT firms, unionized auto manufacturing, and the financial sector, which relied on high skills and peaceful labour relations, a status quo policy and regulatory mix of individualized employment relations and limited union bargaining rights provided the best context to address competitive market conditions. Moreover, unlike British Columbia, no long-term, "all-business" coalition emerged in Ontario to advance labour policy reforms. As a result, the Liberal Party could adopt an electoral strategy that involved IT and unionized construction firms as well as a wider producer coalition that was largely neutral towards existing labour policy and employment standards, and that sought to uphold current frameworks to either retain access to skilled labour or to ensure little conflict within workplaces.

Second, supporting this wider strategy were Liberal efforts to secure the backing of unionized construction workers and unionized education workers in the province. The strong neoliberal turn in the 1990s had led construction workers and teachers in Ontario to seek new alliances with the Liberal Party with the hope that a new government would overturn previous Conservative policies (Schuetze et al. 2011; Walchuk 2010). Parts of the Canadian Auto Workers union (CAW), facing membership decline and under pressure to adapt new strategies, also began to propose the necessity of strategic voting to keep the Conservative Party from returning to office. In shifting away from their traditional alliance with the New Democratic Party in Ontario, autoworkers sought a more consensual labour environment and more strategic investments in the auto sector to retain unionized auto manufacturing plants in Ontario (Stanford 2010). At the same time, teachers pushed for new funding and a wide range of program support within schools as well as reforms to the Colleges of Teachers.

Under this coalition, unions provided a range of support for the Liberal Party, and in return, the Liberal Party proposed to make selective reforms or introduce new policies that would provide a new "balance" to the education, auto, and construction sectors (Walchuk 2010). Beginning in 2003, the Working Families Coalition provided campaign support, political donations, and television advertisements that backed the Liberal Party during election campaigns. Most significant were the funds raised by the unions for partisan television advertisements that underlined the negative consequences of a Conservative government for workers in Ontario (Urquhart 2007). Equally significant was that union financial contributions to the Liberal Party began to exceed those to the NDP in 2003 and continued to do so until 2011. Unlike the Liberal Party in BC or the Conservative Party in Newfoundland and Labrador, this level of union campaign support was unique to Ontario and marked a fundamental departure of union-NDP ties elsewhere in Canada (Savage 2010).

Third, the Liberal government appealed to – and won over – a broad range of middle- and low-income constituencies and interests in key urban areas such as Toronto. Unlike in BC, where with rising income inequality and declining voter turnout, the BC Liberal Party sought to build a programmatic platform that appealed primarily to upper- and middle-income earners in high-income districts, in Ontario the Liberal Party sought to also capture low- and median-income suburban ridings, especially in the ridings that comprised the Greater Toronto Area – a key to capturing electoral power in Ontario (Boudreau, Keil, and Young 2009). As table 8.1 demonstrates, while the Conservatives and Liberals routinely split the support of the highest-income ridings in the province, the Liberals regularly captured the majority of the lowest-income ridings in the province, including all those in the GTA, at the expense of the Conservatives and the NDP – the party most associated with redistributive policies and social program spending.

Table 8.1. Ontario voting and income polarization, 2003–2011

		2003	2007	2011	Total
Top 12 Wealthiest	Liberal	6	6	5	17
Electoral Districts	PC	4	6	6	16
	NDP	0	0	1	1
Bottom 12 Wealthiest	Liberal	10	11	9	30
Electoral Districts	PC	0	0	1	1
	NDP	0	1	1	2

Note: As the result of district restructuring, only ten ridings are counted for 2003, and eleven for 2011.
Source: Statistics Canada, "Federal Electoral District Profile, 2006 Census," catalogue no. 92-595-XWE, 26 June 2008. Based on median household income.

Top median-income electoral ridings, 2003–11: Oakville, Halton, Carleton-Mississippi Mills, Nepean-Carleton, Newmarket, Ancaster, Whitby-Oshawa, Wellington-Halton Hills, Oakridges-Markham, St. Paul, Pickering-Ajax, Essex

Bottom median-income electoral ridings, 2003–11: York West, York South-Weston, Scarborough-Agincourt, Hamilton Centre, Scarborough-Guildwood, Scarborough-Rouge River, Scarborough Centre, Davenport, Scarborough Southwest, York Centre, Don Valley East, Prince Edward-Hastings

---

The success of the Liberals in winning over parts of these "outsider" constituencies did not rely on traditional redistribution policies. Despite commitments to reducing child poverty and improving training to low-income individuals, the Liberals did not notably expand social spending in the province, nor did their policies improve income redistribution (Mackenzie 2010). Moreover, unlike in Newfoundland and Labrador, where the Conservative Party and government officials were tightly tied to regional boards and councils, there were no such institutions playing a mediating political role between low-income ridings and governing officials in Ontario. Nor is there evidence to suggest that low-income neighbourhoods in the GTA were as fiscally conservative as those in high-income ridings. International Social Survey data reveal that 70 per cent of households with family incomes under $65,000 believed that government definitely should reduce income differences between rich and poor.

Evidence does suggest that low-income support for the Liberals came from policies focused on the suburbs that developed elementary and secondary education, as well as infrastructure and transportation investments that would expand asset wealth in housing while providing new opportunities for affordable housing (Hulchanski 2010; Winfield 2006). Over the course of the 1990s and first decade of 2000, the fastest population growth came in the expanding suburbs of the GTA. The majority of residents who came to live in these regions and neighbourhoods were low-income families, racialized immigrants, and second-generation immigrants (Galabuzi 2006). Seeking economic opportunities, housing, and educational opportunities for children, immigrant families and second-generation citizens moved in large numbers into inner and outer suburban Toronto.

But rather than develop a comprehensive set of solutions to the mounting problems of poverty and low-wage work that immigrants and racialized minorities faced, the Liberals developed an economic model that supported home ownership and the growth in house prices that delivered satisfaction to a number of suburban voters for government performance (Hulchanski 2010). The policies for this new growth model included a new gas tax that prioritized transit development in the suburbs, streamlining of environmental assessments for new high-density condominium developments, and new funding for highway and infrastructure development in the region – all policies that proved popular with voters throughout the first decade of 2000.

For homeowners in the GTA, these policies contributed to more than doubling house prices in most parts of the GTA between 2000 and 2012 (RBC-Pembina Institute 2013). Low-income groups who rented and relied on public transportation were the losers of this model (Hulchanski 2010). For those who owned housing, Liberal development policies provided a key source of asset growth, particularly in a period of high asset-price inflation. These housing and infrastructure policies ensured broad support in the GTA for Liberal policies.

This balancing of policy choices was in many ways similar to other Third Way governments such as the British Labour Party under Tony Blair or Gerhard Schroeder's Social Democrats in Germany (Huo 2009). In all three cases, governments represented a wide range of diverse views, loosely centred on economic advancement and educational opportunities as keys for employment growth. In Ontario, the Liberal Party highlighted how individual success could be achieved through hard work, but only with a "ladder of opportunity" comprising public investments in education and training (Coulter 2009). The Liberal government of Ontario was little interested in pursuing legislative reform that could potentially raise wages, nor – outside of taking steps to address child poverty in 2008 – would it pursue the underlying issues driving low-wage work, poverty, and social exclusion, if that meant increasing taxes or reforming labour legislation in a way that business opposed. Indeed, Labour Ministry officials in the Liberal government commented that no substantive reforms were possible without business support and the development of a "balanced" consensus that kept industry in Ontario (Ontario Labour Ministry official).

However, even though the Ontario Liberal government did not seek to de-regulate bargaining and employment regulations, their Third Way approach had negative consequences for the labour market and labour policy. In par-ticular, the pursuit of economic growth in the absence of institutional com-mitments to better jobs, higher minimum wages, or unionized employment meant that firms were allowed to operate with restricted wage costs and flex-ible employment strategies as top priorities. Moreover, in a context of mas-sive industrial restructuring and the rapid growth of low-wage private service industries, the loss of good unionized jobs was compounded by the growth of non-standard jobs with low wages. And with the decline of unions, and the lack of policies that would have reduced that decline, the effects were felt not only in the economic sphere, but also in Ontario politics, with organized labour increasingly unable to effectively advance the interests of workers across the province.

Policy Drift and Low-Wage Work in Ontario

Throughout the post-war period, shifts in governing parties traditionally meant shifts in macroeconomic and social policies, with left parties favouring lower interest rates and mildly expansionary policies, and right parties utilizing tax reductions and limited increases to spending during economic upswings and contractionary policies during downturns in the market (Hibbs 1987). How-ever, with changes to the operation of parties and the growing influence of business, recent critical political economy suggests that there is less partisan difference between parties, and when new governments are elected, they more typically leave policies in place or enact only minor reforms in order to retain a more business-friendly economic environment (Glyn 2006; Hacker and Pier-son 2010b; Hassel and Schelke 2013). Such a theoretical perspective appears equally true of Ontario, especially in its tax and transfer policies. But in labour policies and regulations under the Conservative (1993–2003) and Liberal ad-ministrations (2003–11), the parties may have agreed on the necessity of low labour costs, but differed in tone and approach.

In the early 1990s, the Conservative government claimed that the province's slow growth was the consequence of its industrial relations and employment regulations, and sought to reduce the scope of unions while reforming em-ployment standards to improve labour market flexibility (Klassen and Had-dow 2006). When the Liberal government came to power in 2003, more labour-friendly legislation was introduced, and improvements were made to the minimum wage and employment standards, but in many cases, these re-forms did little more than chip away at the edges of Conservative policy. In other cases, the Liberal government simply bowed to pressure and killed legis-lation aimed at improving wage and workplace protection.

Such government actions – and inactions – not only continued to undercut the ability of unions to organize new workers and slowly eroded their bargaining power throughout the province. This policy stance also wore away at wage and employment protections for low-paid workers, with few of the Liberal policy changes closing loopholes in employment standards, improving enforcement, or regulating employers in their use of non-standard employment contracts with low wages and no benefits. It was in this context of policy "reform" in the 1990s followed by policy "drift" over the first decade of 2000 that firms routinely sought to maintain profitability through quick adjustments in their labour forces and labour costs, and workers were left to deal with the consequences of employers' increasing resort to low-wage work, non-standard employment contracts, and non-unionized positions.

Drift in Labour Relations and Labour Law

The original drafters of the original Ontario Labour Relations Acts (OLRA) in the 1940s and 1950s intended to follow the federal government's lead and create a rough balance of power between employers and unions, and in so doing, stabilize employment relations and limit strikes (Smith 2008). To achieve these goals, they formalized certification procedures, instituted bargaining procedures, and legalized strikes. The OLRA did effectively limit militancy by the 1960s (Wells 1995). But it also allowed unions to grow, gave them a voice in the day-to-day operations of their firms, and forced the management of companies – with the exception of those in the mining industry – to respect collective agreements (Eidlin 2015).

Legislation enacted by the Conservative government in 1995 and 2000 weakened these rights, and Liberal reforms in the first decade of 2000 did little to alter this legal context. As a consequence of this shift and drift in labour law and regulation, businesses in Ontario increasingly went on the offensive against unions over the course of the 1990s and the first decade of 2000. This "drift" in Ontario's industrial relations framework – and the increasing incidence of employers circumventing or shedding collective bargaining structures – can be seen in several key aspects, most notably in certification procedures, changes in the labour boards' powers to ensure "fair and effective" outcomes during strikes or changes of employers, and in the failure to adopt basic collective bargaining rights for agricultural workers in the province (Lebi and Mitchell 2003; Slinn 2004).

Prior to 1995, the oversight of a card-based certification system for unions to organize new workers and the use of remedial interim orders against employers who engaged in discriminatory practices such as firing or disciplining workers engaged in organizing drives, were the two key regulatory means that the provincial labour board used in providing "fair, effective, and expeditious methods of dispute resolution." With Bill 7, the Conservative government rewrote the OLRA, narrowing the purpose of the act to simply "facilitating collective bargaining between employers and trade unions" in the most expeditious manner. In 2005, with Bill 144, the Liberal government again provided card certification to unions in the construction industry, and it also reinstated labour board powers to make remedial reinstatements of workers. However, the reforms did not fundamentally change the balance of power between unions and employers during certification or address changes to how employers have adopted far more aggressive positions opposing unions during organizing drives.

The result was a dramatic decline in the number of attempts by unions to certify new workers and an equally sharp decline in the success rate of new certifications. In the early 1990s, unions filed on average more than a thousand new certification applications and were successful in 73 per cent of their attempts. By the late 1990s, those numbers had fallen to 721 with a 61 per cent success rate (Slinn 2004). And between 2004 and 2010, they fell even further to 670 new annual applications with a success rate of only 55 per cent (OLRB 2011).

The evidence suggests that such a decline – despite the interest of workers in union representation (Campolieti, Gomez, and Gunderson 2011) – meant that unions were seldom able to win better wages and benefits for workers in Ontario. The decline in certifications also suggests that mandatory voting did not work well for workers to fully exercise their rights to freedom of association, instead allowing substantial unlawful employer resistance with few – if any – adequate remedies or penalties (Bartkiw 2008). But under the pressure of employers opposing reforms, the Liberal government refused to consider improving or extending card certification to address growing problems – a case of upholding a policy even while the number of atypical and irregular workers grew and the demand for unionization remained high.

Another area where government intervened to allow the erosion of collective bargaining institutions was in legislation regarding strikes and successor rights – despite alternatives introduced by the opposition NDP and the labour movement. In Ontario in the wake of the financial crisis (2008–12), for example, with agreements about to expire, no fewer than twenty employers in the manufacturing and mining industries demanded major concessions that unions were unable to accept (Ferguson, Benzie, and Talaga 2012; Peters 2010; USW 2011). Forced to strike, or faced with an employer lockout, unions were left at a major disadvantage when employers moved to replace union strikers and continued to operate as "business as usual." In contrast to other provincial jurisdictions such as British Columbia and Quebec (as well as all West European countries), which had put firm restrictions on employer use of replacement workers during strikes because of the economic and social turmoil that typically results, Ontario governments continued to back employer demands to retain the right to use replacement workers during strikes, and to terminate striking workers after six months.

With the global downturn in markets after 2008, a number of firms – especially those under new corporate or new private equity management – took advantage of this policy to hire replacement workers and run their operations for the duration of the strike or lockout (OFL 2011; Peters 2010). Because the hiring of replacement workers always operates to the extreme detriment of a union local, especially as strikes or lockouts drag out for six months or more, employers routinely used the advantage of the law to demand concessions, and when this failed, move operations to non-union jurisdictions. In five of the strikes/lockouts since 2009, firms (e.g., Caterpillar) simply closed and reopened in the United States with non-union operations. In others, the legislation contributed to an environment in which employers were able to bargain wage and benefit concessions from unions under threat of closure and job loss (United Steelworkers 2015; Peters 2010).

Such problematic outcomes, together with the law's general concern with the protection of property rights, made strikes increasingly risky strategies for unions and workers. With powerful corporations regularly able to operate despite the presence of a picket line at their facilities, a number of employers obtained injunctions against mass picketing and fired strikers who they deemed to have engaged in "illegal" activities on the picket line. However, when unions brought the issue of the lack of balance in the OLRA in regards to strikes and the power of employers to terminate striking workers after six months to the legislature, the Liberal government refused to act. Between 2004 and 2011, the NDP moved three private member's bill in the Ontario legislature that would have banned the use of replacement workers during strikes or that would have permitted interest arbitration after sixty days. In each case, despite protests, labour lobbies, and wider public campaigns, the Liberal government simply refused to enact any policy changes, as such a move they believed would give an unfair advantage to striking workers (Peters 2010).

A comparable policy stance of blocking labour reforms was taken by the Liberal government on union successor rights in the private service sector, where companies as in cleaning, food, building maintenance, and security services routinely bid on contracts, but if firms or clients chose another service provider, there were no successor rights provisions for the unionized employees, and workers lost their bargained rights or their jobs. This opening for service employers to change their ownership status through subcontracting arrangements first appeared in 1995, when the Conservative government removed a number of successor rights provisions from the OLRA for both public and private sector employees, on the grounds that this would provide greater "flexibility" for employers and promote economic prosperity (Jain and Muthu 1997). In 2004, the Liberal government restored successor rights for public sector employees in public enterprises that were sold, providing for the continuity of collective agreement coverage. Successor rights were also improved for other workers when businesses were sold, allowing for collective bargaining rights to continue with the change in ownership.

However, in the case of private service contractors and unionized and non-unionized service employees, the Liberal government did not make any amendments. And over the next decade, despite a growing number of notable cases where private employers used these contracting provisions to restructure, fire workers, and then rehire workers at lower wages and often with no benefits (as well as efforts by unions and the opposition NDP to draw attention to these problems and make legislative changes), the Liberal government declined to reform the legislation (Workers' Action Centre 2015). With the rapid expansion of the business service industry, the numbers of workers in the sector grew by 40 per cent between 2000 and 2014. But the legislative exemption left many part-time, casual, and self-employed workers vulnerable to abuse as service employers routinely "flipped" contracts and changed their subcontracting arrangements in order to keep pay low and terminate unwanted workers – both unionized and not (Mojtehedzadeh 2015a, 2015c).

A final case of drift in labour law and Ontario collective bargaining institutions' lack of inclusiveness can be seen in the Agricultural Employees Protection Act (AEPA). This act – passed first in 2002 – faced numerous Supreme Court challenges and was also subject to union interventions and public advocacy campaigns, academic studies, and international rulings on its numerous problems, exemptions, and failures to uphold basic rights and standards for domestic and foreign agricultural workers. Yet it still witnessed the Conservative and then the Liberal provincial governments upholding the act – as a separate piece of legislation outside of the OLRA – in order to maintain the agricultural sector's competitiveness and its "unique" time-sensitive production and distribution processes (Fudge 2012; Tucker 2012).

Both the federal and provincial governments – and finally the Supreme Court – held that the special agricultural act did provide the opportunity for workers to form an employees association and represent their views and was therefore in line with freedom of association rights, even though it did not provide workers the right to strike or seek arbitration. The federal government claimed that its rules for the Seasonal Agricultural Worker Program (SAWP) provided protection for standard employee contracts, while the Liberal Ministry of Agriculture maintained that the AEPA, along with employment standards (even with exemptions for agriculture that included the non-application of minimum wage and overtime laws) and a special agricultural tribunal, provided adequate access to regulatory enforcement for workers to ensure disputes with employers would be heard (Binford 2013; Law Commission of Ontario 2012).

However, as recent academic studies have argued, neither legislation nor employment standards effectively upheld a basic floor of labour rights for workers, nor did they allow workers the basic freedoms to exercise their rights (Preibisch 2012; Tucker 2012). While wages for workers were typically at the minimum rate, there was no overtime pay and third-party agents working for employers routinely charged workers fees. In addition, the wages of workers were reduced significantly by transportation costs, meal and accommodation expenses, and numerous taxes and deductions for social programs to which they had no access (Wells et al. 2014). Nor did the AEPA address the greatest source of vulnerability faced by seasonal workers – tied work permits (Law Commission of Ontario 2012). These work permits restricted workers to employment with only one employer and put workers in precarious situations, often fearing termination, repatriation, or non-contract renewal if they engaged in union organizing or brought complaints about breaches of employment standards or health and safety violations to employers (Hennebry 2012).

The result was poverty-level incomes for workers upon their return to Mexico and the Caribbean (Binford 2013), as well as significant risk of occupational injuries, diseases, and in some cases, death (Prebisch and Hennebry 2011) for which workers had no benefits or adequate incomes to address. While the 18,000 seasonal workers in Ontario, in theory, had the right to voice concerns about workplace issues, the reality was that the threat of repatriation was often enough to effectively deny workers open avenues of legal support under provincial law. This policy weakness, combined with the lack of functioning unions on farms across Ontario, not only left employers with significant control over working conditions and accommodation, and it also left workers open to exploitation by aggressive employers who cheated workers out of wages, provided inadequate accommodation, and initiated harsh work schedules (Preibisch 2012).

Such policy actions and inactions on labour legislation had uneven effects for workers across Ontario. Even though traditional bargaining arrangements proved reasonably resilient for public sector workers (where bargaining coverage remained high) and for large MNCs, as in the auto sector (where layoffs and plant closures were negotiated between employers and unions), in many other parts of the private sector a wider process of institutional weakening and narrowing of employment rights took place. With the ability to avoid unions or to shed collective agreements through closure and restructuring, employers were increasingly able to operate outside of stable collective bargaining structures, and collective agreements increasingly lost their equalizing powers across the labour market. The failure to update labour board powers, the continuation of mandatory voting procedures, and the legal capacity for employers to resort to replacement workers and to avoid successor rights all made it more difficult for unions to organize and pursue industrial action.

The overall consequences were substantial and often negative. The gaps in labour market regulation allowed more employers to use non-unionized workers and non-standard forms of work to lower labour costs in response to fluctuations of demand. At the same time, the numerous exemptions in employment standards, as well as their limited enforcement, increasingly gave employers (particularly agricultural employers) the option of using non-standard employment as their preferred strategy for hiring and firm operation – an option that led many firms to follow a "low-road" labour market strategy including low pay and non-standard jobs. Workers in Ontario were thus not only hurt by major changes in the economy like the growth of non-standard jobs; they were also hobbled by a legislative framework that failed to protect them against the anti-union activities of employers, subcontractors, temporary agencies, or managers of small firms.

Employment Standards and the Regulation of Non-standard Work and Low-Wage Options for Employers

In the liberal market economies of Canada, Great Britain, and the United States, it has long been commonplace for firms to undertake fast adjustments, structural changes, and job layoffs to respond to changes in market conditions and finance (Amable 2003; Moody 2007). When faced with new competitors or a sudden economic downturn, the most typical response of North American firms has been to increase capital intensity, lay off or outsource workers, and subsequently step up the intensity of work while extending hours.

But in recent decades, with the growth of global value chains and new financial pressures, employers have also begun to resort to non-standard forms of work across the business cycle to lower labour costs – all while using non-standard hires to lower their social contributions and avoid the separation costs typically required by collective agreements or basic employment law (Appelbaum 2010; Bosch, Mayhew, and Gautié 2010). The chief reason why firms have sought to expand the "flexibility" of their workforces has been to further reduce labour costs and escape the pressures of market competition by hiring cheaper workers.

But how far and fast employers have been able to shift to cheaper labour and exit from more inclusive labour relations systems or basic employment standards has continued to vary (Gautie and Schmitt 2010). Most important to this variation in wages and job quality has been the inclusiveness and coverage of collective bargaining systems and the quality of employment-related policies ranging from minimum wages to employment protection, to working conditions and social wages such as paid leave and pensions (Battle 2011; ILO 2012b; Schulten 2014). In Ontario, as well, employment standards played an increasingly significant regulatory role, providing the basic floor for wages and rights for all workers, but most significantly for the non-unionized employees

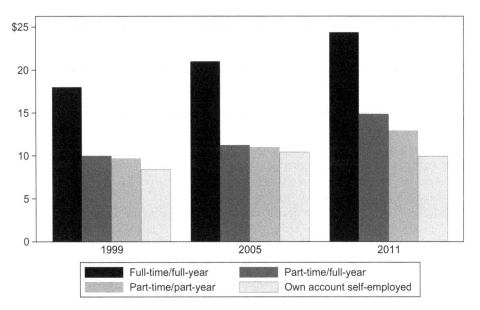

Figure 8.7. Ontario non-standard employment and wage penalties, 1999–2011 (median hourly wages)
Source: Author's figures from custom request, Statistics Canada, Survey of Labour and Income Dynamics and Survey of Consumer Finances, "Percentage of Workers with Low Annual Earnings and Low Hourly Wages, Canada and Provinces," table C685593.

who accounted for more than 80 per cent of the labour market. However, with growing employer efforts to evade institutional constraints while limiting the impacts of employment standards on work, the Employment Standards Act was increasingly unable to limit firms' ability to lower wage and reduce employment security. With Conservative efforts to deregulate employment standards in the province and the subsequent Liberal government undertaking few reforms, the result was a deterioration of job quality, the ongoing high incidence of low-wage work, and a widening of the earnings gap between high- and low-paid workers.

As noted above, the increase in non-standard forms of employment was considerable, with non-standard jobs growing faster than full-time, full-year jobs in Ontario over the course of the late 1990s and the first decade of 2000. Overall growth in part-time and temporary employment increased by 25 per cent between 1999 and 2011. In contrast, full-time work expanded only by 15 per cent (Tiessen 2014). As figure 8.7 demonstrates, there was a clear economic reason to explain this increase – wage costs. Throughout the first decade of 2000, employers routinely paid part-time and temporary employees as well as the own-account self-employed little more than half the rate of a full-time, full-year worker.

Motivated by the drive to cut costs, employers increasingly used lower-paid non-standard workers to perform tasks across a range of industries. Moreover, as the low pay, inadequate benefits, and variable hours were unattractive to native-born and established workers in Ontario, firms increasingly relied on immigrants, especially recent immigrants, to fill these jobs (Noack and Vosko 2011). Those working in own-account self-employed jobs fared the worst, with hourly median wages falling to only 40 per cent of those in full-time, full-year employment by 2011, approximately twenty-five cents less than the official minimum of the time. Even those workers in part-time and part-year jobs – more typically covered by minimum wage legislation – were paid far less by employers, generally receiving hourly wages that were only 52–5 per cent of what a full-time, full-year worker was paid.

In addition, by using non-standard employees, employers could realize other cost savings. For example, by hiring more part-time and temporary workers, employers could refuse to extend private health and pension benefits, or provide for paid time away from duty or severance pay (UNIFOR 2015). The Conference Board of Canada estimated that employers typically have benefit costs in addition to wages that average another 10 per cent more per full-time employee, half of which is to cover federally mandated programs for pensions, employment insurance, and worker's compensation premiums (Conference Board of Canada 2012).

However, unlike in many European countries – but similar to the United States – many social benefits in Ontario such as private drug and eyeglass coverage, dental care, and paid sick leave are not legally regulated. Consequently, many private sector employers frequently exclude low-paid, part-time, or temporary workers from non-wage benefits. In Ontario, only 50 per cent of employers regularly provided for other health, dental, and drug insurance for employees, and only one-fifth extended benefits to their non-unionized, part-time, and temporary employees (Hurley and Guindon 2008; Workers' Action Centre 2007). Using non-standard employees in this way to avoid supplementary costs, it is estimated that firms could regularly save another 2–5 per cent from their total payroll.

Ontario's minimum wage did little to change these employers' strategies or improve wage and earning distribution. In the 1960s and 1970s, Ontario's minimum wage rose above the poverty line (Hennessy, Tiessen, and Yalnizyan 2013). But by the first decade of 2000, after the Conservative government had frozen it for eight years (1995–2003), the minimum wage was only 42 per cent of the median wage in Ontario – well below a poverty wage threshold of 50 per cent of the median wage. The Liberal government took a different approach, arguing that there were normative and economic reasons to increase the minimum wage, and from 2004 to 2011 government increased the minimum wage by 50 per cent. These increases did nothing, however, to reduce the proportion of workers below the low-pay threshold or to moderate employer strategies that relied on low-wage costs.

The minimum wage did increase relative to the median wage and to the wages of full-time, full-year workers. By 2011, for example, the minimum wage was 49 per cent of Ontario's median wage of $20.24 – just below a poverty wage threshold (Minimum Wage Advisory Panel 2014). However, the increases in the minimum wage were not particularly efficient in reducing the overall number of workers with low wages. Indeed, the number of low-wage workers (with wages below two-thirds of the median wage of a full-time worker) continued to slowly rise from 39.6 per cent of the workforce in 2005 to 40.6 per cent in 2011. Nor did it reduce the number of workers in minimum wage jobs, which increased dramatically (Block 2015). Between 1997 and 2011, the share of workers earning the minimum wage in Ontario increased nearly four-fold from 2.4 per cent of all employees to 9.6 per cent in 2011.

This increase suggests that the most typical employer response to increases in the minimum wage was not to heighten their rates of pay more broadly in order to attract and retain more workers, but rather to hire more workers at low rates of pay. Consequently, the low – and inadequate – increases to the minimum wage did not lead to significant improvement to standards of living for workers. Rather, employers adapted human resource strategies that limited the impacts of minimum wages increases – above all, by reducing the differentials between wage rates and low-skill jobs at the bottom of their wage structures. The result was the ongoing incidence of high rates of low-wage work in the province.

Another key factor for the rise of low-wage work in the province was the lack of improvements to ESA legislation and the inadequate resources devoted to enforcement. Employment standards in Ontario, as in other provinces, have long been intended to improve the job security of workers and constrain employers from engaging in practices that undermine basic worker wages, rights, and conditions at work (Thomas 2009). But as studies by the Law Commission of Ontario on precarious work and the Employment Standards Act (ESA) have noted, over the course of the first decade of 2000, the ESA increasingly failed to uphold a basic floor of rights, lacked direct enforcement, and provided few mechanisms for wider education or ensuring employer compliance (Law Commission of Ontario 2012).

One problem that the Liberal government failed to address was the numerous special rules and exemptions that failed to provide adequate protection for all workers – many of which were introduced by the previous Conservative administration in the 1990s (Thomas 2009). Small businesses with fewer than fifty employees remained exempt from many of the sections of the act, while employers in the agricultural, construction, restaurant, accommodation, and information technology sectors were not subject to rules on overtime, rest periods, and pay. In other cases, workers in various forms of non-standard employment did not qualify for certain protections because they had insufficient hours or their employment was intermittent. The result, the Law Commission of Ontario concluded, was a "legislative framework that no longer meets its objective in providing a basic floor of minimum rights for all workers" (Law Commission of Ontario 2012).

Another problem that government officials fell short on was employers' increasing use of temporary and self-employment contracts to avoid ESA legislation. Over the course of the 1990s and the first decade of 2000, employers in Ontario – most notably in construction and private services such as cleaning, clerical, and security – rapidly adopted flexible work and contract arrangements in order to lower costs while covering a greater number of hours (Noack and Vosko 2011; Workers' Action Centre 2015). In theory, the ESA was designed to ensure minimum wages and basic terms and conditions of employment for workers hired under these more "flexible'" arrangements. But in reality, firms routinely misclassified workers as self-employed in order to lower wages and avoid paying overtime, benefits, and payroll taxes (Law Commission of Ontario 2012). While temporary agencies not only charged workers fees, they also had workers sign employment contracts that denied them the right to severance and vacation pay, and until 2009 effectively denied them opportunities for full-time employment by charging employers an additional fee if they sought to hire a temporary agency worker into a full-time job (Workers' Action Centre 2015). Such loopholes in the ESA left workers with little legal protection against low wages, dismissal, or unequal treatment.

Finally, government officials were unable to cope with the large number of complaints or adopt effective enforcement procedures that ensured employer compliance (Thomas 2009). And ultimately by 2010, the Liberal government adopted a "soft" law approach that put more responsibility on workers to resolve their problems directly with employers before going forward with an employment standards complaint (Gellatly et al. 2011). Many of the problems of enforcing employment standards stemmed from the inadequate resources at the disposal of the Ministry of Labour, which was unable to cope with the thousands of complaints each year (Vosko 2013).

This lack of resources meant that some 45 per cent of the more than twenty thousand annual complaints were not investigated, while other worker complaints were dealt with only after delays of many months. Violations such as employers failing to pay the minimum wage, overtime, termination, or vacation pay, or failing to pay workers for all the hours they worked, were widespread, with workplace "blitz" inspections by ministry officials discovering that many employers often contravened ESA legislation (Law Commission of Ontario 2012). However, while the ministry did recover unpaid wages and ESA entitlements (in a few cases through negotiation and the brokering of settlements between employers and workers), ministry prosecutions of employers for violating the act averaged less than 2 per cent of total claims, and the typical fine was no more than $360. For many worker advocates, such low levels of direct enforcement – along with the minimal penalties that were settled, with employers often paying less than was claimed owing – hardly deterred employers looking to save on labour costs by avoiding the regulations in the ESA (Workers' Action Centre 2011).

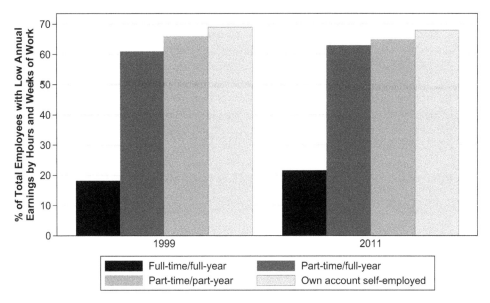

Figure 8.8. Non-standard employment and low-wage work in Ontario, 1999–2011 (% workers below low-wage threshold of two-thirds median hourly wage of full-time/full-year workers)
Source: Author's figures from custom request, Statistics Canada, Survey of Labour and Income Dynamics and Survey of Consumer Finances, "Percentage of Workers with Low Annual Earnings and Low Hourly Wages, Canada and Provinces," table C685593.

This neglect of employment standards – along with the weakness of collective bargaining – appears to have strongly contributed to an ongoing high incidence of low pay in the province. Not only did the provincial minimum wage remain low relative to the median wage, but the enforcement of labour laws and regulations was also weak, and there were numerous loopholes and exemptions in the ESA that employers could use. For workers at the bottom of the labour market, with few protective institutions, little bargaining power, and few opportunities to exercise their voice over wages and working conditions, the result was the continuing expansion of low-wage jobs.

Over the course of the first decade of 2000, while the labour market grew by more than one million workers, employers continued to resort to a number of "exit" options from collective bargaining agreements and provincial labour laws and regulations. With the Liberal government doing little to plug gaps in coverage or improve the inclusiveness of employment standards and collective bargaining, firms cut costs and managed demand fluctuations through the use of part-time and temporary workers. As figure 8.8 demonstrates, over the course of the first decade of 2000, employers consistently used part-time and contract self-employed workers as key sources of cheap labour. While businesses slowly increased their numbers of full-time workers with low-wage to 22 per cent, it was their extensive use of non-standard workers at low wages that was central to their operating strategies of flexibility and low costs. Thus, unlike in BC, where the government's active deregulation of bargaining and employment standards expanded low-wage work, in Ontario institutional neglect – often under the pressure of employers – was the key contributing factor to the erosion of job quality and compensation standards for workers.

Inter-union Conflict and Organized Labour's Response

In response to employers' aggressive efforts to restructure and impose different forms of flexibility, Ontario's labour unions employed a range of strategies – original and traditional, innovative and intensive – in their attempts to improve the prospects for wages, working conditions, and public policy. But in contrast to the 1960s and 1970s, when unions organized workers, launched thousands of strikes, and developed political organizations to push for broad economic reforms, and the late 1990s, when they mobilized against the Conservative government's policy reforms, Ontario's public and private sector unions either pursued a repertoire of new political and social mobilization strategies in isolation from one another, or simply enacted a far more defensive set of strategic options throughout the first decade of 2000 under the Liberal administration. Common tactics included new partnership arrangements with employers and governments, greater attention to public advocacy campaigns, increased attempts at community support, and experimentation with new forms of international cooperation.

These approaches were adopted and brought to the forefront of union efforts for pragmatic reasons: to cope with globalization, the opposition of employers, as well as address legal protections that were often inadequate, if not hostile to labour rights (Fairbrother and Yates 2003). Many unions, especially in the public sector, hoped that their more pragmatic bargaining and campaign tactics would make up for declining levels of strikes and organizing, while retaining some influence on the wider workforce and public officials (Ontario OFL labour official; Ontario retired public sector labour staff). Labour also engaged with innovative strategies such as advocacy campaigns or new community and social justice mobilization efforts with the expectation that even modest political success could spur rank-and-file mobilization and go on to spark new organizing and community support.

But faced with declining memberships and a growing number of employer assaults on wages and the lack of supportive public policies and institutions, Ontario's labour movement found it difficult to develop province-wide strategies that improved their collective bargaining leverage. Most difficult for the labour movement were the marked ideological differences that inhibited cooperation and strategic coherence. In chapter 3 I argued that labour movements face greater problems in developing, organizing, and mobilizing strategies when they encounter inter-union conflict. In Ontario, this appears to be particularly true, for despite having the largest membership and the greatest concentration of staff and resources, the provincial labour movement often found it difficult to maintain a common set of priorities that improved organizing, raised political turnout, or swayed public opinion on income inequality or the role of unions in society. Unlike in British Columbia, where the majority of unions were affiliated with the provincial federation of labour and retained financial and institutional support with the NDP, in Ontario the lack of inter-union solidarity and its attendant problems created another set of political hurdles that contributed to labour policy "drift" in Ontario.

Much as in British Columbia and other provinces, through the 1970s and 1980s, Ontario unions, led by the autoworkers, the Canadian Union of Public Employees, and the Canadian Postal Workers, provided widespread financial and membership support for the New Democratic Party at both the federal and provincial levels (Archer 1990). But in the late 1980s and 1990s, this relationship began to fray in a number of provinces including Ontario, in large part because even though unions increased their electoral activity and support of the NDP – in many cases helping secure NDP electoral victories – unions were not able to translate these efforts into increases in union membership, improvements to collective bargaining, or stronger political influence (Pilon, Ross, and Savage 2010). In Ontario, some of these difficulties in union-party relations were initially put to rest with the election of an NDP government in 1990 – the first in the province's history. But in the face of a recession and growing deficit, there were increasingly sharp disagreements between unions and the NDP government over policy and legislation. Unions looked for job protection, job creation, and improvements to public services and income transfer programs, and received some labour policy reform. But when the NDP government embarked on deficit reduction and public sector wage freezes and layoffs, unions split over the policy, with many leaving the party, and others simply offering little support to the party in subsequent elections.

In the late 1990s, the Conservative labour policy reforms affected all unions in the private and public sector alike, and there was wider union agreement to initiate a provincial "Days of Action" strategy that included protests and rotating strikes in major cities across the province (Camfield 2000; Ontario retired union staff official). Generally, unions across the public and private sector worked well together in trying to mobilize wider public opinion against the reforms, and educate members on government changes negatively affecting rights to organize, the representation of workers, and health and safety (Ontario retired union researcher). The hope was that these political actions would help educate workers, help build political solidarity across the labour movement, and ultimately support the effort to remove the Conservatives from office. Undertaking such "Days of Action" was also important as unions officials were shut out of institutionalized channels of influence on the government and had no openings to lobby public officials on policy.

However, by 1999, a number of unions withdrew from the wider provincial strategy on the grounds that it was not the best use of resources, while others withdrew out of the fear that such public protests were damaging the public image of unions (Ontario retired union president, private sector). Consequently, union leadership in several key private and public sector unions felt that strategic voting and the support of Liberal and NDP candidates in key contested ridings would provide the best opportunity to defeat the Conservative government and reverse its policy changes (Walchuk 2010). In the 1999 election, the new union emphasis on strategic voting did not bear winning results. But in the 2003 election, under the Working Families Coalition, strategic voting did contribute to the election of a Liberal government, with unions contributing thousands of dollars and a number of unionized public sector members working on behalf of the Liberal Party. With the election victory of the Liberal government in 2003, the Ontario labour movement, which had never been that unified in its politics or goals, further fragmented on ideological and strategic lines.

Many unions adopted a more independent, autonomous stance towards the NDP and began pragmatic support, bargaining, and compromise with the Liberal Party and Liberal candidates. For example, the building trades and public sector unions were the biggest supporters of the Liberal Party. However by 2006, many union–party relationships had frayed. Most notable was the erosion of the NDP relationship with the Canadian Auto Workers, one of the founding unions of the party in the 1960s, which resulted in the expulsion of the CAW's leader from the NDP and subsequently to the CAW disaffiliating from the NDP in 2006, and CAW locals backing Liberal candidates (Savage 2010). Other unions retained their party links but in many cases reduced their financial support for the party and instead used their funds for a wider range of political interventions. But without wider agreement on basic political goals, leaders of unions increasingly went their own way with their own bargaining and political strategies. While this provided for autonomy and a few new experiments in political advocacy, the lack of consensus fundamentally undermined wider union cooperation on organizing, wider policy campaigns for increasing the minimum wage, and development of a unified training strategy that ensured the growth of unionized jobs across the province.

One such tactic that public sector and construction unions did develop in this context of political fragmentation within the labour movement was more "partnership-oriented" or "pragmatic" relations with governments and employers (Camfield 2011a). Fearing job losses and worrying that strikes would have little impact and even less public support, a number of unions looked to foster a rough accommodation and coordination with employers. The goal was to meet employer demands for flexibility in wages, hours, and hiring, and in return seek contractual guarantees from employers for financing, investment, and jobs. In high-wage and high-capital industries such as auto, steel, primary metals, mining, and machinery (which have felt the effects of competition and corporate restructuring the hardest), many locals have begun to focus on improving the competitive position of the company, giving wage, pension, and job concessions while accepting speed-up, job-loading, contracting out, longer hours, and two-tier agreements for new hires (Bruno 2005; Peters 2010). In the public sector as well, unions such as the provincial government employees' unions and the nursing associations attempted to protect jobs and adequate retirement packages in response to government demands for cuts and modernization through "flexicurity" arrangements that expanded part-time and temporary employment, and provided more opportunities for governments to contract out (Camfield 2011b; Rose 2007).

A second noteworthy response was labour's efforts to counter the rise of low-wage and precarious employment through long-term corporate and community outreach organizing campaigns. With the rapid spread of Walmart and low-wage work by foreign migrant workers in agriculture, the United Food and Commercial Workers (UFCW), for example, began to undertake comprehensive political and community campaigns in their efforts to organize workers. To improve the conditions of foreign agricultural workers, most notably in Southern Ontario, the UFCW has opened outreach offices and provided education, worker aid, and organizing support among Canada's agricultural workers. Through provincial advocacy campaigns as well as a series of court challenges, the UFCW had forced industrial farmers to provide basic necessities like clean water and bathrooms (Basok 2009; Walchuk 2009). And in 2008, the UFCW launched organizing drives on farms in Ontario. While it did not succeed in certifying farm workers, it did build up wider community support for the UFCW's efforts to organize low-wage agricultural workers and improve the contracts offered to seasonal foreign workers.

A third approach saw public sector unions like CUPE working with a host of community groups in order to publicly advocate and lobby against the privatization of services in health care, electricity, and pension financing (Camfield

2011a; Tattersall 2010; Swift and Stewart 2005). Organized in reaction to government efforts to lower labour costs and undermine public sector bargaining power, at their most successful, these community-based advocacy campaigns hired coordinators, retained significant organizational strength for more than a year, and often put pressure on politicians during elections and public hearings into proposed legislative reform. Based on leveraging wider public support to influence government and ministerial officials, such coalitions have varied from short to long term and have been successfully used by unions to oppose legislation as well as to build support for basic democratic principles. The Ontario Health Coalition early in the first decade of 2000 developed a network of over four hundred community organizations and played a key role in labour mobilizations to combat government plans for the privatization of health care in Ontario (Tattersall 2010).

A fourth approach was the efforts of unions such as the Steelworkers (USW) to forge international mergers and international framework agreements in order to counter the power and reach of transnational firms (Bronfenbrenner 2007). Traditionally, in the majority of advanced capitalist countries, large domestic companies generally exported to foreign markets, and unions sought to bargain to protect domestic jobs and wages. Now this has changed. Not only do Western firms have global operations, but there are many more foreign transnational companies from the developing world in Canada pushing for wage and benefit concessions.

In dealing with the global mining giants Vale and Rio Tinto, as well as US Steel in Hamilton, Ontario (2009–11), the USW used its global alliances to help coordinate international campaigns intended to publicize how these global firms were operating and with what consequences (Peters 2010). Emphasizing the importance and impact of strikes and lockouts to the company's financial backers, shareholders, and customers, the USW attempted to bring financial pressure on the company. And relying on their union allies or NGOs abroad to initiate actions against companies, the USW sought to bring policymakers into the equation, with the expectation that government officials would pressure the MNCS to return to the bargaining table and offer more than ongoing requests for concessions.

Added to these initiatives were traditional labour strategies of mobilizing membership through protests, job actions, bargaining campaigns, and lobbying. In the wake of the financial crisis in 2008, for example, unions undertook dozens of demonstrations and rallies to voice their displeasure and educate members and the general public. Unions started education and outreach campaigns to explain current conditions and ongoing strategies. The CAW backed workplace occupations and blockades to demonstrate the union's ability to mobilize members in workplace actions (Rosenfeld 2009). CUPE coordinated province-wide planning meetings for workplace actions (Gindin and Hurley

2010; Evans 2011). In turn, unions used these opportunities to lobby governments and emphasize the importance of public support for industrial sectors and the benefits of good jobs with stable incomes.

In initiating such actions over the first decade of 2000, unions often accepted and acknowledged their limits in holding the line on concessions (Albo, Gindin, and Panitch 2010). Many realized bargaining power was weak, and in an age of globalization, employers could unilaterally determine investment and employment decisions (Murnighan and Stanford 2013). Still, by launching public campaigns, new organizing drives, and mobilizing community coalitions, unions sought to demonstrate to government and employers alike that they still had the ability to resist the harshest demands. They also hoped to show their members that unions still had the collective power to influence the course of events.

The Fragmentation of Organized Labour and Its Constraints on Countervailing Power

Despite these recent efforts, the balance of power continued to shift against organized labour and workers across Ontario. Inequality went up. The rich got richer, and the political equilibrium became far more responsive to the economic needs of upper-income Ontarians and wealthy homeowners. However, even as union leaders and activists throughout Ontario recognized many of these problems, there was little or no consensus on how to deal with them, and even though some unions engaged in innovative political campaigns and solidarity actions with civil society groups, the lack of political consensus and institutional solidarity constrained the development of new political views and lines of action for wider social mobilization.

Job loss in the unionized manufacturing sector aggravated the inability of the labour movement to develop more comprehensive policies, fundamentally changing the nature of the labour movement and its priorities. In the 1970s, manufacturing, resource, and construction unions covered nearly 50 per cent of their sectors. Pattern agreements often set the standards for wages and benefits that other non-unionized employers had to follow, and manufacturing unions such as the autoworkers and steelworkers took the lead in economic bargaining and political mobilization. But by 2009, private sector unionization was in free fall and pattern bargaining was a thing of the past. And where historically, private sector unions had played led in the labour movement, public sector unions – often with better-educated, more professional, and higher-income members – had the larger memberships, financial resources, and greater sway in public debate.

The ongoing decline in union coverage and union membership in much of the private sector had cumulative impacts on the ability of organized labour to improve jobs and policy. Organizing, deindustrialization, and the loss of union members created a harsh new reality for unions – the fewer the number of union members, the greater the cost per member to organize the vast non-union sector and to support political campaigns. Within private sector unions, this proved an insurmountable problem (Ontario union organizer, private sector). In looking at costly long-term corporate campaigns or organizing low-wage private service sector workers, most unions adopted more cost-conscious and conservative approaches (Yates 2007). Some pursued mergers to boost membership. Others focused only on certifying new members in large workplaces and continued to rely on the traditional model of "hotshop" organizing. But many simply shifted organizing to large workplaces with more permanent workforces, as the costs – and potential for failure – were too high in small workplaces with temporary workers (Ontario union organizer, private sector 2).

The result was not only the ongoing decline in new union member certifications, which fell by 50 per cent between 1992–5 and 2005–10. But also given the new make-up of the labour movement and the splits inside the Ontario Federation of Labour, there was little political will or interest in undertaking wider advocacy and organizing campaigns on behalf of low-wage workers (Ontario retired public sector labour staff). Despite awareness of the need for greater coordination among unions to target low-wage and non-standard workers, there was no consensus within the labour movement on financing the wider training of activists, the support for community activists or centres, or the creation of an institute that would support research into key targeted sectors for new organizing.

In the United States, and in British Columbia, central labour federations led in the establishment of organizing institutes that targeted employers across sectors in key geographic locales in order to establish master contracts (Fletcher and Gapasin 2008). But at the Ontario Federation of Labour, after a conference to discuss new organizing strategies, it was decided that unions would not back such an initiative in Ontario and unions would continue to organize as before – within their own jurisdictions and organizers (retired Ontario union staff official). The lack of consensus among leaders – most notably in public sector unions that were concerned with the use of resources directed towards non-unionized workers – was one reason for the failure of this effort at taking on new strategies for organizing (Ontario retired union president, private sector).

The new emphasis on public campaigns by individual unions also proved a poor substitute for wider campaigns that targeted government policies, mobilized workers and community activists, and initiated reforms that posed a significant threat to the stability of policy status quo. In the past, strikes gave unions the opportunities to involve members in setting priorities, building workplace unity, setting up and delivering membership communication and action networks, and undertaking public advocacy campaigns that built public support (La Botz 2005; Bronfenbrenner et al. 1998). But with the decline in strikes, and the increasing use of advocacy campaigns, unions found it far harder to mobilize and educate members, and campaigns often did little to build community links (Peters 2010). Apart from the very successful health and anti-privatization campaigns, many other union efforts at advocacy campaigning were often little more than the distribution of flyers, an afternoon rally, and email distributed to members (Ontario public sector union leader 1). Local leaders and members were seldom given extensive education, many members seldom participated, and campaigns seldom had the scale, community bridge builders, and coalition structures necessary to influence governments or employers (Shantz 2009).

Making matters more difficult were the disagreements at the Ontario Federation of Labour (OFL) that limited input into wider community campaigns. During the course of the first decade of 2000, few community activists viewed the OFL as a resource, instead more commonly turning to the Toronto District Labour Council for support (Ontario community activist). But with few financial or staff resources, the district labour council was unable to offer the resources and time commitment necessary to undertake a citywide campaign on employment standards and low-wage work in the province. With the election of a new OFL president in 2009, who was committed to a social unionism and community mobilizing perspective, there was the expectation that the OFL would undertake province-wide advocacy campaigns and set up community support committees for social justice projects (Ontario community activist). But divisions between leaders at the OFL quickly limited the capacities of the federation to take on this role (Ontario retired union staff official). A number of leading public sector unions quickly withdrew their annual contributions to the OFL. Others simply refused to participate in OFL activities that were not "membership related" or that were critical of the government. Consequently, even though the OFL made efforts to publicize low-wage issues in the province and campaigned for wider labour reforms, the lack of resources and staff seriously limited the ability of the labour organization to get their message out or build wider community support.

Moreover, with the divisions among unions over political strategy and mobilizing issues, proponents of new cross-border corporate and bargaining campaigns were unable to command sufficient organization, revenues, or numbers to provide a wider basis for mobilization. Thus international campaigns and their associated union alliances remained generally undeveloped, with little muscle to protect workers during strikes or in bargaining. The USW, for example, launched international corporate campaigns during their long strike against Vale and the lockout of workers at US Steel in Hamilton. Yet despite having the most global alliances and community networks of any private sector union in the world, in neither case was the USW able to influence corporate behaviour or public debate. In Sudbury, the USW was forced to accept major concessions on bonuses, layoffs, pensions, and bumping rights, as well as the loss of over three hundred members (Peters 2010). In Hamilton, the lockout ended with similar job and pension concessions, only to see US Steel lay off all of its 800 employees eleven months later.

Finally, the political divisions within the provincial labour movement did nothing to improve the mobilization of members or reverse the decline of voter turnout, especially in low-income ridings. Beginning in the 2003 election campaign, the move by a number of unions to officially back the Liberal Party boosted union financial involvement and provided key advertising resources in strategic ridings throughout the province (Walchuk 2010). But it did little for the development of wider member involvement in politics or for the development of a message that resonated more widely with citizens. Traditionally, the role of organized labour as an equalizing political force depended on its ability to encourage members to volunteer their time and effort to work for candidates and educate community members. But with the split in organized labour and the shift to strategic voting, unions found it increasingly difficult to articulate clear political messages to members or to the wider public. In some unions, the shift to strategic voting led to a rapid decline of member turnout and support for political events (Ontario retired union researcher). In others, it meant little political discussion and less political education by union staff (Ontario retired public sector union staff).

The political differences also meant it was difficult for the provincial labour movement to claim to represent the mass of middle-class workers or the growing low-wage workforce (Gindin 2011). Rather, with some unions supporting the Liberal Party, these unions were often seen as favoured "insiders" unfairly protected from the pains of globalization and business competition. Consequently, rather than aspire to becoming union members, more workers came to envy and resent the relative advantages of unionized workers (Walkom 2010) or to distrust unions (Frangi and Hennebert 2015). At the same time, with the fragmentation of labour and the loss of union members, unions had fewer resources for political activity. The result was that as income inequality rose, unions were unable to overcome the ongoing decline in voter turnout, which by 2011 had fallen to a record low of 48 per cent.

Professionals, better-educated, and union members with higher incomes, were all more likely to vote and to participate in political activities (Bryson et al. 2013), especially in high-income ridings in Toronto and Ottawa (Ontario NDP staff researcher). But in low-income ridings (most notably in former manufacturing hubs of Ontario with long-time support of the NDP), even where ridings were targeted by the NDP as winnable, voting turnout continued to decline. Similarly, in low-income ridings in Toronto where the Liberal Party won, the influence of strategic voting campaigns and union support were often minimal, as traditional party apparatuses were used in the campaigns and there was no coordination of resources. The outcome was thus one very similar to that in the United States (Rosenfeld 2014), where the ability of unions to increase turnout fell dramatically in former manufacturing strongholds, and many low-income Ontarians were left without the organizational ties and networks that would allow them to learn more about politics or to participate in elections.

Such reversals contributed significantly to policy "drift" in Ontario – with unions split, lacking the resources, or on the defensive, they were unable to stop the decline in union density or the loss of thousands of union jobs through the championing of workers' interests or more strategic political interventions. Moreover, given the political divides among unions, new campaigns did not halt the fall-off of political influence. Nor did individual union alliances limit employer efforts at restructuring and the worsening of wages and benefits for the majority of workers.

These setbacks mattered greatly for issues of economic inequality. Unions once acted as a strong countervailing force to the influence of business and the wealthy in Ontario's political economy. But over the course of the first decade of 2000, the Ontario labour movement faced a steep decline in its bargaining power with employers, and an even steeper fall-off of its political influence (Camfield 2011a). More and more, with the erosion of bargaining coverage, Ontario's unions were forced to simply defend the gains of their current membership at the cost of building a larger labour movement. More and more, the loss of members drained needed financial resources and the unionized memberships necessary to strengthen collective bargaining, while making unions increasingly wary of the prospects of strikes that could actually pressure governments and make employers listen. More and more, the political divides among unions limited their coordination and undermined their ability to build wider political campaigns or mobilize citizens during elections.

As figure 8.9 shows, over the course of the 1990s and first decade of 2000, these divides made it difficult for unions to counter the impacts of inequality. With few consistent or wide-reaching ties to communities across Ontario or the GTA region, the labour movement in Ontario was unable to educate, mobilize, or engage the many citizens who were marginalized and left with few opportunities beyond insecure employment and low-wage work. This not only left many unions politically weaker, able to place only intermittent pressure on governments and MNCs. It also left many unions more vulnerable to employer attack and government inaction.

Thus, rather than a "virtuous circle" of strategies and gains, Ontario unions found themselves enclosed in "vicious circles" – where government neglect, job loss, and employer opposition shrank union capacities and demobilized the workforce, and in turn seriously undermined any future possibilities for organizing success and building political influence. Absent a strong political

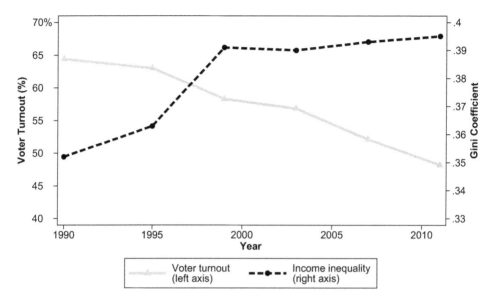

Figure 8.9. Income inequality and voting turnout in Ontario, 1990–2011
Sources: Statistics Canada, CANSIM table 202-705; Elections Ontario, "Historical Voter Turnout"; Sharpe and Capeluck (2012).

constituency like organized labour, business and industry were largely free to continue exerting their undue influence on Ontario public policy and block improvements to collective bargaining and employment standards. For Ontario's unions and non-unionized workforce, the political implications of such setbacks were often profound – more low-wage work, the erosion of common standards of living, and increasing limits on unions' abilities to counteract the increasing inequality in political participation.

Drift in the Wake of the Financial Crisis

The financial crisis and the recession that followed (2008–11) had similarly serious consequences on many high-quality jobs as well as Ontario's labour movement (Albo, Gindin, and Panitch 2010). With the rapid fall-off of financial markets in North America and Western Europe, the demand for Canadian exports plummeted. Across Canada, from late 2008 to November 2009 firms laid off more than 450,000 full-time workers, the majority in manufacturing and natural resources in Ontario. At the same time, businesses large and small launched new initiatives to undermine collective agreements, fissure their workforces, and extract greater increases in productivity.

Many firms quickly made "quantity" adjustments in the size of their workforces. In auto, for example, car sales plummeted in 2008–9 to their lowest level in decades, and the Big Three automakers responded by shutting down four plants. Auto parts manufacturers folded many more plants, and with the bankruptcy of General Motors and Chrysler in 2009, over thirty thousand auto jobs were lost in the assembly and auto parts industry. In mining, global giants Vale and Xstrata laid off hundreds of workers as the downturn worsened. Vale then fought a twelve-month strike with the United Steelworkers Local 6500 that resulted in major wage concessions by the local, the retirement of another 10 per cent of their unionized labour force, and the continuing widespread use of part-time contractors (Peters 2010).

Then as financial markets and major corporations were bailed out with new government policies of "quantitative easing" that purchased trillions of dollars in debt, firms used their new cash holdings to invest in bonds, stocks, and money markets, or redirected new investments to mergers and acquisitions in South-East Asia and Latin America (Peters 2017). Investments in stock and money markets soared, leading to rapidly growing investment returns for top income earners. But corporate profitability also soon improved as firms shed high-wage earners in leading industrial economies, replacing them with more precariously employed workers in supplier networks or with low-wage workforces in non-OECD countries (OECD 2012). Indeed, throughout the crisis in North America and in its immediate aftermath, the major labour market trend was the ongoing expansion of non-standard contracts.

Organized labour in Ontario was unable to influence these trends of aggressive corporate restructuring, declining unionized jobs, and fewer full-time jobs. In auto, the CAW did respond to plant bankruptcies and closures with dramatic actions – including plant occupations – to fight for severance benefits for the affected workers (Murnighan and Stanford 2013). But because they were losing members, the far more typical response of unions in the auto, steel, and forestry industries was to focus on improving the competitive position of the company in return for job commitments to diminishing members.

Typically, this involved unions accepting wage and job concessions while accepting speed-up, job-loading, and longer hours in return for the protection of a dwindling core number of jobs. Concessions became central to union plans for labour-management cooperation, and workers were often forced to go along because of threats of plant closures, downsizing, or the failure of the company to secure new products – especially true in auto, but also mining, and steel in the wake of the crisis (Anastakis 2019).

In the public sector, too, the Liberal government continued with its plan to "modernize" Ontario along "Third Way" lines by downloading the costs of government from capital to the middle and working classes through tax reductions on business and the wealthy, as well as tax "relief," government subsidy, and policy support for corporations and finance. The most significant was the government's new "Open for Business" plan that phased-in a permanent reduction in corporate income tax from 14 to 10 per cent by 2013 at a cost of some $4.5 billion. To this was added the elimination of capital tax for corporate assets, as well as numerous proposals for business deregulation to foster "competitiveness."

Such proposals were critical in commercializing regulations or in providing more opportunities for business to self-regulate (Fanelli and Thomas 2011). But more importantly, for Toronto's financial sector, the tax cuts provided important stepping stones to the recovery of high-end executive compensation. In 2011, only two years after the financial collapse, top bank executives were again earning more than $10 million in compensation with the return of rising stock and equity prices (Robertson 2011a, 2011b). Indeed, with the rapid bounce back in financial and stock market trading, the top 10 per cent of income earners quickly took in 85 per cent of all capital gains from the TSX (which traded over a trillion dollars annually), the $3 trillion pension industry, and the trillion-dollar bond and money markets.

In contrast, those in low-wage work with uncertain, unstable, and insecure employment conditions were left to bear the risks of government policies that did little to protect workers on the job and employers who were to quick exploit regulatory loopholes. By 2015, nearly three million workers in Ontario were in non-standard contracts ranging from part-time to casual employment to own-account self-employed. Most notably in low-wage private service sectors such as accommodation and food, wholesale and retail, as well as business, building, and cleaning services, more than 70 per cent of the workers in these sectors were earning less than $17,500 annually. Most at risk of relegation to working poverty were women, racialized minorities, and immigrants (Stapleton 2019). Lacking sick days, basic enforcement of employment standards, and job security, these workers were forced to cope with growing levels of insecurity and uncertainty – on and off the job (Vosko et al. 2020).

But following upon their earlier modest efforts to improve basic employment standards – or at least to make the appearance of improving jobs and working conditions – the governments of McGuinty and his successor, Kathleen Wynne, embarked upon a four-year policy review beginning with the Minimum Wage Advisory Panel (2013), then initiating a Changing Workplace Review (2015), before culminating in Bill 148, the "Fair Workplaces, Better Jobs Act." Throughout this process, government-appointed panels heard of the many problems facing workers on the jobs from the lack of union representation, to workers' lack of regular schedules and work hours, to the need for greater enforcement and penalties. And in 2017, under the pressure of labour and community groups fighting for a living wage, Bill 148 raised the province's minimum wage from $11.60 to $14.00 per hour in 2018 (Evans, Fanelli,

McDowell 2021). It also introduced a minimal number of sick days, emergency leave, and greater schedule regulations.

However, after the years of discussion, reports, and consultations, the improvements to workplaces and employment contracts were short lived. With the election of a new Conservative government only three months after the introduction of Bill 148, the vast majority of the numerous provisions were repealed and future minimum wage increases were halted. This left Ontario's workers in the same position as they had been in for the previous decades – subject to numerous non-standard work arrangements, with few if any social protections, and no policies or regulations that would enhance the quality of non-standard work.

Conclusion

Such patterns of labour policy change in Ontario can be characterized as a case of "drift," which saw the erosion of collective bargaining coverage and a growing number of low-wage workers, often in non-standard employment, with little protection. Consistent with a post-democratic logic, even though there were few direct reforms or employer efforts to rewrite bargaining legislation and employment regulation in a more business-friendly manner from 2003 to 2011, government also took no action to improve redistribution or wages, fearing the consequences on competitiveness in the province. Only in the wake of the financial crisis did the Liberal government begin to study the possibility of improving wages and employment regulations in the province. But not until 2017 were these reforms put in place, and the subsequent Conservative government quickly repealed them. Consequently, the more typical policy pattern was one of change occurring more gradually and slowly; collective bargaining coverage declining slowly in the 1990s and early in the first decade of 2000, and then more rapidly in the wake of the financial crisis and the subsequent rise of unemployment throughout Canada and the United States.

However, it is important to emphasize that the policy drift in the province involved instances of deliberate political inaction, as firms and government actors put off reforms that would improve bargaining and employment regulations. Firms and employer associations lobbied government, provided policy advice, and campaigned widely against proposed labour reforms. Debates in Ontario on increases to the minimum wage throughout the first decade of 2000 routinely saw business associations publicly oppose increases on economic grounds. And more recently, in response to the Liberal government's 2015 Ontario Changing Workplaces Consultation, the CFIB called for no increase in the "regulatory or compliance burden" on business and insisted that all current exemptions in the ESA be retained.

But the politics that allowed the continued erosion of collective bargaining and employment standards in Ontario was more complex than critical political economy arguments about neoliberalism and deregulation in North America have often suggested. Unlike in many provinces and states, even if the Liberal government was closely tied to business through political finance and policy development, its electoral coalition also included construction, public sector, and some auto unions. In addition, IT, finance, and developers were less concerned with the deregulation and flexibility of labour markets than they were with broader tax breaks, infrastructure, and policy support. This cross-class coalition of support for the party thus provided an opening for the government to promote "balance" between employer and union interests while at the same time marginally improving certification procedures for construction unions and raising the minimum wage.

The politics of labour policy thus did not take the form of wholesale reform of collective bargaining and employment institutions as in British Columbia. Nor did Ontario's Liberal government follow the path of Newfoundland and Labrador in attempting to renew and update collective bargaining legislation or improve public sector services and employment. Rather, after more wide-ranging employer-friendly reforms in the 1990s, in Ontario in the first decade of 2000 under a Liberal administration, public officials did not seek to restructure or undermine labour policies and laws. Instead, they remained focused on preventing reforms that would address the erosion in union coverage and the deepening of low-wage and non-standard work throughout the province. Most notably, they upheld the idea of "fairness and balance," which meant maintaining the status quo of employer-dominated workplace bargaining while doing even less to uphold or enforce minimal employment standards. As a consequence, labour market change advanced incrementally, as employment shifted from unionized industrial and resource-based jobs into low-end manufacturing and private services, where employers could use the loopholes and exit options available to them within employment regulations to expand their low-wage workforces.

9 Conclusion: Rethinking the Political Economy of Inequality

It is ironic that over the past decade, despite a financial crisis caused by the deregulation of finance and the massive over-expansion of credit and debt markets, public officials in Canada and many other advanced industrial countries have carried on as before. Rather than more closely regulate banks and the financial sector, public officials have continued to emphasize the importance of "light touch" regulation in order to expand global finance and bank profits. At the same time, even though it has been clear that citizens had nothing to do with causing the financial crisis, officials and politicians have frequently recast it as one of public finances and the need for citizens to make do with less – including lower wages, fewer public services, and poorer labour protections. It is also deeply problematic that policymakers have often promoted such policies in the face of dramatic changes in the real-world distribution of income that have largely benefitted the very wealthy few at the expense of jobs and incomes for the vast majority of workers.

Certainly, as we have seen, there are excellent reasons for why this strange – and seemingly counter-intuitive – turn of events has occurred. Economic business and financial interests have become far more powerful. Citizens and organized labour have often been marginalized in the policy process. And the policy and institutional frameworks that ensured greater equality and a wider sharing of prosperity in the past have been fundamentally overhauled to the benefit of business or left to decline. But conventional social science and economics have also failed in large measure to come to grips with many of the major transformations to politics, economics, finance, and policy of the last thirty years.

Rather than assess how political power and distributional issues are key to macroeconomic outcomes, economists have too often clung to neoclassical models that assume that all productivity increases – and policies that improve unit profits at the expense of unit increases to wages – will automatically lead to better wages. Similarly, rather than explore changes to capital and financial markets, corporate finance and operation – and their wide-ranging impacts – many social scientists have continued to insist that "external" market forces associated with technological change and trade are the only sources of rising income inequality. And even when social scientists have pointed to the decline in the power of unions to mitigate job loss as a key driver of rising inequality, they have often ignored the enhanced role of state intervention in markets and how it has given finance and business increased power and prominence.

The broad purpose of this book has been to address these gaps. It has examined the politics behind financialization and labour market deregulation in Canada. Looking at the policy choices of public officials, this study has asked, Why did government officials pursue competitiveness through supply-side policies such as financial deregulation, pension reform, trade liberalization, and tax cuts? And at the same time, why did policymakers engage in labour market deregulation even as they so heavily backed firm efforts to expand, restructure, and boost their profitability?

Of most interest has been exploring which political and policy factors were most likely to determine the strategies that promoted the opening and globalization of financial markets and corporate financialization, as well as what factors help us account for how and why Canada's provincial governments have sought to lower labour costs and create greater flexibility for employers while maintaining labour peace.

In examining these interconnected questions, I have argued that the sources of rising inequality are to be found in the politics and power dynamics of organized economic interests and how they have changed policies and institutions to prioritize corporate power and financial expansion, while driving wider labour market deregulation. Indeed, I have claimed if we are to best understand how and why income has been so regularly redistributed to those at the top, we need to pay close attention to how many of the basic features of business, government, and labour have recently changed, and changed in ways that benefitted the few at the cost of the many.

In this final chapter, I analyse what we have learnt about financialization and labour market deregulation within a post-democracy framework. First I will review my empirical findings in light of recent comparative studies and underscore the importance of organizational shifts to political economies in explaining the government tendency to support finance-led growth models and deregulation. In the following section, I review institutional and policy alternatives to low-wage work and rising income inequality, a number of which can be found in other advanced economies, others that must pushed forward to address the challenge of climate change. I conclude by highlighting the need for a politics willing to constrain financial markets and the power of business, as well as a revitalized politics that develops laws and policies that can reverse rising labour market inequalities.

Updating Our Understanding of Income Distribution and Income Inequality

Peter Hall and Jonah Levy have identified several new state missions in the advanced economies, ranging from "making systems of social protection and labour markets more employment friendly" to "repairing the main varieties of capitalism" (Hall 2015; Levy 2006). In Levy's terms, many of the new policies and priorities of advanced capitalist countries are now "market-supporting" types of intervention, as distinct from the market-steering of the post-war period. Capitalist economies based on private ownership of the means of production, distribution, and exchange have always maintained owners' right to dispose of their property and to employ labour on terms that subordinate those employed to direction and control by management.

But throughout the post-war period and up until the late 1970s, the state played a very different role in regulating financial markets as well as employment relations, as governments often put serious constraints on firms investing overseas, as well as corresponding restraints on investment and money entering their country, in order to boost and regulate economic growth in the national interest. So too public officials under the pressure of trade unions and parties of the Left bolstered the rights of employees against employers by legislating collective bargaining frameworks and employment protection regulations, all of which were designed in large measure to ensure more efficient working relations between business and labour while increasing economic prosperity and stabilizing economic demand (Sassoon 2010; Western 1997).

However, recent emphasis on supply-side economic reforms and financial system overhauls has reversed these roles. Now governments often side with corporations and investors, while backing employers' rights, limiting labour regulations, and reforming industrial relations systems in order to expand flexibility (Baccaro and Avdagic 2014; Crouch 2014). So too the introduction of "pro-growth" economic models has been fundamental to the financialization of economies and the introduction of new financial and shareholder models for conducting business. These changes have created contemporary firms that are not only more global. Such policy overhauls were also fundamental in creating finance-led corporate models focused on cost-cutting and reducing labour costs through outsourcing and off-shoring, downsizing and concessions, as well as "flexible" employment relations and the "fissuring" of employment contracts.

In this book, I have traced these changes to a new politics of inequality – a politics focused on financial liberalization and labour market deregulation – and how they have played key roles in reversing the distribution of labour incomes in economies upwards to a wealthy few – most notably in Canada and the United States (Flaherty 2015; Hein 2015; Piketty 2014). Joseph Stiglitz has characterized such processes as the "victory of the rentiers" (Stiglitz 2013).

Notwithstanding the many variations of these processes across North America and Western Europe, it is clear that the victory of the "rentiers" has had profound distributional consequences, with top income earners capturing increasingly disproportionate shares of economic reward, and with workers left with stagnating wages, low-wage work, and growing levels of insecurity.

What do such arguments mean for comparative and critical political economy? Five conclusions stem from this analysis of the political determinants of income inequality and the redistribution of income from labour to capital.

I.   *Financialization, employer politics, and business political power are critical to the ongoing rise in inequality and the worsening of jobs and wages.*

Over the past decade, critical political economy has provided new insights into neoliberalism. Key to these insights has been much better understandings of how changes to global credit systems, corporate finance and operation have widened inequality, as well as how the political actions of business and employers have remade public policy for a wealthy few. Whereas neoclassical economic models continue to theorize that all productivity gains lead to increases in wages and improvements to jobs – while largely ignoring the role of monetary and financial systems – critical scholarship has highlighted how the politics and public policies surrounding finance and labour market deregulation have been key to explaining why the owners of capital and financial assets have been the major beneficiaries of "pro-growth" economic reforms.

In addition, whereas varieties-of-capitalism studies have continued to explain comparative policy differences primarily in terms of employer organizations and the economic coordinating capacities of business, critical scholarship has instead emphasized the activism of business in backing political parties, lobbying governments, and funding policy networks. In this perspective, firms are never neutral, nor are they uninterested political actors. Rather, as scholars such as Crouch (2011) and Hacker and Pierson (2010a) have pointed out, legislators are often most responsive to business leaders when firms and business lobbies drive agenda-setting processes, shape wider perceptions of policy reform, and work behind the scenes to help parties or individuals win office. Varieties-of-capitalism studies and neoclassical economic theory have often missed these points and the fact that markets on their own seldom share their benefits equally. So to understand recent changes to the economy and labour markets, a focus on post-democracy – and how politics and governments is again falling under the influence of business and the wealthy – is essential.

However, my argument adds two qualifications to recent critical literatures. First, to understand the new emergence of jobs with inequality, critical arguments need to pay more attention to financialization and how pro-growth officials have worked with industry and financial insiders to ensure that private debt and credit markets are now centre-stage in growth models around the world. It is how such neoliberal policies have transformed finance that allows us to explain how capitalism has entered a new phase, transforming how industry operates and recasting how unions, labour laws, and employment regulation function.

More than ever, the financialization of advanced capitalist economies puts investment banks, hedge and mutual funds, pension managers, and many other financial actors in the driver's seat. More and more, dominant financial actors are able to draw rents from their ownership of assets and their roles in capital and financial markets. At the same time, financialization has redrawn the basic operating procedures and priorities of corporations and their supplier networks, with new logics and governance models focused on profitmaking from financial channels that make businesses less willing and less able to pay. Such financialization allows us to account for the consistent and systematic downward mobility of organized labour and the exploitation of an increasingly precarious labour force. Just as important, these political economic dynamics also help us explain "trickle-up" economics, and why inequality has risen so dramatically at the top for the wealthy few, with widespread deleterious impacts for the rest of the workforce.

Second, to understand contemporary shifts in political power and post-democracy, it is important that future scholarship examine more closely how financially oriented business lobbying and business political activity actually takes place, and how much political coordination among businesses is required for its effectiveness. As my case studies show, even though the political influence of financial power-holders is widespread and growing as part of wider post-democracy trends, there are still important divides among economic sectors on the necessity of labour reform. In BC, firms established a broad coalition to pressure the government and were able to push through wholesale reforms. In contrast, in Ontario, employer groups were among the best organized and most politically active. But without an overarching coalition to direct reform and manage political differences, employers could only continue to block any reforms that would improve minimum wages or shore up employment standards.

As these experiences suggest, if political economists are to get a better handle on post-democracy and the determinants of recent reform models and approaches, they need to pay more attention to how financialization informs the political activities of business, but also to how and why employers act collectively within political circles and with what policy goals in mind. Business associations might act as willing partners with government, accepting government regulation and government involvement in preventing crashes, promoting consensus, and coordinating economic development. But business communities with new financial resources and financial pressures can also seek a radical change in direction, with new coalitions and sectors developing organizational resources to attack government policies and foster widespread opposition.

II. *Labour union solidarity and coordination is necessary but not sufficient for countering neoliberal reforms and developing progressive alternative policies.*

My analysis underscores how financialization and labour market deregulation have greatly increased employers' power over workers and unions. This can be seen in the ability of financially minded corporations to gain profits from financial investments and move jobs and investments around the globe. But also in how financialization has created supply chains that pressure firms and suppliers – large and small – to aggressively pursue concessions in wages and benefits while expanding part-time and temporary labour forces, most notably in the labour-intensive private service industries, but also in agriculture, construction, and natural resource sectors. Such developments – alongside government reform efforts and the widespread failure to uphold labour laws and regulations – have seriously constrained the power and capacities of unions to counter firms and financialization.

As the case studies here suggest, however, unions have not lain down, even managing in a few places to resist and intervene, organize to protect public services, return organizing rights in construction, or win new access and oversight over training. Unions in Newfoundland and Labrador were also able to work with the Conservative government to advance more egalitarian bargaining and training policies. This suggests that, even in the most difficult circumstances, unions can still play a role in mitigating neoliberal reforms and can be effective in enforcing laws and holding government to account when employers operating within financially driven production networks seek to skirt laws and regulations.

The Ontario case, however, clearly underscores the limited power of organized labour when unions are divided by politics and strategy. In this situation, unions lacked many of the necessary resources to influence politics and policymaking. Above all, they lacked the ability to undertake longer-term strategic innovation in organizing, building community alliances, or establishing coherent political coalitions that could influence legislators. In contrast, in Newfoundland and Labrador, even though there were no formal ties to political parties of the left or right, the coordination and cooperation of the labour movement was critical in winning over government support for maintaining labour and employment policies that would benefit the majority of workers in the province. This suggests that the broader strategies for building labour solidarity within political jurisdictions can influence policy, and that there are ways for labour movements to shift law and policy to more egalitarian ends.

However, this is only a first step. Many labour scholars have written of the importance of union renewal as well as greater democracy and membership activism within unions as the path to stronger and more influential labour movements. But as the case studies here suggest, of equal importance to future research and thinking is how unions interact with one another, and especially how they cooperate and coordinate in trying to influence governments, parties, and communities in order to challenge political authorities.

Simply looking at individual union cases of renewal, however valuable that may be in understanding associational change within unions, is of little value in answering the question of why some labour movements have retained sway on governments and others have not. Understanding how unions build solidarity and wield political power across issues and elections – within the labour movement and with workers and citizens more generally – is key to explaining why some are active participants in vibrant social movements and others are left fighting rearguard actions for their very survival.

Equally important are the questions of what kind of labour politics and to what ends. The post-war order was shaped in large measure by how organized labour and workers more generally challenged the reigning practices of free market competition – whether by winning new labour laws and new public policies like health care, or by unions initiating nation-wide or industry-wide strikes in the name of socialist or democratic alternatives. These actions opened the universe of political possibility.

However, as the case studies demonstrate, this is no longer the case. Unions and provincial labour movements are often sidelined by the power of financialized industries and instead focused on protecting members and upholding existing laws and regulations – not extending them or building a wider popular sovereignty over the economy and government. How and why unions and labour movements are – or are not – trying to rebuild their political cultures and egalitarian goals in the face of post-democracy and financialization is a critical issue for future research.

III. *Political parties and their interconnections with business and finance are central to the development and implementation of labour market deregulation.*

The role of political parties in imposing neoliberalism and labour market deregulation is also essential for our understanding of policy outcomes and employment. Comparative political economists as well as political scientists more generally have long been interested in whether government partisanship – i.e., whether governments are of the Left or Right – has mattered to the pattern of policy reforms that have emerged over the past thirty years. But as we have seen, it is not simply the ideology of the governing party that has influenced the scope and direction that labour law and policy reform have taken.

In British Columbia, for example, the policies of the Campbell Liberal government undermined collective bargaining and employment standards in the province. In contrast, interventions of the Williams Conservative government in Newfoundland and Labrador were crucial to brokering a deal between oil companies, construction, and unionized workers in supporting coordinated bargaining and the development of training policies. This suggests that government partisanship is of little analytical value by itself in understanding government responses to labour market reform. Rather, as this study has illustrated, what has mattered most to policymaking are the deeper strategies that parties deploy in response to business and the diminishing minority of active citizens, as well as their considerations of what is required to appeal to this minority and achieve electoral success.

As Crouch and other scholars critical of current political arrangements have argued, in order to explain how far and how fast parties have adopted neoliberal policy platforms, it is more useful to examine how political parties have shifted their ideological platforms in a more pro-market direction in response to business lobbying and business connections, as well as to declining rates of electoral participation that have narrowed their electoral calculations substantively.

More than ever, parties are tightly tied to business elites who themselves are highly politically minded and very well organized. In British Columbia, for example, the Campbell Liberals adopted aggressive reform positions across all key areas of labour market policy, and ended any routine political exchange, in response to party transformations that prioritized business and strategic considerations and the preferences of affluent voters in high-income constituencies, in a situation where only half of citizens voted.

But it is also important to keep in mind the long-term variation in corporate ties to political parties. Critical political economists often have very stylized conceptions of the ties between parties and business that overlook the changing relationships between the two. Comparative political economists often look in more detail at the institutions that link business and government, but do so in a static manner that typically ignores real-world political developments. A more developed political economy perspective will require a far more sophisticated assessment of the various aspects of business mobilization (party finance, lobbying, public advocacy, and operation of government programs), while paying greater analytic attention to how parties respond and provide opportunities for business to expand its long-term influence.

As the Newfoundland case here demonstrates, even in pluralist political systems, with powerful economic players, there are avenues for labour and government exchange, and for labour-citizen interaction to influence centre-right parties. Understanding when and where these connections between labour movements, citizens, and government officials can be developed in North America, and what prospects there are for different kinds of political unionism, is a subject that scholars of labour revitalization need to consider more carefully.

IV. *Post-democracy and the deepening of neoliberalism have required the mobilization of affluent and secure citizens. Governments may be restrained from taking such actions by other institutional avenues of citizen access. But policy trends are moving towards a concentration of economic and political power and the decline of citizen voice and citizen input.*

The political actors and coalitions that figure most prominently in my causal analysis are business and the affluent. Only in Newfoundland and Labrador did unions and wider citizen interests play a role in maintaining bargaining arrangements as well as in crafting a new training policy. Elsewhere, unions were often forced into fights that produced little beyond symbolic recognition. The sole exception was in Ontario, where unionized construction workers were able to pressure the Liberal government to reinstate organizing rights that had been rescinded by the previous administration. Just as notable were how low-wage workers and the working poor had few political resources and little influence on policymakers.

Such a view of the political bases – and biases – of governments clearly differs from many of the standard treatments of politics and recent comparative political economy studies. In median voter explanations, it is said that governments respond to shifts among a plurality of voters and that there is a level playing field for all interests in policymaking.

But as a post-democracy perspective highlights, with half of voters withdrawing from political involvement in many Canadian provinces, the electoral pool narrows significantly, and low-income and middle-class citizens increasingly forfeit their voice on policymaking through conventional electoral channels. Financialization and labour market deregulation have not only created a "flexible" workforce. They have also helped disaggregate the wider citizenry, leaving many without the resources, security, or shared interests necessary to effectively engage in democratic politics.

It is these new politics of inequality that drive agendas today, making contemporary politics very different from that of the past, with newly recast political configurations pushing governments in a far more unequal direction, leaving the majority of citizens poorer and far less economically secure and protected on the job.

V. *Analyses of labour market deregulation and economic financialization need to pay far more attention to the long-term incremental changes in democratic politics, and to how political choices foster long-term economic change that increases elite power and undermines egalitarian policies and the collective actions of workers and citizens alike.*

It is my hope that the research strategy adopted here has demonstrated the value to be derived from abandoning the typical comparative scholarship emphasis on "historical legacies," "institutions," and "ruptures" for understanding courses of neoliberal reform (Mahoney and Rueschemeyer 2003). Instead, I have argued that scholars would benefit far more by adopting a nuanced comparative analysis that includes the long-term impacts of economic developments and policy reforms on economic interests, citizen participation, and political mobilization – most particularly the ways in which long-term policy shifts in finance and labour law and policy can reverse (and have reversed) the balance of power between employers and workers, as well as between governments and the majority of citizens.

Comparative political economists have not been wrong to highlight how actors' preferences are often shaped by their domestic institutional configurations. On the contrary, the ways that business, labour, and citizens' interests have been influenced by their political economies' institutional set-up and outcomes continued to play a part in political economic adjustment. As Kathleen Thelen (2014) has argued, the interplay of institutional change and political coalitions has been central to shaping policy responses of growth and labour market regulation over the past generation.

The problem comes when a focus on the short term – and institutional change and comparative advantage – comes at the expense of a broader and longer-term focus on the actual organizational dynamics of political change. If the arguments in this book are correct, the policy choices of reform, drift, and stasis were far less historically constrained than the dominant paradigms on path dependency would lead us to think.

The policy preferences and reform strategies of public officials were shaped largely by the incremental change to the capacities of business interests, organized labour, and citizens brought about by public policies. Elections offered the window of opportunity for enduring labour law and policy change or to simply continue blocking and ignoring updates to labour institutions and policy. But financialization and labour market deregulation were critical to each of these processes.

Financialization introduced new logics to business demands for flexibility while providing resources to make their voice heard. As the very richest catapulted to heights of wealth beyond their dreams, they became less interested in compromise or in policies that would promote democracy or wider prosperity. In contrast, labour movements were fundamentally weakened over the years, and citizens were cut out of policymaking through flexible labour markets and deregulation, often leading to disillusionment with the democratic process.

Scholars interested in the dynamics of neoliberalism, how it emerges, and how it deepens, need to take these long-term impacts seriously. Only by considering the dynamics between politics, finance, business, and labour markets can scholars begin to grasp how major businesses and financiers not only have greater motivation, but also greater opportunities and increasing wealth to pursue and win policy reforms in their own narrow short-term interest.

Countering Jobs with Inequality

Can these trends be reversed? Is it inevitable that post-democracy continues to erode the jobs and incomes of the many for the benefit of the few? Is "jobs with inequality" the best that citizens can hope for? Growing awareness of inequality, its consequences, and the range of policy solutions available might suggest that there are not only problems with the current economic system, but that there is also a growing understanding and interest in governments taking action to counter the widening income gap.

Over the past few years, in the wake of the financial crisis, the Organisation for Economic Cooperation and Development, for example, has published numerous reports on the deepening of income inequality and low-wage work and the need for regulatory changes that will improve jobs and incomes (OECD 2011a, 2014a, 2015a). The International Monetary Fund similarly has shifted some of its policy stances, advocating for institutional solutions that ensure that economic growth is more broadly shared and that governments lead in supporting education and skills training through public investment. Reducing inequality and improving economic growth, they now claim, are "two sides of the same coin" (Berg and Ostry 2011; Dabla-Norris, Kochhar et al. 2015). Even the World Economic Forum, an informal institution made up of global experts, considers that growing inequality poses the greatest risk to the world (World Economic Forum 2014). Such shifts in views by important institutions to more balanced policy positions underscores how widespread a problem inequality has become, and how pressing the need is for a new policy agenda to address its many aspects.

The Occupy Wall Street movement also highlighted how widespread public antipathy has become towards income inequality and the influence of moneyed interests over politics (Hardt and Negri 2011). In the aftermath of the economic crisis of 2008–9, global protests erupted in 2011–12 targeting policies that supported banks while failing to protect people's jobs and homes. The protests captured the public perception that many public policies have been reshaped to the benefit of the wealthy few (Gitlin 2012). By undertaking this activism, protestors brought the problems of inequality into the public eye, where many have begun to realize that rising inequality is not simply a result of impersonal market forces, but rather a symptom of a politics that too often favours the few at the expense of the vast majority of working people (Stiglitz 2013).

Such developments have led to a resurgence of interest in inequality and contributed to a growing sense that just and egalitarian solutions are not only wanted, but also needed. In policy circles, inequality has now entered the academic lexicon at levels from the international to the local, and across fields from the economic to the political and the social (Atkinson 2015; Piketty 2014). More and more scholars, researchers, and activists are highlighting the problem of inequality and the necessity for more worker-friendly laws and policies because of the political and social benefits that high wages and redistributive tax and transfer systems provide to citizens.

Health researchers Kate Pickett and Richard Wilkinson (2010), for example, have demonstrated how inequality is damaging the social fabric of many societies, and how better work and social policies are essential to reversing the mushrooming of health and social problems that plague unequal societies. Only public policies that reinstate progressive taxation and limit corporate power, they argue, will create the stable economies that generate prosperity for all citizens.

Labour market researchers and sociologists have also shown the benefits of higher rates of unionization, progressive labour laws, and better public social and training programs. The ten-year comparative Sage research program on low-wage work concluded that countries with strong collective bargaining systems were critical to ensuring income equality and reducing low-wage work (Gautie and Schmitt 2010). But just as important in countries where bargaining systems were not as comprehensive, governments whose policies supported high minimum and median wages were also able to minimize wage inequality and the impacts of low pay (Schmitt 2012; Schulten 2014). In the circumstances of rising inequality, economists such as Robert Reich (2015) and the Nobel Prize–winning Joseph Stiglitz (2010, 2013) and many others are advocating labour-supportive reforms, from strong labour laws and collective bargaining institutions, to income-supporting employment insurance systems, and restrictions on working hours and arbitrary dismissal. Public pensions that provide stable incomes in retirement are also a necessity to create economies that work for citizens rather than business elites.

Finally, public policy research has underscored the necessity of economic reforms that limit the power of multinational corporations and major financial actors and markets. Such economic reforms must prioritize shared prosperity, overhaul the financial sector, and incentivize environmental sustainability

(Pettifor 2017; Stiglitz 2015). Reforms must also ensure that monopolies do not stifle innovation, and that they prevent the too-common outcome of massive concentrations of economic power generating massive political clout (Crouch 2013). Anti-trust laws provide one set of solutions for these problems. But the direct public ownership of shares also provides a public counterweight to unregulated misuses of corporate power (Baker 2017). Other reforms worth pursuing include proposals such as rewriting corporate charters to institute wider priorities of work, environmental sustainability, and communities, as well as the election of workers to corporate boards (Warren 2018; Ferreras 2017).

Equally important will be reforms to monetary and credit systems and the reintroduction of public control and regulation over banks and financial actors that are argued to be "too big to fail" (Stiglitz 2015). The necessity of limiting bank size, rebuilding public control over private finance, as well as separating banking and commerce are initiatives more urgent than ever before. There are also growing calls to re-establish public banks and public credit institutions (Stiefmueller 2018). Also required are new international frameworks that limit the leverage of major financial institutions, regulate or ban shadow banking, and place environmental goals in financial charters (Stiefmueller 2017). In addition, alternative forms of economic financial institutions such as cooperatives, credit unions, not-for-profits, and worker-controlled pension funds that meet common needs and keep wealth within communities, are likewise essential for "de-growth" and more sustainable ways of living (Chivers 2015; Victor 2008). Unless public financial institutions and public enterprises for governments and people alike are developed, there will be no serious counter to the power of financialization and corporate globalization today.

As recent progressive scholars and public policy researchers have argued, all these reforms are needed to restore economies to good health and improve the working conditions of the majority of citizens. Strong people-oriented, economic policies, alongside labour laws, bargaining institutions, and employment protection are essential to moderate the excesses of capitalism and curb the worst tendencies of global competition. They are also critical to reducing the risk to the economic health of the world and redistributing the income necessary for securing environmentally sustainable development.

Mobilizing against Post-Democracy and Organizing for Equality

But as I have shown throughout this book, the problem is not in lack of progressive policy options or evidence that supports the benefits of worker-friendly and democratic policies for societies and economies. The problem is in politics – and above all, the power of business and finance to influence democracy and public policy.

Today, many businesses have the power to simply threaten to relocate to friendlier regulatory environments. Firms and financial actors also have the billions necessary to regularly back political campaigns, lobby, conduct advocacy and advertising campaigns, and fund research that supports their interest. In contrast, organized labour in Canada and the United States especially face many problems in reconstituting itself into an organized political force that can mobilize citizens and counterbalance corporate interests in public debate or political engagement (Peters 2012b; Rosenfeld 2014). An equally large challenge is that many social democratic parties have argued that labour laws and employment protections are no longer needed and can therefore be dropped from their political agenda (Evans and Schmidt 2012; Keating and McCrone 2013; Sassoon 2010).

Countering these problems will certainly be a challenge for workers and citizens. But as the history of the past century has shown, these hurdles are not insurmountable (Hacker and Pierson 2016; Sassoon 2010). During the Great Depression and in the wake of the Second World War, citizens mobilized and agitated for democratic reforms, and this "countervailing power" won huge reforms that regulated business and led to a new post-war "settlement" that oversaw an expanding economy that distributed income widely.

Today, in the wake of the financial and COVID-19 crises, there is reason to believe that changing economic circumstances have again provided openings for citizens to find common cause. Similar to the depression of the 1930s, the financial crisis has called into question many of the nostrums of globalization and liberalization (Crouch 2011). There is also great potential for coalition building among small investors and homeowners, salaried employees and hourly workers, around new policies that would limit corporate subsidies and tax breaks. Broad support could also be found for promoting campaign finance reform that would restrain the influence of money in politics.

The environment and climate change too provide a new potential galvanizing issue around which community and labour organizations can build a broader popular movement for more universal public policy demands and progressive democratic governance. Given that lowering carbon emissions to meet current international treaty standards will require infrastructure and energy changes on an enormous scale, then citizens, climate groups, and organized labour will have to continue working together if they are to achieve the economic transformation and job creation necessary to achieve environmental sustainability (Stroud et al. 2015). The scale of the "leap" required to make renewable energy a reality for industrial economies also suggests this can be accomplished only through government investment, planning, and global cooperation (Klein 2014). This need for government involvement should give more than a few corporations reason to reconsider their opposition to public-led transition models, as well as to think seriously about the new opportunities that a "green" economy offers business across all sectors and countries. And already broader inclusionary "Blue-Green" alliances have formed across North America and Western Europe that have led to new renewable energy initiatives, new energy programs, and commitments to political action to address global warming (Hampton 2015; Räthzel and Uzzell 2012).

Last, the labour movement still represents one of the best options for generating the dialogue needed, and the organizing required, to create more economically and environmentally sustainable models (Gumbrell-McCormick and Hyman 2013). While not the only source of countervailing power to global inequality or global warming, unions remain the largest and best-resourced civil society associations that citizens have to represent their interests. Unions still seek to reduce inequality and stabilize the macroeconomy through collective bargaining and egalitarian social policies. Unions are also the most diverse organizations that represent workers from all backgrounds – regardless of skill level, gender, ethnicity, or occupation – in seeking better rights in workplaces, better incomes for citizens, and a voice for workers in their workplaces and in the wider society.

But as in the 1930s, corporations and finance today have much power, and workers very little. Progressive proposals meet fierce resistance, and governments often seek to marginalize civil society opponents, while business-funded think tanks and commentators act with new intensity in attacking even the most modest of proposals for progressive labour, environmental, or social policy reform – especially those proposed by organized labour. The central political story of the New Deal, the Second World War, and the post-war period was the emergence of democracy and citizen involvement through unions, interest groups, and political parties in response to war, social upheaval, and global crisis (Western 1997). But today, organized business and financial interests shape politics and policy through their vast array of associations and ties to political parties – a situation reminiscent of the early twentieth century.

To tackle these challenges, workers and citizens have been trying to find ways to build membership and power. Unions are now using new organizing models, labour-community coalitions, worker centres, and community unions to gain new members, advocate for rights, and educate people on the problems of inequality and climate change. Unions are also working with community groups, students, environmentalists, and housing activists to block pipelines, campaign for a green economy, and expand opportunity for citizens through better climate mitigation and renewable energy policies. These developments all share the goal of unions and citizens working on issues beyond wages and working conditions, looking for common interests between workers and community members, and growing citizen power through direct action or political reform (Luce 2014). They are also evidence of the breadth and extent of oppositional politics within and across societies today – the oppositional politics that has always been so central to the widening of democracy in the past, and that today help citizens find a wider common good, despite the fragmentation of their everyday work lives (Tilly and Tarrow 2015).

There is no quick fix on the horizon. Activists and labour organizers face the challenge of organizing and retaining the resources necessary to maintain a foothold in politics long enough to make politicians listen. But if the right policy battles are chosen – ones that change not only programs but also the way people think and act – and if social movements can find a common purpose in rebuilding and reinventing democracy for all, then citizens can get their troubled democracies back on track. Organized labour is one of the most likely associations to have the power and capacity to do this work, in alliance with other movements or with political parties. But for a more egalitarian society to emerge, tremendous political will and organizing are required among citizens and social movements.

On their own, labour markets do not ensure living wages, decent benefits, or long-term security. Nor do "free" markets and firm competition in any way guarantee that income will be distributed in ways that promote a stable economy – let alone one that is environmentally sustainable. Restoring democracy and tackling inequality in workplaces and governments will thus have to take place on multiple fronts. Yet central to this restoration must be replacing "jobs with inequality" with "good jobs and green jobs for all." Equally critical is that citizens develop the countervailing powers necessary to create governments that act for the common good and that foster broad environmentally sustainable prosperity. A serious challenge to financialization, deregulation, and post-democracy will require nothing less.

Appendix A: Data Definitions and Sources

To assess outcomes and sequences of change to inequality and labour markets, I draw on a range of new economic and income data, as well as measurements of income inequality. Examinations of income inequality are often only as good as the data, and over the past decade, researchers have made great strides in digging deeper into income and tax statistics to develop a better sense of how wide the income gap is growing within societies (Atkinson 2015; Atkinson and Piketty 2007). For many years, discussions of income inequality in Canada typically focused only on the Gini coefficient, which – as a single-number summary of inequality between 0 and 100 – provides an approximate sense of how full-time workers and their families are faring, what taxes and transfers are doing to marginally reduce inequality, and how Canada compares. But as recent scholarship has pointed out, analysis that relies only on Gini coefficients gives little sense of just how unequal a country has become or how rapidly inequality has risen in recent decades with the growth in non-standard employment.

Accordingly, in looking to build on recent inequality research, I rely heavily on three new sets of data. The first comes from Statistics Canada T1 tax file data and examines what has happened to all household market and after-tax and transfer incomes from the top to the bottom. This allows us to assess not only what has happened to so many low-income households. It also permits us to see clearly what has happened to the incomes of the top 1 per cent, and the very top 0.1 and 0.01 per cent of families and earners. I also rely heavily on Statistics Canada Survey of Labour and Income Dynamics (SLID) and Survey of Consumer Finances to see what has happened to all working families in the labour force. Second, the Canadian Centre for Policy Alternatives (CCPA) likewise generously shared decile income data for working families across Canada for the 1990s and the first decade of 2000. Since wages make up the vast majority of household income, any examination of what has happened to household incomes across the income distribution gives a far sharper sense of who has gained or who has lost from economic growth over the past few decades.

Third, I employ data from the SLID and the Canadian Income Survey (CIS) to examine what has happened to individual jobs and to gain a far more nuanced understanding of how many were in low-wage work (defined as earning two-thirds or less of the hourly wage of a full-time worker, or earning less than 50 per cent of what a full-time, full-year worker earned annually). These statistics may have imperfections – above all, that some of this data collection was discontinued after 2011 and that CIS data do not always capture those precariously employed throughout the year – but they do shed much light on the extent of income inequality at the bottom of Canada's labour market.

Finally, this book relies on data from the Organization of Economic Cooperation and Development (OECD) and the International Social Survey Programs. Interested readers can check OECD and the International Social Survey Program for further reference. Below, however, I describe key features from the custom tabulations for low-wage work, income inequality, and working poverty, as well as fuller description of the data for provincial electoral data.

Data for Computation of Low-Wage Work and the Working Poor

Although there is no strict definition of low-wage (or low-pay) work across countries, the now standard international definition set by the OECD defines low pay as less than two-thirds of median earnings for full-time workers. This definition is used by a number of countries, with variants examining hourly earnings, and monthly and annual incomes.

However, there is still a divergence in definitions of which workers are considered when calculating the percentage of workers in low pay, and whether calculations are based on hourly wages or market income. In Canada, low pay has typically been defined only in relation to full-time workers and to those with hourly wage earnings (LaRochelle-Côté and Dionne 2009). However, as Eurostat has noted, by excluding part-time and temporary workers from the calculation of the number of low-wage workers, this underestimates the incidence of low pay. The more narrow definition based only on hourly wage earnings also excludes the many workers who have been defined as "self-employed" by employers in contract positions, as well as the many workers who are paid on temporarily by the day, week, month, or project.

To address these problems, my custom tabulation follows Eurostat in defining low pay as all workers, regardless of employment status, earning less than two-thirds of median hourly earnings of a full-time/full-year worker. This definition includes full-time, part-time, temporary, and self-employed workers. Notably, where I diverge from standard definitions of low pay is including unincorporated self-employed workers without employees. Typically, many of the self-employed are mis-classified as self-employed when they have no control over workplace and are unincorporated. As the bulk of the unincorporated self-employed work in construction, cleaning services, private security, and low-end manufacturing, rather than in professional occupations, it is clear that the mis-classification has been widespread over the past decade or more.

For the analysis of low-wage work in the book, I utilized the Survey of Labour and Income Dynamics, the Survey of Consumer Finances, and the Canada Income Survey. The SLID data provide clear tabulations for those working in full-time/full-year employment and for those in other part-time, temporary, and contract arrangements. Self-employment hourly income was calculated on a combination of tax returns, work weeks, and daily work hours. Self-employment hourly wages were then averaged and weighted across the different work contexts. It is important to note the significant break that occurs in 2011 with the discontinuation of the SLID. The CIS, which replaced it, does not include all workers who are temporarily employed throughout the year. Rather, based on weekly surveys, the CIS counts only workers in work that week. With regular churn among non-standard employees, however, this can lead to more than one million workers being missed in the survey. This creates issues in comparison of low-wage non-standard work across time periods.

Definitions of "working poverty" or the "working poor" are equally diverse. But to capture a better sense of annual incomes for workers and the extent of low-wage work, I have expanded upon the Statistics Canada definition that more typically considers only family incomes, covers workers who have had a job for at least one month, and have a family income that is below 50 per cent of median earnings. My definition more closely applies the Norwegian and German definitions of "working poor" by considering all individual dependent employees and own-account self-employed who have 50 per cent or less of earnings of a full-time/full-year worker. This better captures the divide between those in full-time work and non-standard employment and provides a far more comprehensive assessment of the depth of low-wage work in the labour force.

Using these definitions, I have used SLID, the Survey of Consumer Finances, and CIS data for custom tabulations of hourly and annual incomes covering union and non-union workers, gender, and immigration by sector. I also requested custom tabulations for low-wage work by province, applying these definitions to provincial and national earnings to capture local labour conditions, as well as how the province compares to national developments.

Data for Computation of Top Income Inequality

Over the past couple of decades, there has been a great improvement in data and data availability for research on top income inequality. The World Top Incomes Database led by Anthony Atkinson and Facundo Alvaredo has now become the standard for tracking income shares of the top 1 per cent of earners, primarily through the use of tax data. Canada's contribution to has been made by Michael Veall of McMaster University, and he has also generously shared with me his other unpublished data on individual top income earnings and provincial top income inequality.

But to better track how incomes have changed more broadly, I have relied on a custom request to Canada's Income Statistics Division using the tax data of family filers (T1FF). Typically tax data requests have been only on individual earners. However, this overlooks the ways that income is shared among family earners, especially for tax purposes. Tracking developments of family incomes – before and after taxes and transfers – also provides a better way of understanding what has happened to household incomes, as household income has grown very differently from real GDP per capita (Crettaz 2013; Marx and Nolan 2012; Stiglitz, Sen, and Fitoussi 2009).

My custom tabulation included market incomes and after-tax and transfer incomes for the top 1, top 0.1, and top 0.01 per cent of family earners, including capital gains, investment income, rental, and partnership income. It excluded census families with zero and negative incomes, making the tabulation focus more specifically on those active in the workforce. But to see the effects of total taxes and transfers on incomes, the tabulation also included other private pension income, disability saving plans, spousal and child support payments, and other taxable income.

New wealth data have also begun to track the growing concentration of total assets within nations and across the globe. Wealth includes the value of businesses, savings, and investments as personal homes and valuables held by households. Income is one factor in accounting for rising inequality. But how personal wealth ownership has so rapidly increased and been redistributed to those at the top also poses long-term problems for economic growth and stability (Credit Suisse 2013). Led by James Davies (University of Western Ontario), Roberto Lluberas (University of Uruguay), and Anthony Shorrocks (Global Economic Perspectives), Credit Suisse has begun to compile global and national wealth data, which has been recently compiled in the Global Wealth Handbook. Anthony Shorrocks has generously shared all their Canadian data on high net-worth individuals with me.

Data for Computation of Household Income Inequality

For income inequality across households, I have used several indicators. For the correlation between wider inequality and voting turnout, I have relied on Statistics Canada for its calculation of the Gini coefficient. Market income is known to have the most direct impact on citizen resources and participation. Voter turnout averages were calculated using a lagged average, based on the assumption that changes to income inequality would have longer-term impacts on voting behaviour. This follows other studies that have adopted a similar methodology (Mahler 2008).

Other income inequality on D90:D50 and D90:20 income ratios is extracted from a custom tabulation of economic families conducted by the Canadian Centre of Policy Alternatives. Unlike the more traditional 90:10 ratios that are used by the Organisation for Economic Cooperation and Development to measure earnings inequality in the workforce, in Canada the earnings of the bottom 10 per cent of the workforce are so low and so inconsistent that they wildly skew any longer-term trends.

Family calculations by decile capture much of the developments that households experienced across the income distribution, and also do much to include the effects of second, third, or more earners in attempting to cope with insecure employment and low-paying jobs. The custom tabulation here calculates incomes after tax and transfers incomes of families, providing a broad-ranging picture of family earnings, and wider trends of inequality between top-, middle-, and low-income earners.

Data for Computation of Voting Turnout

Provincial voting turnout data was extracted from provincial election agencies (note: weblinks for government agencies change frequently):

BC: "BC Voter Participation: 1983 to 2013," https://www.elections.bc.ca/docs/stats/bc-voter-participation-1983-2013.pdf

Newfoundland and Labrador: "Election Reports – 1999, 2003, 2007, 2011," https://www.elections.gov.nl.ca/elections/resources/ereports.html.

Ontario: "Results Overview – Graphics and Charts," https://results.elections.on.ca/en/graphics-charts.

Data for Computation of Voting and Income Polarization

For provincial tables assessing the relationship between income and party support, I employed provincial elections and provincial statistic databases to assess high- and low-income voting patterns. District restructuring in each province led to a low number of changes for ridings in each province. New and old districts were then assessed for income levels. Resulting districts were retained if they maintained low- or high-income characteristics.

For BC, median incomes for districts was extracted from: Elections BC: "2001 Electoral District Profiles," https://elections.bc.ca/resources/statistics/, and

BC: "2006 Census: Provincial Electoral Districts" http://www.llbc.leg
.bc.ca/public/PubDocs/bcdocs/453011/index.htm.

For Newfoundland and Labrador, data on income from communities were
compiled from Statistics Canada, Community Accounts, Community Profiles and NL Community Accounts (https://nl.communityaccounts.ca
/tablesand charts.asp?_=vb7En4WVgbOxz7Zj). The five largest communities in each provincial district were selected, after which median incomes
were then averaged and weighted for each district to estimate income
levels.

For Ontario, median incomes for districts were calculated using Statistics
Canada, Federal Electoral District profiles, Federal Electoral District
(FED) Profile, 2006 Census, Statistics Canada catalogue no. 92-595-XWE,
released 26 June 2008, based on median household income. Federal data
were used as provincial and federal district ridings were coterminous
2003–15, with the exception of districts in Northern Ontario. Census
profiles of Northern Ontario were then examined to determine median
incomes.

Data for Computation of Political Party Revenues and Expenditures

Provincial electoral data vary in depth and category breakdowns. For BC I used
annual political party statements from the Elections BC website "Financial Reports and Political Contributions" (https://contributions.electionsbc.gov.bc.ca
/pcs/). Financial reports are available online beginning only in 2001. Business
and union contributions were then separated from all contribution lists. A similar extraction of business contributions from contribution lists was undertaken
for Newfoundland and Labrador, where annual reports for each political party
were extracted from "Political Finance Reports" (https://www.elections.gov
.nl.ca/elections/resources/gereports.html), and business and union contributions separated from annual party reports. For Ontario, I relied on a political
finance dataset provided by Robert MacDermid, York University, who has broken down political finance and expenditures for all parties 1999–2011 based on
submitted reports to the Ontario Election Finances Commission.

Appendix B: Interview Sources by Case

British Columbia

Date	Affiliation
6 September 2012	BC independent labour researcher 1
7 September 2012	BC union staff official 1, private sector
8 September 2012	BC retired union official 2, private sector
9 September 2012	BC retired union president 1, private sector
11 September 2012	BC labour leader 1
11 September 2012	BC Ministry of Labour official 1
12 September 2012	BC independent public policy researcher 1
12 September 2012	BC independent public policy researcher 2
13 September 2012	BC union staff official 2, private sector
13 September 2012	BC retired business consultant
14 September 2012	BC journalist
14 September 2012	BC retired Liberal Party official
15 September 2012	BC retired business lawyer
17 September 2012	BC union president 1, private sector
17 September 2012	BC member of the legislative assembly
18 September 2012	BC Ministry of Jobs, Tourism, and Skills official
19 September 2012	BC union president, public sector

Newfoundland and Labrador

Date	Affiliation
24 October 2011	NL labour leader
25 October 2011	NL union staff official 1, private sector
26 October 2011	NL union president 1, private sector

27 October 2011	NL union executive, public sector
27 October 2011	NL union staff official, public sector
1 November 2011	NL union president 2, private sector
2 November 2011	NL Ministry of Fisheries official
2 November 2011	NL Agency of Labour Relations official
15 November 2011	NL municipal official
3 December 2011	NL Ministry of Finance official
2 August 2015	NL regional councillor

Ontario

Date	Affiliation
9 August 2012	Ontario NDP staff researcher
10 August 2012	Ontario retired union researcher
11 August 2012	Ontario NDP MPP
20 August 2012	Ontario public sector union leader 1
23 August 2012	Ontario Ministry of Labour official
28 August 2012	Ontario retired Ministry of Labour official
30 August 2012	Ontario Ministry of Community and Social Services official
7 May 2013	Ontario OFL labour official
8 May 2013	Ontario retired public sector labour staff
9 May 2013	Ontario retired Ontario union president, private sector
10 May 2013	Ontario union organizer, private sector 1
10 May 2013	Ontario union organizer, private sector 2
11 May 2013	Ontario retired union staff official
15 May 2013	Ontario community activist

Appendix C: Methods and Research Design

Finally, I will say a few words about methodology. Exploring the components of political economy is often complex – especially when tackling recent changes to finance and corporate operation as well as democracy. Consequently, to develop my arguments about how the politics of income distribution is related to financialization, firm operation, and labour market deregulation, this book employs a multidimensional approach rooted in comparative historical analysis.

In broad terms, my research goal is to trace organizational and institutional change over time to understand the causes and contrasts in income inequality and labour market change. Political struggles over policy are always a blend of what has happened before and what can be done in the present. So in developing my arguments about financialization and post-democracy, I seek to analyse the degree of consistency – or "congruence" – between my theoretical assumptions and the observed levels of policy change and market inequality. Such a congruence method is often used for comparative case studies, as it offers flexibility in assessing political economic theories and testing their ability to explain outcomes (George and Bennett 2005).

In examining three distinct but closely interrelated causal mechanisms (financialization, labour market deregulation, and post-democracy), I adopt a research framework that focuses on the interaction of economic and political spheres across national and international boundaries. Most accounts of inequality are nationally focused. However, my explanation emphasizes that the sources of financialization have originated from domestic political economic structures and larger developments in the United States and the global economy.

To clarify the relative strength of any of these individual factors in understanding financialization, I first detail the bundle of international and national factors necessary to explain the new dominance of finance, and the subsequent reforms to corporate finance, ownership, and governance in Canada and other advanced industrial economies. This requires attention to evidence across global markets and over time, and testing to explore whether there has been a broad convergence toward financialization with related impacts on labour markets and income distribution across Canada.

To accomplish this task, I rely on quantitative indicators of the economic and financial system to provide probabilistic assessments of causal propositions. From the statistical figures, comparative tables, scatterplots, and cross-tabulations that present data over time at the national level, we can see if there are consistent patterns of association between variables, and if so then we might conclude that the causal variables at work are closely related – that is, whether there is "congruence" between the theory and the evidence. In adopting this research design, I look to evaluate the relationships between financialization and inequality by estimating some of the average effects of changes to corporate finance and governance on manufacturing and service employment, public sector jobs, and income inequality across Canada. In tracking these developments, I use univariate distributions to explore the central tendencies in financial indicators in Canada and other developed economies. I also rely on cross-tabulations to measure the association between financialization and labour market outcomes.

I also use comparative scatterplots to look for regular patterns of association between variables across countries, and how Canada compares. Here, the design of these tables is to address the question whether economic changes are associated with inegalitarian labour market trends across countries, or whether Canada has features that follow trends common to other liberal market economies. These are especially useful, for in contrast to larger econometric regressions, scatterplots are direct and provide a much easier way to interpret data through bivariate correlations. If these relationships are strong, then logically we should see consistent trends and bivariate correlations relating financial and corporate developments to rising inequality, the erosion of good jobs, and the rise of low-wage work across numerous sectors of the economy.

While these data can show correlations between developments like financialization and inequality, I look to supplement this analysis by drawing on extensive secondary literature, business reports, not-for-profit analyses, and OECD research for my analysis of key firm and labour market developments in leading economic sectors in Canada and internationally. This evidence is important, as it provides another avenue to further assess the central theoretical propositions of this study. By assessing Canada and three of its provinces as case studies for the development of financialization and inegalitarian labour market trends, this allows a probing of the sequence of changes to public policy, global financial markets, international finance, and corporate operation. If my theoretical argument is correct, we should expect significant economic policy reforms to trade and investment policy, corporate taxation, pension reform, and banking and mortgage market liberalization to foster widespread economic transformation. Additionally, I employ quantitative indicators to examine recent financial and corporate developments and to further query whether recent economic developments in the Canadian context match those of causal propositions central to this study.

For example, in tracking changes to financialization and corporate operation in chapters 3 and 4, I rely heavily on recent OECD statistics, as well as data from the International Monetary Fund, the World Bank, and Statistics Canada. Jordan Brennan of UNIFOR very generously shared data on the financial assets of the top multinationals operating in Canada based on Compustat, the most comprehensive business database available. Overall, this analysis of secondary materials and other "grey" literature provides another body of evidence that contributes to conclusions about the effects of financialization on corporate operation and labour market inequality.

In addition, while I am interested in tracing common political and economic dynamics at the national and international level that might account for the convergence of countries towards financialization and greater inequality, I also wish to consider reasons for variation in labour law and employment policy and their frequent ineffectiveness. Here, because of Canada's uniquely decentralized federalism, and the extensive role of provincial governments in labour market regulation, I turn my focus to provincial developments and in-depth case study analysis of the impacts of post-democracy.

Thus, to analyse the casual effects of political developments on labour market inequality, and whether they have varied systematically, I employ "process tracing" – a second common comparative method. Often used by comparative social scientists, this method seeks to develop a historical narrative of the detailed causal processes involved in specific cases and assess such developments against known theoretical explanations (Mahoney and Rueschemeyer 2003). In this book I use process tracing and detailed narrative to explore the causes that can lead from post-democratic political developments to labour market deregulation and inequality across three of Canada's provinces.

Given the hypothesized variations in post-democratic changes to business, parties, unions, and voter preferences and norms, I claim that how such causal processes interact should amplify and accelerate policy change in specific neoliberal political contexts while diminishing or delaying reforms in others. In mapping out the role of finance and firms in rising inequality across Canada, I also theorize there is a specific repertoire of post-democratic developments provincially that are consistent with the extent and intensity of neoliberal policy reforms. If politics and different political coalitions are indeed key to understanding labour market reforms, we should see consistent evidence between the hypothesized mechanisms and the processes, sequences, and outcomes. In assessing this argument, I rely on many government documents, policy reports, and secondary literature on economic and political developments to ask whether these causal processes are evident in my provincial cases.

As I discuss in appendix A, to gauge long-term causal changes to voting turnout and political finance, I have turned to provincial electoral commissions. Additionally, to examine changes to voter preferences and voter turnout, I have relied on the International Social Survey Programme to investigate topics for political science research such as distributive preferences and trust in government. For evaluating developments and reforms to collective bargaining, certifications, labour law changes, and employment standards reforms, I have relied on the annual publications of provincial labour boards, updates from provincial ministries responsible for labour issues, and special commissions addressing labour and wage-related issues. While unfortunately these data do not cover the entire period from 1990 to 2010, they often provide insight into comparable changes across the first decade of 2000 in Canada.

Moreover, to better understand how political events contributed to policy reform – or the blocking or renewal of labour laws and employment policies – in each of the three provinces, I conducted interviews with provincial government and union officials, addressing public and private sector developments (appendix B). These interviews provided insight into the political dynamics of inequality and the role of organized interests and citizens. But interviews with current or recently retired government officials and deputy ministers working on collective bargaining and employment standards, as well as those working on training and labour market reactivation programs, retired union officials, and staff of the major provincial unions, as well as other academic experts and other non-governmental researchers, was essential in understanding provincial politics and law and policy change.

References

Aalbers, Manuel. 2016. *The Financialization of Housing: A Political Economy Approach.* New York: Routledge.

– 2017. "Corporate Financialization." In *The International Encyclopedia of Geography*, 1–11. Oxford: Wiley.

Acharya, Ram C., Someshwar Rao, Subrata Bhattacharjee, and Leila Wright. 2010. "Outward FDI from Canada and Its Policy Context." *Transnational Corporations Review* 2 (3): 28–43. https://doi.org/10.1080/19186444.2010.11658248.

Adler, Lee, Maite Tapia, and Lowell Turner. 2014. *Mobilizing against Inequality: Unions, Immigrant Workers, and the Crisis of Capitalism.* Ithaca, NY: Cornell University Press.

Adsera, Alicia, and Barry Chiswick. 2006. "Divergent Patterns in Immigrant Earnings Across Euro Destinations." In *Immigration and the Transformation of Europe*, edited by C. Parsons and T.M. Smeeding, 85–110. New York: Cambridge University Press.

Aggarwal, Reena, Isil Erel, Miguel Ferreira, and Pedro Matos. 2011. "Does Governance Travel around the World? Evidence from Institutional Investors." *Journal of Financial Economics* 100 (1): 154–81. https://doi.org/10.1016/j.jfineco.2010.10.018.

Agriculture and Agri-Food Canada. 2013. *An Overview of the Canadian Agriculture and Agri-Food System 2013.* Ottawa: Department of Agriculture and Agri-Food Canada.

Aguilera, Ruth V., and Gregory Jackson. 2010. "Comparative and International Corporate Governance." *Academy of Management Annals* 4 (1): 485–556. https://doi.org/10.1080/19416520.2010.495525.

Alavarez-Medina, Lourdes, and Jorge Carrillo. 2014. "Restructuring of the Automotive Industry in the North American Free Trade Agreement (NAFTA) Region from 2007 to 2011." *International Review of Management and Business Research* 3 (4): 2120–30. https://www.irmbrjournal.com/papers/1421125971.pdf.

Albo, Greg, Sam Gindin, and Leo Panitch. 2010. *In and Out of Crisis: The Global Financial Meltdown and Left Alternatives.* Oakland, CA: PM.

Alepin, Brigitte. 2012. *Bill Gates, Pay Your Fair Share of Taxes ... like We Do!* Toronto: James Lorimer.

Allen, Jason, and Ying Liu. 2007. "Efficiency and Economies of Scale of Large Canadian Banks." *Canadian Journal of Economics/Revue canadienne d'économique* 40 (1): 225–44. https://doi.org/10.1111/j.1365-2966.2007.00406.x.

Allen, Robert. C. 1986. "Growth and Flucuations in the B.C. Economy." In *Restraining the Economy: Social Credit Economic Policies for B.C. in the Eighties*, edited by R.C. Allen and G. Rosenbluth. Vancouver: New Star Books.

Alvaredo, Facundo, Anthony B. Atkinson, Thomas Piketty, and Emmanuel Saez. 2013. "The Top 1 Percent in International and Historical Perspective." *Journal of Economic Perspectives* 27 (3): 3–20. https://doi.org/10.1257/jep.27.3.3.

Alvaredo, Facundo, Lucas Chancel, Thomas Piketty, Emmanuel Saez, and Gabriel Zucman. 2017. *World Inequality Report 2018*. Paris: World Inequality Lab.

– 2018. *World Inequality Report 2018*. Paris: World Wealth and Income Database.

Amable, Bruno. 2003. *The Diversity of Modern Capitalism*. New York: Oxford University Press.

– 2009. "Structural Reforms in Europe and the (In)coherence of Institutions." *Oxford Review of Economic Policy* 25 (1): 17–39. http://doi.org/10.1093/oxrep/grp001.

Anastakis, Dimitry. 2005. *Auto Pact: Creating a Borderless North American Auto Industry, 1960–1971*. Toronto: University of Toronto Press.

– 2019. "A Neoliberal Pause? The Auto and Manufacturing Sectors in Ontario since Free Trade." In *Divided Province: Ontario Politics in the Age of Neoliberalism*, edited by G. Albo and B. Evans, 103–29. Montreal and Kingston: McGill-Queen's University Press.

Anderson, Christopher J., and Pablo Beramendi. 2008. "Income Inequality, and Electoral Participation." In *Democracy, Inequality, and Representation in Comparative Perspective*, edited by P. Beramendi and C.J. Anderson, 3–24. New York: Russell Sage Foundation.

Anderson, Cameron, and Laura B. Stephenson, eds. 2010. *Voting Behaviour in Canada*. Vancouver: University of British Columbia Press.

Angevine, Gerry, and Miguel Cervantes. 2010. *Global Petroleum Survey 2010*. Vancouver: Fraser Institute.

Appelbaum, Eileen. 2010. "Institutions, Firms, and the Quality of Jobs in Low-Wage Labor Markets." In *Low-Wage Work in the Wealthy World.*, edited by J. Gautié and J. Schmitt, 185–210. New York: Russell Sage Foundation.

– 2017. "Domestic Outsourcing, Rent-Seeking, and Increasing Inequality." *Review of Radical Political Economics* 49 (6): 513–28. http://doi.org/10.1177/0486613417697121.

Appelbaum, Eileen, A. Bernhardt, and R.J. Murnane, eds. 2003. *Low-Wage America: How Employers Are Reshaping Opportunity in the Workplace*. New York: Russell Sage Publications.

Arcand, Alan, Michael Burt, and Todd Crawford. 2012. *Fuel for Thought: The Economic Benefit of Oil Sands Investment for Canada's Regions*. Toronto: Conference Board of Canada.

Archer, Keith. 1990. *Political Choices and Electoral Consequences: A Study of Organized Labour and the New Democratic Party*. Montreal and Kingston: McGill-Queen's University Press.

Archer, Simon. 2011. "Pension Funds as Owners and as Financial Intermediaries: A Review of Recent Canadian Experience." In *The Embedded Firm: Corporate Governance, Labor, and Finance Capitalism*, edited by C. Williams and P. Zumbansen, 177–204. New York: Cambridge University Press.

Armingeon, Klaus, and Giuliano Bonoli, eds. 2006. *Adopting Post-War Social Policies to New Social Risks*. New York: Routledge.

Arrighi, Giovanni. 2010. *The Long Twentieth Century: Money, Power, and the Origins of Our Times*. New York: Verso.

Arrowsmith, James. 2013. "Working Time in Europe." In *The Transformation of Employment Relations in Europe*, edited by J. Arrowsmith and V. Pulignano, 111–32. New York: Routledge.

Atkinson, Anthony B. 2009. "Factor Shares: The Principal Problem of Political Economy?" *Oxford Review of Economic Policy* 25 (1): 3–16. http://doi.org/10.1093/oxrep/grp007.

– 2015. *Inequality: What Can Be Done?* Cambridge, MA: Harvard University Press.

Atkinson, Anthony B., and Thomas Piketty, eds. 2007. *Top Incomes over the Twentieth Century: A Contrast between Continental European and English-Speaking Countries*. New York: Oxford University Press.

– eds. 2010. *Top Incomes: A Global Perspective*. New York: Oxford University Press.

Atkinson, Anthony B., Thomas Piketty, and Emmanuel Saez. 2011. "Top Incomes in the Long Run of History." *Journal of Economic Literature* 49 (1): 3–71. http://doi.org/10.1257/jel.49.1.3.

Atkinson, Michael, Dustin Rogers, and Sara Olfert. 2016. "Better Politicians: If We Pay, Will They Come?" *Legislative Studies Quarterly* 41 (2): 361–91. https://doi.org/10.1111/lsq.12117.

Atlantic Provinces Economic Council. 2011. *How Atlantic Canada's Economy Is Adapting to New Global Realities*. Halifax: Atlantic Provinces Economic Council.

Autor, D., L. Katz, and M. Kearny. 2005. "Trends in U.S. Wage Inequality: Reassessing the Revisionists." NBER Working Paper. Washington, DC: National Bureau of Economic Research.

Baccaro, Lucio, and Sabina Avdagic. 2014. "The Future of Employment Relations in Advanced Capitalism: Inexorable Decline?" In *The Oxford Handbook of Employment Relations: Comparative Employment Systems*, edited by A. Wilkinson, G. Wood, and R. Deeg, 701–26. New York: Oxford University Press. https://doi.org/10.1093/oxfordhb/9780199695096.013.031.

Baccaro, Lucio, and Chris Howell. 2011. "A Common Neoliberal Trajectory: The Transformation of Industrial Relations in Advanced Capitalism." *Politics and Society* 39 (4): 521–63. https://doi.org/10.1177/0032329211420082.

– 2017. *European Industrial Relations: Trajectories of Neoliberal Transformation*. New York: Cambridge University Press.

Bach, Stephen, and Lorenzo Bordogna. 2011. "Varieties of New Public Management or Alternative Models? The Reform of Public Service Employment Relations in Industrialized Democracies." *International Journal of Human Resource Management* 22 (11): 2281–94. http://doi.org/10.1080/09585192.2011.584391.

Bach, Steffen, Rebecca Givan, and John Forth. 2009. "The Public Sector in Transition." In *The Evolution of the Modern Workplace*, edited by W. Brown, A. Bryson, J. Forth, and K. Whitfield, 307–31. New York: Cambridge University Press.

Baker, Dean. 2009. *Plunder and Blunder: The Rise and Fall of the Bubble Economy.* Sausalito, CA: PoliPoint.

– 2017. *Rigged: How Globalization and the Rules of the Modern Economy Were Structured to Make the Rich Richer.* Washington, DC: Center for Economic and Policy Research.

Bank of Canada. 2004. *Financial System Review*, June. Ottawa: Bank of Canada.

– 2009. *Annual Report 2009.* Ottawa: Bank of Canada.

Banting, Keith, and John Myles. 2014. *Inequality and the Fading of Redistributive Politics.* Vancouver: UBC Press.

Barker, Roger M. 2010. *Corporate Governance, Competition, and Political Parties: Explaining Corporate Governance Change in Europe.* New York: Oxford University Press.

Barnes, Trevor, and Roger Hayter. 1992. "'The Little Town That Did': Flexible Accumulation and Community Response in Chemainus, British Columbia." *Regional Studies* 26 (7): 647–63. http://doi.org/10.1080/00343409212331347281.

Bartkiw, Timothy. 2008. "Manufacturing Descent? Labour Law and Union Organizing in the Province of Ontario." *Canadian Public Policy* 34 (1): 111–31. https://doi.org/10.3138/cpp.34.1.111.

Bartram, Timothy, Brendan Boyle, Pauline Stanton, John Burgess, and Anthony McDonell. 2015. "Multinational Enterprises and Industrial Relations: A Research Agenda for the 21st Century." *Journal of Industrial Relations* 57 (2): 127–45. https://doi.org/10.1177%2F0022185614564379.

Basok, Tanya. 2009. *Tortillas and Tomatoes: Transmigrant Mexican Harvesters in Canada.* Montreal and Kingston: McGill-Queen's University Press.

Bassanini, Andrea, Luca Nunziata, and Danielle Venn. 2009. "Job Protection Legislation and Productivity Growth in OECD Countries." *Economic Policy* 58 (1): 349–402. http://doi.org/10.1111/j.1468-0327.2009.00221.x.

Batt, Rosemary, and Eileen Appelbaum. 2013. "The Impact of Financialization on Management and Employment Outcomes." SSRN. http://ssrn.com/abstract=2235748.

– 2014. *Private Equity at Work: When Wall Street Manages Main Street.* New York: Russell Sage Publications.

Battle, Ken. 2011. *Restoring Minimum Wages in Canada.* Ottawa: Caledon Institute of Social Policy.

Baud, Céline, and Cédric Durand. 2012. "Financialization, Globalization, and the Making of Profits by Leading Retailers." *Socio-Economic Review* 10 (2): 241–66. http://doi.org/10.1093/ser/mwr016.

BC Campaign 2000. *2010 Child Poverty Report Card.* Vancouver: BC Campaign 2000. https://firstcallbc.org/wordpress/wp-content/uploads/2015/08/2010-BC-Child -Poverty-Report-Card-FirstCall-2010-11.pdf.

BC Liberal Party. 2001. *A New Era for British Columbia.* Vancouver: BC Liberals.

BC Ministry of Jobs, Tourism and Innovation. 2012. *2012/13–2014/15 Service Plan.* Victoria: Ministry of Jobs, Tourism, and Innovation.

BC Ministry of Labour and Citizens' Services. 2007. *2007/08–2009/10 Service Plan.* Victoria: BC Ministry of Labour and Citizens' Services.

BC Ministry of Skills Development and Labour. 2002. *Bill 48 Employment Standard Amendment Act 2002.* Victoria: Queen's Printer.

Beaudry, Paul, and David A. Green. 2005. "Changes in U.S. Wages, 1976–2000: Ongoing Skill Bias or Major Technological Change?" *Journal of Labor Economics* 23 (3): 609–48. http://doi.org/10.1086/430288.

Bedard-Page, Guillaume, Annick Demers, Eric Tuer, and Miville Tremblay. 2016. "Large Canadian Public Pensions: A Financial System Perspective." *Bank of Canada: Financial System Review* June, 33–8.

Beers, David. 2005. "The Big Swerve." In *Liberalized: The Tyee Report on British Columbia under Gordon Campbell's Liberals*, edited by D. Beers. Vancouver: New Star Books.

Behrens, Martin, and Reinhard Dribbusch. 2013. "Anti-Unionism in a Coordinated Market Economy." In *Global Anti-Unionism: Nature, Dynamics, Trajectories, and Outcomes*, edited by T. Dundon and G. Gall, 83–103. New York: Palgrave Macmillan.

Bell, Brian D., and John Van Reenen. 2013. "Extreme Wage Inequality: Pay at the Very Top." *American Economic Review* 103 (3): 153–7. http://doi.org/10.1257/aer .103.3.153.

Bellamy Foster, John, and Hannah Holleman. 2010. "The Financial Power Elite." *Monthly Review* 62 (1). http://doi.org/10.14452/MR-062-01-2010-05_1.

Belman, Dale, and Allen Smith. 2008. "Reconstructing Construction Unionism: Beyond Top Down and Bottom Up." Alfred B. Sloan Foundation Industry Studies. Boston: Sloan Foundation.

Beramendi, Pablo, and Christopher J. Anderson, eds. 2008. *Democracy, Inequality, and Representation: A Comparative Perspective*. New York: Russell Sage Foundation.

Beramendi, Pablo, and Thomas R. Cusack. 2008. "Economic Institutions, Partisanship, and Inequality." In *Democracy, Inequality and Representation: A Comparative Perspective*, edited by C.J. Anderson and P. Beramendi, 127–68. New York: Russell Sage Foundation.

Beramendi, Pablo, Silja Hausermann, Herbert Kitschelt, and Hanspeter Kriesi. 2015. "Introduction: The Politics of Advanced Capitalism." *The Politics of Advanced Capitalism*, edited by P. Beramendi, S. Hausermann, H. Kitschelt, and H. Kriesi, 1–68. New York: Cambridge University Press.

Berg, Andrew G., and Jonathon D. Ostry. 2011. "Inequality and Unsustainable Growth: Two Sides of the Same Coin?" IMF Staff Discussion Note. New York: International Monetary Fund.

Bermeo, Nancy, and Jonas Pontusson, eds. 2012. *Coping with Crisis: Government Reactions to the Great Recession*. New York: Russell Sage Foundation.

Bernhardt, Annette, Heather Boushey, Laura Dresser, and Chris Tilly, eds. 2008. *The Gloves Off Economy: Problems and Possibiities at the Bottom of America's Labor Market*. Ithaca, NY: Cornell University Press.

Bieling, Hans-Jürgen. 2006. "EMU, Financial Integration and Global Economic Governance." *Review of International Political Economy* 13 (3): 420–48. https://doi.org/10.1080/09692290600769286.

– 2013. "European Financial Capitalism and the Politics of (De-)financialization." *Competition & Change* 17 (3): 283–98. http://doi.org/10.1179/1024529413Z.00000000038.

Binford, Leigh. 2013. *Tomorrow We're All Going to the Harvest: Temporary Foreign Worker Programs and Neoliberal Political Economy*. Austin: University of Texas Press.

Birch, Kean, and Matti Siemiatycki. 2016. "Neoliberalism and the Geographies of Marketization: The Entangling of State and Markets." *Progress in Human Geography* 40 (2): 177–98. https://doi.org/10.1177%2F0309132515570512.

Bittner, Amanda, and Elizabeth Goodyear-Grant. 2013. "A Laggard No More? Women in Newfoundland and Labrador Politics." In *The Representation of Women in Canadian Legislatures*, edited by L. Trimble, J. Arscott, and M. Tremblay, 115–34. Vancouver: UBC Press.

Bittner, Amanda, and Royce Koop, eds. 2011. *Parties, Elections, and the Future of Canadian Politics*. Vancouver: University of British Columbia Press.

Blackburn, Robin. 2002. *Banking on Death: Or, Investing in Life – The History and Future of Pensions*. New York: Verso.

– 2011. *Age Shock: How Finance Is Failing Us*. New York: Verso.

Blake, Donald. 1996. "The Politics of Polarization: Parties and Elections in BC." In *Politics, Policy and Government in BC*, edited by R.K. Carty, 67–85. Vancouver: University of British Columbia Press.

Block, Sheila. 2015. *A Higher Standard: The Case for Holding Low-Wage Employers in Ontario to a Higher Standard*. Toronto: Canadian Centre for Policy Alternatives.

Blyth, Mark. 2013. *Austerity: The History of a Dangerous Idea*. New York: Oxford University Press.

Boardman, Anthony E., and Aidan R. Vining. 2012. "A Review and Assessment of Privatization in Canada." SPP Research Papers, School of Public Policy. Calgary: University of Calgary Press.

Boeri, Tito, Agar Brugiavini, and Lars Calmfors, eds. 2001. *The Role of Unions in the Twenty-First Century*. New York: Oxford University Press.

Boeri, Tito, and Jan van Ours. 2013. *The Economics of Imperfect Labor Markets*. Princeton, NJ: Princeton University Press.

Boileau, David, and Aaron Sydor. 2011. *Global Value Chains in Canada*. Ottawa: Global Affairs Canada.

Bonica, Adam, Nolan McCarty, Keith T. Poole, and Howard Rosenthal. 2013. "Why Hasn't Democracy Slowed Rising Inequality?" *Journal of Economic Perspectives* 27 (3): 103–24. https://doi.org/10.1257/jep.27.3.103.

Bordo, Michael D., Angela Redish, and Hugh Rockoff. 2015. "Why Didn't Canada Have a Banking Crisis in 2008 (or in 1930, or 1907, or …)?" *Economic History Review* 68 (1): 218–43. https://doi.org/10.1111/1468-0289.665.

Boreham, Gordon F. 1989. "The Rise of Non-Bank Financial Conglomerates: A Major Trend in the Unfolding Financial Services Sector of the Canadian Economy." *Service Industries Journal* 9 (4): 90–105. https://doi.org/10.1080/02642068900000064.

Borghi, Roberto Alexandre Zanchetta, Fernando Sarti, and Marcos Antonio Macedo Cintra. 2013. "The 'Financialized' Structure of Automobile Corporations in the 2000s." *World Review of Political Economy* 4 (3): 387–409. http://doi.org/10.13169 /worlrevipoliecon.4.3.0387.

Borjas, George. 2015. *Labor Economics*. 7th ed. New York: McGraw Hill Education.

Bortolotti, Bernardo, and Domenico Siniscalco. 2004. *The Problems of Privatization: An International Analysis*. New York: Oxford University Press.

Bosch, Gerhard, Steffen Lehndorff, and Jill Rubery. 2009. "European Employment Models in Flux: Pressures for Change and Prospects for Survival and Revitalization." In *European Employment Models in Flux: A Comparison of Institutional Change in Nine European Countries*, edited by G. Bosch, S. Lehndorff, and J. Rubery, 1–56. New York: Palgrave Macmillan.

Bosch, Gerhard, Ken Mayhew, and Jérôme Gautié. 2010. "Industrial Relations, Legal Regulations, and Wage Setting." In *Low-Wage Work in the Wealthy World*, edited by J. Gautié and J. Schmitt, 91–146. New York: Russell Sage Foundation.

Boudarbat, Brahim, Thomas Lemieux, and Craig Riddell. 2010. "The Evolution of the Returns to Human Capital in Canada, 1980–2005." IZA Discussion Papers. Bonn: IZA.

Boudreau, Julie-Anne, Roger Keil, and Doug Young. 2009. *Changing Toronto: Governing Urban Neoliberalism*. Toronto: University of Toronto Press.

Boulay, Eric. 2010. "The Evolution of the Global Financial Crisis and Cross-Border Financial Activity, 2007–2010." Canadian Economic Observer. Ottawa: Statistics Canada.

Boyer, Robert, and Daniel Drache, eds. 1996. *States against Markets: The Limits of Globalization*. New York: Routledge.

Brakman, S., Harry Garretsen, and Charles van Marrewijk. 2005. "Cross-Border Mergers and Acquisitions: On Revealed Comparative Advantage and Merger Waves." Tinbergen Institute Discussion Paper, TI 2008-013. http://dx.doi .org/10.2139/ssrn.870389.

Brady, David. 2009. *Rich Democracies, Poor People: How Politics Explain Poverty*. New York: Oxford University Press.

Brady, David, and Ryan Denniston. 2006. "Economic Globalization, Industrialization, and Deindustrialization in Affluent Democracies." *Social Forces* 85: 297–329. https://doi.org/10.1353/sof.2006.0117.

Brandolini, Andrea, and Timothy M. Smeeding. 2008. "Inequality Patterns in Western Democracies: Cross-Country Differences and Changes over Time." In *Democracy, Inequality, and Representation: A Comparative Perspective*, edited by P. Beramendi and C.J. Anderson, 25–61. New York: Russell Sage Foundation.

Brean, Donald. 2003. "Financial Liberalization in Canada: Historical, Institutional and Economic Perspectives." In *Critical Issues in International Financial Reform*, edited by A. Berry and G. Indart, 125–52. New Brunswick, NJ: Transaction Publishers.

Breau, Sébastien. 2007. "Income Inequality across Canadian Provinces in an Era of Globalization: Explaining Recent Trends." *Canadian Geographer/Le Geographe canadien* 51 (1): 72–90. http://doi.org/10.1111/j.1541-0064.2007.00166.x.

Breau, Sébastien, and David L. Rigby. 2010. "International Trade and Wage Inequality in Canada." *Journal of Economic Geography* 10 (1): 55–86. https://doi.org/10.1093/jeg/lbp016.

Brennan, Jordan. 2012. *A Shrinking Universe: How Concentrated Corporate Power Is Shaping Income Inequality in Canada.* Ottawa: Canadian Centre for Policy Alternatives.

– 2014. *The Creation of a Shared Prosperity in Canada: Unions, Corporations, and Countervailing Power.* Ottawa: Canadian Centre for Policy Alternatives.

– 2015. *Ascent of Giants. NAFTA, Corporate Power, and the Growing Income Gap.* Ottawa: Canadian Centre for Policy Alternatives.

Brenner, Robert. 2002. *The Boom and the Bubble: The US in the World Economy.* New York: Verso.

British Columbia Business Summit. 2000. "Summit Highlights." Vancouver.

British Columbia Fair Wages Commission. 2018. *BC Fair Wages Commission Report and Recommendations to the Minister of Labour.* First Report. *The Transition to a $15 Minimum Wage and Subsequent Increases.* Vancouver.

British Columbia Fiscal Review Panel. 2001. *British Columbia Fiscal Forecast and Issues 2001/02 to 2003/04.* Victoria: BC Ministry of Finance.

British Columbia Ministry of Skills Development and Labour. 2004. *A Human Resource Strategy for British Columbia.* Victoria: Queen's Printer.

Bronfenbrenner, Kate. 2007. *Global Unions: Challenging Transnational Capital through Cross-Border Campaigns.* Ithaca, NY: Cornell University Press.

Bronfenbrenner, Kate, Sheldon Friedman, Richard W. Hurd, Rudolph Oswald, and Ronald L. Seeber, eds. 1998. *Organizing to Win: New Research on Union Strategies.* Ithaca, NY: Cornell University Press.

Brooks, Neil. 2016. "Policy Forum: The Case against Boutique Tax Credits and Similar Tax Expenditures." *Canadian Tax Journal/Revue Fiscale Canadienne* 64 (1): 65–133.

Brownlee, Jamie. 2005. *Ruling Canada: Corporate Cohesion and Democracy.* Halifax: Fernwood Publishing.

Brownsey, Keith, and Michael Howlett, eds. 1992. *The Provincial State: Politics in Canada's Provinces and Territories.* Mississauga, ON: Copp Clark Pitman.

Bruff, Ian, Matthias Ebenau, and Christian May, eds. 2015. *New Directions in Comparative Capitalisms Research: Critical and Global Perspectives.* London: Palgrave MacMillan.

Bruno, Robert. 2005. "USWA-Bargained and State-Oriented Responses to the Recurrent Steel Crisis." *Labor Studies Journal* 30 (1): 67–91. https://doi.org/10.1177%2F0160449X0503000105.

Bryson, Alex, Rafael Gomez, Tobias Kretschmer, and Paul Willman. 2013. "Workplace Voice and Civic Engagement: What Theory and Data Tell Us about Unions and Their Relationship to the Democratic Process." *Osgoode Hall Law Journal* 50 (4): 965–98.

Buchanan, Bonnie G. 2016. *Securitization and the Global Economy: History and Prospects for the Future.* New York: Palgrave Macmillan.

Burgar, Joanna, and Martin Monkman. 2010. *Who Heads to the Polls? Exploring the Demographics of Voters in British Columbia.* Victoria: BC Stats.

Cadigan, Sean T. 2009. *Newfoundland and Labrador: A History.* Toronto: University of Toronto Press.

– 2010. "Organizing Offshore: Labour Relations, Industrial Pluralism, and Order in the Newfoundland and Labrador Oil Industry, 1997–2006." In *Work on Trial: Cases in Context*, edited by J. Fudge and E. Tucker, 143–71. Toronto: Osgoode Society and Irwin.

– 2012. "Boom, Bust and Bluster: Newfoundland and Labrador's 'Oil Boom' and Its Impacts on Labour." In *Boom, Bust and Crisis: Labour, Corporate Power and Politics in Canada*, edited by J. Peters, 68–83. Halifax: Fernwood Publishing.

Cafruny, Alan W., Leila Simona Talani, and Gonzalo Pozo Martin, eds. 2016. *The Palgrave Handbook of Critical International Political Economy.* London: Palgrave MacMillan.

Caledon Institute of Social Policy. 2009. *Newfoundland and Labrador: Innovative Strategies in Government-Community Collaboration.* Ottawa: Caledon Institute of Social Policy.

Calmès, Christian. 2004. *Regulatory Changes and Financial Structure: The Case of Canada.* Ottawa: Bank of Canada.

Calmès, Christian, and Ying Liu. 2009. "Financial Structure Change and Banking Income: A Canada-US Comparison." *Journal of International Financial Markets, Institutions and Money* 19 (1): 128–39. http://doi.org/10.1016/j.intfin.2007.09.003.

Calmès, Christian, and Raymond Théoret. 2013. "Market-Oriented Banking, Financial Stability and Macro-Prudential Indicators of Leverage." *Journal of International Financial Markets, Institutions and Money* 27:13–34. https://doi.org/10.1016/J.INTFIN.2013.07.004.

Cameron, Grant. 2004. "Diverse Coalition Opposes Changes to Ontario's Labour Relations Act." *Daily Commercial News and Construction Record* 77 (245): 21 December.

Camfield, David. 2000. "Assessing Resistance in Harris's Ontario, 1995–1999." In *Restructuring and Resistance: Canadian Public Policy in an Age of Global Capitalism*, edited by M. Burke, C. Mooers, and J. Shields, 306–17. Halifax: Fernwood Publishing.

– 2006. "Neoliberalism and Working-Class Resistance in British Columbia: The Hospital Employee's Union Struggle, 2002–2004." *Labour/Le Travail* 57 (Spring): 9–41. URI: https://id.erudit.org/iderudit/llt57_1art01.

– 2011a. *Canadian Labour in Crisis: Reinventing the Workers' Movement*. Halifax: Fernwood Publishing.

– 2011b. "The 'Great Recession,' the Employers' Offensive and Canadian Public Sector Unions." *Socialist Studies/Etudes Socialistes* 7 (1/2): 95–115. https://doi.org/10.18740/S4M887.

Campbell, Bruce. 2013. *The Petro-Path Not Taken: Comparing Norway with Canada and Alberta's Management of Petroleum Wealth*. Ottawa: Canadian Centre for Policy Alternatives.

Campolieti, Michele, Rafael Gomez, and Morley Gunderson. 2011. "What Accounts for the Representation Gap? Decomposing Canada-US Differences in the Desire for Collective Voice." *Journal of Industrial Relations* 53 (4): 425–49. http://doi.org/10.1177/0022185611409111.

Canada, Statistics. 2009. *The Indebtedness and Liquidity of Non-Financial Corporations*. Ottawa: Statistics Canada.

Canada–Newfoundland and Labrador Offshore Petroleum Board. 2010. Resource Management Statistics 2010. Total production. https://www.cnlopb.ca/information/statistics/.

Canada NewsWire. 2004. "Business Leaders Form Coaltion to Oppose Changes to Ontario Labour Relations Act." Canada Newswire, 16 December.

Canadian Association of Petroleum Producers. 2010. *Newfoundland and Labrador's Oil and Natural Gas Exploration and Production Industry Contributing to a Strong Provincial Economy*.

Canadian Automotive Partnership Council. 2013. *A Call to Action: II. A Report by the Manufacturing Competitiveness Committee of the Canadian Automotive Partnership Council*. Ottawa: Canadian Automotive Partnership Council.

Canadian HR Reporter. 2013. "Migrant Workers Account for Most New Jobs," 13 May. https://www.hrreporter.com/news/hr-news/migrant-workers-account-for-most-new-jobs-clc/279481.

Canadian Labour Congress. 2009. *Recession Watch Issue 3*. Ottawa: Canadian Labour Congress, Social and Economic Policy Department.

Canadian Restaurant and Foodservices Association. 2005. *Submission to Standing Committee on Social Policy 2005-Apr-26: Bill 144, Labour Relations Statute Law Amendment*. Toronto: Legislative Assembly of Ontario.

Card, David, Thomas Lemieux, and W. Craig Riddell. 2003. "Unionization and Wage Inequality: A Comparative Study of the US, the UK, and Canada." National Bureau of Economic Research. https://www.nber.org/papers/w9473.

Carmichael, Jeffrey, and Michael Pomerleano. 2002. *The Development and Regulation of Non-Bank Financial Institutions*. New York: World Bank.

Carre, Francoise, Chris Tilly, Maarten van Klaveren, and Dorothea Voss-Dahm. 2010. "Retail Jobs in Comparative Perspective." In *Low-Wage Work in the Wealthy World*, edited by J. Gautié and J. Schmitt, 211–68. New York: Russell Sage Foundation.

Carroll, Bill. 2017. "Canada's Carbon-Capital Elite: A Tangled Web of Corporate Power." *Canadian Journal of Sociology* 42 (3): 225–60. http://doi.org/10.29173/cjs28258.

Carroll, William K. 1989. "Neoliberalism and the Recomposition of Finance Capital in Canada." *Capital & Class* 13 (2): 81–112. http://doi.org/10.1177/030981688903800106.

– 2007. "From Canadian Corporate Elite to Transnational Capitalist Class: Transitions in the Organization of Corporate Power." *Canadian Review of Sociology/Revue de sociologie* 44 (3): 265–88. http://doi.org/10.1111/j.1755-618X.2007.tb01186.x.

– 2008. "The Corporate Elite and the Transformation of Finance Capital: A View from Canada." *Sociological Review* 56:44–63. http://doi.org/10.1111/j.1467-954X.2008.00761.x.

Carter, Angela. 2011. "Environmental Policy in a Petro-State: The Resource Curse and Political Ecology in Canada's Oil Frontier." PhD diss., Cornell University, Ithaca, NY.

– 2016. "The Petro-Politics of Environmental Regulation in the Tar Sands." In *First World Petro-Politics: Political Ecology and Governance in Alberta*, edited by L.B.M. Adkin, N. Krogman, and R. Haluza-Delay, 152–89. Toronto: University of Toronto Press.

– 2020. *Fossilized: Environmental Policy in Canada's Petro-Provinces*. Vancouver: UBC Press.

Carter, Angela, Gail Fraser, and Anna Zalik. 2017. "Environmental Policy Convergence in Canada's Fossil Fuel Provinces? Regulatory Streamlining, Impediments, and Drift." *Canadian Public Policy* 43 (1): 61–76. http://doi.org/10.3138/cpp.2016-041.

Carter, Angela, John Peters, and Sean Cadigan. 2014. "The Political Economy of the Labour Market in Newfoundland and Labrador." In *First among Unequals: The Premier, Politics, and Policy in Newfoundland and Labrador*, edited by A. Marland and M. Kerby, 247–64. Montreal and Kingston: McGill-Queen's University Press.

Carter, Tom. 2015. "The Canadian Housing Market: No Bubble? No Meltdown?" In *Global Housing Markets: Crises, Policies, and Institutions*, edited by A. Bardhan, R. Edelstein, and C. Kroll, 511–34. Hoboken, NJ: John Wiley and Sons.

Cassels Brock and Blackwell LLP. 2009. "Restructuring Chrysler and General Motors." In *Chambers Client Report*. Toronto: Cassels Brock and Blackwell LLP.

Castles, Francis G. 2004. *The Future of the Welfare State: Crisis Myths and Crisis Realities*. New York: Oxford University Press.

Castles, Stephen. 2006. "Guestworkers in Europe: A Resurrection?" *International Migration Review* 40 (4): 741–66. https://doi.org/10.1111/j.1747-7379.2006.00042.x.

Castles, Stephen, Hein De Haas, and Mark J. Miller. 2014. *The Age of Migration: International Population Movements in the Modern World.* 5th ed. New York: Guilford.

CBC. 2013. "Retirement Savings in Canada: By the Numbers," 4 January. https://www.cbc.ca/news/business/taxes/retirement-savings-in-canada-by-the-numbers-1.1303371.

CCPA. 2007. *Ontario Alternative Budget 2007: No Time to Lose – An Action Blueprint for Ontario.* Toronto: Canadian Centre for Policy Alternatives.

Cecchetti, Stephen G., and Enisse Kharroubi. 2013. "Why Does Financial Sector Growth Crowd Out Real Economic Growth?" BIS Working Papers. Basel, CH: Bank for International Settlements.

Celik, Serdar, and Mats Isaksson. 2014. "Institutional Investors and Ownership Engagement." *OECD Journal: Financial Market Trends*, 19 March, 93–114. http://doi.org/10.1787/fmt-2013-5jz734pwtrkc.

Centre for Constitutional Studies. 2007. *Health Services and Support: Facilities Subsector Bargaining Assn.* Edmonton: Centre for Constitutional Studies, University of Alberta.

Cerny, Philip G. 2010. "The Competition State Today: From *raison d'État* to *raison du Monde.*" *Policy Studies* 31 (1): 5–21. http://doi.org/10.1080/01442870903052801.

Cervantes, Miguel, and Fred McMahon. 2009. *Survey of Mining Companies: 2008/2009.* Vancouver: Fraser Institute.

CFIB. 2004. "CFIB Submission to the Ontario Ministry of Labour on 'Ending the 60-Hour Work Week.'" Toronto: Canadian Federation of Independent Business.

Chapman, James, Stephanie Lavoie, and Lawrence Schembri. 2011. "Emerging from the Shadows: Market-Based Financing in Canada." *Bank of Canada: Financial System Review* (June), 29–38.

Chase, Kerry A. 2003. "Economic Interests and Regional Trading Arrangements: The Case of NAFTA." *International Organization* 57 (1): 137–74. http://doi.org/10.1017/S0020818303571053.

– 2004. "From Protectionism to Regionalism: Multinational Firms and Trade-Related Investment Measures." *Business and Politics* 6 (2): 1–36. http://doi.org/10.2202/1469-3569.1067.

– 2009. *Trading Blocs: States, Firms, and Regions in the World Economy.* Ann Arbor: University of Michigan Press.

Chivers, Danny. 2015. *No-Nonsense Guide to Renewable Energy: Cleaner, Fairer Ways to Power the Planet.* Oxford: New Internationalist Publications.

Chown Oved, Marco. 2016a. "Loopholes Costing Canada Billions in Lost Revenue." *Toronto Star*, 17 June.

– 2016b. "Tax Loopholes Cost Canada Billions in Lost Revenue." *Toronto Star*, 17 June.

– 2018. "CRA Conducts First Major Raid Related to Panama Paper Leaks." *Toronto Star*, 15 February.

Citizenship and Immigration Canada. 2011. *Facts and Figures: Immigration Overview*. Ottawa: Citizenship and Immigration Canada.

– 2013. *Facts and Figures 2013*. Ottawa: Citizenship and Immigration Canada.

Clapp, Jennifer, and Eric Helleiner. 2012. "Troubled Futures? The Global Food Crisis and the Politics of Agricultural Derivatives Regulation." *Review of International Political Economy* 19 (2): 181–207. http://doi.org/10.1080/09692290.2010 .514528.

Clark, Gordon, Ashby Monk, and Courtney Monk. 2007. *Defined Benefit Coverage and Funding in Ontario: Local Experiences in a Global Context*. Oxford: Oxford University Centre for the Environment.

Clarke, Judith, Marsha Courchane, Cynthia Holmes, and Tsur Somerville. 2010. 'The Subprime Crisis: Weathering the Storm in the U.S., Canada, and Australia." Conference paper presented at Annual Meeting of the American Real Estate and Urban Economics Association. Atlanta, GA, January.

Clarke, Sean, and Lydia Couture. 2017. "Real Growth of Canadian Manufacturing since 2000." *Economic Insights*. Ottawa: Statistics Canada.

Clarkson, Stephen. 2002. *Uncle Sam and Us: Globalization, Neoconservatism, and the Canadian State*. Toronto: University of Toronto Press.

– 2008. *Does North America Exist? Governing the Continent after NAFTA and 9/11*. Toronto: University of Toronto Press.

Clausing, Kimberley. 2016. "The Nature and Practice of Tax Competition." In *Global Tax Governance*, edited by P. Dietsch and T. Rixen, 27–55. Colchester, UK: ECPR.

Clemens, Jason, and Joel Emes. 2001. "Returning British Columbia to Prosperity." In *Public Policy Sources*, 3–125. Vancouver,: Fraser Institute.

Close, David, Penelope M. Rowe, and Carla J. Wheaton. 2007. *Planning the Future of Rural Newfoundland and Labrador by Engaging the Public: From the Strategic Social Plan to the Rural Secretariat*. St. John's: Values Added Community-University Research Alliance, Community Services Council. http://envision.ca/pdf /cura/Planning_Future_Rural_NL_Jan08_07.pdf.

CMHC. 2009. *Canadian Housing Observer*. Ottawa: Canadian Mortgage and Housing Corporation. https://publications.gc.ca/collections/collection_2010/schl-cmhc/nh1 -1/NH1-1-2009-eng.pdf.

Coalition of BC Businesses. 2002. "Coalition of BC Businesses: Labour Policy Position Paper." Vancouver.

– 2011. *Labour Policies That Work: A New Vision for BC*. Vancouver: Coalition of BC Businesses.

Coates, David. 2014. "Studying Comparative Capitalisms by Going Left and by Going Deeper." *Capital and Class* 38 (1): 18–30. https://doi.org/10.1177%2F0309816813 510372.

Cobb, J. Adam. 2016. "How Firms Shape Income Inequality." *Academy of Management Review* 41 (2): 324–48. http://doi.org/10.5465/amr.2015.0364.

Cobham, Alex, and Petr Jansky. 2015. "Measuring Misalignment: The Location of US Multinationals' Economic Activity versus the Location of Their Profits." ICTD Working Paper 42. Brighton, UK: International Centre for Tax and Development.

Coe, Neil, Karen P. Lai, and Dariusz Wójcik. 2014. "Integrating Finance into Global Production Networks." *Regional Studies* 48 (5): 761–77. https://doi.org/10.1080 /00343404.2014.886772.

Coe, Neil, and Henry Wai-Chung Yeung. 2015. *Global Production Networks: Theorizing Economic Development in an Inter-Connected World.* New York: Oxford University Press.

Cohen, Marjorie Griffin. 2012. *BC Disadvantage for Women: Earnings Compared with Other Women in Canada.* Vancouver: Canadian Centre for Policy Alternatives.

Cohen, Marjorie Griffin, and Marcy Cohen. 2004. *A Return to Wage Discrimination: Pay Equity Losses through the Privatization of Health Care.* Vancouver: Canadian Centre for Policy Alternatives BC Office.

Coleman, William, and Tony Porter. 2003. "'Playin' Along': Canada and Global Finance." In *Changing Canada: Political Economy as Transformation*, edited by W. Clement and L. Vosko, 241–64. Montreal and Kingston: McGill-Queen's University Press.

Commission of Inquiry Respecting the Muskrat Falls Project. 2018. *Final Report.* St. John's. https://www.muskratfallsinquiry.ca/.

Commission of the Reform of Ontario's Public Services. 2012. *Public Services for Ontarians: A Path to Sustainability and Excellence.* Toronto: Ontario Ministry of Finance.

Competition Policy Review Panel. 2007. *Sharpening Canada's Competitive Edge.* Ottawa: Industry Canada.

– 2008. *Compete to Win: Final Report – June 2008.* Ottawa: Industry Canada.

Conference Board of Canada. 2012. *Benefits Benchmarking 2012.* Toronto: Conference Board of Canada.

– 2013. *The Private Equity Experience of Canadian Business.* Toronto: Conference Board of Canada.

– 2014. *The Private Equity Experience of Canadian Business.* Toronto: Conference Board of Canada.

– 2017. *Canadian Tax Avoidance: Examining the Potential Tax Gap.* Toronto: Conference Board of Canada.

Congressional Budget Office. 2017. *International Comparisons of Corporate Income Tax Rates.* Washington, DC: Congress of the United States.

Cooper, Morgan C. 2000. *Labour Relations Proceses on Offshore Oil and Gas Fabrication and Construction Projects.* St. John's: Labour Relations Board.

Coulter, Kendra. 2009. "Deep Neoliberal Integration: The Production of Third Way Politics in Ontario." *Studies in Political Economy* 83 (Spring): 191–208. https://doi .org/10.1080/19187033.2009.11675061.

CPP Investment Board. 2005. *Annual Report.* Toronto: Canada Pension Plan Investment Board.

Credit Suisse. 2013. *Global Wealth Report 2013*. Zurich: Credit Suisse AG.

– 2015. *Global Wealth Handbook 2015*. London: Credit Suisse.

Crettaz, Eric. 2013. "A State-of-the-Art Review of Working Poverty in Advanced Economies: Theoretical Models, Measurement Issues, and Risk Groups." *Journal of European Social Policy* 23 (4): 347–62. http://doi.org/10.1177/0958928713507470.

Cribb, Robert, and Marco Chown Oved. 2017. "Snow Washing: Canada Is the World's New Tax Haven." *Toronto Star*, 25 January.

Crompton, Rosemary. 2006. *Employment and the Family*. New York: Cambridge University Press.

Cross, P. 2008. "The Role of Natural Resources in Canada's Economy." *Canadian Economic Observer*, catalog no. 11-010-X (November), 3.1–3.10.

Cross, Philip. 2010. "Year-End Review of 2009." *Canadian Economic Observer*. Ottawa: Statistics Canada.

– 2015. *Unearthing the Full Economic Impact of Canada's Natural Resources*. Ottawa: Macdonald-Laurier Institute.

Crouch, Colin. 2006. *Post-Democracy*. Malden, MA: Polity.

– 2009. "Privatised Keynesianism: An Unacknowledged Policy Regime." *British Journal of Politics and International Relations* 11, 382–99. https://doi.org/10.1111/j.1467-856X.2009.00377.x.

– 2010. "The Global Firm: The Problem of the Giant Firm in Democratic Capitalism." In *The Oxford Handbook of Business and Government*, edited by G. Wilson, W. Grant, and D. Coen, 148–72. New York: Oxford University Press. https://doi.org/10.1093/oxfordhb/9780199214273.001.0001.

– 2011. *The Strange Non-Death of Neo-Liberalism*. Malden, MA: Polity.

– 2013. *Making Capitalism Fit for Society*. Malden, MA: Polity.

– 2014. "The Neo-Liberal Turn and the Implications for Labour." In *The Oxford Handbook of Employment Relations: Comparative Employment Relations*, edited by A. Wilkinson, G. Wood, and R. Deeg, 589–614. New York: Oxford University Press.

– 2015. *Governing Social Risks in Post-Crisis Europe*. Northampton, MA: Edward Elgar Publishing.

Culpepper, Pepper D. 2011. *Quiet Politics and Business Power: Corporate Control in Europe and Japan*. New York: Cambridge University Press.

Cusack, Thomas R., Torben Iversen, and Phillip Rehm. 2008. "Economic Shocks, Inequality, and Popular Support for Redistribution." In *Democracy, Inequality and Representation: A Comparative Perspective*, edited by C.J. Anderson and P. Beramendi, 203–31. New York: Russell Sage Foundation.

Cushman and Wakefield Lepage. 2007. *Marketbeat: Vancouver Industrial Report*. Vancouver, BC: Cushman and Wakefield Lepage.

Dabla-Norris, Era, Kalpana Kochhar, Nujin Suphaphiphat, and Evridiki Tsounta. 2015. "Causes and Consequences of Income Inequality: A Global Perspective." IMF Staff Discussion Note. New York: International Monetary Fund.

Dahl, Robert. 1982. *Dilemmas of Pluralist Democracy*. New Haven, CT: Yale University Press.

Daniels, Gary, and John McIlroy, eds. 2008. *Trade Unions in a Neo-Liberal World: The Politics of Contemporary British Trade Unionism*. London: Routledge.

Darcillon, Thibault. 2015. "How Does Finance Affect Labor Market Institutions? An Empirical Analysis in 16 OECD Countries." *Socio-Economic Review* 13 (3): 477–504. https://doi.org/10.1093/ser/mwu038.

Daudey, Emilie, and Cecilia García-Peñalosa. 2007. "The Personal and the Factor Distributions of Income in a Cross-Section of Countries." *Journal of Development Studies* 43 (5): 812–29. https://doi.org/10.1080/00220380701384406.

Davis, Gerald F. 2009. *Managed by Markets: How Finance Reshaped America*. New York: Oxford University Press.

– 2013. "After the Corporation." *Politics and Society* 41 (2): 283–308. http://doi.org/10.1177/0032329213483110.

– 2016. *The Vanishing American Corporation*. Oakland, CA: Berrett-Koehler.

Davis, Gerald F., and Suntae Kim. 2015. "Financialization of the Economy." *Annual Review of Sociology* 41:203–21. https://doi.org/10.1146/annurev-soc-073014-112402.

Day, Suzanne, April Girard, Laureen Snider, and Jordan Watters. 2009. "Rightsizing Regulation: The Competition Act, 1975–2005." *Canadian Journal of Law and Society* 24 (1): 47–67. https://doi.org/10.1017/S0829320100009765.

Deakin, Simon, and Antoine Rebérioux. 2009. "Corporate Governance, Labour Relations and Human Resource Management in the UK and France: Convergence or Divergence?" In *Does Company Ownership Matter?* edited by J-P. Touffut, 234–52. Cheltenham, UK: Edward Elgar Publishing.

Deaton, Richard. 1989. *The Political Economy of Pensions: Power, Politics, and Social Change in Canada, Great Britain, and the United States*. Vancouver: University of British Columbia Press.

Deer, Carolyn. 2000. *Net Gains: Linking Fisheries Management, International Trade and Sustainable Development*. Cambridge: IUCN – The World Conservation Union.

Del Boca, Daniela, and Cecile Wetzels, eds. 2007. *Social Policies, Labour Markets, and Motherhood: A Comparative Analysis of European Countries*. New York: Cambridge University Press.

DeMara, Bruce. 2004. "Lobbying Changes with the Times." *Toronto Star*, 12 October.

De Mooij, Ruud A. 2012. "Tax Biases to Debt Finance: Assessing the Problem, Finding Solutions." *Fiscal Studies* 33 (4): 489–512. https://doi.org/10.1111/j.1475-5890.2012.00170.x.

Dencker, John C., and Chichun Fang. 2016. "Rent Seeking and the Transformation of Employment Relationships: The Effect of Corporate Restructuring on Wage Patterns, Determinants, and Inequality." *American Sociological Review* 81 (3): 467–87. https://doi.org/10.1177%2F0003122416642419.

Deneault, Alain. 2015. *Canada: A New Tax Haven*. Vancouver: Talon Books.

Deneault, Alain, and William Sacher. 2010. *Imperial Canada Inc.: Legal Haven of Choice for the World's Mining Industries*. Vancouver: Talon Books.

Denk, Oliver. 2015. "Financial Sector Pay and Labour Income Inequality." OECD Economics Department Working Papers. Paris: OECD.

Department of Finance, Government of Newfoundland and Labrador. 2011. "Wide Range of Initiatives Provide Assistance to People Who Need It Most." News release. http://www.releases.gov.nl.ca/releases/2011/fin/0303n08.htm.

Department of Human Resources, Labour and Employment. 2005. *Reducing Poverty in Newfoundland and Labrador: Working towards a Solution*. St. John's: Government of Newfoundland and Labrador.

– 2009. *Empowering People, Engaging Community, Enabling Success*. St. John's: Government of Newfoundland and Labrador.

Detzer, Daniel, and Eckhard Hein. 2014. "Financialisation and the Financial and Economic Crisis: The Case of Germany. ." IPE Working Papers. 44/2014. Berlin: Berlin School of Economics and Law, Institute for International Political Economy.

Deutsche Bundesbank. 2014. *Private Debt* – Status Quo, *Need for Adjustment and Policy Implications*. Monthly report. Cologne. https://www.bundesbank.de /resource/blob/622260/a5162703e1eafd6f2a918d046f86ee9a/mL/2014-01-privat -debt-data.pdf.

Devereux, Michael, Katarzyna Habu, Strahil Lepove, and Giorgia Maffini. 2016. *G20 Corporation Tax Ranking*. Oxford: Oxford University Centre for Business Taxation.

Dicken, Peter. 2015. *Global Shift: Mapping the Changes Contours of the World Economy*. 7th ed. New York: Sage Publications.

Dickie, Patrick. 2005. *The Crisis in Union Organizing under the BC Liberals*. Vancouver: Hastings Labour Law Office.

Dionne, George, and Tarek Harchaoui. 2007. "Banks' Capital, Securitization, and Credit Risk: an Empirical Evidence." MPRA Paper. 56693, Munich: University Library of Munich.

Dobbin, Murray. 1998. *The Myth of the Good Corporate Citizen*. Toronto: Stoddart.

Doellgast, Virginia, Nathan Lillie, and Valeria Pulignano, eds. 2018. *Reconstructing Solidarity: Labour Unions, Precarious Work, and the Politics of Institutional Change in Europe*. New York: Oxford University Press.

Dorfmann, Jessica. 2015. "New Wealth Seeks a 'Home': The Global Rise of the Hedge City." *Harvard International Review* 36 (3): 4–6.

Duménil, G., and D. Lévy. 2004. *Capital Resurgent: Roots of the Neoliberal Revolution*. Cambridge, MA: Harvard University Press.

– 2011. *The Crisis of Neoliberalism*. Cambridge, MA: Harvard University Press.

Dundon, Tony, and Gregory Gall, eds. 2013. *Global Anti-Unionism: Nature, Dynamics, Trajectories, and Outcomes*. New York: Palgrave Macmillan.

Duprey, Thibaut, Tim Grieder, and Dylan Hogg. 2017. "Recent Evolution of Canada's Credit-to-GDP Gap: Measurement and Interpretation." *Bank of Canada Staff Analytical Notes*, Ottawa: Bank of Canada. https://doi.org/10.34989/san-2017-25.

Dupuis, Mathieu, John Peters, and Phillippe J. Scrimger. 2020. "Financialization and Union Decline in Canada: The Influence on Sectors and Core Industries." *Competition & Change* 24 (3–4): 268–90. https://doi.org/10.1177/1024529420930323.

Durand, Cedric. 2017. *Fictitious Capital: How Finance Is Appropriating Our Future.* New York: Verso.

Dribbusch, Heiner, and Peter Birke. 2019. *Trade Unions in Germany: Challenges in a Time of Transition.* Dusseldorf: Friedrich-Ebert-Stiftung, International Policy Analysis.

Dupuis, Mathieu, John Peters, and Phillippe J. Scrimger. 2020. "Financialization and Union Decline in Canada: The Influence on Sectors and Core Industries." *Competition & Change* 24 (3–4): 268–90. https://doi.org/10.1177 /1024529420930323.

Durufle, Gilles. 2009. *Why Venture Capital Is Essential to the Canadian Economy: The Impact of Venture Capital on the Canadian Economy.* Toronto: Canada's Venture Capital and Private Equity Association. http://en.ebdata.com/wp-content /uploads/2012/04/CVCA_VC_Impact_Study_Jan_2009_Final_English.pdf.

Ebbinghaus, Bernhard. 2015. "The Privatization and Marketization of Pensions in Europe: A Double Transformation Facing the Crisis." European Policy Analysis 1 (1): 56–73. https://doi.org/10.18278/epa.1.1.5.

Economic Policy Institute. 2015. *Top CEOs Make 300 Times More Than Typical Workers.* Washington, DC: Economic Policy Institute.

Economist. 2014. "The Repurchase Revolution." 12 September.

Edwards, Tony J. 2013. "Control over Employment Practice in Multinationals: Subsidiary Functions, Corporate Structures, and National Systems." *ILR Review* 66 (3): 670–95. http://doi.org/10.1177/001979391306600305.

Egan, David. 2001. *State of the BC Seafood Industry Report: BC Seafood Summit.* Vancouver: PricewaterhouseCoopers.

Eidlin, Barry. 2015. "Class vs. Special Interest: Labor, Power, and Politics in the United States and Canada in the Twentieth Century." *Politics and Society* 43 (2): 181–211. https://doi.org/10.1177/0032329215571280.

– 2018. *Labor and the Class Idea in the United States and Canada.* Cambridge: Cambridge University Press.

Elections BC. 2001–10. *Financial Reports and Political Contributions System.* Victoria: Elections BC.

Elections BC. n.d. "General Election Statistics in Comparison, 1928–2009." Vancouver: Elections BC. https://elections.bc.ca/resources/statistics/.

Elections Ontario. n.d. "Graphics & Charts – Historical Voter Turnout." Toronto: Elections Ontario. https://results.elections.on.ca/en/graphics-charts.

Emmenegger, Patrick. 2014. *The Power to Dismiss: Trade Unions and the Regulation of Job Security in Western Europe.* New York: Oxford University Press.

Emmenegger, Patrick, and Romana Careja. 2012. "From Dilemma to Dualization: Social and Migration Policies in the 'Reluctant Countries of Immigration.'" In

The Age of Dualization, edited by P. Emmenegger, S. Hausermann, B. Palier, and M. Seeleib-Kaiser, 124–50. New York: Oxford University Press.

Emmenegger, Patrick, Silja Hausermann, Bruno Palier, and Martin Seeleib-Kaiser. 2011. "Why We Grow More Unequal." In *The Age of Dualization: The Changing Face of Inequality in De-industrializing Societes*, edited by P. Emmenegger, S. Hausermann, B. Palier, and M. Seeleib-Kaiser, 3–26. New York: Oxford University Press.

– eds. 2012. *The Age of Dualization: The Changing Face of Inequality in De-industrializing Societies*. New York: Oxford University Press.

Engelen, Ewald, Ismail Erturk, Julie Froud, Sukhdev Johal, Adam Leaver, Michael Moran, Adriana Nilsson, and Karel Williams. 2011. *After the Great Complacence: Financial Crisis and the Politics of Reform*. New York: Oxford University Press.

Epstein, Gerald. 2005. "Introduction: Financialization and the World Economy." In *Financialization and the World Economy*, edited by G. Epstein, 3–18. Northampton, MA: Edward Elgar.

– 2015. "Financialization: There's Something Happening Here." Working Paper Series. Amherst, MA: Political Economy Research Institute – University of Massachusetts Amherst.

Erwin, Steve. 2005. "Premier Denies Former Advisor-Turned-Lobbyist Contacted Him over Nukes." Canadian Press NewsWire, 5 December.

Esping-Anderson, Gosta. 1999. *Social Foundations of Post-Industrial Economies*. New York: Oxford University Press.

Etchemendy, Sebastian. 2011. *Models of Economic Liberalization*. New York: Cambridge University Press.

European Commission. 2012. *Tackling the Financial Crisis: Banks*. Brussels: European Commission.

Evans, Bryan. 2011. "The Politics of Public Sector Wages: Ontario's Social Dialogue for Austerity." *Socialist Studies/Études socialistes* 7 (1/2): 171–90.

– 2013. "When Your Boss Is the State: The Paradoxes of Public Sector Work." In *Public Sector Unions in the Age of Austerity*, edited by S. Ross and L. Savage, 18–30. Halifax: Fernwood Publishing.

Evans, Bryan, Carlo Fanelli, and Tom McDowell. 2021. "Resisting Low-Wage Work: The Struggle for Living Wages." In *Rising Up: The Fight for Living Wage Work in Canada*, edited by B. Evans, C. Fanelli, and T. McDowell, 3–28. Vancouver: University of British Columbia Press.

Evans, Bryan, and Stephen McBride, eds. 2017. *The Austerity State*. Toronto: University of Toronto Press.

Evans, Bryan, and Charles W. Smith. 2015a. "The Transformation of Ontario Politics: The Long Ascent of Neoliberalism." In *Transforming Provincial Politics: The Political Economy of Canada's Provinces and Territories in the Neoliberal Era*, edited by B. Evans and C.W. Smith, 162–91. Toronto: University of Toronto Press.

– eds. 2015b. *Transforming Provincial Politics: The Political Economy of Canada's Provinces and Territories in the Neoliberal Era*. Toronto: University of Toronto Press.

Fairbrother, Peter. 2014. "Unions: Practices and Prospects." In *The Oxford Handbook of Employment Relations: Comparative Employment Systems*, edited by A. Wilkinson, G. Wood, and R. Deeg, 637–54. New York: Oxford University Press.

Fairbrother, Peter, and Charlotte A.B. Yates, eds. 2003. *Trade Unions in Renewal: A Comparative Study*. New York: Continuum.

Fairey, David. 2005. *Eroding Worker Protections: British Columbia's New "Flexible" Employment Standards*. Vancouver: Canadian Centre Policy Alternatives BC Office.

Fairey, David B. 2009. "Exclusion of Unionized Workers from Employment Standards Law." *Relations industrielles/Industrial Relations* 64 (1): 112–33.

Fairey, David, Christina Hanson, Glen MacInnes, Arlene Tigar McLaren, Gerardo Otero, Kerry Prebisch, and Mark Thompson. 2008. *Cultivating Farmworker Rights: Ending the Exploitation of Immigrant and Migrant Farmworkers in BC*. Vancouver: Canadian Centre for Policy Alternatives BC Office.

Fairey, David, John Peters, and Tom Sandborn. 2012. "The 'Biggest Roll Back of Worker Rights in Canadian History': The Campbell Government and Labour Market Deregulation in British Columbia." In *Boom, Bust, and Crisis: Work and Labour in 21st Century Canada*, edited by J. Peters, 104–24. Halifax: Fernwood Publishing.

Fanelli, Carlo, and Mark Thomas. 2011. "Austerity, Competitiveness, and Neoliberalism Redux: Ontario Responds to the Great Recession." *Socialist Studies* 7 (1/2): 141–70. http://doi.org/10.18740/S4BS31.

Fattouh, Bassam, Lutz Kilian, and Lavan Mahadeva. 2013. "The Role of Speculation in Oil Markets: What Have We Learned so Far?" *Energy Journal*, 34 (3): 7–33. http://doi.org/10.5547/01956574.34.3.2.

Ferguson, Charles. 2012. *Inside Job: The Financiers Who Pulled Off the Heist of the Century*. London: Oneworld Publications.

Ferguson, Niall. 2008. *The Ascent of Money: A Financial History of the World*. New York: Penguin.

Ferguson, Rob, Robert Benzie, and Tanya Talaga. 2012. "Caterpillar Closes Electro-Motive Plant in London." *Toronto Star*, 3 February.

Fernandez, Rodrigo, and Manuel Aalbers. 2016. "Financialization and Housing: Between Globalization and Varieties of Capitalism." *Competition and Change* 22 (2): 71–88. https://doi.org/10.1177/1024529415623916.

Ferreras, Isabelle. 2017. *Firms as Political Entities: Saving Democracy through Economic Bicameralism*. Cambridge: Cambridge University Press.

Flaherty, Eoin. 2015. "Top Incomes under Finance-Driven Capitalism, 1990–2010: Power Resources and Regulatory Orders." *Socio-Economic Review* 13 (3): 417–47. https://doi.org/10.1093/ser/mwv011.

Fletcher, Bill, and Fernando Gapasin. 2008. *Solidarity Divided: The Crisis in Organized Labor and a New Path towards Social Justice*. Berkeley: University of California Press.

Fligstein, Neil, and Taekjin Shin. 2007. "Shareholder Value and the Transformation of the U.S. Economy, 1984–2000." *Sociological Forum* 22 (4): 399–424. https://doi.org/10.1111/j.1573-7861.2007.00044.x.

Forhoohar, Rana. 2016. *Makers and Takers: The Rise and Fall of American Business.* New York: Crown Publishing.

Fossum, John Erik. 1997. *Oil, the State, and Federalism: The Rise and Demise of Petro-Canada as a Statist Impulse.* Toronto: University of Toronto Press.

Foster, Jason, and Bob Barnetson. 2015. "Exporting Oil, Importing Labour, and Weakening Democracy: The Use of Foreign Migrant Workers in Alberta." In *Alberta Oil and the Decline of Democracy in Canada*, edited by M. Shrivstava and L. Stefanick. Edmonton: Athabasca University Press.

Fougère, Maxime. 2002. "RRSP Savings and the Aging of the Baby Boom Generation." *Canadian Tax Journal* 50 (2): 524–49. https://heinonline.org/HOL/LandingPage? handle=hein.journals/cdntj50&div=31&id=&page=.

Frangi, Lorenzo, and Marc-Antonin Hennebert. 2015. "Expressing Confidence in Unions in Quebec and Other Canadian Provinces." *Relations industrielle/Industrial Relations* 70 (1): 131–56. https://doi.org/10.7202/1029283ar.

Fraser Institute. 1999. *Challenging Perceptions: Twenty-Five Years of Influential Ideas, 1974–1999.* Vancouver: Fraser Institute.

– 2001. *Annual Report.* Vancouver: Fraser Institute.

Freeman, Richard. 2008. *Labor Market Institutions around the World.* London: London School of Economic and Political Science, Centre for Economic Performance.

Frege, Carola M., and John Kelly, eds. 2004. *Varieties of Unionism: Strategies for Union Revitalization in a Globalizing Economy.* New York: Oxford University Press.

Friendly, Martha, and Susan Prentice. 2009. *About Canada: Childcare.* Halifax: Fernwood Publishing.

Fritzell, Johan. 1993. "Income Inequality Trends in the 1980s: A Five-Country Comparison." *Acta Sociologica* 36 (1): 47–62. http://doi.org/10.1177/000169939303 600104.

Froud, Julie, Sukhdev Johal, Adam Leaver, and Karel Williams. 2006. *Financialization and Strategy: Narrative and Numbers.* New York: Routledge.

Fuchs, Doris. 2007. *Business Power in Global Governance.* Boulder, CO: Lynne Rienner Publishers.

Fudge, Judy. 2007. "The New Discourse of Labour Rights: From Social to Fundamental Rights." *Comparative Labour Law and Policy Journal* 29 (1): 29–66.

– 2012. "Constitutional Rights, Collective Bargaining and the Supreme Court of Canada: Retreat and Reversal in the Fraser Case." *Industrial Law Journal* 41 (1): 1–29. http://doi.org/10.1093/indlaw/dwr026.

Fudge, Judy, and Kendra Strauss, eds. 2014. *Temporary Work, Agencies, and Unfree Labour: Insecurity in the New World of Work.* New York: Routledge.

Fusco, Leah. 2007. "Offshore Oil: An Overview of Development in Newfoundland and Labrador." St. John's: Memorial University of Newfoundland. http://www.ucs .mun.ca/~oilpower/documents/NL%20oil%207-25-1.pdf.

Galabuzi, Grace-Edward. 2006. *Canada's Economic Apartheid: The Social Exclusion of Racialized Groups in the New Country.* Toronto: Canadian Scholars' Press.

Gall, Gregory, Richard Hurd, and Adrian Wilkinson, eds. 2011. *The International Handbook of Labour Unions: Responses to Neo-Liberalism*. Northhampton, MA: Edward Elgar.

Galt, Virginia. 1992. "Business Finds Solidarity in War of Ideologies." *Globe and Mail*, 4 February.

Garrett, Geoffrey. 1998. *Partisan Politics in the Global Economy*. New York: Cambridge University Press.

Gautie, Jerome, and John Schmitt, eds. 2010. *Low-Wage Work in the Wealthy World*. New York: Russell Sage Foundation.

Gellatly, Mary, John Grundy, Kiran Mirchandani, Adam Perry, Mark Thomas, and Leah Vosko. 2011. "'Modernizing' Employment Standards? Administrative Efficiency, Market Regulation, and the Production of the Illegitimate Claimant in Ontario, Canada." *Economic and Labour Relations Review* 22 (2): 81–106. https://doi.org/10.1177/103530461102200205.

Genschel, Phillip, and Peter Schwarz. 2013. "Tax Competition and Fiscal Democracy." In *Politics in the Age of Austerity*, edited by A. Schafer and W. Streeck, 59–83. Malden, MA: Polity.

George, Alexander L., and Andrew Bennett. 2005. *Case Study and Theory Development in the Social Sciences*. Boston: MIT Press.

George, Susan. 2015. *Shadow Sovereigns: How Global Corporations Are Seizing Power*. Malden, MA: Polity.

Gertel, Jörg, and Sarah Ruth Sippel. 2016. "The Financialization of Agriculture and Food." In *International Handbook of Rural Studies*, edited by M. Shucksmith and D. Brown. 215–26. New York: Routledge.

Ghosh, Jayati, James Heintz, and Robert Pollin. 2012. "Speculation on Commodities Futures Markets and Destabilization of Global Food Prices: Exploring the Connections." *International Journal of Health Services* 42 (3): 465–83. http://doi.org/10.2190/HS.42.3.f.

Gilens, Martin. 2012. *Affluence and Influence: Economic Inequality and Political Power in America*. Princeton, NJ: Princeton University Press.

Gindin, Sam. 2011. "Unionism, Austerity, and the Left." *Bullet*, 10 May.

Gindin, Sam, and Michael Hurley. 2010. "The Public Sector: Searching for a Focus." *Bullet*, 15 May.

Gitlin, Tood. 2012. *Occupy Nation: The Roots, the Spirit, and the Promise of Occupy Wall Street*. New York: Itbooks/Harper Collins.

Gittell, Jody Hoffer, Kim Cameron, Sandy Lim, and Victor Rivas. 2006. "Relationships, Layoffs, and Organizational Resilience: Airline Industry Responses to September 11." *Journal of Applied Behavioral Science* 42 (3): 300–29. http://doi.org/10.1177/0021886306286466.

Gkanoutas-Leventis, Angelos, and Anastasia Nesvetailova. 2015. "Financialisation, Oil and the Great Recession." *Energy Policy* 86:891–902.

Glassner, Vera, Maarten Keune, and Paul Marginson. 2011. "Collective Bargaining in a Time of Crisis: Developments in the Private Sector in Europe." *Transfer: European Review of Labour and Research* 17 (3): 303–22. https://doi.org/10.1177/1024258911406378.

Globe and Mail. 2002. "Campbell's Breach." 30 January.

Glyn, Andrew. 2006. *Capitalism Unleashed: Finance Globalization and Welfare*. New York: Oxford University Press.

Godechot, Olivier. 2012. "Is Finance Responsible for the Rise in Wage Inequality in France?" *Socio-Economic Review* 10 (3): 447–70. http://doi.org/10.1093/ser/mws003.

– 2016. "Financialization Is Marketization! A Study of the Respective Impacts of Various Dimensions of Financialization on the Increase in Global Inequality." *Sociological Science* 3:495–519. http://doi.org/10.15195/v3.a22.

Gospel, Howard, and Andrew Pendleton, eds. 2005. *Corporate Governance and Labour Management: An International Comparison*. New York: Oxford University Press.

Gospel, Howard, Andrew Pendleton, and Sigurt Vitols. 2013. *Financialization, New Investment Funds, and Labour: An International Comparison*. New York: Oxford University Press.

Government of Newfoundland and Labrador. 2008. "Budget Highlights," 29 April. http://www.budget.gov.nl.ca/Budget2008/highlights.htm.

– 2009. "Budget 2009: Budget Highlights." http://www.budget.gov.nl.ca/budget2009/highlights/default.htm.

Goyer, Michel. 2009. "Varieties of Institutional Investors and National Models of Capitalism: The Transformation of Corporate Governance in France and Germay." In *European Corporate Governance: Readings and Perspectives*, edited by T. Clarke and J.-F. Chanlat, 233–52. New York: Routledge.

Grady, Jo, and Melanie Simms. 2018. "Trade Unions and the Challenge of Fostering Solidarities in an Era of Financialisation." *Economic and Industrial Democracy* 40 (3): 490–510. https://doi.org/10.1177%2F0143831X18759792.

Graham, Nicholas, Shannon Daub, and Bill Carroll. 2017. *Mapping Political Influence: Political Donations and Lobbying by the Fossil Fuel Industry*. Vancouver: Canadian Centre for Policy Alternatives.

Gravelle, Toni, Timothy Grieder, and Stephanie Lavoie. 2013. "Monitoring and Assessing Risks in Canada's Shadow Banking Sector." *Financial System Review* (June), 55–63.

Gray, Jeff. 2011. "Invasion of the Giant Law Firms." *Globe and Mail*, 15 March.

– 2014. "Bay Street Law Firm Denies Allegations of Conflict of Interest in GM Lawsuit." *Globe and Mail*, 10 September.

Green, David, and Benjamin Sand. 2015. "Has the Canadian Labour Market Polarized?" In *Income Inequality: The Canadian Story*, edited by D. Green, C. Riddell, and F. St-Hilaire, 217–28. Montreal: Institute for Research on Public Policy.

Greer, Ian, and Virginia Doellgast. 2017. "Marketization, Inequality, and Institutional Change: Toward a New Framework for Comparative Employment Relations." *Journal of Industrial Relations* 59 (2): 192–208. https://doi.org/10.1177/0022185616673685.

Griffin Cohen, Marjorie, and Seth Klein. 2011. "Poverty Reduction in British Columbia? How 'The Best Place on Earth' Keeps People Poorest." *Canadian Review of Social Policy* 65–6.

Grimshaw, Damian, Stefania Marino, Dominique Anxo, Jérôme Gautié, Laszlo Neumann, and Claudia Weinkopf. 2018. "Negoiating Better Conditions for Workers during Austerity in Europe." In *Reconstructing Solidarity: Labour Unions, Precarious Work and the Politics of Institutional Change in Europe*, edited by V. Doellgast, N. Lillie, and V. Pulignano, 42–62. New York: Oxford University Press.

Grossman, Emiliano, and Cornelia Woll. 2013. "Saving the Banks: The Political Economy of Bailouts." *Comparative Political Studies* 47 (4): 1–27. https://doi.org/10.1177/0010414013488540.

Gumbrell-McCormick, Rebecca, and Richard Hyman. 2013. *Trade Unions in Western Europe*. New York: Oxford University Press.

Gunnoe, Andrew. 2014. "The Political Economy of Institutional Landownership: Neorentier Society and the Financialization of Land." *Rural Sociology* 79 (4): 478–504. https://doi.org/10.1111/ruso.12045.

– 2016. "The Financialization of the US Forest Products Industry: Socio-Economic Relations, Shareholder Value, and the Restructuring of an Industry." *Social Forces* 94 (3): 1075–101. https://doi.org/10.1093/sf/sov108.

Guttmann, Robert. 2016. *Finance-Led Capitalism: Shadow Banking, Re-Regulation, and the Future of Global Markets*. New York: Palgrave Macmillan.

Haberly, Daniel, and Dariusz Wójcik. 2014. "Tax Havens and the Production of Offshore FDI: An Empirical Analysis." *Journal of Economic Geography* 15 (1): 75–101. https://doi.org/10.1093/jeg/lbu003.

Hacker, Jacob, and Paul Pierson. 2010a. *Winner-Take-All Politics: How Washington Made the Rich Richer, and Turned Its Back on the Middle Class*. New York: Simon & Schuster.

– 2010b. "Winner-Take-All Politics: Public Policy, Political Organization, and the Precipitous Rise of Top Incomes in the United States." *Politics and Society* 38 (2): 152–204. http://doi.org/10.1177/0032329210365042.

Hacker, Jacob S. 2006. *The Great Risk Shift: The Assault on American Jobs, Families, Health Care, and Retirement and How You Can Fight Back*. Oxford: Oxford University Press.

Hacker, Jacob S., Suzanne Mettler, and Dianne Pinderhughes. 2007. "Inequality and Public Policy." In *Inequality and American Democracy*, edited by L.R. Jacobs and T. Skocpol, 156–213. New York: Russell Sage Foundation.

Hacker, Jacob S., and Paul Pierson. 2005. *Off Center: The Republican Revolution and the Erosion of American Democracy*. New Haven, CT: Yale University Press.

– 2016. *American Amnesia: How the War on Government Led Us to Forget What Made America Prosper*. New York: Simon and Schuster.

Hall, Peter A. 2015. "The Changing Role of the State in Liberal Market Economies." In *The Oxford Handbook of Transformations of the State*, edited by S. Leibfred, E. Huber, M. Lange, J.D. Levy. and J.D. Stephens, 426–44. New York: Oxford University Press.

Hall, Peter A., and David Soskice, eds. 2001. *Varieties of Capitalism: The Institutional Foundations of Comparative Advantage*. New York: Cambridge University Press.

Hamann, Kerstin, and John Kelly. 2004. "Unions as Political Actors: A Recipe for Revitalization?" In *Varieties of Unionism: Strategies for Union Revitalization in a Globalizing Economy*, edited by C.M. Frege and J. Kelly, 93–116. New York: Oxford University Press.

– 2010. *Parties, Elections, and Social Pacts*. New York: Routledge.

– 2011. *Parties, Elections, and Policy Reforms in Western Europe*. New York: Routledge.

Hampton, Paul. 2015. *Workers and Trade Unions for Climate Solidarity: Tackling Climate Change in a Neoliberal World*. New York: Routledge.

Hancké, Bob, Martin Rhodes, and Mark Thatcher. 2008. "Introduction: Beyond Varieties of Capitalism." In *Beyond Varieties of Capitalism: Conflict, Contradiction, and Complementarities in the European Economy*, edited by B. Hancké, M. Rhodes, and M. Thatcher, 3–38. New York: Oxford University Press.

Handler, Joel. 2004. *Social Citizenship and Workfare in the United States and Western Europe*. New York: Cambridge University Press.

Hardt, Michael, and Antonio Negri. 2011. "The Fight for 'Real Democracy' at the Heart of Occupy Wall Street." *Foreign Affairs* no. 11 (October) Snapshot.

Harvey, David. 2006. *A Brief History of Neoliberalism*. New York: Oxford University Press.

– 2010. *The Enigma of Capital and the Crises of Capitalism*. London: Profile Books.

Harvey, Geraint, and Peter Turnbull. 2015. "Can Labor Arrest the 'Sky Pirates'? Transnational Trade Unionism in the European Civil Aviation Industry." *Journal of Labor History* 56 (3): 308–26. http://doi.org/10.1080/0023656X.2015.1042775.

Hassel, Anke, Marek Naczyk, and Tobias Wiß. 2019. "The Political Economy of Pension Financialisation: Public Policy Responses to the Crisis." *Journal of European Public Policy* 26 (4): 483–500. https://doi.org/10.1080/13501763.2019.1575455.

Hassel, Anke, and Waltrud Schelke. 2013. "The Policy Consensus Ruling European Political Economy: The Political Attraction of Discredited Economics." *Global Policy* 3 (1): 16–27. https://doi.org/10.1111/1758-5899.12012.

Hausermann, Silja. 2010. *The Politics of Welfare State Reform in Continental Europe*. New York: Cambridge University Press.

Hay, Colin. 2009. "Good Inflation, Bad Inflation: The Housing Boom, Economic Growth and the Disaggregation of Inflationary Pressures in the UK and Ireland." *British Journal of Politics and International Relations* 11 (3): 461–78. https://doi.org/10.1111/j.1467-856X.2009.00380.x.

Hay, Colin, and Daniel Wincott. 2012. *The Political Economy of Welfare Capitalism.* New York: Palgrave Macmillan.

Hayter, Roger. 2000. *Flexible Crossroads: The Restructuring of British Columbia's Forest Economy.* Vancouver: UBC Press.

– 2003. "'The War in the Woods': Post-Fordist Restructuring, Globalization, and the Contested Remapping of British Columbia's Forest Economy." *Annals of the Association of American Geographers* 93 (3): 706–29. https://doi.org/10.1111 /1467-8306.9303010.

Hayter, Rodger, and T.J. Barnes. 1992. "Labour Market Segmentation, Flexibility, and Recession: A British Columbian Case Study." *Environment and Planning C: Government and Policy* 10 (3): 333–53. http://doi.org/10.1068/c100333.

Healey, Joseph F., Andi Stepnick, and Eileen O'Brien. 2018. *Race, Ethnicity, Gender, and Class: The Sociology of Group Conflict and Change.* Thousand Oaks, CA: Sage Publications.

Hein, Eckhard. 2015. "Finance-Dominated Capitalism and Re-distribution of Income: A Kaleckian Perspective." *Cambridge Journal of Economics* 39 (3): 907–34.

Hein, Eckhard, Daniel Detzer, and Nina Dodig. 2016. *Financialisation and the Financial and Economic Crises: Country Studies.* Cheltenham, UK: Edward Elgar Publishing.

Heisz, Andrew. 2015. "Trends in Income Inequality in Canada and Elsewhere." In *Income Inequality: The Canadian Story,* edited by D. Green, C. Riddell, and F. St-Hilaire, 77–102. Montreal: Institute for Reseach on Public Policy.

Helleiner, Eric. 1994. *States and the Reemergence of Global Finance: From Bretton Woods to the 1990s.* Ithaca, NY: Cornell University Press.

– 1995. "Explaining the Globalization of Financial Markets: Bringing States Back In." *Review of International Political Economy* 2 (2): 315–41. https://doi.org /10.1080/09692299508434322.

Hellowell, Mark, and Allyson Pollock. 2007. *Private Finance and Public Deficits: A Report on the Costs of PFI and its Impact on Health Services in England.* Edinburgh: Centre for International Public Health Policy.

Hemerijck, Anton. 2012. *Changing Welfare States.* New York: Oxford University Press.

Hemingway, Alex, and David Macdonald. 2018. "Whose Wealth Is It Anyway? BC's Top 10 Billionaires and the Rest of US." Policy Note. Vancouver: Canadian Centre for Policy Alternatives. https://www.policynote.ca/bc-billionaires/.

Hennebry, Jenna. 2012. *Permanently Temporary? Agricultural Migrant Workers and Their Integration in Canada.* Montreal: Institute for Research on Public Policy.

Hennessy, Trish, Kaylie Tiessen, and Armine Yalnizyan. 2013. *Making Every Job a Good Job: A Benchmark for Setting Ontario's Minimum Wage.* Toronto: Canadian Centre for Policy Alternatives.

Hermann, Christoph. 2014. "Structural Adjustment and Neoliberal Convergence in Labour Markets and Welfare: The Impact of the Crisis and Austerity Measures on European Economic and Social Models." *Competition & Change* 18 (2): 111–30. http://doi.org/10.1179/1024529414Z.00000000051.

Hermann, Christoph, and Jörg Flecker, eds. 2012. *Privatization of Public Services: Impacts for Employment, Working Conditions, and Service Quality in Europe.* New York: Routledge.

Herrnson, Paul. 2008. *Congressional Elections: Campaigning at Home and in Washington.* 5th ed. Washington, DC: CQ.

Heyes, Jason, and Paul Lewis. 2013. "Employment Protection under Fire: Labour Market Deregulation and Employment in the European Union." *Economic and Industrial Democracy* 35 (4):1–21. http://doi.org/10.1177/0143831X13491842.

Hibbs, Douglas A. 1987. *The Political Economy of Industrial Democracies.* Cambridge, MA: Harvard University Press.

Hillel, Inez. 2020. *Holes in the Social Safety Net: Poverty, Inequality, and Social Assistance in Canada.* Ottawa: Centre for the Study of Living Standards. http://www.csls.ca/reports/csls2020-02.pdf.

Hobsbawm, Eric. 1995. *The Age of Extremes 1914–1991.* London: Abacus.

Hodge, Graeme, and Diana Bowman. 2006. "The 'Consultocracy': The Business of Reforming Government." In *Privatization and Market Development: Global Movements in Public Policy Ideas*, edited by G. Hodge, 97–126. Northampton, MA: Edward Elgar.

Holmes, John. 2015. "Labour Relations and Human Resource Management in the Automotive Industry: North American Perspectives." In *The Global Automotive Industry*, edited by P. Nieuwenhuis and P. Wells, 67–82. Hoboken: Wiley Online Library. https://doi.org/10.1002/9781118802366.ch7.

Holmes, John, and Austin Hracs. 2010. "The Transportation Equipment Industry." In *What Do We Know? What Do We Need to Know? The State of Canadian Research on Work, Employment, and Climate Change*, edited by C. Lipsig-Mumme, 127–46. Toronto: York University Press.

Hood, Christopher. 2011. *The Blame Game: Spin, Bureaucracy, and Self-Preservation in Government.* Princeton, NJ: Princeton University Press.

Hopkin, Jonathan, and Julia Lynch. 2016. "Winner-Take-All Politics in Europe? European Inequality in Comparative Perspective." *Politics & Society* 44 (3): 335–43. http://doi.org/10.1177/0032329216656844.

Horn, Laura. 2012. *Regulating Corporate Governance in the EU.* Basingstoke, UK: Palgrave Macmillan.

House, John Douglas. 2002. *The Challenge of Oil: Newfoundland's Quest for Controlled Development.* St. John's, NL: Institute of Social and Economic Research, Memorial University of Newfoundland.

– 2003. "Does Community Really Matter in Newfoundland and Labrador? The Need for Supportive Capacity in the New Regional Economic Development." In *Retrenchment and Regeneration in Rural Newfoundland*, edited by R. Byron, 226–67. Toronto: University of Toronto Press.

Howell, Chris. 2005. *Trade Unions and the State: The Construction of Industrial Relations in Britain, 1890–2000.* Princeton, NJ: Princeton University Press.

– 2015. "The Changing Relationship between Labor and the State in Contemporary Capitalism." *Law, Culture and the Humanities* 11 (1): 6–16. https://doi.org/10.1177/1743872112448362.

– 2016. "Regulating Class in the Neoliberal Era: The Role of the State in the Restructuring of Work and Employment Relations." *Work, Employment & Society* 30, no. 4, 573–89. http://doi.org/10.1177/0950017015595954.

Huber, Evelyne, and John D. Stephens. 2001. *Development and Crisis of the Welfare State: Parties and Policies in Global Markets*. Chicago: University of Chicago Press.

Huizinga, H., and L. Jonung, eds. 2005. *The Internationalization of Foreign Ownership in Europe*. New York: Cambridge University Press.

Hulchanski, David J. 2010. *The Three Cities within Toronto: Income Polarization among Toronto's Neighbourhoods, 1970–2005*. Toronto: Cities Centre, University of Toronto.

Humphreys, Macartan, Jeffrey D. Sachs, and Joseph E. Stiglitz. 2007. *Escaping the Resource Curse*, edited by M. Humphreys, J.D. Sachs and J.E. Stiglitz. New York: Columbia University Press.

Huo, Jingjing. 2009. *Third Way Reforms: Social Democracy after the Golden Age*. New York: Cambridge University Press.

Hurley, Jeremiah, and G. Emmanuel Guindon. 2008. "Private Health Insurance in Canada." CHEPA Working Paper Series. Hamilton, ON: Centre for Health Economics and Policy Analysis.

Hyde, Allen, Todd Vachon, and Michael Wallace. 2018. "Financialization, Income Inequality, and Redistribution in 18 Affluent Democracies, 1981–2011." *Social Currents* 5 (2): 193–211. https://doi.org/10.1177%2F2329496517704874.

Hyman, Richard. 2008. "The State in Industrial Relations." In *The Sage Handbook of Industrial Relations*, edited by E. Heery, N. Bacon, P. Blyton, and J. Fiorito, 258–84. Thousand Oaks, CA: Sage Publications.

Ibsen, Christian Lyhne, and Kathleen Thelen. 2017. "Diverging Solidarity: Labor Strategies in the New Knowledge Economy." *World Politics* 69 (3): 409–47. https://doi.org/10.1017/S0043887117000077.

IGOPP. 2012. *Pay for Value: Cutting the Gordian Knot of Executive Compensation*. Montreal: Institute for Governance of Private and Public Organizations.

ILO. 2011a. *Global Wage Report 2010/11*. Geneva: International Labor Organization.

– 2011b. "A Review of Global Fiscal Stimulus." EC-IILS Joint Discussion Paper Series no. 5. Geneva: ILO/International Institute for Labour Studies.

– 2012a. *Global Wage Report 2012/13: Wages and Equitable Growth*. Geneva: International Labor Organization.

– 2012b. *World of Work Report 2012*. Geneva: ILO.

– 2014. *Global Wage Report 2014/15: Wages and Income Inequality*. Geneva: International Labor Organization.

IMF. 2010. *World Economic Outlook 2010: Recovery, Risk, and Rebalancing*. New York: International Monetary Fund.

– 2014a. Canada: Financial System Stability Assessment. In *IMF Country Report*. New York, NY: International Monetary Fund.

– 2014b. *Global Financial Stability Report: Risk Taking, Liquidity, and Shadow Banking*. New York: International Monetary Fund.

– 2016. *The World Economic Outlook*. Washington, DC: International Monetary Fund.

– 2017. *Global Financial Stability Report*. New York: International Monetary Fund.

Industry Canada. 2009. *Ontario Economic Overview*. February 2009 Update. Ottawa: Industry Canada.

– 2010. *Ontario Economic Overview*. February 2010 Update. Ottawa: Industry Canada.

Ingham, Geoffrey. 2013. *Capitalism: With a New Postscript on the Financial Crisis and Its Aftermath*. New York: John Wiley & Sons.

Innovation, Science and Economic Development Canada. 2009. *Survey of Innovation and Business Strategy (SIBS) 2009*. Ottawa: ISEDC.

Ivanova, Iglika. 2010. *BC's Shrinking Public Sector*. Vancouver: Canadian Centre for Policy Alternatives.

– 2016. *Working Poverty in Metro Vancouver*. Vancouver: Canadian Centre for Policy Alternatives.

Ivanova, Iglika, and Seth Klein. 2012. *Working for a Living Wage 2012 Update*. Vancouver: Canadian Centre for Policy Alternatives.

Iversen, Torben. 2006. *Capitalism, Democracy, and Welfare*. New York: Cambridge University Press.

Jackson, Andrew. 1999. "The Free Trade Agreement: A Decade Later." *Studies in Political Economy* 58 (1): 141–60.

– 2010. *Work and Labour in Canada: Critical Issues*. 2nd ed. Toronto: Canadian Scholars' Press.

Jackson, Andrew, and Sylvain Schetagne. 2010. *Is EI Working for Canada's Unemployed?* Ottawa: Canadian Centre for Policy Alternatives.

Jacobs, Lawrence R., and Theda Skocpol, eds. 2005. *Inequality and American Democracy*. New York: Russell Sage Foundation.

Jacobs, Lawrence R., and Joe Soss. 2010. "The Politics of Inequality in America: A Political Economy Framework." *Annual Review of Political Science* 13:341–64. https://doi.org/10.1146/annurev.polisci.041608.140134.

Jacoby, Sanford. 2005. "Corporate Governance and Employees in the United States." In *Corporate Governance and Labour Management: An International Comparison*, edited by H. Gospel and A. Pendleton, 33–58. New York: Oxford University Press.

Jaehrling, Karen, and Philippe Mehaut. 2013. "'Varieties of Institutional Avoidance': Employers' Strategies in Low-Waged Service Sector Occupations in France and Germany." *Socio-Economic Review* 11 (4): 687–710.

Jain, Harish, and S. Muthu. 1997. "Ontario Labour Law Reforms: A Comparative Study of Bill 40 and Bill 7." *Canadian Labour and Employment Law Journal* 4:311–30.

Jensen, Michael C. 1989. "Eclipse of the Public Corporation." *Harvard Business Review* (September–October): 61–74.

Jessop, Bob. 2013. "Putting Neoliberalism in Its Time and Place: A Response to the Debate." *Social Anthropology/Anthropologie sociale* 21 (1): 65–74. https://doi.org /10.1111/1469-8676.12003.

– 2016. "The Heartlands of Neoliberalism and the Rise of the Austerity State." In *The Handbook of Neoliberalism*, edited by K. Birch, S. Springer, and J. MacLeavy, 410–22. New York: Routledge.

Jog, Vijay, and Jack Mintz. 2013. "Sovereign Wealth and Pension Funds Controlling Canadian Businesses: Tax Policy Implications." *The School of Public Policy SPP Research Papers, University of Calgary* 6, no. 5.

Johansson, Bjorn. 2009. "Sales Abroad by Canadian Foreign Affiliates." Issue Brief, Department of Foreign Affairs and International Trade, 9 September. Ottawa: Office of the Chief Economist.

Jung, Jiwook. 2014. "Shareholder Value and Workforce Downsizing, 1981–2006." *Social Forces* 93 (4): 1335–68. http://doi.org/10.1093/sf/sou108.

Jung, Jiwook, and Frank Dobbin. 2014. "Finance and Institutional Investors." In *The Oxford Handbook of The Sociology of Finance*, edited by K. Knorr Cetina and A. Preda, 52–74. New York: Oxford University Press.

Juravich, Tom. 2007. "Beating Global Capital: A Framework and Method for Union Strategic Research and Campaigns." In *Global Unions: Challenging Transnational Capital through Cross-Border Campaigns*, edited by K. Bronfenbrenner, 16–39. Ithaca, NY: Cornell University Press.

Kallbeberg, Arne L. 2011. *Good Jobs, Bad Jobs: The Rise of Polarized and Precarious Employment Systems in the United States, 1970s to 2000s*. New York: Russell Sage Foundation.

– 2018. *Precarious Lives: Job Insecurity and Well-being in Rich Semocracies*. New York: John Wiley & Sons.

Kaplan, Steven, and Joshua Rauh. 2013. "It's the Market: The Broad-Based Rise in the Return to Top Talent." *Journal of Economic Perspectives* 27 (3): 35–56. https:// doi.org/10.1257/jep.27.3.35.

Kaplan, Steven, and Per Stromberg. 2009. "Leveraged Buyouts and Private Equity." *Journal of Economic Perspectives* 23 (Winter): 121–46. https://doi.org/10.1257 /jep.23.1.121.

Karl, Terry Lynn. 1997. *The Paradox of Plenty: Oil Booms and Petro-States*. Berkeley, CA: University of California Press.

Keating, Michael and David McCrone, eds. 2013. *The Crisis of Social Democracy in Europe*. Edinburgh: Edinburgh University Press.

Kelly, John. 1998. *Rethinking Industrial Relations: Mobilization, Collectivism, and Long Waves*. London: Routledge.

Kelly, Nathan. 2009. *The Politics of Income Inequality in the United States*. New York: Cambridge University Press.

Kent Baker, H., Bin Chang, Shantanu Dutta, and Samir Saadi. 2013. "Canadian Corporate Payout Policy." *International Journal of Managerial Finance* 9 (3): 164–84. https://doi.org/10.1108/IJMF-03-2012-0040.

Kerby, Matthew. 2009. "Worth the Wait: Determinants of Ministerial Appointment in Canada, 1935–2008." *Canadian Journal of Political Science* 42 (3): 593–611. https://doi.org/10.1017/S0008423909990424.

Kerstetter, Steve. 2010. *A Closer Look at Low Wages in BC*. Vancouver: Canadian Centre for Policy Alternatives.

Keune, Maarten, and Kurt Vandaele. 2013. "Wage Regulation in the Private Sector: Moving Further Away from a 'Solidaristic Wage Policy'?" In *The Transformation of Employment Relations in Europe*, edited by J. Arrowsmith and V. Pulignano, 104–26. New York: Routledge.

Kinderman, Daniel. 2005. "Pressure from Without, Subversion from Within: The Two-Pronged German Employer Offensive." *Comparative European Politics* 3 (4): 432–63. http://doi.org/10.1057/palgrave.cep.6110064.

– 2016. "Challenging Varieties of Capitalism's Account of Business Interests: Neoliberal Think-tanks, Discourse as a Power Resource and Employers' Quest for Liberalization in Germany and Sweden." *Socio-Economic Review* 15 (3): 587–613. http://doi.org/10.1093/ser/mww040.

King, Desmond, and David Rueda. 2008. "Cheap Labor: The New Politics of 'Bread and Roses' in Industrial Democracies." *Perspectives on Politics* 6 (2): 279–97. https://doi.org/10.1017/S1537592708080614.

Klassen, Thomas, and Rodney Haddow. 2006. *Partisanship, Globalization, and Canadian Labour Market Policy*. Toronto: University of Toronto Press.

Klein, Naomi. 2014. *This Changes Everything: Capitalism vs the Climate*. Toronto: Alfred A. Knopf.

Knafo, Samuel, and Sahil Jai Dutta. 2019. "The Myth of the Shareholder Revolution and the Financialization of the Firm." *Review of International Political Economy* 27 (2): 1–24. http://doi.org/10.1080/09692290.2019.1649293.

Knutsen, Oddbjørn. 2006. *Class Voting in Western Europe: A Comparative Longitudinal Study*. Lanham, MD: Lexington Books.

Kochan, Thomas A., and Christine A. Riordan. 2016. "Employment Relations and Growing Income Inequality: Causes and Potential Options for Its Reversal." *Journal of Industrial Relations* 58 (3) 419–40. http://doi.org/10.1177/0022185616634337.

Kohler, Karsten, Alexander Guschanski, and Engelbert Stockhammer. 2019. "The Impact of Financialisation on the Wage Share: A Theoretical Clarification and Empirical Test." *Cambridge Journal of Economics* 43 (4): 937–74. https://doi.org/10.1093/CJE%2FBEZ021.

Kollmeyer, Christopher. 2009. "Explaining Deindustrialization: How Affluence, Productivity Growth, and Globalization Diminish Manufacturing Employment." *American Journal of Sociology* 114 (6): 1644–74. https://doi.org/10.1086/597176.

– 2018. "Trade Union Decline, Deindustrialization, and Rising Income Inequality in the United States, 1947 to 2015." *Research in Social Stratification and Mobility* 57:1–10. https://doi.org/10.1016/j.rssm.2018.07.002.

Kollmeyer, Christopher, and John Peters. 2019. "Financialization and the Decline of Organized Labor: A Study of 18 Advanced Capitalist Countries, 1970–2012." *Social Forces* 98 (1): 1–30. https://doi.org/10.1093/sf/soz041.

Konings, Martijn. 2011. *The Development of American Finance*. New York: Cambridge University Press.

Konzelmann, Suzanne, and Marc Fovargue-Davies, eds. 2013. *Banking Systems in the Crisis: The Faces of Liberal Capitalism*. Oxford: Routledge.

Konzelmann, Suzanne, Marc Fovargue-Davies, and Frank Wilkinson. 2013. "The Return of 'Financialized' Liberal Capitalism." In *Banking Systems in the Crisis: The Faces of Liberal Capitalism*, edited by S. Konzelmann and M. Fovargue-Davies, 32–56. New York: Routledge.

Koopman, Robert, William Powers, Zhi Wang, and Shang-Jin Wei. 2010. *Give Credit Where Credit Is Due: Tracing Value Added in Global Production Chains*. Working Paper 16426. Cambridge, MA: National Bureau of Economic Research.

KPMG. 2012. *Competitive Alternatives 2012 Special Report: Focus on Tax*. New York: KPMG.

Krippner, Greta R. 2011. *Capitalizing on Crisis: The Political Origins of the Rise of Finance*. Cambridge, MA: Harvard University Press.

Kristal, Tali. 2010. "Good Times, Bad Times: Postwar Labor's Share of National Income in Capitalist Democracies." *American Sociological Review* 75 (5): 729–63. https://doi.org/10.1177%2F0003122410382640.

Kus, Basak. 2013. "Financialisation and Income Inequality in OECD Nations: 1995–2007." *Economic and Social Review* 43 (4): 477–95. https://www.esr.ie/article/view/34.

Kwon, Roy. 2018. "How Do Neoliberal Policies Affect Income Inequality? Exploring the Link between Liberalization, Finance, and Inequality." *Sociological Forum* 33 (3): 643–65. https://doi.org/10.1111/socf.12438.

Labban, Mazen. 2010. "Oil in Parallax: Scarcity, Markets, and the Financialization of Accumulation." *Geoforum* 41 (4): 541–52. http://doi.org/10.1016/j.geoforum.2009.12.002.

La Botz, Dan. 2005. "Strikes." In *A Troublemaker's Handbook*, edited by J. Slaughter. Detroit, MI: Labor Education and Research Project.

Lane, Christel, and Geoffrey Wood, eds. 2012. *Capitalist Diversity and Diversity within Capitalism*. New York: Routledge.

Lapavitsas, Costas. 2014. *Profiting without Producing: How Finance Exploits Us All*. New York: Verso.

LaRochelle-Côté, Sébastien, and Claude Dionne. 2009. "International Differences in Low-Paid Work." *Perspectives on Labour and Income*. Ottawa: Statistics Canada. https://www150.statcan.gc.ca/n1/pub/75-001-x/2009106/article/10894-eng.htm.

LaRochelle-Côté, Sébastien, and Jason Gilmore. 2009. "Canada's Employment Downturn." *Perspectives on Labour and Income*. Ottawa: Statistics Canada. https://www150.statcan.gc.ca/n1/en/pub/75-001-x/2009112/pdf/11048-eng.pdf?st=qx8pkdNj.

Laux, Jeanne Kirk, and Maureen Appel Molot. 1988. *State Capitalism: Public Enterprise in Canada*. Ithaca, NY: Cornell University Press.

Lavoie, Marc. 2011. "The Global Financial Crisis: Methodological Reflections from a Heterodox Perspective." *Studies in Political Economy* 88 (1): 35–57. https://doi.org/10.1080/19187033.2011.11675008.

Lavoie, Marc, and Mario Seccareccia. 2006. "The Bank of Canada and the Modern View of Central Banking." *International Journal of Political Economy* 35 (1): 44–61. https://doi.org/10.2753/IJP0891-1916350103.

– 2014. "Reciprocal Influences: A Tale of Two Central Banks on the North American Continent." *International Journal of Political Economy* 42 (3): 63–83. https://doi.org/10.2753/IJP0891-1916420304.

Law Commission of Ontario. 2012. *Vulnerable Workers and Precarious Work*. Toronto: Law Commission of Ontario.

Lazonick, William. 2011. "From Innovation to Financialization: How Shareholder Value Ideology Is Destroying the US Economy." In *The Handbook of the Political Economy of Financial Crises*, edited by M. Wolfson and G.A. Epstein, 491–511. New York: Oxford University Press.

– 2014. "Profits without Prosperity." *Harvard Business Review* 92 (9): 46–55.

– 2017. "The New Normal Is 'Maximizing Shareholder Value': Predatory Value Extraction, Slowing Productivity, and the Vanishing American Middle Class." *International Journal of Political Economy* 46 (4): 217–26. https://doi.org/10.1080/08911916.2017.1407736.

Lazonick, William, and Mary O'Sullivan. 2000. "Maximizing Shareholder Value: A New Ideology for Corporate Governance." *Economy and Society* 29 (1): 13–35. https://doi.org/10.1080/030851400360541.

Lebi, Ron, and Elizabeth Mitchell. 2003. "The Decline in Trade Union Certification in Ontario: The Case for Restoring Remedial Certification." *Canadian Labour and Employment Law Journal* 10:473–99.

Lee, Marc. 2014. *Path to Prosperity? A Closer Look at British Columbia's Natural Gas Royalties and Proposed LNG Income Tax*. Vancouver: Canadian Centre for Policy Alternatives.

– 2016. *Getting Serious about Affordable Housing*. Vancouver: Canadian Centre for Policy Alternatives.

Lee, Marc, and Brock Ellis. 2013. *Canada's Carbon Liabilities: The Implications of Stranded Fuel Assets for Financial Markets and Pension Funds*. Vancouver: Canadian Centre for Policy Alternatives.

Lee, Marc, Iglika Ivanova, and Seth Klein. 2011. *BC's Regressive Tax Shift: A Decade of Diminishing Tax Fairness, 2000 to 2010*. Vancouver: Canadian Centre for Policy Alternatives.

Lee, Marc, and Seth Klein. 2020. *Winding Down BC's Fossil Fuel Industries*. Vancouver: Canadian Centre for Policy Alternatives.

Lehman Schlozman, Kay, Sidney Verba, and Henry E. Brady. 2012. *The Unheavenly Chorus: Unequal Political Voice and the Broken Promise of American Democracy*. Princeton, NJ: Princeton University Press.

Lehndorff, Steffen, ed. 2012. *The Triumph of Failed Ideas: European Models of Capitalism in the Crisis*. Brussels: European Trade Union Institute.

Lemieux, Thomas, and Craig Riddell. 2016. "Who Are Canada's Top 1 Per Cent?" In *Income Inequality: The Canadian Story*, edited by D. Green, C. Riddell, and F. St-Hilaire, 103–55. Montreal: Institute for Research on Public Policy.

Lethbridge, Jane. 2005. *Care Services in Europe*. Greenwich, UK: Public Services International Research Unit. https://gala.gre.ac.uk/id/eprint/3761/1/PSIRU_9489 _-_2005-02-H-Care_services_in_Europe.pdf.

2008. *Changing Care Services and Labour Markets*. Greenwich: Public Services International Research Unit. https://gala.gre.ac.uk/id/eprint/2977/

Levesque, Christian, and Gregor Murray. 2010. "Understanding Union Power: Resources and Capabilities for Renewing Union Capacity." *Transfer: European Review of Labour and Research* 16 (3) 333–50. https://doi.org/10.1177%2F1024258910373867.

Levy, Jonah D. 2006. *The State after Statism: New State Activities in the Age of Liberalization*. Cambridge, MA: Harvard University Press.

Ley, David. 2017. "Global China and the Making of Vancouver's Residential Property Market." *International Journal of Housing Policy* 17 (1): 15–34. https://doi.org /10.1080/14616718.2015.1119776.

Leys, Colin. 2003. *Market-Driven Politics: Neoliberal Democracy and the Public Interest*. New York: Verso.

Lightman, Naomi, and Luann Good Gingrich. 2013. "The Intersecting Dynamics of Social Exclusion: Age, Gender, Race and Immigrant Status in Canada's Labour Market." *Canadian Ethnic Studies* 44 (3): 121–45. http://doi.org/10.1353/ces.2013.0010.

Lilley, Wayne. 2006. *Magna Cum Laude: How Frank Stronach Became Canada's Best-Paid Man*. Toronto: McClelland and Stewart.

Lin, Ken-Hou. 2016. "The Rise of Finance and Firm Employment Dynamics." *Organization Science* 27 (4): 972–88. https://doi.org/10.1287/orsc.2016.1073.

Lin, Ken-Hou, and Megan Tobias Neely. 2020. *Divested: Inequality in Financialized America*. Oxford: Oxford University Press, USA.

Lin, Ken-Hou, and Donald Tomaskovic-Devey. 2013. "Financialization and U.S. Income Inequality, 1970–2008." *American Journal of Sociology* 118 (5): 1284–329. http://doi.org/10.1086/669499.

Lindvall, Johannes. 2010. *Mass Unemployment and the State*. New York: Oxford University Press.

Little, Bruce. 2008. *Fixing the Future: How Canada's Usually Fractious Governments Worked Together to Rescue the Canada Pension Plan*. Toronto: University of Toronto Press.

Liu, Ying, Eli Papakirykos, and Mingwei Yuan. 2004. *Market Valuation and Risk Assessment of Canadian Banks.* Ottawa: Bank of Canada.

Livingstone, David W., Dorothy E. Smith, and Warren Smith, eds. 2014. *Manufacturing Meltdown: Reshaping Steel Work.* Halifax: Fernwood Publishing.

Locke, Wade. 2006. "Economics of Newfoundland and Labrador's Offshore Oil Industry: Separating Fact from Myth." Newfoundland and Labrador Oil and Gas Industry Association Annual Conference, St. John's, NL, 22 June.

– 2010. *Do Newfoundland and Labrador Royalties Subsidize Offshore Oil and Gas Investments?* St. John's, NL: Harris Centre.

Longhurst, Andrew, Sage Ponder, and Margaret McGregor. 2020. "Labor Restructuring and Nursing Home Privatization in British Columbia Canada." In *The Privatization of Care: The Case of Nursing Homes*, edited by P. Armstrong and H. Armstrong, 102–22. New York: Routledge.

Luce, Stephanie. 2014. *Labor Movements: Global Perspectives.* Malden, MA: Polity.

Luchak, Andrew A. 2003. "Newfoundland and Labrador: Shifting Tides." In *Beyond the National Divide: Regional Dimensions of Industrial Relations*, edited by M. Thompson and J.B. Rose. Montreal and Kingston: McGill-Queen's University Press.

Lund, Susan, Eckart Windhagen, James Manyika, Philipp Härle, Jonathan Woetzel, and Diana Goldshtein. 2017. *The New Dynamics of Financial Globalization.* Washington: McKinsey Global Institute.

Macaire, Simone, Udo Rehfeldt, Maurice Brand, and Catherine Sauviat. 2002. "Industrial Relations Aspects of Mergers and Acquisitions." Brussels: European Foundation for the Improvement of Living and Working Conditions. http://www.eurofound.europa.eu/eiro/2001/02/study/tn0102401s.htm.

MacDermid, Robert. 2009. "Ontario Political Parties in the Neo-Liberal Age." Paper presented at Canadian Political Science Association Annual General Meeting, 29 May, Ottawa.

– 2011. *Funding Ontario Political Parties: 2004 to 2011.* Toronto: Vote Ontario.

Mackenzie, Hugh. 2008. *The Great CEO Pay Race: Over before It Begins.* Ottawa: Canadian Centre for Policy Alternatives.

– 2010. "Steering Ontario out of Recession." OAB 2010: Technical Paper. Toronto: Canadian Centre for Policy Alternatives.

– 2012. *Canada's CEO Elite 100: The 0.01%.* Ottawa: Canadian Centre for Policy Alternatives.

– 2016. *Staying Power: CEO Pay in Canada.* Ottawa: Canadian Centre for Policy Alternatives.

– 2017. *Throwing Money at the Problem: 10 Years of Executive Compensation.* Ottawa: Canadian Centre for Policy Alternatives.

MacLeod, Andrew. 2008. "Pat Kinsella's Bumpy Career." *Tyee*, 16 June.

MacPhail, Fiona, and Paul Bowles. 2008. *Improving the Economic Security of Casual Workers in BC.* Vancouver: Canadian Centre for Policy Alternatives.

Mahler, Vincent. 2008. "Electoral Turnout and Income Redistribution by the State: A Cross-National Analysis of the Developed Democracies." *European Journal of Political Research* 47 (2): 161–83. http://doi.org/10.1111/j.1475-6765.2007.00726.x.

Mahoney, James. 2003. "Knowledge Accumulation in Comparative Historical Research." In *Comparative Historical Analysis in the Social Sciences*, edited by J. Mahoney and Dietrich Rueschemyer, 131–74. New York: Cambridge University Press.

Mahoney, James, and Dietrich Rueschemeyer, eds. 2003. *Comparative Historical Analysis in the Social Sciences*. New York: Cambridge University Press.

Mair, Peter. 2013. *Ruling the Void: The Hollowing of Western Democracy*. New York: Verso.

Marginson, Paul. 2015. "Coordinated Bargaining in Europe: From Incremental Corrosion to Frontal Assault?" *European Journal of Industrial Relations* 21 (2): 97–114. https://doi.org/10.1177/0959680114530241.

Marshall, Dale, and Jodi-Lyn Newnham. 2004. *Running on Empty: Shifting to a Sustainable Energy Plan for BC*. Vancouver: Canadian Centre Policy Alternatives BC Office and David Suzuki Foundation.

Marshall, Katherine. 2009. "The Family Work Week." *Perspectives on Labour and Income*. Ottawa: Statistics Canada. https://www150.statcan.gc.ca/n1/pub/75-001-x/2009106/article/10894-eng.htm.

Martin, Cathie Jo, and Duane Swank. 2012. *The Political Construction of Business Interests*. New York: Cambridge University Press.

Martineau, Fasken. 2012. *Listing on TSX: What You Need to Know*. Toronto: Fasken Martineau.

Marx, Ive, and Brian Nolan. 2014. "In-Work Poverty." In *Reconciling Work and Poverty Reduction*, edited by B. Cantillon and F. Vandenbroucke, 131–56. New York: Oxford University Press.

Marx, Paul, and Werner Eichhorst. 2012. "Whatever Works: Dualization and the Service Economy in Bismarckian Welfare States." In *The Age of Dualization: The Changing Face of Inequality in Deindustrializling Societies*, edited by P. Emmenegger, S. Hausermann, B. Palier, and M. Seeleib-Kaiser, 73–99. New York: Oxford University Press.

Mason, Geoff, and Weimar Salverda. 2010. "Low Pay, Working Conditions, and Living Standards." In *Low-Wage Work in the Wealthy World*, edited by J. Gautié and J. Schmitt, 35–90. New York: Russell Sage Foundation.

McAdam, Doug, and Hilary Shaffer Boudet. 2012. *Putting Social Movements in Their Place*. New York: Cambridge University Press.

McAlevey, Jane. 2015. "The Crisis of New Labor and Alinsky's Legacy: Revisiting the Role of Organic Grassroots Leaders in Building Powerful Organizations and Movements." *Politics and Society* 43 (3): 415–41. https://doi.org/10.1177%2F0032329215584767.

– 2020. *A Collective Bargain: Unions, Organizing, and the Fight for Democracy*. New York: HarperCollins.

McBride, Stephen. 2005. *Paradigm Shift: Globalization and the Canadian State*. Halifax: Fernwood Publishing.

McBride, Stephen, and Kathleen Mcnutt. 2007. "Devolution and Neoliberalism in the Canadian Welfare State: Ideology, National and International Conditioning Frameworks, and Policy Change in British Columbia." *Global Social Policy* 7 (2): 177–201. http://doi.org/10.1177/1468018107078161.

McBride, Stephen, and Heather Whiteside. 2011. *Private Affluence, Public Austerity: Economic Crisis and Democratic Malaise in Canada*. Halifax: Fernwood Publishing.

McCabe, Brian J. 2016. *No Place like Home: Wealth, Community, and the Politics of Homeownership*. Oxford: Oxford University Press.

McKinsey and Company. 2010. *Private Equity Canada 2010*. Toronto: McKinsey& Company.

McLaren, Brian, and Jason Pollard. 2009. "Restructuring of the Boreal Forest and the Forest Sector in Newfoundland, Canada." *Forestry Chronicle* 85 (5): 772–82. https://doi.org/10.5558/tfc85772-5.

McMartin, Will. 2004. "Alberta's Posse in BC." *Tyee*, 23 November.

– 2005a. "Conjuring a $5 Billion 'NDP' Deficit." In *Liberalized: The Tyee Report on British Columbia under Gordon Campbell's Liberals*, edited by D. Beers. Vancouver: New Star Books.

– 2005b. "Did Liberals 'Fix' BC's Economy?" In *Liberalized: The Tyee Report on British Columbia under Gordon Campbell's Liberals*, edited by D. Beers. Vancouver: New Star Books.

– 2010a. "Accenture's BC Hydro Contract Way over Budget." *Tyee*, 21 June.

– 2010b. "Plutonic Tops List of Power Firms Donating to Libs." *Tyee*, 12 April.

– 2011. "First to Profit from $1 Billion Smart Meter Program." *Tyee*, 7 March.

McMichael, Philip. 2012. "The Land Grab and Corporate Food Regime Restructuring." *Journal of Peasant Studies* 39 (3–4): 681–701. http://doi.org/10.1080/03066150.2012.661369.

– 2013. "Value-Chain Agriculture and Debt Relations: Contradictory Outcomes." *Third World Quarterly* 34 (3): 671–90. http://doi.org/10.1080/01436597.2013.786290.

Mendelson, Michael. 2005. *Financing the Canada and Quebec Pension Plans*. Washington, DC: AARP Public Policy Institute.

Menz, George. 2010. "Employers, Trade Unions, Varieties of Capitalism and Labour Migration Policies." In *Labour Migration in Europe*, edited by A. Caviedes and G. Menz, 25–53. New York: Palgrave MacMillan.

Mercille, Julien, and Enda Murphy. 2017. "What Is Privatization? A Political Economy Framework." *Environment and Planning A* 49 (5): 0308518X1668908. http://doi.org/10.1177/0308518X16689085.

Messacar, Derek. 2017. *Trends in RRSP Contributions and Pre-Retirement Withdrawals, 2000 to 2013*. Ottawa: Statistics Canada.

Meyer, Brett. 2019. "Financialization, Technological Change, and Trade Union Decline." *Socio-Economic Review* 17 (3): 477–502. https://doi.org/10.1093/ser/mwx022.

Milberg, William, and Deborah Winkler. 2013. *Outsourcing Economics: Global Value Chains in Capitalist Development.* New York: Cambridge University Press.

Milkman, Ruth. 2013. "Back to the Future? US Labour in the New Gilded Age." *British Journal of Industrial Relations* 51 (4): 645–65. https://doi.org/10.1111/bjir.12047.

Milkman, Ruth, and Kim Voss, eds. 2004. *Rebuilding Labor: Organizing and Organizers in the New Union Movement.* Ithaca, NY: Cornell University Press.

Milley, Peter. 2008. *Newfoundland Forest Sector Strategy: Final report.* Corner Brook: Submitted by Halifax Global to Forestry Services Branch, DNR, Government of Newfoundland.

Milway, James, Sana Nisar, Claurelle Poole, and Ying Yang. 2007. *Assessing Toronto's Financial Services Cluster.* Toronto: Institute for Competitiveness and Prosperity.

Minimum Wage Advisory Panel. 2014. *Report and Recommendations to the Minister of Labour.* Toronto: Queen's Printer for Ontario.

Mintz, Jack, and Duanjie Chen. 2010. "Taxing Canada's Cash Cow: Tax and Royalty Burdens on Oil and Gas Investments." SPP Briefing Papers. Calgary: University of Calgary, School of Public Policy.

– 2012. "Capturing Economic Rents from Resources through Royalties and Taxes." SPP Research Papers. Calgary: University of Calgary, School of Public Policy.

Modjeski, Morgan, and Ashley Gaboury. 2009. "Builders Real Estate Firms Gave Big to BC Liberals." *Tyee,* 8 May.

Mojtehedzadeh, Sara. 2015a. "Contract Flipping Leaves York Transit Employees Feeling like 'Temporary Workforce.'" *Toronto Star,* 15 October.

– 2015b. "Ontario's Temp Agencies, Then and Now." *Toronto Star,* 10 May.

– 2015c. "Pearson Workers Fear Good Jobs in Peril over Contract-Flipping." *Toronto Star,* 11 June.

Molina, Oscar, and Martin Rhodes. 2008. "The Political Economy of Adjustment in Mixed Market Economies: A Study of Spain and Italy." In *Beyond Varieties of Capitalism: Conflict, Contradiction, and Complementarities in the European Economy,* edited by B. Hancké, M. Rhodes, and M. Thatcher, 223–54. New York: Oxford University Press.

Moody, Kim. 1997. *Workers in a Lean World.* New York: Verso.

– 2007. *US Labor in Trouble and Transition: The Failure of Reform from Above, the Promise of Revival from Below.* New York: Verso.

– 2017. *On New Terrain: How Capital Is Reshaping the Battleground of Class War.* Chicago: Haymarket Books.

Moomaw, W., T. Griffin, K. Kurczak, and J. Lomax. 2012. "The Critical Role of Global Food Consumption Patterns in Achieving Sustainable Food Systems and Food for All." A UNEP Discussion Paper, edited by U.N.E. Programme. Paris.

Moran, Michael. 2009. *Business, Politics, and Society.* New York: Oxford University Press.

Moreira, Amilcar, and Ivar Lodemel. 2014. "Governing Activation in the 21st Century." In *Activation or Workfare? Governance and Neoliberal Convergence,* edited by A. Moreira and I. Lodemel, 289–326. New York: Oxford University Press.

Morrissey, Alisha 2007. "Unemployment Rate 13.2%. National Average 5.9%. A Number for All Seasons." *Telegram*, 17 December.

Moschonas, Gerasimos. 2002. *In the Name of Social Democracy: The Great Transformation: 1945 to the Present*. New York: Verso.

Mueller, Michael, and Andre Usche. 2016. "Towards More Resilient Markets: Over-the-Counter Derivatives Reform in Canada." *Financial System Review*, December, 53–65. Ottawa: Bank of Canada.

Mugge, Daniel. 2010. *Widen the Market, Narrow the Competition: Banker Interests and the Making of a European Capital Market*. Colchester, UK: ECPR.

Munnell, Alicia, and Steven Sass. 2006. *Social Security and the Stock Market: How the Pursuit of Market Magic Shapes the System*. Kalamazoo, MI: W.E. Upjohn Institute for Employment Research.

Murnighan, Bill, and Jim Stanford. 2013. "'We Will Fight This Crisis': Auto Workers Resist an Industrial Meltdown." In *From Crisis to Austerity: Neoliberalism, Labour and the Canadian State*, edited by T. Fowler. Ottawa: Red Quill Books.

Murphy, Fidelma, and Terrence McDonough. 2012. "US Auto Companies' Ownership and Control of Production in Mexico's 'Maquiladoras.'" *Cambridge Journal of Regions, Economy and Society* 5 (3): 413–34. http://doi.org/10.1093/cjres/rss014.

Murphy, Kevin. 2013. "Executive Compensation: Where We Are and How We Got There." In *Handbook of the Economics of Finance*. Vol. 2, edited by G. Constantinides, M. Harris, and R. Stultz, 211–356. Amsterdam: Elsevier Science.

Murray, Grant, Barbara Neis, and Johan P. Johnsen. 2006. "Lessons Learned from Reconstructing Interactions between Local Ecological Knowledge, Fisheries Science, and Fisheries Management in the Commercial Fisheries of Newfoundland and Labrador, Canada." *Human Ecology* 34 (4): 549–71.

Murray, Gregor, and Joelle Cuillerier. 2009. "The Sky Is Not Falling: Unionization, Wal-Mart, and First-Contract Arbitration in Canada." *Just Labour: A Canadian Journal of Work and Society* 15, special edition, 78–98.

Natural Resources Canada. 2008. *Mineral Trade Information Bulletin August 2008*. Ottawa: Natural Resources Canada.

– 2014. *Our Resources, New Frontiers: Overview of Competitiveness in Canada's Natural Resources Sector*. Ottawa: Natural Resources Canada.

Nau, Michael 2013. "Economic Elites, Investments, and Income Inequality." *Social Forces* 92 (2): 437–61. http://doi.org/10.1093/sf/sot102.

Neilson, David, and Thomas Stubbs. 2016. "Competition States in the Neoliberal Era." *Competition and Change* 20 (2): 122–44. https://doi.org/10.1177/1024529415623917.

Neis, Barbara, and Robert Kean. 2003. "Why Fish Stocks Collapse: An Interdisicplinary Approach to the Problem of 'Fishing Up.'" In *Retrenchment and Regeneration in Rural Newfoundland*, edited by R. Byron, 65–102. Toronto: University of Toronto Press.

Newman, Peter. 1998. *Titans: How the New Canadian Business Establishment Seized Power*. Toronto: Penguin Books.

Nicholls, Christopher. 2006. "The Characteristics of Canada's Capital Markets and the Illustrative Case of Canada's Legislative Response to Sarbanes-Oxley." In *Maintaining a Competitive Capital Market in Canada*. Vol. 4. Toronto: Task Force to Modernize Securities Legislation in Canada.

Nikiforuk, Andrew. 2008. *Tar Sands: Dirty Oil and the Future of a Continent*. Toronto: Greystone Books.

NL Department of Finance. 2006. *The Economic Review: 2006*. St. John's, NL: Government of Newfoundland and Labrador.

– 2008. *The Economic Review: 2008*. St. John's, NL: Government of Newfoundland and Labrador.

– 2010. *The Economic Review: 2010*. St. John's, NL: Government of Newfoundland and Labrador.

NL Department of Human Resources, Labour and Employment. 2011. *Newfoundland and Labrador Labour Market Outlook 2020*. St. John's, NL: Department of Human Resources.

Noack, Andrea, and Leah Vosko. 2011. *Precarious Jobs in Ontario: Mapping Dimensions of Labour Market Insecurity by Workers' Social Location and Context*. Toronto: Law Commission of Ontario.

Norris, David G. 2003. "The Fiscal Position of Newfoundland and Labrador." In *Royal Commission on Renewing and Strengthening Our Place in Canada*. St. John's: Office of the Queen's Printer.

Noseworthy, John. 2009. *Summary: Report of the Auditor General to the House of Assembly: Reviews of Departments and Crown Agencies for the Year Ended 31 March 2009*. St. John's, NL: Auditor General of Newfoundland and Labrador.

Oakley, James C. 2012. *Review of Special Project Order Legislation in Newfoundland and Labrador*. St. John's, NL: NL Ministry Responsible for the Labour Relations Agency.

OECD. 1994. *The OECD Jobs Study: Facts, Analysis, Strategies*. Paris: OECD.

– 2004. *Employment Outlook: Boosting Jobs and Incomes*. Paris: OECD.

– 2006. *Employment Outlook: Boosting Jobs and Incomes*. Paris: OECD.

– 2008. *Growing Unequal: Income Distribution and Poverty in OECD Countries*. Paris: OECD.

– 2009. *Global Value Chains (GVCs): Canada*. Paris: OECD Publishing.

– 2010. *OECD Economic Outlook* 2010/1, no. 87, May. Paris: OECD.

– 2011a. *Divided We Stand: Why Inequality Keeps Rising*. Paris: OECD.

– 2011b. *The Role of Institutional Investors in Promoting Good Corporate Governance*. Paris: OECD.

– 2012. *Employment Outlook 2012*. Paris: OECD Publishing.

– 2013. *Education at a Glance 2013*. Paris: OECD Publishing.

– 2014a. *Tackling High Inequalities, Creating Opportunities for All*. Paris: OECD Publishing.

– 2014b. *Trends in Top Income and Their Taxation*. Paris: OECD Publishing.
– 2015a. *In It All Together: Why Less Inequality Benefits All*. Paris: OECD Publishing.
– 2015b. *OECD Employment Outlook 2014*. Paris: OECD Publishing.
– 2016. *OECD Business and Finance Outlook 2016*. Paris: OECD Publishing.
– 2018. *Education at a Glance*. Paris: OECD Publishing.
2019. *Global Pension Statistics* Paris: OECD.
Oesch, Daniel. 2006. *Redrawing the Class Map: Stratification and Institutions in Germany, Britain, Sweden, and Switzerland*. London: Palgrave Macmillan.
Office of Consumer Affairs. 2013. "Major Actors with the Canadian Retail Marketplace." *Consumer Trends Update*. Ottawa: Innovation, Science, and Economic Development.
Office of the Auditor General, Government of Newfoundland and Labrador. 2006. *2006 Report on the Audit of the Financial Statements of the Province*. St. John's.
Omarova, Saule, Cynthia Williams, Lissa Lankin Broome, and John Conley. 2013. "The United States: 'With Freedom and Liberty for All.'" In *Banking Systems in the Crisis: The Faces of Liberal Capitalism*, edited by S. Konzelmann and M. Fovargue-Davies, 57–79. New York: Routledge.
Ommer, Rosemary E., and the Coasts under Stress Research Project Team. 2007. *Coasts under Stress: Restructuring and Social-Ecological Health*. Montreal and Kingston: McGill-Queen's University Press.
Ontario Chamber of Commerce. 2013. *Public Sector Problems, Private Sector Solutions: Transforming Government*. Toronto: Ontario Chamber of Commerce.
Ontario Federation of Labour. 2011. *Closing of Brantford's ECP Factory the Disgracful Result of Premier's Inaction*. Toronto: OFL.
Ontario Labour Relations Board. 2011. "Ontario Labour Relations Board 2011." In *Annual Report*. Toronto: OLRB.
Ontario Liberal Party. 2003. *Choose Change*. Toronto: Ontario Labour Party.
– 2007. *Moving Forward Together*. Toronto: Ontario Labour Party.
– 2011. *Forward Together*. Toronto: Ontario Labour Party.
Orhangazi, Ozgur. 2008. *Financialization and the US Economy*. Northampton, MA: Edward Elgar Publishing.
Osberg, Lars. 2008. *A Quarter Century of Economic Inequality: 1981–2006*. Ottawa: Canadian Centre for Policy Alternatives.
Oxfam America. 2004. *Like Machines in the Fields: Workers without Rights in American Agriculture*. Boston: Oxfam America.
Oxfam GB. 2016. *Tax Battles: The Dangerous Global Race to the Bottom on Corporate Tax*. Oxford: Oxfam.
Page, Benjamin, and Lawrence R. Jacobs. 2009. *Class War? What Americans Really Think about Economic Inequality*. Chicago: University of Chicago Press.
Palan, Ronen, Richard Murphy, and Christian Chavagneux. 2013. *Tax Havens: How Globalization Really Works*. Ithaca, NY: Cornell University Press.
Palley, Thomas I. 2013. *Financialization: The Economics of Finance Capital Domination*. London: Palgrave Macmillan UK.

Panitch, Leo, and Sam Gindin. 2013. *The Making of Global Capitalism*. New York: Verso.

Panitch, Leo, and Donald Swartz. 2003. *From Consent to Coercion: The Assault on Trade Union Freedoms*. 3rd ed. Aurora, ON: Garamond.

– 2013. "The Continuing Assault on Public Sector Unions." In *Public Sector Unions in the Age of Austerity*, edited by S. Ross and L. Savage. Halifax: Fernwood Publishing.

Parfitt, Ben. 2017. *The Great Log Export Drain*. Vancouver,: Canadian Centre for Policy Alternatives.

Peck, Jamie. 2001. *Workfare States*. New York: Guilford Publications.

– 2010. *Constructions of Neoliberal Reason*. New York: Oxford University Press.

Pedersini, Roberto. 2006. "Relocation of Production and Industrial Relations." Brussels: European Foundation for the Improvement of Living and Working Conditions. https://air.unimi.it/handle/2434/10625.

Peirce, Jon, and Karen Bentham. 2009. *Canadian Industrial Relations*. 3rd ed. Toronto: Pearson/Prentice Hall.

Peters, John. 2010. "Down in the Vale: Corporate Globalization, Unions on the Defensive, and the USW Local 6500 Strike in Sudbury, 2009–2010." *Labour/Le Travail* 66 (Fall): 73–106.

– 2011. "The Rise of Finance and the Decline of Organised Labour in the Advanced Capitalist Countries." *New Political Economy* 16 (1): 73–99. https://doi.org/10.1080/13563461003789746.

–, ed 2012a. *Boom, Bust, and Crisis: Work and Labour in 21st Century Canada*. Halifax: Fernwood Publishing.

– 2012b. "Free Markets and the Decline of Unions and Good Jobs." In *Boom, Bust and Crisis: Labour, Corporate Power and Politics in Canada*, edited by J. Peters, 16–53. Halifax: Fernwood Publishing.

– 2012c. "Neoliberal Convergence in North America and Western Europe: Fiscal Austerity, Privatization, and Public Sector Reform." *Review of International Political Economy* 19 (2): 208–35. http://doi.org/10.1080/09692290.2011.552783.

– 2017. "Post-Democracy and the Politics of Inequality: Explaining Policy Responses to the Financial Crisis and the Great Recession." In *The Austerity State*, edited by S. McBride and B.M. Evans, 44–73. Toronto: University of Toronto Press.

2018. "The Ontario Growth Model: The 'End of the Road' or a 'New Economy'?" In *Divided Province: Ontario Politics in the Age of Neoliberalism*, edited by G. Albo and B. Evans, 43–76. Montreal and Kingston: McGill-Queen's University Press.

Pettifor, Ann. 2017. *The Production of Money: How to Break the Power of Bankers*. New York: Verso Books.

Phalippou, Ludovic, Christian Rauch, and Marc Umber. 2016. *Private Equity Portfolio Company Fees*. Oxford: Oxford University, Frankfurt School of Finance and Management.

Phillips, Stephen. 2010. "Party Politics in British Columbia: The Persistence of Polarization." In *British Columbia Politics and Government*, edited by M. Howlett, D. Pilon, and T. Summerville. Toronto: Emond Montgomery.

Piazza, James A. 2002. *Going Global: Unions and Globalization in the United States, Sweden, and Germany*. Lanham, MD: Lexington Books.

Pickett, Kate, and Richard Wilkinson. 2010. *The Spirit Level: Why Equality Is Better for Everyone*. New York: Penguin Books USA.

Pierson, Paul. 2001. *The New Politics of the Welfare State*. New York: Oxford University Press.

2003. "Big, Slow-Moving, and Invisible: Macrosocial Processes in the Study of Comparative Politics." In *Comparative Historical Analysis in the Social Sciences*, edited by J. Mahoney and Dietrich Rueschmeyer, 131–74. New York: Cambridge University Press.

Pierson, Paul, and Theda Skocpol, eds. 2007. *The Transformation of American Politics: Activist Government and the Rise of Conservatism*. Princeton, NJ: Princeton University Press.

Piketty, Thomas. 2014. *Capital in the Twenty-First Century*. Cambridge, MA: Harvard University Press.

Pilon, Dennis, Stephanie Ross, and Larry Savage. 2010. "Solidarity Revisited: Organized Labour and the New Democratic Party." *Canadian Political Science Review* 5 (1): 20–37. https://ojs-test.unbc.ca/index.php/cpsr/article/view/291.

Plewa, Piotr. 2007. "The Rise and Fall of Temporary Foreign Worker Policies: Lessons for Poland." *International Migration* 45 (2): 3–36.

Pollitt, Christopher, and Geert Bouckaert. 2004. *Public Management Reform: A Comparative Analysis*. 2nd ed. New York: Oxford University Press.

Pollock, Allyson M., and Colin Leys. 2005. *NHS Plc: The Privatisation of Our Health Care*. New York: Verso.

Pontusson, Jonas. 2005. *Inequality and Prosperity: Social Europe vs. Liberal America*. Ithaca, NY: Cornell University Press.

Pontusson, Jonas, and David Rueda. 2008. "Inequality as a Source of Political Polarization: A Comparative Analysis of Twelve OECD Countries." In *Democracy, Inequality, and Representation*, edited by P. Beramendi and C. Anderson, 312–53. New York: Russell Sage Foundation. http://www.jstor.org/stable/10.7758/9781610440448.

Porter, Tony. 2004. *Globalization and Finance*. Malden, MA: Polity.

– 2014. "Canada, the FSB, and the International Institutional Response to the Current Crisis." In *Crisis and Reform: Canada and the International Financial System*, edited by R. Medhora and D. Rowlands, 71–86. Montreal and Kingston: McGill-Queen's University Press.

Poulantzas, Nicos. 1978. *Political Power and Social Classes*. London: Verso.

Preibisch, Kerry. 2010. "Pick-Your-Own Labor: Migrant Workers and Flexibility in Canadian Agriculture." *International Migration Review* 44 (2): 404–11. https://doi.org/10.1111/j.1747-7379.2010.00811.x.

– 2012. "Migrant Workers and Changing Work-Place Regimes in Contemporary Agricultural Production in Canada." *International Journal of Sociology of Agriculture and Food* 19 (1): 62–82. https://doi.org/10.48416/ijsaf.v19i1.237.

Prebisch, Kerry, and Leigh Binford. 2007. "Interrogating Racialized Global Labour Supply: An Exploration of the Ethnic Replacement of Foreign Agricultural Workers in Canada." *Canadian Review of Sociology and Anthropology* 44 (1): 5–36. https://doi.org/10.1111/j.1755-618X.2007.tb01146.x.

Prebisch, Kerry, and Jenna Hennebry. 2011. "Temporary Migration, Chronic Effects: The Health of International Migrant Workers." *Canadian Medical Association Journal* 183 (9): 1033–8. https://doi.org/10.1503%2Fcmaj.090736.

Preqin. 2015. *Private Equity in Europe*. London. https://docs.preqin.com/reports/Preqin-European-Private-Equity-June-2015.pdf.

– 2016a. *2016 Preqin Global Hedge Fund Report*. New York: Preqin.

– 2016b. 2016 *Preqin Global Private Equity and Venture Capital Report*. London: Preqin.

PricewaterhouseCoopers. 2009. *Canadian Mining Taxation: 2009 Toronto*. Toronto: PricewaterhouseCoopers.

– 2010a. *Canadian Annual Energy Survey 2010 Edition: Survey of 2009 Results*. Toronto: PricewaterhouseCoopers.

– 2010b. *Mine Back to the Boom: Review of Global Trends in the Mining Industry – 2010*. Toronto: PricewaterhouseCoopers.

Progressive Conservative Party of NL. 2003. *Our Blueprint for the Future*. St. John's, NL: PC Party.

– 2007. *Proud, Strong, Determined: The Future Is Ours*. St. John's, NL: PC Party.

Pulignano, Valeria, and Maarten Keune. 2014. "Understanding Varieties of Flexiblity and Security in Multi-nationals: Product Markets, Institutions Variation, and Local Bargaining." *European Journal of Industrial Relations* 21 (1): 5–21. https://doi.org/10.1177/0959680114527880.

Puri, Poonam. 2012. "'Bank Bashing' Is a Popular Sport." In *Banking Systems in Crisis: The Faces of Liberal Capitalism*, edited by S. Konzelmann and M. Fovargue-Davies, 155–85. New York: Routledge.

PWC. 2010. *Report 6: Economic Impact of the 2010 Olympic and Paralympic Winter Games on British Columbia and Canada*. Vancouver: PricewaterhouseCoopers.

– 2011. *Forging Ahead: The Mining Industry in British Columbia*. Vancouver: PricewaterhouseCoopers.

– 2012. *Oil and Gas Taxation in Canada*. Toronto: PricewaterhouseCoopers.

Radetizki, Marian. 2010. *A Handbook of Primary Commodities in the Global Economy*. New York: Cambridge University Press.

Räthzel, Nora, and David Uzzell. 2012. *Trade Unions in the Green Economy: Working for the Environment*. New York: Routledge.

RBC Economics. 2012. *Vancouver's Housing Market: Moderation in Store*. Vancouver: RBC.

RBC-Pembina Institute. 2013. *Priced Out: Understanding the Factors Affecting Home Prices in the GTA*. Toronto: Pembina Institute.

Red Seal Secretariat. 2014. *Apprenticeship Completion, Certification, and Outcomes*. Gatineau, QC: Employment and Social Development Canada.

Rehm, Phillip, Jacob S. Hacker, and Mark Schlesinger. 2012. "Insecure Alliances: Risk Inequality and the Support for the Welfare State." *American Political Science Review* 106 (2): 386–406. https://doi.org/10.1017/S0003055412000147.

Reich, Robert. 2016. *Saving Capitalism: For the Many, Not the Few*. New York: Alfred A. Knopf.

Richardson, Jack. 1992. "Free Trade: Why Did it Happen?" *Canadian Review of Sociology/Revue canadienne de sociologie* 29 (3): 307–28. https://doi.org/10.1111/j.1755-618X.1992.tb02441.x.

RMS Review Committee. 2005. *Report of the Chairman Raw Material Sharing Review Committee*. St. John's, NL: Department of Fisheries and Aquaculture.

Roberts, Anthony, and Roy Kwon. 2017. "Finance, Inequality and the Varieties of Capitalism in Post-Industrial Democracies." *Socio-Economic Review* 15 (3): 511–38. https://doi.org/10.1093/ser/mwx021.

Roberts, Paul. 2009. *The End of Food*. New York: Houghton Mifflin Harcourt.

Roberts, Wayne. 2013. *The No-Nonsense Guide to World Food*. Toronto: Between the Lines.

Robertson, Grant. 2011a. "CIBC's McGaughey Gets 50% Raise." *Globe and Mail*, 17 March.

– 2011b. "Scotiabank's Rick Waugh Earns $10.7 Million." *Globe and Mail*, 4 March.

Rogenmoser, Frederic, Martine Lauzon, and Leo-Paul Lauzon. 2012. *Le réel taux d'imposition de grandes entreprises canadiennes: du mythe à la réalité*. Montreal: Le Laboratoire d'études socio-économiques de l'UQAM.

Rose, Joseph B. 2007. "Canadian Public Sector Unions at the Crossroads." *Journal of Collective Negotiations* 31 (7): 183–98. http://doi.org/10.2190/CN.31.3.a.

Rosenfeld, Herman. 2009. "The North American Auto Industry in Crisis." *Monthly Review* 61, no. 2, 18–36. https://doi.org/10.14452/MR-061-02-2009-06_2.

Rosenfeld, Jake. 2014. *What Unions No Longer Do*. Cambridge, MA: Harvard University Press.

Ross, Michael L. 2012. *The Oil Curse: How Petroleum Wealth Shapes the Development of Nations*. Princeton, NJ: Princeton University Press.

Ross, Stephanie. 2013. "Social Unionism and Union Power in Public Sector Unions." In *Public Sector Unions in the Age of Austerity*, edited by S. Ross and L. Savage, 9–17. Halifax: Fernwood Publishing.

Ross, Stephanie, and Larry Savage, eds. 2012. *The Politics of Labour in Canada*. Halilfax: Fernwood Publishing.

– eds. 2013. *Public Sector Unions in the Age of Austerity, Labour in Canada*. Halifax: Fernwood Publishing.

Ross, Stephanie, Larry Savage, Errol Black, and Jim Silver. 2015. *Building a Better World: An Introduction to the Labour Movement in Canada*. Halifax: Fernwood Publishing.

Rutherford, Tod, and John Holmes. 2014. "Manufacturing Resiliency: Economic Restructuring and Automotive Manufacturing in the Great Lakes Region."

Cambridge Journal of Regions, Economy and Society 7 (3): 359–78. http://doi.org
/10.1093/cjres/rsu014.

Rydqvist, Kristian, Joshua Spizman, and Ilya Strebulaev. 2011. "The Evolution of
Aggregate Stock Ownership." CFS Working Paper. Frankfurt: Center for Financial
Studies.

Sachs, Jeffrey D., and Andrew M. Warner. 2001. "The Curse of Natural Resources."
European Economic Review 45 (4–6): 827–38. http://doi.org/10.1016/S0014
-2921(01)00125-8.

Saez, Emmanuel, and Michael R. Veall. 2005. "The Evolution of High Incomes in
North America: Lessons from the Canadian Evidence." *American Economic Review*
95 (3): 831–49. https://doi.org/10.1257/0002828054201404.

Saez, Emmanuel, and Gabriel Zucman. 2019. *The Triumph of Injustice: How the Rich
Dodge Taxes and How to Make Them Pay*. New York: W.W. Norton.

Salverda, Weimar, and Christina Haas. 2014. "Earnings, Employment, and Income
Inequality." In *Changing Inequalities in Rich Countries*, edited by W. Salverda,
B. Nolan, D. Checchi, I. Marx, A. McKnight, I. Toth, and H. van de Werhorst,
49–81. New York: Oxford University Press.

Salverda, Weimar, Brian Nolan, Daniele Checchi, Ive Marx, Abigail McKnight, Gyorgy
Toth, and Herman van de Werhorst, eds. 2014. *Changing Inequaities in Rich Countries:
Analytical and Comparative Perspectives*. New York: Oxford University Press.

Salverda, Wiemer, Brian Nolan, and Timothy M. Smeeding. 2009. *The Oxford
Handbook of Economic Inequality*. Oxford: Oxford University Press.

Sandborn, Tom. 2008. "Foreign Farm Workers Unionize: A First in BC." *Tyee*, 21 August.
– 2010. "The Biggest Rollback of Worker Rights in Canadian History." *Tyee*,
7 September.

Sassoon, Donald. 2010. *One Hundred Years of Socialism*. London: I.B. Tauris.

Savage, Larry. 2010. "Contemporary Party-Union Relations in Canada." *Labor Studies
Journal* 35 (1): 8–26. http://doi.org/10.1177/0160449X09353028.

Schafer, Armin, and Wolfgang Streeck, eds. 2013. *Politics in the Age of Austerity*.
Malden, MA: Polity.

Scheur, Steen. 2007. "Dilemmas of Collectivism: Danish Trade Unions in the Twenty-
First Century." *Journal of Labor Research* 28 (2): 233–54. https://link.springer.com
/article/10.1007/BF03380044.

Schmidt, Ingo, and Bryan Evans. 2012. *Social Democracy after the Cold War*.
Edmonton, AB: Athabasca University Press.

Schmitt, John. 2012. *Low-Wage Lessons*. Washington, DC: Center for Economic and
Policy Research.

Schuetze, Hans, Larry Kuehn, Adam Davidson-Harden, Daniel Schurgensky, and
Nadya Weber. 2011. "Globalization, Neoliberalism, and Schools: The Canadian
Story." In *Educating the Global Citizen – In the Shadow of Neoliberalism: Thirty
Years of Educational Reform in North America*, edited by L. Olmos, C. Alberto
Torres, and R. Van Heertum. Oak Park, IL: Bentham Science Publishers.

Schulten, Thorsten. 2014. *Minimum Wage Regimes in Europe – And What Germany Can Learn from Them*. Berlin: Friedrich-Ebert-Stiftung.

Schwartz, Harold, and Leonard Seabrooke. 2008. "Varieties of Residential Capitalism in the International Political Economy: Old Welfare States and the New Politics of Housing." *Comparative European Politics* 6 (3): 237–61.

Schwartz, Herman. 2009. *Subprime Nation: American Power, Global Capital, and the Housing Bubble*. Ithaca, NY: Cornell University Press.

Seccareccia, Mario. 2012. "Financialization and the Transformation of Commercial Banking: Understanding the Recent Canadian Experience before and during the International Financial Crisis." *Journal of Post Keynesian Economics* 35 (2): 277–300. https://doi.org/10.2753/PKE0160-3477350206.

Seguin, Marc-Andre. 2013. "Shell Companies: Blinders On." *National Magazine,* June.

Shantz, Jeff. 2009. "The Limits of Social Unionism in Canada." *Working USA: The Journal of Labor and Society* 12 (1): 113–29. https://doi.org/10.1111/j.1743-4580 .2008.01222.x.

Shaoul, Jean, Anne Stafford, and Pamela Stapleton. 2007. "Partnerships and the Role of Financial Advisors: Private Control over Public Policy." *Policy and Politics* 35 (3) 479–95. http://doi.org/10.1332/030557307781571678.

Sharma, Nandita. 2005. *Home Economics: Nationalism and the Making of "Migrant Workers" in Canada*. Toronto: University of Toronto Press.

Sharpe, Andrew, and Evan Capeluck. 2012. *The Impact of Redistribution on Income Inequality in Canada and the Provinces, 1981–2010*. Ottawa: Centre for the Study of Living Standards.

Shaxson, Nicholas. 2012. *Treasure Islands: Tax Havens and the Men Who Stole the World.* New York: Random House.

– 2018. *The Finance Curse: How Global Finance Is Making Us All Poorer*. London: Penguin Books.

Siegel, Donald, Mike Wright, and Igor Filatotcheve. 2011. "Private Equity, LBOs, and Corporate Governance: International Evidence." *Corporate Governance: An International Review* 19 (3): 185–94. https://doi.org/10.1111/j.1467-8683 .2010.00842.x.

Siemiatycki, Elliot. 2012. "Forced to Concede: Permanent Restructuring and Labour's Place in the North American Auto Industry." *Antipode: A Radical Journal of Geography* 44 (2): 453–73. https://doi.org/10.1111/j.1467-8330.2010 .00863.x.

– 2012. "Forced to Concede: Permanent Restructuring and Labour's Place in the North American Auto Industry." *Antipode* 44 (2): 453–73. https://doi.org/10.1111 /j.1467-8330.2010.00863.x.

Sjoberg, Ola. 2009. "Corporate Governance and Earnings Inequality in the OECD Countries, 1979–2000." *European Sociological Review* 25 (5): 519–33. https://doi .org/10.1093/esr/jcn069.

Skerrett, Kevin. 2017. "Canada's Public Pension Funds: The 'New Masters of the (Neoliberal) Universe." In *The Contradictions of Pension Fund Capitalism*, edited by K. Skerrett, J. Weststar, S. Archer, and C. Roberts, 121–54. Ithaca, NY: Cornell University Press.

Skerrett, Kevin, Chris Roberts, Johanna Weststar, and Simon Archer, eds. 2018. *The Contradictions of Pension Fund Capitalism*. Ithaca, NY: Cornell University Press.

Skocpol, Theda. 2003. *Diminished Democracy: From Membership to Management in American Civic Life*. Norman: University of Oklahoma Press.

Skocpol, Theda, and Vanessa Williamson. 2012. *The Tea Party and the Remaking of Republican Conservatism*. New York: Oxford University Press.

Slinn, Sara. 2004. "The Effect of Compulsory Certification Votes on Certification Applications in Ontario: An Empirical Analysis." *Canadian Labour and Employment Law Journal* 10: 367–97.

– 2008. "No Right (to Organize) without a Remedy: Evidence and Consequences of the Failure to Provide Compensatory Remedies for Unfair Labour Practices in British Columbia." *McGill Law Journal* 53:688–737.

Smith, Charles W. 2008. "The Politics of Ontario Labour Relations Act: Business, Labour, and Government in the Consolidation of Post-War Industrial Relations, 1949–1961." *Labour/Le Travail* 62 (Fall): 109–51. URI: https://id.erudit.org/iderudit /llt62art04.

Sorbara, Greg. 2014. *The Battlefield of Ontario Politics*. Toronto: Dundurn.

Soss, Joe, and Lawrence R. Jacobs. 2009. "The Place of Inequality: Non-Participation in the American Polity." *Political Science Quarterly* 124 (1): 95–125. https://doi .org/10.1002/j.1538-165X.2009.tb00643.x.

Spitz-Oener, A. 2006. "Technical Change, Job Tasks, and Rising Educational Demands: Looking outside the Wage Structure." *Journal of Labor Economics* 24 (2): 235–70. http://doi.org/10.1086/499972.

Springer, Simon, Kean Birch, and Julie MacLeavy. 2016. *Handbook of Neoliberalism*. New York: Routledge.

Standing, Guy. 2002. *Beyond the New Paternalism: Basic Security as Equality*. New York: Verso.

– 2011. *The Precariat: The New Dangerous Class*. New York: Bloomsbury Academic.

– 2016. *The Corruption of Capitalism: Why Rentiers Thrive and Work Does Not Pay*. London: Biteback Publishing.

Stanford, Jim. 1999. *Paper Boom: Why Real Prosperity Requires a New Approach to Canada's Economy*. Ottawa: Canadian Centre for Policy Alternatives/James Lorimer.

– 2008. "Staples, Deindustrialization, and Foreign Investment: Canada's Economic Journey Back to the Future." *Studies in Political Economy* 82 (Autumn): 7–34. https://doi.org/10.1080/19187033.2008.11675062.

– 2010. "The Geography of Auto Globalization and the Politics of Auto Bailouts." *Cambridge Journal of Regions, Economy and Society* 3:383–405. https://doi.org /10.1093/cjres/rsq025.

– 2011. *Having Their Cake and Eating It Too. Business Profits, Taxes, and Investment in Canada: 1961 through 2010*. Ottawa: Canadian Centre for Policy Alternatives.

Stapleton, John. 2019. *The Working Poor in the Toronto Region*. Toronto: Metcalf Foundation. https://metcalffoundation.com/publication/the-working-poor-in-the -toronto-region-a-closer-look-at-the-increasing-numbers/.

Statistics Canada. 2017. "Household Income in Canada: Key Results from the 2016 Census." *Daily*. Ottawa: Statistics Canada.

Stiefmueller, Christian. 2017. *Ten Years After: The 2017 Banking Package: One Step Forward, Two Steps Back*. Brussels: Finance Watch.

– 2018. *Ten Years After: Back to Business as Usual*. Brussels: Finance Watch.

Stiglitz, Joseph E. 2006. *Making Globalization Work*. New York: W.W. Norton.

– 2010. *Freefall: America, Free Markets, and the Sinking of the World Economy*. New York: W.W. Norton.

– 2013. *The Price of Inequality: How Today's Divided Society Endangers Our Future*. New York: W.W. Norton.

– 2015. *Rewriting the Rules of the American Economy: An Agenda for Growth and Shared Prosperity*. New York: W.W. Norton.

– 2017. *Globalization and Discontents Revisited: Anti-Globalization in the Era of Trump*. New York: W.W. Norton.

Stiglitz, Joseph E., Amartya Sen, and Jean-Paul Fitoussi. 2009. *Report by the Commission on the Measurement of Economic Performance and Social Progress*. Paris.

Stinson, Jane, Nancy Pollak, and Marcy Cohen. 2005. *The Pains of Privatization: How Contracting Out Hurts Health Support Workers, Their Families, and Health Care*. Vancouver: Canadian Centre for Policy Alternatives BC Office.

Stockhammer, Engelbert. 2013a. "Financialization, Income Distribution and the Crisis." In *Financial Crisis, Labour Markets and Institutions*, edited by S. Fadda and P. Tridico, 98–119. New York: Routledge.

– 2013b. *Why Have Wage Shares Fallen? A Panel Analysis of the Determinants of Functional Income Distribution*. Conditions of Work and Employment and Series. Geneva: International Labour Organization.

– 2015. "Rising Inequality as a Cause of the Present Crisis." *Cambridge Journal of Economics* 39 (3): 935–58.

Strange, Susan. 1996. *The Retreat of the State: The Diffusion of Power in the World Economy*. New York: Cambridge University Press.

– Streeck, Wolfgang. 2014. *Buying Time: The Delayed Crisis of Democratic Capitalism*. New York: Verso.

Stroud, Dean, Peter Fairbrother, Claire Evans, and Joanne Blake. 2015. "Governments Matter for Capitalist Economies: Regeneration and Transition to Green and Decent Jobs." *Economic and Industrial Democracy*, 39 (1): 87–108. https://doi.org/10.1177 /0143831X15601731.

Swank, Duane. 2002. *Global Capital, Political Institutions, and Policy Change in Developed Welfare States*. New York: Cambridge University Press.

Sweeney, Brendan. 2010. *Comparing Employment Relations in a Cross-Border Region: The Case of Cascadia's Forest Products Industry*, Kingston, ON: Queen's University, PhD, Department of Geography.

Swift, Jamie, and Keith Stewart. 2005. "Union Power: The Charged Politics of Electricity in Ontario." *Just Labour: A Canadian Journal of Work and Society* 5 (Winter): 14–22.

Tattersall, Amanda. 2010. *Power in Coalition: Strategies for Strong Unions and Social Change*. Ithaca, NY: Cornell University Press.

– 2015. *Narrative Report on Canada*. Chelsam, UK: Tax Justice Network.

Taylor, Amy, Matthew Bramley, and Mark Winfield. 2005. *Government Spending on Canada's Oil and Gas Industry: Undermining Canada's Kyoto Commitment*. Edmonton, AB: Pembina Institute.

Taylor, Amy, and Marlo Raynolds. 2006. *Thinking like an Owner: Overhauling the Royalty and Tax Treatment of Alberta's Oil Sands*. Edmonton, AB: Pembina Institute.

Teles, Steven M. 2009. *The Rise of the Conservative Legal Movement: The Battle for Control of the Law*. Princeton, NJ: Princeton University Press.

Telegram. 2008. "Unemployment Rate Expected to Dip: BMO," 16 February.

Thelen, Kathleen. 2012. "Varieties of Capitalism: Trajectories of Liberalization and the New Politics of Social Solidarity." *Annual Review of Political Science* 15:137–59. https://doi.org/10.1146/annurev-polisci-070110-122959.

– 2014. *Varieties of Liberalisation and the New Politics of Social Solidarity*. New York: Cambridge University Press.

Thomas, Mark. 2009. *Regulating Flexibility: The Political Economy of Employment Standards*. Montreal and Kington: McGill-Queen's University Press.

Thomas, Mark, and Steven Tufts. 2016. "Austerity, Right Populism, and the Crisis of Labour in Canada." *Antipode* 48 (1): 212–30. https://doi.org/10.1111/anti.12162.

Thompson, Paul. 2013. "Financialization and the Workplace." *Work, Employment & Society* 27 (3): 472–88. https://doi.org/10.1177%2F0950017013479827.

Tiessen, Kaylie. 2014. *Seismic Shift: Ontario's Changing Labour Market*. Toronto: Canadian Centre for Policy Alternatives.

Tilly, Charles, and Sidney G. Tarrow. 2015. *Contentious Politics*. New York: Oxford University Press.

Tobin, Anne-Marie. 1992. "Delay Planned Labour Law Changes, Says Coalition Group." *Ottawa Citizen*, 4 February.

Tomaskovic-Devey, Donald, Ken-Hou Lin, and Nathan Meyers. 2015. "Did Financialization Reduce Economic Growth?" *Socio-Economic Review* 13 (3): 525–48.

Tomlinson, Kathy. 2017. "British Columbia: The 'Wild West' of Fundraising." *Globe and Mail*, 10 March. https://www.theglobeandmail.com/news/investigations/wild -west-bc-lobbyists-breaking-one-of-provinces-few-political-donationrules /article34207677/.

Toninelli, Pierangelo Maria, ed. 2000. *The Rise and Fall of State-Owned Enterprise in the Western World*. New York: Cambridge University Press.

Tooze, Adam. 2018. *Crashed: How a Decade of Financial Crisis Changed the World*. New York: Penguin Random House.

Toronto Financial Services Alliance. 2016. *Review of the Federal Financial Sector Framework*. Toronto. https://www.canada.ca/content/dam/fin/migration/consultresp/pdf-ssge-sefc/ssge-sefc-61.pdf.

Toronto Life. 2011. "The Loaded List. We Catalogue the Astronomical Salaries of Toronto's Ruling Class," 9 November.

Torys LLP. 2016. *Private Equity in Focus*. Toronto: Torys LLP.

Tucker, E. 2008. "The Constitutional Right to Bargain Collectively: The Ironies of Labour History in the Supreme Court of Canada." *Labour/Le Travail* 61 (Spring). URI: https://id.erudit.org/iderudit/llt61pre01.

– 2012. "Farm Worker Exceptionalism: Past, Present, and the Post-Fraser Future." In *Constitutional Labour Rights in Canada: Farm Workers and the Fraser Case*, edited by F. Faraday, J. Fudge, and E. Tucker. Toronto: Irwin Law.

Uguccioni, James, Andrew Sharpe, and Alexander Murray. 2016. *Labour Productivity and the Distribution of Real Earnings in Canada, 1976–2014*. Ottawa: Centre for the Study of Living Standards.

UN Department of Economic and Social Affairs. 2010. *Trends in Sustainable Development: Chemicals, Mining, Transport, and Waste Management*. New York: UN Division for Sustainable Development.

UNIFOR. 2015. *Building Balance, Fairness, and Opportunity in Ontario's Labour Market*. Toronto: UNIFOR.

United Nations Conference of Trade and Development (UNCTAD). 2009a. *Trade and Development Report, 2009*. New York: UNCTD.

– 2009b. *World Investment Report 2009*. New York: United Nations.

– 2012. *World Investment Report 2012*. New York: United Nations.

– 2013. *World Investment Report*. New York: United Nations.

– 2016. *World Investment Report 2016*. New York: United Nations.

United Steelworkers. 2015. *Submission by the United Steelworkers: Ontario's Changing Workplaces Review Consultation Process*. Toronto: United Steelworkers.

Upchurch, Martin, Graham Taylor, and Andrew Mathers. 2009. *The Crisis of Social Democratic Trade Unionism in Western Europe, Contemporary Employment Relations Series*. Surrey, UK: Ashgate Publishing.

Urquhart, Ian. 2007. "Tory Faces Union Ad Campaign." *Toronto Star*, 15 June.

USW. 2011. "Banning Replacement Workers: It Will Happen Eventually." United Steelworkers District 6. Toronto, 11 April.

vander Ploeg, Casey, and Jack Vicq. 2011. *A Tax Framework for Saskatchewan's Continuing Prosperity*. Calgary: Canada West Foundation.

van der Ploeg, Fredrick, and Steven Poelhekke. 2009. "Volatility and the Natural Resource Curse." *Oxford Economic Papers* 61 (4): 727–60. http://doi.org/10.1093/oep/gpp027.

van der Zwan, Natascha. 2014. "Making Sense of Financialization." *Socio-Economic Review* 12 (1): 99–129. http://doi.org/10.1093/ser/mwt020.

Van Harten, Peter. 2004. "Strategy Corp Home to Divine Crop of Insiders, Lobbyists Can Negotiate Hall of Power." *Hamilton Spectator*, 24 January.

Veall, Michael R. 2012. "Top Income Shares in Canada: Recent Trends and Why They Might Matter." *Canadian Journal of Economics* 45 (4): 1247–72.

Victor, Peter A. 2008. *Managing without Growth: Slower by Design, Not Disaster.* Cheltenham, UK: Edward Elgar Publishing.

Visser, Jelle. 2019. *Trade Unions in the Balance.* Geneva: International Labour Organization, Bureau for Workers' Activities (ACTRAV). https://etufegypt.com/wp-content/uploads/2019/10/wcms_722482.pdf.

Vodden, Kelly. 2008. *New Spaces, Ancient Places: Collaborative Governance and Sustainable Development on Canada's Coasts.* Vancouver: Geography, Simon Fraser University.

– 2010. "Heroes, Hope, and Resource Development in Canada's Periphery: Lessons from Newfoundland and Labrador." In *The Next Rural Economies: Constructing Rural Place in Global Economies,* edited by G. Halseth, S. Markey, and D. Bruce. Oxfordshire, UK: CABI International.

Volscho, Thomas W., and Nathan J. Kelly. 2012. "The Rise of the Super-Rich Power Resources, Taxes, Financial Markets, and the Dynamics of the Top 1 Per Cent, 1949 to 2008." *American Sociological Review* 77 (5): 679–99. https://doi.org/10.1177/0003122412458508.

Vosko, Leah, ed. 2006a. *Understanding Labour Market Insecurity in Canada.* Montreal and Kingston: McGill-Queen's University Press.

– ed. 2006b. *Precarious Employment: Understanding Labour Market Insecurity in Canada.* Montreal and Kingston: McGill-Queen's University Press.

– 2013. "'Rights without Remedies': Enforcing Employment Standards in Ontario by Maximizing Voice among Workers in Precarious Jobs." *Osgoode Hall Law Journal* 50 (4): 845–74.

Vosko, Leah, and the Closing the Enforcement Gap Research Group. 2020. *Closing the Enforcement Gap: Improving Employment Standards Protections for People in Precarious Jobs.* Toronto: University of Toronto Press.

Vosko, Leah, Martha MacDonald, and Iain Campbell, eds. 2009. *Gender and the Contours of Precarious Employment.* London: Routledge.

Vosko, Leah, and Mark Thomas. 2014. "Confronting the Employment Standards Enforcement Gap: Exploring the Potential for Union Engagement with Employment Law in Ontario, Canada." *Journal of Industrial Relations* 56 (5): 631–52. http://doi.org/10.1177/0022185613511562.

Wailes, Nick, Chris Wright, Greg Bamber, and Russell Lansbury. 2016. "Introduction: An Internationally Comparative Approach to Employment Relations." In *International and Comparative Employment Relations: National Regulation, Global Changes,* edited by N. Wailes, C. Wright, G. Bamber, and R. Lansbury, 1–19. Thousand Oaks, CA: Sage Publications.

Walchuk, Bradley. 2009. "Ontario's Agriculture Workers and Collective Bargaining: A History of Struggle." *Just Labour: A Canadian Journal of Work and Society* 14 (Autumn): 150–63.

– 2010. "Changing Union-Party Relations in Canada: The Rise of the Working Families Coalition." *Labor Studies Journal* 35 (1): 27–50. http://doi.org/10.1177/0160449X09353036.

Walkom, Thomas. 2010. "The Art of Reverse Class Resentment." *Toronto Star*, 27 February.

Walks, Alan. 2014. "Canada's Housing Bubble Story: Mortgage Securitization, the State, and the Global Financial Crisis," *International Journal of Urban and Regional Research* 38 (1): 256–84. https://doi.org/10.1111/j.1468-2427.2012.01184.x.

Walks, Alan, and Brian Clifford. 2015. "The Political Economy of Mortgage Securitization and the Neoliberalization of Housing Policy in Canada." *Environment and Planning A* 47 (8): 1624–42. https://doi.org/10.1068%2Fa130226p.

Wallace, Iain. 1996. "Restructuring in the Canadian Mining and Mineral-Processing Industries." In *Canada and the Global Economy: The Geography of Structural and Technological Change*, edited by J.H. Britton. Toronto: University of Toronto Press.

Wang, Lu, and Callie Bost. 2014. *S&P 500 Companies Spend Almost All Profits on Buybacks*. New York: Bloomberg.

Warner, Kris. 2013. "The Decline of Unionization in the United States: Some Lessons from Canada." *Labour Studies Journal* 38 (2): 110–38. http://doi.org/10.1177/0160449X13490801.

Warren, Elizabeth. 2018. "Companies Shouldn't Be Accountable Only to Shareholders." *Wall Street Journal*, 14 August.

Watt, Andrew. 2008. "The Impact of Private Equity on European Companies and Workers: Key Issues and a Review of the Evidence." *Industrial Relations Journal* 39 (6): 548–68. https://doi.org/10.1111/j.1468-2338.2008.00505.x.

Watts, Michael. 2014. "Oil Frontiers: The Niger Delta and the Gulf of Mexico." In *Oil Culture*, edited by R. Barrett and D. Worden. Minneapolis: University of Minnesota Press.

Weil, David. 2014. *The Fissured Workplace: Why Work Became So Bad for So Many and What Can Be Done to Improve It*. Cambridge, MA: Harvard University Press.

Weis, Anthony John. 2007. *The Global Food Economy: The Battle for the Future of Farming*. London: Zed Books.

Wells, Don. 1995. "Origins of Canada's Wagner Model of Industrial Relations: The United Auto Workers in Canada and the Supression of 'Rank and File' Unionism, 1936–1953." *Canadian Jounal of Sociology* 20 (2): 193–225.

– 2016. "Living Wage Campaigns and Building Communities." *Alternate Routes: A Journal of Critical Social Research* 27:235–46. http://www.alternateroutes.ca/index.php/ar/article/view/22400.

Wells, Don, Janet McLaughlin, Andre Lyn, and Aaron Diaz Mendiburo. 2014. "Sustaining Precarious Transnational Families: The Significance of Remittances from Canada's Seasonal Agricultural Workers Program." *Just Labour* 22 (Autumn): 144–67.

Western, Bruce. 1997. *Between Class and Market: Postwar Unionization in the Capitalist Democracies*. Princeton, NJ: Princeton University Press.

Whiteside, Heather. 2015. *Purchase for Profit: Public-Private Partnerships and Canada's Public Health System*. Toronto: University of Toronto Press.

Whitfield, Dexter. 2001. *Public Services or Corporate Welfare: Rethinking the Nation State in the Global Economy*. Sterling, VA: Pluto.

– 2012. *In Place of Austerity: Reconstructing the Economy, State and Public Services*. Nottingham, UK: Spokesman Books.

Whittaker, Julie M., and Katelin P. Isaacs. 2013. *Unemployment Insurance: Legislative Issues in the 113th Congress*. Washington: Congressional Research Service. https://ecommons.cornell.edu/xmlui/bitstream/handle/1813/78673/CRS _Unemployment_Insurance.pdf?sequence=1.

Wickham, James. 2016. *Unequal Europe: Social Divisions and Social Cohesion in an Old Continent*. New York: Routledge.

Wilks, Stephen. 2013. *The Political Power of the Business Corporation*. Northampton, MA: Edward Elgar Publishing.

Willis Towers Watson. 2020. *Global Pension Assets Study – 2020*. Surrey: Thinking Ahead Institute. https://www.thinkingaheadinstitute.org/research-papers /global-pension-assets-study-2020/.

Winfield, Mark. 2006. *Building Sustainable Urban Communities in Ontario: A Provincial Progress Report*. Toronto: Pembina Institute.

Wolff, Edward. 2015. "Inequality and Rising Profitability in the United States, 1947–2012." *International Review of Applied Economics* 29 (6): 741–69. https:// doi.org/10.1080/02692171.2014.956704.

Wood, James D.G. 2017. "The Effects of the Distribution of Mortgage Credit on the Wage Share: Varieties of Residential Capitalism Compared." *Comparative European Politics* 15 (6): 819–47. https://doi.org/10.1057/s41295-016-0006-5.

Workers' Action Centre. 2007. *Working on the Edge*. Toronto: Workers' Action Centre.

– 2011. *Unpaid Wages, Unprotected Workers: A Survey of Employment Standards Violations*. Toronto: Worker's Action Centre.

– 2015. *Still Working on the Edge: Building Decent Jobs from the Ground Up*. Toronto: Worker's Action Centre.

World Economic Forum. 2014. *Global Risks 2014*. Geneva: World Economic Forum.

Wray, L. Randall. 2011. "Minsky's Money Manager Capitalism and the Global Financial Crisis." *International Journal of Political Economy* 40 (2): 5–20. https:// doi.org/10.2753/IJP0891-1916400201.

Wren, Anne. 2013. "Introduction: The Political Economy of the Post-Industrial Age." In *The Political Economy of the Service Transition*, edited by A. Wren, 1–72. New York: Oxford University Press.

Yakabuski, Konrad. 2013. "Income Inequality in Canada: What's the Problem." *Globe and Mail*, 18 November. https://www.theglobeandmail.com/news/national/time-to-lead/income-inequality-in-canada-whats-the-problem/article15470499/.

Yalnizyan, Armine. 2009. *Exposed: Revealing Truths about Canada's Recession*. Ottawa: Canadian Centre for Policy Alternatives.

Yalnizyan, Armine. 2010. *The Rise of Canada's Richest 1%. In Growing Gap*. Ottawa: Canadian Centre for Policy Alternatives.

Yates, Charlotte A.B. 2007. "Missed Opportunities and Forgotten Futures: Why Union Renewal in Canada Has Stalled." In *Trade Union Revitalisation: Trends and Prospects in 34 Countries*, edited by C. Phelan, 57–74. Bern: Peter Lang Publishers.

Young, Nathan, and Ralph Matthews. 2007. "Resource Economies and Neoliberal Experimentation: The Reform of Industry and Community in British Columbia." *Area, Royal Geographical Society* 39 (2): 176–85.

Young Chang, Bo, Michaeal Januska, Gitanjali Kumar, and Andre Usche. 2016. "Monitoring Shadow Banking in Canada: A Hybrid Approach." *Financial System Review* (December): 23–37.

Zucman, Gabriel, Teresa Lavender Fagan, and Thomas Piketty. 2015. *The Hidden Wealth of Nations: The Scourge of Tax Havens*. Chicago: University of Chicago Press.

Index

Accenture, 199

accommodation sector: in BC, 207; employment standards, 207; exemptions from ESA, 315; low-wage employment in, 117–18, 232; non-standard employment in, 126; part-time employment in, 117, 226; seasonal employment in, 226

affluence. *See* wealthy

Agricultural Employees Protection Act (AEPA), 295–6, 310

agricultural sector: AEPA and, 310–11; agribusiness boom, 124; in BC, 185; business associations and, 293, 294–6; capital investment in, 124; employment standards, 310–11; financialization and growth of, 122; financialization of, 124–5; flexibility in, 185; globalization and growth of, 54; in Ontario, 302; service industries in, 125; support/service industries, 126; TNCs in, 125; and unions, 311

agricultural workers: Agricultural Workers Alliance, 218; in BC, 206, 215; and collective bargaining, 295; employees' associations, 310–11; employment standards for, 295, 311; exemptions from ESA, 315; foreign temporary workers, 288; immigrant, 215; as low-skilled, 125; low-wage employment in, 54, 126–9, 288; migrant labour, 125–7; minimum standards/protections for, 206; minimum wage for, 218–19; in Ontario, 294–6; in Quebec, 295; repatriation of, 311; right to strike, 295; temporary, 206; temporary employment of, 126, 161; temporary foreign workers, 215; TFWs in, 127–9; unionization, 218–19, 294–6. *See also* temporary foreign workers (TFWs)

Amazon, 50

Apple, 50, 171

Aquilini, Francesco, 198

Aquilini Development Group, 198

Aramark, 212

Arrighi, Giovanni, 33–4

assets: in auto sector, 107; business reliance on, 9; capital tax on, 330; expansion of income-producing, 132–3; for financial investments vs. business operations, 52; of financial sector, 132–3; firms as, 46; growth, and top earners/incomes, 133; international liberalization and, 94–5; NFC reliance on, 79–80; prioritization of speculation in, 35;

Milton Keynes UK
Ingram Content Group UK Ltd.
UKIIW011254210424
441408UK00003B/39/J